Middle School 2-1
학교시험 완벽대비

KB100593

1학기 전과정

적중"100 plus

영어 기출문제집

중2
지학 | 민찬규

Best Collection

구성과 특징

교과서의 주요 학습 내용을 중심으로 학습 영역별 특성에 맞춰 단계별로 다양한 학습 기회를 제공하여 단원별 학습능력 평가는 물론 중간 및 기말고사 시험 등에 완벽하게 대비할 수 있도록 내용을 구성

Words & Expressions

Step1 Key Words 단원별 핵심 단어 설명 및 풀이
Key Expression 단원별 핵심 숙어 및 관용어 설명
Word Power 반대 또는 비슷한 뜻 단어 배우기
English Dictionary 영어로 배우는 영어 단어

Step2 실력평가 단원별 수시평가 대비 주관식, 객관식 문제풀이

Step3 서술형 대비 학업성취도 및 수행능력평가 대비 서술형 문제풀이

Conversation

Step1 핵심 의사소통 의사소통에 필요한 주요 표현 방법 요약
핵심 Check 기본적인 표현 방법 및 활용능력 확인

Step2 대화문 익히기 상황에 따른 대화문 활용 및 연습

Step3 기본평가 시험대비 기초 학습 능력 평가

Step4 실력평가 단원별 수시평가 대비 주관식, 객관식 문제풀이

Step5 서술형 대비 학업성취도 및 수행능력평가 대비 서술형 문제풀이

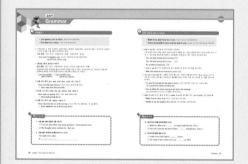

Grammar

Step1 주요 문법 단원별 주요 문법 사항과 예문을 알기 쉽게 설명
핵심 Check 기본 문법사항에 대한 이해 여부 확인

Step2 기본평가 시험대비 기초 학습 능력 평가

Step3 실력평가 단원별 수시평가 대비 주관식, 객관식 문제풀이

Step4 서술형 대비 학업성취도 및 수행능력평가 대비 서술형 문제풀이

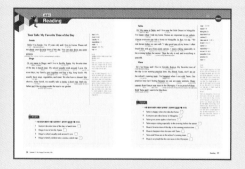

Reading

Step1 구문 분석 단원별로 제시된 문장에 대한 구문별 분석과 내용 설명
확인문제 문장에 대한 기본적인 이해와 인지능력 확인

Step2 확인학습A 빈칸 채우기를 통한 문장 완성 능력 확인

Step3 확인학습B 제시된 우리말을 영어로 완성하여 작문 능력 키우기

Step4 실력평가 단원별 수시평가 대비 주관식, 객관식 문제풀이

Step5 서술형 대비 학업성취도 및 수행능력평가 대비 서술형 문제풀이
교과서 구석구석 교과서에 나오는 기타 문장까지 완벽 학습

Composition

   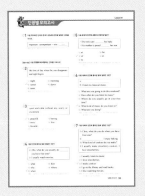

|영역별 핵심문제|

단어 및 어휘, 대화문, 문법, 독해 등 각 영역별 기출문제의 출제 유형을 분석하여 실전에 대비하고 연습할
수 있도록 문제를 배열

|서술형 실전 및 창의사고력 문제|

학교 시험에서 점차 늘어나는 서술형 시험에 집중 대비하고 고득점을 취득하는데 만전을 기하기 위한
학습 코너

|단원별 예상문제|

기출문제를 분석한 후 새로운 시험 출제 경향을 더하여 새롭게 출제될 수 있는 문제를 포함하여 시험에 완벽
하게 대비할 수 있도록 준비

|단원별 모의고사|

영역별, 단계별 학습을 모두 마친 후 실전 연습을 위한 모의고사

on the textbook. .... 교과서 파헤치기

- **단어Test1~2** 영어 단어 우리말 쓰기와 우리말을 영어 단어로 쓰기

- **대화문Test1~2** 대화문 빈칸 완성 및 전체 대화문 쓰기

- **본문Test1~5** 빈칸 완성, 우리말 쓰기, 문장 배열연습, 영어 작문하기 복습 등 단계별 반복 학습을
  통해 교과서 지문에 대한 완벽한 습득

- **구석구석지문Test1~2** 지문 빈칸 완성 및 전문 영어로 쓰기

Lesson 1

New Beginnings

 의사소통 기능

- 주의 끌기
  You know what?

- 의도 표현하기
  I'm thinking of learning *taekwondo*.

언어 형식

- One ... The other ~
  I have two pets. **One** is a dog. **The other** is a cat.

- If 조건절
  If you exercise every day, you will become healthier.

Words & Expressions

Key Words

- **art** [ɑːrt] 명 미술, 예술
- **beef** [biːf] 명 소고기
- **bite** [bait] 동 물다 명 물린 자국
- **break** [breik] 동 깨뜨리다, 부수다
- **care** [kɛər] 명 주의, 조심
- **clean** [klin] 동 청소하다, 깨끗하게 하다
- **cupcake** [kʌ́pkèik] 명 컵케이크
- **dear** [diər] 형 친애하는
- **decide** [disáid] 동 결정하다
- **during** [djúəriŋ] 전 ~ 동안
- **email** [íːmèil] 동 이메일을 보내다
- **fall** [fɔːl] 명 가을
- **false** [fɔːls] 형 틀린, 거짓의
- **funny** [fʌ́ni] 형 재미있는, 익살맞은
- **habit** [hǽbit] 명 습관
- **handle** [hǽndl] 명 손잡이
- **healthy** [hélθi] 형 건강한, 튼튼한
- **hobby** [hábi] 명 취미
- **hold** [hould] 동 잡다, 쥐다
- **homeroom teacher** 담임 선생님
- **jogging** [dʒágiŋ] 명 달리기
- **kind** [kaind] 명 종류

- **lie** [lai] 동 거짓말을 하다
- **nail** [neil] 명 손톱
- **past** [pæst] 명 과거
- **personal** [pə́rsənl] 형 개인적인
- **planet** [plǽnit] 명 행성
- **print** [print] 동 인쇄하다
- **soon** [suːn] 부 곧
- **spring** [spriŋ] 명 봄
- **smart** [smɑːrt] 형 똑똑한, 명석한
- **space** [speis] 명 우주
- **sure** [ʃuər] 형 확실한, 확신하고 있는
- **ticket** [tíkit] 명 표, 입장권
- **tip** [tip] 명 조언, 정보
- **toy** [tɔi] 명 장난감
- **traffic** [trǽfik] 명 교통
- **truth** [truːθ] 명 사실, 진실
- **try** [trai] 동 시도하다
- **upset** [ʌ́pset] 형 화난, 속상한
- **vacation** [veikéiʃən] 명 방학
- **vegetable** [védʒətbl] 명 야채
- **wish** [wiʃ] 명 소망
- **yoga** [jóugə] 명 요가

Key Expressions

- **be interested in** ~에 흥미가 있다
- **be into** ~에 열중하다
- **break a bad habit** 나쁜 습관을 버리다
- **by the way** 그건 그렇고, 그런데
- **change into** ~로 변하다
- **come true** 실현되다
- **do one's best** 최선을 다하다
- **each other** 서로
- **hear from** ~로부터 소식을 듣다

- **It's time to** ~할 때다
- **make changes** 변화를 이루다
- **not ~ anymore** 더 이상 ~하지 않다
- **on one's way home** 집에 오는 길에
- **take a class** 수업을 듣다
- **take care** 몸 건강해, 잘 있어
- **these days** 요즈음에
- **those days** 그 당시에
- **think of** ~할 생각이다

Words Power

※ 서로 반대되는 뜻을 가진 어휘

- □ **healthy** 건강한 ↔ **unhealthy** 건강하지 못한
- □ **funny** 재미있는 ↔ **boring** 지겨운, 지루한
- □ **private** 사적인, 사사로운 ↔ **public** 공공의
- □ **clean** 깨끗한 ↔ **dirty** 더러운
- □ **lie** 거짓말 ↔ **truth** 진실, 사실
- □ **true** 사실인, 참인 ↔ **false** 거짓의

- □ **buy** 사다 ↔ **sell** 팔다
- □ **honest** 정직한 ↔ **dishonest** 정직하지 못한
- □ **smart** 영리한, 똑똑한 ↔ **foolish** 어리석은
- □ **thin** 얇은 ↔ **thick** 두꺼운
- □ **save** 저축하다 ↔ **waste** 낭비하다
- □ **wet** 젖은 ↔ **dry** 마른

English Dictionary

- □ **art** 미술
  → the methods and skills used for painting, sculpting, drawing, etc.
  회화, 조각, 그리기 등에 사용되는 기법이나 기술

- □ **beef** 소고기
  → meat from a cow
  소에서 나는 고기

- □ **bite** 물다
  → to press down on or cut into someone or something with the teeth
  치아로 누군가나 무엇인가를 누르거나 베다

- □ **decide** 결정하다
  → to make a choice about something
  무언가에 대해 선택을 하다

- □ **handle** 손잡이
  → a part that is designed especially to be grasped by the hand
  특히 손에 의해 쥐어질 수 있도록 고안된 부분

- □ **homeroom teacher** 담임 선생님
  → a teacher in charge of a class
  학급을 담당하는 교사

- □ **nail** 손톱
  → the hard covering at the end of a finger or toe
  손가락이나 발가락의 끝을 덮고 있는 딱딱한 부분

- □ **personal** 개인적인
  → belonging or relating to a particular person
  특정한 개인에게 속하거나 관련된

- □ **planet** 행성
  → a large, round object in space that travels around a star
  별 주위를 도는 우주의 크고 둥근 물체

- □ **traffic** 교통
  → the movement of vehicles or pedestrians through an area or along a route
  한 지역을 통과하거나 길을 따라 가는 자동차나 보행자들의 움직임

- □ **try** 시도하다
  → to do or use something in order to find out if you like it
  당신이 좋아하는지를 알아내기 위해 무언가를 사용하거나 하다

- □ **wish** 소망
  → a feeling of wanting to do or have something
  무언가를 하고 싶거나 갖고 싶은 감정

서답형

01 다음 짝지어진 단어의 관계가 같도록 빈칸에 알맞은 말을 쓰시오.

> funny : boring = _____ : public

중요

02 다음 중 밑줄 친 부분의 뜻풀이가 바르지 않은 것은?

① She used to bite <u>nails</u>. 손톱
② Jupiter is the biggest <u>planet</u> in the solar system. 우주
③ I <u>decided</u> to become an English teacher. 결심했다
④ Minju is working for a <u>toy</u> store. 장난감
⑤ I missed the train because of a <u>traffic</u> jam. 교통

03 다음 주어진 문장의 밑줄 친 handle(s)의 의미와 같은 의미로 쓰인 것은?

> My special cup has two <u>handles</u>.

① I can't <u>handle</u> this matter anymore.
② I'm not sure if I can <u>handle</u> this car.
③ I don't expect you can <u>handle</u> this problem.
④ My department <u>handles</u> the information you need.
⑤ She grasped the <u>handle</u> of the knife.

04 다음 문장에 공통으로 들어갈 말을 고르시오.

> • Would you do me a favor? I need to hammer the _____ on the wall.
> • I have cut my _____ too close.
> • My sweater was caught on the _____.

① net ② needle ③ pin
④ nail ⑤ toe

서답형

05 다음 문장의 빈칸에 들어갈 말을 보기에서 골라 알맞은 형태로 쓰시오.

> ┤ 보기 ├
> make changes / hear from /
> be into / be interested in

(1) I _____ _____ _____ playing soccer these days.
(2) My brother _____ _____ playing computer games.
(3) Have you _____ _____ Sumi recently?
(4) She made lots of efforts to _____ _____.

중요

06 다음 문장에 공통으로 들어갈 말을 고르시오.

> • I know the answer. It's on the _____ of my tongue.
> • How much should I give as a _____?
> • Could you give me a useful _____ on how to spend time wisely?

① advice ② information
③ edge ④ tip
⑤ fee

01 다음 짝지어진 단어의 관계가 같도록 빈칸에 알맞은 말을 쓰시오.

> clean : dirty = true : _____

[02~03] 다음 영영풀이에 해당하는 말을 쓰시오.

02

> a teacher in charge of a class
>
> ➡ _____

03

> a large, round object in space that travels around a star
>
> ➡ _____

04 다음 우리말과 일치하도록 주어진 단어를 알맞게 배열하여 완성하시오.

(1) 집에 오는 길에 우유 좀 사다 주겠니?
(way / home / milk / for / you / me / your / on / would / buy)

➡ _____

(2) 변화를 이루기 위해 새로운 프로그램을 사용할 때이다.
(make / time / it's / a / program / to / use / to / changes / new)

➡ _____

(3) 그는 더 이상 컴퓨터 수업을 듣지 않는다.
(class / anymore / he / the / doesn't / computer / take)

➡ _____

05 다음 우리말에 맞게 빈칸에 알맞은 말을 쓰시오.

(1) 나는 나쁜 습관을 그만 두기 위해 노력하고 있다.
➡ I'm trying to _____ _____ _____ _____.

(2) 그건 그렇고, 내가 너를 위해 이 책을 샀어.
➡ _____ _____ _____, I bought this book for you.

(3) 나는 너의 소망이 이루어지길 바란다.
➡ I hope your wish _____ _____.

(4) 주제에 대해 토론해 볼 시간이다.
➡ _____ _____ _____ discuss the topic.

06 다음 문장의 빈칸에 들어갈 말을 〈보기〉에서 골라 쓰시오.

> ┤ 보기 ├
> handles   kind   bite   wish

(1) I often _____ my nails when I feel nervous.
(2) What _____ of music do you like most?
(3) I _____ I can make lots of friends.
(4) A pot usually has two _____.

07 다음 문장의 빈칸에 들어갈 말을 순서대로 쓰시오.

> • I hope to hear (A)_____ my daughter soon.
> • (B)_____ the way, why do we get together?
> • It can change (C)_____ a different style of clothes.

➡ (A) _____, (B) _____, (C) _____

Conversation

1 주의 끌기

You know what? (너 그거 아니?)

■ 대화에서 상대방이 자기의 말에 귀를 기울이도록 주의를 끌기 위한 표현으로 새로운 사실이나 놀라운 일을 소개하거나 또는 새로운 주제로 이야기를 시작할 때 'You know what?'을 이용하여 상대방의 주의를 끌 수 있다.

주의 끌기의 여러 가지 표현

• You know what? (너 그거 아니?)
• Guess what? (있잖아.)
• Look! (여기 봐!)
• Listen. (들어 봐.)

핵심 Check

1. 다음 우리말과 일치하도록 빈칸에 알맞은 말을 쓰시오.

   A: _____ _____ _____? I'm thinking of taking a Chinese class. (그거 아니? 나 중국어 수업을 들을까 생각 중이야.)

   B: That's great.

2. 다음 우리말과 일치하도록 빈칸에 알맞은 말을 쓰시오.

   A: _____ _____? I decided to learn swimming. (있잖아. 나 수영을 배우기로 결심했어.)

   B: Sounds great.

3. 다음 우리말과 일치하도록 빈칸에 알맞은 말을 쓰시오.

   A: _____ You should clean your room before going out. (여기 봐! 너는 외출 전에 네 방을 치워야 해.)

   B: I see. I _____ to clean everything now. (알겠어요. 제가 지금 모두 치울 것을 약속해요.)

② 의도 표현하기

I'm thinking of learning *taekwondo*. (나는 태권도를 배울 생각이야.)

■ 'I'm thinking of ~'는 '나는 ~할 생각이다'라는 뜻으로 '의도'를 나타낼 때 쓰는 표현이다. 이 표현은 'I'm planning to ~'로 바꿔 쓸 수 있다. of 뒤에는 명사(구)나 동명사가 오지만 'I'm planning to ~'를 쓸 때는 뒤에 동사원형을 사용한다는 점에 유의한다.

의도 표현하기

- I'm thinking of saving money. (나는 돈을 저금할 생각이야.)
- I'm planning to learn yoga. (나는 요가를 배울 계획이다.)
- I'm going to take a badminton class. (나는 배드민턴 수업을 들을 거야.)
- I will keep a diary in English. (나는 영어로 일기를 쓸 거야.)
- I made a plan to go jogging in the morning. (나는 아침에 조깅을 갈 계획을 세웠다.)

핵심 Check

4. 다음 우리말과 일치하도록 빈칸에 알맞은 말을 쓰시오.

   A: What are you going to do this weekend? (이번 주말에 무엇을 할 예정이니?)

   B: _____ _____ _____ visit my grandfather. (나는 할아버지 댁을 방문할 계획이야.)

5. 다음 우리말과 일치하도록 빈칸에 알맞은 말을 쓰시오.

   A: _____ _____ _____ keep a diary in English. (나는 영어로 일기를 쓸 거야.)

   B: Why did you _____ to do that? (왜 너는 그렇게 하기로 결심했니?)

6. 다음 우리말과 일치하도록 빈칸에 알맞은 말을 쓰시오.

   A: _____ _____ _____ _____ *bulgogi* for dinner. (나는 저녁으로 불고기를 요리할 생각이야.)

   B: Oh, can you make it by yourself? (오. 너 혼자서 그것을 만들 수 있니?)

A. Listen and Speak 2-A

Jane: Minsu, Sujin and I ❶are thinking of starting a club.

Minsu: Really? What kind of club?

Jane: We want to learn about stars and ❷planets. So, we're thinking of starting a space science club.

Minsu: ❸Sounds good. How often are you going to meet?

Jane: Maybe once a week.

Minsu: I see. Where will you meet?

Jane: In Room 101. Minsu, do you want to join our club?

Minsu: Yes, ❹I'm interested in space, too.

Jane: 민수야, 수진이와 나는 동아리를 만들 생각이야.
Minsu: 정말? 어떤 종류의 동아리야?
Jane: 우리는 별과 행성에 대해 알고 싶어. 그래서 우주 과학 동아리를 만들 생각이야.
Minsu: 그거 멋지다. 얼마나 자주 모일 예정이니?
Jane: 아마도 일주일에 한 번쯤.
Minsu: 그렇구나. 어디에서 모일 거니?
Jane: 101호에서. 민수야, 우리 동아리에 가입할래?
Minsu: 응, 나도 우주에 관심 있어.

❶ 'be thinking of ~'는 '~할 생각이야'라는 의미로 '의도'를 나타낸다.
❷ planet: 행성
❸ (That) Sounds good. = That's wonderful. = What a great idea!
❹ be interested in ~: ~에 관심이 있다

Check(√) True or False

(1) Sujin and Jane want to learn about stars and planets.   T ☐ F ☐

(2) Minsu is thinking of starting a new club.   T ☐ F ☐

B. Real Life Communication

Emily: ❶You know what, Junsu? I'm thinking of taking a painting class.

Junsu: Really? Why did you ❷decide to ❸take a painting class, Emily?

Emily: Because I want to go to an art high school.

Junsu: Are you thinking of becoming an artist in the future?

Emily: I hope so. I'm interested in painting pictures.

Junsu: That's great. I hope your wish ❹comes true.

Emily: Thanks. ❺I'll do my best.

Emily: 준수야, 그거 아니? 나는 미술 수업을 들을 생각이야.
Junsu: 정말? 왜 미술 수업을 들으려고 결심했니, Emily?
Emily: 예술 고등학교에 가고 싶어서야.
Junsu: 장래에 미술가가 될 생각이니?
Emily: 그러고 싶어. 나는 그림 그리는 것에 흥미가 있어.
Junsu: 그거 잘 됐다. 네 꿈이 이뤄지길 바라.
Emily: 고마워. 최선을 다할 거야.

❶ 상대방의 주의를 끌기 위해 사용하는 표현이다.
❷ decide to: ~하기로 결심하다
❸ take a class: 수업을 듣다
❹ come true: 실현되다
❺ do one's best: 최선을 다하다

Check(√) True or False

(3) Emily is interested in painting pictures.   T ☐ F ☐

(4) Junsu wants to be an artist in the future.   T ☐ F ☐

Listen and Speak 1 A

Brian: Julia, how was your winter vacation?

Julia: It was great. ❶You know what? I ❷took *muay thai* lessons ❸during the vacation.

Brian: That's amazing. I didn't know that you ❹ were interested in *muay thai*.

Julia: Yes. ❺It was really fun.

Brian: Really? I want ❻to try ❼it.

❶ You know what?: '너 그거 아니?'라는 뜻으로 상대방의 주의를 끌고자 할 때 사용한다. 이 다음에는 말하고자 하는 새로운 사실이 나온다.

❷ take a lesson: 수업을 듣다

❸ during은 '~ 동안에'라는 의미로 뒤에 기간을 나타내는 명사가 이어진다.

❹ be interested in: ~에 관심이 있다

❺ it은 *muay thai*를 가리킨다.

❻ want의 목적어로 to부정사가 쓰이고 있다. try는 '한 번 해보다'의 의미이다.

❼ it은 *muay thai*를 가리킨다.

Listen and Speak 2 B

Alex: Mom, I made *bulgogi* at school today. ❶I'm thinking of cooking *bulgogi* for dinner.

Mom: That ❷sounds great, Alex.

Alex: Do we have ❸any vegetables at home, Mom? ❹ What about beef?

Mom: We have ❺some vegetables, but we don't have beef. I'll buy ❻some for you ❼on my way home.

Alex: Great.

❶ I'm thinking of ~: '나는 ~할 생각이야'라는 뜻으로, '의도'를 나타내는 표현이다. 'I'm planning to ~'로 바꾸어 쓸 수 있다. of 뒤에는 (동)명사(구)가 오지만, to 다음에는 동사원형이 온다.

❷ 감각동사(sound) 다음에 형용사(great)가 보어로 나왔다.

❸ 의문문이므로 any가 쓰였다.

❹ What about ~?: '~는 어때요?'라는 뜻으로 여기서는 '소고기는 있어요?'라는 뜻이다.

❺ 긍정문이므로 some이 쓰였다.

❻ 여기서 some은 대명사로 '약간의 소고기'를 의미한다.

❼ on one's way home: 집에 오는 길에

Listen and Speak 1 B

Jimin: You know what, Tim? Mr. Smith is my ❶ homeroom teacher ❷this year.

Tim: That's great, Jimin. His science class last year was ❸a lot of fun.

Jimin: Who's your homeroom teacher this year?

Tim: It's Ms. Kim. She's a new teacher.

Jimin: What does she teach?

Tim: She teaches ❹art.

❶ homeroom teacher: 담임 선생님

❷ this year: 올해

❸ a lot of는 수(= many)와 양(= much) 두 가지의 경우 모두 쓰인다.

❹ 과목 명 앞에서 관사는 생략한다.

Real Life Communication

Sue: You know what? Jenny's family is going to move to Japan.

Jack: Is that right? Jenny didn't tell me about ❶it.

Sue: She learned about ❶it just last week and she's very ❷upset now.

Jack: I can understand her feelings. I am going to ❸miss her so much.

Sue: ❹Me, too. She said she would ❺keep in touch with us.

❶ it은 일본으로 이사 가는 것을 가리킨다.

❷ upset : 속상한

❸ miss는 '그리워하다'라는 의미로 쓰였다.

❹ Me, too. = So am I.: 나도 그래.

❺ keep in touch: 연락하다

● 다음 우리말과 일치하도록 빈칸에 알맞은 말을 쓰시오.

Listen & Speak 1 A

Brian: Julia, how was your winter vacation?

Julia: It was great. _____ _____ _____? I took *muay thai* lessons during the vacation.

Brian: That's amazing. I didn't know that _____ _____ _____ _____ *muay thai*.

Julia: Yes. It was really fun.

Brian: Really? I want to try it.

 해석

Brian: Julia, 네 겨울 방학은 어땠니?
Julia: 좋았어. 그거 아니? 나는 방학 동안 무에타이 수업을 받았어.
Brian: 그거 멋지다. 나는 네가 무에타이에 관심이 있는지 몰랐어.
Julia: 응. 아주 재미있었어.
Brian: 그래? 나도 해 보고 싶다.

Listen & Speak 1 B

Jimin: You know what, Tim? Mr. Smith is my _____ _____ this year.

Tim: That's great, Jimin. His science class last year was a lot of _____.

Jimin: Who's your homeroom teacher this year?

Tim: It's Ms. Kim. She's a new teacher.

Jimin: _____ _____ _____ _____?

Tim: She teaches _____.

Jimin: 그거 아니, Tim? Smith 선생님이 올해 우리 반 담임 선생님이야.
Tim: 그거 잘됐다, 지민아. 작년 Smith선생님의 과학 수업은 아주 재미있었어.
Jimin: 올해 너희 반 담임 선생님은 누구니?
Tim: 김 선생님이야. 그녀는 새로 오신 선생님이야.
Jimin: 그분은 어떤 과목을 가르치시니?
Tim: 미술을 가르치셔.

Listen & Speak 2 A

Jane: Minsu, Sujin and I _____ _____ _____ _____ a club.

Minsu: Really? _____ _____ _____ _____?

Jane: We want to learn about _____ and _____. So, we're thinking of starting a space science club.

Minsu: Sounds good. How often are you going to meet?

Jane: Maybe _____ _____ _____.

Minsu: I see. Where will you meet?

Jane: In Room 101. Minsu, do you want to join our club?

Minsu: Yes, _____ _____ _____ space, too.

Jane: 민수야, 수진이와 나는 동아리를 만들 생각이야.
Minsu: 정말? 어떤 종류의 동아리야?
Jane: 우리는 별과 행성에 대해 배우고 싶어. 그래서 우주 과학 동아리를 만들 생각이야.
Minsu: 그거 멋지다. 얼마나 자주 모일 예정이니?
Jane: 아마도 일주일에 한 번쯤.
Minsu: 그렇구나. 어디에서 모일 거니?
Jane: 101호에서. 민수야, 우리 동아리에 가입할래?
Minsu: 응, 나도 우주에 관심 있어.

Listen & Speak 2 B

Alex: Mom, I made *bulgogi* at school today._____ _____ _____ *bulgogi* for dinner.

Mom: That sounds great, Alex.

Alex: Do we have any vegetables at home, Mom? _____ _____ _____?

Mom: We have some vegetables, but we don't have beef. _____ _____ _____ _____ _____ _____ _____.

Alex: Great.

Alex: 엄마, 오늘 학교에서 불고기를 만들었어요. 오늘 저녁으로 불고기를 요리할 생각이에요.
Mom: 그거 멋지구나, Alex.
Alex: 집에 채소 있어요, 엄마? 소고기는요?
Mom: 채소는 좀 있는데 소고기는 없어. 집에 오는 길에 좀 사올게.
Alex: 좋아요.

Real Life Communication A

Emily: You know what, Junsu? _____ _____ _____ _____ a _____ _____.

Junsu: Really? Why did you _____ to take a painting class, Emily?

Emily: Because _____ _____ _____ _____ _____ _____ _____ _____ _____.

Junsu: Are you thinking of becoming an _____ in the future?

Emily: I hope so. I'm interested in painting pictures.

Junsu: That's great. I hope your wish _____ _____.

Emily: Thanks. I'll _____ _____ _____.

Emily: 준수야, 그거 아니? 나는 미술 수업을 들을 생각이야.
Junsu: 정말? 왜 미술 수업을 들으려고 결심했니, Emily?
Emily: 예술 고등학교에 가고 싶어서야.
Junsu: 장래에 미술가가 될 생각이니?
Emily: 그러고 싶어. 나는 그림 그리는 것에 흥미가 있어.
Junsu: 그거 잘 됐다. 네 꿈이 이뤄지길 바라.
Emily: 고마워. 최선을 다할 거야.

Real Life Communication B

Sue: You know what? Jenny's family is going to _____ to Japan.

Jack: Is that right? Jenny didn't tell me about it.

Sue: She learned about it just last week and she's very _____ now.

Jack: _____ _____ _____ _____ _____ _____ _____. I am going to miss her so much.

Sue: Me, too. She said she would _____ _____ _____ us.

Sue: 있잖아, Jenny 가족이 일본으로 이민을 간대.
Jack: 정말이야? Jenny가 그것에 관해 얘기하지 않았는데.
Sue: Jenny도 지난주에야 알았어. 그래서 지금 매우 기분이 안 좋아.
Jack: 나는 Jenny의 기분을 이해할 수 있어. Jenny가 정말 그리울 거야.
Sue: 나도 그래. Jenny는 우리와 계속 연락할 거라고 했어.

01 다음 대화의 우리말을 주어진 단어를 사용하여 영작하시오.

> A: 너 그거 아니? I'm thinking of buying a bike. (what)
> B: Why did you decide to do that?

➡ _____ ?

02 다음 대화가 자연스럽게 이어지도록 순서대로 배열하시오.

You know what? Jenny's family is going to move to Japan.

> (A) Me, too. She said she would keep in touch with us.
> (B) Is that right? Jenny didn't tell me about it.
> (C) She learned about it just last week and she's very upset now.
> (D) I can understand her feelings. I am going to miss her so much.

➡ _____

[03~04] 다음 대화를 읽고 물음에 답하시오.

Jimin: You know what, Tim? Mr. Smith is my homeroom teacher this year.
Tim: That's great, Jimin. His science class last year was a lot of fun.
Jimin: (A)올해 너의 반 담임 선생님은 누구니?
Tim: It's Ms. Kim. She's a new teacher.
Jimin: What does she teach?
Tim: She teaches art.

03 위 대화에서 (A)의 우리말을 영어로 쓰시오.

➡ _____

04 위 대화의 내용과 일치하지 <u>않는</u> 것은?

① Jimin의 올해 담임 선생님은 Mr. Smith이다.
② Mr. Smith는 과학 선생님이다.
③ Tim은 작년에 Mr. Smith에게 과학을 배웠다.
④ Ms. Kim은 미술 선생님으로 새로 왔다.
⑤ Jimin과 Tim은 서로 같은 반이 되었다.

[01~02] 다음 대화를 읽고 물음에 답하시오.

Brian: Julia, (A)[what / how] was your winter vacation?

Julia: It was great. You know what? I took *muay thai* lessons during the vacation.

Brian: That's (B)[amazing / amazed]. I didn't know that you were (C)[interesting / interested] in *muay thai*.

Julia: Yes. It was really fun.

Brian: Really? I want to try it.

01 위 대화의 괄호 (A)~(C)에 알맞은 말로 바르게 짝지어진 것은?

	(A)	(B)	(C)
①	what	amazing	interesting
②	what	amazed	interested
③	how	amazed	interesting
④	how	amazing	interested
⑤	how	amazing	interesting

02 위 대화의 내용과 일치하지 <u>않는</u> 것은?

① Julia는 겨울 방학을 잘 보냈다.
② Julia는 겨울 방학에 무에타이 수업을 들었다.
③ Brian은 Julia가 무에타이에 관심이 있다는 것을 알고 있었다.
④ Julia는 무에타이 수업이 재미있었다.
⑤ Brain은 무에타이를 한 번 해보고 싶어 한다.

03 다음 대화가 자연스럽게 이어지도록 순서대로 배열하시오.

Emily: You know what, Junsu? I'm thinking of taking a painting class.

(A) Are you thinking of becoming an artist in the future?
(B) Because I want to go to an art high school.
(C) That's great. I hope your wish comes true.
(D) I hope so. I'm interested in painting pictures.
(E) Really? Why did you decide to take a painting class, Emily?

Emily: Thanks. I'll do my best.

➡ _____

[04~05] 다음 대화를 읽고 물음에 답하시오.

Jimin: (A) Mr. Smith is my homeroom teacher this year.

Tim: (B) That's great, Jimin. His science class last year was a lot of fun.

Jimin: (C) Who's your homeroom teacher this year?

Tim: (D) It's Ms. Kim. She's a new teacher.

Jimin: (E) What does she teach?

Tim: She teaches art.

04 위 대화의 (A)~(E) 중 주어진 문장이 들어가기에 적절한 곳은?

You know what?

① (A)　② (B)　③ (C)　④ (D)　⑤ (E)

05 위 대화를 읽고 대답할 수 <u>없는</u> 것은?

① Who is Jimin's homeroom teacher?
② What did Tim learn from Mr. Smith?
③ What is Ms. Kim going to teach?
④ How was Ms. Kim's class last year?
⑤ Who is the new teacher?

[06~07] 다음 대화를 읽고 물음에 답하시오.

Sue: You know what? Jenny's family is going to move to Japan.

Jack: Is that right? Jenny didn't tell me about it.

Sue: She learned about it just last week and she's very upset now.

Jack: I can understand her feelings. I am going to miss her so much.

Sue: Me, too. She said she would (A)_____ us.

서답형

06 위 대화의 빈칸 (A)에 '~와 연락하다'를 의미하는 숙어를 4 단어로 완성하시오.

➡ _____

07 위 대화를 통해 알 수 있는 Jenny의 심경으로 적절한 것은?

① pleased   ② nervous
③ frustrated   ④ lonely
⑤ excited

[08~09] 다음 대화를 읽고 물음에 답하시오.

Alex: Mom, I made *bulgogi* at school today. I'm thinking ⓐof cooking *bulgogi* for dinner.

Mom: ⓑThat sounds great, Alex.

Alex: Do we have any vegetables ⓒat home, Mom? What ⓓabout beef?

Mom: We have some vegetables, but we don't have beef. I'll buy some for you ⓔin my way home.

Alex: Great.

서답형

08 위 대화의 밑줄 친 ⓐ~ⓔ 중 어법상 틀린 것을 찾아 바르게 고쳐 쓰시오.

➡ _____

09 위 대화를 읽고 대답할 수 없는 것은?

① What did Alex make at school?
② What is Alex planning to make for dinner?
③ What does Alex need to cook *bulgogi*?
④ To cook *bulgogi*, what doesn't Alex have?
⑤ Where is Alex's mom now?

[10~12] 다음 대화를 읽고 물음에 답하시오.

Jane: Minsu, Sujin and I are thinking of starting a club.

Minsu: Really? What kind of club?

Jane: We want to learn about stars and planets. So, we're thinking of starting a space science club.

Minsu: Sounds good. (A)_____

Jane: Maybe once a week.

Minsu: I see. Where will you meet?

Jane: In Room 101. Minsu, do you want to join our club?

Minsu: Yes, I'm interested in space, too.

서답형

10 위 대화의 빈칸 (A)에 들어갈 말을 주어진 단어를 모두 사용 하여 완성하시오.

┌── 보기 ──┐

to are meet how going often you

➡ _____

서답형

11 About what do Sujin and Jane want to learn in a space science club?

➡ _____

서답형

12 What is Minsu interested in?

➡ _____

[01~03] 다음 대화를 읽고 물음에 답하시오.

Brian: Julia, how was your winter vacation?
Julia: It was great. You know what? I took *muay thai* lessons during the vacation.
Brian: That's amazing. I didn't know that you were interested in *muay thai*.
Julia: Yes. It was really fun.
Brian: Really? I want to try (A)it.

01 위 대화의 밑줄 친 (A)it이 가리키는 것을 영어로 쓰시오.

➡ _____

02 What did Julia do during the winter vacation?

➡ _____

03 What was Julia interested in?

➡ _____

04 다음 주어진 문장에 이어질 대화가 자연스럽게 이어지도록 순서대로 배열하시오.

> You know what? Mr. Smith is my homeroom teacher this year.

> (A) She teaches art.
> (B) What does she teach?
> (C) It's Ms. Kim. She's a new teacher.
> (D) Who's your homeroom teacher this year?
> (E) That's great. His science class last year was a lot of fun.

➡ _____

05 다음 대화의 우리말을 주어진 단어를 이용하여 영작하시오.

> A: You know what? 나는 요가를 배울 생각이야. (am, think, learn)
> B: I think it's good for your health.

➡ _____

06 다음 대화의 내용과 일치하도록 민수의 일기를 완성하시오.

> Jane: Minsu, Sujin and I are thinking of starting a club.
> Minsu: Really? What kind of club?
> Jane: We want to learn about stars and planets. So, we're thinking of starting a space science club.
> Minsu: Sounds good. How often are you going to meet?
> Jane: Maybe once a week.
> Minsu: I see. Where will you meet?
> Jane: In Room 101. Minsu, do you want to join our club?
> Minsu: Yes, I'm interested in space, too.

⬇

> Wed, March 27th, 2019
> Today, Jane told me about starting a space science club. Sujin and she were interested in (A)_____, so they wanted to make a space science club. They were planning to meet (B)_____ in (C)_____. It sounded good. So, I decided to join the club. I'm really looking forward to learning about space.

➡ (A) _____ (B) _____
   (C) _____

Grammar

1 One ... The other ~

- I have two pencils. **One** is short and **the other** is long. 내게는 연필 두 자루가 있다. 하나는 짧고 다른 하나는 길다.

- There are three umbrellas. **One** is yellow, **another** is blue, and **the other** is black. 우산이 세 개 있다. 하나는 노란색이고, 또 다른 하나는 파란색이고, 남은 하나는 검정색이다.

■ 둘 중에 하나를 가리킬 때에 'one'을 쓰고 남은 하나를 가리킬 때 'the other'를 쓴다. '하나는 …', '나머지 다른 하나는 ~'이라는 뜻으로 사용된다.

- There are two balls. **One** is baseball. **The other** is basketball. 공이 두 개 있다. 하나는 야구공이다. 나머지 다른 하나는 농구공이다.

■ 셋을 지칭할 때에는 제일 처음 가리키는 것을 'one', 그 다음으로 가리키는 것을 'another', 마지막으로 남은 하나를 가리킬 때에는 'the other'를 쓴다. 'the other+복수명사'가 올 경우 'the others'로 대명사화 할 수 있다.

- I'm fixing three cars. **One** is a truck. **Another** is a minivan. **The other** is a sports car.
  나는 차 세 대를 고치는 중이야. 한 대는 트럭이야. 다른 한 대는 미니밴이야. 나머지 한 대는 스포츠카야.

■ 지칭하는 것이 복수일 때에는 'some'을 쓰고, 이미 언급한 것과는 다른 것을 묶어서 이야기할 때에는 'other+복수명사'를 쓴다.

- **Some** students want to be teachers. **Other** students(= Others) want to be politicians.
  몇몇 학생들은 선생님이 되기를 원한다. 다른 학생들은 정치인이 되기를 원한다.

- The persons in the lounge have different jobs. **One** is a dentist. **Some** people are tennis players. **Others** are chefs.
  라운지에 있는 사람들은 여러 가지 직업을 가지고 있다. 한 사람은 치과의사이다. 몇몇 사람들은 테니스 선수들이다. 다른 사람들은 요리사이다.

핵심 Check

1. 다음 우리말과 같도록 빈칸에 알맞은 말을 쓰시오.

(1) 그녀에게는 책 두 권이 있다. 한 권은 소설이고, 나머지 한 권은 잡지이다.

➡ She has two books. _____ is a novel and _____ is a magazine.

(2) 사과 다섯 개가 있다. 하나는 엄마 것이다. 다른 하나는 내 것이다. 나머지 모두는 아빠 것이다.

➡ There are five apples. _____ is Mom's. _____ is mine. _____ are Dad's.

(3) 몇몇 책은 과학에 관한 것이고, 다른 책들은 영화에 관한 것이다.

➡ _____ are about science, and _____ are about movies.

② If가 이끄는 조건절

- **If** you meet him, you will like him. 네가 그를 만난다면, 너는 그를 좋아할 거야.
- **If** you have some time tomorrow, what will you do? 내일 시간이 좀 있으면, 넌 뭘 할 거야?

■ 조건의 부사절에서는 현재시제를 사용하여 미래를 나타내며 '만약 ~라면'이라고 해석한다.

- **If** he goes by taxi, he will get there soon. 그가 택시를 타고 간다면, 그곳에 곧 도착할 거야.
- **If** you are hungry, she will make you a pizza. 네가 배고프다면, 그녀가 너에게 피자를 만들어 줄 거야.

■ 때를 나타내는 부사절에서도 현재시제를 사용하여 미래를 나타낸다.

- We will go out **after** we finish watching this movie. 이 영화를 보는 걸 끝낸 후에 우리는 나갈 것이다.

■ If절이 명사 역할을 하는 경우도 있다. 명사절을 이끄는 접속사 if와 부사절을 이끄는 접속사 if의 쓰임을 구별하자. 명사절을 이끄는 접속사 if의 경우 '~인지 아닌지'로 해석하며 미래를 나타낼 때에는 미래시제를 써야 한다.

- I wonder **if** you **will accept** the offer. 나는 네가 그 제안을 받아들일지 궁금해.
- No one can tell **if** he **will** really **sign** the contract or not.
  그가 정말 그 계약서에 서명할지 서명하지 않을지는 아무도 알 수 없다.
- I can't decide **if** I **will take** a vacation with her or not.
  나는 그녀와 휴가를 갈지 안 갈지 결정할 수 없어.

■ If ~ not은 '만약 ~하지 않으면'의 의미인 Unless로 쓸 수 있다. Unless 역시 조건절이므로 현재시제로 미래를 나타낸다.

- **If** you **don't hurry**, you will miss the train. 서두르지 않으면 그 기차를 놓칠 거야.
  = **Unless** you **hurry**, you will miss the train.

핵심 Check

2. 다음 우리말과 같도록 빈칸에 알맞은 말을 쓰시오.

(1) 그들이 일찍 도착한다면, 우리는 일찍 떠날 거야.

➡ If they _____ early, _____ _____ leave early.

(2) 네가 그의 파티에 오지 않는다면, 그는 아주 슬플 거야.

➡ _____ you come to his party, he _____ _____ very sad.

(3) 나는 네가 여행에서 돌아왔는지 알고 싶어.

➡ I want to know _____ you came back from the trip.

01 다음 문장에서 어법상 <u>어색한</u> 부분을 바르게 고쳐 쓰시오.

(1) If you will tell me the truth, I won't tell it to anyone.

_____ ➡ _____

(2) Some people like oranges. Another people like apples.

_____ ➡ _____

(3) I don't know if she practices hard tomorrow.

_____ ➡ _____

(4) There are two seats. One is mine and other is yours.

_____ ➡ _____

02 다음 빈칸에 알맞은 말을 쓰시오.

(1) If it _____ tomorrow, I will lend you my umbrella.
(2) She is holding two cameras. _____ is mine, and _____ is hers.
(3) _____ you wake up early, you will be late for the meeting.
(4) I bought five skirts. One is red, _____ is pink, and _____ are white.

03 다음 우리말에 맞게 주어진 어구를 바르게 배열하시오. (필요하다면 단어를 추가할 것)

(1) 어떤 꽃들은 흰색이고, 또 다른 꽃들은 노란색이다.
   (flowers / are / yellow / white / some / are / and / others)
   ➡ _____

(2) 만약 네가 이 잡지를 원한다면, 내가 그것을 네게 빌려줄게.
   (want / lend / you / to / if / this magazine / I / it / you)
   ➡ _____

(3) 너는 두 개의 시계를 가지고 있잖아. 하나는 여기에 있어. 다른 하나는 어디에 있니?
   (two watches / have / one / you / here / the other / is / where / is)
   ➡ _____

(4) 네가 이기면, 우리는 행복할 거야. (if / be / you / we / win / happy)
   ➡ _____

01 다음 빈칸에 들어갈 말로 어법상 적절한 것을 <u>모두</u> 고르시오.

_____ I can see you arrive here safely, I won't leave.

① Unless　　② Because　　③ Although
④ Until　　⑤ Since

02 다음 빈칸에 들어갈 말로 가장 적절한 것은?

A: What is the difference between these two bikes?
B: Well, this one is more comfortable than _____.

① some　　② another　　③ other
④ one　　⑤ the other

03 다음 빈칸에 들어갈 말이 바르게 짝지어진 것은?

If you _____ a problem, we _____ it later.

① will have – will discuss
② had – can solve
③ have had – discuss
④ have – will discuss
⑤ have – discuss

서답형
04 다음 빈칸에 알맞은 말을 쓰시오.

Mr. Robinson has three daughters. _____ is a teacher, _____ is a pianist, and _____ is a writer.

➡ _____

05 다음 우리말을 영어로 바르게 옮긴 것은?

네가 하나를 선택하면, 내가 남은 하나를 선택할게.

① If you choose it, I will choose another.
② If you choose one, I will choose other.
③ If you will choose one, I will choose the other.
④ If you will choose it, I will choose another.
⑤ If you choose one, I will choose the other.

06 다음 중 어법상 바르지 <u>않은</u> 것은?

There ①are many people ②downstairs. ③Some want to have peach juice, ④other want to have lemonade. If you want me ⑤to ask what the others want to have, I will.

07 다음 중 밑줄 친 if의 쓰임이 나머지와 <u>다른</u> 하나는?

① If anyone finds it, I will call you.
② You will regret if you don't listen to me.
③ It is hard to tell if he liked it or not.
④ She will stay longer if you ask her to.
⑤ If the tree is cut, we will plant another one.

서답형
08 주어진 어구를 이용하여 다음 우리말을 영어로 쓰시오.

네게 시간이 있다면, 내 부탁 하나 들어주겠니?
(have time / do / a favor)

➡ _____

09 다음 중 어법상 옳은 것은?

① Please move your car because you are blocking another cars.

② Unless you are not an expert, it is difficult to do the job.

③ If I make some mistakes, can you help me?

④ Angela has three necklaces. One is short and the other are long.

⑤ I wonder if you buy a lap top computer this weekend.

서답형
10 주어진 단어를 활용하여 밑줄 친 우리말을 8 단어로 이루어진 문장으로 쓰시오.

> This copy machine is broken. 다른 복사기가 있는지 혹시 아니? (know / if / there / one)

➡ _____

중요
11 다음 빈칸에 공통으로 들어갈 말은?

> • I will go skiing _____ it snows this weekend.
> • Can you tell me _____ James will join the party tonight?

① because   ② while   ③ if
④ unless   ⑤ although

중요
12 다음 중 빈칸에 들어갈 말이 바르게 짝지어진 것은?

> There are two cats under the tree. _____ is sleeping, and _____ is playing with a ball.

① It – another   ② The one – other
③ One – two   ④ One – the other
⑤ One - another

서답형
13 다음 빈칸에 알맞은 말을 쓰시오.

> I got three letters. _____ was from my grandfather. _____ was from my brother. _____ was from my girlfriend.

➡ _____

14 다음 중 밑줄 친 부분과 바꾸어 쓸 수 있는 것은?

> I bought a blue hat but I want to buy a different one.

① one   ② it   ③ the other
④ other   ⑤ another

중요
15 다음 중 밑줄 친 부분이 문맥이나 어법상 옳은 것은?

① If they will throw a party, will they invite Tom?

② Some people like bowling and another like badminton.

③ Let me know if you will be there.

④ If you say sorry, Mom will be upset.

⑤ This shirt is too bright. Can you show me the other one in this size?

서답형
16 다음 빈칸 ⓐ~ⓔ에 알맞은 말을 쓰시오.

> Look at your hand. You have five fingers. ⓐ_____ is your thumb. ⓑ_____ is your index finger. ⓒ_____ is your middle finger. ⓓ_____ is your ring finger. And ⓔ_____ finger is your little finger.

➡ ⓐ: _____ ⓑ: _____ ⓒ: _____
ⓓ: _____ ⓔ: _____

서답형

17 주어진 단어를 이용하여 다음 우리말을 영어로 쓰시오.

> 만약 그녀가 널 초대하면, 너는 그 파티에 갈거니? (invite / go) (if로 시작할 것)

➡ _____

18 다음 빈칸에 들어갈 말로 가장 적절한 것은?

> A: What are you doing?
> B: I'm watching Timmy. He is writing something with one hand, and holding a hamburger with _____ .

① the others   ② another
③ the other   ④ one hand
⑤ other

서답형

19 두 문장의 의미가 같도록 빈칸에 알맞은 말을 쓰시오.

> If you don't read the book carefully, you will not pass the test.
> = _____ you read the book carefully, you will not pass the test.

➡ _____

중요

20 다음 중 빈칸에 들어갈 말이 바르게 짝지어진 것은?

> If you look at _____ side of the coin, you _____ a small castle on it.

① other – will discover
② another – discover
③ the other – discovered
④ another – discovered
⑤ the other – will discover

21 다음 빈칸에 들어갈 말로 가장 적절한 것은?

> Jenny has two sisters. _____

① One is taller than another.
② She is taller than others.
③ One is taller than the other.
④ She is taller than other.
⑤ One is taller than others.

중요

22 다음 빈칸에 들어갈 말이 바르게 짝지어진 것은?

> Many students have their favorite K-pop idols. These students often show their love in various ways. _____ scream wildly at concerts. _____ wait hours just to see their stars.

① One – The other   ② Some – Others
③ Few – Others   ④ Some – Another
⑤ One – Others

23 다음 빈칸에 가장 적절한 것은?

> I have been to two cities. One is Busan and _____ is Seoul.

① it   ② others   ③ other
④ another   ⑤ the other

서답형

24 적절한 부정대명사를 이용하여 다음 우리말을 영어로 쓰시오. (8 letters)

> 어떤 사람들은 파란색을 좋아하고, 어떤 사람들은 초록색을 좋아한다.

➡ _____

01 괄호 안에 주어진 동사를 이용하여 다음 우리말을 영어로 쓰시오.

> A: I think I left my lip balm at your house. Have you seen it?
>
> B: No, but 내가 그것을 찾으면, 네게 말해 줄게. (find, tell)

➡ _____

02 다음 빈칸에 알맞은 말을 쓰시오.

> Ms. Jefferson has five children. One of them has red hair. _____ children have brown hair.

➡ _____

03 다음 주어진 문장과 같은 의미의 문장을 쓰시오.

> If it doesn't rain tomorrow, I will play tennis with my friends.
> = _____ _____ _____ tomorrow, I will play tennis with my friends.

➡ _____

04 주어진 어구를 활용하여 다음 우리말을 두 개의 문장으로 쓰시오.

> 내일 몸이 좋지 않으면, 집에 머물 거야. (feel well / stay / at)

➡ _____

➡ _____

05 주어진 단어를 활용하여 다음 우리말을 영어로 쓰시오.

> 나는 두 개의 언어를 말할 수 있다. 하나는 한국어이고, 다른 하나는 영어이다. (speak / language)

➡ _____

06 괄호 안에 주어진 동사를 어법에 맞게 쓰시오.

> A: What are you going to do this weekend?
>
> B: My sister is going to come home this weekend. So if she (come) home early, I (go) shopping with her.

➡ _____

07 주어진 동사를 이용하여 다음 우리말을 영어로 쓰시오.

> 만약 네가 Jerry를 본다면, 너는 그를 좋아할 거야. (see / like)

➡ _____

08 빈칸에 알맞은 말을 쓰시오.

> I have been in only three cities since I came to the United States. _____ is Chicago, and _____ is San Francisco, and _____ is Miami.

➡ _____

09 주어진 어구를 어법에 맞게 빈칸에 각각 쓰시오.

> another   the other   the others
> one   some   other   others

(1) _____ people prefer classic music, but _____ prefer pop music.

(2) Molly has two goals in her life. _____ is to become a famous singer. _____ is to read many books.

(3) Jason got _____ birthday presents from his family. _____ is a computer. _____ is a bike. _____ is a long padding coat.

(4) There are ten bananas on the table. _____ is mine. _____ are yours.

(5) Some students like to study English, but _____ students like to study math.

(6) I lost my pencil, so I have to buy _____ one.

(7) In summer, _____ friends want to go to the beach, _____ want to go to the mountains.

10 두 개의 문장을 연결하여 자연스러운 하나의 문장으로 만드시오.

> • You cheat on the test.
> • You have a car.
> • You don't wear a helmet.

> • You will be hurt.
> • You will get caught.
> • Will you take me to the airport?

➡ _____

➡ _____

➡ _____

11 다음 빈칸에 적절한 것을 쓰시오.

> There were ten chairs in the room, but I can count only five now. Where are _____?

➡ _____

12 괄호 안에 주어진 단어를 활용하여 빈칸 ⓐ와 ⓑ에 알맞은 말을 쓰고, 빈칸 ⓒ에는 적절한 부정대명사를 쓰시오.

> A: What will do you if it rains after school?
> B: If ⓐ_____ (rain) after school, I ⓑ_____ (use) one of my umbrellas. Actually, I have two umbrellas.
> A: Then, can you borrow me ⓒ_____ one?
> B: Sure.

➡ ⓐ_____ ⓑ_____ ⓒ_____

13 다음 글을 읽고 물음에 완전한 문장의 영어로 답하시오.

> Helen took a cookie from the cookie jar and ate it. Then she took the other one and ate it, too. There were no more cookies in the cookie jar.

Q: How many cookies were there in the cookie jar?

➡ _____

14 다음 빈칸에 알맞은 말을 쓰시오.

> There are two boys. _____ is wearing glasses and _____ is tall.

➡ _____

My New Changes

My friend Eric and I made some interesting changes during the
My friend와 Eric은 동격으로 동일 인물을 나타냄 ~ 동안(숫자를 포함하지 않은 특정 기간)
vacation. We emailed each other and talked about our changes.

Dear Eric,

It's a beautiful spring in Seoul. The last winter vacation was a great
날씨, 날짜, 거리, 명암 등을 나타내는 비인칭 주어 it
time for me. I made two personal changes during the vacation. One is
나에게 two changes 중 하나를 가리키며 '하나'라는 뜻을 나타냄
my new hobby. It's making cupcakes. Making my own cupcakes is a
=My new hobby 동명사(보어) 동명사(주어) 동명사 주어는 단수 취급
lot of fun. The other change is breaking one of my bad habits. In the
two changes 중 나머지를 가리키며 '나머지 다른'이란 뜻을 나타냄
past, I often bit my nails. Now I don't anymore. I feel great about the
빈도부사로 일반동사 bite 앞에 위치. bite–bit–bitten 'not ~ anymore'는 '더 이상 ~ 않다'는 뜻이며, Now I don't bite my nails anymore.에서 bite my nails를 생략한 문장이다
changes I made. If you try to make some changes, I'm sure you'll feel
앞에 관계대명사 목적격 that[which] 생략 =I'm sure (that)~: ~을 확신한다
great like me. I hope to hear from you soon.
~처럼 hope의 목적어

Your friend, Junho.
친한 친구 사이의 편지글의 마무리 말

---

make changes: 변화를 이루다

email: 이메일을 보내다

each other: 서로

personal: 개인적인

break a bad habit: 나쁜 습관을 그만두다

bite: 깨물다

nail: 손톱

not ~ anymore: 더 이상 ~하지 않다

hear from: ~로부터 연락을 받다

 확인문제

- 다음 문장이 본문의 내용과 일치하면 T, 일치하지 않으면 F를 쓰시오.

1 Junho isn't good at making cupcakes. ☐

2 Junho used to bite his nails. ☐

3 Junho feels great about not biting his nails. ☐

4 Junho doesn't like making his own cupcakes so much. ☐

Dear Junho,

In Sydney, it's fall in March. You talked about your changes in your email. Now, it's time to talk about my new changes.

These days, I'm into 3D printing. I printed two things with a 3D printer. One is a model of my dream car. If the traffic is heavy, it will change into a flying car. The other is a special cup for my grandfather. He can't hold his cup well because he's sick. My special cup has three handles, so it is easy to hold. My grandfather is very happy. By the way, I want to try your cupcakes some day, Junho.

Take care.

Best wishes,

Eric.

It's time to ~: ~할 때다
these days: 요즘에는
be into: ~에 빠져 있다
traffic: 교통
change into: ~로 변하다
handle: 손잡이
by the way: 그건 그렇고
take care: 잘 있어

확인문제

- 다음 문장이 본문의 내용과 일치하면 T, 일치하지 않으면 F를 쓰시오.

1 Eric wrote the email in March. ☐

2 Eric wants to talk about his new changes. ☐

3 Eric printed three things with a 3D printer. ☐

4 A flying car is Eric's dream car. ☐

5 Eric made the special cup for his grandmother. ☐

6 Eric's grandfather is healthy. ☐

● 우리말을 참고하여 빈칸에 알맞은 말을 쓰시오.

1 My friend Eric and I _____ _____ _____ _____ the vacation.

2 We _____ _____ _____ and _____ _____ our changes.

3 _____ Eric,

4 _____'s a beautiful _____ _____ Seoul.

5 _____ _____ _____ _____ was a great _____ for me.

6 I _____ two _____ _____ _____ the vacation.

7 _____ is my new hobby.

8 It's _____ cupcakes.

9 _____ my _____ cupcakes _____ a lot of fun.

10 _____ _____ _____ is _____ one of my bad habits.

11 In the past, I _____ _____ my nails.

12 Now I _____ _____.

13 I _____ _____ _____ the changes I _____.

14 _____ you _____ _____ _____ some changes, I'm sure you _____ _____ great _____ me.

15 I hope to _____ _____ you soon.

16 Your _____, Junho.

1 내 친구 Eric과 나는 방학 동안 흥미로운 변화가 있었다.

2 우리는 서로에게 이메일을 보냈고 우리의 변화에 관해 이야기했다.

3 안녕 Eric,

4 서울은 아름다운 봄이야.

5 지난 겨울 방학은 나에게 멋진 시간이었어.

6 나는 방학 동안 두 가지 개인적인 변화가 있었어.

7 하나는 나의 새로운 취미야.

8 그것은 컵케이크를 만드는 거야.

9 나만의 컵케이크를 만드는 것은 정말 재미있어.

10 나머지 다른 변화는 나의 나쁜 습관 중 하나를 없애는 거야.

11 예전에 나는 종종 손톱을 물어뜯곤 했어.

12 이제 나는 더 이상 그러지 않아.

13 나는 내가 만든 변화가 정말 기분 좋아.

14 만약 네가 변화하려고 노력한다면, 너도 나처럼 기분이 좋을 거라고 확신해.

15 곧 소식 전해 줘.

16 너의 친구 준호가

17 _____ Junho,

18 _____ Sydney, _____'s fall _____ March.

19 You talked _____ your _____ in your email.

20 Now, it's _____ _____ _____ _____ my new changes.

21 _____ _____, I'm _____ 3D printing.

22 I printed _____ _____ _____ a 3D printer.

23 _____ is a model of my _____ _____.

24 _____ the traffic _____ _____, it _____ _____ _____ a flying car.

25 _____ _____ is a special cup _____ my grandfather.

26 He can't _____ his cup _____ because he's _____.

27 My special cup has _____ _____, so it is easy _____ _____.

28 My grandfather is very _____.

29 _____ _____ _____, I want _____ _____ your cupcakes some day, Junho.

30 _____ _____.

31 Best _____, Eric.

---

17 안녕 준호,

18 시드니에서는 3월이 가을이야.

19 너는 이메일에서 너에게 일어난 변화들을 말해 주었지.

20 이제 나의 새로운 변화를 말해 줄 차례야.

21 요즈음, 나는 3D 프린팅에 빠져 있어.

22 나는 3D 프린터로 2가지를 인쇄했어.

23 하나는 나의 꿈의 자동차의 모형이야.

24 교통이 혼잡할 때, 그것은 날 수 있는 차로 바뀌어.

25 나머지 다른 하나는 우리 할아버지를 위한 특수 컵이야.

26 할아버지는 편찮으셔서 컵을 잘 들지 못하셔.

27 나의 특수 컵은 손잡이가 3개 있어서 들기 쉬워.

28 할아버지는 아주 행복해 하셔.

29 그건 그렇고, 너의 컵케이크를 언젠가 먹어 보고 싶다, 준호야.

30 잘 지내.

31 행운을 빌어, Eric

● 우리말을 참고하여 본문을 영작하시오.

1 내 친구 Eric과 나는 방학 동안 흥미로운 변화가 있었다.

➡ _____

2 우리는 서로에게 이메일을 보냈고 우리의 변화에 관해 이야기했다.

➡ _____

3 안녕 Eric,

➡ _____

4 서울은 아름다운 봄이야.

➡ _____

5 지난 겨울 방학은 나에게 멋진 시간이었어.

➡ _____

6 나는 방학 동안 두 가지 개인적인 변화가 있었어.

➡ _____

7 하나는 나의 새로운 취미야.

➡ _____

8 그것은 컵케이크를 만드는 거야.

➡ _____

9 나만의 컵케이크를 만드는 것은 정말 재미있어.

➡ _____

10 나머지 다른 변화는 나의 나쁜 습관 중 하나를 없애는 거야.

➡ _____

11 예전에 나는 종종 손톱을 물어뜯곤 했어.

➡ _____

12 이제 나는 더 이상 그러지 않아.

➡ _____

13 나는 내가 만든 변화가 정말 기분 좋아.

➡ _____

14 만약 네가 변화하려고 노력한다면, 너도 나처럼 기분이 좋을 거라고 확신해.

➡ _____

15 곧 소식 전해 줘.

➡ _____

16 너의 친구 준호가

➡ _____

17 안녕 준호,

➡ _____

18 시드니에서는 3월이 가을이야.

➡ _____

19 너는 이메일에서 너에게 일어난 변화들을 말해 주었지.

➡ _____

20 이제 나의 새로운 변화를 말해 줄 차례야.

➡ _____

21 요즈음, 나는 3D 프린팅에 빠져 있어.

➡ _____

22 나는 3D 프린터로 2가지를 인쇄했어.

➡ _____

23 하나는 나의 꿈의 자동차의 모형이야.

➡ _____

24 교통이 혼잡할 때, 그것은 날 수 있는 차로 바뀌어.

➡ _____

25 나머지 다른 하나는 우리 할아버지를 위한 특수 컵이야.

➡ _____

26 할아버지는 편찮으셔서 컵을 잘 들지 못하셔.

➡ _____

27 나의 특수 컵은 손잡이가 3개 있어서 들기 쉬워.

➡ _____

28 할아버지는 아주 행복해 하셔.

➡ _____

29 그건 그렇고, 너의 컵케이크를 언젠가 먹어 보고 싶다, 준호야.

➡ _____

30 잘 지내.

➡ _____

31 행운을 빌어, Eric.

➡ _____

[01~06] 다음 글을 읽고 물음에 답하시오.

My friend Eric and I made some interesting changes during the vacation. We emailed each other and talked about our changes.

Dear Eric,

(A)It's a beautiful spring in Seoul. The last winter vacation was a great time for me. I made two personal changes during the vacation. (B)[It / One] is my new hobby. It's making cupcakes. Making my own cupcakes (C)[is / are] a lot of fun. ⓐ_____ change is breaking one of my bad (D)[habit / habits]. In the past, I often bit my nails. Now I don't anymore. I feel great about (a)내가 만든 변화. If you try to make some changes, I'm sure you'll feel great like me. I hope to hear ⓑ_____ you soon.
Your friend, Junho.

서답형

01 빈칸 ⓐ에 알맞은 말을 쓰시오.

➡ _____

02 다음 중 빈칸 ⓑ에 들어갈 말과 같은 것은?

① She is thinking _____ taking a trip to Europe.
② Jerry called his father _____ his way home.
③ Are you interested _____ breaking your bad habit?
④ Listen _____ what others say carefully.
⑤ Where did you come _____?

서답형

03 밑줄 친 우리말 (a)를 영어로 쓰시오.

➡ _____

04 다음 중 밑줄 친 (A)와 쓰임이 같은 것끼리 바르게 묶은 것은?

Ⓐ It is getting dark outside. Let's go home.
Ⓑ It is four kilometers from the school to my house.
Ⓒ It is climbing up the tree.
Ⓓ It is important to always tell the truth to your friend.
Ⓔ It is eight o'clock already.

① Ⓐ, Ⓑ, Ⓒ
② Ⓒ, Ⓓ, Ⓔ
③ Ⓑ, Ⓓ, Ⓔ
④ Ⓐ, Ⓑ, Ⓔ
⑤ Ⓐ, Ⓒ, Ⓓ

중요

05 (B)~(D)에서 어법상 옳은 것끼리 바르게 짝지은 것은?

① It – is – habit
② It – are – habit
③ One – is – habit
④ One – is – habits
⑤ One – are – habits

06 위 글의 내용과 일치하지 않는 것은?

① The writer is Junho.
② The writer made two changes.
③ Changes were made during the vacation.
④ The writer and Eric didn't contact each other.
⑤ The writer wrote the email in spring.

[07~14] 다음 글을 읽고 물음에 답하시오.

Dear Junho,

In Sydney, it's fall in March. You talked about your changes in your email. Now, it's time to talk about my new changes. These days, I'm ⓐ_____ 3D printing. I printed two things with a 3D printer. One is a model of my dream car. If the traffic is heavy, it will change ⓑ_____ a (A)_____ car. The other is a special cup for my grandfather. He can't hold his cup well ⓒ_____ he's sick. My special cup has three handles, so ⓓit is easy to hold. My grandfather is very happy. ⓔ By the way, I want (B)_____ your cupcakes some day, Junho.

Take care.

Best wishes,

Eric.

07 다음 중 빈칸 ⓐ와 ⓑ에 공통으로 들어갈 말은?

① on ② about ③ into
④ by ⑤ from

08 다음 중 빈칸 ⓒ에 들어갈 말로 가장 적절한 것은?

① if ② so ③ because
④ when ⑤ although

서답형

09 주어진 단어를 어법에 맞게 빈칸 (A)와 (B)에 각각 쓰시오.

(fly / try)

➡ (A)_____ (B)_____

서답형

10 밑줄 친 ⓓ가 가리키는 것은?

➡ _____

11 다음 중 밑줄 친 ⓔ의 의미로 가장 적절한 것은?

① 집에 가는 길에 ② 그 길목에서
③ 그건 그렇고 ④ 길옆에서
⑤ 혹시

12 위 글의 내용과 일치하지 않는 것은?

① 준호의 편지에 대한 Eric의 답장이다.
② Eric은 3D 프린터로 꿈의 자동차 모형을 인쇄하였다.
③ Eric이 만든 컵은 손잡이가 3개 있다.
④ Eric이 만든 컵은 들기 쉽다.
⑤ Eric은 준호에게 컵케이크를 보내달라고 요청하고 있다.

13 다음 빈칸에 들어갈 말로 가장 적절한 것은?

According to the letter, it is thought that Junho's email was about _____.

① how he spent his time with his family
② some changes he made
③ how to make cupcakes
④ why he wanted to buy a 3D printer
⑤ changes in our environment

서답형

14 다음은 Eric이 자신의 컵을 소개하는 글이다. 위 글의 내용에 맞게 빈칸에 알맞은 말을 쓰시오.

This cup is very special. I made it for _____ _____. It has _____ _____. So it is easy to hold this _____.

➡ _____

[15~21] 다음 글을 읽고 물음에 답하시오.

My friend Eric and I made some ⓐ_____ changes during the vacation. We emailed each other and talked ⓑ_____ our changes.

Dear Eric,

It's a beautiful spring in Seoul. The last winter vacation was a great time for me. ① I made two personal changes during the vacation. ② One is my new hobby. ③ Making my own cupcakes is a lot of fun. ④ The other change is (A)_____. ⑤ In the past, I often bit my nails. Now I don't anymore. I feel great about the changes I made. If you try to make some changes, I'm sure you'll feel great like me. I hope (B) to hear from you soon.
Your friend, Junho.

15 ①~⑤ 중 주어진 문장이 들어가기에 가장 적절한 곳은?

It's making cupcakes.

①   ②   ③   ④   ⑤

16 빈칸 ⓐ와 ⓑ에 들어갈 말이 바르게 짝지어진 것은?

① interesting – in
② interested – with
③ interesting – about
④ interest – to
⑤ interested – into

서답형

17 다음 단어를 바르게 배열하여 빈칸 (A)를 채우시오. (하나의 단어를 어법에 맞게 변형하시오.)

habits / break / one / my / of / bad

➡ _____

18 다음 중 위 글을 읽고 답할 수 없는 것은?

① Who is Eric?
② To whom did Junho write the email?
③ How does Junho feel about making his own cupcakes?
④ Why did Junho bite his nails so much?
⑤ What is Junho's new hobby?

서답형

19 다음과 같이 풀이되는 단어를 위 글에서 찾아 쓰시오.

(1)

the hard covering at the end of a finger

➡ _____

(2)

the time before the present, and the things that have happened

➡ _____

서답형

20 위 글의 내용에 맞게 대화의 빈칸을 채우시오.

Amelia: Junho, how do you feel about the changes you made?

Junho: _____ _____ _____

➡ _____

21 다음 중 밑줄 친 (B)와 그 쓰임이 같은 것은?

① We will be glad to see you again.
② I decided to become a lawyer.
③ She felt sorry not to be honest with her friend.
④ Do you have a friend to trust?
⑤ Is there anyone to help you?

[22~26] 다음 글을 읽고 물음에 답하시오.

Dear, Junho,

In Sydney, it's fall in March. You talked about your changes in your email. Now, it's time (A)[talking / to talk] about my new changes. These days, ⓐI'm into 3D printing. I printed two things with a 3D printer. One is a model of my dream car. If the traffic is heavy, it will (B)[change / change into] a flying car. The other is a special cup for my grandfather. He can't hold his cup well because he's sick. My special cup has three handles, so it is easy (C)[holding / to hold]. My grandfather is very happy. By the way, I want to try your cupcakes some day, Junho.

Take care.

Best wishes,

Eric.

22 (A)~(C) 중 어법상 옳은 것끼리 바르게 짝지은 것은?

① talking – change – holding
② to talk – change into – holding
③ talking – change into – to hold
④ to talk – change into – to hold
⑤ talking – change – to hold

23 서답형 How many handles does Eric's cup have? Answer in English with a full sentence.

➡ _____

24 밑줄 친 ⓐ의 의미로 가장 적절한 것은?

① I look into a 3D printer.
② I would like to have a 3D printer.
③ I am interested in making a 3D printer.
④ I imagine 3D printing.
⑤ I am crazy about 3D printing.

25 서답형 주어진 어구를 사용하여 다음 물음에 12 단어로 이루어진 하나의 문장으로 답하시오.

Q: Why did Eric make a special cup for his grandfather? (wanted to help / because / hold)

➡ _____

_____

26 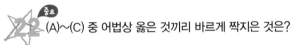 위 글의 내용과 일치하지 않는 것은?

① It is a letter written by Eric.
② Eric is writing about his new changes.
③ Eric printed two things with his 3D printer.
④ Eric's grandfather is sick.
⑤ Eric's grandfather doesn't like the special cup that much.

27 주어진 문장과 자연스럽게 이어지도록 (A)~(C)를 바르게 나열한 것은?

It's a beautiful spring in Seoul. The last winter vacation was a great time for me.

(A) If you try to make some changes, I'm sure you'll feel great like me. I really think so.
(B) The other change is breaking one of my bad habits. In the past, I often bit my nails. Now I don't anymore. I feel great about the changes I made.
(C) I made two personal changes during the vacation. One is my new hobby. It's making cupcakes. Making my own cupcakes is a lot of fun.

① (A)-(C)-(B)   ② (B)-(A)-(C)
③ (B)-(C)-(A)   ④ (C)-(A)-(B)
⑤ (C)-(B)-(A)

[01~08] 다음 글을 읽고 물음에 답하시오.

My friend Eric and I made some interesting changes during the vacation. (A)우리는 서로에게 이메일을 보냈다 and talked about our changes.

Dear Eric,
It's a beautiful spring in Seoul. The last winter vacation was a great time for me. I made two personal changes during the vacation. ⓐ_____ is my new hobby. It's making cupcakes. Making my own cupcakes is a lot of fun. ⓑ_____ change is breaking one of my bad habits. In the past, I often bit my nails. ⓒNow I don't anymore. I feel great about the changes I made. If you try to make some changes, I'm sure you'll feel great like me. I hope to hear from you soon.
Your friend, Junho.

01 밑줄 친 우리말 (A)를 영어로 쓰시오.

➡ _____

02 빈칸 ⓐ와 ⓑ에 알맞은 어구를 쓰시오.

➡ ⓐ_____ ⓑ_____

03 밑줄 친 ⓒ를 완전한 문장으로 쓰시오.

➡ _____

04 According to the passage, where does Junho live? Answer in English with a full sentence.

➡ _____

05 위 글의 내용에 맞게 대화의 빈칸을 채우시오.

Jenny: Junho, do you have a _____ _____ that you want to _____?
Junho: I had it before. But I broke it.

➡ _____

06 위 글의 내용에 맞게 대화의 빈칸에 알맞은 말을 쓰시오.

Julia: Junho, what are you doing?
Junho: I am _____ _____ _____ _____. It is my new hobby.
Julia: Is there _____ hobby?
Junho: Yes, there is.

➡ _____

07 위 글의 표현을 참고하여 다음 우리말을 영어로 쓰시오.

너의 나쁜 습관 중 하나를 없앤다면, 너는 기분이 좋을 거야.

➡ _____

08 괄호 안에 주어진 단어를 사용하여 다음 물음에 완전한 문장의 영어로 답하시오.

Q: Why does Junho say that the last winter vacation was a great time for him?
A: _____
_____ (because, vacation)

[09~17] 다음 글을 읽고 물음에 답하시오.

Dear Junho,

In Sydney, it's fall in March. You talked about your changes in your email. Now, it's time to talk about my new changes. These days, I'm into 3D printing. I printed two things with a 3D printer. One is a model of my dream car. ⓐIf the traffic will be heavy, it will change into a flying car. ⓑ나머지 다른 하나는 우리 할아버지를 위한 특수 컵이야. He can't hold his cup well because he's sick. ⓒ My special cup has three handles, so it is easy to hold. My grandfather is very happy. By the way, I want to try your cupcakes some day, Junho.

Take care.

Best wishes,

Eric.

09 다음은 Eric이 친구들에게 할 수 있는 말이다. 밑줄 친 우리말을 영어로 쓰시오.

> Eric: I made a special cup for my grandfather. 네가 이 컵을 들면, 너는 이 컵이 들기 쉽다는 것을 알게 될 거야.

➡ _____

10 Where and when did Eric write the letter? Answer in English with a full sentence.

➡ _____

11 밑줄 친 ⓐ에서 어법상 틀린 것을 바르게 고치고, 그렇게 고친 이유를 서술하시오.

➡ _____ ➡ _____

➡ 이유: _____

12 다음은 Eric이 만든 컵을 본 할아버지의 반응이다. 괄호 안에 주어진 단어를 어법에 맞게 고쳐 쓰고, 빈칸에 들어갈 말은 위 글에서 찾아 쓰시오.

> Grandfather: Eric, I (satisfy) this cup. I feel _____ .

➡ _____

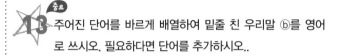

13 주어진 단어를 바르게 배열하여 밑줄 친 우리말 ⓑ를 영어로 쓰시오. 필요하다면 단어를 추가하시오..

> (my / other / cup / grandfather / a / is / special / for)

➡ _____

14 What is Eric into these days? Answer in English with a full sentence.

➡ _____

15 주어진 단어를 사용하여 밑줄 친 ⓒ와 같은 의미의 문장을 쓰시오.

> (because)

➡ _____

16 What do they talk about through email? Answer in English with a full sentence.

➡ _____

17 According to the passage, what can Junho make? Answer in English with a full sentence.

➡ _____

Real Life Communication - Step 2

A: You know what? I'm thinking of keeping a diary in English.
그거 아니?   동명사(전치사의 목적어)

B: Why did you decide to do that?
          결심하다   = keep a diary in English

A: It's because I want to be good at English writing.
     because+주어+동사   ~를 잘하다

B: That's great.

구문해설 • think of: ~에 대해 생각하다 • keep a diary: 일기를 쓰다 • decide: 결심하다

A: 그거 아니? 나는 영어로 일기를 쓸 생각이야.
B: 왜 그런 결심을 했어?
A: 왜냐하면 영어 쓰기를 잘하고 싶기 때문이야.
B: 멋지다.

My Writing Portfolio

Dear me,

You are very smart and funny. However, you still want to make two changes,
                                그러나   want의 목적어

don't you? One is to have more good friends. The other is to become healthier.
부가의문문   (둘 중에서) 하나는   나머지 다른 하나

Here are my tips for your wishes. If you are nicer to others and eat more
my tips에 수의 일치   조건의 부사절에서 현재시제로 미래를 나타냄 =other people

vegetables, you'll make these changes.

Love, Me

구문해설 • still: 아직, 여전히 • change: 변화 • healthier: 더 건강한 • tip: 조언 • wish: 소망

나에게

너는 매우 영리하고 재미있어. 하지만 너는 아직 두 가지 변화를 이루고 싶어 해, 그렇지 않니? 하나는 더 많은 좋은 친구를 사귀는 거야. 다른 하나는 더 건강해지는 거야. 여기 너의 소망을 위한 조언이 있어. 다른 사람들에게 더 친절하고 더 많은 채소를 먹는다면, 너는 이러한 변화들을 이룰 수 있을 거야.

사랑하는,

내가

Words in Action B

Bobo is my pet dog. She has two brothers. One is black. The other is white.
                          둘 중 첫 번째로 언급하는 것을 one   나머지 하나를 언급하는 것은 the other이다.

She has two toys. One is a ball. The other is a plastic duck. She has two habits.

One is watching TV. The other is sleeping on my chair.
      동명사(is의 보어)   동명사

구문해설 • pet: 애완동물 • plastic: 플라스틱 • habit: 습관

보보는 내 애완견이다. 그녀는 남동생이 둘 있다. 하나는 검정색이다. 다른 하나는 하얀색이다. 그녀는 장난감이 두 개 있다. 하나는 공이다. 다른 하나는 플라스틱 오리이다. 그녀는 두 가지 습관이 있다. 하나는 TV를 보는 것이다. 다른 하나는 내 의자 위에서 자는 것이다.

01 다음 우리말에 맞게 빈칸에 알맞은 말을 쓰시오.

(1) 그는 재즈 음악에 열중해 있다.

➡ He _____ _____ jazz music.

(2) 내가 집에 가는 길에 빵을 살게.

➡ I'll buy some bread _____ _____

_____ _____.

(3) 그녀는 아들한테 소식을 듣기를 기다리고 있어.

➡ She is waiting to _____ _____

her son.

02 다음 중 밑줄 친 부분의 뜻풀이가 바르지 않은 것은?

① The rumor is proved to be false.

사실의

② She made me laugh with a funny story.

재미있는

③ How was your summer vacation? 휴가

④ I'm not sure if I can make it, but I'll try.

시도하다

⑤ Hold the baby in your arms. 안다

03 다음 우리말을 주어진 단어를 이용하여 영작하시오.

(1) 나는 나의 나쁜 습관을 그만두기로 결심했다.

(decide, break)

➡ _____

(2) 나는 시험에 통과하기 위해 최선을 다할 것이

다. (do, pass, test)

➡ _____

(3) 그는 골프에 열중하고 있다. (playing, into)

➡ _____

04 다음 문장에 공통으로 들어갈 말을 고르시오.

• Did your dog _____ you?

• I'm hungry. Let's grab a _____.

• Tom has an itchy hand because of a

mosquito _____.

① eat   ② beat

③ bite   ④ catch

⑤ bend

05 다음 주어진 문장의 밑줄 친 kind와 같은 의미로 쓰인

것은?

What kind of music do you like?

① They didn't sell that kind of cake.

② My grandmother has a kind heart.

③ Somi is a very kind and helpful person.

④ Thank you for your kind comments.

⑤ Let's make a kind and safe society.

06 다음 대화의 빈칸에 들어갈 말로 어색한 것은?

A: What is your plan for this weekend,

Sejun?

B: _____

① I'm thinking of visiting my grandparents.

② I'm planning to play soccer with my

friends.

③ I'm going to have dinner with my uncles.

④ I have a plan to do my homework.

⑤ I planted trees in the garden.

[07~09] 다음 대화를 읽고 물음에 답하시오.

Brian: Julia, ⓐhow was your winter vacation?

Julia: It was great. (A)그거 아니? I took *muay thai* lessons ⓑfor the vacation.

Brian: That's ⓒamazing. I didn't know that you were ⓓinterested in *muay thai*.

Julia: Yes. It was really fun.

Brian: Really? I want ⓔto try it.

07 위 대화의 밑줄 친 (A)의 우리말을 3단어를 사용하여 영어로 쓰시오.

➡ _____

08 위 대화의 밑줄 친 ⓐ~ⓔ 중 어법상 어색한 것을 찾아 바르게 고치시오.

➡ _____

09 위 대화를 읽고 대답할 수 <u>없는</u> 것은?

① What did Julia learn during the winter vacation?

② How were *muay thai* lessons?

③ What was Julia interested in?

④ What does Brian want to try?

⑤ What class did Brian take during the winter vacation?

10 다음 대화가 자연스럽게 이어지도록 순서대로 배열하시오.

(A) That sounds great.

(B) We have some vegetables, but we don't have beef. I'll buy some for you on my way home.

(C) Do we have any vegetables at home? What about beef?

(D) I made *bulgogi* at school today. I'm thinking of cooking *bulgogi* for dinner.

➡ _____

[11~13] 다음 대화를 읽고 물음에 답하시오.

Jane: Minsu, (A)Sujin and I are thinking of starting a club.

Minsu: Really? What kind of club?

Jane: We want to learn about stars and planets. So, we're thinking of starting a space science club.

Minsu: Sounds good. How often are you going to meet?

Jane: Maybe once a week.

Minsu: I see. Where will you meet?

Jane: In Room 101. Minsu, do you want to join our club?

Minsu: Yes, I'm interested in space, too.

11 위 대화에서 다음의 영영풀이가 가리키는 말을 찾아 쓰시오.

a large, round object in space that travels around a star

➡ _____

12 밑줄 친 (A)와 바꾸어 쓸 수 <u>없는</u> 것은?

① Sujin and I are planning to start a club.

② Sujin and I are going to start a club.

③ Sujin and I are into starting a club.

④ Sujin and I are considering starting a club.

⑤ Sujin and I will start a club.

13 위 대화의 내용과 일치하지 <u>않는</u> 것은?

① Sujin and Jane are thinking of starting a club.

② Jane and Sujin are interested in learning about stars and planets.

③ Jane and Sujin are planning to meet once a month.

④ The members of the space science club will meet in Room 101.

⑤ Minsu wants to join the space science club.

[14~15] 다음 대화를 읽고 물음에 답하시오.

Jimin: You know what, Tim? Mr. Smith is my homeroom teacher this year.

Tim: That's great, Jimin. His science class last year was a lot of fun.

Jimin: Who's your homeroom teacher this year?

Tim: It's Ms. Kim. She's a new teacher.

Jimin: What does she teach?

Tim: She teaches art.

14 According to Tim, how was Mr. Smith's class last year?

➡ _____

15 What are Tim and Jimin going to learn from the new teacher?

➡ _____

Grammar

16 다음 빈칸에 가장 적절한 것은?

> Hawaii is a popular tourist destination.
> Italy is _____ popular tourist destination.

① other
② the other
③ another
④ others
⑤ one

17 다음 중 어법상 바르지 <u>않은</u> 것은?

> ①Will you ②give this message ③to her ④if Susan ⑤will come back?

①　　②　　③　　④　　⑤

18 다음 중 밑줄 친 부분을 대신하여 쓸 수 있는 것은?

> Some of the birds are flying. Other birds are sitting on a fence.

① Another
② The other
③ The others
④ Others
⑤ Other

19 주어진 단어를 이용하여 다음 우리말을 영어로 쓰시오.

> 내게는 세 명의 외국인 친구가 있다. 한 명은 일본에서 왔고, 다른 두 명은 프랑스에서 왔다.
> (have / foreign / from)

➡ _____
_____

20 다음 중 if의 쓰임이 같은 것끼리 바르게 묶인 것은?

> ⓐ Robert will be here on time if he doesn't miss the bus.
> ⓑ If you don't mind, I will pay for it.
> ⓒ I wonder if there is some food in the refrigerator.
> ⓓ If you need lots of paper, I will give you some.
> ⓔ How can I know if someone is my true friend or not?

① ⓐⓑⓒ, ⓓⓔ
② ⓐⓑⓓ, ⓒⓔ
③ ⓐⓒⓓ, ⓑⓔ
④ ⓐⓓⓔ, ⓑⓒ
⑤ ⓐⓑⓒⓓⓔ

21 다음 중 어법상 바르지 <u>않은</u> 것은?

> ①Some of ②his books ③are novels and　④others ⑤are all comics.

22 주어진 단어를 바르게 배열하여 다음 우리말을 영어로 쓰시오.

> 최선을 다하지 않는다면, 너는 아무것도 성취할 수 없을 거야. (unless로 시작할 것)
> (anything / unless / not / achieve / you / will / you / your / do / best)

➡ _____
_____

23 다음 대화의 빈칸에 들어갈 말로 가장 적절한 것은?

> A: What are your two daughters doing now?
> B: _____

① One is sleeping, and another is listening to music.
② A daughter is cleaning her room, and the others is hanging out with her friend.
③ One is answering a phone, and other is doing her homework.
④ One is baking bread, and one is playing a computer game.
⑤ One is watching TV, and the other is reading a book.

24 주어진 어구를 이용하여 다음 우리말을 두 개의 영어 문장으로 쓰시오. (부사절을 주절의 앞에 쓸 것)

> 따뜻한 옷을 입지 않으면, 너는 감기에 걸릴 거야. (wear / clothes / catch a cold)

➡ _____
➡ _____

25 다음 빈칸에 들어갈 말을 바르게 짝지은 것은?

> There are three balls in the box. _____ is blue. _____ is red. _____ is gray.

① It – The other – Other
② It – The other – The other
③ One – Another - Another
④ One – Another – The other
⑤ One – Other – The other

26 주어진 단어를 어법에 맞게 활용하여 다음 우리말을 영어로 쓰시오. (if로 시작할 것)

> 네가 매일 조깅하러 가면, 너는 더 건강해 질 거야. (go / jog / get / healthy)

➡ _____

Reading

[27~30] 다음 글을 읽고 물음에 답하시오.

My friend Eric and I made some interesting changes ⓐ_____ the vacation. We emailed ① each other and talked about our changes.

Dear Eric,
It's a beautiful spring ②in Seoul. The last winter vacation was a great time for me. I made ⓑ_____ personal changes during the vacation. One is my new hobby. It's making cupcakes. Making my own cupcakes is a lot of fun. ③The other is breaking one of my bad habits. In the past, I often ④bite my nails. Now I don't ⑤anymore. I feel great about the changes I made. ⓒ만약 네가 변화하려고 노력한다면, I'm sure you'll feel great like me. I hope to hear from you soon.
Your friend, Junho.

27 다음 중 빈칸 ⓐ에 들어갈 말과 같은 것은?

① I'm going away _____ a few days.
② We only saw her once _____ our stay in Korea.
③ I've studied English _____ three hours.
④ They went down to the sea _____ a day.
⑤ Helen stayed there _____ a couple of weeks.

28 빈칸 ⓑ에 들어갈 말로 가장 적절한 것은?

① a great deal of   ② a number of
③ a couple of   ④ a lot of
⑤ so much

29 주어진 단어를 바르게 배열하여 밑줄 친 ⓒ를 영어로 옮기시오.

(changes / if / make / you / some / try / to)

➡ _____

30 밑줄 친 ①~⑤ 중 어법상 바르지 <u>않은</u> 것은?

①   ②   ③   ④   ⑤

[31~34] 다음 글을 읽고, 물음에 답하시오.

Dear Junho,

In Sydney, it's fall in March. You talked about your changes in your email. Now, it's time to talk about my new changes. These days, I'm into 3D printing. I printed two things with a 3D printer. One is a model of my dream car. If the traffic is heavy, it will change into a flying car. The other is a special cup for my grandfather. He can't hold his cup well because he's sick. My special cup has three handles, so it is easy to hold. My grandfather is very happy. By the way, I want to try your cupcakes some day, Junho.

Take care.

Best wishes,

Eric.

31 다음 중 위 글을 읽고 답할 수 <u>없는</u> 것은?

① What did Junho talk about in his email?
② What season is it in Sydney in March?
③ What does Eric want to talk about in his email?
④ When does Eric's dream car change into a flying car?
⑤ Why is Eric's grandfather sick?

32 다음 빈칸에 해당하는 단어를 위 글에서 찾아 쓰시오.

A _____ is the part that is designed especially to be grasped by the hand.

➡ _____

33 위 글의 내용에 맞게 빈칸에 알맞은 말을 쓰시오.

Eric lives in _____. He is interested _____ _____ _____.

➡ _____

34 Write the reason why Eric's special cup is easy to hold. Use the word 'because.'

➡ _____

[01~02] 다음 대화를 읽고 물음에 답하시오.

Alex: Mom, I made *bulgogi* at school today. I'm thinking of cooking *bulgogi* for dinner.
Mom: That sounds great, Alex.
Alex: Do we have any vegetables at home, Mom? What about beef?
Mom: We have some vegetables, but we don't have beef. I'll buy some for you on my way home.
Alex: Great.

출제율 90%

01 위 대화의 표현을 사용하여 다음 주어진 문장을 영작하시오.

나는 도서관에 가는 길에 Mike를 만났다.

➡ _____

출제율 95%

02 위 대화의 내용과 일치하지 <u>않는</u> 것은?

① Alex is planning to make *bulgogi* for dinner.
② Alex needs some vegetables and beef to make *bulgogi*.
③ Alex has some vegetables at home.
④ Alex's mom is thinking of buying some beef for Alex.
⑤ Alex and his mom are talking in the kitchen together.

[03~05] 다음 대화를 읽고 물음에 답하시오.

Emily: You know what, Junsu? I'm thinking of taking a painting class.
Junsu: Really? Why did you decide to take a painting class, Emily?
Emily: Because I want to go to an art high school.
Junsu: Are you thinking of becoming an artist in the future?

Emily: I hope so. I'm interested in painting pictures.
Junsu: That's great. (A)_____
Emily: Thanks. I'll do my best.

출제율 100%

03 위 대화의 빈칸 (A)에 들어갈 말을 〈보기〉에 주어진 단어를 배열하여 완성하시오.

┌─ 보기 ─┐
true / hope / your / I / wish / comes
└────────┘

➡ _____

출제율 86%

04 What does Emily want to be in the future?

➡ _____

출제율 90%

05 What is Emily planning to do to go to an art high school?

➡ _____

[06~07] 다음 대화를 읽고 물음에 답하시오.

A: You know what? (A)나는 영어로 일기를 쓸 생각이야. (think, keep)
B: Why did you (B)decide to do that?
A: It's because I want to be good at English writing.
B: That's great.

출제율 90%

06 위 대화의 (A)를 주어진 단어를 이용하여 영작하시오.

➡ _____

출제율 95%

07 위 대화의 밑줄 친 (B)와 바꾸어 쓸 수 있는 것은?

① determine   ② refuse
③ postpone   ④ delay
⑤ bite

[08~09] 다음 대화를 읽고 물음에 답하시오.

Sue: You know what? Jenny's family is going to move to Japan.

Jack: Is that right? Jenny didn't tell me about it.

Sue: She learned about it just last week and she's very upset now.

Jack: I can understand her feelings. I am going to miss her so much.

Sue: (A)Me, too. She said she would keep in touch with us.

08 위 대화의 밑줄 친 (A)와 바꾸어 쓸 수 있는 것은?

① So do I.
② So am I.
③ Nether do I.
④ Neither am I.
⑤ Nether did I.

09 위 대화의 내용과 일치하지 않는 것은?

① Jenny의 가족이 일본으로 이민을 갈 예정이다.
② Jenny는 Jack에게 이민 가는 것에 대해 이야기하지 않았다.
③ Jenny는 지금 Jack에게 매우 화가 나 있다.
④ Jenny는 일본에서도 Sue와 Jack에게 연락할 것이다.
⑤ Jack은 Jenny의 심정을 이해한다.

10 다음 대화가 자연스럽게 이어지도록 순서대로 배열하시오.

(A) Really? I want to try it.
(B) Yes. It was really fun.
(C) That's amazing. I didn't know that you were interested in *muay thai*.
(D) How was your winter vacation?
(E) It was great. You know what? I took *muay thai* lessons during the vacation.

➡ _____

11 다음 빈칸에 가장 적절한 것은?

This hat is not good for me. Show me _____.

① other one
② the others
③ another
④ others
⑤ one

12 다음 문장의 빈칸에 들어갈 말로 가장 적절한 것은?

_____ into reading, there will be many interesting books you can borrow anytime.

① When you will be
② If you are
③ Though you are
④ Because you were
⑤ If you will be

13 빈칸에 들어갈 말이 바르게 짝지어진 것은?

- Cindy invited five friends to her party. But only two of them came. _____ didn't came.
- There are many students in the classroom. Some study Korean, _____ study English.

① The other – other
② Others – others
③ The others – the others
④ The other – others
⑤ The others – others

14 주어진 단어를 이용하여 다음 빈칸에 알맞은 말을 쓰시오. *출제율 90%*

> lend / pay

> A: I have to buy some chocolate for Valentine's Day. But I am short of money.
> B: How much?
> A: About ten dollars. If you _____ _____ ten dollars, I _____ _____ you back tomorrow.

➡ _____

15 주어진 단어를 이용하여 각 빈칸에 적절한 문장을 쓰시오. *출제율 85%*

> • There are three colors that I really like.
> • _____ (blue).
> • _____ (hot pink).
> • _____ (yellow).

➡ _____ ➡ _____
➡ _____

16 다음 우리말을 영어로 바르게 옮긴 것은? *출제율 90%*

> 내가 그것들 중 하나를 사용하면, 네가 나머지 하나를 쓸 거니?

① If I use one of them, do you use the other?
② If I use one, will you use the others?
③ If I use one of them, will you use the other?
④ If I use one of them, do you use others?
⑤ If I use one, will you use another?

[17~20] 다음 글을 읽고 물음에 답하시오.

My friend Eric and I made some ①interesting changes during the vacation. We emailed each ⓐ_____ and talked about our changes.

Dear Eric,
It's a beautiful spring in Seoul. The last winter vacation was ②a great time for me. I made two personal changes during the vacation. One is my new hobby. It's ⓑ_____ cupcakes. ⓒ_____ my own cupcakes is ③a lot of fun. The other change is ⓓ_____ one of my bad habits. In the past, I often bit my nails. Now I ④am not anymore. I feel great about the changes I made. If you try to make some changes, I'm sure you ⑤will feel great like me. I hope to hear from you soon.
Your friend, Junho.

17 다음 중 빈칸 ⓐ에 들어갈 말과 같은 것은? *출제율 95%*

① Can you show me _____ color of this scarf?
② There are two people. One is sitting, and _____ is cleaning.
③ Some friends want to eat pizza, and _____ friends want to eat noodle.
④ One of my three dolls is new, and _____ are a little old.
⑤ Some people have brown hair, but _____ have black hair.

18 주어진 동사를 빈칸 ⓑ~ⓓ에 문맥과 어법에 맞게 쓰시오. *출제율 90%*

> (make / break)

➡ ⓑ _____ ⓒ _____
ⓓ _____

19 ①~⑤ 중 어법상 어색한 것을 골라 바르게 고치시오.

＿＿＿＿＿＿＿ ➡ ＿＿＿＿＿＿＿

20 위 글의 내용과 일치하지 않는 것은?

① Junho made personal changes during the winter vacation.

② Eric is Junho's friend.

③ Junho wrote a letter to Eric in winter.

④ Junho can make his own cupcakes.

⑤ Junho used to bite his nails.

[21~25] 다음 글을 읽고, 물음에 답하시오.

Dear Junho,

In Sydney, it's fall in March. You talked about your changes in your email. Now, it's time ①to talk about my new changes. These days, I'm into 3D printing. I printed two things ②with a 3D printer. One is a model of my dream car. If the traffic is (A)[light / heavy], it will change into a flying car. ③The others is a (B)[common / special] cup for my grandfather. He can't hold his cup well (C) [because / unless] he's sick. My special cup has three handles, so it is easy ④to hold. My grandfather is very happy. ⑤By the way, I want to try your cupcakes some day, Junho.

Take care.

Best wishes,

Eric.

21 ①~⑤ 중 어법상 바르지 않은 것은?

①　　②　　③　　④　　⑤

22 (A)~(C)에서 글의 흐름상 적절한 것끼리 바르게 묶인 것은?

① light – common – because

② heavy – common – unless

③ light – special – because

④ heavy – special – because

⑤ light – special – unless

23 What did Eric print with a 3D printer? Answer in English with a full sentence.

➡ ＿＿＿＿＿＿＿＿＿＿＿＿＿＿＿

＿＿＿＿＿＿＿＿＿＿＿＿＿＿＿＿

24 According to the passage, what does Eric want to try some day? Answer in English with a full sentence.

➡ ＿＿＿＿＿＿＿＿＿＿＿＿＿＿＿

25 위 글의 내용으로 보아 대답할 수 없는 질문은?

① What did Junho talk about in his email?

② What is Eric talking about?

③ What is Eric interested in now?

④ What is Eric print with a 3D printer?

⑤ When will Eric eat Junho's cupcakes?

[01~03] 다음 대화를 읽고 물음에 답하시오.

> **Alex:** Mom, I made *bulgogi* at school today. (A)오늘 저녁으로 불고기를 요리할 생각이에요. (think, *bulgogi*, cook)
>
> **Mom:** That sounds great, Alex.
>
> **Alex:** Do we have any vegetables at home, Mom? What about beef?
>
> **Mom:** We have some vegetables, but we don't have beef. I'll buy some for you on my way home.
>
> **Alex:** Great.

01 위 대화의 (A)의 우리말을 주어진 표현을 이용하여 영작하시오.

➡ _____

02 What does Alex need to cook *bulgogi*?

➡ _____

03 What is Alex's mom going to do for Alex?

➡ _____

04 괄호 안에 주어진 어구를 이용하여 다음 대화를 완성하시오.

> **A:** Do you see the two people in the kitchen? What are they doing?
>
> **B:** (making food / washing the dishes)

➡ _____

05 두 개의 문장을 연결하여 자연스러운 하나의 문장으로 만드시오.

> • You need it.
> • You want her to help you.
> • Your alarm clock is out of order.

> • She will help you.
> • You can have it.
> • I will buy you a new one.

➡ _____

➡ _____

➡ _____

06 주어진 문장과 같은 의미의 문장을 두 개 쓰시오.

> Listen carefully, or you won't know what to do.

➡ _____

➡ _____

07 다음 빈칸에 알맞은 말을 쓰시오.

> I have three cats. _____ has blue eyes. _____ have yellow eyes.

➡ _____

08 괄호 안에 주어진 단어를 어법에 맞게 쓰시오.

> A: If you (finish) your homework early, what (do, you)?
> B: I (clean) my room if I (finish) my homework early.

➡ _____

[09~11] 다음 글을 읽고 물음에 답하시오.

Dear Eric,

It's a beautiful spring in Seoul. The last winter vacation was a great time for me. I made two <u>person</u> changes during the vacation. One is my new hobby. It's making cupcakes. Making my own cupcakes is a lot of fun. The other change is breaking one of my bad habits. In the past, I often bit my nails. Now I don't anymore. I feel great about the changes I made. If you try to make some changes, I'm sure you'll feel great like me. I hope to hear from you soon.

Your friend, Junho.

09 위 글의 밑줄 친 person을 알맞은 형으로 고치시오.

➡ _____

10 적절한 대명사를 이용하여 다음 물음에 답하시오.

> Q: How does Junho feel about the changes he made?

➡ _____

11 위 글의 내용을 참고하여 대화의 빈칸을 알맞게 채우시오.

> Jason: How did you spend your last winter vacation?
> Junho: I spent my vacation _____ two personal changes.
> Jason: Oh, really? What was that?
> Junho: _____ is making cupcakes and _____ _____ is _____ my bad habit.
> Jason: That sounds great.

➡ _____

[12~13] 다음 글을 읽고 물음에 답하시오.

Dear Junho,

In Sydney, it's fall in March. You talked about your changes in your email. Now, it's time to talk about my new changes. These days, I'm into 3D printing. I printed two things with a 3D printer. One is a model of my dream car. (A)<u>교통이 혼잡하면, 그것은 날 수 있는 차로 바뀌어.</u> The other is a special cup for my grandfather. He can't hold his cup well because he's sick. My special cup has three handles, so it is easy to hold. My grandfather is very happy. By the way, I want to try your cupcakes some day, Junho.

Take care.

Best wishes,

Eric.

12 주어진 단어를 이용하여 밑줄 친 우리말 (A)를 영어로 쓰시오.

> (if / heavy / change)

➡ _____

13 위 글의 내용에 맞게 다음 물음에 완전한 문장의 영어로 답하시오.

> Q: How does Eric's cup look?

➡ _____

01 다음 대화의 내용과 일치하도록 Jack의 일기를 완성하시오.

> **Sue:** You know what? Jenny's family is going to move to Japan.
>
> **Jack:** Is that right? Jenny didn't tell me about it.
>
> **Sue:** She learned about it just last week and she's very upset now.
>
> **Jack:** I can understand her feelings. I am going to miss her so much.
>
> **Sue::** Me, too. She said she would keep in touch with us.

> Monday, April 1st, 2019
>
> Today, I heard that (A)_____. I was so surprised because Jenny did not tell me about it at all. Sue said that (B)_____ because her family didn't tell her about it until last week. I understood how she felt. Anyway, I'll miss her so much and (C)_____ with her.

02 다음 <보기>와 같이 두 가지 사물이나 사람을 설명하는 문장을 쓰시오.

> ═══ 보기 ═══
>
> There are two people at the table. One is a man. The other is a woman.

(1) _____

(2) _____

(3) _____

(4) _____

(5) _____

03 다음 단어를 이용하여 <보기>와 같이 내일 계획을 쓰시오.

> ═══ 보기 ═══
>
> If it is cloudy tomorrow, I will cancel my appointment.
> sunny   windy   rainy   hot

(1) _____

(2) _____

(3) _____

(4) _____

단원별 모의고사

1 다음 짝지어진 단어의 관계가 같도록 빈칸에 알맞은 말을 쓰시오.

> clean : dirty = _____ : true

2 다음 영영풀이에 해당하는 말을 고르시오.

> a part that is designed especially to be grasped by the hand

① barrier
② handle
③ hold
④ grip
⑤ container

3 다음 주어진 우리말과 일치하도록 빈칸을 완성하시오.

(1) 그들이 무엇이라 이야기하든 그것은 진실이다.
➡ It is the _____ no matter what they say.

(2) 손톱은 네게 건강에 관한 많은 것을 이야기해 줄 수 있다.
➡ The _____ can tell you many things about your health.

(3) 제가 개인적인 의견을 드려도 될까요?
➡ Can I give you my _____ opinion?

4 다음 문장의 빈칸에 들어갈 말을 보기에서 골라 알맞은 형태로 쓰시오.

> ┤ 보기 ├
> break a bad habit / come true / not
> ~ anymore / take a class

(1) I believe your dreams _____ _____.
(2) I decided to _____ a yoga _____.
(3) They are _____ children _____.
(4) She started to keep a diary to _____
_____ _____ _____.

[05~08] 다음 대화를 읽고 물음에 답하시오.

Emily: You know (A)[what / why], Junsu? (a) <u>나는 미술 수업을 들을 생각이야.</u>

Junsu: Really? Why did you decide to take a painting class, Emily?

Emily: (B)[Because of / Because] I want to go to an art high school.

Junsu: Are you thinking of becoming an (C)_____ in the future?

Emily: I hope so. I'm (D)[interested / interesting] in painting pictures.

Junsu: That's great. I hope your wish comes true.

Emily: Thanks. I'll do my best.

5 위 대화의 괄호 (A), (B) 및 (D)에 들어갈 말로 바르게 짝지어진 것은?

	(A)	(B)	(D)
①	what	Because of	interested
②	what	Because	interested
③	what	Because of	interesting
④	why	Because	interesting
⑤	why	Because of	interesting

6 위 대화의 빈칸 (C)에 다음 영영 풀이가 가리키는 말을 쓰시오.

> a person who creates works of art, especially paintings or drawings

➡ _____

7 위 대화의 밑줄 친 (a)의 우리말을 영작하시오.

➡ _____

08 위 대화의 내용과 일치하지 <u>않는</u> 것은?

① Emily는 미술 수업을 들으려고 생각 중이다.
② Emily는 예술 고등학교에 가고 싶어 한다.
③ Emily는 그림 그리는 것에 관심이 있다.
④ Junsu는 Emily가 최선을 다하기를 바란다.
⑤ Emily는 미래에 미술가가 되기를 희망한다.

[09~10] 다음 대화를 읽고 물음에 답하시오.

Jane: Minsu, Sujin and I are thinking of starting a club.
Minsu: Really? What kind of club?
Jane: We want to learn about stars and planets. So, we're thinking of starting a space science club.
Minsu: Sounds good. How often are you going to meet?
Jane: Maybe once a week.
Minsu: I see. Where will you meet?
Jane: In Room 101. Minsu, do you want to join our club?
Minsu: Yes, ⓐ<u>나도 우주에 관심이 있어</u>.

09 위 대화의 밑줄 친 ⓐ의 우리말을 영작하시오.

➡ _____

10 How often are the members of the space science club going to meet?

➡ _____

[11~12] 다음 대화를 읽고, 물음에 답하시오.

Sue: (A) You know what? Jenny's family is going to move to Japan.
Jack (B) Is that right? Jenny didn't tell me about it.
Sue: (C) She learned about it just last week and she's very upset now.

Jack: (D) I am going to miss her so much.
Sue: (E) Me, too. She said she would keep in touch with us.

11 위 대화의 (A)~(E) 중 주어진 문장이 들어가기에 가장 적절한 곳은?

I can understand her feelings.

① (A)   ② (B)   ③ (C)   ④ (D)   ⑤ (E)

12 위 대화를 통해 대답할 수 <u>없는</u> 것은?

① Why is Jenny upset now?
② Where is Jenny's family going to move?
③ When did Jenny learn about her move?
④ Who will keep in touch with Jenny?
⑤ Why does Jenny's family want to move?

13 다음 중 어법상 바르지 <u>않은</u> 것은?

① There were two pears on the table, and one is here. Where is the other?
② Unless you don't use soap, your clothes won't get clean.
③ I'm not sure if they will want me to teach them.
④ If you wake up early, will you wake me up?
⑤ A student left alone. The other students went home.

14 다음 빈칸에 가장 적절한 것은?

> I have two candy bars. I want only one of them. Would you like _____ ?

① other one
② another one
③ the other one
④ the others
⑤ others

15 주어진 단어를 사용하여 다음 우리말을 영어로 쓰시오.

> Kevin은 나머지 다른 소년들과는 달라요.
> (different from)

➡ _____

16 주어진 어구를 바르게 배열하여 다음 우리말을 영어로 쓰시오. (하나의 단어를 두 번 쓸 것)

> 만약 네가 택시를 탄다면, 10분밖에 안 걸릴 거야.
> (10 minutes / if / only / you / take / will / it / a taxi)

➡ _____

17 다음 중 어법상 바르지 않은 것은?

> Emily bought two dresses. ①One is red, and ②another is blue. She really ③likes the dresses, so she wants ④to buy ⑤ another one.

[18~21] 다음 글을 읽고 물음에 답하시오.

> Dear Eric,
> It's a beautiful spring in Seoul. The last winter vacation was a great time for me. I made two personal changes during the vacation. One is my new hobby. It's ⓐmaking cupcakes. Making my own cupcakes is a lot of fun. ⓑ The other is breaking one of my bad habits. In the past, I often bit my nails. Now I don't anymore. I feel great about the changes I made. If you try to make some changes, I'm sure you'll feel great like me. I hope to hear from you soon.
> Your friend, Junho.

18 밑줄 친 ⓐ와 쓰임이 다른 것은?

① Computers play an important role in making films.
② By making conversation, people become friends.
③ The girl is making a box.
④ My goal is making a cake for her birthday present.
⑤ I want you to stop making trouble now.

19 위 글을 읽고 답할 수 없는 것은?

① How did Junho spend his last winter vacation?
② When did Junho write the letter?
③ How many changes did Junho make?
④ What did Junho use to bite?
⑤ How does Junho feel about Eric?

20 밑줄 친 ⓑ가 의미하는 것을 구체적으로 쓰시오.

➡ _____

21 위 글의 내용에 맞게 빈칸에 알맞은 말을 쓰시오.

In the email, Junho is mainly talking about _____ _____ _____ _____.

[22~25] 다음 글을 읽고 물음에 답하시오.

Dear Junho,
In Sydney, it's fall in March. You talked about your changes in your email. Now, it's time ⓐ_____ about my new changes. These days, I'm into 3D printing. I printed two things with a 3D printer. One is a model of my dream car. If the traffic is heavy, it will change into a ⓑ_____ car. The other is a special cup for my grandfather. He can't hold his cup well ⓒ_____ he's sick. My special cup has three handles, so it is easy to hold. My grandfather is very happy. By the way, I want to ⓓtry your cupcakes some day, Junho.
Take care.
Best wishes,
Eric.

22 주어진 동사를 어법에 맞게 빈칸 ⓐ와 ⓑ에 각각 쓰시오.

(talk / fly)

➡ ⓐ: _____ ⓑ: _____

23 다음 중 빈칸 ⓒ에 들어갈 말과 같은 말이 들어가는 것은?

① Some people like juice, _____ others don't.
② He is quite strong _____ he is old.
③ I wonder _____ he is at home.
④ You will miss the bus _____ you walk more quickly.
⑤ I couldn't sleep last night _____ I was so afraid.

24 다음 중 밑줄 친 ⓓ의 의미로 가장 적절한 것은?

① test   ② taste   ③ wear
④ see   ⑤ attempt

25 다음 중 위 글의 내용과 일치하는 것의 개수는?

ⓐ Junho lives in Sydney.
ⓑ Eric wrote the email in fall.
ⓒ Eric wrote about 3D printing.
ⓓ Eric bought a car.
ⓔ Junho talked about his cupcakes in his email.

① 1개   ② 2개   ③ 3개
④ 4개   ⑤ 5개

Lesson 2

Better Safe Than Sorry

 의사소통 기능

- 걱정 표현하기
  I'm worried about my leg.

- 충고하기
  You should clean your room.

 언어 형식

- 의문사＋to부정사
  I don't know **what to do**.

- 관계대명사
  Here are some tips **which** can be helpful.

교과서
Words & Expressions

Key Words

- **amazing** [əméiziŋ] 형 놀라운
- **avoid** [əvɔ́id] 동 방지하다, 막다, 피하다
- **break** [breik] 동 깨다, 부수다, 부서지다
- **by** [bai] 전 ~까지
- **cover** [kʌ́vər] 동 씌우다, 덮다
- **dangerous** [déindʒərəs] 형 위험한
- **decide** [disáid] 동 결정하다, 결심하다
- **disaster** [dizǽstər] 명 재난, 재해
- **earthquake** [ə́ːrθkweik] 명 지진
- **elevator** [éləvèitər] 명 승강기
- **empty** [émpti] 형 비어 있는, 빈
- **escape** [iskéip] 동 탈출하다
- **fall** [fɔːl] 동 넘어지다
- **floor** [flɔːr] 명 바닥, 마루
- **follow** [fálou] 동 따르다, 따라가다
- **forget** [fərgét] 동 잊어버리다
- **hurt** [həːrt] 동 다치게 하다, 아프게 하다
- **injury** [índʒəri] 명 상처, 부상
- **knife** [naif] 명 칼
- **low** [lou] 형 낮은
- **medicine** [médisn] 명 약
- **might** [mait] 조 ~할 수 있다
- **natural disaster** 자연 재해

- **prepare** [pripέər] 동 준비하다, 대비하다
- **pole** [poul] 명 기둥, 장대
- **program** [próugræm] 명 (방송) 프로그램
- **protect** [prətékt] 동 보호하다
- **rule** [ruːl] 명 법칙, 규칙
- **safety** [séifti] 명 안전
- **scary** [skɛ́əri] 형 두려운, 무서운
- **serious** [síəriəs] 형 심각한
- **shake** [ʃeik] 명 흔들림, 떨림 동 흔들다
- **situation** [sìtʃuéiʃən] 명 상황
- **slip** [slip] 동 미끄러지다
- **slippery** [slípəri] 형 미끄러운
- **solve** [salv] 동 해결하다
- **sore** [sɔːr] 형 아픈
- **space** [speis] 명 공간
- **stair** [stɛər] 명 계단
- **strange** [streindʒ] 형 이상한, 낯선
- **strike** [straik] 동 발생하다
- **survive** [sərváiv] 동 살아남다, 생존하다
- **throat** [θrout] 명 목구멍
- **wet** [wet] 형 젖은
- **wipe** [waip] 동 닦다
- **worry** [wə́ːri] 명 걱정, 근심 동 걱정하다

Key Expressions

- **a little** 약간, 좀
- **be worried about** ~에 대해 걱정하다
- **feel better** (기분이) 나아지다
- **get out of** (~에서) 나가다, 떠나다
- **hold on to** ~을 꼭 잡다
- **keep ~ in mind** ~을 기억하다

- **one by one** 하나씩, 차례차례
- **stay away from** ~에서 떨어져 있다
- **take a rest** 휴식을 취하다
- **take cover** 숨다
- **these days** 요즘
- **Why don't you ~?** ~하는 것이 어때?

Word Power

※ 서로 반대되는 뜻을 가진 어휘

- **empty** 비어 있는 ↔ **full** 가득 찬
- **prepared** 준비된 ↔ **unprepared** 준비되지 않은
- **low** 낮은 ↔ **high** 높은
- **wet** 젖은 ↔ **dry** 건조한

- **forget** 잊어버리다 ↔ **remember** 기억하다
- **cover** 덮다, 씌우다 ↔ **uncover** 덮개를 벗기다
- **safe** 안전한 ↔ **dangerous** 위험한
- **strange** 낯선 ↔ **familiar** 친근한, 친숙한

※ 자연 재해를 가리키는 어휘

- **earthquake** 지진
- **flood** 홍수
- **hurricane** 허리케인
- **drought** 가뭄

- **storm** 폭풍
- **typhoon** 태풍
- **tsunami** 쓰나미
- **tornado** 토네이도

English Dictionary

- **avoid** 방지하다, 막다, 피하다
  → to stay away from; to prevent the occurrence of something bad, unpleasant, etc.
  떨어져 있다; 나쁘거나 좋지 않은 무언가가 발생하는 것을 막다

- **break** 깨다, 부수다
  → to separate something into parts or pieces often in a sudden and forceful or violent way, to cause to separate into two or more pieces
  두 개 또는 그 이상의 조각들로 분리되도록 하기 위해 갑자기 강압적인 또는 폭력적인 방식으로 무언가를 조각나게 하거나 분리시키다

- **disaster** 재난, 재해
  → something such as a flood, tornado, fire, plane crash, etc. that happens suddenly and causes much suffering or loss to many people
  갑자기 일어나 많은 사람들에게 많은 고통이나 손실을 야기하는 홍수, 토네이도, 화재, 비행기 사고 등과 같은 것

- **earthquake** 지진
  → a shaking of a part of the Earth's surface that often causes great damage
  종종 큰 피해를 야기하는 지구 표면의 한 부분의 흔들림

- **empty** 비어 있는, 빈
  → not having any people, and not occupied; containing nothing
  어떤 사람도 있지 않고, 점유되지 않은; 아무것도 포함하지 않은

- **fall** 넘어지다
  → to come or go down suddenly from a standing position
  서 있는 자세에서 갑자기 밑으로 가다

- **follow** 따르다
  → to move behind someone or something and go where they go
  어떤 사람이나 어떤 것의 뒤에서 움직이며 그들이 가는 곳으로 가다

- **forget** 잊어버리다
  → to be unable to think of or remember something
  무언가를 생각해 내지 못하거나 기억하지 못하다

- **hurt** 다치게 하다
  → to cause pain or injury to yourself, someone else, or a part of your body
  당신 자신이나 다른 누군가 또는 자신의 신체의 한 부분에 상처를 입히거나 고통을 야기시키다

- **injury** 상처, 부상
  → harm or damage; an act or event that causes someone or something to no longer be fully healthy or in good condition
  해 또는 손상; 누군가나 무언가가 더 이상 건강하거나 좋은 상태가 되지 못 하도록 하는 행동이나 사건

- **pole** 기둥, 막대
  → a long, thin stick made of wood or metal, used to hold something up
  무언가를 떠받치기 위해 사용되는 나무나 금속으로 만들어진 길고 가는 막대

- **protect** 보호하다
  → to keep someone or something from being harmed, lost, etc.
  누군가나 무언가를 손상되거나 상실되는 것으로부터 막다

- **safety** 안전
  → the state of not being dangerous or harmful
  위험하거나 해롭지 않은 상태

- **shake** 흔들림, 떨림
  → short, quick movement back and forth or up and down
  앞뒤로 또는 위아래로 짧고 빠른 움직임

01 다음 짝지어진 단어의 관계가 같도록 빈칸에 알맞은 말을 쓰시오.

> low: high = _____ : full

02 다음 우리말에 맞게 빈칸에 알맞은 말을 쓰시오.

(1) 건강이 재산보다 낫다는 것을 기억해라.

➡ _____ _____ _____ that good health is above wealth.

(2) 나는 장난감을 하나씩 상자에 넣었다.

➡ I put the toys into the box _____

_____ _____.

(3) 나는 이것보다 약간 더 긴 것을 원해요.

➡ I want _____ _____ longer than this one.

(4) 큰 개에게서 떨어져 있어라.

➡ _____ _____ _____ the big dog.

03 다음 중 밑줄 친 부분의 뜻풀이가 바르지 <u>않은</u> 것은?

① Shake the bottle before you drink it.
흔들다

② He was disappointed with an empty box.
비어 있는

③ Minho is suffering from a serious illness.
경미한

④ This village was damaged by a powerful earthquake. 지진

⑤ I was worried about the injury on my head. 상처

04 다음 문장의 빈칸에 들어갈 말을 보기에서 골라 쓰시오.

┤ 보기 ├

slip / shake / escape / follow

(1) She was lucky to _____ from the burning car.

(2) You should _____ the safety rules.

(3) Be careful not to _____ on the ice.

(4) Suddenly, her hands began to _____.

05 다음 주어진 문장의 밑줄 친 pole의 의미와 같은 의미로 쓰인 것은? (2개)

> Hold on to the pole or the tree.

① We will soon reach the North Pole.

② Walk straight until you see a pole with a sign.

③ The man is locking his bike to the pole.

④ Do you know who is the first person to discover the South Pole?

⑤ A compass shows the magnetic pole.

06 다음 영영풀이가 가리키는 것을 고르시오.

> something such as a flood, tornado, fire, plane crash, etc. that happens suddenly and causes much suffering or loss to many people

① drought   ② disaster

③ earthquake   ④ volcano

⑤ tsunami

01 다음 짝지어진 단어의 관계가 같도록 빈칸에 알맞은 말을 쓰시오.

> wet : dry = _____ : dangerous

02 다음 우리말과 일치하도록 주어진 어구를 모두 배열하여 영작하시오.

(1) 나는 영어 시험을 걱정하고 있다.
(about / the / exam / I'm / English / worried)
➡ _____

(2) 너는 계단에서 걸어야 한다.
(walk / stairs / on / you / should / the)
➡ _____

(3) 차에서 나올 때, 네 머리를 조심해라.
(the car / of / head / watch / you / your / get / when / out)
➡ _____
_____

(4) 너는 문을 닫을 때 손을 조심해야 한다.
(should / the / door / when / you / close / your / hand / you / watch)
➡ _____
_____

03 다음 대화의 (A)~(C)에 들어갈 말을 고르시오.

> Sujin: It's raining. I'm worried (A)[about / of] our picnic in the afternoon.
> Mom: It is going to rain (B)[from / until] late afternoon today. You should go (C)[one / another] day.
> Sujin: You're right, Mom. I'll call my friend and choose another day.

➡ (A) _____, (B) _____, (C) _____

04 다음 문장의 빈칸에 들어갈 말을 순서대로 쓰시오.

> • Keep his advice (A)_____ your mind.
> • You should stay away (B)_____ wild animals.
> • I called their names one (C)_____ one

➡ (A) _____ (B) _____ (C) _____

05 다음 우리말에 맞게 빈칸에 알맞은 말을 쓰시오.

(1) 나는 이 곡을 좋아해, 왜냐하면 이 곡은 나의 기분이 나아지게 만들기 때문이야.
➡ I like this song because it makes me _____ _____.

(2) 비가 오기 시작했을 때, 나는 나무 아래로 숨었다.
➡ When it started to rain, I _____ _____ under the tree.

(3) 지진은 자연 재해의 한 형태이다.
➡ An _____ is one type of the _____ _____.

06 다음 문장의 빈칸에 들어갈 말을 〈보기〉에서 골라 쓰시오.

> ┤ 보기 ├
> hold on to / stay away from / get out of / take cover / feel better

(1) _____ _____ _____ the fireplace.
(2) _____ _____ _____ the pole not to fall down.
(3) I decided to move to _____ _____ _____ the city.
(4) The thieves tried to _____ _____ behind the tree.

교과서

Conversation

걱정 표현하기

> **I'm worried about my leg.** 나는 내 다리가 걱정돼.

■ 'I'm worried about ~'은 걱정을 나타내는 표현으로 '나는 ~을 걱정하고 있다'라는 뜻이다. about 다음에는 걱정에 해당하는 명사 형태의 표현을 사용한다. 걱정을 나타낼 때, 'I'm concerned about ~' 또는 'I'm anxious about ~'으로 나타낼 수 있다.

걱정 표현하기

I'm worried about the exam. (나는 시험을 걱정하고 있어.)

I'm anxious about my sore throat. (나는 아픈 목이 걱정이야.)

I'm concerned about my red eyes. (나는 충혈된 눈이 걱정이야.)

핵심 Check

1. 다음 우리말과 일치하도록 빈칸에 알맞은 말을 쓰시오.

   A: _____ _____ _____ my bad cold. (나는 심한 감기를 걱정하고 있어.)

   B: I think you need to take some medicine. (나는 네가 약을 좀 먹을 필요가 있다고 생각해.)

2. 다음 우리말과 일치하도록 빈칸에 알맞은 말을 쓰시오.

   A: _____ _____ _____ because I'll be with you. (내가 너와 함께 있을 테니 걱정 마.)

   B: Thank you so much. (정말 고마워요.)

3. 다음 우리말과 일치하도록 빈칸에 알맞은 말을 쓰시오.

   A: _____ _____ _____ pimples on my face. (나는 얼굴에 여드름이 나서 걱정이에요.)

   B: Why don't you go see a doctor? (의사에게 가보는 게 어때?)

② 충고하기

You should clean your room. 너는 네 방을 청소해야 해.

■ 충고하기

'You should ~'는 충고를 할 때 쓰는 표현으로 '너는 ~해야 해'라는 뜻이다. 'Why don't you ~?', 'How[What] about ~ing?' 또는 'You'd better ~'와 바꿔 쓸 수 있다.

충고하기

You should exercise. (너는 운동을 해야 해.)

Why don't you wear a helmet? (헬멧을 쓰는 게 어때?)

How about walking on the stairs? (계단에서는 걷는 게 어때?)

You'd better watch your step. (발밑을 조심하는 게 좋아.)

He advised her to take an umbrella. (그는 그녀에게 우산을 가져가라고 조언했다.)

I think you need to go see a doctor. (나는 네가 의사에게 가 볼 필요가 있다고 생각해.)

핵심 Check

4. 다음 우리말과 일치하도록 빈칸에 알맞은 말을 쓰시오.

A: It's snowing a lot outside. (밖에 눈이 많이 오고 있어.)

B: _____ _____ wear a heavy coat. (너는 두꺼운 코트를 입어야 해.)

5. 다음 우리말과 일치하도록 빈칸에 알맞은 말을 쓰시오.

A: I'm going to ride my bike. (나는 자전거를 타려고 해.)

B: _____ _____ _____ wear a helmet? (헬멧을 쓰는 게 어때?)

6. 다음 우리말과 일치하도록 빈칸에 알맞은 말을 쓰시오.

A: I hurt my leg, so I can't walk. (다리를 다쳐서 걸을 수가 없어요.)

B: _____ _____ _____ _____ _____ call an ambulance. (나는 우리가 구급 차를 불러야 할 필요가 있다고 생각해.)

A. Listen and Speak 1-B

Brian: What are you watching?

Jane: It's a program about earthquakes.

Brian: ❶Sounds interesting. ❷I'm worried about earthquakes ❸these days.

Jane: Me, too. This program has some helpful tips.

Brian: Really? What does it say?

Jane: When things start to shake, you need to ❹take cover under a table.

Brian: Oh, I didn't know ❺that.

Brian: 무엇을 시청하고 있니?
Jane: 지진에 관한 프로그램이야.
Brian: 그거 재미있겠다. 나는 요즘 지진이 걱정돼.
Jane: 나도 그래. 이 프로그램에는 도움이 되는 몇 가지 조언이 있어.
Brian: 그래? 뭐라고 하는데?
Jane: 물건들이 흔들리기 시작하면 탁자 아래에 숨어야 해.
Brian: 아, 그건 몰랐어.

❶ (That) Sounds interesting.: 재미있겠네. sound 다음에는 형용사가 보어로 와서 '~처럼 들리다'라는 뜻을 갖는다.
❷ I'm worried about ~: ~을 걱정하고 있다
❸ these days: 요즘
❹ take cover: 숨다
❺ that은 흔들리기 시작할 때, 탁자 아래로 숨을 필요가 있다는 것을 가리킨다.

Check(√) True or False

(1) Jane got helpful tips from the program about earthquakes.　　T ☐ F ☐

(2) When things start to shake, people should take cover under a table.　　T ☐ F ☐

 B. Real Life Communication

Brian: There was ❶a big fire at the city library yesterday.

Mina: Yes, I heard about it. I was worried about the people ❷there.

Brian: Don't worry. Everybody was okay. ❸They all followed the safety rules.

Mina: Really? What are the rules?

Brian: You need to cover your nose and mouth with a wet towel. Then ❹ stay low and escape.

Mina: Oh, I didn't know that.

Brian: You should ❺keep that in mind. It might be helpful some day.

Brian: 어제 시립 도서관에 큰 불이 났어.
Mina: 응, 그것에 대해 들었어. 거기 있었던 사람들이 걱정 됐어.
Brian: 걱정하지 마. 모두들 무사했어. 사람들이 모두 안전 규칙을 따랐대.
Mina: 정말? 그게 뭔데?
Brian: 젖은 수건으로 코와 입을 가려야 해. 그 다음, 몸을 낮게 유지하고 탈출하는 거야.
Mina: 아, 그건 몰랐어.
Brian: 넌 그것을 명심해야 해. 언젠가 도움이 될 수도 있어.

❶ a big fire: 큰 화재, fire는 셀 수 없는 명사이지만 사건이나 사고를 나타낼 때는 하나의 사건으로 보아 단수로 취급할 수 있다.
❷ there=at the city library
❸ They all: 그들은 모두(They와 all은 동격) / safety rules: 안전 규칙
❹ stay는 be동사와 같이 불완전동사로 형용사 low를 보어로 취하고 있다.
❺ keep ~ in mind: ~을 기억하다

Check(√) True or False

(3) Brian tells Mina what to do during a fire.　　T ☐ F ☐

(4) Many people were hurt because of a big fire at the city library yesterday.　　T ☐ F ☐

Listen and Speak 1-A

Tom: Yujin, ❶what's wrong?

Yujin: ❷I'm worried about my leg. It hurts a lot.

Tom: ❸Why don't you ❹go see a doctor?

Yujin: I'm going to go after school today.

Tom: I hope you ❺feel better soon.

Yujin: ❻I hope so, too.

❶ what's wrong?: 무슨 일이니?(= what's the matter?)
❷ I'm worried about ~: 나는 …에 관해 걱정이다
❸ Why don't you ~?: ~하는 것이 어때?
❹ go see a doctor 의사에게 가 보다 (= go and see a doctor)
❺ feel better: 나아지다
❻ I hope so= I hope (that) I feel better

Listen and Speak 2-B

Emily: What time is the movie?

Tom: It starts at 4:30.

Emily: Oh, no. We only ❶have 20 minutes left.
Let's run!

Tom: No! You ❷might fall and ❸hurt yourself.
You should walk on the stairs.

Emily: You're right. We can be ❹a little late.

Tom: Yes. ❺Better safe than sorry.

❶ have 20 minutes left: 20분 남다(left는 leave의 과거분사)
❷ might는 조동사로 '~일지도 모른다'를 뜻한다. may보다 약한 가능성을 나타낼 때 쓰인다
❸ hurt oneself: 다치다
❹ a little: 약간
❺ 후회하는 것보다는 안전한 것이 더 낫다.

Listen and Speak 2-A

Jack: Dad, I'm going out to play basketball with Minu.

Dad: Did you ❶finish cleaning your room?

Jack: No, not yet. Can I do it later?

Dad: No. ❷You should clean your room first.

Jack: Okay. I'll clean my room and then play basketball.

Dad: Good. ❸Don't forget to be home ❹by six o'clock.

Jack: Okay.

❶ finish는 동명사를 목적어로 취한다.
❷ 'You should ~'는 '너는 ~해야 한다'의 뜻으로 충고하는 표현이다.
❸ 'Don't forget'은 Remember와 같은 의미로 '~할 것을 잊지 마'라는 의미이다.
/ be home: 집에 오다
❹ by: ~까지는(not later than a specified time)

Let's Check

Sujin: It's raining. ❶I'm worried about our picnic in the afternoon.

Mom: It is going to rain ❷until late afternoon today. ❸You should go another day.

Sujin: You're right, Mom. I'll call my friend and choose another day.

❶ 오후의 소풍에 대해 걱정을 나타낸다.
❷ until: ~까지
❸ 다른 날로 소풍 갈 것을 충고한다.

● 다음 우리말과 일치하도록 빈칸에 알맞은 말을 쓰시오.

Listen & Speak 1 A

Tom: Yujin, what's wrong?

Yujin: _____ _____ _____ my leg. It hurts a lot.

Tom: _____ _____ _____ go see a doctor?

Yujin: I'm going to go after school today.

Tom: I hope _____ _____ _____ soon.

Yujin: I hope so, too.

Listen & Speak 1 B

Brian: What are you watching?

Jane: It's a program about _____.

Brian: _____ _____. _____ _____ _____ these days.

Jane: Me, too. This program has some _____ _____.

Brian: Really? What does it say?

Jane: When things start to _____, you need to _____ _____ under a table.

Brian: Oh, I didn't know that.

Listen & Speak 2 A

Jack: Dad, I'm going out to play basketball with Minu.

Dad: Did you _____ _____ _____ _____?

Jack: No, _____ _____. Can I do it later?

Dad: No. _____ _____ _____ _____ _____ _____.

Jack: Okay. I'll clean my room and then play basketball.

Dad: Good. _____ _____ to be home by six o'clock.

Jack: Okay.

해석

Tom: 유진아, 무슨 일이야?
Yujin: 내 다리가 걱정돼서. 많이 아프거든.
Tom: 병원에 가보는 게 어때?
Yujin: 오늘 방과 후에 갈 거야.
Tom: 곧 괜찮아지기를 바라.
Yujin: 나도 그러길 바라.

Brian: 무엇을 시청하고 있니?
Jane: 지진에 관한 프로그램이야.
Brian: 그거 재미있겠다. 나는 요즘 지진이 걱정돼.
Jane: 나도 그래. 이 프로그램에는 도움이 되는 몇 가지 조언이 있어.
Brian: 그래? 뭐라고 하는데?
Jane: 물건들이 흔들리기 시작하면 탁자 아래에 숨어야 해.
Brian: 아, 그건 몰랐어.

Jack: 아빠, 저 민우와 농구하러 나갈 거예요.
Dad: 네 방 청소는 끝냈니?
Jack: 아니요, 아직 안했어요. 나중에 해도 돼요?
Dad: 아니. 너는 네 방을 먼저 청소해야 해.
Jack: 알았어요. 방을 청소하고 농구할게요.
Dad: 착하구나. 6시까지 집에 오는 것 잊지 마라.
Jack: 알겠어요.

Listen & Talk 2 B

Emily: What time is the movie?

Tom: It starts at 4:30.

Emily: Oh, no. We only have 20 minutes _____. Let's run!

Tom: No! _____ _____ _____ _____ _____ _____.

　　　You should walk _____ _____ _____.

Emily: You're right. We can be _____ _____ _____.

Tom: Yes. _____ _____ _____ _____.

해석

Emily: 영화는 몇 시에 하니?
Tom: 4시 30분에 시작해.
Emily: 이런. 우리 20분밖에 남지 않았어. 뛰자!
Tom: 안 돼! 넘어져서 다칠 수 있어. 계단에서는 걸어가야 해.
Emily: 네 말이 맞아. 우리 좀 늦을 수도 있겠어.
Tom: 그래. 후회하는 것보다 안전한 게 낫지.

Real Life Communication

Brian: There was _____ _____ _____ at the city library yesterday.

Mina: Yes, I heard about it. _____ _____ _____ _____ _____ _____ _____.

Brian: Don't worry. Everybody was okay. They all followed the _____ rules.

Mina: Really? What are the rules?

Brian: You need to _____ your nose and mouth _____ _____ _____ _____. Then _____ _____ and _____.

Mina: Oh, I didn't know that.

Brian: You should _____ _____ _____ _____. It might be helpful some day.

Brian: 어제 시립 도서관에 큰 불이 났어.
Mina: 응, 그것에 대해 들었어. 거기 있었던 사람들이 걱정 됐어.
Brian: 걱정하지 마. 모두들 무사했어. 사람들이 모두 안전 규칙을 따랐대.
Mina: 정말? 그게 뭔데?
Brian: 젖은 수건으로 코와 입을 가려야 해. 그 다음, 몸을 낮게 유지하고 탈출하는 거야.
Mina: 아, 그건 몰랐어.
Brian: 넌 그것을 명심해야 해. 언젠가 도움이 될 수도 있어.

Let's Check

Sujin: It's raining. I'm worried about _____ _____ in the afternoon.

Mom: It is going to rain _____ _____ _____ today. _____ _____ _____ _____ _____.

Sujin: You're right, Mom. I'll call my friend and _____ _____ _____.

Sujin: 비가 와요. 오후에 있을 소풍이 걱정 돼요.
Mom: 오늘 오후 늦게까지 비가 올 거야. 다른 날 소풍 가는 것이 좋을 것 같구나.
Sujin: 맞아요, 엄마. 친구에게 전화해서 다른 날을 정해야겠어요.

01 다음 대화의 밑줄 친 (A)와 바꾸어 쓸 수 있는 것을 모두 고르시오.

> A: (A)I'm worried about my sore throat.
> B: Why don't you take some medicine?
> A: Okay. I'll try.

① I'm surprised at my sore throat.

② I'm relieved due to my sore throat.

③ I'm concerned about my sore throat.

④ I'm satisfied with my sore throat.

⑤ I'm anxious about my sore throat.

02 다음 대화가 자연스럽게 이어지도록 배열하시오.

Tom: Yujin, what's wrong?

> (A) I hope so, too.
> (B) I'm going to go after school today.
> (C) Why don't you go see a doctor?
> (D) I hope you feel better soon.
> (E) I'm worried about my leg. It hurts a lot.

➡ _____

[03~04] 다음 대화를 읽고 물음에 답하시오.

Emily: What time is the movie?
Tom: It starts at 4:30.
Emily: Oh, no. We only have 20 minutes left. Let's run!
Tom: No! You might fall and hurt yourself. You should walk on the stairs.
Emily: You're right. We can be a little late.
Tom: Yes. (A)후회하는 것보다 안전한 게 낫지.

03 다음 주어진 영영풀이가 가리키는 말을 위 대화에서 찾아 쓰시오.

> to come or go down suddenly from a standing position

➡ _____

04 위 대화의 밑줄 친 (A)의 우리말을 4 단어를 사용하여 영어로 쓰시오.

➡ _____

Conversation 시험대비 실력평가

[01~03] 다음 대화를 읽고 물음에 답하시오.

Tom: Yujin, (A)_____

Yujin: I'm worried about my leg. It hurts a lot.

Tom: (B)Why don't you go see a doctor?

Yujin: I'm going to go after school today.

Tom: I hope you feel better soon.

Yujin: I hope so, too.

01 위 대화의 빈칸 (A)에 들어갈 말로 <u>어색한</u> 것은?

① what happened?

② what's the matter?

③ what's wrong?

④ what's the matter with you?

⑤ what are you doing?

02 위 대화의 밑줄 친 (B)와 바꾸어 쓸 수 <u>없는</u> 것은?

① What about going to see a doctor?

② You had better go see a doctor.

③ I think you should see a doctor.

④ How about going to see a doctor?

⑤ Why didn't you go see a doctor?

03 위 대화에서 Yujin의 심경으로 적절한 것은?

① calm   ② nervous

③ anxious   ④ pleased

⑤ lonely

[04~06] 다음 대화를 읽고 물음에 답하시오.

Brian: What are you watching?

Jane: It's a program about earthquakes.

Brian: Sounds interesting. I'm worried about earthquakes these days.

Jane: (A)Me, too. This program has some helpful tips.

Brian: Really? What does it say?

Jane: When things start to shake, (B)_____.

Brian: Oh, I didn't know that.

04 위 대화의 밑줄 친 (A)와 바꾸어 쓸 수 있는 것은?

① So am I.   ② So do I.

③ Neither did I.   ④ Neither am I.

⑤ Neither do I.

서답형

05 위 대화의 빈칸 (B)에 들어갈 말을 보기에 주어진 어구를 모두 배열하여 완성하시오.

┌─ 보기 ─┐

cover   need   a table   take

you   to   under

└────────┘

➡ _____

중요

06 위 대화의 내용과 일치하지 <u>않는</u> 것은?

① Jane은 지진에 관한 프로그램을 보고 있다.

② Brian과 Jane은 요즘 지진에 대해 걱정하고 있다.

③ Jane은 프로그램에서 지진에 관한 유용한 정보를 얻었다.

④ 지진 발생시, 탁자 아래에 숨어야 한다.

⑤ 물건이 흔들리기 시작할 때, 물건을 탁자 아래로 옮겨야 한다.

[07~09] 다음 대화를 읽고 물음에 답하시오.

> Jack: Dad, I'm going out to play basketball with Minu.
> Dad: Did you finish cleaning your room?
> Jack: No, not yet. Can I do it later?
> Dad: No. You should clean your room first.
> Jack: Okay. I'll clean my room and then play basketball.
> Dad: Good. Don't forget to be home by six o'clock.
> Jack: Okay.

서답형

07 What is Jack going to do with Minu?

➡ _____

서답형

08 What did Jack's dad tell him to do before going out?

➡ _____

서답형

09 By what time should Jack return home?

➡ _____

[10~11] 다음 대화를 읽고 물음에 답하시오.

> Emily: What time is the movie?
> Tom: It starts at 4:30.
> Emily: Oh, no. We only have 20 minutes left. Let's run!
> Tom: No! You might fall and hurt yourself. You should walk on the stairs.
> Emily: You're right. We can be a little late.
> Tom: Yes. (A)_____

10 위 대화의 빈칸 (A)에 들어갈 말로 적절한 것은?

① Will is power.
② Better safe than sorry.
③ A sound mind in a sound body.
④ A friend in need is a friend indeed.
⑤ No smoke without fire.

11 위 대화의 내용과 일치하지 <u>않는</u> 것은?

① The movie will start at 4:30.
② It's 4:10 now.
③ Emily is in a hurry not to be late for the movie.
④ Tom advises Emily not to run on the stairs.
⑤ Tom prefers being on time to being safe.

[12~13] 다음 대화를 읽고 물음에 답하시오.

> Brian: There was a big fire at the city library yesterday.
> Mina: Yes, I heard about it. I was worried about the people there.
> Brian: Don't worry. Everybody (A)[was / were] okay. They all followed the safety rules.
> Mina: Really? What are the rules?
> Brian: You need (B)[covering / to cover] your nose and mouth with a wet towel. Then (C)[stay / staying] low and escape.
> Mina: Oh, I didn't know that.
> Brian: You should keep that in mind. It might be helpful some day.

서답형

12 위 대화의 괄호 (A)~(C)에서 적절한 것을 골라 쓰시오.

➡ (A) _____ (B) _____ (C) _____

13 위 대화의 내용과 일치하지 <u>않는</u> 것은?

① 어제 시립 도서관에서 큰 불이 있었다.
② Mina는 도서관에 있던 사람들을 걱정했다.
③ 도서관에 있던 사람들은 모두 안전 규칙을 따랐다.
④ 화재 시 젖은 수건으로 코와 입을 가려야 한다.
⑤ 화재 시 똑바로 서서 탈출해야 한다.

01 다음 대화가 자연스럽게 이어지도록 순서대로 배열하시오.

Dad, I'm going out to play basketball with Minu.

> (A) No, not yet. Can I do it later?
> (B) No. You should clean your room first.
> (C) Did you finish cleaning your room?
> (D) Good. Don't forget to be home by six o'clock.
> (E) Okay. I'll clean my room and then play basketball.

➡ _____

[02~03] 다음 대화를 읽고 물음에 답하시오.

Emily: What time is the movie?
Tom: It starts at 4:30.
Emily: Oh, no. We only have 20 minutes left. Let's run!
Tom: No! You might fall and hurt yourself. (A)You should walk on the stairs. (why)
Emily: You're right. We can be a little late.
Tom: Yes. Better safe than sorry.

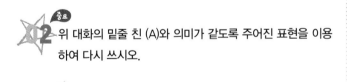 **02** 위 대화의 밑줄 친 (A)와 의미가 같도록 주어진 표현을 이용하여 다시 쓰시오.

➡ _____

03 Why did Tom tell Emily not to run on the stairs?

➡ _____

[04~07] 다음 대화를 읽고 물음에 답하시오.

Brian: There was a big fire at the city library yesterday.
Mina: Yes, I heard about it. I was worried about the people there.
Brian: Don't worry. Everybody was okay. They all followed the safety rules.
Mina: Really? What are the rules?
Brian: You need to cover your nose and mouth with a wet towel. Then stay low and escape.
Mina: Oh, I didn't know that.
Brian: You should keep (A)that in mind. It might be helpful some day.

04 What happened at the city library yesterday?

➡ _____

05 Why didn't everyone get hurt at the big fire?

➡ _____

06 위 대화의 밑줄 친 (A)가 가리키는 내용을 우리말로 간략히 설명하시오.

➡ _____

07 다음 대화의 빈칸에 들어갈 말을 보기에 주어진 어구를 모두 배열하여 완성하시오.

> A: I heard about your accident. I was worried about you.
> B: Thanks. I hurt my hand, but it's not serious. I'll be okay.
> A: Good. _____
> B: You're right. I will.

> ┤ 보기 ├
> the door / watch / your / hands / you / close / should / you / when

➡ _____
_____

Grammar

교과서

1 의문사+to부정사

> • I don't know **what to do**. 나는 무엇을 해야 할지 모르겠어.
> • She asked me **how to make** the cake. 그녀는 나에게 그 케이크를 만드는 법을 물었다.

■ '의문사+to부정사'는 문장 속에서 명사구로 주어, 목적어, 보어 역할을 한다. 해당하는 의문사는 what, when, where, how, which, who, whom 등이 있으며, 'where to go'는 '어디로 가야 할지'와 같이 의문사와 동사의 의미를 넣어 해석한다.

- Can you tell me **where to find** the hotel? 어디에서 그 호텔을 찾을지 말해줄래?
- **How to teach** students is important. 학생들을 가르치는 방법은 중요하다.
- Did you decide **whom to invite**? 누구를 초대할지 결정했니?
- I didn't tell you **when to sleep**. 네가 언제 자야 할지 나는 말하지 않았어.

■ '의문사+to부정사'는 '의문사+주어+should+동사원형'으로 바꾸어 쓸 수 있다.

- Julia told me **what to do**. (= Julia told me what I should do.) Julia는 내게 무엇을 해야 할지 말해주었다.
- Let me show you **how to do** it. (= Let me show you how you should do it.) 네가 그것을 어떻게 해야 하는지 내가 보여줄게.
- Let's choose **what to eat** for lunch. (= Let's choose what we should eat for lunch.) 점심으로 무엇을 먹을지 선택하자.

핵심 Check

1. 다음 우리말과 같도록 빈칸에 알맞은 말을 쓰시오.

(1) 나는 자동차를 운전하는 방법을 몰라.

➡ I don't know _____ _____ _____ a car.

= I don't know _____ _____ _____ _____ a car.

(2) 우리는 언제 떠날지 몰라.

➡ We don't know _____ _____ _____.

= We don't know _____ _____ _____ _____.

(3) 나는 누구를 믿어야 할지 모르겠어.

➡ I don't know _____ _____ _____.

= I don't know _____ _____ _____ _____.

2 관계대명사

> • Bradley is my friend **who** lives in Mexico. Bradley는 멕시코에 사는 내 친구이다.
>
> • The woman you saw yesterday is my aunt. 네가 어제 본 그 여자는 내 숙모야.

■ 관계대명사는 두 개의 문장을 하나로 이어주는 접속사 역할을 하면서 동시에 명사 역할을 한다. 본래 문장에서 주격으로 쓰인 명사는 주격 관계대명사로, 소유격으로 쓰인 명사는 소유격 관계대명사로, 목적격으로 쓰인 명사는 목적격 관계대명사로 바꾸어준다.

- • I thanked the woman. She found me my wallet.

   = I thanked the woman **who** found me my wallet.

- • The pants were on the bed. I washed them.

   = The pants **which** I washed were on the bed.

■ 선행사에 따라서 사용되는 관계대명사의 종류는 다음과 같으며, 목적격 관계대명사와 '주격 관계대명사+be동사'는 생략 가능하다.

	주격	소유격	목적격
사람	who	whose	whom[who]
사물	which	whose[of which]	which

- • Tell me about the famous people **who[whom]** you became friends with in Yale.
   네가 예일 대학에 있을 때 친구가 된 유명한 사람들에 대해 말해줘.

- • I know a dentist **whose** daughters are twins. 나는 쌍둥이 딸을 가진 치과의사를 안다.

- • The movie **which** we booked yesterday was canceled. 우리가 어제 예약한 영화는 취소되었다.

■ 관계대명사 that은 who와 which를 대신하여 사용될 수 있으며 소유격은 없다. 단, 선행사가 '사람+사물'인 경우에는 반드시 that을 쓰며, 선행사가 'the+최상급', 'the+서수', 'the only', 'the very', 'the same'의 수식을 받거나, 선행사가 '-thing', '-body', '-one'으로 끝나는 경우 관계대명사 that을 쓰는 경우가 많다.

- • The woman **that[who/whom]** I called yesterday had a nice voice. 내가 어제 통화했던 여자는 예쁜 목소리를 가졌다.

- • Cathy is the only friend **that** I can tell my secrets. Cathy는 내 비밀을 말할 수 있는 유일한 친구이다.

핵심 Check

2. 다음 우리말과 같도록 빈칸에 알맞은 말을 쓰시오.

(1) 경주에서 진 그 소녀는 비참했다.

➡ The girl _____ lost the race was miserable.

(2) 나는 그의 누나가 매우 키가 큰 남자를 안다.

➡ I know the man _____ _____ is very tall.

01 다음 문장에서 어법상 어색한 부분을 바르게 고쳐 쓰시오.

composer: 작곡가

(1) Some people don't know when quit.

_____ ➡ _____

(2) I stayed in the room and which was very beautiful.

_____ ➡ _____

(3) I'm not sure which way to going.

_____ ➡ _____

(4) Do you know the song who the famous composer wrote?

_____ ➡ _____

02 다음 주어진 단어를 어법에 맞게 빈칸에 쓰시오.

(1) They taught me _____ _____ _____. (how / read)
(2) Look at the boys who _____ playing the guitar on the stage. (be)
(3) Jimmy took care of a dog _____ tail was hurt. (who)
(4) I don't know _____ _____ _____ the question. (who / ask)

03 다음 우리말에 맞게 주어진 어구를 바르게 배열하시오. (필요하면 단어를 추가하거나 변형할 것)

(1) 언제 오실지 알려 드리겠습니다.

(come / I / when / you / let / will / know)

➡ _____

(2) 갖고 싶은 것이 있어?

(have / there / to / is / you / anything / that / want)

➡ _____

(3) 나는 그 기계를 사용하는 방법을 몰라.

(the machine / I / use / know / how / don't)

➡ _____

(4) 나는 어느 유명한 작가가 쓴 책을 읽었다.

(write / read / I / a famous writer / a book / which)

➡ _____

01 다음 빈칸에 들어갈 말로 가장 적절한 것은?

> • I don't know _____ to submit.
> 어느 것을 제출해야 할지 모르겠어.

① when   ② how   ③ which
④ who   ⑤ where

02 다음 중 빈칸에 들어갈 말이 나머지 넷과 <u>다른</u> 하나는?

① She is a woman _____ lives in Tokyo.
② I don't know _____ to talk to.
③ I know a girl _____ goal is to win the race.
④ There lived a boy _____ thought himself an angel.
⑤ The girl _____ hates to be alone is happy now.

03 다음 주어진 우리말을 영어로 바르게 옮긴 것은?

> 나는 어디서부터 시작해야 할지 모르겠어.

① I don't know when to start.
② I don't know how to do.
③ I don't know who to start.
④ I don't know where to start.
⑤ I don't know what to do.

04 다음 두 개의 문장을 하나의 문장으로 만드시오.

> The man lives here. He is cleaning the house.

➡ _____

05 다음 문장과 같은 의미의 문장은?

> Tell me where I should park this car.

① Would you tell her where to park this car?
② Can you tell me where to park this car?
③ Will you tell him how to park this car?
④ Could you tell me when to park this car?
⑤ Tell me whose car to park.

06 다음 빈칸에 알맞은 말을 <u>모두</u> 고르시오.

> Yesterday, I met the boy _____ you were interested in.

① that   ② whose   ③ which
④ who   ⑤ whom

07 다음 빈칸에 들어갈 말이 바르게 짝지어진 것은?

> • Let me know _____ to begin.
> • Do you know the boy _____ is wearing a blue shirt?

① when – whom   ② that – that
③ who – who   ④ when – that
⑤ how – whose

08 주어진 문장과 같은 의미의 문장을 쓰시오.

> Let me know where I should get off.

➡ _____

09 다음 빈칸에 공통으로 들어갈 말은?

> • Helen advised me _____ to buy.
> • This is the box _____ Jason was looking for.

① that　　② of which　　③ who
④ which　　⑤ whose

10 다음 중 나머지 넷과 쓰임이 <u>다른</u> 하나는?

① Please tell me <u>that</u> it doesn't matter.
② Why do you think <u>that</u> he did it?
③ It is a fact <u>that</u> she can dance.
④ It is said <u>that</u> time is money.
⑤ There was a boy <u>that</u> had a beautiful voice.

11 중요 다음 중 어법상 옳은 것을 바르게 묶은 것은?

> ⓐ Do you know how make an apple pie?
> ⓑ They were invited to the party which was very boring.
> ⓒ The man who is singing on the stage is my boyfriend.
> ⓓ Did you find the key was on the sofa?
> ⓔ I'm not sure what to do next.

① ⓐ, ⓒ, ⓓ　　　　② ⓑ, ⓓ, ⓔ
③ ⓐ, ⓑ, ⓓ　　　　④ ⓑ, ⓒ, ⓔ
⑤ ⓒ, ⓓ, ⓔ

서답형
12 다음 문장을 같은 의미가 되도록 빈칸에 알맞은 말을 쓰시오.

> • The pen is mine. It is on the desk.
> = The pen _____ is mine.

➡ _____

13 다음 중 어법상 바르지 <u>않은</u> 것은?

> The man ①<u>who</u> ②<u>is</u> standing over there ③<u>tell</u> me ④<u>to do</u> something. But I don't know ⑤<u>what to do</u> first.

14 중요 다음 중 어법상 옳은 문장은?

① They are not sure when should ask him.
② Jason is the only friend which I trust.
③ You didn't tell me where go.
④ The woman who I saw was your teacher.
⑤ I have a puppy that are three years old.

15 다음 밑줄 친 부분 중 생략할 수 <u>없는</u> 것은?

① Do you use the pen <u>that</u> you borrowed from me?
② The movie <u>that</u> you talked about is very interesting.
③ You can tell me anything <u>that</u> you want to talk about.
④ Julia has four books <u>that</u> are very interesting.
⑤ The tip of the brush <u>that</u> you gave me is very soft.

서답형
16 to부정사와 주어진 단어를 활용하여 다음 우리말을 영어로 쓰시오.

> 무엇을 주문해야 할지 모르겠어.
> (order)

➡ _____

17 다음 빈칸에 들어갈 말이 바르게 짝지어진 것은?

> The film _____ made people all over the world surprised _____ made by a famous director.

① that – are
② who – were
③ whose – is
④ whom – was
⑤ which – was

18 다음 주어진 문장과 같은 의미의 문장을 고르시오.

> He doesn't know how he should behave.

① He wants to know what to behave.
② He doesn't know how to behave.
③ He can't know when to behave.
④ He doesn't know where to behave.
⑤ He wants to know which to behave.

19 다음 빈칸에 공통으로 들어갈 말은?

> • Did you kick the ball _____ was in my room?
> • Have you seen the girls _____ always do something together?

① who
② that
③ which
④ whose
⑤ whom

20 다음 우리말을 영어로 옮길 때 빈칸에 알맞은 말을 쓰시오.

> • 나에게 공원으로 가는 길을 물어본 그 남자는 어디로 가야 할지 몰랐어.
> = The man _____ _____ _____ the way to the park didn't know _____ _____ _____ .

➡ _____

21 다음 중 밑줄 친 관계대명사의 쓰임이 바른 것은?

① Jenny liked the movie <u>whom</u> she saw with her friends.
② The cake <u>whose</u> he made was really delicious.
③ The pants <u>that</u> she is wearing are new.
④ Do you know that man <u>whom</u> swims so well?
⑤ We eat the vegetables <u>who</u> we grew in the yard.

22 다음 우리말을 영어로 옮길 때 빈칸에 알맞은 말을 쓰시오.

> 어디에서 만날지 결정하자.
> = Let's decide _____ .

➡ _____

23 다음 두 문장을 한 문장으로 만들 때 빈칸에 알맞은 것을 <u>모두</u> 고르시오.

> I bought a book from the boy. He was talking with my sister.
> = I bought a book from the boy _____

① whose was talking with my sister.
② he was talking with my sister.
③ which was talking with my sister.
④ talking with my sister.
⑤ who was talking with my sister.

24 빈칸에 알맞은 말을 쓰시오.

> I don't know _____ to do.
> = I don't know what I _____ .

➡ _____

01 〈보기〉의 문장과 관계대명사를 이용하여 빈칸을 알맞게 채우시오. (that은 쓰지 말 것)

┌─ 보기 ─
• They were painted by your mom.
• They want to be rich.
• It is very useful for you.
• The person is visiting a place for pleasure and interest.
└

(1) A tourist is someone _____

_____.

(2) What happened to the pictures _____

_____?

(3) There are many people _____.

(4) She will give you a tip _____

_____.

02 다음 문장이 서로 같은 의미가 되도록 빈칸에 알맞은 말을 쓰시오.

(1) She asked me where she should find the bathroom.

= She asked me _____.

(2) It's up to you to decide what you should do next.

= It's up to you to decide _____

_____.

(3) I haven't decided which class I should sign up for.

= I haven't decided _____

_____.

03 다음 우리말을 주어진 단어를 이용하여 영어로 쓸 때 빈칸을 알맞게 채우시오.

┌
나는 졸업 후에 무엇을 해야 할지 확실히 모르겠어.
(to / graduation)
└

➡ I'm not sure _____

04 다음 빈칸에 공통으로 들어갈 말을 쓰시오.

┌
• I don't know _____ to speak to.
• He is the man _____ everyone respects.
└

➡ _____

05 주어진 단어를 바르게 배열하여 다음 우리말을 영어로 쓰시오. 필요하다면 단어를 변형하시오.

┌
안녕이라고 말하는 방식은 문화마다 다르다.
(cultures / how / different / hello / in / to / vary / say)
└

➡ _____

06 다음 두 문장을 하나의 문장으로 쓰시오.

┌
• There are children.
• They are playing in the garden.
└

➡ _____

07 다음 대화의 빈칸을 어법에 맞게 채우시오.

┌
A: Do you know _____ _____ _____ ?
B: Yes, I do. Mom said we should go to the park.
└

➡ _____

08 다음 중 서로 관련 있는 문장을 연결하여 하나의 문장으로 쓰시오. 관계대명사 that은 사용하지 마시오.

> • The apartment is no longer available.
> • The boy is now in the hospital.
> • Do you want to buy the pictures?
> • Bruno Mars is a singer.
> • I must thank the people.
> • An artist is a person.

> • They are very expensive.
> • He is very popular all over the world.
> • He cut his finger.
> • He or she draws or paints pictures as a job.
> • It was empty.
> • They congratulated me.

➡ _____

➡ _____

➡ _____

➡ _____

➡ _____

➡ _____

09 다음 빈칸에 알맞은 말을 쓰시오.

> **A:** I don't know what I should do for the project.
> **B:** Do you see the man _____ is writing something? He is the manager. He will tell you _____ _____ _____.

10 다음 빈칸에 알맞은 말을 쓰시오.

> • There are many people.
> • They are doing their best.
> = There are many people _____
>   _____ _____ their best.
> = There are many people _____ their best.

11 다음 우리말을 영어로 옮길 때 빈칸에 알맞은 말을 쓰시오.

> • 이 책은 그것을 읽는 사람들에게 어떻게 생각해야 할지를 가르쳐 줘.
> = This book teaches people _____
>   _____ _____ _____
>   _____ _____.

12 다음 대화의 빈칸에 알맞은 말을 쓰시오.

> **Carrie:** A police officer helped you. Did you thank her?
> **Jason:** Yes, I thanked the police officer _____ _____ _____.

13 적절한 관계대명사와 주어진 단어를 이용하여 다음 우리말을 영어로 쓰시오.

> 읽고 있던 책을 다 읽었니? (finish)

➡ _____

14 다음 우리말을 두 가지의 영어 문장으로 쓰시오.

> 나는 뭐라고 말해야 할지 모르겠어.

➡ _____

➡ _____

Reading

Prepare for the shake

Do you know what to do when an earthquake strikes? Take this quiz
　　　　　　　'의문사+to부정사'로 know의 목적어

and think about how to be safe during this kind of natural disaster.
　　　　　　　　'의문사+to부정사'로 about의 목적어　while (×)

1. When things start to shake, run outside quickly. (O / ×)
　　　　　　　~하기 시작하다

2. Stay away from windows. (O / ×)
　　~에서 떨어져 있다

3. Use the stairs to get out of buildings. (O / ×)
　　　　　　　　　~에서 나가다

4. When you are outside, hold on to a pole or a tree. (O / ×)
　　　　　　밖에 있다　　~을 꼭 잡다

How did you do on the quiz? Can you survive an earthquake safely?

Here are some safety tips which can be helpful in an earthquake. Let's
Here is/are ~ : 여기에 ~이 있다　주격 관계대명사(that으로 바꿔 쓸 수 있다)

check them one by one and learn what to do.
　　　　하나씩　　　　무엇을 할지(=what we should do)

shake: 흔들림, 떨림	
earthquake: 지진	
strike: 발생하다	
disaster: 재난	
stay away from: ~에서 떨어져 있다	
stair 계단	
hold on to: ~을 꼭 잡다	
pole: 기둥	
survive: 살아남다	
safely: 안전하게	
safety: 안전	

 확인문제

● 다음 문장이 본문의 내용과 일치하면 T, 일치하지 않으면 F를 쓰시오.

1　The passage is about how to be safe in an earthquake. ☐

2　There are some safety tips to survive in all kinds of natural disasters. ☐

3　We can learn what we should do during an earthquake. ☐

4　The following passage will be about people who survived an earthquake. ☐

Don't run outside when things are shaking. Find a table or a desk and

때를 나타내는 부사절로 'things are shaking'은 현재진행형이 사용되어 '물건들이 흔들리고 있을 때'라는 뜻이다.

take cover under it. You can hold on to the legs to protect yourself.

to부정사의 부사적 용법 '~하기 위해서' 재귀대명사의 재귀적 용법(주어와 목적어가 같을 때 목적어로 재귀대명사 사용)

Also, stay away from windows. They can break during an earthquake

~에서 떨어져 있어라   =Windows

and hurt you.

You can go outside when the shaking stops. To get out of buildings,

to부정사의 부사적 용법 '~하기 위해서'

don't use the elevator. Take the stairs. It's much safer.

부정명령문   비교급 강조 부사 '훨씬'

Once you are outside, find an empty space that is far from buildings.

일단 ~하면   주격 관계대명사 ~에서 멀다

There may be people who want to hold on to a pole or a tree, but think

추측을 나타내는 조동사 주격 관계대명사(that으로 바꿔 쓸 수 있다)

again. That's a bad idea because it can fall on you.

=To hold on to a pole or a tree

Earthquakes can strike anytime. They can be scary experiences for

언제든지

everyone. So learn how to be safe in an earthquake. You can avoid

'how+to부정사' 안전할 방법

injuries and protect yourself. Follow these tips and be safe!

take cover: 숨다
protect: 보호하다
break: 깨다, 부수다, 부서지다
hurt: 다치다
once: 한 번; 일단 ~하면
outside: 밖에, 밖으로
empty: 비어 있는
space: 공간, 공터
avoid: 방지하다
pole: 기둥
scary: 무서운
experience: 경험
injury: 상처, 부상

확인문제

● 다음 문장이 본문의 내용과 일치하면 T, 일치하지 않으면 F를 쓰시오.

1 If things are still shaking, you should run outside as fast as possible. ☐

2 When things are shaking, it is good to take cover under a table or a desk. ☐

3 Staying close to the window is not a good idea. ☐

4 When the shaking stops, we should be indoors. ☐

5 Holding on to a pole or a tree is a bad idea. ☐

• 우리말을 참고하여 빈칸에 알맞은 말을 쓰시오.

_____ for the shake

1 Do you know _____ _____ _____ when an earthquake _____?

2 _____ this quiz and think about _____ _____ _____ safe _____ this kind of natural disaster.

3 When things start _____ _____, run outside _____. (o / x)

4 _____ _____ from windows. (o / x)

5 _____ the stairs _____ _____ _____ _____ buildings. (o / x)

6 _____ you are outside, _____ _____ _____ a pole or a tree. (o / x)

7 _____ did you do _____ the quiz?

8 Can you _____ _____ _____?

9 _____ _____ some safety tips _____ can be _____ in an earthquake.

10 Let's check _____ _____ _____ _____ and learn _____ _____.

11 Don't run outside _____ _____ _____ _____.

12 _____ a table or a desk and _____ under it.

13 You can hold on to the legs _____ _____.

14 Also, _____ _____ windows.

15 _____ can break _____ an earthquake and hurt you.

16 You can _____ _____ when _____ _____.

지진을 대비하라

1 지진이 발생할 때 해야 할 일을 알고 있습니까?

2 이 퀴즈를 풀며 이러한 종류의 자연 재해가 발생하는 동안 어떻게 해야 안전할 수 있는지를 생각해 보세요.

3 물건들이 흔들리기 시작하면, 빨리 밖으로 뛰어나가세요.

4 창문으로부터 멀리 떨어지세요.

5 건물에서 나갈 때는 계단을 이용하세요.

6 밖에 나가서는 기둥이나 나무를 붙들고 있으세요.

7 퀴즈가 어떠셨나요?

8 당신은 지진에서 안전하게 살아남을 수 있나요?

9 여기에 지진 발생 시 도움이 될 수 있는 안전 지침이 있습니다.

10 하나하나 확인하면서 무엇을 해야 하는지를 배워 봅시다.

11 물건들이 흔들리기 시작할 때 밖으로 뛰어나가지 마세요.

12 탁자나 책상을 찾아서 그 밑에 숨으세요.

13 자신을 보호하기 위해 탁자나 책상 다리를 붙들고 있으세요.

14 또한, 창문으로부터 멀리 떨어지세요.

15 지진이 일어나는 동안 창문들이 깨져 다칠 수 있으니까요.

16 흔들림이 멈추었을 때 밖으로 나가도 됩니다.

17 _____ _____ _____ _____ buildings, don't use the

elevator.

18 _____ the stairs.

19 It's _____ _____ .

20 _____ you are outside, _____ _____ _____ _____

that _____ far _____ buildings.

21 There may be people _____ _____ _____ _____

_____ _____ a pole or a tree, _____ think again.

22 That's a bad idea _____ _____ can _____ _____ you.

23 _____ can strike _____ .

24 _____ can be _____ _____ for everyone.

25 So learn _____ _____ _____ _____ in an earthquake.

26 You can _____ _____ and _____ _____ .

27 _____ these tips and _____ safe!

17 건물에서 나가기 위해 엘리베이터를 이용하지 마세요.

18 계단을 이용하세요.

19 그것이 훨씬 더 안전합니다.

20 일단 밖으로 나가면. 건물로부터 멀리 떨어진 공터를 찾으세요.

21 기둥이나 나무를 꼭 잡고 있으려는 사람들이 있을 수 있지만. 다시 생각해 보세요.

22 그것이 당신 위로 넘어질 수 있으므로 그것은 좋지 않은 생각입니다.

23 지진은 언제든지 발생할 수 있습니다.

24 지진은 모두에게 무서운 경험일 것입니다.

25 따라서 지진이 날 때 안전을 지키는 법을 배우세요.

26 부상을 방지하고 자신을 보호할 수 있습니다.

27 이 지침을 따르고 안전을 지키세요!

- 우리말을 참고하여 본문을 영작하시오.

1 지진이 발생할 때 해야 할 일을 알고 있습니까?

➡ _____

2 이 퀴즈를 풀며 이러한 종류의 자연 재해가 발생하는 동안 어떻게 해야 안전할 수 있는지를 생각해 보세요.

➡ _____

3 물건들이 흔들리기 시작하면, 빨리 밖으로 뛰어나가세요.

➡ _____

4 창문으로부터 멀리 떨어지세요.

➡ _____

5 건물에서 나갈 때는 계단을 이용하세요.

➡ _____

6 밖에 나가서는 기둥이나 나무를 붙들고 있으세요.

➡ _____

7 퀴즈가 어떠셨나요?

➡ _____

8 당신은 지진에서 안전하게 살아남을 수 있나요?

➡ _____

9 여기에 지진 발생 시 도움이 될 수 있는 안전 지침이 있습니다.

➡ _____

10 하나하나 확인하면서 무엇을 해야 하는지를 배워 봅시다.

➡ _____

11 물건이 흔들리기 시작할 때 밖으로 뛰어나가지 마세요.

➡ _____

12 탁자나 책상을 찾아서 그 밑에 숨으세요.

➡ _____

13 자신을 보호하기 위해 탁자나 책상 다리를 붙들고 있으세요.

➡ _____

14 또한, 창문으로부터 멀리 떨어지세요.

➡ _____

15 지진이 일어나는 동안 창문들이 깨져 다칠 수 있으니까요.

➡ _____

16 흔들림이 멈추었을 때 밖으로 나가도 됩니다.

➡ _____

17 건물에서 나가기 위해 엘리베이터를 이용하지 마세요.

➡ _____

18 계단을 이용하세요.

➡ _____

19 그것이 훨씬 더 안전합니다.

➡ _____

20 일단 밖으로 나가면, 건물로부터 멀리 떨어진 공터를 찾으세요.

➡ _____

21 기둥이나 나무를 꼭 잡고 있으려는 사람들이 있을 수 있지만, 다시 생각해 보세요.

➡ _____

22 그것이 당신 위로 넘어질 수 있으므로 그것은 좋지 않은 생각입니다.

➡ _____

23 지진은 언제든지 발생할 수 있습니다.

➡ _____

24 지진은 모두에게 무서운 경험일 것입니다.

➡ _____

25 따라서 지진이 날 때 안전을 지키는 법을 배우세요.

➡ _____

26 부상을 방지하고 자신을 보호할 수 있습니다.

➡ _____

27 이 지침을 따르고 안전을 지키세요!

➡ _____

01 자연스러운 글이 되도록 (A)~(D)를 바르게 나열한 것은?

> Here are some safety tips which can be helpful in an earthquake.

(A) You can hold on to the legs to protect yourself. Also, stay away from windows.

(B) Don't run outside when things are shaking. Find a table or a desk and take cover under it.

(C) They can break during an earthquake and hurt you.

(D) Let's check them one by one and learn what to do.

① (B)-(D)-(A)-(C)　② (B)-(A)-(C)-(D)

③ (C)-(B)-(A)-(D)　④ (D)-(A)-(B)-(C)

⑤ (D)-(B)-(A)-(C)

[02~05] 다음 글을 읽고 물음에 답하시오.

Do you know ⓐwhat you should do when an earthquake strikes? Take this quiz and think about how to be safe ⓑ_____ this kind of natural disaster.

1. When things start to shake, run outside quickly. (O / X)

2. Stay away from windows. (O / X)

3. Use the stairs to get out of buildings. (O / X)

4. When you are outside, hold on to a pole or a tree. (O / X)

서답형
02 밑줄 친 ⓐ를 대신하여 쓸 수 있는 말을 다음 빈칸에 쓰시오.

➡ _____ _____ _____

중요
03 다음 중 빈칸 ⓑ에 들어갈 말로 가장 적절한 것은?

① at　② during　③ by

④ on　⑤ for

서답형
04 다음과 같이 풀이되는 단어를 위 글에서 찾아 쓰시오.

> short, quick movement back and forth or up and down

➡ _____

05 What is the quiz about?

① when to go if you are in trouble

② where to go when you feel alone

③ what to do when you feel scared

④ how to go to the safest place in the world

⑤ what to do when an earthquake strikes

[06~10] 다음 글을 읽고 물음에 답하시오.

How did you do on the quiz? Can you ⓐsurvive an earthquake safely? Here ⓑ_____ some safety tips ⓒ_____ can be helpful in an earthquake. Let's check them one ⓓ_____ one and learn what to do.

06 다음 중 밑줄 친 ⓐ의 의미로 가장 적절한 것은?

① find a hiding place

② affect someone in a bad way

③ remain alive

④ keep someone from being harmed

⑤ break something into parts

서답형
07 be동사의 알맞은 형태를 빈칸 ⓑ에 쓰시오.

➡ _____

---

08 빈칸 ⓒ에 들어갈 말로 적절한 것을 **모두** 고르시오.

① who ② whom ③ that
④ which ⑤ whose

09 다음 중 빈칸 ⓓ에 들어갈 말과 같은 말이 들어가는 것은?

① We left _____ 3 o'clock.
② Are you interested _____ painting?
③ I know that she traveled _____ bus.
④ The shop is crowded _____ tourists.
⑤ They look forward _____ seeing each other again.

10 다음은 위 글의 앞에 나온 내용을 설명한 문장이다. 빈칸에 알맞은 말을 쓰시오. (2단어)

• Before the passage, there was _____ which we should take.

➡ _____

[11~16] 다음 글을 읽고 물음에 답하시오.

Here are some safety tips which can be helpful in an earthquake. Let's check them ⓐ_____ and learn what to do.
① Don't run outside when things are shaking. ② Find a table or a desk and take cover under ⓑit. ③ You can hold on to the legs ⓒto protect yourself. ④ They can break during an earthquake and hurt you. ⑤

11 빈칸 ⓐ에 들어갈 말로 가장 적절한 것은?

① case by case ② side by side
③ little by little ④ day by day
⑤ one by one

12 밑줄 친 ⓑ가 가리키는 것을 위 글에서 찾아 쓰시오.

➡ _____

13 ①~⑤ 중 다음 주어진 문장이 들어가기에 가장 적절한 곳은?

Also, stay away from windows.

① ② ③ ④ ⑤

14 위 글의 내용을 참고하여 다음 빈칸에 알맞은 말을 어법에 맞게 쓰시오.

To protect yourself, you should find a table or a desk _____ _____ you can hold on to and take cover _____ _____.

15 다음 중 밑줄 친 ⓒ와 쓰임이 같은 것은?

① I want you to come back to me.
② Is it possible to be safe during an earthquake?
③ Emilia went out to buy some snacks.
④ They hoped to visit there again.
⑤ Do you have something to write with?

16 다음 중 글의 내용과 일치하는 것은?

① Running outside during an earthquake is helpful.
② It is good to stand still when things are shaking.
③ You should hold on to your legs.
④ Putting your things under a table or a desk is important.
⑤ Standing near the window can hurt you.

Reading **87**

[17~21] 다음 글을 읽고 물음에 답하시오.

You can go outside when the shaking stops. (A)[Getting / To get] out of buildings, don't use the elevator. Take the stairs. It's (B)[very / much] safer. Once you are outside, find an empty space that is far from buildings. There may be people ⓐ_____ want to hold on to a pole or a tree, but think again. That's a bad idea (C)[because of / because] it can fall on you.

17 빈칸 ⓐ에 들어갈 말로 적절한 것을 모두 고르시오.

① which   ② whom   ③ who
④ that   ⑤ whose

18 (A)~(C)에서 어법상 옳은 것끼리 바르게 짝지은 것은?

① Getting – very – because of
② To get – very – because
③ Getting – much – because of
④ To get – much – because
⑤ Getting – much – because

서답형
19 위 글의 내용에 맞게 다음 대화의 빈칸에 알맞은 말을 쓰시오.

A: Now, we can get out of this building.
B: What makes you think so?
A: It's because _____ _____ .

20 다음 중 위 글의 내용과 일치하지 않는 것은?

① If the shaking stops, we can go outside.
② It is not a good idea to use the elevator.
③ You should stand still near the building.
④ It is possible that a pole falls on you.
⑤ The empty space should be far from buildings.

서답형
21 다음과 같이 풀이되는 단어를 위 글에서 찾아 쓰시오.

not having any people; containing nothing

➡ _____

[22~26] 다음 글을 읽고 물음에 답하시오.

(A)_____ .
Here are some tips. Let's learn (B)what to do and be (C)_____!
A wet floor can be dangerous. People might slip and fall. So you should wipe up the water on the floor. Broken glass can be also dangerous. You should clean up the broken glass because people might step on the broken glass.

서답형
22 다음 두 문장을 하나의 문장으로 만들어 빈칸 (A)에 쓰시오.

• There are many situations.
• They can be dangerous.

➡ _____

23 밑줄 친 (B)를 대신하여 쓸 수 있는 것은?

① what you do
② what we learn
③ what we should do
④ what you have
⑤ what we should get

서답형
24 빈칸 (C)에는 본문에 있는 한 단어의 반의어가 들어간다. (C)에 들어갈 알맞은 말을 쓰시오.

➡ _____

서답형

25 According to the writer, what can be dangerous to people? Answer in English with a full sentence.

➡ _____

_____

중요

26 위 글의 내용과 일치하는 것은?

① People like to slip on the floor.

② If a floor is wet, you should wipe it up.

③ It is hard to say that a wet floor is dangerous.

④ People can fall on broken glass.

⑤ We should be careful about glass.

[27~32] 다음 글을 읽고 물음에 답하시오.

You can go outside when the shaking stops. To get out of buildings, don't use the elevator. Take the stairs. It's much ①safer. Once you are ②outside, find an empty space that is far from buildings. There may be people who want to hold (A)_____ to a pole or a tree, but think again. That's a ③fine idea because it can fall (B)_____ you.

Earthquakes can strike anytime. They can be ④scary experiences for everyone. So learn (C)_____ to be safe in an earthquake. You can avoid injuries and protect yourself. Follow these tips and ⑤be safe!

27 빈칸 (A)와 (B)에 공통으로 들어갈 말로 가장 적절한 것은?

① in   ② toward   ③ on

④ by   ⑤ with

중요

28 다음 중 빈칸 (C)에 들어갈 말과 같은 것은?

① _____ time is it now?

② _____ beautiful the flower is!

③ _____ do you do for a living?

④ _____ a scary moment it was!

⑤ _____ makes you say so?

중요

29 ①~⑤ 중 글의 흐름상 어색한 것은?

①   ②   ③   ④   ⑤

30 다음 중 위 글에서 반의어를 찾을 수 없는 것은?

① inside   ② full   ③ close to

④ dangerous   ⑤ prevent

서답형

31 위 글의 내용에 맞게 다음 대화의 빈칸을 알맞게 채우시오.

A: I don't know _____ out of the building.

B: We'd better _____ _____ _____.
I heard that it is safer than using the elevator.

서답형

32 Once you are outside, what should you look for? Answer in English with a full sentence.

➡ _____

[01~04] 다음 글을 읽고 물음에 답하시오.

Do you know what to do when an earthquake strikes? Take this quiz and think about ⓐ_____ during ⓑthis kind of natural disaster.
1. When things start ⓒ_____, run outside quickly. (○ / ✕)
2. Stay away from windows. (○ / ✕)
3. Use the stairs to get out of buildings. (○ / ✕)
4. When you are outside, hold on to a pole or a tree. (○ / ✕)

⭐**01** 주어진 단어를 어법에 맞게 활용하여 빈칸 ⓐ에 쓰시오.

(how / safe)

➡ _____

02 밑줄 친 ⓑ가 가리키는 것을 위 글에서 찾아 쓰시오.

➡ _____

⭐**03** 주어진 동사를 어법에 맞게 빈칸 ⓒ에 쓰시오.

shake

➡ _____

04 다음과 같이 풀이되는 단어를 위 글에서 찾아 쓰시오.

to affect someone or something suddenly in a bad way, to cause damage or harm to someone or something

➡ _____

[05~07] 다음 글을 읽고 물음에 답하시오.

How did you do on the quiz? Can you survive an earthquake safely? ⓐHere are some safety tips which can be helpful in an earthquake. Let's check ⓑthem one by one and learn ⓒwhat to do.

05 밑줄 친 ⓐ를 두 개의 문장으로 풀어 쓰시오.

➡ _____

➡ _____

⭐**06** 밑줄 친 ⓑ가 가리키는 것을 위 글에서 찾아 쓰시오.

➡ _____

07 적절한 조동사를 이용하여 밑줄 친 ⓒ와 같은 의미의 문장을 쓰시오.

➡ _____

[08~10] 다음 글을 읽고 물음에 답하시오.

Here ⓐ_____ some safety tips which can be helpful in an earthquake. Let's check them one by one and ⓑ_____ what to do.

Don't run outside when things are shaking. Find a table or a desk and take cover under it. You can hold on to the legs ⓒ_____ yourself. ⓓAlso, stay away from windows. They can break during an earthquake and hurt you.

08 주어진 동사를 문맥과 어법에 맞게 빈칸 ⓐ, ⓑ, ⓒ에 쓰시오.

(protect / learn / be)

➡ ⓐ_____ ⓑ_____ ⓒ_____

09 적절한 관계대명사를 이용하여 밑줄 친 ⓓ를 하나의 문장으로 쓰시오.

➡ _____

_____

10 주어진 단어를 바르게 배열하여 다음 물음에 답하시오.

Q: Why is taking cover under a table helpful?

A: (things / and / tables / fall / because / desks / us / when / protect / can)

➡ _____

[11~17] 다음 글을 읽고 물음에 답하시오.

You can go outside when the shaking stops. To get out of buildings, don't use the elevator. Take the stairs. It's much safer. Once you are outside, (A)_____. There may be people who want to hold on to a pole or a tree, but think again. That's a bad idea because it can fall on you.

Earthquakes can strike anytime. They can be scary experiences for everyone. So learn how to be safe in an earthquake. You can avoid injuries and protect yourself. Follow these tips and be safe!

11 다음 두 문장을 하나의 문장으로 연결하여 빈칸 (A)에 쓰시오.

• Find an empty space.
• It is far from buildings.

➡ _____

12 글의 내용에 맞게 다음 빈칸에 알맞은 말을 쓰시오.

Q: When can you go outside?

A: _____, we can go outside.

➡ _____

13 글의 내용에 맞게 빈칸에 알맞은 말을 쓰시오.

_____ _____ _____ is much safer than _____ _____ _____.

14 글의 내용에 맞게 다음 물음에 답하시오.

Q: Why is holding on to a pole or a tree a bad idea?

A: It's because _____.

➡ _____

15 지진으로 인한 흔들림이 멈춘 후 하지 말아야 할 두 가지 행동을 주어진 단어를 이용하여 쓰시오.

don't

➡ _____
➡ _____

16 주어진 단어를 활용하여 위 글의 주제를 쓰시오.

(how / to / during)

➡ _____

17 위 글의 내용에 맞게 다음 빈칸에 알맞은 말을 쓰시오.

Because earthquakes can be scary experiences for everyone, we must _____ _____ _____ _____ _____ _____ _____ .

Real Life Communication B

A: I heard about your accident. I was worried about you.
　　　　　~에 대해 들었다　　　　　　　　~에 대해 걱정하다 (= be anxious about = be concerned about)

B: Thanks. I hurt my hand, but it's not serious. I'll be okay.
　　　　　　　다치다

A: Good. You should watch your hands when you close the door.
　　　　　　충고 표현 '너는 ~해야 한다'　　　　　　　　　~할 때

B: You're right. I will.
　　　=That's right.

구문해설　• accident: 사고　• serious: 심각한　• close: 닫다

A: 네 사고에 대해 들었어. 네가 걱정되었어.

B: 고마워. 손을 다쳤지만 심각하지 않아. 괜찮을 거야.

A: 다행이야. 문을 닫을 때 손을 조심해야 해.

B: 맞아. 그럴게.

Culture & Life

When an earthquake struck in Italy in 2016, people found Georgia thanks to
　　　　　　　　　　　　　넓은 장소와 연도 앞에 전치사 in

Leo, a dog. Leo found the eight-year-old girl 16 hours after the earthquake
동격 (Leo라는 개)　　　　　　　　　　　　　~한지 16시간이 지나

struck.

구문해설　• strike: (일이) 발생하다　• thanks to: ~ 덕분에　• find: 발견하다

2016년 이탈리아에 지진이 발생했을 때, 사람들은 Leo라는 개 덕분에 Georgia를 발견했다. Leo는 지진 발생 후 16시간이 지나 그 8살짜리 소녀를 발견했다.

Culture & Life Project

Here are the items for our survival bag. We packed some food and water. We
여기에 ~이 있다　　　　　　　　　　　　　　　약간의

need them to survive. We also packed some matches that might be helpful in
=food and water to부정사의 부사적 용법 중 목적(~하기 위해서)　　　　주격 관계대명사

disasters. We put medicine in the bag, too. We might need it for injuries.
　　　　　　　　　　　　　또한　　　~일지도 모르다 medicine

구문해설　• survival bag: 생존 가방　• pack: ~을 싸다　• match: 성냥　• disaster: 재난　• injury: 부상

여기 우리의 생존 가방에 들어갈 물품이 있습니다. 우리는 약간의 음식과 물을 챙겼습니다. 우리는 생존하기 위해서 그것들이 필요합니다. 우리는 또한 재난 발생 시 유용할 수 있는 성냥을 챙겼습니다. 가방에 약품도 넣었습니다. 부상 당했을 때 필요할 수 있습니다.

영역별 핵심문제

01 다음 중 나머지 네 개의 단어들을 포함할 수 있는 것은?

① flood
② drought
③ earthquake
④ disaster
⑤ storm

02 다음 영영풀이가 가리키는 것을 고르시오.

> the state of not being dangerous or harmful

① safety
② pole
③ hazard
④ elevator
⑤ occasion

03 다음 중 밑줄 친 부분의 뜻풀이가 바르지 <u>않은</u> 것은?

① The floor is wet and <u>slippery</u>.
　　　　　　　　　부드러운
② I have a really <u>sore</u> throat. 아픈
③ There is not enough <u>space</u> between the desk and the bed.　공간
④ I heard about the news of the <u>disaster</u>.
　　　　　　　　　　　　재난
⑤ You should always wear a helmet for the <u>safety</u>. 안전

04 다음 문장에 공통으로 들어갈 말을 고르시오.

> • My parents worked hard to _____ my tuition fee.
> • Jack _____ed his mouth with his hands.
> • Emma designed the _____ of this book.

① cost
② avoid
③ head
④ fix
⑤ cover

05 다음 문장의 빈칸에 들어갈 말을 보기에서 골라 쓰시오.

> ┤ 보기 ├
> take a rest / keep in mind / one by one / why don't you

(1) _____ _____ _____ that it's better to be safe than sorry.
(2) Children are getting off the bus _____ _____ _____ .
(3) You'd better _____ _____ _____ during the break time.
(4) _____ _____ _____ go see a doctor?

06 다음 우리말을 주어진 단어를 이용하여 영작하시오.

(1) 너는 네 모자를 꼭 잡아야 한다. (should / hold / hat / to)
　➡ _____
(2) 나는 혼잡한 장소에서 떨어져 있기 위해 노력했다. (stay / places / away / crowded)
　➡ _____
(3) 내 남동생은 자동차 뒤에 숨었다. (younger / behind / took)
　➡ _____

[07~08] 다음 대화를 읽고 물음에 답하시오.

Tom: Yujin, what's wrong?
Yujin: (A) It hurts a lot.
Tom: (B) Why don't you go see a doctor?
Yujin: (C) I'm going to go after school today.
Tom: (D) I hope you feel better soon.
Yujin: (E) I hope so, too.

07 위 대화의 (A)~(E) 중 다음 문장이 들어가기에 적절한 곳은?

> I'm worried about my leg.

① (A) ② (B) ③ (C) ④ (D) ⑤ (E)

08 위 대화를 읽고 대답할 수 <u>없는</u> 것은?

① What's the matter with Yujin?
② Where does Yujin hurt?
③ What is Yujin going to do after school?
④ What does Tom hope for now?
⑤ Why didn't Yujin go see a doctor?

[09~11] 다음 대화를 읽고 물음에 답하시오.

Jack: Dad, I'm going out to play basketball with Minu.
Dad: Did you finish cleaning your room?
Jack: No, not yet. Can I do it later?
Dad: No. (A)_____
Jack: Okay. I'll clean my room and then play basketball.
Dad: Good. (B)Don't forget to be home by six o'clock. (remember)
Jack: Okay.

09 위 대화의 빈칸 (A)에 들어갈 말로 나머지와 의도가 <u>다른</u> 것은?

① You should clean your room first.
② I think you ought to clean your room first.
③ You'd better clean your room first.
④ If I were you, I'd clean your room first.
⑤ Why didn't you clean your room first?

10 위 대화의 밑줄 친 (B)와 의미가 같도록 주어진 표현을 사용하여 다시 쓰시오.

➡ _____

11 위 대화의 내용과 일치하지 <u>않는</u> 것은?

① Jack은 Minu와 농구하기 위해 외출할 예정이다.
② Jack은 방청소를 끝내지 않았다.
③ Jack의 아버지는 Jack에게 방청소부터 할 것을 충고하였다.
④ Jack은 6시까지 귀가할 것이다.
⑤ Jack은 Minu와 농구를 한 후 방청소를 하기로 아버지와 약속하였다.

[12~14] 다음 대화를 읽고 물음에 답하시오.

Brian: What are you watching?
Jane: It's a program about earthquakes.
Brian: Sounds (A)[interesting / interested]. I'm (B)[worrying / worried] about earthquakes these days.
Jane: Me, too. This program has some helpful tips.
Brian: Really? What does it say?
Jane: When things start to shake, you need to take (C)[cover / to cover] under a table.
Brian: Oh, I didn't know that.

12 위 대화의 (A)~(C)에 들어갈 알맞은 말을 고르시오.

➡ (A) _____, (B) _____, (C) _____

13 What are Brian and Jane worried about these days?

➡ _____

14 According to the program, what should you do when the earthquake occurs?

➡ _____

[15~16] 다음 대화를 읽고 물음에 답하시오.

> Emily: What time is the movie?
> Tom: (A) It starts at 4:30.
> Emily: (B) Oh, no. We only have 20 minutes left. Let's run!
> Tom: (C) You should walk on the stairs.
> Emily: (D) You're right. We can be a little late.
> Tom: (E) Yes. Better safe than sorry.

15 위 대화의 (A)~(E) 중 주어진 문장이 들어가기에 적절한 곳은?

> No! You might fall and hurt yourself.

① (A) ② (B) ③ (C) ④ (D) ⑤ (E)

16 위 대화의 내용과 일치하도록 빈칸을 완성하시오.

> Although Tom and Emily were late a little for the movie, they agreed that there was nothing more important than _____.

Grammar

17 다음 빈칸에 적절하지 <u>않은</u> 것은?

> The man _____ is sitting there.

① for whom I was looking
② whom I was looking for
③ I was looking for
④ that I was looking for
⑤ for I was looking

18 다음 중 우리말을 영어로 바르게 옮기지 <u>않은</u> 것은?

① Julie는 그 열쇠를 어디에 두어야 할지 확신하지 못해.
→ Julie isn't sure where to put the key.
② 나는 기타 치는 방법을 배우고 싶어.
→ I want to learn how to play the guitar.
③ 친구가 유명한 배우인 그 여자를 아니?
→ Do you know the woman who friend is a famous actor?
④ 많은 학생들이 존경하는 그 선생님은 나의 아버지이다.
→ The teacher whom in many students look up to is my father.
⑤ 나는 그곳에 언제 갈지 결정 못하겠어.
→ I can't decide when to go there.

19 다음 대화의 밑줄 친 ⓑ와 같은 표현을 빈칸 ⓐ에 쓰시오.

> A: Did you answer the question?
> B: No, I didn't. I don't know ⓐ_____.
> Do you have any idea ⓑ<u>what I should say</u>?

➡ _____

20 다음 빈칸에 들어갈 말이 바르게 짝지어진 것은?

> • What is the title of the book _____ cover is colorful?
> • What is the title of the book _____ you bought last week?

① which – that
② that – which
③ whose – which
④ whose – whose
⑤ whose – whom

21 다음 중 어법상 바르지 <u>않은</u> 것은?

> The man ①who ②was wearing a blue suit ③showed me ④where I should ⑤to wash my hands.

22 다음 빈칸에 공통으로 들어갈 말로 가장 적절한 것은?

> • The chair _____ you made is very comfortable.
> • I can't decide _____ dress to buy.

① that　　② who　　③ whose
④ which　　⑤ what

23 다음 빈칸에 적절한 말로 옳은 것을 <u>모두</u> 고르시오.

> The people _____ gathered together are the guests of the party.

① which　　② who　　③ that
④ whose　　⑤ whom

24 주어진 단어와 to부정사를 활용하여 다음 우리말을 영어로 쓰시오.

> 너는 너의 돈을 현명하게 쓰는 법을 알아야 해.
> (should / know / use / to / wisely)

➡ _____

25 다음 중 밑줄 친 부분의 쓰임이 <u>다른</u> 하나는?

① He is not the man <u>who</u> will betray us.
② The boys <u>who</u> took my class are noisy.
③ Do you know the girl <u>who</u> Kevin likes?
④ Jake is the child <u>who</u> had lunch with my son.
⑤ I don't know <u>who</u> he is.

26 적절한 관계사를 이용하여 다음 두 문장을 하나의 문장으로 쓰시오.

> • Where is the ketchup?
> • It was in the refrigerator.

➡ _____

27 빈칸에 공통으로 들어갈 말로 가장 적절한 것은?

> • Mike, _____ do you think about learning it?
> • Please inform me _____ to do next.

① who　　② when　　③ where
④ how　　⑤ what

28 다음 빈칸에 알맞은 말을 쓰시오.

> I can't decide _____ _____ _____ _____.
> 나는 무엇에 대하여 쓸지 결정할 수 없어.

Reading

[29~31] 다음 글을 읽고 물음에 답하시오.

> Do you know what to do when an earthquake strikes? Take this quiz and think about ⓐ _____ to be safe during this kind of natural disaster.
> 1. When things start to shake, run outside quickly. (o / x)
> 2. Stay away from windows. (o / x)
> 3. Use the stairs to get out of buildings. (o / x)
> 4. When you are outside, hold on to a pole or a tree. (o / x)
>
> ⓑ_____ did you do on the quiz? Can you survive an earthquake safely? Here are some safety tips which can be helpful in an earthquake. Let's check them one by one and learn what to do.

29 다음 중 ⓐ와 ⓑ에 공통으로 들어갈 말로 가장 적절한 것은?
(대·소문자 무시)

① when   ② what   ③ how
④ where   ⑤ who

30 다음 중 위 글의 내용과 일치하는 것은?

① The passage is about living without natural disasters.
② The quiz is not helpful at all.
③ The writer wants to talk about some safety tips.
④ The quiz is about how to plant trees.
⑤ We can survive an earthquake easily.

31 다음 우리말에 맞게 빈칸에 알맞은 말을 쓰시오.

> • 글쓴이가 우리와 함께 확인하기를 원하는 안전 지침은 지진 발생 시 도움이 될 수 있다.
> = Some _____ _____ _____ the writer wants to check with us _____ _____ _____ in an earthquake.

[32~33] 다음 글을 읽고 물음에 답하시오.

Here are some safety tips which can be helpful in an earthquake. Let's check them one by one and learn what to do.

Don't run outside when things are shaking. Find a table or a desk and take cover under it. You can hold on to the legs to protect yourself. ⓐ_____, stay away from windows. They can break during an earthquake and hurt you.

32 빈칸 ⓐ에 들어갈 말로 가장 적절한 것은?

① However   ② Therefore
③ Moreover   ④ Likewise
⑤ On the other hand

33 다음 중 글의 내용과 일치하지 <u>않는</u> 것은?

① The writer gives us a few safety tips for an earthquake.
② The writer wants readers to check the tips one by one.
③ When things are shaking, we should find a table or a desk.
④ We should jump on the table in an earthquake.
⑤ The writer tells us not to run outside in an earthquake.

[34~35] 다음 글을 읽고 물음에 답하시오.

You can go outside when the shaking stops. ⓐ <u>To get</u> out of buildings, don't use the elevator. Take the stairs. It's much safer. Once you are outside, find an empty space that is far from buildings. There may be people who want to hold on to a pole or a tree, but think again. That's a bad idea because it can fall on you.

34 다음 중 밑줄 친 ⓐ와 쓰임이 같은 것은?

① I want <u>to have</u> some pizza.
② Julia came here <u>to meet</u> me.
③ Do you need anything <u>to wear</u>?
④ It is nice <u>to see</u> you again.
⑤ They encouraged me <u>to try</u> it again.

35 다음 중 글의 내용과 일치하는 것은?

① We can go out anytime we want.
② Using the elevator is safe when we get out of buildings.
③ Taking the stairs is not as safe as using the elevator.
④ When we are outside, we'd better be in an empty space.
⑤ We should not think twice when we want to hold on to something.

01 출제율 90%

다음 대화가 자연스럽게 이어지도록 순서대로 배열하시오.

> (A) You're right. I will.
> (B) I heard about your accident. I was worried about you.
> (C) Thanks. I hurt my hand, but it's not serious. I'll be okay.
> (D) Good. You should watch your hands when you close the door.

➡ _____

02 출제율 90%

주어진 단어를 바르게 배열하여 문장을 완성하시오. 필요하다면 단어를 추가하시오.

> A director of a film _____.
> (what / is / a person / do / who / the actors / tells)

➡ _____

[03~04] 다음 대화를 읽고 물음에 답하시오.

> Tom: Yujin, what's wrong?
> Yujin: (A)내 다리가 걱정돼. It hurts a lot.
> Tom: Why don't you go see a doctor?
> Yujin: I'm going to go after school today.
> Tom: (B)_____
> Yujin: I hope so, too.

03 출제율 85%

위 대화의 우리말 (A)를 영작하시오.

➡ _____

04 출제율 90%

위 대화의 빈칸 (B)에 들어갈 말을 보기에 주어진 단어를 모두 배열하여 완성하시오.

> ┤ 보기 ├
> hope / feel / I / soon / better / you

➡ _____

[05~06] 다음 대화를 읽고 물음에 답하시오.

> Brian: What are you watching?
> Jane: It's a program about earthquakes.
> Brian: Sounds interesting. I'm worried about earthquakes these days.
> Jane: Me, too. This program has some (A) helpful tips.
> Brian: Really? What does it say?
> Jane: When things start to shake, you need to take cover under a table.
> Brian: Oh, I didn't know that.

05 출제율 100%

위 대화의 밑줄 친 (A)와 바꾸어 쓸 수 있는 것은?

① useful   ② handy
③ friendly   ④ generous
⑤ convenient

06 출제율 90%

위 대화의 내용과 일치하도록 Jane의 일기를 완성하시오.

> Mon, April 29th. 2019.
> Today, I watched a program about (A)_____. Because I was concerned about (A)_____ these days, it was so interesting. While I was watching the program, I talked with Brian and gave him (B)_____ for the earthquake safety. The program said that when things around us start to shake, (C)_____.

➡ (A) _____
➡ (B) _____
➡ (C) _____

[07~08] 다음 대화를 읽고 물음에 답하시오.

Jack: Dad, I'm going out ⓐto play basketball with Minu.
Dad: Did you finish ⓑto clean your room?
Jack: No, ⓒnot yet. Can I do it later?
Dad: No. You should clean your room first.
Jack: Okay. I'll clean my room and then ⓓplay basketball.
Dad: Good. Don't forget ⓔto be home by six o'clock.
Jack: Okay.

출제율 95%

07 위 대화의 밑줄 친 ⓐ~ⓔ 중 어법상 **틀린** 것을 찾아 바르게 고치시오.

➡ _____

출제율 90%

08 위 대화를 읽고 대답할 수 **없는** 것은?

① What is Jack going to do with Minu?
② What does Jack's dad ask him to do before going out?
③ Why does Jack want to clean his room later?
④ What should Jack remember to do?
⑤ By when should Jack be home?

[09~10] 다음 대화를 읽고 물음에 답하시오.

Brian: There was a big fire at the city library yesterday.
Mina (A) Yes, I heard about it. I was worried about the people there.
Brian: (B) Don't worry. Everybody was okay. They all followed the safety rules.
Mina (C) Really? What are the rules?
Brian: (D) Then stay low and escape.
Mina (E) Oh, I didn't know that.
Brian: ⓐ_____ It might be helpful some day.

출제율 85%

09 위 대화의 빈칸 ⓐ에 들어갈 말을 보기에 주어진 단어를 모두 배열하여 완성하시오.

┌─ 보기 ─────────────────────────┐
should / keep / mind / in / you / that
└───────────────────────────────┘

➡ _____

출제율 90%

10 위 대화의 (A)~(E) 중 주어진 문장이 들어가기에 적절한 곳은?

You need to cover your nose and mouth with a wet towel.

① (A) ② (B) ③ (C) ④ (D) ⑤ (E)

출제율 100%

11 빈칸에 공통으로 들어갈 말은?

• The problem is not _____ easy.
• Everything _____ you cooked for me is very delicious.
• I think _____ he wants you to take the taxi.

① what ② who ③ that
④ which ⑤ whom

출제율 90%

12 다음 중 뜻이 같은 문장이 **아닌** 것은?

① The girl is showing him where to dig.
 = The girl is showing him where he should dig.
② I know the man. I admire his goal.
 = I know the man who I admire.
③ Tell me when to stand up.
 = Tell me when I should stand up.
④ He called the girl. She lives in Canada.
 = He called the girl who lives in Canada.
⑤ Susan met a girl. Her name is Linda.
 = Susan met a girl whose name is Linda.

13 다음 대화의 빈칸에 알맞은 말을 쓰시오.

> A: I don't know where I should go.
> B: Don't worry. I will explain to you
> _____ _____ _____ .

14 다음 중 어법상 옳은 것을 바르게 묶은 것은?

> ⓐ The music which I listened to last night was popular in the 2000s.
> ⓑ The dress Amelia is wearing is mine.
> ⓒ In our town, there are people don't have their own gardens.
> ⓓ Thomas actually enjoyed playing the game we did it together.
> ⓔ Mr. Thomson teaches a subject which I am really into.

① ⓐ, ⓑ, ⓓ
② ⓐ, ⓑ, ⓔ
③ ⓑ, ⓒ, ⓓ
④ ⓑ, ⓒ, ⓔ
⑤ ⓒ, ⓓ, ⓔ

15 다음 중 어법상 바르지 않은 것은?

① The man is holding a mug that is expensive.
② People who do taekwondo wear white uniforms.
③ Bradley wanted me to tell him where to park the car.
④ It teaches you how you to protect yourself.
⑤ The students who won the group jump rope felt excited.

16 다음 빈칸에 공통으로 들어갈 말은?

> • The couple _____ adopted the child are happy now.
> • The goldfish _____ is in the fishbowl looks so cute.

① which
② that
③ whom
④ what
⑤ whose

17 주어진 단어를 활용하여 다음 우리말을 영어로 쓰시오.

> 나와 함께 대화를 나눈 그 사람은 내게 좋은 조언을 해주었다.
> (talk with / give / advice)

➡ _____

_____

[18~20] 다음 글을 읽고 물음에 답하시오.

How did you do on the quiz? Can you survive an earthquake safely? Here are some safety tips ⓐ_____ can be helpful in an earthquake. Let's check (A)[it / them] one by one and learn what to do.

Don't run outside when things are shaking. Find a table or a desk and take cover under it. You can hold on to the legs to protect (B)[you / yourself]. Also, stay away from windows. They can break (C)[during / while] an earthquake and hurt you.

18 다음 중 빈칸 ⓐ에 들어갈 말과 다른 것은?

① The key _____ you put on the table is lost.
② He bought a bike _____ is similar to mine.
③ Bony is the girl _____ I like most.
④ Do you know the car _____ handle is broken?
⑤ Cathy has a dog _____ looks very cute.

19 (A)~(C) 중 어법상 옳은 것끼리 바르게 짝지은 것은? *출제율 100%*

① it – you – during

② them – you – while

③ them – yourself – during

④ them – yourself – while

⑤ it – you – while

20 다음 대화의 빈칸에 해당하는 말을 위 글에서 찾아 쓰시오. *출제율 90%*

> A: Things start to shake. I think an earthquake strikes. I don't know where to hide.
>
> B: _____.

[21~25] 다음 글을 읽고 물음에 답하시오.

> You can go outside when the shaking stops. To get out of buildings, don't use the elevator. ① Take the stairs. ⓐIt's much safer. Once you are outside, find an empty space ⓑthat is far from buildings. ② There ⓒmay be people who want to ⓓhold on to a pole or a tree, but think again. ③ That's a bad idea (A)because it can fall on you. ④
>
> Earthquakes can strike ⓔanytime. ⑤ So learn how to be safe in an earthquake. You can avoid injuries and protect yourself. Follow these tips and be safe!

21 ①~⑤ 중 주어진 문장이 들어가기에 가장 적절한 곳은? *출제율 95%*

> They can be scary experiences for everyone.

①   ②   ③   ④   ⑤

22 밑줄 친 (A)를 대신하여 쓰일 수 있는 것을 모두 고르시오. *출제율 90%*

① since   ② when   ③ although

④ as   ⑤ while

23 다음 중 위 글을 읽고 답할 수 없는 것은? *출제율 90%*

① When can we go outside?

② How can we get out of buildings safely?

③ Why do people hold on to something?

④ Why is holding on to a tree a bad idea?

⑤ What should we do first once we are outside?

24 위 글의 내용에 맞게 다음 빈칸에 알맞은 말을 쓰시오. *출제율 85%*

> A: I don't know _____ _____ _____ myself when an earthquake strikes.
>
> B: You can protect yourself by following some tips.

25 ⓐ~ⓔ에 대한 설명 중 바른 것은? *출제율 90%*

① ⓐ: 엘리베이터를 이용하는 것을 의미한다.

② ⓑ: 주격 관계대명사로 쓰였으므로 who로 대체 가능하다

③ ⓒ: '~해도 좋다'는 허가를 의미한다.

④ ⓓ: '~을 고수하다'는 의미이다.

⑤ ⓔ: 'at any time'으로 바꾸어 쓸 수 있다.

[01~03] 다음 대화를 읽고 물음에 답하시오.

> **Tom:** Yujin, what's ⓐwrong?
> **Yujin:** I'm ⓑworrying about my leg. It hurts a lot.
> **Tom:** Why don't you go ⓒsee a doctor?
> **Yujin:** I'm going to go after school today.
> **Tom:** I hope you feel ⓓbetter soon.
> **Yujin:** I hope ⓔso, too.

01 위 대화의 밑줄 친 ⓐ~ⓔ 중 어법상 틀린 것을 찾아 바르게 고치시오.

➡ _____

02 What is Yujin concerned about?

➡ _____

03 What is Yujin going to do after school?

➡ _____

04 주어진 단어를 바르게 배열하여 다음 우리말을 영어로 쓰시오.

> 나는 나와 함께 일하는 사람들을 좋아해.
> (with / like / work / I / the people / I / whom)

➡ _____

05 주어진 어구를 이용하여 다음 우리말을 두 가지의 영어 문장으로 쓰시오.

> 졸업 후에 무엇을 해야 할지 나는 잘 모르겠어.
> (graduation)

➡ I'm not sure _____
➡ I'm not sure _____

06 〈보기〉와 같이 하나의 문장을 두 개의 문장으로 쓰시오.

> ┤ 보기 ├
> The people who moved in our apartment enjoy talking loudly in the morning.
> ➡ The people enjoy talking loudly in the morning.
> ➡ They moved in our apartment.

(1) I want to have the cheese cake which is sold only online.

➡ _____
➡ _____

(2) Where is the cap that was in the closet?

➡ _____
➡ _____

07 다음 대화의 우리말을 주어진 단어를 사용하여 영작하시오.

> **A:** I heard about your accident.
> (A)나는 네가 걱정돼. (worried)
> **B:** Thanks. I hurt my hand, but it's not serious. I'll be okay.
> **A:** Good. (B)너는 칼을 사용할 때 손을 조심해야 해. (should, watch, hands, when)

➡ (A) _____
➡ (B) _____

08 다음 빈칸에 알맞은 말을 쓰시오.

> **A:** Can you teach me _____ _____ _____ step by step? Because I am not good at dancing.
> **B:** Oh, sure. I will teach you how you should dance.

You can go outside when the shaking stops. To get out of buildings, don't use the elevator. Take the stairs. It's much safer. Once you are outside, find an empty space that is far from buildings. (A)There may be people who want to hold on to a pole or a tree, but think again. (B)That's a bad idea because it can fall on you.

Earthquakes can (C)_____ anytime. They can be scary experiences for everyone. So learn how to be safe in an earthquake. You can (D)_____ injuries and (E)_____ yourself. (F)_____ these tips and be safe!

09 밑줄 친 (A)를 두 개의 문장으로 나누어 쓰시오.

➡ _____

➡ _____

10 밑줄 친 (B)가 의미하는 것을 우리말로 쓰시오.

➡ _____

11 주어진 동사를 어법과 문맥에 맞게 빈칸 (C)~(F)에 각각 쓰시오.

follow / protect / strike / avoid

➡ (C) _____ (D) _____
　 (E) _____ (F) _____

12 주어진 단어를 바르게 배열하여 다음 물음에 답하시오.

Q: When the shaking stops, how should you get out of buildings?
A: (safer / we / much / is / it / should / because / stairs / the / use)

➡ _____

13 위 글에서 다음 물음에 대한 답을 찾아 완전한 문장의 영어로 답하시오.

Q: What can we learn from the passage?

➡ _____

Here are some safety tips which can be helpful in an earthquake. Let's check them one by one and learn what to do.

Don't run outside when things are shaking. Find a table or a desk and take cover under it. You can hold on to the legs to protect yourself. ⓐ_____, stay away from windows. They can break during an earthquake and hurt you.

14 Write the reason why we need to stay away from windows.

➡ _____

15 위 글의 내용에 맞게 빈칸에 알맞은 말을 위 글에서 찾아 쓰시오.

The tips _____ the writer gives to readers are _____.

➡ _____

01 다음 대화의 내용과 일치하도록 Mina의 일기를 완성하시오.

> Brian: There was a big fire at the city library yesterday.
> Mina: Yes, I heard about it. I was worried about the people there.
> Brian: Don't worry. Everybody was okay. They all followed the safety rules.
> Mina: Really? What are the rules?
> Brian: You need to cover your nose and mouth with a wet towel. Then stay low and escape.
> Mina: Oh, I didn't know that.
> Brian: You should keep that in mind. It might be helpful some day.

> Tue, May 7th, 2019
> I heard that there was a big fire at the city library yesterday. I talked about it with Brian. I was concerned about (A)_____. Brian told me that everybody was safe because (B)_____. Frankly speaking, I didn't know what to do in the event of a fire. Brian told me that I should (C)_____, then stay low and escape. I kept that in mind. Moreover, I decided to study more about the safety rules.

02 주어진 동사와 '의문사+to부정사'를 이용하여 문장을 만드시오.

> prepare / cook / go / meet / buy

(1) _____
(2) _____
(3) _____
(4) _____
(5) _____

03 〈보기〉와 같이 관계대명사를 이용하여 다음 직업을 설명하는 문장을 쓰시오.

> ┌─ 보기 ─
> A carpenter is a person who makes and repairs wooden things.
> pilot / nurse / architect / dentist / farmer

(1) _____
(2) _____
(3) _____
(4) _____
(5) _____

단원별 모의고사

01 다음 영영풀이가 가리키는 것을 고르시오.

> short, quick movement back and forth or up and down

① protect ② hurt ③ shake
④ cover ⑤ change

02 다음 주어진 문장의 밑줄 친 fall과 같은 의미로 쓰인 것은?

> Be careful! You might <u>fall</u> and hurt yourself.

① The leaves were starting to <u>fall</u>.
② I visited Canada in the <u>fall</u> of 2018.
③ Do you love the weather of <u>fall</u>?
④ The <u>fall</u> term just started in the United States.
⑤ Have you ever seen Niagara <u>Falls</u>?

03 다음 문장에 공통으로 들어갈 말을 고르시오.

> • Let's take a _____ . We need to get some rest.
> • If you drop the cup, it'll _____ into pieces.
> • Do you think he can _____ a record at the Olympics?

① escape ② solve ③ break
④ slip ⑤ strike

04 다음 대화가 자연스럽게 이어지도록 순서대로 배열하시오.

> (A) It starts at 4:30.
> (B) You're right. We can be a little late.
> (C) What time is the movie?
> (D) Oh, no. We only have 20 minutes left. Let's run!
> (E) No! You might fall and hurt yourself. You should walk on the stairs.

➡ _____

05 다음 주어진 단어를 이용하여 우리말을 영작하시오.

(1) 어떻게 우리는 자연 재해에 대비할 수 있을까요? (how / prepare / natural)

➡ _____

(2) 지진이 발생할 때, 건물들이 흔들리거나 무너질 수 있다. (strikes / down)

➡ _____

(3) 계단에서 뛰지 마세요. 넘어지거나 다칠 수 있어요. (on / might / get)

➡ _____

[06~08] 다음 대화를 읽고 물음에 답하시오.

Brian: What are you watching?

Jane: It's a program about earthquakes.

Brian: Sounds interesting. I'm worried about earthquakes these days.

Jane: Me, too. This program has some helpful (A)tips.

Brian: Really? What does it say?

Jane: When things start to shake, you need to take cover under a table.

Brian: Oh, I didn't know (B)that.

06 위 대화에서 다음 영영풀이가 가리키는 말을 찾아 쓰시오.

> a shaking of a part of the Earth's surface that often causes great damage

➡ _____

07 위 대화의 밑줄 친 (A)와 바꾸어 쓸 수 있는 것을 모두 고르시오.

① data   ② information
③ guidance   ④ report
⑤ material

08 위 대화의 밑줄 친 (B)가 가리키는 것을 우리말로 20자 이내로 설명하시오.

➡ _____

09 다음 대화의 내용과 일치하도록 빈칸을 완성하시오.

> Jack: Dad, I'm going out to play basketball with Minu.
> Dad: Did you finish cleaning your room?
> Jack: No, not yet. Can I do it later?
> Dad: No. You should clean your room first.
> Jack: Okay. I'll clean my room and then play basketball.
> Dad: Good. Don't forget to be home by six o'clock.
> Jack: Okay.

⬇

> Jack was supposed to (A)_____. His dad told him to (B)_____ first before going out, but he wanted to put it off. But his dad requested him to do it first, so Jack decided to clean his room. Going out to play basketball, Jack promised to (C)_____.

➡ (A) _____
　　(B) _____
　　(C) _____

10 다음 대화의 내용과 일치하지 않는 것은?

> Sujin: It's raining. I'm worried about our picnic in the afternoon.
> Mom: It is going to rain until late afternoon today. You should go another day.
> Sujin: You're right, Mom. I'll call my friend and choose another day.

① 수진은 오후에 있을 소풍을 걱정하고 있다.
② 오늘 오후 늦게까지 비가 올 것이다.
③ 엄마는 다른 날 소풍 가는 것이 좋을 것이라고 충고하였다.
④ 수진은 엄마의 충고를 받아들였다.
⑤ 수진은 친구에게 전화해서 오후에 소풍을 갈 것이다.

11 다음 밑줄 친 ⓐ~ⓔ 중 어색한 것을 골라 바르게 고치시오.

> A: I heard about your ⓐaccidental. I was ⓑworried about you.
> B: Thanks. I hurt my hand, but it's not ⓒserious. I'll be okay.
> A: Good. You should ⓓwatch your hands when you ⓔclose the door.
> B: You're right. I will.

➡ _____

12 다음 중 짝지어진 대화가 어색한 것은?

① A: It's raining a lot outside.
　 B: I think you should take an umbrella.
② A: The floor is slippery.
　 B: I like your bed slippers.
③ A: I'm going to ride my bike.
　 B: How about bring your helmet?
④ A: I have a bad cold.
　 B: Why don't you go see a doctor?
⑤ A: I'm worried about the storm.
　 B: You'd better stay inside.

13 주어진 문장의 빈칸에 들어갈 말과 다른 하나는?

> There were many children _____ knew what to do in the public place.

① Look at the house _____ has large windows.
② Shakespeare wrote many plays _____ are read all over the world.
③ I have two sisters _____ I should take care of.
④ That is the boy _____ sister won the first prize.
⑤ There was a dog _____ was looking after its babies.

14 다음 우리말을 바르게 영작한 것을 모두 고르시오.

> 나는 눈이 큰 저 소녀를 안다.

① I know the girl which has big eyes.
② I know the girl whose eyes are big.
③ I know the girl who is big eyes.
④ I know the girl that eyes are big.
⑤ I know the girl who has big eyes.

15 다음 우리말에 맞게 빈칸에 알맞은 말을 쓰시오.

> 무엇을 먹을지 결정하는 건 쉬운 일이 아니다.
> It is not easy to _____ _____ _____ _____.

16 주어진 단어를 바르게 배열하여 다음 문장을 완성하시오.

> Monday _____ Tuesday.
> (before / that / the / comes / day / is)

➡ _____

17 다음 빈칸에 적절한 관계대명사를 바르게 배열한 것은?

> • I met a boy _____ could speak many languages.
> • This is a picture of my brother _____ life is full of adventure.

① that – whom
② who – that
③ that – whose
④ whose – whose
⑤ what – that

[18~20] 다음 글을 읽고 물음에 답하시오.

> Do you know what to do when an earthquake strikes? Take this quiz and think about how to be safe during this kind of natural disaster.
> 1. When things start to shake, run outside (A)[quick / quickly]. (o / x)
> 2. Stay away (B)[from / in] windows. (o / x)
> 3. Use the stairs (C)[getting / to get] out of buildings. (o / x)
> 4. When you are outside, hold on to a pole or a tree. (o / x)
> How did you do on the quiz? Can you survive an earthquake safely? Here are some safety tips which can be helpful in an earthquake. Let's check them one by one and learn what to do.

18 (A)~(C) 중 어법상 옳은 것끼리 바르게 짝지어진 것은?

① quick – from – getting
② quickly – in – getting
③ quick – in – to getting
④ quickly – from – to get
⑤ quick – in – to get

19 위 글의 내용에 맞게 다음 빈칸에 알맞은 말을 쓰시오.

> _____ the quiz helps us think about
>
> _____ _____ _____ _____
>
> when an earthquake _____.

20 다음 중 위 글의 내용과 일치하지 <u>않는</u> 것은?

① An earthquake is a natural disaster.

② The writer will talk about some safety tips in an earthquake.

③ Safety tips can be useful to readers.

④ The quiz is about safety rules in school.

⑤ By checking the tips, readers can learn what they should do in an earthquake.

[21~23] 다음 글을 읽고 물음에 답하시오.

Don't run outside when things are shaking. Find a table or a desk and take cover under it. You can hold on to the legs to protect yourself. (A)_____, stay away from windows. They can break during an earthquake and hurt you.

You can go outside when the shaking stops. To get out of buildings, don't use the elevator. Take the stairs. It's much safer. Once you are outside, find an empty space that is far from buildings. There may be people who want to hold on to a pole or a tree, but think again. That's a bad idea because it can fall on you.

21 다음 중 빈칸 (A)에 들어갈 말로 가장 적절한 것은?

① However   ② Therefore

③ In addition   ④ In other words

⑤ Otherwise

22 다음 중 위 글의 내용과 일치하는 것의 개수는?

ⓐ Although things stop shaking, you should stay inside.

ⓑ When things are shaking, we should find a table or a desk.

ⓒ Windows can be dangerous during an earthquake.

ⓓ After getting out of buildings, we stay close to the buildings.

ⓔ Finding an empty place is the first thing to do when we are outside.

① 1개   ② 2개   ③ 3개

④ 4개   ⑤ 5개

23 위 글의 내용에 맞도록 다음 물음에 완전한 문장의 영어로 답하시오.

> Q: To protect yourself under a table, what can you hold on to?

➡ _____

[24~25] 다음 글을 읽고 물음에 답하시오.

Darlene Etienne, a 16-year-old girl, survived the earthquake that hit Haiti in 2010. People found her 15 days after the earthquake struck. They think that she possibly survived by (A)_____ bath water.

24 주어진 단어를 어법에 맞게 빈칸 (A)에 쓰시오.

> drink

➡ _____

25 위 글의 내용과 일치하지 <u>않는</u> 것은?

① There was an earthquake in Haiti in 2010.

② Darlene was 16 years old in 2010.

③ Darlene was not found for more than two weeks.

④ Darlene is a survivor from an earthquake.

⑤ The earthquake continued for 15 days.

Happy Others, Happier Me

 의사소통 기능

- 도움 제안하기
  Let me help you.

- 칭찬에 답하기
  I'm glad you like(d) it.

🪶 언어 형식

- 목적격 관계대명사
  Here are two stories **which** I read yesterday.

- to부정사를 목적격보어로 취하는 동사
  She **asked** him **to do** the job.

Words & Expressions

교과서

Key Words

- **activity** [æktívəti] 명 활동
- **arrow** [ǽrou] 명 화살, 화살표
- **avoid** [əvɔ́id] 동 피하다
- **basket** [bǽskit] 명 바구니
- **bus stop** 버스 정류장
- **children's center** 아동 센터
- **coin** [kɔin] 명 동전
- **confusing** [kənfjúːziŋ] 형 혼란스러운
- **danger** [déindʒər] 명 위험
- **decide** [disáid] 동 결심하다
- **different** [dífərənt] 형 다른
- **disappear** [dìsəpíər] 동 사라지다
- **effort** [éfərt] 명 노력
- **explain** [ikspléin] 동 설명하다
- **few** [fju:] 형 몇몇의
- **forget** [fərgét] 동 잊어버리다
- **frame** [freim] 명 틀, 테
- **free** [fri:] 형 무료의
- **glad** [glæd] 형 기쁜
- **hear** [hiər] 동 듣다
- **map** [mæp] 명 지도
- **mentee** [mentí:] 명 멘티

- **mentor** [méntɔːr] 명 멘토
- **need** [ni:d] 동 필요로 하다
- **outside** [áutsàid] 형 바깥의, 외부의
- **pay phone** 공중전화
- **plan** [plæn] 동 …하려고 계획하다
- **plastic bag** 비닐봉지
- **possible** [pásəbl] 형 가능한
- **refrigerator** [rifrídʒərèitər] 명 냉장고
- **rest** [rest] 동 쉬다, 휴식하다
- **say** [sei] 동 (글·글씨 등이) 쓰이다
- **secret** [síːkrit] 명 비밀, 비결 형 비밀의
- **sign** [sain] 명 표지판
- **soap** [soup] 명 비누
- **solution** [səlúːʃən] 명 해결책
- **solve** [sɑlv] 동 해결하다
- **start** [stɑːrt] 동 시작하다
- **sticker** [stíkər] 명 딱지, 스티커
- **street** [stri:t] 명 거리
- **success** [səksés] 명 성공
- **trash** [træʃ] 명 쓰레기
- **volunteer club** 자원 봉사 동아리
- **wonderful** [wʌ́ndərfəl] 형 훌륭한, 굉장한

Key Expressions

- **come up with** (생각을) 찾아내다, 제시하다
- **during the day** 낮 동안
- **give it a try** 시도하다, 한번 해 보다
- **give out** …을 나누어 주다
- **have to** …해야 한다
- **on one's own** 자기 스스로

- **one day** (과거의) 어느 날
- **put up** 설치하다, 세우다
- **stop -ing** …하는 것을 멈추다
- **thanks to** … 덕분에
- **the other day** 며칠 전에, 지난번, 요전에
- **waste one's time** …의 시간을 낭비하다

Word Power

※ 서로 반대되는 뜻을 가진 어휘
- **mentor** 멘토 ↔ **m** □ **same** 같은 ↔ **different** 다른
- **forget** 잊어버리다 ↔ **remember** 기억하다
- **success** 성공 ↔ **failure** 실패
- **start** 시작하다 ↔ **finish** 끝내다
- **danger** 위험 ↔ **safety** 안전

- **outside** 바깥의 ↔ **inside** 안쪽의
- **possible** 가능한 ↔ **impossible** 불가능한
- **free** 한가한 ↔ **busy** 바쁜

※ 동사 – 명사
- **succeed** 성공하다 — **success** 성공
- **fail** 실패하다 — **failure** 실패

- **advise** 충고하다 — **advice** 충고
- **solve** 해결하다 — **solution** 해결

English Dictionary

- **activity** 활동
  → something that is done as work for a particular purpose 특별한 목적을 위한 일로 이루어지는 것
- **arrow** 화살표
  → a mark that is shaped like an arrow and that is used to show direction 화살과 같은 모양으로 방향을 보여주기 위해 사용되는 표시
- **confusing** 혼란스러운
  → difficult to understand 이해하기 어려운
- **disappear** 사라지다
  → to stop being visible 보여지는 것이 멈추다
- **few** 몇몇의
  → not many, but some 많지 않은, 그러나 약간 있는
- **free** 무료의
  → not costing any money 어떠한 돈도 들지 않는
- **hear** 듣다
  → to be aware of sounds with your ears 당신의 귀로 소리를 인식하다
- **map** 지도
  → a drawing or plan of the earth's surface or part of it, showing countries, town, rivers, etc. 국가, 마을, 강 등을 보여주는 지구의 표면 또는 그것의 일부의 그림이나 도면

- **mentee** 멘티
  → a person who is advised and helped by a more experienced person 좀 더 경험이 있는 사람에 의해 조언을 받거나 도움을 받는 사람
- **montor** 멘토
  → someone who teaches or gives help and advice to a less experienced and often younger person 경험이 별로 없거나 종종 어린 사람에게 도움이나 조언을 주거나 가르치는 사람
- **refrigerator** 냉장고
  → a device or room that is used to keep things cold 사물들을 차갑게 유지하기 위해 사용되는 장치나 공간
- **secret** 비밀의
  → kept hidden from others 다른 사람들로부터 숨겨진
- **sign** 표지판
  → a piece of paper, wood, etc., with words or pictures on it that gives information about something 어떤 것에 관한 정보를 제공하는 글귀나 사진들이 위에 있는 종이, 나무 등의 조각
- **success** 성공
  → the correct or desired result of an attempt 어떤 시도의 정확하거나 바람직한 결과
- **start** 시작하다
  → to begin doing or using something 무언가를 하거나 사용하기 시작하다

01 다음 영영풀이가 나타내는 말을 고르시오.

> a drawing or plan of the earth's surface or part of it, showing countries, towns, rivers, etc.

① arrow ② map
③ effort ④ soap
⑤ activity

02 다음 문장에 공통으로 들어갈 말을 고르시오.

> • What does the card _____?
> • Will you _____ what you mean simply?
> • I disagree with what you _____.

① tell ② write
③ say ④ hear
⑤ listen

03 다음 중 밑줄 친 부분의 뜻풀이가 바르지 않은 것은?

① The sign in the store window says 'OPEN'. 서명
② The moon disappeared behind a cloud.
사라졌다
③ Nobody else knows about this place because it's our secret place.
비밀의
④ The arrow on the sign points north.
화살표
⑤ We did a fun activity at an English camp.
활동

04 서답형 다음 짝지어진 단어의 관계가 같도록 빈칸에 알맞은 말을 쓰시오.

> low: high = _____ : safety

05 다음 주어진 문장의 밑줄 친 free와 같은 의미로 쓰인 것은?

> • Hojun and I planned to give out free stickers today.

① I was so happy because I received free tickets.
② Each student has a free choice of course.
③ What do you like to do in your free time?
④ Free speech is one of the features of democracy.
⑤ Let's set free a bird from a cage.

06 서답형 다음 문장의 빈칸에 들어갈 말을 보기에서 골라 쓰시오.

> ┤ 보기 ├
> confusing / secret / soap / decide

(1) The road sign was really _____.
(2) You can _____ if you'll stay here or not.
(3) My sister made the _____ using the natural oil.
(4) The _____ to my health is to exercise regularly.

1 다음 짝지어진 단어의 관계가 같도록 빈칸에 알맞은 말을 쓰시오.

success : failure = possible : _____

02 다음 대화의 빈칸에 보기에 주어진 단어를 알맞게 채워 넣으시오.

| 보기 |
help / try / glad / good / tip

A: I'm not (A)_____ at science. What can I do?

B: Let me (B)_____ you. Why don't you start with easier books?

A: Okay, I'll give it a (C)_____. Thanks for the (D)_____.

B: No problem. I'm (E)_____ you like it.

03 다음 주어진 우리말과 일치하도록 주어진 단어를 모두 배열하여 문장을 완성하시오.

(1) 그는 집 앞에 'For Sale' 표지판을 세웠다.
(a 'For Sale' / put / in / of / his / he / house / up / sign / front)

➡ _____

(2) 나는 그의 도움 덕택에 이 일을 일찍 끝냈다.
(thanks / this / work / earlier / finished / I / his / to / help)

➡ _____

(3) 우리는 우리 스스로 숙제를 해야 한다.
(on / we / own / our / homework / do / our / have / to)

➡ _____

04 다음 우리말에 맞게 빈칸에 알맞은 말을 쓰시오.

(1) 네 도움 덕분에 우리는 그 일을 마칠 수 있었다.
➡ _____ _____ your help, we could finish the work.

(2) 며칠 전에 엄마는 내게 쿠키를 구워 주셨다.
➡ My mother baked cookies for me _____ _____ _____.

(3) 우리 견본을 좀 나누어 주는 게 어때?
➡ Why don't we _____ _____ some samples?

5 다음 문장의 빈칸에 들어갈 말을 보기에서 골라 쓰시오.

| 보기 |
give out / come up with / put up / one day

(1) We'll _____ free umbrellas on a rainy day.

(2) She will _____ a new idea for our club.

(3) We _____ the poster on the window.

(4) _____, all dinosaurs disappeared completely.

06 다음 영영풀이가 나타내는 말을 찾아 쓰시오.

a piece of paper, wood, etc., with words or pictures on it that gives information about something

➡ _____

Conversation

1 도움 제안하기

Let me help you. 내가 도와줄게.

■ 상대방에게 도움을 제안하고자 할 때 'Let me help you.', 'I'll help you.' 또는 'I'll give you a hand.' 등으로 표현할 수 있다.

도움 요청하기

- Would you help me out? (나를 좀 도와주시겠어요?)
- Could you do something for me? (저를 좀 도와주시겠습니까?)
- Would you give me a hand? (저 좀 도와주시겠어요?)
- Would you mind helping me? (좀 도와주시겠습니까?)

도움 제안하기

- Let me help you. (내가 도와줄게.)
- Would you like me to help you? (내가 너를 도와주길 원하니?)
- Do you need any help? (도움이 필요하세요?)
- Can I give you a hand? (도와 드릴까요?)
- May I help you? (제가 도와드릴까요?)
- How can I help you? (무엇을 도와드릴까요?)
- I'll help you. (제가 도와드릴게요.)

핵심 Check

1. 다음 우리말과 일치하도록 빈칸에 알맞은 말을 쓰시오.

   A: I don't have a bottle-opener. I can't open the bottle.

   B: Let ＿＿＿＿ ＿＿＿＿ ＿＿＿＿. (내가 도와드릴게요.)

2. 다음 우리말과 일치하도록 빈칸에 알맞은 말을 쓰시오.

   A: ＿＿＿＿ ＿＿＿＿ ＿＿＿＿ ＿＿＿＿ ＿＿＿＿? (도움이 필요하신가요?)

   B: Yes. I can't fix the light. It's too high.

3. 다음 우리말과 일치하도록 빈칸에 알맞은 말을 쓰시오.

   A: I can't swim here. It's too ＿＿＿＿. (여기서 수영을 못하겠어요. 너무 깊어요.)

   B: ＿＿＿＿ ＿＿＿＿. I'll ＿＿＿＿ ＿＿＿＿. (걱정 마세요. 제가 도와드릴게요.)

② 칭찬에 답하기

I'm glad you like it. 네가 그것을 좋아한다니 나도 기뻐.

■ 'I'm glad you like(d) it.'은 '네가 그것을 좋아한[했]다니 나도 기뻐.' 라는 뜻으로 자신이 상대방에게 해 준 일에 관해 칭찬의 말을 들었을 때 답하는 표현이다.

칭찬에 답하기

• My pleasure. (저도 기뻐요.)

• Not at all. (별 말씀을요.)

• You're welcome. (천만에요.)

• Don't mention it. (별 말씀을요.)

• I'm glad[happy, pleased] to hear that. (그 말을 들으니 기쁩니다.)

• You're so kind to say that. (그렇게 말해 주시다니 참 친절하시군요.)

• Thank you for saying so. (그렇게 말해 주셔서 감사합니다.)

핵심 Check

4. 다음 우리말과 일치하도록 빈칸에 알맞은 말을 쓰시오.

A: It's a wonderful picture. I like it. (훌륭한 그림이야. 나는 그게 마음에 들어.)

B: I'm _____ _____ _____ _____. (네가 그것을 좋아한다니 나도 기뻐.)

5. 다음 우리말과 일치하도록 빈칸에 알맞은 말을 쓰시오.

A: How nice! I really like this scarf. (멋지다! 나 이 스카프가 정말 마음에 들어.)

B: _____ _____. (저도 기뻐요.)

6. 다음 우리말과 일치하도록 빈칸에 알맞은 말을 쓰시오.

A: What a great story! (정말 훌륭한 이야기에요!)

B: Thank you _____ _____ _____. (그렇게 말해 주시니 감사합니다.)

A. Listen and Speak 1 A

Tom: Hojun and I planned to ❶give out free stickers today, but I think he forgot.

Sora: Really? ❷Let me help you then. Why are you going to give out stickers?

Tom: It's part of our ❸volunteer club activity.

Sora: ❹I see. What does this sticker mean?

Tom: It means that when we smile at ❺each other, the world will become a better place.

Sora: That's a wonderful idea.

Tom: 호준이와 나는 오늘 무료 스티커를 나눠주기로 계획 했는데 호준이가 잊어버린 것 같아.
Sora: 그래? 그럼 내가 도와줄 게. 너희는 스티커를 왜 나 눠주려고 하니?
Tom: 그건 우리 자원봉사 동아 리 활동의 일부야.
Sora: 그렇구나. 이 스티커는 무 엇을 의미하니?
Tom: 그건 우리가 서로에게 미 소 지을 때, 세상이 더 좋 은 곳이 될 거라는 의미야.
Sora: 그거 멋진 아이디어구나.

❶ give out: ~을 나누어 주다
❷ Let me help you then.: 그러면 내가 도와줄게.
❸ volunteer club: 자원봉사 동아리
❹ I see.: 알겠어.
❺ each other: 서로

Check(√) True or False

(1) Sora is going to help Tom.　　　　　　　　　　　　　　　T ☐ F ☐

(2) Sora already knew the meaning of the sticker.　　　　　T ☐ F ☐

B. Real Life Communication

Emily: Welcome back, Brian. Are you feeling better?

Brian: Yes, thanks. I tried to study ❶on my own in the hospital, but it was hard.

Emily: Let me help you. ❷Why don't you join my study group?

Brian: Did you start a ❸study group? That's wonderful.

Emily: Thanks. I think that we can learn better when we teach each other.

Brian: I agree. I'll try hard to be a good member. Thanks for helping me.

Emily: You're welcome. ❹I'm glad you like my idea.

Emily: 돌아온 걸 환영해, Brian. 좀 나아졌니?
Brain: 응, 고마워. 나는 병원에 서 혼자 공부하려고 했는 데, 어려웠어.
Emily: 내가 도와줄게. 우리 스 터디 모임에 함께 하는 게 어때?
Brain: 스터디 모임을 시작했 니? 그거 멋지다.
Emily: 고마워. 나는 우리가 서 로를 가르쳐주면 더 잘 배울 수 있을 거라고 생 각해.
Brain: 맞아. 나는 좋은 구성원 이 되려고 열심히 노력할 게. 도와줘서 고마워.
Emily: 천만에. 내 아이디어를 좋아해줘서 나도 기뻐.

❶ on one's own: 자기 스스로
❷ Why don't you ~?: 너는 ~하는 게 어때?
❸ study group: 공부 모임
❹ I'm glad you like my idea.: 상대방의 칭찬에 대답하는 표현이다.

Check(√) True or False

(3) Brian came back to school from the hospital.　　　　　T ☐ F ☐

(4) Brian isn't going to join Emily's study group.　　　　T ☐ F ☐

Listen and Speak 1 B

Mike: Jimin, what are all these things in the box?

Jimin: They're for my ❶mentee at the ❷ children's center. I'm going to give her my old books today.

Mike: Do you teach ❸her every weekend?

Jimin: Yes. I feel happy when I teach her.

Mike: ❹You are a good mentor. Oh, the box looks heavy. Let me help you.

Jimin: Thanks.

❶ mentee (멘티) ↔ mentor (멘토)
❷ children's center: 아동 센터
❸ Jimin의 mentee를 가리킨다.
❹ Jimin을 칭찬하는 표현이다.

Listen and Speak 2 B

Yujin: I read a story about a special boy in India. Do you want to hear about ❶it?

Jack: Sure. Why is he special, Yujin?

Yujin: Many children in his town couldn't go to school and ❷had to work. So he taught ❸them in his house every day.

Jack: That's a great story.

Yujin: I'm glad you like it.

❶ a story about a special boy in India를 가리킨다.
❷ had to: ~해야 했다(have to의 과거형)
❸ many children in his town을 가리킨다.

Listen and Speak 2-A

Alex: Mom, ❶this is for you. I made it with plastic bags.

Mom: That's very cute, Alex. How did you know that I needed a new basket?

Alex: You talked about ❷it when we were having dinner ❸the other day.

Mom: ❹How nice! I really like this basket. It has many different colors.

Alex: I'm glad you like it.

❶ 'This is for you.'는 상대방에게 선물 등을 줄 때 쓰는 표현이다.
❷ a new basket을 가리킨다.
❸ the other day: 며칠 전, 요전날
❹ How nice!: '정말 마음에 든다!'라는 표현으로 감탄문 형식으로 쓰였다. 원래의 표현은 How nice this basket is!이며 '주어+동사' 뒷부분이 생략된 형태이다.

Let's Check

Henry: Your bag looks heavy. Let me help you.

Sujin: Thanks. Where is the ❶bus stop around here?

Henry: ❷It's over there. I'll carry your bag to the bus stop for you.

Sujin: ❸You're very kind.

Henry: ❹No problem. I am going that way, too.

❶ bus stop: 버스 정류장
❷ It's over there.: 그것은 저쪽에 있어.
❸ Henry의 도움에 칭찬하는 표현이다.
❹ '별말씀을요.'의 뜻으로 칭찬에 답하는 표현이다.

● 다음 우리말과 일치하도록 빈칸에 알맞은 말을 쓰시오.

Listen & Speak 1 A

Tom: Hojun and I planned to _____ _____ free stickers today, but I think he forgot.

Sora: Really? _____ _____ _____ _____ _____. Why are you going to give out stickers?

Tom: It's part of our _____ _____ _____.

Sora: I see. What does this sticker _____?

Tom: _____ _____ _____ when we smile at _____ _____, the world will become a _____.

Sora: That's a wonderful idea.

Tom: 호준이와 나는 오늘 무료 스티커를 나눠주기로 계획했는데 호준이가 잊어버린 것 같아.
Sora: 그래? 그럼 내가 도와줄게. 너희는 스티커를 왜 나눠주려고 하니?
Tom: 그건 우리 자원봉사 동아리 활동의 일부야.
Sora: 그렇구나. 이 스티커는 무엇을 의미하니?
Tom: 그건 우리가 서로에게 미소 지을 때, 세상이 더 좋은 곳이 될 거라는 의미야.
Sora: 그거 멋진 아이디어구나.

Listen & Speak 1 B

Mike: Jimin, what are all these things in the box?

Jimin: They're for _____ _____ at the children's center. I'm going to give her my old books today.

Mike: _____ _____ _____ _____ _____ _____?

Jimin: Yes. I feel happy when I teach her.

Mike: _____ _____ _____ _____ _____. Oh, the box looks heavy. Let me help you.

Jimin: Thanks.

Mike: 지민아, 상자에 들어 있는 이게 전부 뭐니?
Jimin: 그건 아동 센터에 있는 내 멘티를 위한 거야. 오늘 내가 보던 책들을 줄 거야.
Mike: 너는 그녀를 주말마다 가르치니?
Jimin: 응. 나는 그녀를 가르칠 때 행복해.
Mike: 넌 좋은 멘토구나. 아, 상자 무거워 보인다. 내가 도와줄게.
Jimin: 고마워.

Listen & Speak 2 A

Alex: Mom, _____ _____ _____ _____. I made it with plastic bags.

Mom: That's very cute, Alex. _____ _____ _____ _____ _____ I needed a new basket?

Alex: You talked about it when we were having dinner _____ _____.

Mom: _____ _____! I really like this basket. It has many different colors.

Alex: _____ _____ _____ _____ _____.

Alex: 엄마, 이거 선물이에요. 제가 비닐봉지로 만들었어요.
Mom: 그것 참 예쁘구나, Alex. 내가 새로운 바구니가 필요한 걸 어떻게 알았니?
Alex: 엄마가 지난번에 저녁 먹을 때 말씀하셨어요.
Mom: 아주 멋지구나! 이 바구니가 아주 좋은 걸. 색깔이 아주 다양하구나.
Alex: 엄마가 좋아하시니 저도 기뻐요.

Listen & Talk 2 B

Yujin: _____ _____ _____ _____ _____ _____ _____ _____ _____ _____ _____. Do you want to hear about it?

Jack: Sure. _____ _____ _____ _____, Yujin?

Yujin: Many children in his town couldn't go to school and _____ _____ _____. So he taught them in his house every day.

Jack: That's a great story.

Yujin: _____ _____ _____ _____.

Yujin: 내가 인도의 특별한 소년에 대한 이야기를 읽었어. 들어 볼래?
Jack: 그래. 왜 그가 특별하다는 거니, 유진아?
Yujin: 그 소년의 마을에 있는 많은 아이들이 학교에 갈 수 없었고 일을 해야만 했어. 그래서 그가 매일 자신의 집에서 아이들을 가르쳤다는 거야.
Jack: 그거 멋진 이야기구나.
Yujin: 네가 좋아하니 나도 기뻐.

Real Life Communication

Emily: Welcome back, Brian. _____ _____ _____ _____?

Brian: Yes, thanks. I tried to study _____ _____ _____ in the hospital, but it was hard.

Emily: _____ _____ _____ _____. Why don't you _____ _____ _____ _____?

Brian: Did you start a study group? That's wonderful.

Emily: Thanks. I think that _____ _____ _____ _____ _____ _____ _____ _____ _____.

Brian: I agree. I'll try hard to be a good member. _____ _____ _____ _____.

Emily: You're welcome. I'm glad you like my idea.

Emily: 돌아온 걸 환영해, Brian. 좀 나아졌니?
Brain: 응, 고마워. 나는 병원에서 혼자 공부하려고 했는데, 어려웠어.
Emily: 내가 도와줄게. 우리 스터디 모임에 함께 하는 게 어때?
Brain: 스터디 모임을 시작했니? 그거 멋지다.
Emily: 고마워. 나는 우리가 서로를 가르쳐주면 더 잘 배울 수 있을 거라고 생각해.
Brain: 맞아. 나는 좋은 구성원이 되려고 열심히 노력할게. 도와줘서 고마워.
Emily: 천만에. 내 아이디어를 좋아해줘서 나도 기뻐.

Let's Check 1

Henry: Your bag _____ _____. _____ _____ _____ _____ _____.

Sujin: Thanks. _____ _____ _____ _____ _____ _____ _____?

Henry: It's over there. I'll carry your bag to the bus stop for you.

Sujin: You're very kind.

Henry: _____ _____. I am going that way, too.

Henry: 가방이 무거워 보이네요. 제가 도와 드릴게요.
Sujin: 고마워요. 이 근처에 버스 정류장이 어디 있나요?
Henry: 저쪽에 있어요. 버스 정류장까지 가방을 들어 드릴게요.
Sujin: 정말 친절하군요.
Henry: 별말씀을요. 저도 그쪽으로 가는 길인 걸요.

[01~02] 다음 대화를 읽고 물음에 답하시오.

> Henry: Your bag looks heavy. (A)Let me help you.
> Sujin: Thanks. Where is the bus stop around here?
> Henry: It's over there. I'll carry your bag to the bus stop for you.
> Sujin: You're very kind.
> Henry: No problem. I am going that way, too.

01 위 대화의 밑줄 친 (A)의 의도로 적절한 것은?

① 도움 요청하기 ② 도움 제안하기
③ 도움 거절하기 ④ 충고 구하기
⑤ 선호 표현하기

02 위 대화의 내용과 일치하지 않는 것은?

① Sujin's bag looked heavy.
② Henry helped Sujin by carrying her bag.
③ Sujin was looking for the bus stop.
④ Henry was going to the taxi stop.
⑤ Sujin appreciated Henry's help.

[03~04] 다음 대화를 읽고 물음에 답하시오.

> Alex: Mom, this is ⓐfor you. I made it ⓑwith plastic bags.
> Mom: That's very cute, Alex. How did you know ⓒwhich I needed a new basket?
> Alex: You talked about it when we were having dinner the ⓓother day.
> Mom: ⓔHow nice! I really like this basket. It has many different colors.
> Alex: I'm glad you like it.

03 위 대화의 밑줄 친 ⓐ~ⓔ 중 어법상 틀린 것을 찾아 바르게 고치시오.

➡ _____

04 위 대화의 내용과 일치하지 않는 것은?

① Alex는 엄마에게 바구니를 만들어 드렸다.
② Alex는 비닐봉지로 바구니를 만들었다.
③ Alex가 만든 바구니는 다양한 색을 갖고 있다.
④ Alex와 엄마는 며칠 전 저녁을 먹기 전 새 바구니를 구매했다.
⑤ 엄마는 Alex의 선물이 마음에 들었다.

01 다음 짝지어진 대화가 어색한 것은?

① A: I can't move the table. Can anybody help me?
B: Let me help you.

② A: What's the matter with you?
B: How can I help you?

③ A: It's hard for me to build the model airplane.
B: I'll help you.

④ A: I can't open the window.
B: Let me give you a hand.

⑤ A: I can't open the bottle.
B: May I help you?

[02~04] 다음 대화를 읽고 물음에 답하시오.

> Tom: Hojun and I planned to give out free stickers today, but I think he forgot.
> Sora: Really? (A)내가 도와줄게.(let) Why are you going to give out stickers?
> Tom: It's part of our volunteer club activity.
> Sora: I see. What does this sticker mean?
> Tom: It means that when we smile at each other, the world will become a better place.
> Sora: (B)_____

02 위 대화의 밑줄 친 (A)의 우리말을 주어진 단어를 사용하여 영작하시오.

➡ _____

03 위 대화의 빈칸 (B)에 들어갈 말로 어색한 것은?

① What a great idea!
② That sounds good.
③ Excellent!
④ What a pity!
⑤ That's a wonderful idea.

04 위 대화의 내용과 일치하도록 빈칸을 완성하시오.

> W: What does the sticker emphasize?
> A: It emphasizes the importance of _____.

[05~06] 다음 대화를 읽고 물음에 답하시오.

> Yujin: I read a story about a special boy in India. Do you want to hear about it? (A)
> Jack: Sure. Why is he special, Yujin? (B)
> Yujin: Many children in his town couldn't go to school and had to work. (C)
> Jack: That's a great story. (D)
> Yujin: I'm glad you like it. (E)

05 다음 (A)~(E) 중 주어진 문장이 들어가기에 적절한 곳은?

> So he taught them in his house every day.

① (A)   ② (B)   ③ (C)   ④ (D)   ⑤ (E)

06 위 대화를 읽고 대답할 수 없는 것은?

① What did Yujin read?
② Why was the boy in India special?
③ What should many children in India do instead of going to school?
④ What did Jack think about the story about a special boy in India?
⑤ What did Yujin do to help many children in India?

서답형

07 다음 대화의 내용과 일치하도록 Mike의 일기를 완성하시오.

> **Mike:** Jimin, what are all these things in the box?
> **Jimin:** They're for my mentee at the children's center. I'm going to give her my old books today.
> **Mike:** Do you teach her every weekend?
> **Jimin:** Yes. I feel happy when I teach her.
> **Mike:** You are a good mentor. Oh, the box looks heavy. Let me help you.
> **Jimin:** Thanks.

> Mon, June 24th, 2019
> Today, I was impressed with Jimin. She teaches (A)_____ at the children's center every weekend. In addition, she was going to give (B)_____ to her mentee. She said that (C)_____ when she taught her. I thought (D)_____.
> The box looked heavy, so I helped her. I think that helping others makes the world a better place.

➡ (A) _____

(B) _____

(C) _____

(D) _____

[08~09] 다음 대화를 읽고 물음에 답하시오.

> **Emily:** Welcome back, Brian. Are you feeling better?
> **Brian:** Yes, thanks. I tried to study on my own in the hospital, but it was hard.
> **Emily:** Let me help you. Why don't you join my study group?
> **Brian:** Did you start a study group? That's wonderful.

> **Emily:** Thanks. I think that we can learn better when we teach each other.
> **Brian:** I agree. I'll try hard to be a good member. Thanks for helping me.
> **Emily:** You're welcome. I'm glad you like my idea.

서답형

08 What did Emily suggest to Brain?

➡ _____

서답형

09 Why did Emily start a study group?

➡ _____

_____

서답형

10 다음 대화가 자연스럽게 이어지도록 순서대로 배열하시오.

> (A) Okay, I'll give it a try. Thanks for the tip.
> (B) I'm not good at science. What can I do?
> (C) No problem. I'm glad you like it.
> (D) Let me help you. Why don't you start with easier books?

➡ _____

[11~12] 다음 대화를 읽고 물음에 답하시오.

> **Aram:** I'm very tired. What should I do?
> **Jack:** Let me help you. I can give you a massage.
> **Aram:** Thank you for your help.
> **Jack:** No problem. I'm glad you liked ⓐit.

서답형

11 위 대화의 밑줄 친 ⓐit이 가리키는 것을 영어로 쓰시오.

➡ _____

서답형

12 What did Jack do to make Aram feel better?

➡ _____

[01~02] 다음 대화를 읽고 물음에 답하시오.

Mike: Jimin, what are all these things in the box?

Jimin: They're for my mentee at the children's center. I'm going to give her my old books today.

Mike: Do you teach her every weekend?

Jimin: Yes. (A)_____

Mike: You are a good (B)m_____. Oh, the box looks heavy. Let me help you.

Jimin: Thanks.

01 다음 빈칸 (A)에 들어갈 말을 보기에 주어진 단어를 모두 배열하여 완성하시오.

┌─ 보기 ─────────────────────────┐
happy / when / I / her / teach / feel / I
└────────────────────────────────┘

➡ _____

02 위 대화의 빈칸 (B)에 주어진 영영 풀이가 가리키는 말을 쓰시오.

┌────────────────────────────────┐
someone who teaches or gives help and advice to a less experienced and often younger person
└────────────────────────────────┘

➡ m_____

[03~04] 다음 대화를 읽고 물음에 답하시오.

Yujin: I read a story about a special boy in India. Do you want to hear about it?

Jack: Sure. Why is he special, Yujin?

Yujin: Many children in his town couldn't go to school and had to work. So he taught (A)them in his house every day.

Jack: That's a great story.

Yujin: I'm glad you like it.

03 위 대화의 밑줄 친 (A)them이 가리키는 것을 영어로 쓰시오.

➡ _____

04 위 대화의 내용과 일치하도록 Jack의 담화를 완성하시오.

┌────────────────────────────────┐
Jack: Today, Yujin told me a great story about (A)_____. I was wondering why she said that (B)_____. Yujin said the boy taught many children in his town who (C)_____ in his house every day. It was a great story.
└────────────────────────────────┘

➡ (A) _____
   (B) _____
   (C) _____

[05~06] 다음 대화를 읽고 물음에 답하시오.

Tom: Hojun and I planned to give out free stickers today, but I think he forgot.

Sora: Really? Let me help you then. Why are you going to give out stickers?

Tom: It's part of our volunteer club activity.

Sora: I see. What does this sticker mean?

Tom: It means that when we smile at each other, the world will become a better place.

Sora: That's a wonderful idea.

05 What is Sora going to do to help Tom?

➡ _____

06 Tom이 준비한 스티커의 의미를 우리말로 20자 내외로 서술하시오.

➡ _____

Grammar

① 목적격 관계대명사

- I have a friend **whom** I want you to meet. 나는 네가 만나보기를 원하는 친구가 한 명 있어.
- The chair **which** you gave to me was broken. 네가 나에게 준 의자가 망가졌어.

■ 관계대명사는 두 개의 문장을 하나로 이어주는 접속사 역할을 하면서 동시에 대명사 역할을 한다. 전치사의 목적어 혹은 동사의 목적어였던 대명사를 목적격 관계대명사로 만들어 문장을 하나로 이어준다.

- There were many people in the cafe **which** we visited last week. 〈동사의 목적어〉 우리가 지난주에 방문한 카페에는 사람이 많았어.

- Those boys **who(m)** the woman is looking after look very cute. 〈전치사의 목적어〉 그 여자가 돌보고 있는 저 소년들은 매우 귀여워 보인다.

■ 목적격 관계대명사 who(m), which는 that으로 대체할 수 있으며, 생략 가능하다. 관계대명사가 전치사의 목적어로 사용된 경우 전치사는 동사 뒤에 그대로 두거나, 전치사를 관계대명사 앞으로 보낼 수 있다.

- Mr. Pang **who(m)** the children love teaches how to swim to them. 그 아이들이 사랑하는 Pang씨는 그들에게 수영하는 방법을 가르친다.

- She never touched food **which** she didn't like. 그녀는 좋아하지 않는 음식에는 손도 대지 않았다.

- The i-pad **which** I got from my father was my birthday present. 내가 아버지로부터 받은 그 아이패드는 내 생일 선물이었어.

- The areas **which** you have mentioned have some problems. 네가 언급한 그 지역에는 몇 가지 문제점이 있어.

- The missing boy **who(m)** people were looking for came home last night. 사람들이 찾던 그 실종 소년이 어젯밤 집으로 왔다.

- Tell me about the people **who(m)** you cared for in the hospital. 네가 병원에서 돌봤던 사람들에 관해 말해줘.

핵심 Check

1. 다음 우리말과 같도록 빈칸에 알맞은 말을 쓰시오.

(1) 이것은 그가 작년에 산 집이다.
➡ This is the house _____ he bought last year.

(2) 나는 모두가 천재라고 생각하는 한 남자를 안다.
➡ I know a man _____ everyone thinks a genius.

② to부정사를 목적격보어로 취하는 동사

- Dan **persuaded** me **to buy** the computer for him. Dan은 내가 그를 위해 컴퓨터를 사도록 설득했다.

- Andrea **expected** us **to welcome** her. Andrea는 우리가 그녀를 환영하리라고 기대했다.

■ '동사+목적어+to V' 형태로 목적어가 to부정사의 주체가 되도록 해석한다.

- I don't **want** her **to see** my portfolio. 나는 그녀가 나의 포트폴리오를 보는 걸 원치 않아.

- Mom **persuaded** me **to do** my homework first. 엄마는 내가 숙제를 먼저 하도록 설득하셨다.

■ to부정사를 목적격보어로 취하는 동사에는 allow, ask, tell, advise, get, force, require, order, persuade, encourage, enable, cause, need, want, help, would like, teach, expect 등이 있다.

- Our teacher **encourages** us **to think** of others before us. 우리 선생님은 우리가 우리보다 타인을 먼저 생각하도록 권장하신다.

- We **would like** you **to have** a cup of tea. 우리는 당신이 차 한 잔 하길 원합니다.

■ to부정사 목적격보어의 부정형은 'not to V'로 표현한다.

- My lawyer **advised** me **not to say a word**. 나의 변호사는 내게 한마디도 하지 말라고 조언했다.

- Dad **ordered** me **not to go** out at night. 아빠는 내게 밤에 나가지 말라고 명령하셨다.

■ make, have, let은 원형부정사를 목적격보어로 취하는 사역동사이다. '목적어가 V하게 하다'로 해석한다.

- She **let** me **go** shopping with my friends. 그녀는 내가 친구들과 함께 쇼핑하러 가게 허락했다.

- What **made** you **break** the promise? 무엇이 너로 하여금 그 약속을 어기게 만든 거야?

핵심 Check

1. 다음 우리말과 같도록 빈칸에 알맞은 말을 쓰시오.

(1) Julia는 우리가 그와 악수하도록 설득했다.

➡ Julia _____ us _____ _____ hands with him.

(2) 나는 그들이 훨씬 더 많이 먹으리라고 예상한다.

➡ I _____ them _____ _____ much more.

(3) 그 여자는 그녀의 아들에게 늦지 말라고 말했다.

➡ The woman _____ her son _____ _____ _____ late.

01 다음 문장에서 어법상 <u>어색한</u> 부분을 바르게 고쳐 쓰시오.

(1) The eggs who I bought are very fresh.

_____ ➡ _____

(2) The building which John built were huge.

_____ ➡ _____

(3) I believe that it will enable us continue this work together.

_____ ➡ _____

(4) Will you allow me to passing, please?

_____ ➡ _____

02 괄호 안에 주어진 단어를 어법에 맞게 빈칸에 쓰시오.

(1) The man whom I fell in love with _____ near my house now. (live)

(2) The race _____ you took part in was very successful. (which)

(3) The police told them _____ calm. (stay)

(4) We encouraged her _____ a new life. (start)

03 주어진 단어를 바르게 배열하여 다음 우리말을 영어로 쓰시오. 필요하다면 단어를 추가하거나 변형하시오.

(1) 이것은 그들이 필요로 했던 테이블이다. (need / this / is / the / they / table)

➡ _____

(2) 그녀는 내가 주관한 어떤 회의에 왔어요. (I / a meeting / she / come / that / run / to)

➡ _____

(3) 우리는 그들이 열심히 일하도록 강요할 수 없어. (hard / can't / them / we / work / force)

➡ _____

(4) 무엇이 네가 그렇게 생각하게 만들었니? (so / think / what / you / make)

➡ _____

01 다음 빈칸에 알맞은 말을 <u>모두</u> 고르시오.

> You can find the things _____ you need in the refrigerator.

① who   ② whom   ③ that
④ which   ⑤ whose

02 다음 빈칸에 들어갈 말로 적절한 것은?

> 이것은 어제 엄마가 내게 사주신 신발이다.
> = These are the shoes _____
>   yesterday.

① whom my mom bought for her
② which I bought for my mom
③ that was bought for my mom
④ which my mom bought for me
⑤ that was bought to me by mom

03 다음 빈칸에 적절하지 <u>않은</u> 것은?

> _____ to save time.

① The plan enabled us
② He wanted me
③ She encouraged us
④ Our boss made us
⑤ Mom advised us

서답형

04 주어진 단어와 적절한 관계대명사를 이용하여 다음 우리말을 영어로 쓰시오.

> 그는 내가 가진 모든 돈을 쓰도록 허락하지 않았다.
> (allow / use / all / have)

➡ _____

_____

05 다음 밑줄 친 부분 중 생략할 수 <u>없는</u> 것은?

① Is she the girl <u>who</u> you talked about?
② The milk <u>which</u> I bought went bad.
③ This is the letter <u>that</u> he sent me.
④ This is the jacket <u>which</u> you brought.
⑤ It is true <u>that</u> he spread the rumor.

06 다음 우리말을 영어로 바르게 옮긴 것은?

> 부산에 있는 작은 가게들은 사람들로 붐빈다.

① Small shops in Busan was crowded with people.
② There were small shops in Busan.
③ Small shops in Busan are crowded with people.
④ Busan has small shops which are run by many people.
⑤ There are small shops in Busan which many people run.

07 다음 중 빈칸에 들어갈 동사 'play'의 형태가 <u>다른</u> 하나는?

① Mom didn't allow me _____ the piano at night.
② My parents encouraged me _____ the flute in front of the guests.
③ We decided _____ soccer after school.
④ Many radio stations refused _____ the music.
⑤ Are you interested in _____ music on the stage?

서답형
08 다음 우리말에 맞게 빈칸에 알맞은 말을 쓰시오.

네가 해야 하는 다음 단계는 그것을 끓이는 것이다.
The next step _____ _____ _____
_____ is _____ _____ it.

09 다음 중 어법상 바르지 않은 것은?

① Some flowers which you picked are on the table.
② Would you like me to speak at the dinner?
③ My advice caused him stop smoking.
④ Is this the yogurt you brought?
⑤ I need you to sign for it.

10 다음 중 어법상 바른 문장의 개수는?

ⓐ The toys in the room is not mine.
ⓑ I don't think that she wanted me do the job.
ⓒ Did you find the key that you were looking for?
ⓓ The car he drives is very old.
ⓔ Ms. Henderson requires us handing in the reports as soon as possible.

① 1개   ② 2개   ③ 3개
④ 4개   ⑤ 5개

11 다음 중 빈칸에 적절하지 않은 것은?

The doctor _____ my dad to drink lots of water.

① advises   ② encourages   ③ tells
④ persuades   ⑤ has

서답형
12 다음 두 문장을 하나의 문장으로 만드시오.

• Do you remember those people?
• You met them on holiday.

➡ _____
_____

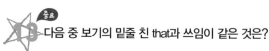
다음 중 보기의 밑줄 친 that과 쓰임이 같은 것은?

┤ 보기 ├
Why aren't you wearing the watch that you borrowed from me?

① Did you know that he came back from Toronto?
② He doesn't know the fact that you don't want to believe it.
③ Most people think that the Beatles is the best pop group.
④ Kelly said that she made some mistakes.
⑤ She is using the pan that I gave to her.

14 다음 중 어법상 옳은 것끼리 바르게 짝지어진 것은?

• A rabbit is an animal [who / which] every child loves.
• Persuade him [tell / to tell] us what he knows.
• He made me [pay / to pay] the bill at the restaurant.

① who – tell – pay
② which – tell – pay
③ who – to tell – to pay
④ which – to tell – pay
⑤ which – to tell – to pay

15 다음 빈칸에 공통으로 들어갈 말로 가장 적절한 것은?

> • Have you noticed _____ many Italian foods have tomatoes in them?
> • The coat _____ the girl is wearing does not look special.

① who   ② which   ③ that
④ whom   ⑤ whose

서답형

16 주어진 단어를 빈칸에 어법에 맞게 쓰시오.

> I want you _____ _____ _____
> _____ _____ because I need a mentor who can help me with math.
> (help / with)

17 다음 중 빈칸에 들어갈 관계대명사의 쓰임이 다른 하나는?

① The students _____ we chose are diligent and honest.
② The candies _____ the shop sells taste good.
③ The performance _____ he saw has been loved by many people.
④ The camera _____ many people love is too expensive.
⑤ A shampoo bottle _____ is in the bathroom is empty.

서답형

18 다음 우리말 의미에 맞게 빈칸에 알맞은 말을 쓰시오.

> 여기에 어제 내가 했던 두 가지 흥미로운 일이 있다.
> Here are two interesting things _____
> _____ _____ _____ .

서답형

19 주어진 단어를 활용하여 다음 빈칸에 알맞은 말을 쓰시오.

> 나가, 그렇지 않으면 우리가 너희를 나가게 만들 거야.
> Get out, or _____ _____
> _____ _____ go out. (force)

서답형

20 주어진 어구를 바르게 배열하여 다음 우리말을 영어로 쓰시오.

> 네가 해서는 안 되는 유일한 것은 다른 사람들이 이야기하는 도중에 끼어드는 것이다.
> (cut in / the only thing / you / while / are talking / others / that / should not do / is / to)

➡ _____
_____

21 다음 중 어법상 바르지 않은 것은?

> Can you ①do me a favor? There ②is ③ one thing ④that I need you ⑤do for me.

22 다음 중 빈칸에 들어갈 말로 가장 적절한 것은?

> My parents would like me _____ with them.

① to living   ② living   ③ live
④ to live   ⑤ lives

서답형

23 다음 빈칸에 알맞은 말을 쓰시오.

> 그는 우리에게 삶을 사랑하도록 가르쳤어요.
> He _____ _____ _____ _____
> life.

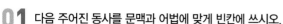

01 다음 주어진 동사를 문맥과 어법에 맞게 빈칸에 쓰시오.

know / clean / be / believe / focus

- The elderly are people who _____ old.
- If you want to learn Hangul, let me _____. I will teach you.
- Do you expect me _____ such a nonsense story?
- Mom got me _____ my room.
- The boss ordered us _____ on the job.

02 다음 대화를 읽고 주어진 단어를 활용하여 Hannah에 관하여 쓰시오.

Clark: Do you know how to play the piano?
Hannah: Yes, I do. My cousin taught me.

(teach / Hannah)

➡ _____

03 주어진 단어를 활용하여 다음 우리말을 영어로 쓰시오.

넌 내가 무엇을 하길 원하는 거야?
(what / want / do)

➡ _____

04 다음 상황을 읽고 빈칸에 알맞은 말을 쓰시오.

There was a girl who listened to music a little loudly in the library. So Peter said to the girl, "Would you turn down the music?"

➡ Peter asked _____

05 다음 보기와 같이 하나의 문장을 두 개의 문장으로 나누시오.

┤ 보기 ├
Have you been to the place which Mary visited last year?
➡ Have you been to the place?
➡ Mary visited the place last year.

(1) Kyle has the money he found on the street.

➡ _____
➡ _____

(2) Is this the book that you are looking for?

➡ _____
➡ _____

06 주어진 단어를 활용하여 James와 Olivia의 대화 내용을 한 문장으로 요약하시오.

Olivia: I have had a stomachache for a few days.
James: Oh, I'm so sorry. Did you see a doctor?
Olivia: No, I didn't.
James: You should see a doctor.

(advise)

➡ _____

07 주어진 단어를 바르게 나열하여 다음 우리말을 영어로 쓰시오. 필요하다면 단어를 변형하시오.

내가 지원했던 그 일자리를 얻길 원해.
(to / apply / I / I / that / the / for / job / get / want)

➡ _____

08 대화를 읽고 주어진 단어를 활용하여 빈칸에 알맞은 말을 쓰시오.

> **Jason:** I want to go shopping with Ann.
> **Mom:** You can go on Monday.

> allow

➡ Jason's mom _____

_____

09 주어진 문장과 같은 의미가 되도록 빈칸에 알맞은 말을 쓰시오.

> Emma asked me, "Can you play the guitar for me?"

➡ Emma asked me _____

10 주어진 단어를 바르게 배열하여 다음 우리말을 영어로 쓰시오. 필요하다면 단어를 추가하거나 변형하시오.

> 그들이 발달시킨 그 기술은 우리가 안전하게 자동차를 운전하는 것을 가능하게 한다.
> (safely / the / technology / a car / that / develop / they / enable / drive / us / have)

➡ _____

_____

11 주어진 단어를 활용하여 다음 우리말을 영어로 쓰시오. 필요하다면 단어를 변형하시오.

> 나는 John이 공원에서 발견했던 그 고양이를 좋아해.
> (like / find / at the park)

➡ _____

12 주어진 단어를 활용하여 빈칸에 알맞은 말을 쓰시오.

> 독감은 사람들에게 두통을 유발할 수 있다.
> The flu can _____
> (cause / have)

➡ _____

13 다음 두 개의 문장을 하나의 문장으로 연결하시오.

(1) Osaka is the city. My sister visited the city last week.

➡ _____

_____

(2) Robert is an actor. We like him very much.

➡ _____

(3) My dad gave me the wallet. I really wanted to have it.

➡ _____

_____

14 다음 우리말을 영어로 쓰시오.

> 내가 할 수 있는 유일한 것은 조용히 하는 거야.
> = The only thing _____ _____
> _____ _____ _____
> _____ _____ .

15 주어진 단어를 바르게 배열하여 문장을 완성하시오.

> Sandra _____ _____ _____
> _____ a good vacation.
> (have / me / told / to)

Reading

교과서

Small but Great Ideas

Here are two stories which I read yesterday. Do you want to hear about them?

목적격 관계대명사(= that) 생략 가능
want의 목적어
= two stories which I read yesterday

Call Someone You Love

Call someone. + You love someone.

New York had many pay phones on its streets. However, nobody really used them. One day, a man came up with an idea. He stuck coins to one of the phones. He also put up a sign that said, "Call Someone You Love." Soon, many people were using the phone.

부정주어로서 문장 전체를 부정의 뜻으로 만들며 '아무도 ~ 않다'라는 뜻
어느 날
stick – stuck – stuck
stick A to B: A를 B에 붙이다
He also put up a sign. + The sign said. "Call Someone (who(m)[that]
You Love."
과거진행형

When they were talking to someone whom they loved, they didn't stop smiling. His idea became a big success. During the day, all the coins disappeared. The man was very happy because his small idea gave happiness to many people.

= that
stop+Ving: V하는 것을 멈추다
이유를 나타내는 접속사
give ~ to ... : ~을 …에게 주다 (3형식)

---

hear: 듣다
pay phone: 공중전화
one day: (과거의) 어느 날
come up with: (생각이) 떠오르다
put up: 세우다
say: (글·글씨 등이) 쓰이다
sign: 표지판
success: 성공
during the day: 낮 동안
disappear: 사라지다

확인문제

● 다음 문장이 본문의 내용과 일치하면 T, 일치하지 않으면 F를 쓰시오.

1 The first story is about what happened in New York. ☐

2 It was hard to see people using a pay phone. ☐

3 The man stuck a coin to some pay phones. ☐

4 People couldn't call someone they loved because they had no coins. ☐

5 It took several days for all the coins to disappear. ☐

The Red Arrow Man

A few years ago, the maps at bus stops in Seoul were very confusing.
몇 년 전에   주어   the maps 수식

They didn't have enough information. People had to ask others to
=The maps   ask ~ to ... : ~에게 ... 해 달라고 요청하다

explain the maps. "Where is this bus stop on the map? Does this bus

go to Gwanghwamun?" Many people often took the wrong bus and
버스를 잘못 탔다

wasted their time.

One day, a young man decided to solve this problem. He bought
(과거의) 어느 날   decided의 목적어

lots of red arrow stickers. Every day he rode his bicycle around the
=many   ride–rode–ridden

city and stuck the stickers on the bus maps. Nobody asked him to do
stick-stuck-stuck

this. He just wanted to help others. Thanks to his effort, people could
버스 지도에 빨간 스티커를 붙이는 일   =other people   ~ 덕분에

understand the maps easily and save time.

arrow: 화살, 화살표
few: 몇몇의
map: 지도
bus stop: 버스 정류장
confusing: 혼란스러운
waste one's time: ~의 시간을 낭비하다
thanks to: ~ 덕택에
understand: 이해하다
easily: 쉽게
save: 절약하다

확인문제

● 다음 문장이 본문의 내용과 일치하면 T, 일치하지 않으면 F를 쓰시오.

1 People in Seoul were confused by the bus maps.

2 The bus maps had plenty of information in the past.

3 There was someone who forced a young man to stick the stickers.

4 What the man wanted to do was to help others.

5 He borrowed some money to buy arrow stickers.

● 우리말을 참고하여 빈칸에 알맞은 말을 쓰시오.

Small but Great Ideas

1 Here _____ two stories _____ I read yesterday.

2 Do you want _____ _____ about _____ ?

3 Call Someone _____ _____ .

4 New York _____ many pay phones on its streets.

5 _____ , _____ really used them.

6 One day, a man _____ _____ _____ an idea.

7 He _____ coins _____ one of the phones.

8 He also _____ _____ a sign _____ _____ , "Call Someone You Love."

9 Soon, many people _____ _____ the phone.

10 _____ they were talking to someone _____ _____ _____ , they didn't stop _____ .

11 His idea became _____ _____ _____ .

12 _____ the day, all the coins _____ .

13 The man was very happy _____ his small idea gave _____ _____ many people.

작지만 위대한 아이디어

1 여기 내가 어제 읽은 이야기가 두 개 있어.

2 들어볼래?

3 당신이 사랑하는 누군가에게 전화하세요.

4 뉴욕에는 길거리에 공중전화가 많이 있었다.

5 그러나 아무도 그것들을 실제로 사용하지는 않았다.

6 어느 날, 한 남자에게 좋은 아이디어가 떠올랐다.

7 그는 공중전화 하나에 동전들을 붙였다.

8 그는 또한 "당신이 사랑하는 사람에게 전화하세요."라고 쓰인 표지판을 설치했다.

9 곧, 많은 사람들이 그 전화기를 사용하고 있었다.

10 그들이 사랑하는 누군가에게 전화하고 있을 때, 그들은 미소 짓기를 멈추지 않았다.

11 그의 아이디어는 커다란 성공이었다.

12 낮 동안, 모든 동전이 사라졌다.

13 그 남자는 자신의 작은 아이디어가 많은 사람에게 행복을 가져다주었기 때문에 매우 행복했다.

14 The Red _____ _____

15 _____ _____ _____ _____, the maps at bus stops in Seoul _____ very _____.

16 They didn't have _____ _____.

17 People had to _____ _____ _____ _____ the maps.

18 "_____ is this bus stop _____ the map? Does this bus _____ _____ Gwanghwamun?"

19 Many people _____ _____ the wrong bus and _____ their time.

20 One day, a young man _____ _____ _____ this problem.

21 He bought _____ _____ _____ _____ _____.

22 Every day he _____ his bicycle _____ the city and _____ the stickers _____ the bus maps.

23 Nobody _____ _____ _____ _____ this.

24 He just _____ _____ _____ others.

25 _____ _____ his effort, people could understand the maps _____ and _____ _____.

---

14 빨간 화살표 청년

15 몇 년 전에, 서울의 버스 정류장의 지도는 매우 혼란스러웠다.

16 지도에는 충분한 정보가 없었다.

17 사람들은 다른 사람들에게 지도를 설명해 달라고 요청해야 했다.

18 "이 버스 정류장은 지도의 어디에 있는 건가요? 이 버스가 광화문으로 가나요?"

19 많은 사람이 종종 버스를 잘못 타서 시간을 낭비하곤 했다.

20 어느 날, 한 젊은 청년이 이 문제를 해결해 보기로 했다.

21 그는 빨간 화살표 스티커를 많이 샀다.

22 매일 그는 자전거를 타고 서울 시내를 돌아다니며 버스 지도에 스티커를 붙였다.

23 아무도 그 청년에게 이 일을 하라고 요청하지 않았다.

24 그는 단지 다른 사람들을 돕고 싶었다.

25 그의 노력 덕분에, 사람들은 지도를 쉽게 이해하고 시간을 절약할 수 있었다.

● 우리말을 참고하여 본문을 영작하시오.

여기 내가 어제 읽은 이야기가 두 개 있어.

1 ➡ _____

들어볼래?

2 ➡ _____

당신이 사랑하는 누군가에게 전화하세요.

3 ➡ _____

뉴욕에는 길거리에 공중전화가 많이 있었다.

4 ➡ _____

그러나 아무도 그것들을 실제로 사용하지는 않았다.

5 ➡ _____

어느 날, 한 남자에게 좋은 아이디어가 떠올랐다.

6 ➡ _____

그는 공중전화 하나에 동전들을 붙였다.

7 ➡ _____

그는 또한 "당신이 사랑하는 사람에게 전화하세요."라고 쓰인 표지판을 설치했다.

8 ➡ _____

곧, 많은 사람들이 그 전화기를 사용하고 있었다.

9 ➡ _____

그들이 사랑하는 누군가에게 전화하고 있을 때, 그들은 미소 짓기를 멈추지 않았다.

10 ➡ _____

그의 아이디어는 커다란 성공이었다.

11 ➡ _____

낮 동안, 모든 동전이 사라졌다.

12 ➡ _____

13 ➡ 그 남자는 자신의 작은 아이디어가 많은 사람에게 행복을 가져다주었기 때문에 매우 행복했다.

➡ _____

14 빨간 화살표 청년

➡ _____

15 몇 년 전, 서울의 버스 정류장의 지도는 매우 혼란스러웠다.

➡ _____

16 지도에는 충분한 정보가 없었다.

➡ _____

17 사람들은 다른 사람들에게 지도를 설명해 달라고 요청해야 했다.

➡ _____

18 "이 버스 정류장은 지도의 어디에 있는 건가요? 이 버스가 광화문으로 가나요?"

➡ _____

19 많은 사람이 종종 버스를 잘못 타서 시간을 낭비하곤 했다.

➡ _____

20 어느 날, 한 젊은 청년이 이 문제를 해결해 보기로 했다.

➡ _____

21 그는 빨간 화살표 스티커를 많이 샀다.

➡ _____

22 매일 그는 자전거를 타고 서울 시내를 돌아다니며 버스 지도에 스티커를 붙였다.

➡ _____

23 아무도 그 청년에게 이 일을 하라고 요청하지 않았다.

➡ _____

24 그는 단지 다른 사람들을 돕고 싶었다.

➡ _____

25 그의 노력 덕분에, 사람들은 지도를 쉽게 이해하고 시간을 절약할 수 있었다.

➡ _____

[01~08] 다음 글을 읽고 물음에 답하시오.

Here are two stories which I read yesterday. Do you want to hear (A)[from / about] ⓐ them?

Call Someone You Love
New York had many pay phones on its streets. ⓑ_____, nobody really used (B)[it / them]. ① One day, a man came up with an idea. He stuck coins to one of the phones. ② He also put up a sign that said, "Call Someone You Love." ③ When they were talking to someone ⓒ_____ they loved, they didn't stop smiling. ④ His idea became a big success. (C)[During / While] the day, all the coins disappeared. ⑤ The man was very happy because his small idea gave happiness ⓓ_____ many people.

서답형
01 밑줄 친 ⓐ가 가리키는 것을 6단어의 영어로 쓰시오.

➡ _____

02 다음 중 빈칸 ⓑ에 들어갈 말로 가장 적절한 것은?

① Therefore   ② As a result
③ In addition   ④ For example
⑤ However

서답형
03 빈칸 ⓒ에 알맞은 말을 모두 쓰시오.

➡ _____

중요
04 다음 중 빈칸 ⓓ에 들어갈 말로 가장 적절한 것은?

① in   ② to   ③ on
④ for   ⑤ by

05 ①~⑤ 중 주어진 문장이 들어가기에 가장 적절한 곳은?

Soon, many people were using the phone.

①   ②   ③   ④   ⑤

중요
06 (A)~(C) 중 어법상 옳은 것끼리 짝지어진 것은?

① from – it – During
② about – it – During
③ from – them – While
④ about – them – During
⑤ from – it – while

07 다음 중 위 글을 읽고 답할 수 있는 것은?

① How many pay phones were there on New York streets?
② Why did nobody use the pay phones?
③ Who stuck coins to a pay phone?
④ How many coins were stuck to a pay phone?
⑤ How many coins did each person use?

서답형
08 주어진 단어를 이용하여 다음 질문에 완전한 문장의 영어로 답하시오.

Q: What did the sign say?
A: _____ (it)

➡ _____

[09~15] 다음 글을 읽고 물음에 답하시오.

The Red Arrow Man

(A)[A few / A little] years ago, the maps ⓐ_____ bus stops in Seoul were very (B)[confusing / confused]. They didn't have enough information. People had to ask others to explain the maps. "Where is this bus stop on the map? Does this bus go to Gwanghwamun?" Many people often took the wrong bus and ⓑ_____ (C)[its / their] time.

One day, a young man decided to solve this problem. He bought lots of red arrow stickers. Every day he rode his bicycle around the city and stuck the stickers on the bus maps. Nobody asked him ⓒto do this. He just wanted to help others. ⓓ_____ his effort, people could understand the maps easily and ⓔsave time.

09 다음 중 빈칸 ⓐ에 들어갈 말과 같은 것은?

① Did you turn _____ the light in the livingroom?
② I was surprised _____ the news.
③ Dad will pick you _____ at five.
④ Please take care _____ yourself.
⑤ Do you mind waiting _____ a little while?

서답형
10 빈칸 ⓑ에 밑줄 친 ⓔ의 반의어를 어법에 맞게 쓰시오.

➡ _____

서답형
11 밑줄 친 ⓒ가 의미하는 것을 우리말로 쓰시오.

➡ _____
  _____

12 다음 중 빈칸 ⓓ에 들어갈 말로 가장 적절한 것은?

① Despite   ② Instead of
③ Thanks to   ④ At last
⑤ Depending on

중요
13 (A)~(C) 중 어법상 옳은 것끼리 짝지어진 것은?

① A few – confusing – its
② A little – confused – its
③ A few – confusing – their
④ A little – confused – their
⑤ A few – confused – their

서답형
14 Write the reason why people often took the wrong bus in Seoul. Use the words 'because', 'there', and 'on the maps.'

➡ _____
  _____

15 다음 중 위 글의 내용과 일치하지 않는 것은?

① People needed some explanation about the maps.
② There were people who took the wrong bus because of the maps.
③ A young man had an idea to solve the problem of the maps.
④ Somebody wanted the young man to stick the stickers.
⑤ A young man used his bicycle in order to stick the stickers.

[16~22] 다음 글을 읽고 물음에 답하시오.

Here are two stories which I read yesterday. Do you want ⓐ _____ about them?

Call Someone You Love
New York had many pay phones ⓑ _____ its streets. However, nobody really used them. One day, a man came up with an idea. He stuck coins to one of the phones. He also put up a sign (A)that said, "Call Someone You Love." (B)Soon, many people were using (C)the phone. When they were ⓒ _____ to someone whom they loved, they didn't stop smiling. His idea became a big success. During the day, all the coins disappeared. The man was very happy because his small idea gave happiness to many people.

서답형

16 주어진 단어를 어법과 문맥에 맞게 빈칸 ⓐ와 ⓒ에 쓰시오.

talk / hear

➡ ⓐ _____ ⓒ _____

17 다음 중 빈칸 ⓑ에 들어갈 말과 같은 것은?

① Are you interested _____ studying English?
② She was not satisfied _____ the result.
③ Ms. Han wanted us to pay attention _____ her class.
④ He likes to take care _____ plants.
⑤ He is the person you can depend _____.

서답형

18 다음과 같이 풀이되는 단어를 위 글에서 찾아 쓰시오.

to stop being visible

➡ _____

19 다음 중 밑줄 친 (A)와 쓰임이 다른 하나는?

① Is he the boy that you talked with?
② The man and his dog that are running together look happy.
③ Do you remember the story that Miranda told you?
④ I want to say that he is my hero.
⑤ Kyle showed me the watch that was really expensive.

20 다음 중 밑줄 친 (B)를 대신하여 쓰일 수 있는 것은?

① For a long time   ② Before long
③ Hardly   ④ Still
⑤ Lately

서답형

21 다음은 밑줄 친 (C)를 설명하는 문장이다. 빈칸에 알맞은 말을 쓰시오.

the phone _____ the man _____ _____ _____.

22 다음 중 위 글의 내용과 일치하지 않는 것은?

① I read a couple of stories yesterday.
② Many pay phones were on the streets in New York.
③ Not everyone used pay phones.
④ A man stuck some coins to a pay phone.
⑤ All the coins were used during the day.

서답형

23 다음 주어진 문장과 자연스럽게 연결되도록 (A)~(C)를 바르게 나열하시오.

> New York had many pay phones on its streets.

(A) He also put up a sign that said, "Call Someone You Love." Soon, many people were using the phone.

(B) However, nobody really used them. One day, a man came up with an idea. He stuck coins to one of the phones.

(C) When they were talking to someone whom they loved, they didn't stop smiling. His idea became a big success.

➡ _____

[24~30] 다음 글을 읽고 물음에 답하시오.

The Red Arrow Man
A few years ago, the maps at bus stops in Seoul were very ⓐ_____ . They didn't have enough information. ⓑPeople had to ask others explain the maps. "Where is this bus stop ⓒ_____ the map? Does this bus go to Gwanghwamun?" Many people often took ①the wrong bus and wasted their time.
One day, a young man decided to ②solve this problem. He bought lots of red arrow stickers. Every day he rode his bicycle around the city and ③stuck the stickers ⓓ_____ the bus maps. ④Nobody asked him to do this. He just wanted to ⑤bother others. Thanks to his effort, people could understand the maps easily and save time.

24 다음 중 빈칸 ⓐ에 들어갈 말로 가장 적절한 것은?

① rare   ② confusing

③ easy   ④ familiar

⑤ common

서답형

25 밑줄 친 ⓑ에서 어법상 바르지 않은 것을 찾아 바르게 고쳐 쓰시오.

➡ _____

26 빈칸 ⓒ와 ⓓ에 공통으로 들어갈 말로 가장 적절한 것은?

① at   ② by   ③ on
④ under   ⑤ about

중요

27 ①~⑤ 중 글의 흐름상 어색한 것은?

①   ②   ③   ④   ⑤

서답형

28 다음 질문에 완전한 문장의 영어로 답하시오.

> Q: What was the problem with the bus maps in Seoul?

➡ _____

29 다음 중 위 글을 읽고 알 수 없는 것은?

① 서울 버스 정류장의 지도에 부족했던 것
② 사람들이 버스를 잘못 탄 이유
③ 광화문으로 가는 버스 번호
④ 청년이 산 스티커 모양
⑤ 청년이 자전거를 타고 돌아다니며 한 일

서답형

30 글의 내용에 맞게 다음 빈칸에 알맞은 말을 쓰시오.

> Thanks to the young man's effort, people in _____ could take the _____ bus and _____ _____.

[01~09] 다음 글을 읽고 물음에 답하시오.

ⓐHere are two stories which I read yesterday. Do you want to hear about them?

ⓑCall Someone You Love
New York had many pay phones on its streets. However, nobody really used ⓒthem. One day, a man came up with an idea. He stuck coins to one of the phones. He also put up a sign that said, "Call Someone You Love." Soon, many people were using the phone. When they were talking to someone whom they loved, ⓓthey didn't stop smiling. His idea became a big success. During the day, all the coins disappeared. The man was very (A)_____ because ⓔhis small idea gave (B)_____ to ⓕmany people.

01 주어진 단어를 어법에 맞게 빈칸 (A)와 (B)에 쓰시오.

> happy

➡ (A) _____ (B)_____

02 적절한 대명사를 이용하여 밑줄 친 ⓐ를 두 개의 문장으로 나누어 쓰시오.

➡ _____

➡ _____

03 밑줄 친 ⓑ에는 생략된 단어가 있다. 생략하지 않은 문장으로 다시 쓰시오.

➡ _____

04 밑줄 친 ⓒ가 가리키는 것을 위 글에서 찾아 쓰시오.

➡ _____

05 주어진 동사를 이용하여 밑줄 친 ⓓ와 같은 의미의 문장을 쓰시오.

> keep

➡ _____

06 다음은 밑줄 친 ⓔ의 의미를 영어로 쓴 것이다. 적절한 관계대명사를 이용하여 빈칸에 알맞은 말을 쓰시오.

> sticking _____ to one of the phones
> _____ _____ _____ _____

07 적절한 관계대명사를 이용하여 밑줄 친ⓕ를 설명하는 문장을 완성하시오.

> many people _____ used the phone with _____.

08 글의 내용에 맞게 다음 대화의 빈칸에 알맞은 말을 쓰시오.

> A: What did a man _____ to one of the pay phones?
> B: He _____ _____ to one of them. I think he wanted people _____ _____ the phone to call _____ _____ they loved.

09 글의 내용에 맞게 다음 빈칸에 알맞은 말을 쓰시오.

> The man stuck coins to one of the phones as well as _____ _____ _____ _____.

[10~18] 다음 글을 읽고 물음에 답하시오.

The Red Arrow Man

A few years ago, the maps at bus stops in Seoul were very confusing. ⓐThey didn't have enough information. People had to ask others to explain the maps. "Where is this bus stop on the map? Does this bus go to Gwanghwamun?" Many people often took the wrong bus and wasted their time.

One day, a young man decided to solve this problem. He bought lots of red arrow stickers. Every day he rode his bicycle around the city and stuck the stickers on the bus maps. ⓑNobody asked him to do this. He just wanted to help others. Thanks to his effort, people could understand the maps easily and save time.

10 밑줄 친 ⓐ가 가리키는 것을 위 글에서 찾아 쓰시오.

➡ _____

11 다음은 밑줄 친 ⓑ와 같은 의미의 문장이다. 적절한 관계대명사를 이용하여 빈칸에 알맞은 말을 쓰시오.

There was no one _____ _____
_____ _____ _____ _____ .

12 Why did people have to ask others to explain the maps at bus stops in Seoul?

➡ It was because _____
_____

13 글의 내용에 맞게 다음 물음에 완전한 문장의 영어로 답하시오.

Q: What did the young man stick on the bus maps?

➡ _____

14 주어진 단어를 이용하여 다음 우리말을 영어로 쓰시오.

그의 노력은 사람들이 지도를 쉽게 이해하는 것을 가능하게 했다. (enable)

➡ _____
_____

15 글의 내용에 맞게 다음 빈칸에 알맞은 말을 쓰시오.

The color of the stickers _____ the young man bought _____ _____ .

16 다음은 위 글을 요약한 것이다. 빈칸에 알맞은 말을 쓰시오.

The bus maps in Seoul were very _____ . So, a young man stuck red arrow stickers on _____ . Thanks to him, people didn't have to _____ their time.

17 주어진 단어를 이용하여 다음 우리말을 영어로 쓰시오.

나는 버스 정류장의 지도들이 충분한 정보를 가지길 원했다. (want)

➡ _____
_____

18 Write the reason why the man stuck red arrow stickers on bus maps every day. Use the phrase 'it's because'.

➡ _____

Real Life Communication B

A: I'm not good at science. What can I do?
be good at: ~을 잘하다

B: Let me help you. Why don't you start with easier books?
~하는 게 어때?(= How about ~?= Let's~)

A: Okay, I'll give it a try. Thanks for the tip.
한번 해 보다

B: No problem. I'm glad you like it.

구문해설 · try: 시도 · tip: 조언

해석

A: 나는 과학을 잘 못해. 어떻게 해야 할까?

B: 내가 도와줄게. 더 쉬운 책으로 시작하는 게 어때?

A: 응, 한번 시도 해볼게. 조언 고마워.

B: 괜찮아. 네가 좋아하니 기뻐.

Let's Write

Be a Mentor!

My name is Semi and I'm in the second grade. I want to help my mentee with
2학년에   to부정사를 목적어로 취하는 동사

her homework. I can meet my mentee after school. I'll ask my mentee to be on
ask+목적어+to부정사: 목적어가 V하도록 요청하다

time. I think a good mentor can be a good friend. So I want to become a good
think의 목적어가 되는 명사절   그래서

friend whom my mentee can trust.
목적격 관계대명사로 생략 가능

구문해설 · grade: 점수, 학년 · mentor: 멘토(경험 없는 사람에게 오랜 기간에 걸쳐 조언과 도움을 베풀어 주는 선배)
· mentee: 멘티(멘토로부터 상담이나 조언을 받는 사람) · after school: 방과 후에
· be on time: 시간을 지키다

멘토가 되세요!

제 이름은 세미이고 저는 2학년입니다. 저는 제 멘티의 숙제를 돕고 싶습니다. 저는 방과 후에 제 멘티를 만날 수 있습니다. 저는 제 멘티에게 시간을 지키라고 요청할 것입니다. 저는 좋은 멘토는 좋은 친구가 될 수 있다고 생각합니다. 그래서 저는 제 멘티가 믿을 수 있는 좋은 친구가 되고 싶습니다.

Culture & Life

Do you see toys inside the bars of soap? Children in South Africa wash their
toys를 수식하는 형용사구

hands more often to get the toys. Washing your hands can prevent many health
to부정사의 부사적 용법 중 '목적'   동명사(주어)

problems. Thanks to this idea, fewer children are getting sick.
~ 덕분에   few의 비교급

구문해설 · bar: 바, 막대 · inside: ~ 안에 · South Africa: 남아프리카 · get: 얻다 · prevent: 예방하다
· get sick: 병에 걸리다

비누들 안에 들어 있는 장난감이 보이나요? 남아프리카의 어린이들은 장난감을 갖기 위해 더 자주 손을 씻습니다. 손을 씻는 것은 많은 건강 문제를 막을 수 있습니다. 이 아이디어 덕분에, 병에 걸리는 어린이들이 줄어들고 있습니다.

영역별 핵심문제

01 다음 영영풀이가 가리키는 것을 고르시오.

> a device or room that is used to keep things cold

① toaster   ② refrigerator

③ closet   ④ stove

⑤ blender

02 다음 중 밑줄 친 부분의 뜻풀이가 바르지 않은 것은?

① They plan to go abroad after graduating from high school. ~할 계획이다

② You need much effort to finish the project. 여유

③ Each student found out a different solution to the problem. 해결책

④ Where should we put our trash? 쓰레기

⑤ I put my jeans in the basket. 바구니

03 다음 우리말에 맞게 빈칸에 알맞은 말을 쓰시오.

(1) 너의 시간을 낭비하지 마라.
➡ Don't _____ _____ _____.

(2) 너는 그 문제를 네 스스로 해결해야 한다.
➡ You should solve the problem _____ _____.

(3) 그는 컴퓨터 게임을 멈추고 나를 바라보았다.
➡ He _____ _____ computer games and looked at me.

04 다음 짝지어진 단어의 관계가 같도록 빈칸에 알맞은 말을 쓰시오.

> teacher : student = mentor : _____

05 다음 문장의 빈칸에 들어갈 말을 보기에서 골라 쓰시오.

> ┤ 보기 ├
> the other day / come up with / on your own

(1) We can _____ _____ _____ creative ideas.

(2) _____ _____ _____ , I came across my English teacher on the street.

(3) I can't believe you made it _____ _____ _____ .

06 다음 주어진 문장의 밑줄 친 rest와 다른 의미로 쓰인 것은?

> • The riders can take a rest at the parking lot.

① It is important for me to have an hour for rest during work.

② We needed a rest for a while because we didn't stop working.

③ You look so tired. Get some rest.

④ You'd better stop singing for a while and try to rest.

⑤ The rest of students spent time reading the books in the library.

Conversation

[07~09] 다음 대화를 읽고 물음에 답하시오.

Tom: Hojun and I planned to give out free stickers today, but I think he forgot.

Sora: Really? (A)Let me help you then. Why are you going to give out stickers?

Tom: It's part of our volunteer club activity.

Sora: I see. What does this sticker mean?

Tom: It means that when we smile at each other, the world will become a better place.

Sora: That's a wonderful idea.

07 위 대화의 밑줄 친 (A)와 바꾸어 쓸 수 있는 것은?

① Can you help me then?
② Let me give you a hand then.
③ I need your help then.
④ Would you help me then?
⑤ I wonder if you can help me then.

08 위 대화에서 다음 영영풀이가 뜻하는 말을 찾아 쓰시오.

a person who does a job without being paid for it

➡ _____

09 위 대화의 내용과 일치하지 <u>않는</u> 것은?

① Hojun과 Tom은 함께 봉사활동을 할 계획이었다.
② Sora가 Hojun 대신 Tom을 도와 줄 것이다.
③ Tom은 무료 스티커를 나누어 줄 계획이다.
④ 스티커는 우리가 서로 웃을 때 세상은 더 좋은 곳이 될 것이라는 것을 의미한다.
⑤ Sora는 Tom과 같은 봉사 동아리에서 활동하고 있다.

[10~12] 다음 대화를 읽고 물음에 답하시오.

Mike: Jimin, what are all these things in the box?

Jimin: (A) I'm going to give her my old books today.

Mike: (B) Do you teach her every weekend?

Jimin: (C) Yes. I feel ⓐhappy when I teach her.

Mike: (D) You are a good mentor. Oh, the box looks heavy. Let me help you.

Jimin: (E) Thanks.

10 위 대화의 (A)~(E) 중 주어진 문장이 들어가기에 적절한 곳은?

They're for my mentee at the children's center.

① (A)　② (B)　③ (C)　④ (D)　⑤ (E)

11 위 대화의 밑줄 친 ⓐ와 바꾸어 쓸 수 <u>없는</u> 것은? (2개)

① delighted　　② pleased
③ joyful　　　④ amazing
⑤ discouraged

12 위 대화의 내용과 일치하지 <u>않는</u> 것은?

① Jimin teaches her mentee at the children's center.
② Jimin is going to give her old books to her mentee.
③ Jimin meets her mentee every weekend.
④ Mike is going to give his hand to Jimin.
⑤ Mike is going to read some books at the children's center.

[13~15] 다음 대화를 읽고 물음에 답하시오.

> Alex: Mom, this is for you. I made it with plastic bags. ⓐ
> Mom: That's very cute, Alex. ⓑ
> Alex: You talked about it when we were having dinner the other day. ⓒ
> Mom: How nice! I really like this basket. It has many different colors. ⓓ
> Alex: I'm glad you like it. ⓔ

13 위 대화의 ⓐ~ⓔ 중 주어진 문장이 들어가기에 적절한 곳은?

> How did you know that I needed a new basket?

① ⓐ   ② ⓑ   ③ ⓒ   ④ ⓓ   ⑤ ⓔ

14 What did Alex make for her mom?

➡ _____

15 When did Alex's mom talk about a new basket?

➡ _____
_____

16 다음 대화가 자연스럽게 이어지도록 순서대로 배열하시오.

> (A) I'm glad you like it.
> (B) That's a great story.
> (C) Sure. Why is he special, Yujin?
> (D) I read a story about a special boy in India. Do you want to hear about it?
> (E) Many children in his town couldn't go to school and had to work. So he taught them in his house every day.

➡ _____

17 다음 빈칸에 들어갈 말로 가장 적절한 것은?

> The man warned us _____ the house. Because the roof of the house leaks.

① buy   ② not buying
③ buying   ④ not to buy
⑤ not to buying

18 다음 빈칸에 알맞은 말을 쓰시오.

> Korea is one of the countries ⓐ_____ lacks water. So teachers advise us ⓑ_____ water when we take a shower. Because saving water is the most important thing that we can do now.

➡ ⓐ _____ ⓑ _____

19 다음 대화의 빈칸에 들어갈 말이 바르게 짝지어진 것은?

> A: I want you _____ me what Katie's favorite flower is.
> B: Tulips are the flowers _____ Katie likes most.

① tell – whose   ② telling – which
③ to tell – that   ④ to tell – what
⑤ telling – what

20 다음 중 빈칸에 공통으로 들어갈 말로 가장 적절한 것은?

> • The novel _____ she wrote ten years ago is going to be published again.
> • Ann, _____ hat do you like better, this or that?

① which   ② that   ③ who
④ whose   ⑤ whom

21 다음 중 어법상 바르지 <u>않은</u> 것은?

① The poor management caused the disease to spread fast.
② Slow music helps us to stay calm and think carefully.
③ The teacher ordered us not to make any troubles.
④ I would like you accept my apology.
⑤ Don't let her stay alone in the park at night.

22 다음 우리말을 영어로 옮길 때 빈칸에 알맞은 말을 쓰시오.

• 그녀에게 이 편지를 복사하라고 요청해 주겠니?
= Can you _____ _____ _____
_____ this letter?

23 다음 중 어법상 바르지 <u>않은</u> 것은?

The bananas ①<u>which</u> my friend ②<u>wanted</u> ③<u>me</u> ④<u>to taste</u> yesterday ⑤<u>was</u> very sweet.

24 밑줄 친 부분 중 생략할 수 <u>없는</u> 것은?

① He is the boy <u>that</u> my mom always compares with me.
② The tree <u>that</u> you planted grows well.
③ Did you think about the suggestion <u>that</u> I made?
④ I want to become a good friend <u>that</u> my friends can trust.
⑤ There are kids <u>that</u> have been left alone all day.

25 다음 빈칸에 적절하지 <u>않은</u> 것은?

My mentor _____ me to do my best.

① persuaded   ② wanted
③ advised   ④ told
⑤ said

Reading

[26~29] 다음 글을 읽고 물음에 답하시오.

Here ①<u>are</u> two stories which I read yesterday. Do you want to hear about them?

Call Someone You Love
New York had many pay phones on its streets. However, (A)[everybody / nobody] really used ②<u>them</u>. One day, a man (B)[came up with / came down with] an idea. He ③<u>stuck</u> coins to one of the phones. He also put up a sign that said, "Call Someone You Love." Soon, many people were ④<u>used</u> the phone. When they were talking to someone ⓐ_____, they didn't stop ⑤<u>smiling</u>. His idea became a big success. During the day, all the coins (C)[appeared / disappeared]. The man was very happy because his small idea gave happiness to many people.

26 알맞은 관계대명사를 이용하여 빈칸 ⓐ에 들어갈 말을 세 단어로 쓰시오.

➡ _____

27 (A)~(C)에서 글의 흐름상 적절한 것끼리 바르게 짝지은 것은?

① everybody – came up with – appeared
② nobody – came up with – disappeared
③ everybody – came down with – appeared
④ nobody – came down with – disappeared
⑤ everybody – came up with – disappeared

28 ①~⑤ 중 어법상 틀린 것을 찾아 바르게 고치시오.

➡ _____

29 다음 중 글을 읽고 답할 수 없는 것은?

① What idea did a man come up with?
② Where were the pay phones in New York?
③ When did people start to use the pay phone?
④ What did people keep doing while using the pay phone?
⑤ How many phone calls did people make?

[30~34] 다음 글을 읽고 물음에 답하시오.

The Red Arrow Man

A few years ago, the maps at bus stops in Seoul were very confusing. They didn't have enough information. People had to ask others (A)_____ the maps. "Where is this bus stop on the map? Does this bus go to Gwanghwamun?" Many people often ⓐtook the wrong bus and wasted their time.

One day, a young man decided (B) _____ this problem. ① Every day he rode his bicycle around the city and stuck the stickers on the bus maps. ② Nobody asked him (C)_____ this. ③ He just wanted to help others. ④ Thanks to his effort, people could understand the maps easily and save time. ⑤

30 주어진 단어를 문맥과 어법에 맞게 빈칸 (A)~(C)에 쓰시오.

(solve / explain / do)

➡ (A) _____ (B) _____ (C) _____

31 ①~⑤ 중 다음 문장이 들어가기에 가장 적절한 곳은?

He bought lots of red arrow stickers.

① ② ③ ④ ⑤

32 다음 중 밑줄 친 ⓐ와 의미가 같은 것은?

① Do you take sugar in your coffee?
② I will take the black jacket.
③ Katherine forgot to take her purse with her.
④ What are you going to take to get there?
⑤ Can you take my hand for a moment?

33 다음 중 위 글의 내용과 일치하지 않는 것은?

① The maps at bus stops in Seoul made people confused a few years ago.
② There wasn't enough information on the maps.
③ People in Seoul took the wrong bus all the time.
④ The young man stuck stickers on his own.
⑤ The man thought that his effort would help other people.

34 위 글의 내용에 맞게 다음 물음에 완전한 문장의 영어로 답하시오.

Q: What happened to people because of the bus maps?

➡ _____
_____

[01~03] 다음 대화를 읽고 물음에 답하시오.

Tom: Hojun and I planned to give out ⓐfree stickers today, but I think he forgot.
Sora: (A) Why are you going to give out stickers?
Tom: (B) It's part of our volunteer club activity.
Sora: (C) I see. What does this sticker mean?
Tom: (D) It means that when we smile at each other, the world will become a better place.
Sora: (E) That's a wonderful idea.

출제율 90%

01 위 대화의 (A)~(E) 중 주어진 문장이 들어가기에 적절한 곳은?

Really? Let me help you then.

① (A)　② (B)　③ (C)　④ (D)　⑤ (E)

출제율 95%

02 위 대화의 밑줄 친 ⓐfree와 같은 의미로 쓰인 것은?

① They are fighting for free speech.
② Jane felt free like a bird.
③ I usually listen to music in my free time.
④ Please feel free to contact me.
⑤ We don't have to pay for the drinks because they're all free.

출제율 90%

03 위 대화를 읽고 대답할 수 없는 것은?

① What did Hojun and Tom plan to do today?
② Why did Tom want to give out stickers?
③ What did the stickers mean?
④ Which club did Tom belong to?
⑤ Why didn't Hojun appear to do his volunteer club activity?

[04~05] 다음 대화를 읽고 물음에 답하시오.

Alex: Mom, this is for you. I made it with plastic bags.
Mom: That's very cute, Alex. How did you know that I needed a new basket?
Alex: You talked about it when we were having dinner the other day.
Mom: (A)How nice! I really like this basket. It has many different colors.
Alex: (B)엄마가 좋아하시니 저도 기뻐요. (glad)

출제율 95%

04 위 대화의 밑줄 친 (A)와 바꾸어 쓸 수 있는 것을 모두 고르시오.

① How nice the basket is!
② How much is it?
③ What do you think about it?
④ How is the basket?
⑤ What a nice basket!

출제율 90%

05 위 대화의 밑줄 친 우리말 (B)를 주어진 단어를 사용하여 영작하시오.

➡ _____

[06~07] 다음 대화를 읽고 물음에 답하시오.

Yujin: I read a story about a special boy in India. Do you want to hear about it?
Jack: Sure. Why is he special, Yujin?
Yujin: Many children in his town couldn't go to school and had to work. So he taught them in his house every day.
Jack: (A)_____
Yujin: I'm glad you like it.

06 위 대화의 빈칸 (A)에 들어갈 말로 <u>어색한</u> 것은?

① It's so touching.

② What a beautiful story!

③ How wonderful it is!

④ That's a great story.

⑤ I'm sorry to hear that.

07 위 대화의 내용과 일치하도록 빈칸을 완성하시오.

Q: Why was the boy in India special?
A: Because he taught (A)_____
_____ who (B)_____
_____ in his house
every day.

[08~10] 다음 대화를 읽고 물음에 답하시오.

Emily: Welcome back, Brian. Are you feeling @better?

Brian: Yes, thanks. I tried to study on my own in the hospital, but it was hard.

Emily: Let me help you. (A)Why don't you join my study group? (how)

Brian: Did you start a study group? That's ⓑwonderful.

Emily: Thanks. I think that we can learn ⓒbetter when we teach each other.

Brian: I ⓓdisagree. I'll try hard to be a good member. Thanks for helping me.

Emily: You're welcome. I'm ⓔglad you like my idea.

08 위 대화의 밑줄 친 (A)와 바꾸어 쓸 수 있는 말을 주어진 단어를 사용하여 쓰시오.

➡ _____

09 위 대화의 밑줄 친 @~ⓔ 중 대화의 흐름상 <u>어색한</u> 말을 찾아 바르게 고치시오.

➡ _____

10 위 대화의 내용과 일치하지 <u>않는</u> 것은?

① Brian은 몸이 좋지 않았었다.

② Emily는 스터디 모임을 시작했다.

③ Emily는 서로 가르쳐 주면 더 잘 배울 수 있을 것이라고 생각한다.

④ Emily는 Brain에게 스터디 모임에 함께 할 것을 제안하였다.

⑤ Brain은 Emily와 함께 병원에서 공부하였다.

11 다음 빈칸에 들어갈 말이 바르게 짝지어진 것은?

• The thing _____ Ann asked me _____ is preparing for the party.

① which – do

② that – doing

③ what – to do

④ which – to do

⑤ that – did

12 다음 우리말을 영어로 옮길 때 빈칸에 들어갈 말로 가장 적절한 것은?

내가 답변해 주기를 원하는 질문이 뭐니?
What is the question _____?

① that you want to ask

② which you want me to answer

③ that you want to answer

④ which I want to answer

⑤ that I want you to answer

13 다음 중 어법상 바르지 <u>않은</u> 것은?

① I want you to consider the option.

② The cup that is on the table is mine.

③ Men who work hard is diligent.

④ Molly will ask you to help her.

⑤ Don't tell me to join the club.

14 주어진 단어를 활용하여 다음 우리말을 영어로 쓰시오. 출제율 85%

> 내가 사고 싶은 차는 미니밴(minivan)이야.
> (that)

➡ _____

15 다음 두 문장을 하나의 문장으로 쓰시오. 출제율 90%

(1) He gave some candies to the little kids. He saw them.

➡ _____

(2) There was a festival. Many people took part in the festival.

➡ _____

(3) The dish was not that expensive. You broke it.

➡ _____

16 다음 상황을 읽고 빈칸에 알맞은 말을 쓰시오. 출제율 95%

> I felt a little cold. When I looked around, I found that the window was open. Jimmy sat next to the window. So I asked Jimmy _____ _____ _____ _____ .

17 다음 중 보기의 밑줄 친 that과 쓰임이 같은 것은? 출제율 100%

> ┌─ 보기 ─┐
> The fact <u>that</u> you lied to me never changes.

① Jack is the man <u>that</u> saved my life.
② The train <u>that</u> you took is slow.
③ I heard the news <u>that</u> you won the game.
④ The pen <u>that</u> you bought is here.
⑤ Always cook the foods <u>that</u> you eat.

[18~21] 다음 글을 읽고 물음에 답하시오.

Here are two stories which I read yesterday. Do you want to hear about them?

Call Someone You Love

New York had many pay phones on its streets. However, nobody really used them. One day, a man came up with an idea. He stuck coins to one of the phones. He also put up a sign ⓐ_____ said, "Call Someone You Love." Soon, many people were using the phone. When they were talking to someone whom they loved, they didn't stop smiling. His idea became a big success. During the day, all the coins disappeared. The man was very happy because his small idea gave happiness to many people.

18 빈칸 ⓐ에 알맞은 말을 모두 쓰시오. 출제율 90%

➡ _____

19 다음 중 글의 내용과 일치하는 것의 개수는? 출제율 95%

> ⓐ There are many public telephones in New York.
> ⓑ People in New York enjoy using a public phone.
> ⓒ It is difficult to know who stuck the coins to the phone.
> ⓓ People used all the coins during the day.
> ⓔ The man thought his idea failed in the end.

① 1개   ② 2개   ③ 3개
④ 4개   ⑤ 5개

20 다음 중 위 글에 이어질 내용으로 가장 적절한 것은?

① what I did yesterday

② another story I wrote

③ another interesting story I heard

④ the other story I read

⑤ other people I called

21 글의 내용에 맞게 빈칸에 알맞은 말을 쓰시오.

> His small idea gave happiness to many people, so _____.

22 주어진 문장과 자연스러운 연결이 되도록 (A)~(D)를 바르게 나열하시오.

> A few years ago, the maps at bus stops in Seoul were very confusing.

(A) "Where is this bus stop on the map? Does this bus go to Gwanghwamun?" Many people often took the wrong bus and wasted their time.

(B) Every day he rode his bicycle around the city and stuck the stickers on the bus maps. Nobody asked him to do this. He just wanted to help others.

(C) One day, a young man decided to solve this problem. He bought lots of red arrow stickers.

(D) They didn't have enough information. People had to ask others to explain the maps.

➡ _____

[23~25] 다음 글을 읽고 물음에 답하시오.

The Red Arrow Man

A few years ago, the maps at bus stops in Seoul were very confusing. They didn't have enough information. People had to ask others to explain the maps. "Where is this bus stop on the map? Does this bus go to Gwanghwamun?" Many people often took the wrong bus and wasted their time.

One day, a young man decided to solve this problem. He bought lots of red arrow stickers. Every day he rode his bicycle around the city and stuck the stickers on the bus maps. Nobody asked him to ⓐdo this. He just wanted to help others. Thanks to his effort, people could understand the maps easily and save time.

23 위 글의 밑줄 친 ⓐdo this가 가리키는 것을 우리말로 간단히 쓰시오.

➡ _____

24 다음 중 위 글의 내용과 일치하지 <u>않는</u> 것은?

① The maps at bus stops in Seoul were not easy to understand.

② The stickers that the man bought were arrow shapes.

③ The young man had his bike.

④ What the man wanted was to help other people.

⑤ The man stuck the stickers every weekend.

25 What happened after the young man's effort? Answer in English with a full sentence.

➡ _____

_____

서술형 실전문제

[01~03] 다음 대화를 읽고 물음에 답하시오.

> Mike: Jimin, what are all these things in the box?
>
> Jimin: They're for my mentee at the children's center. I'm going to give her my old books today.
>
> Mike: Do you teach her every weekend?
>
> Jimin: Yes. I feel happy when I teach her.
>
> Mike: You are a good mentor. Oh, the box looks heavy. Let me help you.
>
> Jimin: Thanks.

01 What is Jimin going to give to her mentee today?

➡ _____

02 중요 How does Jimin feel when she teaches her mentee?

➡ _____

03 What is Mike going to do to help Jimin?

➡ _____

04 다음 빈칸에 알맞은 말을 쓰시오.

> The dentist told me _____ _____ my mouth. But I was so scared that I couldn't open it.

05 주어진 단어를 활용하여 다음 우리말을 영어로 쓰시오.

> 너는 우리가 도서관에서 대출한 그 책을 가지고 있니?
>
> (have / which / check out / from)

➡ _____
_____

06 중요 주어진 단어를 활용하여 다음 문장과 같은 의미의 문장을 쓰시오.

> My mom let me stay out late.
> (allow)

➡ _____

07 다음 상황을 읽고 주어진 단어를 활용하여 빈칸을 알맞게 채우시오.

> Paul: Jimmy, would you get in line, please? We are all waiting in line here.

> ask

➡ Paul _____ .

08 적절한 관계대명사를 이용하여 다음 우리말을 영어로 쓰시오.

> 네가 읽고 있는 책은 흥미롭니?

➡ _____

09 중요 다음 우리말에 맞도록 빈칸에 알맞은 말을 쓰시오.

> 어제 네가 길에서 이야기하고 있었던 소년은 누구였니?
>
> Who was the boy _____ _____ _____ on the street yesterday?

Call Someone You Love

New York had many pay phones on its streets. However, nobody really used them. One day, ⓐa man came up with an idea. He stuck coins ①to one of the ②phones. He also put up a sign that ③said, "Call Someone You Love." Soon, many people were using the phone. When they were talking to someone whom they loved, they didn't stop ④to smile. His idea became ⑤a big success. During the day, all the coins disappeared. The man was very happy because his small idea gave happiness to many people.

10 ①~⑤ 중 어법상 틀린 것을 골라 바르게 고치시오.

➡ _____

11 다음은 밑줄 친 ⓐ와의 대화이다. 빈칸에 알맞은 말을 쓰시오.

> A: What are you doing?
>
> B: I am _____ _____ to this pay phone.
>
> A: Why?
>
> B: It will enable people _____ _____ someone _____ _____. And people will have an interest in using pay phones.
>
> A: What a great idea!

12 글의 내용에 맞도록 다음 물음의 대답을 완성하시오.

> Q: Why was the man happy?
>
> A: It's because _____.

➡ _____

The Red Arrow Man

A few years ago, the maps at bus stops in Seoul were very confusing. They didn't have enough information. People had to ask others to explain the maps. "Where is this bus stop on the map? Does this bus go to Gwanghwamun?" Many people often took the wrong bus and wasted their time.

One day, a young man decided to solve this problem. He bought lots of red arrow stickers. Every day he rode his bicycle around the city and stuck the stickers on the bus maps. Nobody asked him to do this. He just wanted to help others. Thanks to his effort, people could understand the maps easily and save time.

13 다음 우리말에 맞게 빈칸에 알맞은 말을 쓰시오.

> 그가 그 문제를 해결하기 위하여 산 것들은 빨간 화살표 스티커였다.
> The things _____ _____ _____ _____ _____ were red arrow stickers.

14 What did people have to do to take the right bus in Seoul? Answer in English with a full sentence.

➡ _____

01 다음 대화의 내용과 일치하도록 Brian의 일기를 완성하시오.

Emily: Welcome back, Brian. Are you feeling better?
Brian: Yes, thanks. I tried to study on my own in the hospital, but it was hard.
Emily: Let me help you. Why don't you join my study group?
Brian: Did you start a study group? That's wonderful.
Emily: Thanks. I think that we can learn better when we teach each other.
Brian: I agree. I'll try hard to be a good member. Thanks for helping me.
Emily: You're welcome. I'm glad you like my idea.

⬇

Tue, May 28th, 2019
I was happy to come back to school. Emily welcomed me very warmly. We talked about lots of things including study. While I was in the hospital, I tried to study (A)_____ but it was hard. When I talked about it to Emily, she gave me a hand. She suggested (B)_____. She started it because she thought that (C)_____. I agreed to her idea. I decided to (D)_____. I really appreciated her.

02 알맞은 관계대명사를 이용하여 다음 사물이나 직업을 설명하는 문장을 완성하시오.

a painter / a purse / a baker / a chair

(1) _____
(2) _____
(3) _____
(4) _____

03 주어진 동사로 여러 가지 문장을 쓰시오.

ask / encourage / force / enable / allow / tell

(1) _____
(2) _____
(3) _____
(4) _____
(5) _____

단원별 모의고사

01 다음 짝지어진 단어의 관계가 같도록 빈칸에 알맞은 말을 쓰시오.

> same : different = inside : _____

02 다음 영영풀이가 가리키는 것을 고르시오.

> a person who is advised and helped by more experienced person

① mentee
② teacher
③ mentor
④ professor
⑤ president

03 다음 우리말을 주어진 단어를 이용하여 영작하시오.

(1) 박쥐는 대개 낮 동안에 잠을 잔다. (mostly, during)

➡ _____

(2) 나는 나의 엄마에게 전화하기 위해 공중전화를 사용했다. (pay, call, mom)

➡ _____

(3) 그는 회의에서 좋은 아이디어를 생각해 냈다. (came, great)

➡ _____

[04~06] 다음 대화를 읽고 물음에 답하시오.

Alex: Mom, this is for you. I made it with plastic bags.
Mom: That's very cute, Alex. How did you know that I needed a new basket?
Alex: You talked about it when we were having dinner the other day.
Mom: (A)_____ nice! I really like this basket. It has many different colors.
Alex: I'm glad you like it.

04 위 대화의 빈칸 (A)에 알맞은 것은?

① Why
② How
③ What
④ When
⑤ Where

05 위 대화를 통해 알 수 있는 엄마의 심경으로 적절한 것은?

① lonely
② happy
③ nervous
④ upset
⑤ dissatisfied

06 위 대화를 읽고 대답할 수 없는 것은?

① What did Alex make for his mom?
② What did Alex use to make his gift for his mom?
③ How did Alex know that his mother needed a new basket?
④ How did Alex feel when his mother liked his gift?
⑤ Where did Alex learn how to make a basket?

[07~09] 다음 대화를 읽고 물음에 답하시오.

Emily: Welcome back, Brian. Are you feeling better?
Brian: Yes, thanks. I tried to study (A)[of / on] my own in the hospital, but it was hard.
Emily: Let me help you. Why don't you join my study group?
Brian: Did you start a study group? That's wonderful.
Emily: Thanks. I think (B)[which / that] we can learn better when we teach each other.

Brian: I agree. I'll try hard to be a good member. Thanks for helping me.

Emily: (D)_____ I'm glad you (C)[like / to like] my idea.

07 위 대화의 괄호 (A)~(C)에서 알맞은 말을 고르시오.

➡ (A)_____, (B)_____, (C)_____

08 위 대화의 빈칸 (D)에 들어가기에 <u>어색한</u> 것은?

① Don't mention it.
② It's my pleasure.
③ Not at all.
④ You're welcome.
⑤ Don't blame me.

09 위 대화를 읽고 대답할 수 <u>없는</u> 것은?

① What did Brian try to do in the hospital?
② What did Emily start?
③ What did Emily suggest to Brian?
④ What did Emily think about a study group?
⑤ What did Emily and Brain learn in a study group?

[10~11] 다음 대화를 읽고 물음에 답하시오.

Henry: Your bag looks heavy. Let me help you.

Sujin: Thanks. Where is the bus stop around here?

Henry: It's over there. I'll carry your bag to the bus stop for you.

Sujin: You're very kind.

Henry: No problem. I am going that way, too.

10 What was Sujin looking for?

➡ _____

11 How did Henry help Sujin?

➡ _____

12 다음 중 짝지어진 대화가 <u>어색한</u> 것은?

① A: I made this picture frame for you.
   B: Thanks. It's wonderful.
② A: Sounds great. I like your story.
   B: I'm glad you like it.
③ A: You're so kind to say like that.
   B: My pleasure.
④ A: I really appreciate your help.
   B: Don't mention it.
⑤ A: I enjoyed baking this cake for you.
   B: I'm sorry to hear that.

13 다음 중 빈칸에 공통으로 들어갈 말로 가장 적절한 것은?

• The dog _____ you take care of has a long tail.
• The children _____ she is looking at look excited.

① that   ② which   ③ whose
④ who   ⑤ what

14 다음 빈칸에 알맞은 말을 쓰시오.

I don't like to eat vegetables. But my mother wants me _____ _____ them.

15 다음 중 빈칸에 들어갈 말로 적절하지 <u>않은</u> 것은?

> I _____ you to answer the phone.

① would like   ② want

③ ask   ④ allow

⑤ make

16 주어진 어구를 활용하여 다음 우리말을 영어로 쓰시오.

> 나는 많은 사람들이 아주 좋아할 영화를 만들고 싶어.
> (a movie / will love)

➡ _____

17 주어진 어구를 바르게 배열하여 다음 우리말을 영어로 쓰시오. 필요하다면 단어를 추가하시오.

> 그 선생님은 우리에게 정각에 오라고 말씀하셨다.
> (on / the teacher / be / us / time / told)

➡ _____

[18~21] 다음 글을 읽고 물음에 답하시오.

Call Someone You Love
New York had many pay phones on its streets. However, nobody really used them. One day, a man came up with an idea. He stuck coins to one of the phones. He also put up a sign that said, "Call Someone You Love." Soon, many people were using the phone. When they were talking to someone whom they loved, they didn't stop (A)<u>smiling</u>. His idea became a big success. During the day, all the coins disappeared. The man was very happy (B)_____ his small idea gave happiness to many people.

18 밑줄 친 (A)와 쓰임이 <u>다른</u> 하나는?

① I am tired of <u>hearing</u> the noise.

② Do you mind <u>opening</u> the door?

③ Norman finished <u>reading</u> the paper.

④ What are they <u>doing</u> now?

⑤ The boys practiced <u>playing</u> soccer after school.

19 다음 중 빈칸 (B)에 들어갈 말로 적절한 것을 <u>모두</u> 고르면?

① though   ② until   ③ as

④ if   ⑤ because

20 다음 중 글의 내용과 일치하는 것은?

① Everybody used play phones in New York.

② A man stuck coins to a pay phone in New York.

③ A man talked with people about using pay phones.

④ People started to use the pay phone after having a conversation with the man.

⑤ Many coins were left at night.

21 주어진 어구를 바르게 배열하여 위 글을 요약하는 문장을 완성하시오.

> (thanks to / when / someone they loved / many people in New York / a man's idea / became happy / they called).

➡ _____

_____

_____

[22~25] 다음 글을 읽고 물음에 답하시오.

The Red Arrow Man

A few years ago, the maps at bus stops in Seoul (A)[was / were] very confusing. They didn't have enough information. People had to ask others to explain the maps. "Where is this bus stop on the map? Does this bus go to Gwanghwamun?" Many people (B)[often took / took often] the wrong bus and wasted their time.

One day, a young man decided to solve this problem. He bought ⓐ_____ red arrow stickers. Every day he rode his bicycle around the city and stuck (C)[it / them] on the bus maps. Nobody asked him to do this. He just wanted to help others. Thanks to his effort, people could understand the maps easily and save time.

22 다음 중 빈칸 ⓐ에 들어갈 말로 적절하지 <u>않은</u> 것은?

① lots of   ② many

③ a lot of   ④ a number of

⑤ much

23 (A)~(C)에서 어법상 옳은 것끼리 바르게 짝지은 것은?

① was – often took – it

② were – often took – them

③ was – took often – it

④ were – took often – it

⑤ was – took often – them

24 다음 중 위 글을 읽고 답할 수 있는 것의 개수는?

ⓐ What was the matter with the maps at bus stops in Seoul?

ⓑ How many bus stops were there in Seoul a few years ago?

ⓒ What bus did people take to go to Gwanghwamun?

ⓓ What did the man do to solve the problem?

ⓔ Why did people often take the wrong bus?

① 1개   ② 2개   ③ 3개

④ 4개   ⑤ 5개

25 위 글의 내용에 맞게 빈칸에 알맞은 말을 쓰시오.

The young man wanted to help _____

_____ _____ the maps easily.

Lesson 4

For a Healthy Summer

 의사소통 기능

- 유감·동정 표현하기
  I'm sorry to hear that.
- 당부하기
  Make sure you wear a hat.

언어 형식

- something+형용사
  I want **something cold** to drink.
- 현재완료
  I **'ve finished** my dinner.

Words & Expressions

Key Words

- **advice** [ædváis] 명 충고, 조언
- **bite** [bait] 명 (벌레에) 물린 상처 동 (벌레가) 물다
- **brush** [brʌʃ] 동 ~을 닦다
- **blood** [blʌd] 명 피
- **bug** [bʌg] 명 벌레
- **bump** [bʌmp] 명 혹, 타박상
- **buzz** [bʌz] 동 윙윙거리다
- **empty** [émpti] 동 비우다
- **female** [fíːmeil] 형 암컷의, 여성의
- **food poisoning** 식중독
- **happen** [hǽpən] 동 일어나다, 발생하다
- **healthy** [hélθi] 형 건강한
- **itch** [itʃ] 동 가렵다
- **itchy** [itʃi] 형 가려운
- **lay** [lei] 동 (알을) 낳다
- **male** [meil] 형 수컷의, 남성의
- **million** [míljən] 명 100만, 다수
- **miss** [mis] 동 놓치다, 빼먹다
- **mosquito** [məskíːtou] 명 모기
- **pack** [pæk] 동 (가방을) 싸다
- **pointed** [pɔ́intid] 형 뾰족한
- **prevent** [privént] 동 예방하다, 방지하다

- **protein** [próutin] 명 단백질
- **reduce** [ridjúːs] 동 줄이다
- **scratch** [skrætʃ] 동 긁다
- **sense** [sens] 동 느끼다, 감지하다
- **sharp** [ʃɑːrp] 형 날카로운
- **sink** [siŋk] 명 (부엌의) 수채 동 가라앉다
- **sleeve** [sliːv] 명 (옷의) 소매, 소맷자락
- **standing** [stǽndiŋ] 형 괴어 있는
- **stomach** [stʌ́mək] 명 위, 복부, 배
- **strange** [streindʒ] 형 이상한
- **sunburn** [sʌ́nbərn] 명 햇볕에 탐, 그을림
- **sunscreen** [sʌ́nskriːn] 명 자외선 차단제
- **sure** [ʃuər] 형 확실한
- **sweat** [swet] 명 땀 동 땀을 흘리다
- **sweaty** [swéti] 형 땀에 젖은
- **thirsty** [θɔ́ːrsti] 형 목마른
- **tiny** [táini] 형 아주 작은
- **trash** [træʃ] 명 쓰레기
- **useful** [júːsfəl] 형 유용한
- **wipe** [waip] 명 닦아내는 천[솜]
- **worried** [wɔ́ːrid] 형 걱정[근심]하는

Key Expressions

- **at that moment** 그때에
- **do better** 더 잘하다
- **feed on** ~을 먹고살다
- **for a while** 당분간
- **go for a walk** 산책 가다
- **I'd love to** ~하고 싶다

- **keep ... in mind** ~을 명심하다
- **lose (~) by** ~(점, 골 등) 차로 (경기에서) 지다
- **stay away from** ~에서 떨어져 있다, 멀리하다
- **suffer from** ~으로 고통받다
- **take ~ to ...** ~을 …로 데려가다[가져가다]

Word Power

※ 서로 반대되는 뜻을 가진 어휘

□ **male** 수컷의, 남성의 ↔ **female** 암컷의, 여성의

□ **sharp** 예민한, 날카로운 ↔ **dull** 무딘, 둔한

□ **empty** 텅 빈 ↔ **full** 가득 찬

□ **healthy** 건강한 ↔ **unhealthy** 건강하지 못한

□ **tiny** 아주 작은 ↔ **huge** 거대한

□ **useful** 유용한 ↔ **useless** 쓸모없는

※ 질병을 나타내는 어휘

□ **stomachache** 복통

□ **toothache** 치통

□ **cough** 기침

□ **fever** 열

□ **sore throat** 인후염

□ **headache** 두통

□ **cold** 감기

□ **cancer** 암

□ **earache** 귀앓이

□ **runny nose** 콧물

English Dictionary

□ **bite** 물린 상처
→ a wound made by biting
물려서 만들어진 상처

□ **bump** 혹, 타박상
→ an area of skin that is raised because it was hit, bitten, etc.
맞거나 물려서 부푼 피부의 한 부분

□ **buzz** 윙윙거리다
→ to make a low, continuous sound of a flying insect
날아다니는 곤충이 낮고 지속적인 소리를 내다

□ **happen** 일어나다, 발생하다
→ to take place especially without being planned
특히 계획된 것 없이 발생하다

□ **itch** 가렵다
→ to have an unpleasant feeling on your skin that makes you want to scratch
피부 위에 당신이 긁고 싶도록 만드는 불쾌한 느낌을 갖다

□ **lay** (알을) 낳다
→ to produce an egg outside the body
몸 밖에 알을 생산하다

□ **miss** 놓치다, 빼먹다
→ to fail to do, take, make, or have something
무언가를 하거나 가져가거나 만들거나 소유하지 못하다

□ **mosquito** 모기
→ a small flying insect that bites the skin of people and animals to suck their blood
사람이나 동물의 피부를 물어 그들의 피를 빠는 작은 날아다니는 곤충

□ **pack** (가방을) 싸다
→ to put something into a bag so that you can take it with you
무언가를 가방에 넣어 갖고 갈 수 있게 하다

□ **prevent** 방지하다, 막다
→ to stop something from happening or existing
무언가가 발생하거나 존재하는 것을 막다

□ **protein** 단백질
→ a substance found in foods such as meat, milk, eggs, and beans
고기, 우유, 계란, 그리고 콩과 같은 음식에서 발견되는 물질

□ **scratch** 긁다
→ to rub your skin with something sharp
날카로운 무언가로 당신의 피부를 문지르다

□ **sense** 느끼다, 감지하다
→ to become aware of something even though you can't see it, hear it, etc.
비록 당신이 보거나 들을 수 없지만 무언가를 알아차리게 되다

□ **sunburn** 햇볕에 탐, 그을림
→ a condition in which your skin becomes sore and red from too much sunshine
너무 많은 햇빛으로 당신의 피부가 쓰리고 붉어진 상태

Words & Expressions 시험대비 실력평가 Step2

서답형
01 다음 짝지어진 단어의 관계가 같도록 빈칸에 알맞은 말을 쓰시오.

> man : woman = male : _____

서답형
02 다음 영영풀이가 가리키는 것을 고르시오.

> to rub your skin with something sharp

① scratch   ② prevent
③ bite   ④ buzz
⑤ pack

03 다음 중 밑줄 친 부분의 뜻풀이가 바르지 <u>않은</u> 것은?

① Almost 5 <u>million</u> people have watched this program. 백만
② Students learn safety rules to <u>prevent</u> the accident. 예방하다
③ Athletes are working out hard in a <u>sweat</u>. 달콤한
④ I felt hungry and <u>thirsty</u> after walking for an hour. 목마른
⑤ Eggs are one of the major sources of <u>protein</u>. 단백질

서답형
04 다음 우리말에 맞게 빈칸에 알맞은 말을 쓰시오.

(1) 나의 머리에 혹이 있다.
  ➡ There's a _____ on my head.
(2) 등이 가렵다.
  ➡ My back _____.
(3) 나를 위해 내 등을 좀 긁어 주시겠어요?
  ➡ Will you _____ my back for me?

서답형
05 다음 우리말에 맞게 빈칸에 알맞은 말을 쓰시오.

(1) 그 때에, 조그만 무언가가 그에게로 날아왔다.
  ➡ _____ _____ _____, something tiny flew at him.
(2) 나는 공원에 산책하러 갔다.
  ➡ I _____ _____ _____ _____ in the park.
(3) 펭귄은 물고기를 먹고 산다.
  ➡ Penguins _____ _____ fish.

서답형
06 다음 문장의 빈칸에 들어갈 말을 보기에서 골라 쓰시오.

> ─┤ 보기 ├─
> tiny / sweaty / protein / standing / pointed

(1) We were hot and _____ after playing basketball.
(2) This dog's ears are large and _____.
(3) Meat is an excellent source of _____.
(4) She's wearing a dress with a pattern of _____ roses.
(5) We can find mosquitos near _____ water.

07 다음 주어진 문장의 밑줄 친 pointed와 같은 의미로 쓰인 것은?

> I need a <u>pointed</u> pencil to draw a picture.

① He <u>pointed</u> at a spot on the map.
② We don't like being <u>pointed</u> at.
③ My child <u>pointed</u> out animals in the book.
④ This bird has a <u>pointed</u> beak.
⑤ She <u>pointed</u> to the restroom.

01 다음 짝지어진 단어의 관계가 같도록 빈칸에 알맞은 말을 쓰시오.

> tiny : huge = _____ : full

02 다음 영영풀이가 가리키는 것을 쓰시오.

> a small flying insect that bites the skin of people and animals to suck their blood

➡ _____

03 다음 문장의 빈칸에 들어갈 말을 보기에서 골라 쓰시오.

┌─ 보기 ─┐
lay / strange / buzzing / prevent

(1) A mosquito is _____ around me.
(2) Brush your teeth after meals to _____ tooth problems.
(3) Do you know whether the frogs _____ eggs or not?
(4) I met someone _____ on my way home.

04 다음 우리말에 맞게 빈칸에 알맞은 말을 쓰시오.

(1) 나는 네가 다음번에 더 잘할 것이라고 확신한다.
  ➡ I'm sure that you'll _____ _____ next time.
(2) 너의 충고를 명심할게.
  ➡ I'll _____ your advice _____ _____.
(3) 나는 두통으로 고통 받고 있다.
  ➡ I'm _____ _____ the headache.

05 다음 우리말에 맞게 주어진 단어를 사용하여 영작하시오.

(1) 우리 당분간 여기에 머무르는 게 어때? (while, why)
  ➡ _____
(2) 나는 한국으로 돌아가고 싶다. (love, back)
  ➡ _____
(3) 많은 사람들이 식중독으로 고통 받았다. (suffered)
  ➡ _____

06 다음 우리말과 일치하도록 주어진 어구를 모두 배열하여 완성하시오.

(1) 만약 네가 그 개에게서 뼈를 가져가면, 그가 너를 물을 것이다. (if로 시작할 것)
(you / from / he / the bone / if / take / will / bite / the dog / you)
  ➡ _____
(2) 너무 덥고 땀이 나기 때문에 나는 여름을 좋아하지 않는다. (I로 시작할 것)
(don't / get / because / I / sweaty / too / like / hot / summer / I / and)
  ➡ _____
(3) 눈병을 예방하기 위해 항상 비누로 손을 씻어라. (to로 시작할 것)
(prevent / always / an eye disease / with / soap / your / wash / to / hands)
  ➡ _____
_____

Conversation

1 유감 · 동정 표현하기

I'm sorry to hear that. (그것 참 안됐네요.)

■ 'I'm sorry to hear that.'은 '그것 참 안됐네요.'라는 뜻으로 좋지 못한 소식을 들었을 때, 유감이나 동정을 표현하는 말이다.

유감 · 동정 표현하기

- That's too bad. (그것 참 안됐군요.)
- That's a pity. (그것 참 안됐군요.)
- What a pity! (가엾어라!)
- That's terrible. (끔찍한 일이군요.)
- That's a shame. (유감이군요.)

핵심 Check

1. 다음 우리말과 일치하도록 빈칸에 알맞은 말을 쓰시오.

   (1) **A:** I lost my wallet. (나는 지갑을 잃어버렸어요.)

   B: I'm _____ _____ _____ that. (그것 참 안됐군요.)

   (2) **A:** I'm not feeling well. (몸 상태가 좋지 않아요.)

   B: That's _____ _____. (그것 참 안됐군요.)

   (3) **A:** My stomach hurts! I think I have food poisoning. (배가 아파요! 나 식중독인거 같아요!)

   B: _____ _____. How about going to see a doctor? (끔찍한 일이야. 의사에게 가는 게 어때?)

② 당부하기

Make sure you wear a hat. (반드시 모자를 쓰세요.)

■ 'Make sure (that) you ~.'는 '반드시 ~해라.'라는 뜻으로 당부를 하는 표현이다. 비슷한 표현으로 'Make sure to ~. / Don't forget to ~.' 등이 있다. 이에 대한 응답 표현으로 'Okay, I will.' 또는 'I'll keep that in mind.' 등이 있다.

당부하기

• Make sure you wear sunscreen when you go outside.
(밖에 나갈 때 반드시 자외선 차단제를 바르세요.)

• Don't forget to wash your hands before you touch food.
(음식에 손대기 전에 손을 씻는 것을 잊지 마세요.)

• Remember to empty your trash can more often.
(당신의 쓰레기통을 더 자주 비워야 하는 것을 기억하세요.)

• Keep in mind that you should take an umbrella with you.
(우산을 가져가야 한다는 것을 명심하세요.)

핵심 Check

2. 다음 우리말과 일치하도록 빈칸에 알맞은 말을 쓰시오.

(1) A: _____ _____ you avoid standing water. (반드시 괴어 있는 물은 피하세요.)

   B: Okay, I will. (알겠어요. 그렇게 할게요.)

(2) A: _____ _____ to put a green tea bag on the itchy area. (가려운 부위에 녹차 티백을 올려놓는 것을 잊지 마세요.)

   B: Okay, I'll try that. (알겠어요. 시도해 볼게요.)

(3) A: Remember to wear a long sleeve. (긴소매를 입어야 한다는 것을 기억하세요.)

   B: _____ _____ _____ _____ _____. (명심할게요.)

A. Listen & Speak 2 –B

Sujin: Dad, do we have any bug spray?

Dad: Yes, ❶it's under the sink. Why?

Sujin: ❷There are a lot of fruit flies around the trash.

Dad: Oh no! What did you put in the trash?

Sujin: Some fruit waste.

Dad: Fruit flies love sweet things. ❸Make sure you don't put fruit waste in the trash can.

Sujin: I'll keep ❹that in mind. I think we should also empty our trash can more often.

Dad: That's a good idea.

Sujin: 아빠, 우리 벌레 퇴치 스프레이가 있나요?

Dad: 응, 그것은 싱크대 밑에 있단다. 왜?

Sujin: 쓰레기 주변에 많은 초파리가 있어요.

Dad: 오 안돼! 쓰레기에 무엇을 넣었니?

Sujin: 약간의 과일 쓰레기요.

Dad: 초파리는 달콤한 것들을 좋아해. 쓰레기통에 과일 쓰레기를 버리지 않도록 하렴.

Sujin: 명심할게요. 제 생각에 우리는 또한 쓰레기통을 좀 더 자주 비워야 할 것 같아요.

Dad: 좋은 생각이구나.

❶ it은 bug spray를 가리킨다.
❷ there are+복수 명사 / there is+단수 명사
❸ 'Make sure ~'는 '반드시 ~해라.'라는 당부의 표현이다.
❹ that은 과일 쓰레기를 쓰레기통에 넣지 말라는 것을 가리킨다.

Check(√) True or False

(1) The bug spray is under the sink. T ☐ F ☐

(2) Sujin kept in mind that she should not put fruit waste in the trash can. T ☐ F ☐

B. Real Life Communication

Ms. Wheeler: Junsu, ❶what happened to your face?

Junsu: I got a lot of mosquito ❷bites.

Ms. Wheeler: ❸I'm sorry to hear that. How did it happen?

Junsu: It happened when I went camping last weekend.

Ms. Wheeler: Oh dear. Don't scratch ❹them!

Junsu: I know, but ❺they're really itchy.

Ms. Wheeler: Clean ❻them with cool water. That'll help. Also, make sure you wear long sleeves when you go camping.

Junsu: Okay, thank you.

Ms. Wheeler: 준수야, 얼굴이 왜 그러니?

Junsu: 모기에 많이 물렸어요.

Ms. Wheeler: 그것 참 안됐구나. 어쩌다 그랬니?

Junsu: 지난 주말에 캠핑 갔다가 그랬어요.

Ms. Wheeler: 이런 참. 물린 곳을 긁지 마라.

Junsu: 알아요, 하지만 정말 가려워요.

Ms. Wheeler: 물린 곳을 찬물로 닦으렴. 도움이 될 거야. 또한 캠핑 갈 때에는 긴 소매 옷을 입도록 해.

Junsu: 네, 감사합니다.

❶ 'what happened to ~?'는 '~에 무슨 일이 있었니?'라는 의미이다
❷ bite는 (벌레에) 물린 상처를 뜻한다.
❸ I'm sorry to hear that.은 유감이나 동정을 나타내며 'That's too bad.'와 바꾸어 쓸 수 있다.
❹,❺,❻ them과 they 모두 mosquito bites를 가리킨다.

Check(√) True or False

(3) Junsu went camping last weekend. T ☐ F ☐

(4) Junsu suffered from a lot of mosquito bites on his face. T ☐ F ☐

Listen & Speak 1–A (1)

Brian: You look worried, Jimin. ❶What's wrong?

Jimin: I'm worried ❷because my cat is sick.

Brian: I'm sorry to hear that. ❸Why don't you take her to an animal doctor?

Jimin: Okay, I will.

❶ What's wrong?은 '무슨 일이니?'라는 의미로 'What happened?'와 바꾸어 쓸 수 있다.
❷ 'because+주어+동사'로 이어지는 반면에 'because of+명사(구)'가 이어진다.
❸ 'Why don't you ~?'는 '~하는 게 어때?'라고 제안하는 표현이다.

Listen & Speak 1–A (2)

Jane: How was the soccer game with Minsu's class, Alex?

Alex: We ❶lost by three goals.

Jane: I'm sorry to hear that. I hope you ❷do better next time.

Alex: I hope so, too.

❶ lose by ... ···점, ···골 등 차로 (경기에서) 지다
❷ do better: 더 잘하다

Listen & Speak 1-B

Tom: Let's go swimming this weekend, Yujin.

Yujin: I'd love to, but I can't.

Tom: ❶Why not?

Yujin: I have an eye problem. The doctor told me to ❷stop swimming for a while.

Tom: I'm sorry to hear that. Maybe we can go next weekend.

Yujin: I really hope so.

❶ 수영을 못가는 이유를 질문하고 있는 표현이다.
❷ stop+~ing: ~하는 것을 멈추다, stop+to부정사: ~하기 위해 멈추다
   for a while: 당분간

Listen & Speak 2–A (1)

Emma: Tim, look at your face! You got ❶ sunburn.

Tim: Yes, it hurts a lot. I went swimming at the beach without sunscreen.

Emma: Oh dear! ❷Make sure you wear sunscreen next time.

❶ sunburn: 햇볕에 탐, 그을림
❷ 'Make sure ~.'는 당부하는 표현으로 'keep in mind ~', 'Don't forget to ~.' 또는 'Remember ~.'와 바꾸어 쓸 수 있다.

Listen & Speak 2–A (2)

Mom: Hojun, do you want to go shopping with me?

Hojun: Sorry, Mom. I'm going to play baseball with Alex this afternoon.

Mom: Okay. No problem. Just make sure you wear a hat. It's going to be very hot this afternoon.

Hojun: ❶Okay, I will.

❶ 당부하기에 대한 대답으로 'I'll keep that in mind.'로 대답할 수도 있다.

Listen & Speak 2–A (3)

Mike: Did you ❶pack for the school trip tomorrow, Sue?

Sue: Yes. Now I'm checking my list again. I don't want to ❷miss anything.

Mike: Make sure you take an umbrella with you. It might rain tomorrow.

Sue: Okay, thank you.

❶ pack: (가방을) 싸다
❷ miss: 놓치다, 빼먹다

● 다음 우리말과 일치하도록 빈칸에 알맞은 말을 쓰시오.

해석

Listen & Speak 1–A (1)

Brian: You look _____, Jimin. What's wrong?

Jimin: I'm _____ because _____ _____ _____ _____.

Brian: _____ _____ _____ _____ _____. Why don't you take her to an animal doctor?

Jimin: Okay, _____ _____.

Listen & Speak 1–A (2)

Jane: _____ was the soccer game with Minsu's class, Alex?

Alex: We _____ _____ three goals.

Jane: _____ _____ _____ _____ _____. I hope _____ _____ _____ _____ _____.

Alex: I hope so, too.

Listen & Speak 1-B

Tom: Let's go swimming this weekend, Yujin.

Yujin: I'd love to, but _____ _____.

Tom: _____ _____?

Yujin: I have an eye problem. The doctor told me _____ _____ _____ _____ _____ _____.

Tom: I'm sorry to _____ _____. Maybe we can go _____ _____.

Yujin: I really _____ _____.

Listen & Speak 2–A (1)

Emma: Tim, look at your face! You got _____.

Tim: Yes, it hurts _____ _____. I went swimming at the beach _____ _____.

Emma: Oh dear! _____ _____ you wear sunscreen next time.

해석

Listen & Speak 2–A (2)

Mom: Hojun, do you want to go shopping with me?

Hojun: Sorry, Mom. I'm going to play baseball with Alex this afternoon.

Mom: Okay. No problem. _____ _____ _____ _____

_____ _____ _____. It's going to be very hot this afternoon.

Hojun: Okay, _____ _____.

Listen & Speak 2–B

Sujin: Dad, do we have _____ bug spray?

Dad: Yes, it's under _____ _____. Why?

Sujin: There are a lot of _____ _____ around the trash.

Dad: Oh no! What did you _____ in the _____?

Sujin: Some fruit waste.

Dad: Fruit flies love sweet things. _____ _____ _____

_____ _____ _____ _____ _____ _____

_____ _____.

Sujin: I'll _____ that _____ _____. I think we should also

_____ _____ _____ _____ more often.

Dad: That's a good idea.

Real Life Communication

Ms. Wheeler: Junsu, _____ _____ to your face?

Junsu: I got a lot of _____ _____.

Ms. Wheeler: _____ _____ _____ _____ _____. _____

did it happen?

Junsu: It happened when I _____ _____ last weekend.

Ms. Wheeler: Oh dear. _____ _____ _____!

Junsu: I know, but they're really _____.

Ms. Wheeler: Clean them _____ cool water. That'll help. Also,

_____ _____ _____ _____ _____

when you go camping.

Junsu: Okay, thank you.

01 다음 대화의 빈칸에 들어갈 말로 적절한 것은?

> **Jane:** How was the soccer game with Minsu's class, Alex?
> **Alex:** _____
> **Jane:** I'm sorry to hear that. I hope you do better next time.
> **Alex:** I hope so, too.

① We beat his class.

② We lost by three goals.

③ We were so happy to win the game.

④ It was a tough game but we won.

⑤ Minsu was a really good player.

02 다음 대화가 자연스럽게 이어지도록 순서대로 배열하시오.

> (A) Okay, I will.
> (B) Hojun, do you want to go shopping with me?
> (C) Sorry, Mom. I'm going to play baseball with Alex this afternoon.
> (D) Okay. No problem. Just make sure you wear a hat. It's going to be very hot this afternoon.

➡ _____

[03~04] 다음 대화를 읽고 물음에 답하시오.

> **Brian:** You look worried, Jimin. What's wrong?
> **Jimin:** I'm worried because my cat is sick.
> **Brian:** (A)_____ Why don't you take her to an animal doctor?
> **Jimin:** Okay, I will.

03 위 대화의 빈칸 (A)에 들어갈 말로 어색한 것은?

① That's too bad. ② That's really sad.

③ That's a pity. ④ What a relief.

⑤ I'm sorry to hear that.

04 위 대화의 내용과 일치하지 않는 것은?

① Jimin was concerned about her cat.

② Jimin's cat was sick.

③ Brian felt sorry to hear about Jimin's cat.

④ Brian advised Jimin to take her cat to the vet.

⑤ Brian was going to take Jimin to a doctor.

01 다음 대화의 빈칸에 들어갈 말로 <u>어색한</u> 것을 고르시오.

> Emma: Tim, look at your face! You got sunburn.
>
> Tim: Yes, it hurts a lot. I went swimming at the beach without sunscreen.
>
> Emma: Oh dear! _____

① Don't forget to wear sunscreen next time.

② Make sure you wear sunscreen next time.

③ Remember to wear sunscreen next time.

④ Keep in mind that you should wear sunscreen next time.

⑤ You don't have to wear sunscreen next time.

[02~03] 다음 대화를 읽고 물음에 답하시오.

> Tom: (a)<u>Let's go swimming this weekend, Yujin.</u>
>
> Yujin: I'd love to, but I can't.
>
> Tom: Why not?
>
> Yujin: I have an eye problem. (A)_____
>
> Tom: I'm sorry to hear that. Maybe we can go next weekend.
>
> Yujin: I really hope so.

서답형
02 위 대화의 빈칸 (A)에 들어갈 말을 주어진 어구를 모두 배열하여 완성하시오.

┌── 보기 ──┐
for / to / stop / a while / the doctor / me
/ told / swimming
└──────────┘

➡ _____

03 위 대화의 밑줄 친 (a)와 바꾸어 쓸 수 있는 것을 <u>모두</u> 고르시오.

① Why don't we go swimming this weekend, Yujin?

② Do you want to go swimming this weekend, Yujin?

③ How about going swimming this weekend, Yujin?

④ Do you like going swimming this weekend, Yujin?

⑤ Why do you go swimming this weekend, Yujin?

[04~05] 다음 대화를 읽고 물음에 답하시오.

> Brian: You look worried, Jimin. What's wrong?
>
> Jimin: I'm worried because my cat is sick.
>
> Brian: I'm sorry to hear that. (A)<u>Why don't you take her to an animal doctor?</u> (how)
>
> Jimin: Okay, I will.

서답형
04 위 대화의 밑줄 친 (A)와 의미가 같도록 주어진 단어를 활용하여 다시 쓰시오.

➡ _____

05 위 대화에서 Jimin의 심경으로 적절한 것은?

① pleased ② anxious

③ nervous ④ excited

⑤ encouraged

[06~07] 다음 대화를 읽고 물음에 답하시오.

> Mom: Hojun, do you want to go shopping with me?
> Hojun: Sorry, Mom. I'm going to play baseball with Alex this afternoon.
> Mom: Okay. No problem. (A)Just make sure you wear a hat. (mind, should, keep) It's going to be very hot this afternoon.
> Hojun: Okay, I will.

06 위 대화의 밑줄 친 (A)와 의미가 같도록 주어진 단어를 사용하여 다시 쓰시오.

➡ _____

07 위 대화의 내용과 일치하는 것은?

① Hojun wants to go shopping with his mom.
② Hojun is going to play baseball with Alex tomorrow.
③ Hojun's mom kept in mind that she should wear a hat.
④ The weather is going to be bad this afternoon.
⑤ Hojun will wear a hat when he plays baseball with Alex.

[08~10] 다음 대화를 읽고 물음에 답하시오.

> Sujin: Dad, do we have any bug spray?
> Dad: Yes, it's under the sink. Why?
> Sujin: (A) There are a lot of fruit flies around the trash.
> Dad: (B) Oh no! What did you put in the trash?
> Sujin: (C) Some fruit waste.
> Dad: (D) Fruit flies love sweet things. Make sure you don't put fruit waste in the trash can.
> Sujin: (E) I think we should also empty our trash can more often.
> Dad: That's a good idea.

08 위 대화의 (A)~(E) 중 주어진 문장이 들어가기에 가장 적절한 곳은?

> I'll keep that in mind.

① (A) ② (B) ③ (C) ④ (D) ⑤ (E)

09 위 대화에서 다음 영영풀이가 가리키는 말을 찾아 쓰시오.

> to remove everything that is in a container, etc.

➡ _____

10 위 대화의 내용과 일치하도록 아래의 빈칸을 완성하시오.

> <How to prevent fruit flies>
> Don't put (A)_____ in the trash can.
> (B)_____ more often.

[11~12] 다음 대화를 읽고 물음에 답하시오.

> Jane: How was the soccer game with Minsu's class, Alex?
> Alex: (A)We lost by three goals.
> Jane: (B)That's too bad. (hear) I hope you do better next time.
> Alex: I hope so, too.

11 위 대화의 밑줄 친 (A)에서 알 수 있는 Alex의 심경으로 적절한 것은?

① pleased   ② discouraged
③ excited   ④ joyful
⑤ surprised

12 위 대화의 밑줄 친 (B)와 의미가 같도록 주어진 단어를 사용하여 다시 쓰시오.

➡ _____

01 다음 대화의 우리말을 주어진 단어를 사용하여 영어로 옮기시오.

> Sora: You look upset, Minu. What's wrong?
> Minu: I lost my hat. It was my favorite.
> Sora: 그거 참 안됐네요. (sorry) Why don't you go to the Lost and Found Center?
> Minu: That's a good idea.

➡ _____

[02~03] 다음 대화를 읽고 물음에 답하시오.

> Emma: Tim, look at your face! You got sunburn.
> Tim: Yes, it hurts a lot. I went swimming at the beach without sunscreen.
> Emma: Oh dear! _____

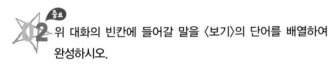 위 대화의 빈칸에 들어갈 말을 〈보기〉의 단어를 배열하여 완성하시오.

┤ 보기 ├
wear / next / sunscreen / make / time / sure / you

➡ _____

03 Why did Tim get sunburn? Answer in English.

➡ _____
_____

[04~05] 다음 대화를 읽고 물음에 답하시오.

> Ms. Wheeler: Junsu, what happened to your face?
> Junsu: I got a lot of mosquito bites.
> Ms. Wheeler: I'm sorry to hear that. How did it happen?

> Junsu: It happened when I went camping last weekend.
> Ms. Wheeler: Oh dear. Don't scratch them!
> Junsu: I know, but they're really itchy.
> Ms. Wheeler: Clean them with cool water. That'll help. Also, make sure you wear long sleeves when you go camping.
> Junsu: Okay, thank you.

04 Where did Junsu get the mosquito bites? Answer in English.

➡ _____

05 위 대화의 내용과 일치하도록 빈칸을 완성하시오.

> When you got bitten by mosquitos
> ■ Make sure _____ .

➡ _____

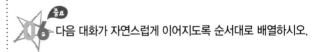 다음 대화가 자연스럽게 이어지도록 순서대로 배열하시오.

> Dad, do we have any bug spray?
> (A) Some fruit waste.
> (B) Yes, it's under the sink. Why?
> (C) Oh no! What did you put in the trash?
> (D) There are a lot of fruit flies around the trash.
> (E) Fruit flies love sweet things. Make sure you don't put fruit waste in the trash can.

➡ _____

Conversation **175**

Grammar

1 **something+형용사**

> • I want to eat **something sweet**. 나는 달콤한 뭔가를 먹고 싶어.
> • Is there **anyone nice** like you? 너처럼 친절한 사람이 있니?

■ '-body, -thing, -one'으로 끝나는 부정대명사는 형용사가 뒤에서 수식한다. 이러한 대명사에는 somebody, something, someone, anybody, anything, anyone, nobody, nothing, no one, everything 등이 있다.

- I need **someone reliable**. 나는 어떤 믿을 만한 사람이 필요해.

- Do you have **anything bigger** than this? 이것보다 더 큰 어떤 것을 가지고 있나요?

- Henna wants **somebody cute** like Tom. Henna는 Tom처럼 귀여운 누군가를 원한다.

- I want to see **something colorful** and **beautiful**. 나는 다채롭고 아름다운 무언가를 보고 싶어.

■ 위의 대명사를 to부정사와 형용사가 동시에 수식할 때 어순은 '대명사+형용사+to부정사'이다.

- She doesn't have **anyone kind to talk** with. 그녀에게는 함께 대화할 친절한 사람이 없어.

- Mike wanted to meet **someone brave to be** admired. Mike는 존경 받을 만한 용감한 누군가를 만나기를 원했다.

- There is **something important to deal** with. 처리해야 할 중요한 무언가가 있다.

핵심 Check

1. 다음 우리말과 같도록 빈칸에 알맞은 말을 쓰시오.

(1) 뜰에 이상한 무언가가 있어.

➡ There is _____ _____ in the yard.

(2) 나는 가지고 놀기에 재미있는 것이 있어.

➡ I have _____ fun _____ _____ _____.

(3) 차가운 마실 것 좀 주시겠어요?

➡ Can I have anything _____ _____ _____?

② 현재완료

- **I have** just **finished** my project. 나는 나의 프로젝트를 막 끝냈어.
- **Have** you **seen** the movie star in person? 너는 그 영화배우를 직접 본 적이 있니?

■ 현재완료는 과거의 사건이 현재까지 영향을 미칠 때 사용한다. 'have[has]+p.p.'의 형태로, 부정형은 'have[has] not+p.p.'이며, 의문형은 'Have[Has]+주어+p.p. ~?'로 나타낸다.

- **I haven't returned** the book yet. 나는 아직 그 책을 반납하지 않았다.
- **Have** you ever **been** to Busan before? 전에 부산에 가 본 적이 있니?

■ 현재완료는 '완료, 경험, 계속, 결과' 네 가지 용법으로 쓰인다. 완료 용법은 'just, already, yet' 등과 같은 부사와 주로 함께 쓰이며, 경험은 'ever, never, once, before' 등과 같은 부사와 함께 쓰인다. 'How long ~?'으로 묻는 질문이나 'for+기간', 'since+특정 시점'은 현재완료의 계속적 용법에 속한다. 결과적 용법은 특별한 부사(구)와 어울리지 않고 과거에 발생한 사건으로 인하여 현재까지 영향을 미치고 있는 상태를 나타낼 때 쓰인다.

- **I have drawn** a picture of myself once. 나는 자화상을 그려 본 적이 한 번 있다.
- **Have** you **caught** a butterfly before? 너는 전에 나비를 잡아 본 적이 있니?
- My grandfather **has owned** the restaurant since 2012. 할아버지는 2012년 이래로 그 식당을 소유하고 계신다.
- Jason **has gone** to Budapest. Jason은 부다페스트에 가고 없다. 〈결과〉

※ have[has] been to와 have[has] gone to의 사용에 유의하자. '~에 가 본 적이 있다'는 경험은 have[has] been to로 표현하고, '~에 가고 없다'는 결과는 have[has] gone to로 표현한다.

■ 현재완료는 과거의 일이 현재까지 영향을 미칠 때 쓰는 시제이므로 과거를 나타내는 부사(구)인 yesterday, last year, ~ago 및 의문부사 when과 함께 쓸 수 없다.

- **I met** Tom last week. 나는 지난주에 Tom을 만났어.
- When **did** you make the cake? 너 그 케이크를 언제 만들었니?

핵심 Check

2. 주어진 동사를 어법에 맞게 쓰시오.

(1) _____ you ever _____ your own ice cream? (make)

(2) I _____ _____ awake since last night. (be)

(3) There _____ _____ a lot of snow on the ground since New Year's Day. (be)

(4) My parents _____ _____ a lot. (travel)

01 다음 문장에서 어법상 <u>어색한</u> 부분을 고치시오.

(1) Is there wrong anything with it?

_____ ➡ _____

(2) I want something to eat healthy.

_____ ➡ _____

(3) They have talked about it last month.

_____ ➡ _____

(4) Jina played the piano since she was a child.

_____ ➡ _____

02 주어진 동사를 현재완료 시제로 어법에 맞게 쓰시오.

(1) He _____ his shoes yet. (polish)

(2) I am looking for Jane. _____ you _____ her today? (see)

(3) There is something I _____ you yet. (tell)

(4) Mona _____ the newspaper. (just, read)

(5) Jack _____ the suit many times. (wear)

03 주어진 단어를 바르게 배열하여 다음 우리말을 영어로 쓰시오. 필요하다면 단어를 변형하거나 추가하시오.

(1) 나는 차가운 마실 것이 필요해. (need / something / I / cold / drink)

➡ _____

(2) 우리는 프랑스에 두 번 가 봤어. (twice / have / we / be / France / to)

➡ _____

(3) 읽기에 재미있는 것이 있니? (read / you / fun / do / anything / have)

➡ _____

(4) 이 게임을 해 본 적이 있니? (play / game / you / have / this / ever)

➡ _____

01 다음 중 빈칸에 들어갈 말로 가장 적절한 것은?

> We _____ Gloria since last year.

① don't meet ② haven't met
③ met ④ will meet
⑤ meet

02 다음 우리말을 영어로 바르게 옮긴 것은?

> 그녀의 어머니는 이전에 한국에 가 본 적이 있다.

① Her mother has gone to Korea before.
② Her mother has been in Korea ago.
③ Her mother has been to Korea before.
④ Her mother has wanted to be in Korea.
⑤ Her mother has visited Korea many times.

03 다음 빈칸에 들어갈 말이 바르게 짝지어진 것은?

> A: Ron _____ away on holiday now.
> B: Oh, where _____ he _____?

① was – has – gone ② be – did – go
③ was – did – go ④ is – has – gone
⑤ is – does – go

서답형
04 주어진 단어를 활용하여 다음 대화의 우리말을 영어로 쓰시오.

> A: 그녀가 나에게 중요한 무언가를 말해 주었어.
>   (something)
> B: What was it?

➡ _____

05 다음 빈칸에 들어갈 말로 가장 적절한 것은?

> 너에게 소개할 특별한 사람이 있어.
> I have _____ .

① to introduce someone special to you
② special someone to introduce to you
③ someone special to introduce to you
④ to introduce special someone to you
⑤ someone special to you to introduce

06 다음 문장의 밑줄 친 부분과 쓰임이 같은 것은?

> Have you ever used this machine?

① My aunt has just knitted a sweater.
② We have already painted the wall.
③ The boy has studied English for a year.
④ They have never ridden a horse.
⑤ How long have you been here?

07 다음 중 어법상 옳은 문장은?

① There is interesting nothing here.
② I have gone to Jeju-do.
③ She said she needed something fun.
④ Have you seen her yesterday?
⑤ We want something to talk.

서답형
08 다음 대화의 우리말을 영어로 쓰시오.

> A: What time are the Kims coming?
> B: 그들은 이미 도착했어.

➡ _____

09 다음 빈칸 (A)~(C)에 들어갈 말이 바르게 짝지어진 것은?

> • Jane ___(A)___ her car key an hour ago.
> • I haven't heard from her ___(B)___ a long time.
> • Jimmy ___(C)___ the book several times until now.

	(A)	(B)	(C)
①	has lost	since	read
②	lost	ago	has read
③	lost	for	has read
④	lost	since	has read
⑤	has lost	since	has read

10 다음 중 어법상 틀린 문장은?

① Ms. Hong has been in Hong Kong for a month.
② Do you have anything interesting to see?
③ I have just finished my report.
④ The students have already packed their bags.
⑤ I think you need something to eat warm.

11 다음 우리말을 영어로 바르게 옮기지 않은 것은?

① 나는 키 큰 누군가가 필요해.
　→ I need someone tall.
② 나는 그녀를 한동안 보지 못했어.
　→ I haven't seen her for a while.
③ 그녀는 어제 새 차를 샀다.
　→ She has bought a new car yesterday.
④ 그는 멍청한 짓을 저질렀다.
　→ He did something stupid.
⑤ Bing 가족은 방금 이곳에 도착했다.
　→ The Bings have just arrived here.

12 주어진 어구를 이용하여 다음 우리말을 영어로 쓰시오.

> 하기에 위험한 것은 없어.
> ➡ There is nothing _____.

13 다음 빈칸에 들어갈 말이 바르게 짝지어진 것은?

> A: Have you _____ finished your homework?
> B: No, I haven't finished it _____.

① since – yet
② already – yet
③ for – since
④ ever – already
⑤ already – ago

14 다음 중 어법상 바르지 않은 것은?

> A: How long ①have you played the piano?
> B: I ②have played the piano ③for 20 years. I ④have learned how to play it ⑤when I was six years old.

①　　②　　③　　④　　⑤

15 다음 빈칸에 들어갈 말이 바르게 짝지어진 것은?

> A: Have you met _____ at the party?
> B: No, I _____ no one yet.

① interesting someone – met
② anyone interesting – met
③ interesting anyone – have met
④ someone interesting – meet
⑤ anyone interesting – have met

16 주어진 단어를 활용하여 다음 우리말을 영어로 쓰시오.

> 나는 함께 일할 근면한 사람이 필요해요.
> (diligent)

➡ _____

다음 빈칸에 들어갈 말이 바르게 짝지어진 것을 고르시오.

> Julia and Grace are very close friends. Julia _____ Grace since she was 12 years old. So Julia _____ Grace very well.

① knows – knows

② knew – knows

③ knew – has known

④ has known – knows

⑤ has known – knew

18 다음 중 어법상 어색한 것은?

① Has anything interesting happened?

② Mary had a date with someone very handsome.

③ I want to try on something larger.

④ There is nothing to eat in the fridge.

⑤ Tell me special everything.

19 다음 밑줄 친 두 문장을 하나의 문장으로 바르게 바꾼 것은?

> A: Where is your sister?
> B: She went out. She is not here.

① She has been here.

② She has not been here.

③ She has gone out.

④ She wasn't here.

⑤ She was here.

서답형

20 주어진 단어를 바르게 배열하여 다음 우리말을 영어로 쓰시오.

> 나는 뭔가 다른 일을 해 보고 싶어.
> (different / do / something / want / I / to)

➡ _____

21 주어진 문장을 영어로 바르게 옮긴 것은?

> 돌보아야 할 사람이 있나요?

① Do you have someone to look at?

② Do you have anyone to look for?

③ Is there someone to take care?

④ Is there anyone to take care of?

⑤ Do you know there is someone to take care of?

22 다음 빈칸에 들어갈 말이 바르게 짝지어진 것은?

> • Tim has been in Seoul _____ last Sunday.
> • Tim has been in Seoul _____ two days.
> • Tim has not left Seoul _____.

① for	since	already
② since	for	yet
③ already	for	already
④ for	since	ago
⑤ since	for	ago

23 다음 중 어법상 바르지 않은 것은?

① I haven't heard from her for a long time.

② Julia has just bought a new house.

③ Robert used the desk for ten years until now.

④ I have seen the ad a lot lately.

⑤ Jacob has been in Canada since October.

서답형

24 주어진 단어를 활용하여 다음 우리말을 영어로 쓰시오.

> 저는 가지고 놀 새로운 것이 필요해요.
> (something / play with)

➡ _____

01 다음 두 문장을 하나의 문장으로 쓰시오.

> It started to rain last night. It still rains.

➡ _____

02 다음 대화의 빈칸에 알맞은 말을 쓰시오.

> A: I have a car.
> B: How long _____ your car?
> A: I _____ it since March.

➡ _____

03 다음 빈칸에 알맞은 말을 세 단어의 영어로 쓰시오.

> There isn't any food in the house. We have got _____ .

➡ _____

04 주어진 단어를 이용하여 어법에 맞게 빈칸에 알맞은 말을 쓰시오.

> A: _____ to Vietnam? (be, ever)
> B: Yes, I have.
> A: When _____ there? (go)
> B: Five years ago.

➡ _____

05 다음 우리말을 영어로 쓰시오.

> 너는 유명한 누군가를 만난 적이 있니?

➡ _____

06 주어진 동사를 문맥이나 어법에 맞게 빈칸에 쓰시오.

> happen   go   have   be   teach

(1) Kyle _____ many different jobs until now.

(2) Your friend was here just now, but I think she _____ somewhere else.

(3) The horrible accident _____ long time ago.

(4) The weather _____ cold for a long time. It's still cold.

(5) My aunt _____ students math in 2015.

07 주어진 단어를 활용하여 다음 밑줄 친 우리말을 영어로 쓰시오.

> I like her. So 나는 그녀의 기분을 다치게 할 어떠한 것도 하고 싶지 않아.
> (want / anything / hurt)

➡ _____

08 다음 대화의 빈칸에 알맞은 말을 쓰시오.

> A: I am so bored. I need something _____ _____ _____ .
> B: How about seeing this movie? I think it will be interesting as much as you want.

09 주어진 단어를 활용하여 다음 대화의 밑줄 친 ⓐ, ⓑ를 어법에 맞게 영어로 쓰시오.

> **A:** ⓐ따뜻한 마실 것이 있나요? (there / drink)
> **B:** ⓑ지금 막 커피를 끓였어요. (make some coffee) Do you want some?
> **A:** Sure.

➡ ⓐ _____

　ⓑ _____

10 주어진 단어를 이용하여 다음 문장을 현재완료 시제로 표현하시오.

> • Amelia moved to this city in 2016.
> • It's the year 2020 now.
> • (for / since)

➡ _____

➡ _____

11 다음 대화의 빈칸에 알맞은 말을 쓰시오.

> **A:** Do you know when Jenny arrived in Canada?
> **B:** I heard that _____ Canada two days ago.
> **A:** Then she _____ in Canada for two days.

12 주어진 단어를 활용하여 다음 우리말을 영어로 쓰시오.

> 그 박물관에 가 본 적이 있니? (ever, be)

➡ _____

13 주어진 단어를 활용하여 다음 우리말을 영어로 쓰시오.

> 그 잡지에는 읽을 만한 중요한 것이 없다. (there / nothing)

➡ _____

14 주어진 단어를 활용하여 다음 밑줄 친 우리말을 영어로 쓰시오.

> **A:** I need to sit down. 편안하게 앉을 만한 것이 있나요? (there / sit on)
> **B:** There is a couch on the corner.

➡ _____

15 다음 대화의 빈칸에 알맞은 말을 세 단어의 영어로 쓰시오.

> **A:** I need something _____.
> **B:** Then, how about wearing my coat? It will make you feel warm.

16 우리말에 맞게 주어진 단어를 활용하여 다음 대화를 영어로 쓰시오.

> **A:** _____
> (너는 영어를 얼마나 오랫동안 배워 왔니?)
> **B:** _____
> (나는 8개월째 영어를 배우고 있어.)
> (learn)

An Interview with Mrs. Mosguito

It was a hot summer evening. Seojun went for a walk in the park.
_{비인칭 주어로 날짜, 요일, 날씨 등을 표현함.}

Soon, he was sweating.
_{과거진행형}

Seojun: I'm thirsty. I want something cold to drink.
_{-body. -thing. -one으로 끝나는 대명사는 형용사가 뒤에서 수식. to drink는 to부정사의 형용사적 용법으로 앞의 something cold를 수식.}

At that moment, something tiny flew at him and bit his arm.
_{tiny는 something을 뒤에서 수식.}

Mrs. Mosquito: Hey, catch me if you can.
_{if you can catch me}

Seojun: Who are you? What have you done to me?
_{have done은 완료 용법의 현재완료}

Mrs. Mosquito: I'm a mosquito. I've just finished my dinner.
_{just는 '방금, 막'이란 뜻으로 현재완료와 함께 쓰임.}

Seojun: Where are you from? How did you find me?

Mrs. Mosquito: I'm from a nearby river. I was looking for some
_{근처의, 가까운 곳의}   _{look for: ~을 찾다}

  blood to drink there. Then I smelled something sweaty
_{to drink는 to부정사의 형용사적 용법으로 some blood를 수식}

  and found you here.

Seojun: How could you smell me from the river?

Mrs. Mosquito: Mosquitoes can sense heat and smell very well.

  That's why we have survived for millions of years.
_{그래서}   _{현재완료(계속)}   _{'for+기간'은 '~ 동안'}

Seojun: Do all mosquitoes drink blood like you?
_{~처럼(전치사)}

Mrs. Mosquito: No. Only female mosquitoes like me drink blood.
_{오직, 단지}

  Male mosquitoes only feed on fruit and plant juice.

 확인문제

- 다음 문장이 본문의 내용과 일치하면 T, 일치하지 않으면 F를 쓰시오.

1 Seojun was sweating and felt thirsty. ☐

2 Mrs. Mosquito came from a nearby river. ☐

3 All mosquitoes drink blood. ☐

mosquito: 모기	
go for a walk: 산책 가다	
sweat: 땀을 흘리다	
buzz: 윙윙거리다	
at that moment: 그때에	
tiny: 아주 작은	
sweaty: 땀 냄새가 나는	
sense: 느끼다, 감지하다	
million: 100만, 다수	
female: 암컷의, 여성의	
male: 수컷의, 남성의	
feed on: ~을 먹고 살다	

Seojun: That's <u>interesting</u>. So why do you drink blood?
흥미를 유발할 때 Ving

Mrs. Mosquito: I need the protein in blood to <u>lay</u> my eggs.
to부정사의 부사적 용법 중 목적(~하기 위해서)을 나타냄.

Seojun: How do you drink blood? Do you have sharp <u>teeth</u>?
tooth의 복수형

Mrs. Mosquito: No, I don't have teeth. But I have a long and pointed mouth. So I can drink your blood easily.

Seojun: After you bit me, I got a bump. <u>It</u> itches.
a bump를 가리킴

Mrs. Mosquito: I'm sorry to hear that. <u>Make sure</u> you don't scratch
to부정사의 부사적 용법 중 감정의 원인: ~해서   당부하는 표현
it. Also, clean <u>it</u> with alcohol wipes.
a bump를 가리킴

Seojun: Alcohol wipes? I've <u>never tried that before</u>.
과거부터 현재까지의 경험을 나타내는 현재완료 구문 '결코 ~한 적이 없다'

Mrs. Mosquito: <u>It</u> will reduce the itchiness.
Cleaning it with alcohol wipes를 가리킴

Seojun: Okay, I'll try <u>that</u> at home. Thanks.
알코올 솜으로 닦는 것

Mrs. Mosquito: I have to go. See you soon.

Seojun: Where are you going?

Mrs. Mosquito: I'm <u>going back to</u> the river.
go back to: ~로 돌아가다

Seojun: Wait! A lot of people <u>have suffered</u> from your bites. How can
과거부터 현재까지 계속되는 상황을 나타내는 현재완료 구문
we prevent <u>them</u>?
= your bites

Mrs. Mosquito: <u>Stay</u> cool and wear long sleeves.
~하게 지내다

Seojun: Thanks. I'll keep your advice in mind.

protein: 단백질
lay: (알을) 낳다
pointed: 뾰족한
bump: 타박상, 혹
itch: 가렵다
scratch: 긁다
wipe: 닦아내는 천이나 솜
suffer from: ~로부터 고통 받다
prevent: ~을 예방하다
sleeve: (옷의) 소매, 소맷자락
keep~in mind: ~을 명심하다

📎 **확인문제**

● 다음 문장이 본문의 내용과 일치하면 T, 일치하지 않으면 F를 쓰시오.

1 In order to lay eggs, mosquitoes need protein. ☐

2 Mosquitoes have many teeth. ☐

3 Mrs. Mosquito wanted Seojun to scratch. ☐

4 Mrs. Mosquito wanted to go back to the river after the conversation. ☐

5 Mrs. Mosquito gave no advice to Seojun. ☐

우리말을 참고하여 빈칸에 알맞은 말을 쓰시오.

1 _____ was a hot summer _____.

2 Seojun _____ _____ _____ _____ in the park.

3 Soon, he was _____.

4 Seojun: I'm _____. I want something _____ _____ _____.

5 At that moment, _____ _____ flew _____ him and _____ his arm.

6 Mrs. Mosquito: Hey, catch me _____ _____ _____.

7 Seojun: Who are you? What _____ _____ _____ to me?

8 Mrs. Mosquito: I'm a mosquito. I've _____ _____ my dinner.

9 Seojun: Where are you _____? _____ did you _____ me?

10 Mrs. Mosquito: I'm _____ a _____ river.

11 I _____ _____ _____ some blood _____ there.

12 Then I smelled _____ _____ and found you here.

13 Seojun: How could you _____ _____ from the river?

14 Mrs. Mosquito: Mosquitoes can _____ _____ and _____ very well.

15 That's _____ we _____ _____ for millions of years.

16 Seojun: Do all mosquitoes drink blood _____ _____?

17 Mrs. Mosquito: No. Only _____ mosquitoes like me _____.

18 Male mosquitoes only _____ _____ fruit and plant juice.

1 무더운 여름날의 저녁이었습니다.

2 서준이는 공원에 산책을 갔습니다.

3 곧, 그는 땀을 흘리고 있었습니다.

4 서준: 목말라. 뭔가 시원한 것을 마시고 싶어.

5 그때에, 뭔가 조그마한 것이 그에게로 날아와서 그의 팔을 물었습니다.

6 모기: 이봐, 나를 잡을 수 있으면 잡아 봐.

7 서준: 너는 누구니? 나한테 무슨 짓을 한 거지?

8 모기: 나는 모기야. 난 방금 저녁 식사를 마쳤어.

9 서준: 너는 어디에서 왔니? 너는 어떻게 나를 찾은 거야?

10 모기: 나는 근처 강에서 왔어.

11 나는 그곳에서 마실 피를 찾던 중이었지.

12 그러다가 땀 냄새를 맡았고, 여기서 너를 발견했어.

13 서준: 너는 어떻게 강에서부터 내 냄새를 맡을 수 있었지?

14 모기: 모기들은 열과 냄새를 매우 잘 감지해.

15 그래서 우리가 수백만 년 동안 살아남은 거야.

16 서준: 모든 모기가 너처럼 피를 마셔?

17 모기: 아니. 오직 나와 같은 암컷 모기만이 피를 마셔.

18 수컷 모기들은 과일과 식물의 즙만을 먹고 살아.

19 Seojun: That's _____. So why do you drink blood?

20 Mrs. Mosquito: I need _____ _____ in blood _____ _____ my eggs.

21 Seojun: _____ do you drink blood? Do you have _____ _____?

22 Mrs. Mosquito: No, I don't have _____.

23 But I have _____ _____ and _____ _____.

24 _____ I can drink your blood _____.

25 Seojun: After you _____ me, I _____ _____ _____. It _____.

26 Mrs. Mosquito: I'm sorry _____ _____ _____.

27 _____ _____ you don't scratch _____.

28 Also, _____ _____ with alcohol wipes.

29 Seojun: Alcohol wipes? I've _____ _____ _____ _____.

30 Mrs. Mosquito: It will reduce _____ _____.

31 Seojun: Okay, I'll _____ _____ at home. Thanks.

32 Mrs. Mosquito: I _____ _____ _____ _____. See you soon.

33 Seojun: _____ are you _____?

34 Mrs. Mosquito: I'm _____ _____ to the river.

35 Seojun: Wait! A lot of people _____ _____ from your bites.

36 How can we _____ _____?

37 Mrs. Mosquito: Stay _____ and _____ long _____.

38 Seojun: Thanks. I'll _____ your advice _____ _____.

19 서준: 그거 재미있네. 그럼 너는 왜 피를 마시는 거야?

20 모기: 알을 낳으려면 핏속의 단백질이 필요해.

21 서준: 너는 피를 어떻게 마시는 거야? 날카로운 이빨이 있니?

22 모기: 아니, 나는 이빨이 없어.

23 하지만 길고 뾰족한 입이 있지.

24 그래서 나는 너의 피를 쉽게 마실 수 있는 거야.

25 서준: 네가 나를 문 다음, 부어오른 자국이 생겼어. 가려워.

26 모기: 그 말을 들으니 미안하군.

27 그것을 긁지 않도록 해.

28 또한, 그것을 알코올 솜으로 닦아.

29 서준: 알코올 솜? 나는 전에 그것을 한 번도 해 보지 않았어.

30 모기: 그것은 가려움을 줄여 줄 거야.

31 서준: 알았어, 집에서 해 볼게. 고마워.

32 모기: 나는 이제 가야겠어. 다음에 보자.

33 서준: 너는 어디로 가는데?

34 모기: 강으로 돌아가려고.

35 서준: 기다려! 많은 사람이 모기에 물려서 괴로워하고 있어.

36 어떻게 하면 모기에 물리는 것을 막을 수 있지?

37 모기: 시원하게 지내고 소매가 긴 옷을 입어.

38 서준: 고마워. 너의 충고를 명심할게.

● 우리말을 참고하여 본문을 영작하시오.

1 무더운 여름날의 저녁이었습니다.
➡ _____

2 서준이는 공원에 산책을 갔습니다.
➡ _____

3 곧, 그는 땀을 흘리고 있었습니다.
➡ _____

4 서준: 목말라. 뭔가 시원한 것을 마시고 싶어.
➡ Seojun: _____

5 그때에, 뭔가 조그마한 것이 그에게로 날아와서 그의 팔을 물었습니다.
➡ _____

6 모기: 이봐, 나를 잡을 수 있으면 잡아 봐.
➡ Mrs. Mosquito: _____

7 서준: 너는 누구니? 나한테 무슨 짓을 한 거지?
➡ Seojun: _____

8 모기: 나는 모기야. 난 방금 저녁 식사를 마쳤어.
➡ Mrs. Mosquito: _____

9 서준: 너는 어디에서 왔니? 너는 어떻게 나를 찾은 거야?.
➡ Seojun: _____

10 모기: 나는 근처 강에서 왔어.
➡ Mrs. Mosquito: _____

11 나는 그곳에서 마실 피를 찾던 중이었지.
➡ _____

12 그러다가 땀 냄새를 맡았고, 여기서 너를 발견했어.
➡ _____

13 서준: 너는 어떻게 강에서부터 내 냄새를 맡을 수 있었지?
➡ Seojun: _____

14 모기: 모기들은 열과 냄새를 매우 잘 감지해.
➡ Mrs. Mosquito: _____

15 그래서 우리가 수백만 년 동안 살아남은 거야.
➡ _____

16 서준: 모든 모기가 너처럼 피를 마셔?
➡ Seojun: _____

17 모기: 아니. 오직 나와 같은 암컷 모기만이 피를 마셔.
➡ Mrs. Mosquito: _____

18 수컷 모기들은 과일과 식물의 즙만을 먹고 살아.
➡ _____

19 서준: 그거 재미있네. 그럼 너는 왜 피를 마시는 거야?

➡ Seojun: _____

20 모기: 알을 낳으려면 핏속의 단백질이 필요해.

➡ Mrs. Mosquito: _____

21 서준: 너는 피를 어떻게 마시는 거야? 날카로운 이빨이 있니?

➡ Seojun: _____

22 모기: 아니, 나는 이빨이 없어.

➡ Mrs. Mosquito: _____

23 하지만 길고 뾰족한 입이 있지.

➡ _____

24 그래서 나는 너의 피를 쉽게 마실 수 있는 거야.

➡ _____

25 서준: 네가 나를 문 다음, 부어오른 자국이 생겼어. 가려워.

➡ Seojun: _____

26 모기: 그 말을 들으니 미안하군.

➡ Mrs. Mosquito: _____

27 그것을 긁지 않도록 해.

➡ _____

28 또한, 그것을 알코올 솜으로 닦아.

➡ _____

29 서준: 알코올 솜? 나는 전에 그것을 한 번도 해 보지 않았어.

➡ Seojun: _____

30 모기: 그것은 가려움을 줄여 줄 거야.

➡ Mrs. Mosquito: _____

31 서준: 알았어, 집에서 해 볼게. 고마워.

➡ Seojun: _____

32 모기: 나는 이제 가야겠어. 다음에 보자.

➡ _____

33 서준: 너는 어디로 가는데?

➡ Seojun: _____

34 모기: 강으로 돌아가려고.

➡ Mrs. Mosquito: _____

35 서준: 기다려! 많은 사람이 모기에 물려서 괴로워하고 있어.

➡ Seojun: _____

36 어떻게 하면 모기에 물리는 것을 막을 수 있지?

➡ _____

37 모기: 시원하게 지내고 소매가 긴 옷을 입어.

➡ Mrs. Mosquito: _____

38 서준: 고마워. 너의 충고를 명심할게.

➡ Seojun: _____

[01~07] 다음 글을 읽고 물음에 답하시오.

It was a hot summer evening. Seojun went for a walk in the park. Soon, he was ⓐ_____.

Seojun: I'm thirsty. I want something (A)[to drink cold / cold to drink].

At that moment, something tiny flew (B)[at / by] him and bit his arm.

Mrs. Mosquito: Hey, catch me ⓑif you can.

Seojun: Who are you? What have you done to me?

Mrs. Mosquito: I'm a mosquito. I've just finished my dinner.

Seojun: ⓒ_____ How did you find me?

Mrs. Mosquito: I'm from a nearby river. I was looking for some blood to drink there. Then I smelled (C)[sweaty something / something sweaty] and found you here.

01 다음과 같이 풀이되는 단어를 빈칸 ⓐ에 어법에 맞게 쓰시오.

to produce a clear liquid from your skin when you are hot or nervous

➡ _____

02 다음 중 밑줄 친 ⓑ와 쓰임이 다른 하나는?

① Call me if you have time.

② If it is fine, we will go out together.

③ Jane wanted to know if you would go with us.

④ I will do that if you want me to do it instead of you.

⑤ If she arrives here in time, there will be no trouble.

03 위 글의 흐름상 빈칸 ⓒ에 들어갈 말로 가장 적절한 것은?

① What did you do?

② Where are you going?

③ Where are you from?

④ Why did you do?

⑤ What happened to you?

04 According to the passage, which one is wrong about Mrs. Mosquito?

① She bit Seojun in the evening.

② She was looking for blood.

③ She drank Seojun's blood.

④ She found Seojun by smelling him.

⑤ She had dinner with Seojun.

05 다음 물음에 완전한 문장의 영어로 답하시오.

Q: What was Mrs. Mosquito doing near the river?

➡ _____

06 (A)~(C)에서 어법상 옳은 것끼리 바르게 짝지어진 것은?

① to drink cold - at - sweaty something

② cold to drink - by - something sweaty

③ cold to drink - at - something sweaty

④ cold to drink - by - sweaty something

⑤ to drink cold - at - something sweaty

07 When and where did the above story happen? Answer in English.

➡ _____

[08~13] 다음 대화를 읽고 물음에 답하시오.

Mrs. Mosquito: I'm ⓐ_____ a nearby river. I was looking for some blood to drink there. Then I smelled something sweaty and found you here.

Seojun: How could you smell me ⓑ_____ the river?

Mrs. Mosquito: Mosquitoes can sense heat and smell very well. That's why we have survived for millions of years.

Seojun: Do all mosquitoes ⓒ_____ like you?

Mrs. Mosquito: No. Only female mosquitoes like me drink blood. Male mosquitoes only feed on fruit and plant juice.

Seojun: That's interesting. So why do you drink blood?

Mrs. Mosquito: I need the protein in blood ⓓto lay my eggs.

08 빈칸 ⓐ와 ⓑ에 공통으로 들어갈 말로 가장 적절한 것은?

① at ② by ③ from
④ on ⑤ in

09 빈칸 ⓒ에 들어갈 말을 위 대화에서 찾아 쓰시오.

➡ _____

10 다음 중 밑줄 친 ⓓ와 쓰임이 같은 것은?

① Do you have a pen to write with?
② It is my duty to tell the truth.
③ We went to the mart to buy a bottle of water.
④ Linda hoped to see him again someday.
⑤ To make people laugh is hard for me.

11 다음 중 위 대화를 읽고 알 수 없는 것은?

① Seojun was sweating when Mrs. Mosquito found him.
② There has been mosquitoes for millions of years.
③ There is protein in human blood.
④ Female mosquitoes lay eggs.
⑤ Female mosquitoes can also feed on plant juice.

12 다음 중 위 대화에 나오는 어휘의 풀이가 아닌 것은?

① to eat something as food
② to produce an egg outside the body
③ wet with sweat
④ to make the low, continuous sound of a flying insect
⑤ a substance found in foods such as meat, milk, eggs, and beans

13 위 대화의 내용에 맞게 빈칸에 알맞은 말을 쓰시오.

Q: Do you know why female mosquitoes drink blood?
A: Yes, I do. It's because _____.

➡ _____

[14~18] 다음 대화를 읽고 물음에 답하시오.

Seojun: That's ①interesting. So why do you drink blood?

Mrs. Mosquito: I need the protein in blood ②to lay my eggs.

Seojun: How do you drink blood? Do you have sharp ③teeth?

Mrs. Mosquito: No, I don't have teeth. But I can drink your blood easily ⓐ_____ I have a long and ④pointed mouth.

Seojun: After you ⑤bite me, I got a bump. It itches.

Mrs. Mosquito: I'm sorry to hear that. Make sure you don't scratch it. Also, clean it with alcohol wipes.

Seojun: Alcohol wipes? ⓑI've never tried that before.

Mrs. Mosquito: ⓒIt will reduce the itchiness.

14 다음 중 빈칸 ⓐ에 들어갈 말로 가장 적절한 것은?

① after   ② since   ③ when

④ so   ⑤ if

15 다음 중 밑줄 친 문장 ⓑ에서 쓰인 현재완료와 그 용법이 같은 것은?

① He has already heard about the party at school.

② They have just arrived from New York.

③ We haven't found the clue yet.

④ Miranda has gone on her summer vacation.

⑤ I have met Frank once in Seoul.

서답형

16 주어진 단어를 활용하여 밑줄 친 ⓒ가 가리키는 것을 쓰시오.

(clean / the bump)

➡ _____

17 위 대화의 밑줄 친 ①~⑤ 중 어법상 바르지 않은 것은?

① ② ③ ④ ⑤

18 다음 중 위 대화를 읽고 답할 수 없는 것은?

① Is there any reason Mrs. Mosquito drinks blood?

② How does Mrs. Mosquito feel after she heard that Seojun got a bump?

③ Where did Mrs. Mosquito bite Seojun?

④ Why did Seojun get a bump?

⑤ Why does Mrs. Mosquito need protein?

[19~24] 다음 대화를 읽고 물음에 답하시오.

Seojun: Alcohol wipes? ⓐI've never tried that before.

Mrs. Mosquito: It will reduce the itchiness.

Seojun: Okay, I'll try that at home. Thanks.

Mrs. Mosquito: I have to go. See you soon.

Seojun: Where are you going?

Mrs. Mosquito: I'm going back to the river.

Seojun: Wait! A lot of people have suffered ⓑ_____ your bites. How can we prevent ⓒthem?

Mrs. Mosquito: Stay cool and wear long sleeves.

Seojun: Thanks. ⓓ너의 충고를 명심할게.

19 다음 중 밑줄 친 ⓐ와 쓰임이 같은 것은?

① I have known her since I was six.

② We haven't seen you for a long time.

③ Jane has studied French since last year.

④ Julia has stayed in California for a year.

⑤ Jason has seen the movie two times.

20 다음 중 빈칸 ⓑ에 들어갈 말과 같은 것은?

① Would you pick _____ the trash, please?

② Don't give _____. You can try it again.

③ Were you surprised _____ the news?

④ I look forward _____ seeing you again.

⑤ Do you know where he came _____?

서답형

21 밑줄 친 ⓒ가 가리키는 것을 위 대화에서 찾아 쓰시오.

➡ _____

서답형

22 주어진 단어를 이용하여 밑줄 친 우리말 ⓓ를 영어로 쓰시오.

> keep, advice

➡ _____

23 다음 중 위 대화의 내용과 일치하지 <u>않는</u> 것은?

① Alcohol wipes can help reduce the itchiness.
② Seojun feels thankful to Mrs. Mosquito.
③ Mrs. Mosquito was from the river.
④ Staying cool helps people to prevent themselves from mosquito bites.
⑤ Seojun will not wear long sleeves to prevent mosquito bites.

서답형

24 '의문사+to부정사'를 이용하여 위 대화의 내용에 맞게 빈칸에 알맞은 말을 쓰시오.

> Mrs. Mosquito advises Seojun on _____ _____ _____ mosquito bites.

[25~28] 다음 글을 읽고 물음에 답하시오.

> My family and I moved to Korea when I was 8. (A)_____ We have visited many great places here. Today is the first day of summer vacation. Tomorrow, we are going to visit Jeju. I have (B)[never gone to / never been to] Jeju. So I'm very (C) [exciting / excited]. I have just finished (D) [packing / to pack], and I'm ready to go. I hope we have a wonderful time in Jeju.
>
> *I = Kate

서답형

25 다음 두 문장을 하나의 문장으로 만들어 빈칸 (A)에 들어갈 말을 쓰시오.

> We moved to Korea six years ago.
> We still live in Korea.

➡ _____

26 다음 중 위 글을 읽고 답할 수 있는 것은?

① How many members are there in Kate's family?
② How many places has Kate visited?
③ When is Kate going to go to Jeju?
④ What is Kate going to do in Jeju?
⑤ How is Kate going to go to Jeju?

27 (B)~(D)에서 어법상 옳은 것끼리 바르게 짝지어진 것은?

① never gone to – exciting – packing
② never been to – exciting – to pack
③ never gone to – excited – packing
④ never been to – excited – packing
⑤ never gone to – excited – to pack

서답형

28 What is Kate going to do on the second day of summer vacation?

➡ _____

[01~04] 다음 글을 읽고 물음에 답하시오.

It was a hot summer evening. Seojun went for a walk in the park. Soon, he was sweating.

Seojun: I'm thirsty. (A)뭔가 차가운 것을 마시고 싶어.

At that moment, something tiny flew at him and bit his arm.

Mrs. Mosquito: Hey, catch me (B)if you can.

Seojun: Who are you? What have you done to me?

Mrs. Mosquito: I'm a mosquito. I've just finished my dinner.

Seojun: Where are you from? How did you find me?

Mrs. Mosquito: I'm from a nearby river. I was looking for some blood to drink there. Then I smelled something sweaty and found you here.

01 밑줄 친 우리말 (A)를 영어로 쓰시오.

➡ _____

02 밑줄 친 (B)를 생략되지 않은 문장으로 쓰시오.

➡ _____

03 According to the passage, what has Mrs. Mosquito done to Seojun? Answer in English with a full sentence.

➡ _____

04 글의 내용에 맞게 빈칸에 알맞은 말을 쓰시오.

Walking in a hot summer made Seojun _____.

[05~08] 다음 대화를 읽고 물음에 답하시오.

Seojun: How do you drink blood? Do you have sharp teeth?

Mrs. Mosquito: No, I don't have teeth. But I have a long and pointed mouth. So I can drink your blood easily.

Seojun: After you bit me, I got a bump. It itches.

Mrs. Mosquito: I'm sorry to hear that. Make sure you don't scratch it. Also, clean it with alcohol wipes.

Seojun: Alcohol wipes? (A)나는 전에 그것을 한 번도 해 보지 않았어.

Mrs. Mosquito: It will reduce the itchiness.

05 다음 빈칸에 적절한 말을 쓰시오.

Cleaning the bump with alcohol wipes will be helpful in _____.

06 주어진 단어를 활용하여 밑줄 친 우리말 (A)를 영어로 쓰시오.

try, that

➡ _____

07 위 대화의 내용에 맞게 빈칸에 알맞은 말을 쓰시오.

When she heard that Seojun got a bump and it itches, Mrs. Mosquito told him not _____. Also she advised him _____.

08 위 대화의 내용에 맞게 빈칸에 알맞은 말을 쓰시오.

The mosquito's mouth is long and _____.

[09~12] 다음 대화를 읽고 물음에 답하시오.

Mrs. Mosquito: Mosquitoes can sense heat and smell very well. That's why we have survived for millions of years.

Seojun: Do all mosquitoes drink blood like you?

Mrs. Mosquito: No. Only female mosquitoes like me drink blood. Male mosquitoes only feed on fruit and plant juice.

Seojun: That's (A)_____. So why do you drink blood?

Mrs. Mosquito: I need the protein in blood to lay my eggs.

9 주어진 단어를 어법에 맞게 빈칸 (A)에 쓰시오.

> (interest)

➡ _____

10 다음 빈칸에 들어갈 말을 위 대화에서 찾아 쓰시오.

> Mrs. Mosquito is talking about what mosquitoes _____ _____, and _____ female mosquitoes drink blood.

11 What does Mrs. Mosquito need to lay her eggs? Answer in English with a full sentence.

➡ _____

12 위 대화의 내용에 맞게 빈칸에 알맞은 말을 쓰시오.

> Hi, we are the mosquito couple. My wife and I eat different things. I eat _____, however, my wife feed on _____.

[13~16] 다음 대화를 읽고 물음에 답하시오.

Seojun: Alcohol wipes? ①I've never tried that before.

Mrs. Mosquito: It will reduce the itchiness.

Seojun: Okay, I'll try that ②at home. Thanks.

Mrs. Mosquito: I ③have to go. See you soon.

Seojun: Where are you going?

Mrs. Mosquito: I'm going back to the river.

Seojun: Wait! (A)많은 사람들이 모기에 물려서 괴로워하고 있어. How can we prevent them?

Mrs. Mosquito: Stay cool and wear ④long sleeves.

Seojun: Thanks. I'll keep your ⑤advise in mind.

13 주어진 어구를 이용하여 밑줄 친 우리말 (A)를 영어로 쓰시오.

> have / suffer from / your bites

➡ _____

14 위 대화의 내용에 맞게 빈칸에 알맞은 말을 쓰시오.

> _____ _____ _____ _____ _____ _____ can prevent people from being bitten by mosquitoes.

15 Where is Mrs. Mosquito from? Answer in English with a full sentence.

➡ _____

16 ①~⑤ 중 어법상 틀린 것을 찾아 바르게 고쳐 쓰시오.

➡ _____

Let's check

Sora: You look upset, Minu. What's wrong?
= What's the matter (with you)?

Minu: I lost my hat. It was my favorite.
잃어버린 모자를 가리킨다.

Sora: I'm sorry to hear that. Why don't you go to the Lost and Found Center?
= How about ~? = What about ~? 모두 제안하는 표현이다.

Minu: That's a good idea.

구문해설 • the Lost and Found Center: 분실물 센터

Sora: 너 속상해 보인다, 민우야. 무슨 일이니?

Minu: 내 모자를 잃어버렸어. 내가 가장 좋아하는 거였는데.

Sora: 그것 참 안됐구나. 분실물 센터에 가보는 게 어때?

Minu: 좋은 생각이다.

Let's Write

Summer Health Guide

Sunburn

Have you ever suffered from sunburn? Here are some useful tips to prevent
경험을 묻는 현재완료   some useful tips에 수일치

sunburn in summer.

1. Wear sunscreen.

2. Wear a hat

Be smart and enjoy the hot weather.
명령문: ~해라

구문해설 • suffer from: ~으로 고통 받다 • here are ~: 여기에 ~이 있다 • prevent: 예방하다
• wear: 바르다

여름철 건강 관리 수칙

햇볕 화상

햇볕 화상으로 고통 받은 적이 있나요? 여기 여름에 햇볕 화상을 예방할 수 있는 유용한 팁이 있습니다.

1. 선크림을 바르세요.

2. 모자를 쓰세요.

현명하게 무더운 날씨를 즐기세요.

Culture & Life

In summer, some people in Korea wear thin and light pants to stay cool.
목적을 나타내는 부사적 용법의 to부정사

They call them "refrigerator pants." Refrigerator pants come in colorful
call: 5형식 동사 them=thin and light pants

patterns. Some of them look very stylish.
look+형용사: ~하게 보이다

구문해설 • thin: 얇은 • light: 가벼운 • call A B: A를 B라고 부르다 • pattern: 무늬 • stylish: 세련된

여름철에 몇몇 한국 사람들은 시원함을 유지하기 위해 얇고 가벼운 바지를 입는다. 그들은 그것을 '냉장고 바지'라고 부른다. 화려한 무늬를 가진 냉장고 바지들이 나온다. 어떤 것들은 매우 세련되어 보인다.

영역별 핵심문제

01 다음 짝지어진 단어의 관계가 같도록 빈칸에 알맞은 말을 쓰시오.

> forget : remember = thick : _____

02 다음 영영풀이가 가리키는 것을 고르시오.

> an area of skin that is raised because it was hit or bitten

① bite   ② sleeve

③ sunburn   ④ bump

⑤ buzz

03 다음 우리말에 맞게 빈칸에 알맞은 말을 쓰시오.

(1) 너는 벽난로에서 떨어져 있어야 한다.

➡ You should _____ _____ _____ the fireplace.

(2) 그녀는 그녀의 장난감을 그녀의 방으로 가져갔다.

➡ She _____ her toy _____ her room.

(3) 우리는 1점 차로 경기에서 졌다.

➡ We _____ the game _____ one point.

04 다음 주어진 우리말에 맞게 영작하시오.

(1) 새들은 곤충을 먹고 산다.

➡ _____

(2) 여왕개미의 일은 알을 낳는 것이다.

➡ _____

(3) 나는 위험을 감지했다. (3 단어)

➡ _____

05 다음 중 밑줄 친 부분의 뜻풀이가 바르지 <u>않은</u> 것은?

① The crocodile has <u>pointed</u> teeth. 뾰족한

② You'd better wear long <u>sleeves</u> when you go camping. 바지

③ This bird can <u>lay</u> one egg a year. 낳다

④ Children are picking up the <u>trash</u> on the road. 쓰레기

⑤ You should wear a hat to avoid a <u>sunburn</u>. 햇볕에 탐

06 다음 주어진 문장의 밑줄 친 <u>lay</u>와 같은 의미로 쓰인 것은?

> Mosquitoes <u>lay</u> eggs in high temperatures.

① These hens are not <u>laying</u> well.

② Did he <u>lay</u> his hand on my shoulder?

③ The hunters are <u>laying</u> a trap in the forest.

④ Mike <u>lay</u> on a sofa.

⑤ She <u>lay</u> in her bed and slept like a baby.

07 다음 문장에 공통으로 들어갈 말을 고르시오.

> • The football player is suffering _____ a knee injury.
> • I tried to stay away _____ flowers because of allergy.

① on   ② for   ③ from

④ by   ⑤ to

Conversation

[08~10] 다음 대화를 읽고 물음에 답하시오.

Ms. Wheeler: Junsu, what happened to your face?

Junsu: I got a lot of mosquito bites.

Ms. Wheeler: I'm sorry to hear that. How did it happen?

Junsu: It happened when I went camping last weekend.

Ms. Wheeler: Oh dear. Don't scratch ⓐthem!

Junsu: I know, but they're really itchy.

Ms. Wheeler: Clean ⓐthem with cool water. That'll help. Also, make sure you wear long sleeves when you go camping.

Junsu: Okay, thank you.

08 위 대화에서 다음 영영풀이가 가리키는 말을 찾아 쓰시오.

to take place especially without being planned

➡ _____

09 위 대화의 밑줄 친 ⓐthem이 공통으로 가리키는 것을 찾아 쓰시오.

➡ _____

10 위 대화의 내용과 일치하지 않는 것은?

① Junsu went camping last weekend.

② Junsu got a lot of mosquito bites on his face.

③ Junsu is suffering from mosquito bites because they are itchy.

④ Junsu should take a shower with cool water not to get bitten by mosquitoes.

⑤ Ms. Wheeler advises Junsu that he should wear long sleeves when he goes camping.

[11~12] 다음 대화를 읽고 물음에 답하시오.

Sujin: Dad, do we have any bug spray?

Dad: Yes, it's under the sink. Why?

Sujin: There ⓐare a lot of fruit flies around the trash.

Dad: Oh no! What did you put ⓑin the trash?

Sujin: Some fruit waste.

Dad: Fruit flies love sweet things. ⓒTo make sure you don't put fruit waste in the trash can.

Sujin: I'll keep ⓓthat in mind. I think we should also ⓔempty our trash can more often.

Dad: That's a good idea.

11 위 대화의 밑줄 친 ⓐ~ⓔ 중 어법상 어색한 것을 골라 바르게 고치시오.

➡ _____

12 위 대화를 읽고 대답할 수 없는 것은?

① What did Sujin put in the trash?

② Where was the bug spray?

③ Why did Sujin need the bug spray?

④ What do fruit flies love?

⑤ What should Sujin do to reduce the trash?

[13~14] 다음 대화를 읽고 물음에 답하시오.

Emma: Tim, look at your face! You got sunburn.

Tim: Yes, it hurts a lot. I went swimming at the beach without sunscreen.

Emma: Oh dear! Make sure you wear sunscreen next time.

13 위 대화에서 다음 영영풀이가 가리키는 말을 찾아 쓰시오.

a condition in which your skin becomes sore and red from too much sunshine

➡ _____

14 What did Emma tell Tim to do?

➡ _____

15 다음 대화의 내용과 일치하도록 Tom의 일기를 완성하시오.

> **Tom:** Let's go swimming this weekend, Yujin.
> **Yujin:** I'd love to, but I can't.
> **Tom:** Why not?
> **Yujin:** I have an eye problem. The doctor told me to stop swimming for a while.
> **Tom:** I'm sorry to hear that. Maybe we can go next weekend.
> **Yujin:** I really hope so.

⬇

> Mon, June 24th, 2019
> Today, I suggested (A)_____ _____ to Yujin. Unfortunately, she said she couldn't join me because of (B)_____. She told me that she should (C)_____. I was sorry to hear that. I hoped we could go together next weekend.

[16~17] 다음 대화를 읽고 물음에 답하시오.

> **Jane:** How was the soccer game with Minsu's class, Alex?
> **Alex:** We lost by three goals.
> **Jane:** I'm sorry to hear that. I hope you do better next time.
> **Alex:** I hope so, too.

16 With whose class did Alex's class play the soccer game?

➡ _____

17 What did Alex hope to do next time?

➡ _____

Grammar

18 다음 우리말을 영어로 옮길 때 빈칸에 들어갈 말로 가장 적절한 것은?

> 그것은 나에게 생각할 다른 무언가를 줄 거야.
> It will give me _____.

① something to think about different
② something different to think with
③ differently thinking about something
④ different something to think
⑤ something different to think about

19 다음 중 어법상 바르지 않은 것은?

> **Joe:** I ①have had ②a cold ③since over a week.
> **Mary:** Why don't you ④go ⑤see a doctor?

①   ②   ③   ④   ⑤

20 다음 우리말을 영어로 바르게 옮기지 않은 것은?

① 나는 재미있는 무언가를 하길 원해.
   → I want to do something fun.
② 그들은 전에 그 박물관에 가 본 적이 있니?
   → Have they been to the museum before?
③ 난 데리고 올 사람이 없어.
   → I have no one to bring.
④ Jason은 여름 휴가 갔어.
   → Jason has gone on summer vacation.
⑤ Jessica는 지난주부터 아파.
   → Jessica was sick since last week.

21 다음 빈칸에 들어갈 말로 적절하지 않은 것은?

> The children have played basketball together _____.

① already   ② before   ③ once
④ many times   ⑤ yesterday

22 주어진 단어를 이용하여 다음 우리말을 영어로 쓰시오.

> 너는 뭔가 이상한 것을 발견했니? (find)

➡ _____

23 다음 문장을 읽고 알 수 있는 것을 <u>모두</u> 고르시오.

> Grace has left the hospital already.

① Grace was in the hospital.
② Grace likes to go to the hospital.
③ Grace has gone to the hospital.
④ Grace is not in the hospital now.
⑤ Grace has been to the hospital several times.

24 다음 문장의 현재완료와 그 쓰임이 <u>다른</u> 하나는?

> Has Sarah started her new job yet?

① I haven't met my new neighbor yet.
② Joe has just read the book.
③ Becky has already had dinner.
④ Mom has driven the car for a month.
⑤ They have already checked the list.

25 다음 문항에서 어법상 <u>틀린</u> 것을 찾아 바르게 고치시오.

> Steve's grandmother has died two years ago.

➡ _____

26 다음 중 어법상 바르지 <u>않은</u> 것은?

① Yuna is cooking something healthy.
② Ian is planning something special for summer.
③ Jiho hasn't cleaned his room yet.
④ Jenny has lost her card the other day.
⑤ I have never learned judo before.

27 주어진 단어를 활용하여 다음 대화의 우리말을 영어로 쓰시오.

> **A:** 영화는 아직 시작하지 않았어. (start)
> **B:** Then how about buying something to eat?

➡ _____

Reading

[28~31] 다음 글을 읽고 물음에 답하시오.

ⓐIt was a hot summer evening. Seojun went for a walk in the park. Soon, he was sweating.

Seojun: I'm thirsty. I want something cold to drink.

At that moment, something tiny flew at him and bit his arm.

Mrs. Mosquito: Hey, catch me if you can.

Seojun: Who are you? ⓑWhat have you done to me?

Mrs. Mosquito: I'm a mosquito. I've just finished my dinner.

Seojun: Where are you from? How did you find me?

Mrs. Mosquito: I'm from a nearby river. I was looking for some blood to drink there. Then I smelled something sweaty and found you here.

28 다음 중 밑줄 친 ⓐ와 쓰임이 <u>다른</u> 하나는?

① <u>It</u> was dark outside.

② <u>It</u> is Sunday today.

③ <u>It</u> was rainy then.

④ <u>It</u> is not my fault.

⑤ <u>It</u> is two miles from here to the beach.

29 다음 중 밑줄 친 문장 ⓑ와 현재완료의 쓰임이 <u>다른</u> 하나는?

① Stella <u>has done</u> her homework already.

② Matt <u>has</u> just <u>met</u> Mina in the church.

③ We <u>have seen</u> this movie before.

④ They <u>have</u> already <u>had</u> lunch.

⑤ <u>Have</u> you <u>finished</u> your homework yet?

30 다음 중 위 글을 읽고 답할 수 <u>없는</u> 것은?

① Why was Seojun sweating?

② How did Seojun feel when he was walking?

③ Where did Mrs. Mosquito come from?

④ Where is Seojun from?

⑤ What did Mrs. Mosquito do to Seojun?

31 Where did Mrs. Mosquito smell something sweaty? Answer in English with a full sentence.

➡ _____

[32~36] 다음 대화를 읽고 물음에 답하시오.

Seojun: That's interesting. So why do you drink blood?

Mrs. Mosquito: I need the protein in blood to lay my eggs. ①

Seojun: How do you drink blood? Do you have sharp teeth?

Mrs. Mosquito: No, I don't have teeth. ② But I have a long and pointed mouth. So I can drink your blood easily. ③

Seojun: After you bit me, I got a bump. It itches.

Mrs. Mosquito: I'm sorry to hear that. ④ Also, clean it with alcohol wipes.

Seojun: Alcohol wipes? I've never tried that before.

Mrs. Mosquito: It will reduce the itchiness. ⑤

Seojun: Okay, I'll try that at home. Thanks.

32 ①~⑤ 중 다음 주어진 문장이 들어가기에 가장 적절한 곳은?

> Make sure you don't scratch it.

①　　　②　　　③　　　④　　　⑤

33 다음 중 위 대화의 내용과 일치하지 <u>않는</u> 것은?

① Seojun wonders why Mrs. Mosquito drinks blood.

② Mrs. Mosquito can drink blood easily with its mouth.

③ Seojun has never cleaned a bump with alcohol wipes before.

④ Seojun wants to know how to use alcohol wipes.

⑤ Mrs. Mosquito bit Seojun.

34 위 대화의 내용에 맞게 다음 빈칸에 알맞은 말을 쓰시오.

> Q: How can Mrs. Mosquito drink blood easily?
>
> A: She can drink blood easily thanks to _____.

35 다음과 같이 풀이되는 단어를 위 대화에서 찾아 쓰시오.

> an area of skin that is raised because it was hit, bitten, etc.

➡ _____

36 According to the dialog, what will Seojun do when he goes home? Answer in English. Use the words 'clean' and 'with.'

➡ _____

01 다음 문장에 공통으로 들어갈 말을 고르시오.

> • Can I use your phone _____ a while?
> • I often go _____ a walk, listening to music.

① from
② by
③ for
④ off
⑤ during

[02~03] 다음 대화를 읽고 물음에 답하시오.

Sujin: Dad, do we have any bug spray?
Dad: Yes, it's under the sink. Why?
Sujin: There are a lot of fruit flies around the trash.
Dad: Oh no! What did you put in the trash?
Sujin: Some fruit waste.
Dad: Fruit flies love sweet things. Make sure you don't put fruit waste in the trash can.
Sujin: I'll keep (A)that in mind. I think we should also empty our trash can more often.
Dad: That's a good idea.

02 위 대화의 밑줄 친 (A)that이 가리키는 내용을 우리말로 간략히 쓰시오.

➡ _____

03 위 대화의 내용과 일치하지 않는 것은?

① Sujin looked for the bug spray because of lots of fruit flies.
② Sujin put some fruit waste in the trash.
③ Fruit flies like sweet things, so Sujin should not put fruit waste in the trash can.
④ It is a good way to empty the trash can more often to prevent fruit flies.
⑤ Sujin makes sure that she should put fruit trash in the trash can.

[04~05] 다음 대화를 읽고 물음에 답하시오.

Jane: (A)[What / How] was the soccer game with Minsu's class, Alex?
Alex: We lost (B)[by / off] three goals.
Jane: I'm sorry to hear that. I hope you do (C) [much / better] next time.
Alex: I hope so, too.

04 위 대화의 (A)~(C)에 들어갈 말로 적절한 것끼리 짝지어진 것은?

	(A)	(B)	(C)
①	What	by	much
②	What	off	much
③	How	by	much
④	How	off	better
⑤	How	by	better

05 위 대화의 내용과 일치하도록 빈칸을 완성하시오.

> Alex was depressed after the soccer game with Minsu's class because his class _____. Jane encouraged him to _____ next time.

[06~08] 다음 대화를 읽고 물음에 답하시오.

Brian: You look ⓐworried, Jimin. What's ⓑwrong?
Jimin: I'm worried ⓒbecause of my cat is sick.
Brian: I'm sorry ⓓto hear that. Why don't you ⓔtake her to an animal doctor?
Jimin: Okay, I will.

06 위 대화의 밑줄 친 ⓐ~ⓔ 중 어법상 어색한 것을 찾아 바르게 고치시오.

➡ _____

07 What's the matter with Jimin?

➡ _____

08 What is Jimin going to do after talking with Brian?

➡ _____

[09~10] 다음 대화를 읽고 물음에 답하시오.

Tom: Let's go swimming this weekend, Yujin.
Yujin: I'd love to, but I can't.
Tom: Why not?
Yujin: I have an eye problem. The doctor told me to stop swimming for a while.
Tom: I'm sorry to hear that. Maybe we can go next weekend.
Yujin: I really hope so.

09 What did Tom suggest to Yujin?

➡ _____

10 Why couldn't Yujin go swimming with Tom?

➡ _____

11 다음 우리말을 주어진 단어를 배열하여 영어로 쓰시오. 필요하다면 단어를 추가하거나 변형하시오.

> 그녀는 그녀를 도울 힘 센 누군가가 필요하다. (her / she / help / need / strong / someone)

➡ _____

12 다음 주어진 문장의 빈칸에 들어갈 말과 같은 말이 들어가는 것은?

> Mr. and Mrs. Hanson have been together _____ they were in college.

① The weather has been fine _____ a long time.
② I have been waiting for the bus _____ fifteen minutes.
③ We haven't eaten anything _____ breakfast.
④ Jacob has known the boys _____ a year.
⑤ They have lived in this town _____ several months.

13 다음 우리말을 영어로 바르게 옮긴 것은?

> 그들은 런던을 방문한 적이 없다.

① They have gone to London.
② They have never gone to London.
③ They have been to London
④ They have never visited London.
⑤ They have just visited London.

14 다음 중 어법상 옳은 문장의 개수는?

> ⓐ Did you see strange anyone on the street?
> ⓑ I'm ready now. I have finished my work.
> ⓒ Where have you been last night?
> ⓓ She said she needed something sweet to eat.
> ⓔ What time did Kelly go out?

① 1개　　　② 2개　　　③ 3개
④ 4개　　　⑤ 5개

15 주어진 단어를 활용하여 빈칸에 알맞은 말을 쓰시오.

> A: What does your friend do?
> B: He is a sculptor. He _____ (win) many prizes for his work.
> A: _____ (you / see) any of his sculptures?
> B: Yes, I _____ (see) some of his works last week.

16 다음 중 현재완료의 용법이 <u>다른</u> 하나는?

① How long have you played the guitar?
② The Roberts have been married for 15 years.
③ Have you known Linda for a long time?
④ This house has been empty for many years.
⑤ Have you ever talked with July seriously?

17 다음 대화의 빈칸에 알맞은 말을 쓰시오.

> A: I want something _____ _____ _____. Do you have anything like that?
> B: I have some cold milk.

[18~20] 다음 글을 읽고 물음에 답하시오.

> Mrs. Mosquito: I'm from a nearby river. I was looking for some blood to drink there. Then I smelled something sweaty and found you here.
> Seojun: How could you smell me from the river?
> Mrs. Mosquito: Mosquitoes can sense heat and smell very well. (A)[That's because / That's why] we have survived (B)[for / since] millions of years.
> Seojun: Do all mosquitoes drink blood like you?
> Mrs. Mosquito: No. Only female mosquitoes like me drink blood. Male mosquitoes only feed on fruit and plant juice.
> Seojun: That's interesting. So why do you drink blood?
> Mrs. Mosquito: I need the protein in blood to (C) [lie / lay] my eggs.

18 (A)~(C)에서 어법상 옳은 것끼리 바르게 짝지어진 것은?

① That's because	for	lay
② That's why	for	lie
③ That's because	since	lay
④ That's why	for	lay
⑤ That's because	since	lie

19 다음 중 위 글의 내용과 일치하지 <u>않는</u> 것은?

① Mrs. Mosquito wanted to drink blood.
② Mrs. Mosquito smelled something sweaty from the nearby river.
③ All mosquitoes drink blood.
④ Female mosquitoes drink blood because they need protein in blood.
⑤ Male mosquitoes eat plant juice as food.

20 위 글의 내용에 맞게 빈칸에 알맞은 말을 주어진 단어를 활용하여 쓰시오.

> Mosquitoes are good at _____ _____ _____ _____. (sense)

[21~25] 다음 글을 읽고 물음에 답하시오.

Seojun: How do you drink blood? Do you have sharp teeth?

Mrs. Mosquito: No, I don't have teeth. But I have a long and pointed mouth. ⓐ_____ I can drink your blood easily.

Seojun: After you bit me, I got ①a bump. ②It itches.

Mrs. Mosquito: I'm sorry to hear that. Make sure you don't scratch ③it. Also, clean ④it with alcohol wipes.

Seojun: Alcohol wipes? ⓑI've never tried that before.

Mrs. Mosquito: ⑤It will reduce the itchiness.

Seojun: Okay, I'll try that at home. Thanks.

Mrs. Mosquito: I have to go. See you soon.

Seojun: Where are you going?

Mrs. Mosquito: I'm going back to the river.

21 다음 중 빈칸 ⓐ에 들어갈 말로 가장 적절한 것은?

① That's because
② However
③ That's why
④ But
⑤ On the other hand

22 다음 중 밑줄 친 ⓑ의 현재완료와 그 쓰임이 다른 하나는?

① Jane has been to France once.
② He has heard the music before.
③ Mina has gone to her home.
④ We have visited there many times.
⑤ Have you played the golf before?

23 밑줄 친 ①~⑤ 중 가리키는 것이 다른 하나는?

①   ②   ③   ④   ⑤

24 다음 중 위 글을 읽고 답할 수 없는 것은?

① Why does Mrs. Mosquito feel sorry?
② What will reduce the itchiness?
③ What is Seojun going to do at home?
④ How long is Mrs. Mosquito's mouth?
⑤ What did Seojun get after Mrs. Mosquito bit him?

25 주어진 어구를 이용하여 다음 물음에 완전한 문장으로 답하시오.

Q: How can you reduce the itchiness when you get a mosquito bite? (the area / with / can)

➡ _____

_____

서술형 실전문제

[01~03] 다음 대화를 읽고 물음에 답하시오.

> Sujin: Dad, do we have any bug spray?
>
> Dad: Yes, it's under the sink. Why?
>
> Sujin: There are a lot of fruit flies around the trash.
>
> Dad: Oh no! What did you put in the trash?
>
> Sujin: Some fruit waste.
>
> Dad: Fruit flies love sweet things. Make sure you don't put fruit waste in the trash can.
>
> Sujin: I'll keep that in mind. I think we should also empty our trash can more often.
>
> Dad: That's a good idea.

01 Where is the bug spray?

➡ _____

02 Why is Sujin looking for the bug spray?

➡ _____

03 What should Sujin do to prevent fruit flies?

➡ _____

_____

04 주어진 단어를 바르게 배열하여 다음 대화를 완성하시오.
(필요하다면 단어를 추가하시오.)

> A: Do you have a special plan for today?
> B: No. (nothing / do / have / special / I)

➡ _____

05 다음 대화가 자연스럽게 이어지도록 순서대로 배열하시오.

> (A) Why not?
> (B) I'd love to, but I can't.
> (C) I have an eye problem. The doctor told me to stop swimming for a while.
> (D) I'm sorry to hear that. Maybe we can go next weekend.
> (E) Let's go swimming this weekend, Yujin.

➡ _____

06 주어진 단어를 활용하여 빈칸에 알맞은 말을 쓰시오.

> A: Do you know Jason's sister?
> B: I _____ (see) her a few times, but I _____ (never / speak) to her until now. _____ (you / ever / speak) to her?
> A: Yes. I _____ (meet) her at a party last month. She is very kind.

07 주어진 단어를 활용하여 다음 우리말을 영어로 쓰시오.

> 나는 함께 얘기할 어떤 재미있는 사람이 필요해.
> (funny / someone)

➡ _____

08 다음 우리말을 6단어의 영어로 이루어진 문장으로 쓰시오.

나는 너에게 결코 거짓말을 한 적이 없어.

➡ _____

09 다음 빈칸에 알맞은 말을 쓰시오.

Nick has been sick _____ a long time.
He has been in the hospital _____ October.

10 다음 빈칸에 알맞은 말을 두 단어로 쓰시오.

Don't do _____.
위험한 일은 하지 마.

[11~16] 다음 대화를 읽고 물음에 답하시오.

Seojun: Who are you? What have you done to me?

Mrs. Mosquito: I'm a mosquito. I've just finished my dinner.

Seojun: ①Where are you from? How did you find me?

Mrs. Mosquito: I'm from ②a nearby river. I ③was looking for some blood to drink there. Then I smelled (A)sweaty something and found you here.

Seojun: How could you smell me from the river?

Mrs. Mosquito: Mosquitoes can sense heat and smell very well. That's why we ④have survived for millions of years.

Seojun: Do all mosquitoes drink blood like you?

Mrs. Mosquito: No. Only female mosquitoes like me ⑤drinks blood. Male mosquitoes only feed on fruit and plant juice.

11 밑줄 친 (A)를 올바르게 고치시오.

➡ _____

12 위 대화의 내용에 맞게 다음 물음에 완전한 문장의 영어로 답하시오.

Q: How did Mrs. Mosquito find Seojun?

➡ _____

13 모기들이 수백만 년 동안 살아남은 이유를 영어로 쓰시오. (8 words)

➡ _____

14 위 대화의 내용에 맞게 다음 빈칸에 알맞은 말을 쓰시오.

A: I got a mosquito bite.
B: Oh, that must be a _____ mosquito. I heard that _____ mosquitoes just eat fruit and plant juice.

15 ①~⑤ 중 어법상 틀린 것을 골라 바르게 고쳐 쓰시오.

➡ _____

16 주어진 단어를 바르게 배열하여 암컷 모기와 수컷 모기의 차이를 한 문장으로 쓰시오.

(on / female / male / feed / mosquitoes / mosquitoes / blood / unlike)

➡ _____
_____

01 다음 대화의 내용과 일치하도록 빈칸을 완성하시오.

> Mike: Did you pack for the school trip tomorrow, Sue?
> Sue: Yes. Now I'm checking my list again. I don't want to miss anything.
> Mike: Make sure you take an umbrella with you. It might rain tomorrow.
> Sue: Okay, thank you.

⬇

> Sue was checking her list again after (A)_____ because she didn't want to miss anything. At that time, Mike reminded her to (B)_____ because it might rain tomorrow.

02 현재완료의 완료, 계속, 경험, 결과 용법을 이용하여 자신의 이야기를 <보기>와 같이 쓰시오.

> ┤ 보기 ├
> • I have just made some cookies.
> • I have driven a car for ten years.
> • I have been to Japan with my family.
> • I have lost my backpack in the zoo.

(1) _____
(2) _____
(3) _____
(4) _____

03 '-body, -thing, -one'으로 끝나는 부정대명사와 주어진 형용사를 이용하여 여름에 할 수 있는 다양한 말을 써 보시오.

> cold   cool   funny   scary

(1) _____
(2) _____
(3) _____
(4) _____

단원별 모의고사

01 다음 문장의 빈칸에 들어갈 말을 보기에서 골라 쓰시오.

┌─ 보기 ┤

at that moment / go for a walk /
keep in mind / lose by

└───────

(1) Ann and Jane usually _____
after meals.
(2) _____, the phone rang.
(3) Tim's team will _____ a
score of 2-1.
(4) _____ that you should wear
the sunscreen.

[02~03] 다음 대화를 읽고 물음에 답하시오.

Tom: Let's go swimming this weekend, Yujin.
Yujin: (A) I'd love to, but I can't.
Tom: (B) Why not?
Yujin: (C) The doctor told me to stop
swimming for a while.
Tom: (D) I'm sorry to hear that. Maybe we can
go next weekend.
Yujin: (E) I really hope so.

02 위 대화의 (A)~(E) 중 주어진 문장이 들어가기에 적절한 곳은?

┌────────────────────┐
│ I have an eye problem. │
└────────────────────┘

① (A) ② (B) ③ (C) ④ (D) ⑤ (E)

03 위 대화의 내용과 일치하지 <u>않는</u> 것은?

① Tom suggested going swimming this
weekend to Yujin.
② Yujin wished to go swimming but she
couldn't.
③ Yujin had an eye problem.
④ The doctor said that Yujin should not
swim for a while.
⑤ Yujin made a plan to go swimming next
weekend.

04 다음 대화의 (A)~(C)에 들어갈 알맞은 말을 고르시오.

Brian: You look (A)[worrying / worried],
Jimin. What's wrong?
Jimin: I'm sad (B)[because / because of]
my cat is sick.
Brian: I'm sorry (C)[hearing / to hear] that.
Why don't you take her to an animal
doctor?
Jimin: Okay, I will.

	(A)	(B)	(C)
①	worrying	because	hearing
②	worrying	because of	hearing
③	worried	because	hearing
④	worried	because of	to hear
⑤	worried	because	to hear

[05~06] 다음 대화를 읽고 물음에 답하시오.

Mike: Did you pack for the school trip
tomorrow, Sue?
Sue: Yes. Now I'm checking my list again. I
don't want to miss anything.
Mike: (A)_____ It might
rain tomorrow.
Sue: Okay, thank you.

05 위 대화의 빈칸에 들어갈 말을 〈보기〉에 주어진 단어를 배열하여 완성하시오.

┌─ 보기 ┤

with / make / you / take / an /
umbrella / you / sure

└───────

➡ _____

06 위 대화를 읽고 대답할 수 <u>없는</u> 것은?

① What is Sue checking now?

② What is Sue going to do tomorrow?

③ What might be the weather like tomorrow?

④ What is Mike asking Sue do to?

⑤ What did Sue miss?

[07~08] 다음 대화를 읽고 물음에 답하시오.

> Amy: I have a mosquito bite. It's really itchy.
>
> Brian: I'm sorry to hear that. Hold a green tea bag on the itchy area. That'll help.
>
> Amy: Okay, I'll try that.
>
> Brian: (A)_____ (prevent) more bites, make sure you stay cool and avoid (B)_____ (sweat).
>
> Amy: Good idea. Thanks.

07 위 대화의 빈칸 (A)와 (B)에 주어진 단어를 직질한 형태로 쓰시오.

➡ (A) _____, (B) _____

08 What can Amy do to relieve the itchiness?

➡ _____

[09~10] 다음 대화를 읽고 물음에 답하시오.

> Ms. Wheeler: Junsu, what happened to your face?
>
> Junsu: (A) I got a lot of mosquito bites.
>
> Ms. Wheeler: (B) How did it happen?
>
> Junsu: (C) It happened when I went camping last weekend.
>
> Ms. Wheeler: (D) Oh dear. Don't scratch them!
>
> Junsu: (E) I know, but they're really itchy.

> Ms. Wheeler: Clean them with cool water. That'll help. Also, make sure you wear long sleeves when you go camping.
>
> Junsu: Okay, thank you.

09 위 대화의 (A)~(E) 중에서 주어진 문장이 들어가기에 적절한 곳을 고르시오.

> I'm sorry to hear that.

① (A)   ② (B)   ③ (C)   ④ (D)   ⑤ (E)

10 위 대화의 내용과 일치하도록 빈칸을 완성하시오.

> Junsu: I'm suffering from (A)_____ _____ on my face. I got them when I went camping last weekend. They are really (B)_____. Ms. Wheeler advised me to (C)_____. Moreover, I keep in mind that (D)_____ _____ when I go camping.

11 다음 대화가 자연스럽게 이어지도록 순서대로 배열하시오.

> (A) I hope so, too.
>
> (B) We lost by three goals.
>
> (C) How was the soccer game with Minsu's class, Alex?
>
> (D) I'm sorry to hear that. I hope you do better next time.

➡ _____

12 다음 주어진 그림을 보고 빈칸에 알맞은 말을 쓰시오.

A: Make sure _____.
B: Okay. I'll keep that in mind.

➡ _____

13 다음 중 어법상 바르지 <u>않은</u> 것은?

① Dan arrived here an hour ago.
② I have read this novel for last Friday.
③ Do you have anything cold to drink?
④ Have you met each other before?
⑤ Clara is drawing something funny.

14 다음 두 문장을 하나의 문장으로 표현하시오.

Claire is studying medicine at the university. She started studying medicine two years ago.

➡ _____

_____

15 다음 빈칸에 들어갈 말로 가장 적절한 것은?

Where _____? I have been looking for you all afternoon.

① are you going
② have you gone
③ have you been
④ were you going
⑤ do you want to go

16 다음 대화의 빈칸에 들어갈 말이 바르게 짝지어진 것은?

A: Would you like something _____?
B: No, thanks. I _____.

① eating – had lunch
② to eat – have just had lunch
③ eating – haven't had lunch yet
④ to eat – didn't have lunch
⑤ to eat – have had lunch an hour ago

17 주어진 단어를 활용하여 다음 우리말을 영어로 쓰시오.

내게는 해야 할 더 중요한 일이 있어요.
(have / important / do)

➡ _____

[18~21] 다음 글을 읽고 물음에 답하시오.

It was a hot summer evening. Seojun went for a walk in the park. Soon, he was sweating.
Seojun: I'm thirsty. I want something cold to drink.
At that moment, (A)뭔가 조그마한 것이 그에게로 날아 왔다 and bit his arm. (tiny, fly)
Mrs. Mosquito: Hey, catch me if you can.
Seojun: Who are you? What have you done to me?
Mrs. Mosquito: I'm a mosquito. I've just finished my dinner.
Seojun: Where are you from? How did you find me?
Mrs. Mosquito: I'm from a nearby river. I was looking for some blood to drink there. Then I smelled something sweaty and found you here.

18 밑줄 친 우리말 (A)를 주어진 단어를 이용하여 영어로 쓰시오.

➡ _____

19 다음 중 위 글의 내용과 일치하지 <u>않는</u> 것은?

① Seojun was walking in the park.

② It happened in a hot summer evening.

③ Mrs. Mosquito bit Seojun's leg.

④ Mrs. Mosquito had dinner by drinking blood.

⑤ Seojun wanted to drink something cold.

20 다음 중 위 글에서 찾아볼 수 <u>없는</u> 것은?

① 무더운 여름날 저녁

② 땀을 흘리는 서준

③ 강에서 마실 물을 찾는 모기

④ 땀 냄새를 감지한 모기

⑤ 갈증을 느끼는 서준

21 다음은 근처 강에서 모기가 한 말이다. 빈칸에 들어갈 말을 위 글에서 찾아 쓰시오.

> Oh, I am so hungry. I need _____ .

➡ _____

[22~25] 다음 글을 읽고 물음에 답하시오.

My family and I moved to Korea when I was 8. We have lived in Korea for 6 years. (A)We have visited many great places here. Today is the first day of summer vacation. Tomorrow, we are going to visit Jeju. I have never been to Jeju. So I'm very excited. I have just finished packing, and I'm ready to go. I hope we have a wonderful time in Jeju.

*I = Kate

22 다음 중 밑줄 친 (A)와 같은 의미의 문장은?

① We have met many people in Korea.

② We have been to many places in Korea.

③ We hoped to go back to the place we lived in.

④ We have gone to many great places in Korea.

⑤ We think there are many great places to see in Korea.

23 다음 중 위 글의 내용과 일치하지 <u>않는</u> 것은?

① Kate lives in Korea with her family.

② Kate moved to Korea six years ago.

③ She is going to visit Jeju.

④ Kate feels excited to visit Jeju.

⑤ Kate has not packed yet.

24 According to the passage, how old is Kate now?

➡ _____

25 위 글의 내용에 맞게 빈칸에 알맞은 말을 쓰시오.

> Kate has lived in Korea _____ she was eight.

INSIGHT
on the textbook

교과서 파헤치기

※ 다음 영어를 우리말로 쓰시오.

01	planet	22	upset
02	bite	23	healthy
03	truth	24	decide
04	soon	25	smart
05	clean	26	personal
06	dear	27	hobby
07	break	28	print
08	during	29	traffic
09	beef	30	tip
10	email	31	fall
11	toy	32	space
12	handle	33	not ~ anymore
13	jogging	34	think of
14	lie	35	by the way
15	nail	36	these days
16	false	37	change into
17	wish	38	come true
18	sure	39	be into
19	try	40	do one's best
20	vacation	41	each other
21	homeroom teacher	42	on one's way home
		43	be interested in

※ 다음 우리말을 영어로 쓰시오.

01	곧	22	거짓말을 하다
02	교통	23	행성
03	조언, 정보	24	깨뜨리다, 부수다
04	틀린, 거짓의	25	물다; 물린 자국
05	똑똑한, 명석한	26	사실, 진실
06	봄	27	방학
07	인쇄하다	28	소고기
08	미술 , 예술	29	틀린, 거짓의
09	건강한, 튼튼한	30	손잡이
10	가을	31	손톱
11	우주	32	장난감
12	결정하다	33	서로
13	종류	34	집에 오는 길에
14	컵케이크	35	~에 열중하다
15	개인적인	36	변화를 이루다
16	잡다, 쥐다	37	실현되다
17	주의, 조심	38	그건 그렇고, 그런데
18	취미	39	더 이상 ~하지 않다
19	화난, 속상한	40	최선을 다하다
20	재미있는, 익살맞은	41	그 당시에
21	야채	42	~로 변하다
		43	~에 흥미가 있다

※ 다음 영영풀이에 알맞은 단어를 <보기>에서 골라 쓴 후, 우리말 뜻을 쓰시오.

1 _____ : meat from a cow: _____

2 _____ : all through a period of time: _____

3 _____ : a teacher in charge of a class: _____

4 _____ : to make a choice about something: _____

5 _____ : to send a message to someone by email: _____

6 _____ : to press down on or cut into someone or something with the teeth: _____

7 _____ : the hard covering at the end of a finger or toe: _____

8 _____ : a feeling of wanting to do or have something: _____

9 _____ : a part that is designed especially to be grasped by the hand: _____

10 _____ : belonging or relating to a particular person: _____

11 _____ : a large, round object in space that travels around a star: _____

12 _____ : an activity that a person does for pleasure when not working: _____

13 _____ : to do or use something in order to find out if you like it: _____

14 _____ : the methods and skills used for painting, sculpting, drawing, etc.:

_____

15 _____ : the movement of vehicles or pedestrians through an area or along a route:

_____

16 _____ : to produce letters, pictures, etc. on paper using a machine that puts ink

on the surface: _____

보기			
traffic	personal	art	print
nail	wish	try	hobby
handle	decide	during	beef
bite	email	planet	homeroom teacher

※ 다음 우리말과 일치하도록 빈칸에 알맞은 말을 쓰시오.

Listen & Speak 1 A

Brian: Julia, _____ was your _____ _____?

Julia: It was great. _____ _____ _____? I took *muay thai* lessons _____ _____ _____.

Brian: That's amazing. I didn't know that _____ _____ _____ _____ *muay thai.*

Julia: Yes. It was _____ _____.

Brian: Really? I _____ _____ _____ it.

Brian: Julia, 네 겨울 방학은 어땠니?
Julia: 좋았어. 그거 아니? 나는 방학 동안 무에타이 수업을 받았어.
Brian: 그거 멋지다. 나는 네가 무에타이에 관심이 있는지 몰랐어.
Julia: 응. 아주 재미있었어.
Brian: 그래? 나도 해 보고 싶다.

Listen & Speak 1 B

Jimin: You _____ _____, Tim? Mr. Smith is my _____ _____ this year.

Tim: That's great, Jimin. _____ _____ _____ last year was _____ _____ _____ _____.

Jimin: Who's your homeroom teacher _____ _____?

Tim: It's Ms. Kim. She's a _____ _____.

Jimin: _____ _____ _____ _____?

Tim: She _____ _____.

Jimin: 그거 아니, Tim? Smith 선생님이 올해 우리 반 담임 선생님이야.
Tim: 그거 잘됐다, 지민아. 작년 Smith 선생님의 과학 수업은 아주 재미있었어.
Jimin: 올해 너희 반 담임 선생님은 누구니?
Tim: 김 선생님이야. 그녀는 새로 오신 선생님이야.
Jimin: 그분은 어떤 과목을 가르치시니?
Tim: 미술을 가르치셔.

Listen & Speak 2 A

Jane: Minsu, Sujin and I _____ _____ _____ _____ _____ a club.

Minsu: Really? _____ _____ _____ _____ _____?

Jane: We want to _____ _____ _____ and _____. So, we're _____ of _____ a space science club.

Minsu: _____ good. _____ _____ are you _____ to meet?

Jane: Maybe _____ _____ _____.

Minsu: I see. Where _____ you _____?

Jane: In Room 101. Minsu, do you _____ _____ _____ _____ _____?

Minsu: Yes, _____ _____ _____ space, _____.

Jane: 민수야, 수진이와 나는 동아리를 만들 생각이야.
Minsu: 정말? 어떤 종류의 동아리야?
Jane: 우리는 별과 행성에 대해 배우고 싶어. 그래서 우주 과학 동아리를 만들 생각이야.
Minsu: 그거 멋지다. 얼마나 자주 모일 예정이니?
Jane: 아마도 일주일에 한 번쯤.
Minsu: 그렇구나. 어디에서 모일 거니?
Jane: 101호에서. 민수야, 우리 동아리에 가입할래?
Minsu: 응, 나도 우주에 관심 있어.

Listen & Speak 2 B

Alex: Mom, I _____ *bulgogi* at school today._____ _____ _____ _____ *bulgogi* _____ _____.

Mom: That _____ _____, Alex.

Alex: Do we have any vegetables _____ _____, Mom? _____ _____ _____?

Mom: We have some _____, but we _____ _____ beef. _____ _____ _____ _____ _____ _____ _____ _____.

Alex: Great.

Real Life Communication A

Emily: You _____ _____, Junsu? _____ _____ _____ _____ a _____ _____.

Junsu: Really? Why did you _____ _____ _____ a painting class, Emily?

Emily: Because _____ _____ _____ _____ _____ _____ _____ _____ _____ _____.

Junsu: _____ you _____ _____ _____ an artist in the future?

Emily: I hope so. I'm _____ _____ _____ pictures.

Junsu: That's great. I hope your wish _____ _____.

Emily: Thanks. I'll _____ _____ _____.

Real Life Communication B

Sue: You know what? Jenny's family is _____ _____ _____ _____ to Japan.

Jack: Is that right? Jenny _____ _____ _____ _____ _____ _____ it.

Sue: She _____ _____ it just last week and she's very _____ now.

Jack: _____ _____ _____ _____ _____ _____ _____. I am _____ _____ _____ her so much.

Sue: Me, too. She said she would _____ _____ _____ _____ us.

Alex: 엄마, 오늘 학교에서 불고기를 만들었어요. 오늘 저녁으로 불고기를 요리할 생각이에요.
Mom 그거 멋지구나, Alex.
Alex: 집에 채소 있어요, 엄마? 소고기는요?
Mom 채소는 좀 있는데 소고기는 없어. 집에 오는 길에 좀 사올게.
Alex: 좋아요.

Emily 준수야, 그거 아니? 나는 미술 수업을 들을 생각이야.
Junsu 정말? 왜 미술 수업을 들으려고 결심했니, Emily?
Emily 예술 고등학교에 가고 싶어서야.
Junsu 장래에 미술가가 될 생각이니?
Emily 그러고 싶어. 나는 그림 그리는 것에 흥미가 있어.
Junsu 그거 잘 됐다. 네 꿈이 이뤄지길 바라.
Emily 고마워. 최선을 다할 거야.

Sue 있잖아, Jenny 가족이 일본으로 이민을 간대.
Jack 정말이야? Jenny가 그것에 관해 얘기하지 않았는데.
Sue Jenny도 지난주에야 알았어. 그래서 지금 매우 기분이 안 좋아.
Jack 나는 Jenny의 기분을 이해할 수 있어. Jenny가 정말 그리울 거야.
Sue 나도 그래. Jenny는 우리와 계속 연락할 거라고 했어.

※ 다음 우리말에 맞도록 대화를 영어로 쓰시오.

해석

Listen & Speak 1 A

Brian: _____

Julia: _____

Brian: _____

Julia: _____

Brian: _____

Brian: Julia, 네 겨울 방학은 어땠니?
Julia: 좋았어. 그거 아니? 나는 방학 동안 무에타이 수업을 받았어.
Brian: 그거 멋지다. 나는 네가 무에타이에 관심이 있는지 몰랐어.
Julia: 응. 아주 재미있었어.
Brian: 그래? 나도 해 보고 싶다.

Listen & Speak 1 B

Jimin: _____

Tim: _____

Jimin: _____

Tim: _____

Jimin: _____

Tim: _____

Jimin: 그거 아니, Tim? Smith 선생님이 올해 우리 반 담임 선생님이야.
Tim: 그거 잘됐다, 지민아. 작년 Smith 선생님의 과학 수업은 아주 재미있었어.
Jimin: 올해 너희 반 담임 선생님은 누구니?
Tim: 김 선생님이야. 그녀는 새로 오신 선생님이야.
Jimin: 그분은 어떤 과목을 가르치시니?
Tim: 미술을 가르치셔.

Listen & Speak 2 A

Jane: _____

Minsu: _____

Jane: _____

Minsu: _____

Jane: _____

Minsu: _____

Jane: _____

Minsu: _____

Jane: 민수야, 수진이와 나는 동아리를 만들 생각이야.
Minsu: 정말? 어떤 종류의 동아리야?
Jane: 우리는 별과 행성에 대해 배우고 싶어. 그래서 우주 과학 동아리를 만들 생각이야.
Minsu: 그거 멋지다. 얼마나 자주 모일 예정이니?
Jane: 아마도 일주일에 한 번쯤.
Minsu: 그렇구나. 어디에서 모일 거니?
Jane: 101호에서. 민수야, 우리 동아리에 가입할래?
Minsu: 응, 나도 우주에 관심 있어.

Listen & Speak 2 B

Alex: _____

_____

Mom: _____

Alex: _____

Mom: _____

_____

Alex: _____

Alex: 엄마, 오늘 학교에서 불고기를 만들었어요. 오늘 저녁으로 불고기를 요리할 생각이에요.
Mom 그거 멋지구나, Alex.
Alex: 집에 채소 있어요, 엄마? 소고기는요?
Mom 채소는 좀 있는데 소고기는 없어. 집에 오는 길에 좀 사올게.
Alex: 좋아요.

Real Life Communication A

Emily: _____

Junsu: _____

Emily: _____

Junsu: _____

Emily: _____

Junsu: _____

Emily: _____

Emily 준수야, 그거 아니? 나는 미술 수업을 들을 생각이야.
Junsu 정말? 왜 미술 수업을 들으려고 결심했니, Emily?
Emily 예술 고등학교에 가고 싶어서야.
Junsu 장래에 미술가가 될 생각이니?
Emily 그러고 싶어. 나는 그림 그리는 것에 흥미가 있어.
Junsu 그거 잘 됐다. 네 꿈이 이뤄지길 바라.
Emily 고마워. 최선을 다할 거야.

Real Life Communication B

Sue: _____

Jack: _____

Sue: _____

Jack: _____

Sue: _____

Sue 있잖아, Jenny 가족이 일본으로 이민을 간대.
Jack 정말이야? Jenny가 그것에 관해 얘기하지 않았는데.
Sue Jenny도 지난주에야 알았어. 그래서 지금 매우 기분이 안 좋아.
Jack 나는 Jenny의 기분을 이해할 수 있어. Jenny가 정말 그리울 거야.
Sue 나도 그래. Jenny는 우리와 계속 연락할 거라고 했어.

※ 다음 우리말과 일치하도록 빈칸에 알맞은 것을 골라 쓰시오.

1 My friend Eric and I _____ some interesting _____ _____ the vacation.
　　A. during　　　　B. changes　　　C. made

2 We _____ each _____ and talked _____ our changes.
　　A. about　　　　B. emailed　　　C. other

3 _____ _____,
　　A. Eric　　　　B. dear

4 _____'s a beautiful _____ _____ Seoul.
　　A. in　　　　B. spring　　　　C. it

5 The _____ winter _____ was a great _____ _____ me.
　　A. for　　　　B. vacation　　　C. time　　　D. last

6 I _____ two _____ changes _____ the vacation.
　　A. during　　　　B. personal　　　C. made

7 _____ is _____ new _____.
　　A. hobby　　　　B. my　　　　C. one

8 It's _____ _____.
　　A. cupcakes　　　B. making

9 _____ my _____ cupcakes _____ a lot of fun.
　　A. is　　　　B. own　　　　C. making

10 The _____ _____ is _____ one of my bad _____.
　　A. habits　　　B. breaking　　　C. change　　　D. other

11 In the _____, I often _____ my _____.
　　A. nails　　　　B. bit　　　　C. past

12 Now I _____ _____.
　　A. anymore　　　B. don't

13 I _____ great _____ the changes I _____.
　　A. made　　　　B. about　　　　C. feel

14 _____ you _____ to make some changes, I'm sure you will _____ great _____ me.
　　A. like　　　　B. feel　　　　C. try　　　D. if

15 I _____ to _____ you soon.
　　A. from　　　　B. hear　　　　C. hope

16 _____ _____, Junho.
　　A. friend　　　　B. your

1 내 친구 Eric과 나는 방학 동안 흥미로운 변화가 있었다.

2 우리는 서로에게 이메일을 보냈고 우리의 변화에 관해 이야기했다.

3 안녕 Eric,

4 서울은 아름다운 봄이야.

5 지난 겨울 방학은 나에게 멋진 시간이었어.

6 나는 방학 동안 두 가지 개인적인 변화가 있었어.

7 하나는 나의 새로운 취미야.

8 그것은 컵케이크를 만드는 거야.

9 나만의 컵케이크를 만드는 것은 정말 재미있어.

10 나머지 다른 변화는 나의 나쁜 습관 중 하나를 없애는 거야.

11 예전에 나는 종종 손톱을 물어뜯곤 했어.

12 이제 나는 더 이상 그러지 않아.

13 나는 내가 만든 변화가 정말 기분 좋아.

14 만약 네가 변화하려고 노력한다면, 너도 나처럼 기분이 좋을 거라고 확신해.

15 곧 소식 전해 줘.

16 너의 친구 준호가

17 _____ _____,

A. Junho   B. dear

18 _____ Sydney, _____'s _____ in March.

A. fall   B. it   C. in

19 You _____ _____ your _____ in your email.

A. changes   B. about   C. talked

20 Now, it's _____ _____ _____ _____ my new changes.

A. about   B. to   C. talk   D. time

21 _____ _____, I'm _____ 3D printing.

A. into   B. days   C. these

22 I _____ two _____ _____ a 3D printer.

A. with   B. things   C. printed

23 _____ is a model _____ my _____ car.

A. dream   B. of   C. one

24 If the _____ is _____, it will _____ _____ a flying car.

A. into   B. change   C. heavy   D. traffic

25 The _____ is a _____ cup _____ my grandfather.

A. for   B. special   C. other

26 He can't _____ his cup well _____ he's _____.

A. sick   B. because   C. hold

27 My special cup has three _____, _____ it is easy _____ _____.

A. hold   B. so   C. to   D. handles

28 _____ grandfather is very _____.

A. happy   B. my

29 _____ the way, I want _____ _____ your cupcakes _____ day, Junho.

A. try   B. by   C. some   D. to

30 _____ _____.

A. care   B. take

31 _____ _____, Eric.

A. wishes   B. best

17 안녕 준호,

18 시드니에서는 3월이 가을이야.

19 너는 이메일에서 너에게 일어난 변화들을 말해 주었지.

20 이제 나의 새로운 변화를 말해 줄 차례야.

21 요즈음, 나는 3D 프린팅에 빠져 있어.

22 나는 3D 프린터로 2가지를 인쇄했어.

23 하나는 나의 꿈의 자동차의 모형이야.

24 교통이 혼잡할 때, 그것은 날 수 있는 차로 바뀌어.

25 나머지 다른 하나는 우리 할아버지를 위한 특수 컵이야.

26 할아버지는 편찮으셔서 컵을 잘 들지 못하셔.

27 나의 특수 컵은 손잡이가 3개 있어서 들기 쉬워.

28 할아버지는 아주 행복해 하셔.

29 그건 그렇고, 너의 컵케이크를 언젠가 먹어 보고 싶다, 준호야.

30 잘 지내.

31 행운을 빌어, Eric.

※ 다음 우리말과 일치하도록 빈칸에 알맞은 말을 쓰시오.

1   My friend Eric and I _____ _____ _____ _____ _____ _____ _____.

2   We _____ _____ _____ and _____ _____ _____.

3   _____ Eric,

4   _____'s a _____ _____ _____ Seoul.

5   _____ _____ _____ _____ was a great _____ for me.

6   I _____ two _____ _____ _____ the vacation.

7   _____ is my _____ _____.

8   It's _____ _____.

9   _____ my _____ cupcakes _____ a _____ of fun.

10   _____ _____ _____ is _____ one of my bad _____.

11   In the _____, I _____ _____ _____ _____.

12   Now I _____.

13   I _____ _____ _____ the _____ I _____.

14   _____ you _____ _____ _____ some changes, I'm _____ you _____ great _____ me.

15   I _____ _____ _____ you soon.

16   _____ _____, Junho.

1 내 친구 Eric과 나는 방학 동안 흥미로운 변화가 있었다.

2 우리는 서로에게 이메일을 보냈고 우리의 변화에 관해 이야기했다.

3 안녕 Eric,

4 서울은 아름다운 봄이야.

5 지난 겨울 방학은 나에게 멋진 시간이었어.

6 나는 방학 동안 두 가지 개인적인 변화가 있었어.

7 하나는 나의 새로운 취미야.

8 그것은 컵케이크를 만드는 거야.

9 나만의 컵케이크를 만드는 것은 정말 재미있어.

10 나머지 다른 변화는 나의 나쁜 습관 중 하나를 없애는 거야.

11 예전에 나는 종종 손톱을 물어뜯곤 했어.

12 이제 나는 더 이상 그러지 않아.

13 나는 내가 만든 변화가 정말 기분 좋아.

14 만약 네가 변화하려고 노력한다면, 너도 나처럼 기분이 좋을 거라고 확신해.

15 곧 소식 전해 줘.

16 너의 친구 준호가.

17 _____ Junho,

18 _____ Sydney, _____'s fall _____ _____.

19 You _____ _____ your _____ in your email.

20 Now, it's _____ _____ _____ _____ my new changes.

21 _____ _____, I'm _____ _____ _____.

22 I _____ _____ _____ _____ a 3D printing.

23 _____ is a _____ _____ my _____ _____.

24 _____ the traffic _____ _____, it _____ _____ _____ _____ _____.

25 _____ _____ is a _____ _____ _____ my grandfather.

26 He _____ _____ his cup _____ _____ he's _____.

27 My special cup has _____ _____, so it is _____ _____ _____.

28 _____ grandfather is very _____.

29 _____ _____ _____, I want _____ _____ your cupcakes _____ _____, Junho.

30 _____ _____.

31 _____ _____, Eric.

17	안녕 준호,
18	시드니에서는 3월이 가을이야.
19	너는 이메일에서 너에게 일어난 변화들을 말해 주었지.
20	이제 나의 새로운 변화를 말해 줄 차례야.
21	요즈음, 나는 3D 프린팅에 빠져 있어.
22	나는 3D 프린터로 2가지를 인쇄 했어.
23	하나는 나의 꿈의 자동차의 모형이야.
24	교통이 혼잡할 때, 그것은 날 수 있는 차로 바뀌어.
25	나머지 다른 하나는 우리 할아 버지를 위한 특수 컵이야.
26	할아버지는 편찮으셔서 컵을 잘 들지 못하셔.
27	나의 특수 컵은 손잡이가 3개 있 어서 들기 쉬워.
28	할아버지는 아주 행복해 하셔.
29	그건 그렇고, 너의 컵케이크를 언젠가 먹어 보고 싶다. 준호야.
30	잘 지내.
31	행운을 빌어, Eric.

※ 다음 문장을 우리말로 쓰시오.

1 My friend Eric and I made some interesting changes during the vacation.
➡ _____

2 We emailed each other and talked about our changes.
➡ _____

3 Dear Eric,
➡ _____

4 It's a beautiful spring in Seoul.
➡ _____

5 The last winter vacation was a great time for me.
➡ _____

6 I made two personal changes during the vacation.
➡ _____

7 One is my new hobby.
➡ _____

8 It's making cupcakes.
➡ _____

9 Making my own cupcakes is a lot of fun.
➡ _____

10 The other change is breaking one of my bad habits.
➡ _____

11 In the past, I often bit my nails.
➡ _____

12 Now I don't anymore.
➡ _____

13 I feel great about the changes I made.
➡ _____

14 If you try to make some changes, I'm sure you'll feel great like me.
➡ _____

15 I hope to hear from you soon.
➡ _____

16 Your friend, Junho.
➡ _____

17 Dear Junho,

➡ _____

18 In Sydney, it's fall in March.

➡ _____

19 You talked about your changes in your email.

➡ _____

20 Now, it's time to talk about my new changes.

➡ _____

21 These days, I'm into 3D printing.

➡ _____

22 I printed two things with a 3D printer.

➡ _____

23 One is a model of my dream car.

➡ _____

24 If the traffic is heavy, it will change into a flying car.

➡ _____

25 The other is a special cup for my grandfather.

➡ _____

26 He can't hold his cup well because he's sick.

➡ _____

27 My special cup has three handles, so it is easy to hold.

➡ _____

28 My grandfather is very happy.

➡ _____

29 By the way, I want to try your cupcakes some day, Junho.

➡ _____

30 Take care.

➡ _____

31 Best wishes, Eric.

➡ _____

※ 다음 괄호 안의 단어들을 우리말에 맞도록 바르게 배열하시오.

1 (friend / my / Eric / and / made / I / interesting / some / changes / vacation. / the / during)
➡ _____

2 (each / we / other / emailed / and / about / talked / changes. / our)
➡ _____

3 (Eric, / Dear)
➡ _____

4 (a / it's / spring / beautiful / Seoul. / in)
➡ _____

5 (last / the / winter / was / vacation / great / a / time / me. / for)
➡ _____

6 (made / I / personal / two / changes / vacation. / the / during)
➡ _____

7 (is / one / new / hobby. / my)
➡ _____

8 (cupcakes. / making / it's)
➡ _____

9 (my / making / own / cupcakes / a / is / lot / fun. / of)
➡ _____

10 (other / the / change / is / breaking / of / one / habits. / bad / my)
➡ _____

11 (past, / the / in / I / bit / often / nails. / my)
➡ _____

12 (I / now / anymore. / don't)
➡ _____

13 (feel / I / great / about / changes / the / made. / I)
➡ _____

14 (you / if / to / try / some / make / changes, / I'm / feel / you'll / sure / me. / like / great)
➡ _____

15 (hope / I / hear / to / soon. / from / you)
➡ _____

16 (Junho. / friend, / your)
➡ _____

1 내 친구 Eric과 나는 방학 동안 흥미로운 변화가 있었다.

2 우리는 서로에게 이메일을 보냈고 우리의 변화에 관해 이야기했다.

3 안녕 Eric,

4 서울은 아름다운 봄이야.

5 지난 겨울 방학은 나에게 멋진 시간이었어.

6 나는 방학 동안 두 가지 개인적인 변화가 있었어.

7 하나는 나의 새로운 취미야.

8 그것은 컵케이크를 만드는 거야.

9 나만의 컵케이크를 만드는 것은 정말 재미있어.

10 나머지 다른 변화는 나의 나쁜 습관 중 하나를 없애는 거야.

11 예전에 나는 종종 손톱을 물어뜯곤 했어.

12 이제 나는 더 이상 그러지 않아.

13 나는 내가 만든 변화가 정말 기분 좋아.

14 만약 네가 변화하려고 노력한다면, 너도 나처럼 기분이 좋을 거라고 확신해.

15 곧 소식 전해 줘.

16 너의 친구 준호가.

17 (Junho, / dear,)

➡ _____

18 (Sydney, / in / fall / it's / March. / in)

➡ _____

19 (talked / you / about / changes / your / email. / in / your)

➡ _____

20 (now, / time / it's / talk / to / about / changes. / new / my)

➡ _____

21 (days, / these / into / I'm / printing. / 3D)

➡ _____

22 (printed / I / things / two / with / printer. / 3D / a)

➡ _____

23 (is / one / model / a / of / car. / dream / my)

➡ _____

24 (the / if / traffic / heavy, / is / will / it / change / into / car. / flying / a)

➡ _____

25 (other / the / is / specail / a / cup / for / grandfather. / my)

➡ _____

26 (can't / he / hold / cup / his / well / he's / sick. / because)

➡ _____

27 (my / cup / special / has / handles, / three / so / is / it / hold. / to / easy)

➡ _____

28 (grandfather / my / is / happy. / very)

➡ _____

29 (the / by / way, / I / to / want / your / try / cupcakes / some / Junho. / day,)

➡ _____

30 (care. / take)

➡ _____

31 (wishes, / Eric / best)

➡ _____

17 안녕 준호,

18 시드니에서는 3월이 가을이야.

19 너는 이메일에서 너에게 일어난 변화들을 말해 주었지.

20 이제 나의 새로운 변화를 말해 줄 차례야.

21 요즈음, 나는 3D 프린팅에 빠져 있어.

22 나는 3D 프린터로 2가지를 인쇄 했어.

23 하나는 나의 꿈의 자동차의 모형이야.

24 교통이 혼잡할 때, 그것은 날 수 있는 차로 바뀌어.

25 나머지 다른 하나는 우리 할아 버지를 위한 특수 컵이야.

26 할아버지는 편찮으셔서 컵을 잘 들지 못하셔.

27 나의 특수 컵은 손잡이가 3개 있 어서 들기 쉬워.

28 할아버지는 아주 행복해 하셔.

29 그건 그렇고, 너의 컵케이크를 언젠가 먹어 보고 싶다. 준호야.

30 잘 지내.

31 행운을 빌어. Eric.

※ 다음 우리말을 영어로 쓰시오.

1 내 친구 Eric과 나는 방학 동안 흥미로운 변화가 있었다.

➡ _____

2 우리는 서로에게 이메일을 보냈고 우리의 변화에 관해 이야기했다.

➡ _____

3 안녕 Eric,

➡ _____

4 서울은 아름다운 봄이야.

➡ _____

5 지난 겨울 방학은 나에게 멋진 시간이었어.

➡ _____

6 나는 방학 동안 두 가지 개인적인 변화가 있었어.

➡ _____

7 하나는 나의 새로운 취미야.

➡ _____

8 그것은 컵케이크를 만드는 거야.

➡ _____

9 나만의 컵케이크를 만드는 것은 정말 재미있어.

➡ _____

10 나머지 다른 변화는 나의 나쁜 습관 중 하나를 없애는 거야.

➡ _____

11 예전에 나는 종종 손톱을 물어뜯곤 했어.

➡ _____

12 이제 나는 더 이상 그러지 않아.

➡ _____

13 나는 내가 만든 변화가 정말 기분 좋아.

➡ _____

14 만약 네가 변화하려고 노력한다면, 너도 나처럼 기분이 좋을 거라고 확신해.

➡ _____

15 곧 소식 전해 줘.

➡ _____

16 너의 친구 준호가.

➡ _____

17 안녕 준호,

➡ _____

18 시드니에서는 3월이 가을이야.

➡ _____

19 너는 이메일에서 너에게 일어난 변화들을 말해 주었지.

➡ _____

20 이제 나의 새로운 변화를 말해 줄 차례야.

➡ _____

21 요즈음, 나는 3D 프린팅에 빠져 있어.

➡ _____

22 나는 3D 프린터로 2가지를 인쇄했어.

➡ _____

23 하나는 나의 꿈의 자동차의 모형이야.

➡ _____

24 교통이 혼잡할 때, 그것은 날 수 있는 차로 바뀌어.

➡ _____

25 나머지 다른 하나는 우리 할아버지를 위한 특수 컵이야.

➡ _____

26 할아버지는 편찮으셔서 컵을 잘 들지 못하셔.

➡ _____

27 나의 특수 컵은 손잡이가 3개 있어서 들기 쉬워.

➡ _____

28 할아버지는 아주 행복해 하셔.

➡ _____

29 그건 그렇고, 너의 컵케이크를 언젠가 먹어 보고 싶다, 준호야.

➡ _____

30 잘 지내.

➡ _____

31 행운을 빌어, Eric.

➡ _____

※ 다음 우리말과 일치하도록 빈칸에 알맞은 말을 쓰시오.

Real Life Communication - Step 2

1. A: You know _____? I'm _____ _____ _____ a diary in English.

2. B: _____ did you _____ _____ _____ that?

3. A: It's _____ I want to _____ _____ _____ English writing.

4. B: That's _____.

1. A: 그거 아니? 나는 영어로 일기를 쓸 생각이야.
2. B: 왜 그런 결심을 했어?
3. A: 왜냐하면 영어 쓰기를 잘하고 싶기 때문이야.
4. B: 멋지다.

My Writing Portfolio

1. _____ me,

2. You are very _____ and _____.

3. _____, you still want to make two changes, _____ _____?

4. _____ is to have more good friends. _____ _____ is to _____ _____.

5. _____ _____ my tips for your _____.

6. If you are _____ _____ _____ and eat more vegetables, you'll _____ _____ _____.

7. _____, Me

1. 나에게,
2. 너는 매우 영리하고 재미있어.
3. 하지만 너는 두 가지 변화를 이루고 싶어 해, 그렇지 않니?
4. 하나는 더 많은 좋은 친구를 사귀는 거야. 다른 하나는 더 건강해지는 거야.
5. 여기 너의 소망을 위한 조언이 있어.
6. 다른 사람들에게 더 친절하게 하고 더 많은 채소를 먹는다면, 너는 이러한 변화들을 이룰 수 있을 거야.
7. 사랑하는, 내가

Words in Action B

1. Bobo is _____ _____ _____.

2. She has _____ _____.

3. _____ is black. _____ _____ is white.

4. She has _____ _____.

5. _____ is a ball. _____ _____ is a plastic duck.

6. She has _____ _____.

7. One is _____ TV. The other is _____ on my chair.

1. 보보는 내 애완견이다.
2. 그녀는 동생이 둘 있다.
3. 하나는 검정색이다. 다른 하나는 하얀색이다.
4. 그녀는 장난감이 두 개 있다.
5. 하나는 공이다. 다른 하나는 플라스틱 오리이다.
6. 그녀는 두 가지 습관이 있다.
7. 하나는 TV를 보는 것이다. 다른 하나는 내 의자 위에서 자는 것이다.

※ 다음 우리말을 영어로 쓰시오.

Real Life Communication - Step 2

1. A: 그거 아니? 나는 영어로 일기를 쓸 생각이야.
➡ _____

2. B: 왜 그런 결심을 했어?
➡ _____

3. A: 왜냐하면 영어 쓰기를 잘하고 싶기 때문이야.
➡ _____

4. B: 멋지다.
➡ _____

My Writing Portfolio

1. 나에게,
➡ _____

2. 너는 매우 영리하고 재미있어.
➡ _____

3. 하지만 너는 두 가지 변화를 이루고 싶어 해, 그렇지 않니?
➡ _____

4. 하나는 더 많은 좋은 친구를 사귀는 거야. 다른 하나는 더 건강해지는 거야.
➡ _____

5. 여기 너의 소망을 위한 조언이 있어.
➡ _____

6. 다른 사람들에게 더 친절하게 하고 더 많은 채소를 먹는다면, 너는 이러한 변화들을 이룰 수 있을 거야.
➡ _____

7. 사랑하는, 내가
➡ _____

Words in Action B

1. 보보는 내 애완견이다.
➡ _____

2. 그녀는 동생이 둘 있다.
➡ _____

3. 하나는 검정색이다. 다른 하나는 하얀색이다.
➡ _____

4. 그녀는 장난감이 두 개 있다.
➡ _____

5. 하나는 공이다. 다른 하나는 플라스틱 오리이다.
➡ _____

6. 그녀는 두 가지 습관이 있다.
➡ _____

7. 하나는 TV를 보는 것이다. 다른 하나는 내 의자 위에서 자는 것이다.
➡ _____

※ 다음 영어를 우리말로 쓰시오.

01 shake _____

02 solve _____

03 empty _____

04 fall _____

05 follow _____

06 strange _____

07 space _____

08 hurt _____

09 floor _____

10 injury _____

11 pole _____

12 knife _____

13 low _____

14 medicine _____

15 safety _____

16 amazing _____

17 break _____

18 scary _____

19 decide _____

20 slip _____

21 strike _____

22 wet _____

23 protect _____

24 escape _____

25 serious _____

26 worry _____

27 avoid _____

28 sore _____

29 dangerous _____

30 slippery _____

31 earthquake _____

32 forget _____

33 disaster _____

34 survive _____

35 get out of _____

36 take cover _____

37 a little _____

38 stay away from _____

39 be worried about _____

40 hold on to _____

41 keep ~ in mind _____

42 feel better _____

43 take a rest _____

※ 다음 우리말을 영어로 쓰시오.

01	씌우다, 덮다
02	닦다
03	탈출하다
04	심각한
05	재난, 재해
06	잊어버리다
07	바닥, 마루
08	아픈
09	방지하다, 막다, 피하다
10	계단
11	~까지
12	걱정, 근심; 걱정하다
13	살아남다, 생존하다
14	준비하다, 대비하다
15	승강기
16	미끄러운
17	위험한
18	보호하다
19	상황
20	지진
21	목구멍

22	(방송) 프로그램
23	안전
24	비어 있는, 빈
25	미끄러지다
26	깨다, 부수다, 부서지다
27	상처, 부상
28	해결하다
29	젖은
30	이상한, 낯선
31	규칙, 법칙
32	공간
33	흔들림, 떨림; 흔들다
34	약
35	휴식을 취하다
36	~에 대해 걱정하다
37	(기분이) 나아지다
38	~을 꼭 잡다
39	~에서 떨어져 있다
40	~을 기억하다
41	하나씩, 차례차례
42	~하는 게 어때?
43	(~에서) 나가다, 떠나다

※ 다음 영영풀이에 알맞은 단어를 <보기>에서 골라 쓴 후, 우리말 뜻을 쓰시오.

1 _____ : to find a way to deal with and end a problem: _____

2 _____ : to keep someone or something from being harmed, lost, etc.: _____

3 _____ : to be unable to think of or remember something: _____

4 _____ : the state of not being dangerous or harmful: _____

5 _____ : to clean or dry something by using a towel, your hand, etc.: _____

6 _____ : not having any people, not occupied; containing nothing: _____

7 _____ : to come or go down suddenly from a standing position: _____

8 _____ : short, quick movement back and forth or up and down: _____

9 _____ : a long, thin stick made of wood or metal, used to hold something up: _____

10 _____ : a shaking of a part of the Earth's surface that often causes great damage: _____

11 _____ : to do what instructions or orders say you should do, to move behind someone or something and go where they go: _____

12 _____ : to stay away from; to prevent the occurrence of something bad, unpleasant, etc.: _____

13 _____ : to cause pain or injury to yourself, someone else, or a part of your body: _____

14 _____ : harm or damage; an act or event that causes someone or something to no longer be fully healthy or in good condition: _____

15 _____ : something such as a flood, tornado, fire, plane crash, etc. that happens suddenly and causes much suffering or loss to many people: _____

16 _____ : to separate something into parts or pieces often in a sudden and forceful or violent way, to cause to separate into two or more pieces: _____

pole	shake	injury	break
safety	wipe	solve	empty
avoid	disaster	follow	hurt
fall	forget	protect	earthquake

※ 다음 우리말과 일치하도록 빈칸에 알맞은 말을 쓰시오.

Listen & Speak 1 A

Tom: Yujin, what's _____?

Yujin: _____ my leg. It _____ _____ _____.

Tom: _____ _____ _____ _____ _____ a doctor?

Yujin: I'm _____ _____ _____ after school today.

Tom: I hope _____ _____ _____ soon.

Yujin: I _____ _____, _____.

Listen & Speak 1 B

Brian: What _____ you _____?

Jane: It's a _____ _____ _____.

Brian: _____ _____. _____ _____ _____ _____ _____ these days.

Jane: _____, _____. This program has some _____ _____.

Brian: Really? What _____ it _____?

Jane: When things _____ _____ _____, you need to _____ _____ under a table.

Brian: Oh, I _____ _____ that.

Listen & Speak 2 A

Jack: Dad, I'm _____ _____ _____ _____ basketball with Minu.

Dad: Did you _____ _____ _____ _____?

Jack: No, _____ _____. Can I do it _____?

Dad: No. _____ _____ _____ _____ _____ _____.

Jack: Okay. I'll _____ my room and then _____ _____.

Dad: Good. _____ _____ to be home _____ _____.

Jack: Okay.

Listen & Speak 2 B

Emily: _____ _____ is the movie?

Tom: It starts at 4:30.

Emily: Oh, no. We only have 20 minutes _____. _____ _____ _____!

Tom: No! _____ _____ _____ _____ _____ _____ _____.

You _____ _____ _____ _____ _____.

Emily: You're _____. We can be _____ _____ _____.

Tom: Yes. _____ _____ _____ _____.

Emily: 영화는 몇 시에 하니?

Tom: 4시 30분에 시작해.

Emily: 이런. 우리 20분밖에 남지 않았어. 뛰자!

Tom: 안 돼! 넘어져서 다칠 수 있어. 계단에서는 걸어가야 해.

Emily: 네 말이 맞아. 우리 좀 늦을 수도 있겠어.

Tom: 그래. 후회하는 것보다 안전한 게 낫지.

Real Life Communication

Brian: There was _____ _____ _____ at the _____ _____ yesterday.

Mina: Yes, I _____ _____ it. _____ _____ _____ _____ _____ _____ _____ _____.

Brian: _____ _____. Everybody was okay. They all _____ the _____ _____.

Mina: Really? _____ are the rules?

Brian: You need to _____ your nose and mouth _____ _____ _____ _____. Then _____ _____ and _____.

Mina: Oh, I _____ _____ that.

Brian: You should _____ _____ _____ _____. It might be _____ _____ _____.

Brian: 어제 시립 도서관에 큰 불이 났어.

Mina: 응, 그것에 대해 들었어. 거기 있었던 사람들이 걱정 됐어.

Brian: 걱정하지 마. 모두들 무사했어. 사람들이 모두 안전 규칙을 따랐대.

Mina: 정말? 그게 뭔데?

Brian: 젖은 수건으로 코와 입을 가려야 해. 그 다음, 몸을 낮게 유지하고 탈출하는 거야.

Mina: 아, 그건 몰랐어.

Brian: 넌 그것을 명심해야 해. 언젠가 도움이 될 수도 있어.

Let's Check

Sujin: It's _____. I'm _____ _____ _____ _____ in the afternoon.

Mom: It is going to rain _____ _____ _____ today. _____ _____ _____ _____ _____.

Sujin: You're right, Mom. I'll _____ my friend and _____ _____ _____.

Sujin: 비가 와요. 오후에 있을 소풍이 걱정 돼요.

Mom: 오늘 오후 늦게까지 비가 올 거야. 다른 날 소풍 가는 것이 좋을 것 같구나.

Sujin: 맞아요, 엄마. 친구에게 전화해서 다른 날을 정해야겠어요.

※ 다음 우리말에 맞도록 대화를 영어로 쓰시오.

Listen & Speak 1 A

Tom: _____

Yujin: _____

Tom: _____

Yujin: _____

Tom: _____

Yujin: _____

Listen & Speak 1 B

Brian: _____

Jane: _____

Brian: _____

Jane: _____

Brian: _____

Jane: _____

Brian: _____

Listen & Speak 2 A

Jack: _____

Dad: _____

Jack: _____

Dad: _____

Jack: _____

Dad: _____

Jack: _____

해석

Tom: 유진아, 무슨 일이야?
Yujin: 내 다리가 걱정돼서. 많이 아프거든.
Tom: 병원에 가보는 게 어때?
Yujin: 오늘 방과 후에 갈 거야.
Tom: 곧 괜찮아지기를 바라.
Yujin: 나도 그러길 바라.

Brian: 무엇을 시청하고 있니?
Jane: 지진에 관한 프로그램이야.
Brian: 그거 재미있겠다. 나는 요즘 지진이 걱정돼.
Jane: 나도 그래. 이 프로그램에는 도움이 되는 몇 가지 조언이 있어.
Brian: 그래? 뭐라고 하는데?
Jane: 물건들이 흔들리기 시작하면 탁자 아래에 숨어야 해.
Brian: 아, 그건 몰랐어.

Jack: 아빠, 저 민우와 농구하러 나갈 거예요.
Dad: 네 방 청소는 끝냈니?
Jack: 아니요, 아직 안했어요. 나중에 해도 돼요?
Dad: 아니. 너는 네 방을 먼저 청소해야 해.
Jack: 알았어요. 방을 청소하고 농구 할게요.
Dad: 착하구나. 6시까지 집에 오는 것 잊지 마라.
Jack: 알겠어요.

Listen & Speak 2 B

Emily: ___
Tom: ___
Emily: ___
Tom: ___
Emily: ___
Tom: ___

Emily: 영화는 몇 시에 하니?
Tom: 4시 30분에 시작해.
Emily: 이런. 우리 20분밖에 남지 않았어. 뛰자!
Tom: 안 돼! 넘어져서 다칠 수 있어. 계단에서는 걸어가야 해.
Emily: 네 말이 맞아. 우리 좀 늦을 수도 있겠어.
Tom: 그래. 후회하는 것보다 안전한 게 낫지.

Real Life Communication

Brian: ___
Mina: ___
Brian: ___
Mina: ___
Brian: ___
Mina: ___
Brian: ___

Brian: 어제 시립 도서관에 큰 불이 났어.
Mina: 응, 그것에 대해 들었어. 거기 있었던 사람들이 걱정 됐어.
Brian: 걱정하지 마. 모두들 무사했어. 사람들이 모두 안전 규칙을 따랐대.
Mina: 정말? 그게 뭔데?
Brian: 젖은 수건으로 코와 입을 가려야 해. 그 다음, 몸을 낮게 유지하고 탈출하는 거야.
Mina: 아, 그건 몰랐어.
Brian: 넌 그것을 명심해야 해. 언젠가 도움이 될 수도 있어.

Let's Check

Sujin: ___
Mom: ___
Sujin: ___

Sujin: 비가 와요. 오후에 있을 소풍이 걱정 돼요.
Mom: 오늘 오후 늦게까지 비가 올 거야. 다른 날 소풍 가는 것이 좋을 것 같구나.
Sujin: 맞아요, 엄마. 친구에게 전화해서 다른 날을 정해야겠어요.

※ 다음 우리말과 일치하도록 빈칸에 알맞은 것을 골라 쓰시오.

1 Do you know _____ _____ do _____ an earthquake _____?
A. strikes   B. when   C. to   D. what

2 _____ this quiz and think about _____ to be safe _____ this kind of natural _____.
A. disaster   B. during   C. how   D. take

3 When _____ start to _____, run _____ quickly. (o / x)
A. outside   B. shake   C. things

4 _____ _____ from windows. (o / x)
A. away   B. stay

5 _____ the stairs to get _____ _____ buildings. (o / x)
A. of   B. out   C. use

6 When you are _____, _____ on to a _____ or a tree. (o / x)
A. pole   B. hold   C. outside

7 _____ did you do _____ the quiz?
A. on   B. how

8 Can you _____ an earthquake _____?
A. safely   B. survive

9 _____ are some _____ tips _____ can be _____ in an earthquake.
A. helpful   B. which   C. safety   D. here

10 Let's _____ them one _____ one and learn _____ to do.
A. what   B. by   C. check

11 Don't _____ outside _____ things are _____.
A. shaking   B. when   C. run

12 _____ a table or a desk and _____ _____ under it.
A. cover   B. take   C. find

13 You can _____ _____ to the legs _____ _____ yourself.
A. protect   B. to   C. on   D. hold

14 Also, _____ _____ _____ windows.
A. from   B. away   C. stay

1 지진이 발생할 때 해야 할 일을 알고 있습니까?

2 이 퀴즈를 풀며 이러한 종류의 자연 재해가 발생하는 동안 어떻게 해야 안전할 수 있는지를 생각해 보세요.

3 물건들이 흔들리기 시작하면, 빨리 밖으로 뛰어나가세요.

4 창문으로부터 멀리 떨어지세요.

5 건물에서 나갈 때는 계단을 이용하세요.

6 밖에 나가서는 기둥이나 나무를 붙들고 있으세요.

7 퀴즈가 어떠셨나요?

8 당신은 지진에서 안전하게 살아남을 수 있나요?

9 여기에 지진 발생 시 도움이 될 수 있는 안전 지침이 있습니다.

10 하나하나 확인하면서 무엇을 해야 하는지를 배워 봅시다.

11 물건들이 흔들리기 시작할 때 밖으로 뛰어나가지 마세요.

12 탁자나 책상을 찾아서 그 밑에 숨으세요.

13 자신을 보호하기 위해 탁자나 책상 다리를 붙들고 있으세요.

14 또한, 창문으로부터 멀리 떨어지세요.

15 They can _____ during an _____ and _____ you.
A. hurt   B. earthquake   C. break

16 You can _____ _____ when the _____ _____.
A. stops   B. shaking   C. outside   D. go

17 To _____ _____ of buildings, _____ _____ the elevator.
A. use   B. don't   C. out   D. get

18 _____ the _____.
A. stairs   B. take

19 It's _____ _____.
A. safer   B. much

20 _____ you are outside, _____ an _____ space that is _____ from buildings.
A. far   B. empty   C. find   D. once

21 There _____ be people who want to _____ on to a _____ or a tree, _____ think again.
A. but   B. pole   C. hold   D. may

22 That's a bad idea _____ it can _____ _____ you.
A. on   B. fall   C. because

23 Earthquakes _____ _____ _____.
A. anytime   B. strike   C. can

24 They can be _____ _____ for _____.
A. everyone   B. experiences   C. scary

25 So learn _____ to be _____ in an _____.
A. earthquake   B. safe   C. how

26 You can _____ _____ and _____ yourself.
A. protect   B. injuries   C. avoid

27 _____ these _____ and be _____!
A. safe   B. tips   C. follow

---

15 지진이 일어나는 동안 창문들이 깨져 다칠 수 있으니까요.

16 흔들림이 멈추었을 때 밖으로 나가도 됩니다.

17 건물에서 나가기 위해 엘리베이터를 이용하지 마세요.

18 계단을 이용하세요.

19 그것이 훨씬 더 안전합니다.

20 일단 밖으로 나가면, 건물로부터 멀리 떨어진 공터를 찾으세요.

21 기둥이나 나무를 꼭 잡고 있으려는 사람들이 있을 수 있지만, 다시 생각해 보세요.

22 그것이 당신 위로 넘어질 수 있으므로 그것은 좋지 않은 생각입니다.

23 지진은 언제든지 발생할 수 있습니다.

24 지진은 모두에게 무서운 경험일 것입니다.

25 따라서 지진이 날 때 안전을 지키는 법을 배우세요.

26 부상을 방지하고 자신을 보호할 수 있습니다.

27 이 지침을 따르고 안전을 지키세요!

※ 다음 우리말과 일치하도록 빈칸에 알맞은 말을 쓰시오.

1 Do you know _____ _____ _____ when an _____ _____?

2 _____ this quiz and think about _____ _____ _____ safe _____ this kind of _____ _____.

3 When things start _____ _____, run outside _____. (o / x)

4 _____ _____ _____ windows. (o / x)

5 _____ the stairs _____ _____ _____ _____ buildings. (o / x)

6 _____ you are _____, _____ _____ _____ a pole or a tree. (o / x)

7 _____ did you do _____ _____ _____?

8 Can you _____ _____ _____ _____?

9 _____ _____ some safety tips _____ can be _____ _____ _____ _____.

10 _____ check _____ _____ _____ and learn _____ _____.

11 _____ run outside _____ _____ _____ _____ _____.

12 _____ a table or a desk and _____ _____ _____ it.

13 You can _____ on to the legs _____ _____ _____.

14 Also, _____ _____ _____ _____.

1 지진이 발생할 때 해야 할 일을 알고 있습니까?

2 이 퀴즈를 풀며 이러한 종류의 자연 재해가 발생하는 동안 어떻게 해야 안전할 수 있는지를 생각해 보세요.

3 물건들이 흔들리기 시작하면, 빨리 밖으로 뛰어나가세요.

4 창문으로부터 멀리 떨어지세요.

5 건물에서 나갈 때는 계단을 이용하세요.

6 밖에 나가서는 기둥이나 나무를 붙들고 있으세요.

7 퀴즈가 어떠셨나요?

8 당신은 지진에서 안전하게 살아 남을 수 있나요?

9 여기에 지진 발생 시 도움이 될 수 있는 안전 지침이 있습니다.

10 하나하나 확인하면서 무엇을 해야 하는지를 배워 봅시다.

11 물건들이 흔들리기 시작할 때 밖으로 뛰어나가지 마세요.

12 탁자나 책상을 찾아서 그 밑에 숨으세요.

13 자신을 보호하기 위해 탁자나 책상 다리를 붙들고 있으세요.

14 또한, 창문으로부터 멀리 떨어지세요.

15 _____ can _____ _____ an earthquake and hurt you.

16 You can _____ _____ when _____ _____ _____.

17 _____ _____ _____ _____ _____ buildings, _____ _____

the elevator.

18 _____ the _____.

19 It's _____ _____.

20 _____ you are outside, _____ _____ _____ _____ _____

that _____ _____ _____ buildings.

21 There may be people _____ _____ _____ _____

_____ _____ a pole or a tree, _____ _____ again.

22 That's a bad idea _____ _____ can _____ _____ you.

23 _____ can _____ _____.

24 They can be _____ _____ _____ _____.

25 So learn _____ _____ _____ _____ _____ in an earthquake.

26 You _____ _____ _____ and _____ _____.

27 _____ _____ _____ and _____ safe!

15 지진이 일어나는 동안 창문들이 깨져 다칠 수 있으니까요.

16 흔들림이 멈추었을 때 밖으로 나가도 됩니다.

17 건물에서 나가기 위해 엘리베이터를 이용하지 마세요.

18 계단을 이용하세요.

19 그것이 훨씬 더 안전합니다.

20 일단 밖으로 나가면, 건물로부터 멀리 떨어진 공터를 찾으세요.

21 기둥이나 나무를 꼭 잡고 있으려는 사람들이 있을 수 있지만, 다시 생각해 보세요.

22 그것이 당신 위로 넘어질 수 있으므로 그것은 좋지 않은 생각입니다.

23 지진은 언제든지 발생할 수 있습니다.

24 지진은 모두에게 무서운 경험일 것입니다.

25 따라서 지진이 날 때 안전을 지키는 법을 배우세요.

26 부상을 방지하고 자신을 보호할 수 있습니다.

27 이 지침을 따르고 안전을 지키세요!

※ 다음 문장을 우리말로 쓰시오.

1 Do you know what to do when an earthquake strikes?

➡ _____

2 Take this quiz and think about how to be safe during this kind of natural disaster.

➡ _____

3 When things start to shake, run outside quickly.

➡ _____

4 Stay away from windows.

➡ _____

5 Use the stairs to get out of buildings.

➡ _____

6 When you are outside, hold on to a pole or a tree.

➡ _____

7 How did you do on the quiz?

➡ _____

8 Can you survive an earthquake safely?

➡ _____

9 Here are some safety tips which can be helpful in an earthquake.

➡ _____

10 Let's check them one by one and learn what to do.

➡ _____

11 Don't run outside when things are shaking.

➡ _____

12 Find a table or a desk and take cover under it.

➡ _____

13 You can hold on to the legs to protect yourself.

➡ _____

14 Also, stay away from windows.

➡ _____

15 They can break during an earthquake and hurt you.

➡ _____

16 You can go outside when the shaking stops.

➡ _____

17 To get out of buildings, don't use the elevator.

➡ _____

18 Take the stairs.

➡ _____

19 It's much safer.

➡ _____

20 Once you are outside, find an empty space that is far from buildings.

➡ _____

21 There may be people who want to hold on to a pole or a tree, but think again.

➡ _____

22 That's a bad idea because it can fall on you.

➡ _____

23 Earthquakes can strike anytime.

➡ _____

24 They can be scary experiences for everyone.

➡ _____

25 So learn how to be safe in an earthquake.

➡ _____

26 You can avoid injuries and protect yourself.

➡ _____

27 Follow these tips and be safe!

➡ _____

※ 다음 괄호 안의 단어들을 우리말에 맞도록 바르게 배열하시오.

1 (know / you / do / what / do / to / when / strikes? / earthquake / an)
➡ _____

2 (this / take / quiz / and / about / think / to / how / be / safe / this / during / kind / disaster. / natural / of)
➡ _____
_____

3 (things / when / to / start / shake, / quickly. / outside / run)
➡ _____

4 (away / stay / windows. / from)
➡ _____

5 (the / use / to / stairs / get / of / out / buildings. / of)
➡ _____

6 (you / when / outside, / are / on / hold / to / pole / a / tree. / a / or)
➡ _____

7 (did / how / do / you / quiz? / on / the)
➡ _____

8 (survive / you / can / an / safely? / earthquake)
➡ _____

9 (are / here / safety / some / tips / which / be / can / in / earthquake. / an / helpful)
➡ _____

10 (check / let's / them / by / one / and / one / learn / do. / to / what)
➡ _____

11 (run / outside / don't / when / shaking. / are / things)
➡ _____

12 (a / find / table / or / desk / a / and / cover / take / it. / under)
➡ _____

13 (can / you / hold / to / on / the / to / legs / yourself. / protect)
➡ _____

14 (stay / also, / windows. / from / away)
➡ _____

1 지진이 발생할 때 해야 할 일을 알고 있습니까?

2 이 퀴즈를 풀며 이러한 종류의 자연 재해가 발생하는 동안 어떻게 해야 안전할 수 있는지를 생각해 보세요.

3 물건들이 흔들리기 시작하면, 빨리 밖으로 뛰어나가세요.

4 창문으로부터 멀리 떨어지세요.

5 건물에서 나갈 때는 계단을 이용하세요.

6 밖에 나가서는 기둥이나 나무를 붙들고 있으세요.

7 퀴즈가 어떠셨나요?

8 당신은 지진에서 안전하게 살아남을 수 있나요?

9 여기에 지진 발생 시 도움이 될 수 있는 안전 지침이 있습니다.

10 하나하나 확인하면서 무엇을 해야 하는지를 배워 봅시다.

11 물건들이 흔들리기 시작할 때 밖으로 뛰어나가지 마세요.

12 탁자나 책상을 찾아서 그 밑에 숨으세요.

13 자신을 보호하기 위해 탁자나 책상 다리를 붙들고 있으세요.

14 또한, 창문으로부터 멀리 떨어지세요.

15 (can / they / break / during / earthquake / and / an / you. / hurt)

➡ _____

16 (go / can / you / outside / when / stops. / shaking / the)

➡ _____

17 (get / to / out / buildings, / of / don't / elevator. / the / use)

➡ _____

18 (stairs. / the / take)

➡ _____

19 (much / it's / safer.)

➡ _____

20 (are / you / once / outside, / an / find / space / empty / that / from / buildings. / far / is)

➡ _____

21 (may / there / be / people / who / to / want / hold / on / to / or / pole / a / tree, / a / again. / but / think)

➡ _____

_____

22 (a / idea / that's / bad / because / can / it / fall / you. / on)

➡ _____

23 (can / earthquakes / anytime. / strike)

➡ _____

24 (can / they / scary / be / everyone. / for / experiences)

➡ _____

25 (learn / so / to / how / safe / be / earthquake. / an / in)

➡ _____

26 (can / you / avoid / injuries / yourself. / and / protect)

➡ _____

27 (these / follow / and / tips / safe! / be)

➡ _____

15 지진이 일어나는 동안 창문들이 깨져 다칠 수 있으니까요.

16 흔들림이 멈추었을 때 밖으로 나가도 됩니다.

17 건물에서 나가기 위해 엘리베이터를 이용하지 마세요.

18 계단을 이용하세요.

19 그것이 훨씬 더 안전합니다.

20 일단 밖으로 나가면, 건물로부터 멀리 떨어진 공터를 찾으세요.

21 기둥이나 나무를 꼭 잡고 있으려는 사람들이 있을 수 있지만, 다시 생각해 보세요.

22 그것이 당신 위로 넘어질 수 있으므로 그것은 좋지 않은 생각입니다.

23 지진은 언제든지 발생할 수 있습니다.

24 지진은 모두에게 무서운 경험일 것입니다.

25 따라서 지진이 날 때 안전을 지키는 법을 배우세요.

26 부상을 방지하고 자신을 보호할 수 있습니다.

27 이 지침을 따르고 안전을 지키세요!

※ 다음 우리말을 영어로 쓰시오.

1 지진이 발생할 때 해야 할 일을 알고 있습니까?

➡ _____

2 이 퀴즈를 풀며 이러한 종류의 자연 재해가 발생하는 동안 어떻게 해야 안전할 수 있는지를 생각해 보세요.

➡ _____

3 물건들이 흔들리기 시작하면, 빨리 밖으로 뛰어나가세요.

➡ _____

4 창문으로부터 멀리 떨어지세요.

➡ _____

5 건물에서 나갈 때는 계단을 이용하세요.

➡ _____

6 밖에 나가서는 기둥이나 나무를 붙들고 있으세요.

➡ _____

7 퀴즈가 어떠셨나요?

➡ _____

8 당신은 지진에서 안전하게 살아남을 수 있나요?

➡ _____

9 여기에 지진 발생 시 도움이 될 수 있는 안전 지침이 있습니다.

➡ _____

10 하나하나 확인하면서 무엇을 해야 하는지를 배워 봅시다.

➡ _____

11 물건이 흔들리기 시작할 때 밖으로 뛰어나가지 마세요.

➡ _____

12 탁자나 책상을 찾아서 그 밑에 숨으세요.

➡ _____

13 자신을 보호하기 위해 탁자나 책상 다리를 붙들고 있으세요.

➡ _____

14 또한, 창문으로부터 멀리 떨어지세요.

➡ _____

15 지진이 일어나는 동안 창문들이 깨져 다칠 수 있으니까요.

➡ _____

16 흔들림이 멈추었을 때 밖으로 나가도 됩니다.

➡ _____

17 건물에서 나가기 위해 엘리베이터를 이용하지 마세요.

➡ _____

18 계단을 이용하세요.

➡ _____

19 그것이 훨씬 더 안전합니다.

➡ _____

20 일단 밖으로 나가면, 건물로부터 멀리 떨어진 공터를 찾으세요.

➡ _____

21 기둥이나 나무를 꼭 잡고 있으려는 사람들이 있을 수 있지만, 다시 생각해 보세요.

➡ _____

22 그것이 당신 위로 넘어질 수 있으므로 그것은 좋지 않은 생각입니다.

➡ _____

23 지진은 언제든지 발생할 수 있습니다.

➡ _____

24 지진은 모두에게 무서운 경험일 것입니다.

➡ _____

25 따라서 지진이 날 때 안전을 지키는 법을 배우세요.

➡ _____

26 부상을 방지하고 자신을 보호할 수 있습니다.

➡ _____

27 이 지침을 따르고 안전을 지키세요!

➡ _____

※ 다음 우리말과 일치하도록 빈칸에 알맞은 말을 쓰시오.

Real Life Communication B

1. A: I _____ _____ your accident. I _____ _____ _____ you.

2. B: Thanks. I _____ my hand, but it's _____ _____. I'll be okay.

3. A: Good. You _____ _____ your hands _____ you _____ the door.

4. B: You're _____. I _____.

1. A: 네 사고에 대해 들었어. 나는 너를 걱정했어.
2. B: 고마워. 손을 다쳤지만 심각하지 않아. 괜찮을 거야.
3. A: 다행이야. 문을 닫을 때 손을 조심해야 해.
4. B: 맞아. 그럴게.

Culture & Life

1. _____ an earthquake _____ in Italy in 2016, people found Georgia _____ _____ Leo, a dog.

2. Leo _____ the eight-year-old girl 16 hours _____ _____ _____ _____.

1. 2016년 이탈리아에 지진이 발생했을 때, 사람들은 Leo라는 개 덕분에 Georgia를 발견했다.
2. Leo는 지진 발생 후 16시간이 지나 이 8살짜리 소녀를 발견했다.

Culture & Life Project

1. _____ _____ the items for _____ _____ _____.

2. We _____ _____ _____ and water.

3. We _____ them _____ _____.

4. We also _____ some _____ that might be helpful _____ _____.

5. We _____ medicine _____ the bag, _____.

6. We might _____ it for _____.

1. 여기 우리의 생존 가방에 들어갈 물품이 있습니다.
2. 우리는 약간의 음식과 물을 챙겼습니다.
3. 우리는 생존하기 위해서 그것들이 필요합니다.
4. 우리는 또한 재난 발생 시 유용할 수 있는 성냥을 챙겼습니다.
5. 가방에 약품도 넣었습니다.
6. 부상당했을 때 필요할 수 있습니다.

※ 다음 우리말을 영어로 쓰시오.

Real Life Communication B

1. A: 네 사고에 대해 들었어. 나는 너를 걱정했어.

   ➡ _____

2. B: 고마워. 손을 다쳤지만 심각하지 않아. 괜찮을 거야.

   ➡ _____

3. A: 다행이야. 문을 닫을 때 손을 조심해야 해.

   ➡ _____

4. B: 맞아. 그럴게.

   ➡ _____

Culture & Life

1. 2016년 이탈리아에 지진이 발생했을 때, 사람들은 Leo라는 개 덕분에 Georgia를 발견했다.

   ➡ _____

2. Leo는 지진 발생 후 16시간이 지나 이 8살짜리 소녀를 발견했다.

   ➡ _____

Culture & Life Project

1. 여기 우리의 생존 가방에 들어갈 물품이 있습니다.

   ➡ _____

2. 우리는 약간의 음식과 물을 챙겼습니다.

   ➡ _____

3. 우리는 생존하기 위해서 그것들이 필요합니다.

   ➡ _____

4. 우리는 또한 재난 발생 시 유용할 수 있는 성냥을 챙겼습니다.

   ➡ _____

5. 가방에 약품도 넣었습니다.

   ➡ _____

6. 부상당했을 때 필요할 수 있습니다.

   ➡ _____

※ 다음 영어를 우리말로 쓰시오.

01 rest _____

02 avoid _____

03 pay phone _____

04 activity _____

05 arrow _____

06 danger _____

07 say _____

08 effort _____

09 success _____

10 possible _____

11 volunteer club _____

12 plan _____

13 solution _____

14 mentee _____

15 wonderful _____

16 street _____

17 explain _____

18 confusing _____

19 refrigerator _____

20 need _____

21 forget _____

22 trash _____

23 secret _____

24 disappear _____

25 different _____

26 frame _____

27 outside _____

28 children's center _____

29 coin _____

30 solve _____

31 map _____

32 free _____

33 plastic bag _____

34 sign _____

35 come up with _____

36 during the day _____

37 on one's own _____

38 give it a try _____

39 put up _____

40 stop -ing _____

41 thanks to _____

42 have to _____

43 one day _____

※ 다음 우리말을 영어로 쓰시오.

01 딱지, 스티커 _____

02 바구니 _____

03 동전 _____

04 표지판 _____

05 혼란스러운 _____

06 비밀; 비밀의 _____

07 해결하다 _____

08 몇몇의 _____

09 버스 정류장 _____

10 아동 센터 _____

11 사라지다 _____

12 틀, 테 _____

13 무료의 _____

14 비누 _____

15 기쁜 _____

16 듣다 _____

17 지도 _____

18 다른 _____

19 멘토 _____

20 바깥의, 외부의 _____

21 비닐봉지 _____

22 쓰레기 _____

23 냉장고 _____

24 설명하다 _____

25 노력 _____

26 결심하다 _____

27 피하다 _____

28 쓰레기 _____

29 위험 _____

30 쉬다, 휴식하다 _____

31 성공 _____

32 공중전화 _____

33 해결책 _____

34 잊어버리다 _____

35 며칠 전에, 지난번 _____

36 ~을 나누어 주다 _____

37 (생각을) 찾아내다, 제시하다 _____

38 낮 동안 _____

39 ~하는 것을 멈추다 _____

40 자기 스스로 _____

41 설치하다, 세우다 _____

42 ~ 덕분에 _____

43 시도하다, 한번 해 보다 _____

※ 다음 영영풀이에 알맞은 단어를 <보기>에서 골라 쓴 후, 우리말 뜻을 쓰시오.

1 _____ : not many, but some: _____

2 _____ : difficult to understand: _____

3 _____ : to begin doing or using something: _____

4 _____ : to stop being visible: _____

5 _____ : not costing any money: _____

6 _____ : kept hidden from others: _____

7 _____ : something that is done as work for a particular purpose: _____

8 _____ : to be aware of sounds with your ears: _____

9 _____ : the correct or desired result of an attempt: _____

10 _____ : a device or room that is used to keep things cold: _____

11 _____ : a mark that is shaped like an arrow and that is used to show direction:

   _____

12 _____ : a person who is advised and helped by more experienced person:

   _____

13 _____ : a piece of paper, wood, etc., with words or pictures on it that gives information

   about something: _____

14 _____ : to stop working or doing an activity for a time and sit down or lie down

   to relax: _____

15 _____ : a drawing or plan of the earth's surface or past of it, showing countries,

   towns, rivers, etc.: _____

16 _____ : someone who teaches or gives help and advice to a less experienced and

   often younger person: _____

보기			
start	activity	mentor	few
map	confusing	sign	refrigerator
hear	free	arrow	mentee
disappear	secret	rest	success

※ 다음 우리말과 일치하도록 빈칸에 알맞은 말을 쓰시오.

Listen & Speak 1 A

Tom: Hojun and I _____ _____ _____ _____ free stickers today, but I _____ he _____ .

Sora: Really? _____ _____ _____ _____ _____ . Why are you _____ to _____ _____ stickers?

Tom: It's _____ of our _____ _____ _____ .

Sora: I see. What does this sticker _____ ?

Tom: _____ _____ _____ when we _____ _____ _____ , the world will _____ _____ _____ _____ .

Sora: That's a _____ _____ .

Listen & Speak 1 B

Mike: Jimin, what are all these things _____ _____ _____ ?

Jimin: They're for _____ _____ at the children's center. I'm _____ _____ _____ her my old books today.

Mike: _____ _____ _____ _____ _____ _____ _____ ?

Jimin: Yes. I _____ _____ when I _____ her.

Mike: _____ _____ _____ _____ _____ _____ . Oh, the box _____ _____ . _____ me _____ you.

Jimin: Thanks.

Listen & Speak 2 A

Alex: Mom, _____ _____ _____ _____ _____ . I _____ it _____ plastic bags.

Mom: That's very cute, Alex. _____ _____ _____ _____ _____ _____ I _____ a new basket?

Alex: You _____ _____ it when we were having dinner _____ _____ _____ .

Mom: _____ _____ ! I really like this basket. It has _____ _____ _____ .

Alex: _____ _____ _____ _____ _____ _____ .

Listen & Speak 2 B

Yujin: _____ _____ _____ _____ _____ _____
_____ _____ _____ _____ . Do you want to _____
_____ it?

Jack: Sure. _____ _____ _____ _____ , Yujin?

Yujin: Many children in his town _____ _____ to school and
_____ _____ _____ . So he _____ them in his house
_____ _____ .

Jack: That's a _____ _____ .

Yujin: _____ _____ _____ _____ _____ .

Yujin: 내가 인도의 특별한 소년에 대한 이야기를 읽었어. 들어 볼래?
Jack: 그래. 왜 그가 특별하다는 거니, 유진아?
Yujin: 그 소년의 마을에 있는 많은 아이들이 학교에 갈 수 없었고 일을 해야만 했어. 그래서 그가 매일 자신의 집에서 아이들을 가르쳤다는 거야.
Jack: 그거 멋진 이야기구나.
Yujin: 네가 좋아하니 나도 기뻐.

Real Life Communication

Emily: Welcome back, Brian. _____ _____ _____ _____ ?

Brian: Yes, thanks. I _____ _____ study _____ _____
_____ in the hospital, _____ it was hard.

Emily: _____ _____ _____ _____ . Why don't you _____
_____ _____ _____ ?

Brian: Did you start a _____ _____ ? That's wonderful.

Emily: Thanks. I think that _____ _____ _____ _____
_____ _____ _____ _____ _____ .

Brian: I agree. I'll _____ _____ to be a good member. _____
_____ _____ _____ .

Emily: You're _____ . I'm _____ you _____ my idea.

Emily: 돌아온 걸 환영해, Brian. 좀 나아졌니?
Brian: 응, 고마워. 나는 병원에서 혼자 공부하려고 했는데, 어려웠어.
Emily: 내가 도와줄게. 우리 스터디 모임에 함께 하는 게 어때?
Brian: 스터디 모임을 시작했니? 그거 멋지다.
Emily: 고마워. 나는 우리가 서로를 가르쳐주면 더 잘 배울 수 있을 거라고 생각해.
Brian: 맞아. 나는 좋은 구성원이 되려고 열심히 노력할게. 도와줘서 고마워.
Emily: 천만에. 내 아이디어를 좋아해 줘서 나도 기뻐.

Let's Check 1

Henry: Your bag _____ _____ . _____ _____ _____
_____ .

Sujin: Thanks. _____ _____ _____ _____ _____
_____ _____ ?

Henry: It's _____ _____ . I'll _____ your bag to the bus stop for
you.

Sujin: You're _____ _____ .

Henry: _____ _____ . I am _____ that way, _____ .

Henry: 가방이 무거워 보이네요. 제가 도와 드릴게요.
Sujin: 고마워요. 이 근처에 버스 정류장이 어디 있나요?
Henry: 저쪽에 있어요. 버스 정류장까지 가방을 들어 드릴게요.
Sujin: 정말 친절하군요.
Henry: 별말씀을요. 저도 그쪽으로 가는 길인 걸요.

※ 다음 우리말에 맞도록 대화를 영어로 쓰시오.

Listen & Speak 1 A

Tom: _____

Sora: _____

Tom: _____

Sora: _____

Tom: _____

_____

Sora: _____

Tom: 호준이와 나는 오늘 무료 스티커를 나눠주기로 계획했는데 호준이가 잊어버린 것 같아.
Sora: 그래? 그럼 내가 도와줄게. 너희는 스티커를 왜 나눠주려고 하니?
Tom: 그건 우리 자원봉사 동아리 활동의 일부야.
Sora: 그렇구나. 이 스티커는 무엇을 의미하니?
Tom: 그건 우리가 서로에게 미소 지을 때, 세상이 더 좋은 곳이 될 거라는 의미야.
Sora: 그거 멋진 아이디어구나.

Listen & Speak 1 B

Mike: _____

Jimin: _____

_____

Mike: _____

Jimin: _____

Mike: _____

Jimin: _____

Mike: 지민아, 상자에 들어 있는 이게 전부 뭐니?
Jimin: 그건 아동 센터에 있는 내 멘티를 위한 거야. 오늘 내가 보던 책들을 줄 거야.
Mike: 너는 그녀를 주말마다 가르치니?
Jimin: 응. 나는 그녀를 가르칠 때 행복해.
Mike: 넌 좋은 멘토구나. 아, 상자 무거워 보인다. 내가 도와줄게.
Jimin: 고마워.

Listen & Speak 2 A

Alex: _____

Mom: _____

Alex: _____

Mom: _____

Alex: _____

Alex: 엄마, 이거 선물이에요. 제가 비닐봉지로 만들었어요.
Mom: 그것 참 예쁘구나, Alex. 내가 새로운 바구니가 필요한 걸 어떻게 알았니?
Alex: 엄마가 지난번에 저녁 먹을 때 말씀하셨어요.
Mom: 아주 멋지구나! 이 바구니가 아주 좋은 걸. 색깔이 아주 다양하구나.
Alex: 엄마가 좋아하시니 저도 기뻐요.

Listen & Speak 2 B

Yujin: _____

Jack: _____

Yujin: _____

  _____

Jack: _____

Yujin: _____

Yujin: 내가 인도의 특별한 소년에 대한 이야기를 읽었어. 들어 볼래?

Jack: 그래. 왜 그가 특별하다는 거니, 유진아?

Yujin: 그 소년의 마을에 있는 많은 아이들이 학교에 갈 수 없었고 일을 해야만 했어. 그래서 그가 매일 자신의 집에서 아이들을 가르쳤다는 거야.

Jack: 그거 멋진 이야기구나.

Yujin: 네가 좋아하니 나도 기뻐.

Real Life Communication

Emily: _____

Brian: _____

Emily: _____

Brian: _____

Emily: _____

Brian: _____

Emily: _____

Emily: 돌아온 걸 환영해, Brian. 좀 나아졌니?

Brian: 응, 고마워. 나는 병원에서 혼자 공부하려고 했는데, 어려웠어.

Emily: 내가 도와줄게. 우리 스터디 모임에 함께 하는 게 어때?

Brian: 스터디 모임을 시작했니? 그거 멋지다.

Emily: 고마워. 나는 우리가 서로를 가르쳐주면 더 잘 배울 수 있을 거라고 생각해.

Brian: 맞아. 나는 좋은 구성원이 되려고 열심히 노력할게. 도와줘서 고마워.

Emily: 천만에. 내 아이디어를 좋아해 줘서 나도 기뻐.

Let's Check 1

Henry: _____

Sujin: _____

Henry: _____

Sujin: _____

Henry: _____

Henry: 가방이 무거워 보이네요. 제가 도와 드릴게요.

Sujin: 고마워요. 이 근처에 버스 정류장이 어디 있나요?

Henry: 저쪽에 있어요. 버스 정류장까지 가방을 들어 드릴게요.

Sujin: 정말 친절하군요.

Henry: 별말씀요. 저도 그쪽으로 가는 길인 걸요.

※ 다음 우리말과 일치하도록 빈칸에 알맞은 것을 골라 쓰시오.

1 Here _____ two stories _____ I _____ yesterday.
A. read　　　　　B. which　　　　　C. are

2 Do you _____ to _____ _____ them?
A. about　　　　　B. hear　　　　　C. want

3 _____ Someone _____ _____.
A. Love　　　　　B. You　　　　　C. Call

4 New York _____ many _____ phones _____ its _____.
A. streets　　　　　B. on　　　　　C. pay　　　　　D. had

5 _____, _____ really _____ them.
A. used　　　　　B. nobody　　　　　C. however

6 _____ day, a man came _____ _____ an idea.
A. with　　　　　B. up　　　　　C. one

7 He _____ coins _____ one _____ the phones.
A. of　　　　　B. to　　　　　C. stuck

8 He also _____ _____ a sign _____ said, "Call Someone You Love."
A. that　　　　　B. up　　　　　C. put

9 Soon, _____ people _____ _____ the phone.
A. using　　　　　B. were　　　　　C. many

10 _____ they were _____ to someone _____ they loved, they didn't stop _____.
A. smiling　　　　　B. whom　　　　　C. talking　　　　　D. when

11 _____ idea _____ a big _____.
A. success　　　　　B. became　　　　　C. his

12 _____ the day, _____ the coins _____.
A. disappeared　　　　　B. all　　　　　C. during

13 The man was very happy _____ his small idea _____ _____ to many people.
A. happiness　　　　　B. gave　　　　　C. because

1 여기 내가 어제 읽은 이야기가 두 개 있어.

2 들어볼래?

3 당신이 사랑하는 누군가에게 전화하세요.

4 뉴욕에는 길거리에 공중전화가 많이 있었다.

5 그러나 아무도 그것들을 실제로 사용하지는 않았다.

6 어느 날, 한 남자에게 좋은 아이디어가 떠올랐다.

7 그는 공중전화 하나에 동전들을 붙였다.

8 그는 또한 "당신이 사랑하는 사람에게 전화하세요."라고 쓰인 표지판을 설치했다.

9 곧, 많은 사람들이 그 전화기를 사용하고 있었다.

10 그들이 사랑하는 누군가에게 전화하고 있을 때, 그들은 미소 짓기를 멈추지 않았다.

11 그의 아이디어는 커다란 성공이었다.

12 낮 동안, 모든 동전이 사라졌다.

13 그 남자는 자신의 작은 아이디어가 많은 사람에게 행복을 가져다 주었기 때문에 매우 행복했다.

14 The Red _____ _____

    A. Man   B. Arrow

15 A _____ years _____, the maps at bus stops in Seoul _____ very _____.

    A. confusing   B. were   C. ago   D. few

16 They _____ have _____ _____.

    A. information   B. enough   C. didn't

17 People _____ to ask _____ to _____ the maps.

    A. explain   B. others   C. had

18 "_____ is this bus stop _____ the map? Does this bus _____ _____ Gwanghwamun?"

    A. to   B. go   C. on   D. where

19 Many people _____ _____ the wrong bus and _____ their time.

    A. wasted   B. took   C. often

20 _____ day, a young man _____ _____ _____ this problem.

    A. solve   B. to   C. decided   D. one

21 He _____ _____ of red _____ stickers.

    A. arrow   B. lots   C. bought

22 Every day he _____ his bicycle _____ the city and _____ the stickers _____ the bus maps.

    A. on   B. stuck   C. around   D. rode

23 Nobody _____ him _____ _____ this.

    A. do   B. to   C. asked

24 He _____ wanted to _____ _____.

    A. others   B. help   C. just

25 _____ to his effort, people _____ understand the maps _____ and _____ time.

    A. save   B. easily   C. could   D. thanks

14 빨간 화살표 청년

15 몇 년 전에, 서울의 버스 정류장의 지도는 매우 혼란스러웠다.

16 지도에는 충분한 정보가 없었다.

17 사람들은 다른 사람들에게 지도를 설명해 달라고 요청해야 했다.

18 "이 버스 정류장은 지도의 어디에 있는 건가요? 이 버스가 광화문으로 가나요?"

19 많은 사람이 종종 버스를 잘못 타서 시간을 낭비하곤 했다.

20 어느 날, 한 젊은 청년이 이 문제를 해결해 보기로 했다.

21 그는 빨간 화살표 스티커를 많이 샀다.

22 매일 그는 자전거를 타고 서울 시내를 돌아다니며 버스 지도에 스티커를 붙였다.

23 아무도 그 청년에게 이 일을 하라고 요청하지 않았다.

24 그는 단지 다른 사람들을 돕고 싶었다.

25 그의 노력 덕분에, 사람들은 지도를 쉽게 이해하고 시간을 절약할 수 있었다.

※ 다음 우리말과 일치하도록 빈칸에 알맞은 말을 쓰시오.

1 Here _____ two stories _____ I _____ yesterday.

2 Do you want _____ _____ _____ them?

3 _____ Someone _____ _____.

4 New York _____ many _____ _____ on its streets.

5 _____, _____ really _____ them.

6 One day, a man _____ _____ _____ an idea.

7 He _____ _____ _____ one of the phones.

8 He also _____ _____ a sign _____ _____, "_____ Someone You _____."

9 Soon, _____ people _____ _____ the phone.

10 _____ they _____ _____ to someone _____ _____ _____, they _____ _____ _____.

11 His idea _____ _____ _____ _____.

12 _____ _____ _____, all the coins _____.

13 The man was very happy _____ his small idea _____ _____ _____ many people.

1 여기 내가 어제 읽은 이야기가 두 개 있어.

2 들어볼래?

3 당신이 사랑하는 누군가에게 전화하세요.

4 뉴욕에는 길거리에 공중전화가 많이 있었다.

5 그러나 아무도 그것들을 실제로 사용하지는 않았다.

6 어느 날, 한 남자에게 좋은 아이디어가 떠올랐다.

7 그는 공중전화 하나에 동전들을 붙였다.

8 그는 또한 "당신이 사랑하는 사람에게 전화하세요."라고 쓰인 표지판을 설치했다.

9 곧, 많은 사람들이 그 전화기를 사용하고 있었다.

10 그들이 사랑하는 누군가에게 전화하고 있을 때, 그들은 미소 짓기를 멈추지 않았다.

11 그의 아이디어는 커다란 성공이었다.

12 낮 동안, 모든 동전이 사라졌다.

13 그 남자는 자신의 작은 아이디어가 많은 사람에게 행복을 가져다주었기 때문에 매우 행복했다.

14 The _____ _____ _____

15 _____ _____ _____ _____, the maps at bus stops in Seoul _____ very _____.

16 They _____ _____ _____ _____.

17 People had to _____ _____ _____ _____ the maps.

18 "_____ is this bus stop _____ _____ _____? Does this bus _____ _____ Gwanghwamun?"

19 Many people _____ _____ _____ _____ _____ and _____ their time.

20 One day, a young man _____ _____ _____ this problem.

21 He bought _____ _____ _____ _____ _____.

22 _____ _____ he _____ his bicycle _____ the city and _____ the stickers _____ the bus maps.

23 Nobody _____ _____ _____ _____ this.

24 He just _____ _____ _____ others.

25 _____ _____ _____ _____, people _____ _____ the maps _____ and _____.

14 빨간 화살표 청년

15 몇 년 전에, 서울의 버스 정류장의 지도는 매우 혼란스러웠다.

16 지도에는 충분한 정보가 없었다.

17 사람들은 다른 사람들에게 지도를 설명해 달라고 요청해야 했다.

18 "이 버스 정류장은 지도의 어디에 있는 건가요? 이 버스가 광화문으로 가나요?"

19 많은 사람이 종종 버스를 잘못 타서 시간을 낭비하곤 했다.

20 어느 날, 한 젊은 청년이 이 문제를 해결해 보기로 했다.

21 그는 빨간 화살표 스티커를 많이 샀다.

22 매일 그는 자전거를 타고 서울 시내를 돌아다니며 버스 지도에 스티커를 붙였다.

23 아무도 그 청년에게 이 일을 하라고 요청하지 않았다.

24 그는 단지 다른 사람들을 돕고 싶었다.

25 그의 노력 덕분에, 사람들은 지도를 쉽게 이해하고 시간을 절약할 수 있었다.

※ 다음 문장을 우리말로 쓰시오.

1 ▶ Here are two stories which I read yesterday.

➡ _____

2 ▶ Do you want to hear about them?

➡ _____

3 ▶ Call Someone You Love

➡ _____

4 ▶ New York had many pay phones on its streets.

➡ _____

5 ▶ However, nobody really used them.

➡ _____

6 ▶ One day, a man came up with an idea.

➡ _____

7 ▶ He stuck coins to one of the phones.

➡ _____

8 ▶ He also put up a sign that said, "Call Someone You Love."

➡ _____

9 ▶ Soon, many people were using the phone.

➡ _____

10 ▶ When they were talking to someone whom they loved, they didn't stop smiling.

➡ _____

11 ▶ His idea became a big success.

➡ _____

12 ▶ During the day, all the coins disappeared.

➡ _____

13 ▶ The man was very happy because his small idea gave happiness to many people.

➡ _____

14 The Red Arrow Man

➡ _____

15 A few years ago, the maps at bus stops in Seoul were very confusing.

➡ _____

16 They didn't have enough information.

➡ _____

17 People had to ask others to explain the maps.

➡ _____

18 "Where is this bus stop on the map? Does this bus go to Gwanghwamun?"

➡ _____

19 Many people often took the wrong bus and wasted their time.

➡ _____

20 One day, a young man decided to solve this problem.

➡ _____

21 He bought lots of red arrow stickers.

➡ _____

22 Every day he rode his bicycle around the city and stuck the stickers on the bus maps.

➡ _____

23 Nobody asked him to do this.

➡ _____

24 He just wanted to help others.

➡ _____

25 Thanks to his effort, people could understand the maps easily and save time.

➡ _____

※ 다음 괄호 안의 단어들을 우리말에 맞도록 바르게 배열하시오.

1 (are / here / stories / two / I / which / yesterday. / read)

➡ _____

2 (you / do / to / want / them? / about / hear)

➡ _____

3 (You / Call / Love / Someone)

➡ _____

4 (York / New / many / had / phones / pay / streets. / its / on)

➡ _____

5 (nobody / however, / used / them. / really)

➡ _____

6 (day, / one / man / a / up / came / idea. / with / an)

➡ _____

7 (stuck / he / to / coins / of / one / phones. / the)

➡ _____

8 (also / he / up / put / sign / a / said, / that / "Call / You / Love." / Someone)

➡ _____

9 (many / soon, / people / using / were / phone. / the)

➡ _____

10 (were / they / when / talking / someone / to / whom / loved, / they / smiling. / stop / didn't / they)

➡ _____

11 (idea / his / became / success. / big / a)

➡ _____

12 (day, / the / during / the / all / disappeared. / coins)

➡ _____

13 (man / the / very / was / happy / because / small / his / idea / happiness / gave / people. / many / to)

➡ _____
_____

1 여기 내가 어제 읽은 이야기가 두 개 있어.

2 들어볼래?

3 당신이 사랑하는 누군가에게 전화하세요.

4 뉴욕에는 길거리에 공중전화가 많이 있었다.

5 그러나 아무도 그것들을 실제로 사용하지는 않았다.

6 어느 날, 한 남자에게 좋은 아이디어가 떠올랐다.

7 그는 공중전화 하나에 동전들을 붙였다.

8 그는 또한 "당신이 사랑하는 사람에게 전화하세요."라고 쓰인 표지판을 설치했다.

9 곧, 많은 사람들이 그 전화기를 사용하고 있었다.

10 그들이 사랑하는 누군가에게 전화하고 있을 때, 그들은 미소 짓기를 멈추지 않았다.

11 그의 아이디어는 커다란 성공이었다.

12 낮 동안, 모든 동전이 사라졌다.

13 그 남자는 자신의 작은 아이디어가 많은 사람에게 행복을 가져다 주었기 때문에 매우 행복했다.

14 (Arrow / The / Man / Red)

➡ _____

16 (few / ago, / a / years / the / maps / bus / at / stops / Seoul / in / confusing. / very / was)

➡ _____

15 (didn't / they / have / information. / enough)

➡ _____

17 (had / people / ask / to / others / explain / to / maps. / the)

➡ _____

18 (is / "where / bus / this / stop / the / on / map? // this / go / does / bus / Gwanghwamun?" / to)

➡ _____

19 (people / many / took / often / wrong / the / bus / and / time / their / wasted)

➡ _____

20 (day, / one / young / a / man / to / decided / problem. / this / solve)

➡ _____

21 (bought / he / of / lots / red / stickers. / arrow)

➡ _____

22 (day / every / rode / he / bicycle / his / the / around / city / and / stuck / stickers / on / the / maps. / bus / the)

➡ _____

23 (asked / to / nobody / this. / do / him)

➡ _____

24 (just / wanted / he / others. / help / to)

➡ _____

25 (to / thanks / effort, / his / could / people / understand / maps / the / easily / time. / save / and)

➡ _____

14 빨간 화살표 청년

15 몇 년 전에, 서울의 버스 정류장의 지도는 매우 혼란스러웠다.

16 지도에는 충분한 정보가 없었다.

17 사람들은 다른 사람들에게 지도를 설명해 달라고 요청해야 했다.

18 "이 버스 정류장은 지도의 어디에 있는 건가요? 이 버스가 광화문으로 가나요?"

19 많은 사람이 종종 버스를 잘못 타서 시간을 낭비하곤 했다.

20 어느 날, 한 젊은 청년이 이 문제를 해결해 보기로 했다.

21 그는 빨간 화살표 스티커를 많이 샀다.

22 매일 그는 자전거를 타고 서울 시내를 돌아다니며 버스 지도에 스티커를 붙였다.

23 아무도 그 청년에게 이 일을 하라고 요청하지 않았다.

24 그는 단지 다른 사람들을 돕고 싶었다.

25 그의 노력 덕분에, 사람들은 지도를 쉽게 이해하고 시간을 절약할 수 있었다.

※ 다음 우리말을 영어로 쓰시오.

1 여기 내가 어제 읽은 이야기가 두 개 있어.

➡ _____

2 들어볼래?

➡ _____

3 당신이 사랑하는 누군가에게 전화하세요.

➡ _____

4 뉴욕에는 길거리에 공중전화가 많이 있었다.

➡ _____

5 그러나 아무도 그것들을 실제로 사용하지는 않았다.

➡ _____

6 어느 날, 한 남자에게 좋은 아이디어가 떠올랐다.

➡ _____

7 그는 공중전화 하나에 동전들을 붙였다.

➡ _____

8 그는 또한 "당신이 사랑하는 사람에게 전화하세요."라고 쓰인 표지판을 설치했다.

➡ _____

9 곧, 많은 사람들이 그 전화기를 사용하고 있었다.

➡ _____

10 그들이 사랑하는 누군가에게 전화하고 있을 때, 그들은 미소 짓기를 멈추지 않았다.

➡ _____

11 그의 아이디어는 커다란 성공이었다.

➡ _____

12 낮 동안, 모든 동전이 사라졌다.

➡ _____

13 그 남자는 자신의 작은 아이디어가 많은 사람에게 행복을 가져다 주었기 때문에 매우 행복했다.

➡ _____

14 빨간 화살표 청년

➡ _____

15 몇 년 전, 서울의 버스 정류장의 지도는 매우 혼란스러웠다.

➡ _____

16 지도에는 충분한 정보가 없었다.

➡ _____

17 사람들은 다른 사람들에게 지도를 설명해 달라고 요청해야 했다.

➡ _____

18 "이 버스 정류장은 지도의 어디에 있는 건가요? 이 버스가 광화문으로 가나요?"

➡ _____

19 많은 사람이 종종 버스를 잘못 타서 시간을 낭비하곤 했다.

➡ _____

20 어느 날, 한 젊은 청년이 이 문제를 해결해 보기로 했다.

➡ _____

21 그는 빨간 화살표 스티커를 많이 샀다.

➡ _____

22 매일 그는 자전거를 타고 서울 시내를 돌아다니며 버스 지도에 스티커를 붙였다.

➡ _____

23 아무도 그 청년에게 이 일을 하라고 요청하지 않았다.

➡ _____

24 그는 단지 다른 사람들을 돕고 싶었다.

➡ _____

25 그의 노력 덕분에, 사람들은 지도를 쉽게 이해하고 시간을 절약할 수 있었다.

➡ _____

※ 다음 우리말과 일치하도록 빈칸에 알맞은 말을 쓰시오.

Real Life Communication B

1. A: I'm _____ _____ _____ science. _____ can I do?
2. B: _____ _____ _____ you. _____ _____ you start

   with easier books?
3. A: Okay, I'll _____ _____ _____ _____. Thanks for the

   tip.
4. B: No _____. I'm _____ you like it.

1. A: 나는 과학을 잘 못해. 어떻게 해야 할까?
2. B: 내가 도와줄게. 좀 더 쉬운 책으로 시작하는 게 어때?
3. A: 응, 한번 시도해 볼게. 조언 고마워.
4. B: 괜찮아. 네가 좋아하니 기뻐.

Let's Write

1. _____ a Mentor!
2. My name is Semi and I'm _____ _____ _____ _____.
3. I _____ _____ _____ my mentee _____ her homework.
4. I _____ _____ my mentee _____ _____.
5. I'll _____ my mentee _____ _____ on time.
6. I _____ a good mentor _____ _____ a good friend.
7. So I want to become a good friend _____ _____ _____

   _____ _____.

1. 멘토가 되세요!
2. 제 이름은 세미이고 저는 2학년입니다.
3. 저는 제 멘티의 숙제를 돕고 싶습니다.
4. 저는 방과 후에 제 멘티를 만날 수 있습니다.
5. 저는 제 멘티에게 시간을 지키라고 요청할 것입니다.
6. 저는 좋은 멘토는 좋은 친구가 될 수 있다고 생각합니다.
7. 그래서 저는 제 멘티가 믿을 수 있는 좋은 친구가 되고 싶습니다.

Culture & Life

1. Do you _____ toys _____ the bars of soap?
2. Children in South Africa _____ _____ _____ more often

   _____ _____ the toys.
3. _____ your hands _____ _____ many health problems.
4. _____ _____ this idea, _____ children are _____ _____.

1. 비누 안에 들어 있는 장난감이 보이나요?
2. 남아프리카의 어린이들은 장난감을 갖기 위해 더 자주 손을 씻습니다.
3. 손을 씻는 것은 많은 건강 문제를 막을 수 있습니다.
4. 이 아이디어 덕분에, 아픈 어린이들이 줄어들고 있습니다.

※ 다음 우리말을 영어로 쓰시오.

Real Life Communication B

1. A: 나는 과학을 잘 못해. 어떻게 해야 할까?
➡ _____

2. B: 내가 도와줄게. 좀 더 쉬운 책으로 시작하는 게 어때?
➡ _____

3. A: 응, 한번 시도해 볼게. 조언 고마워.
➡ _____

4. B: 괜찮아. 네가 좋아하니 기뻐.
➡ _____

Let's Write

1. 멘토가 되세요!
➡ _____

2. 제 이름은 세미이고 저는 2학년입니다.
➡ _____

3. 저는 제 멘티의 숙제를 돕고 싶습니다.
➡ _____

4. 저는 방과 후에 제 멘티를 만날 수 있습니다.
➡ _____

5. 저는 제 멘티에게 시간을 지키라고 요청할 것입니다.
➡ _____

6. 저는 좋은 멘토는 좋은 친구가 될 수 있다고 생각합니다.
➡ _____

7. 그래서 저는 제 멘티가 믿을 수 있는 좋은 친구가 되고 싶습니다.
➡ _____

Culture & Life

1. 비누 안에 들어 있는 장난감이 보이나요?
➡ _____

2. 남아프리카의 어린이들은 장난감을 갖기 위해 더 자주 손을 씻습니다.
➡ _____

3. 손을 씻는 것은 많은 건강 문제를 막을 수 있습니다.
➡ _____

4. 이 아이디어 덕분에, 아픈 어린이들이 줄어들고 있습니다.
➡ _____

※ 다음 영어를 우리말로 쓰시오.

01	strange	_____
02	pointed	_____
03	sweat	_____
04	bug	_____
05	scratch	_____
06	thirsty	_____
07	miss	_____
08	protein	_____
09	empty	_____
10	sleeve	_____
11	female	_____
12	prevent	_____
13	sense	_____
14	food poisoning	_____
15	mosquito	_____
16	stomach	_____
17	blood	_____
18	happen	_____
19	sweaty	_____
20	itch	_____
21	lay	_____

22	worried	_____
23	sunscreen	_____
24	male	_____
25	advice	_____
26	million	_____
27	tiny	_____
28	pack	_____
29	buzz	_____
30	reduce	_____
31	itchy	_____
32	bump	_____
33	trash	_____
34	useful	_____
35	at that moment	_____
36	stay away from	_____
37	feed on	_____
38	suffer from	_____
39	keep ~ in mind	_____
40	lose (~) by	_____
41	go for a walk	_____
42	for a while	_____
43	I'd love to	_____

※ 다음 우리말을 영어로 쓰시오.

01 걱정[근심]하는

02 자외선 차단제

03 벌레

04 줄이다

05 쓰레기

06 100만, 다수

07 식중독

08 암컷의, 여성의

09 땀에 젖은

10 가렵다

11 수컷의, 남성의

12 (알을) 낳다

13 땀; 땀을 흘리다

14 햇볕에 탐, 그을림

15 날카로운

16 놓치다, 빼먹다

17 긁다

18 뾰족한

19 이상한

20 단백질

21 (옷의) 소매, 소맷자락

22 피

23 비우다

24 모기

25 위, 복부, 배

26 목마른

27 혹; 타박상

28 유용한

29 예방하다, 방지하다

30 아주 작은

31 충고, 조언

32 (가방을) 싸다

33 윙윙거리다

34 가려운

35 당분간

36 ~으로 고통받다

37 더 잘하다

38 ~을 먹고살다

39 ~을 명심하다

40 산책 가다

41 그때에

42 ~에서 떨어져 있다

43 ~을 …로 데려가다

※ 다음 영영풀이에 알맞은 단어를 <보기>에서 골라 쓴 후, 우리말 뜻을 쓰시오.

1 _____ : any small insect: _____

2 _____ : a wound made by biting: _____

3 _____ : to stop something from happening or existing: _____

4 _____ : to fail to do, take, make, or have something: _____

5 _____ : an area of skin that is raised because it was hit, bitten, etc.: _____

6 _____ : to rub your skin with something sharp: _____

7 _____ : to produce an egg outside the body: _____

8 _____ : a substance found in foods such as meat, milk, eggs, and beans:

   _____

9 _____ : to make a low, continuous sound of a flying insect: _____

10 _____ : to take place especially without being planned: _____

11 _____ : to make something smaller in size, amount, number, etc.: _____

12 _____ : to have an unpleasant feeling on your skin that makes you want to

   scratch: _____

13 _____ : to put something into a bag so that you can take it with you: _____

14 _____ : a condition in which your skin becomes sore and red from too much

   sunshine: _____

15 _____ : a small flying insect that bites the skin of people and animals to suck

   their blood: _____

16 _____ : to become aware of something even though you can't see it, hear it, etc.:

   _____

보기			
pack	mosquito	prevent	protein
bump	buzz	scratch	bite
sense	itch	happen	reduce
miss	lay	sunburn	bug

※ 다음 우리말과 일치하도록 빈칸에 알맞은 말을 쓰시오.

Listen & Speak 1-A (1)

Brian: You _____ _____, Jimin. What's _____?

Jimin: I'm _____ because _____ _____ _____ _____.

Brian: _____ _____ _____ _____ _____ . _____ _____ _____ _____ her to an animal doctor?

Jimin: Okay, _____ _____.

Brian: 너 걱정 있어 보여, 지민아. 무슨 일이니?
Jimin: 내 고양이가 아파서 걱정돼.
Brian: 그것 참 안됐구나. 고양이를 수의사에게 데려가는 것이 어때?
Jimin: 응, 그럴게.

Listen & Speak 1-A (2)

Jane: _____ was the soccer game with Minsu's _____, Alex?

Alex: We _____ _____ three goals.

Jane: _____ _____ _____ _____ _____. I hope _____ _____ _____ _____.

Alex: I _____ _____, _____.

Jane: 민수네 반과의 축구 시합은 어땠니, Alex?
Alex: 우리가 세 골 차로 졌어.
Jane: 그것 참 안됐구나. 다음번엔 네가 더 잘하길 바라.
Alex: 나도 그러길 바라.

Listen & Speak 1-B

Tom: _____ _____ _____ this weekend, Yujin.

Yujin: I'd _____ _____, but _____ _____.

Tom: _____ _____?

Yujin: I have an eye problem. The doctor told me _____ _____ _____ _____.

Tom: I'm _____ _____ _____ _____. Maybe we _____ _____ _____ _____.

Yujin: I really _____ _____.

Tom: 이번 주말에 수영하러 가자, 유진아.
Yujin: 나도 그러고 싶지만, 그럴 수 없어.
Tom: 왜 그럴 수 없어?
Yujin: 내 눈에 문제가 있어. 의사 선생님이 내게 당분간 수영을 중단하라고 말씀하셨어.
Tom: 그것 참 안됐구나. 아마 우리는 다음 주말에나 갈 수 있겠구나.
Yujin: 나는 정말 그러길 바라.

Listen & Speak 2-A (1)

Emma: Tim, _____ _____ your face! You got _____.

Tim: Yes, it _____ _____ _____. I _____ _____ at the beach _____ _____.

Emma: Oh dear! _____ _____ you _____ _____ next time.

Emma: Tim, 네 얼굴을 보렴! 햇볕에 심하게 탔구나.
Tim: 네, 매우 아파요. 저는 선크림을 바르지 않고 해변으로 수영하러 갔어요.
Emma: 이런 참! 다음번엔 꼭 선크림을 바르도록 해.

Listen & Speak 2-A (2)

Mom: Hojun, do you want to _____ _____ with me?

Hojun: Sorry, Mom. I'm _____ _____ _____ baseball with Alex this afternoon.

Mom: Okay. No problem. _____ _____ _____ _____

_____ _____ _____. It's _____ _____ _____

_____ _____ this afternoon

Hojun: Okay, _____ _____.

Listen & Speak 2-B

Sujin: Dad, do we have _____ bug spray?

Dad: Yes, it's _____ _____ _____. Why?

Sujin: There are a lot of _____ _____ _____ the trash.

Dad: Oh no! What did you _____ in the _____?

Sujin: Some _____ _____.

Dad: Fruit flies love sweet things. _____ _____ _____

_____ _____ _____ _____

_____ _____.

Sujin: I'll _____ that _____ _____. I think we _____

_____ _____ _____ _____ _____ more often.

Dad: That's a _____ _____.

Real Life Communication

Ms. Wheeler: Junsu, _____ _____ to your face?

Junsu: I got _____ _____ _____ _____ _____ _____.

Ms. Wheeler: _____ _____ _____ _____ _____ _____.

_____ did it happen?

Junsu: It happened when I _____ _____ last weekend.

Ms. Wheeler: Oh dear. _____ _____ _____ _____!

Junsu: I know, but they're really _____.

Ms. Wheeler: Clean them _____ cool water. That'll help. Also,

_____ _____ _____ _____ _____ _____ _____

_____ when you _____ _____.

Junsu: Okay, _____ _____.

Mom: 호준아, 나랑 장보러 갈래?
Hojun: 미안해요, 엄마. 저는 오후에 Alex와 야구할 거예요.
Mom: 알았어. 괜찮다. 모자를 꼭 쓰도록 해. 오후에 매우 더워질 거야.
Hojun: 네, 그럴게요.

Sujin: 아빠, 우리 벌레 퇴치 스프레이가 있나요?
Dad: 응, 그것은 싱크대 밑에 있단다. 왜?
Sujin: 쓰레기 주변에 많은 초파리가 있어요.
Dad: 오 안돼! 쓰레기에 무엇을 넣었니?
Sujin: 약간의 과일 쓰레기요.
Dad: 초파리는 달콤한 것들을 좋아해. 쓰레기통에 과일 쓰레기를 버리지 않도록 하렴.
Sujin: 명심할게요. 제 생각에 우리는 또한 쓰레기통을 더 자주 비워야 할 것 같아요.
Dad: 좋은 생각이구나.

Ms. Wheeler: 준수야, 얼굴이 왜 그러니?
Junsu: 모기에 많이 물렸어요.
Ms. Wheeler: 그것 참 안됐구나. 어쩌다 그랬니?
Junsu: 지난 주말에 캠핑 갔다가 그랬어요.
Ms. Wheeler: 이런 참. 물린 곳을 긁지 마라.
Junsu: 알아요, 하지만 정말 가려워요.
Ms. Wheeler: 물린 곳을 찬물로 닦으렴. 도움이 될 거야. 또한 캠핑 갈 때에는 긴 소매 옷을 입도록 해.
Junsu: 네, 감사합니다.

※ 다음 우리말에 맞도록 대화를 영어로 쓰시오.

Listen & Speak 1-A (1)

Brian: _____

Jimin: _____

Brian: _____

Jimin: _____

Listen & Speak 1-A (2)

Jane: _____

Alex: _____

Jane: _____

Alex: _____

Listen & Speak 1-B

Tom: _____

Yujin: _____

Tom: _____

Yujin: _____

Tom: _____

Yujin: _____

Listen & Speak 2-A (1)

Emma: _____

Tim: _____

Emma: _____

해석

Brian: 너 걱정 있어 보여, 지민아. 무슨 일이니?
Jimin: 내 고양이가 아파서 걱정돼.
Brian: 그것 참 안됐구나. 고양이를 수의사에게 데려가는 것이 어때?
Jimin: 응, 그럴게.

Jane: 민수네 반과의 축구 시합은 어땠니, Alex?
Alex: 우리가 세 골 차로 졌어.
Jane: 그것 참 안됐구나. 다음번엔 네가 더 잘하길 바라.
Alex: 나도 그러길 바라.

Tom: 이번 주말에 수영하러 가자, 유진아.
Yujin: 나도 그러고 싶지만, 그럴 수 없어.
Tom: 왜 그럴 수 없어?
Yujin: 내 눈에 문제가 있어. 의사 선생님이 내게 당분간 수영을 중단하라고 말씀하셨어.
Tom: 그것 참 안됐구나. 아마 우리는 다음 주말에나 갈 수 있겠구나.
Yujin: 나는 정말 그러길 바라.

Emma: Tim, 네 얼굴을 보렴! 햇볕에 심하게 탔구나.
Tim: 네, 매우 아파요. 저는 선크림을 바르지 않고 해변으로 수영하러 갔어요.
Emma: 이런 참! 다음번엔 꼭 선크림을 바르도록 해.

Listen & Speak 2-A (2)

Mom: _____

Hojun: _____

Mom: _____

_____

Hojun: _____

Mom: 호준아, 나랑 장보러 갈래?
Hojun: 미안해요, 엄마. 저는 오후에 Alex와 야구할 거예요.
Mom: 알았어. 괜찮다. 모자를 꼭 쓰도록 해. 오후에 매우 더워질 거야.
Hojun: 네, 그럴게요.

Listen & Speak 2-B

Sujin: _____

Dad: _____

Sujin: _____

Dad: _____

Sujin: _____

Dad: _____

_____

Sujin: _____

Dad: _____

Sujin: 아빠, 우리 벌레 퇴치 스프레이가 있나요?
Dad: 응, 그것은 싱크대 밑에 있단다. 왜?
Sujin: 쓰레기 주변에 많은 초파리가 있어요.
Dad: 오 안돼! 쓰레기에 무엇을 넣었니?
Sujin: 약간의 과일 쓰레기요.
Dad: 초파리는 달콤한 것들을 좋아해. 쓰레기통에 과일 쓰레기를 버리지 않도록 하렴.
Sujin: 명심할게요. 제 생각에 우리는 또한 쓰레기통을 더 자주 비워야 할 것 같아요.
Dad: 좋은 생각이구나.

Real Life Communication

Ms. Wheeler: _____

Junsu: _____

Ms. Wheeler: _____

Junsu: _____

Ms. Wheeler: _____

Junsu: _____

Ms. Wheeler: _____

_____

Junsu: _____

Ms. Wheeler: 준수야, 얼굴이 왜 그러니?
Junsu: 모기에 많이 물렸어요.
Ms. Wheeler: 그것 참 안됐구나. 어쩌다 그랬니?
Junsu: 지난 주말에 캠핑 갔다가 그랬어요.
Ms. Wheeler: 이런 참. 물린 곳을 긁지 마라.
Junsu: 알아요, 하지만 정말 가려워요.
Ms. Wheeler: 물린 곳을 찬물로 닦으렴. 도움이 될 거야. 또한 캠핑 갈 때에는 긴 소매 옷을 입도록 해.
Junsu: 네, 감사합니다.

※ 다음 우리말과 일치하도록 빈칸에 알맞은 것을 골라 쓰시오.

1 _____ was a _____ summer _____ .
A. hot   B. it   C. evening

2 Seojun went _____ a _____ _____ the park.
A. for   B. in   C. walk

3 _____ , he was _____ .
A. sweating   B. soon

4 Seojun: I'm _____ . I want _____ _____ to _____ .
A. something   B. thirsty   C. cold   D. drink

5 _____ that moment, _____ _____ flew at him and _____ his arm.
A. bit   B. tiny   C. something   D. at

6 Mrs. Mosquito: Hey, _____ me _____ you _____ .
A. catch   B. can   C. if

7 Seojun: Who are you? What _____ _____ _____ to me?
A. done   B. have   C. you

8 Mrs. Mosquito: I'm a mosquito. I've _____ _____ my dinner.
A. finished   B. just

9 Seojun: Where are you _____ ? _____ did you _____ me?
A. find   B. from   C. how

10 Mrs. Mosquito: I'm _____ a _____ river.
A. nearby   B. from

11 I was _____ _____ some blood _____ drink there.
A. looking   B. to   C. for

12 Then I smelled _____ _____ and _____ you here.
A. found   B. sweaty   C. something

13 Seojun: How _____ you _____ me _____ the river?
A. smell   B. from   C. could

14 Mrs. Mosquito: Mosquitoes can _____ and _____ very well.
A. smell   B. heat   C. sense

15 That's _____ we have _____ _____ millions of years.
A. for   B. why   C. survived

16 Seojun: Do _____ mosquitoes drink blood _____ ?
A. like   B. all   C. you

17 Mrs. Mosquito: No. Only _____ mosquitoes like me _____ .
A. female   B. blood   C. drink

18 Male mosquitoes only _____ _____ fruit and _____ juice.
A. on   B. feed   C. plant

---

1 무더운 여름날의 저녁이었습니다.

2 서준이는 공원에 산책을 갔습니다.

3 곧, 그는 땀을 흘리고 있었습니다.

4 서준: 목말라. 뭔가 시원한 것을 마시고 싶어.

5 그때에, 뭔가 조그마한 것이 그에게로 날아와서 그의 팔을 물었습니다.

6 모기: 이봐, 나를 잡을 수 있으면 잡아 봐.

7 서준: 너는 누구니? 나한테 무슨 짓을 한 거지?

8 모기: 나는 모기야. 난 방금 저녁 식사를 마쳤어.

9 서준: 너는 어디에서 왔니? 너는 어떻게 나를 찾은 거야?

10 모기: 나는 근처 강에서 왔어.

11 나는 그곳에서 마실 피를 찾던 중이었지.

12 그러다가 땀 냄새를 맡았고, 여기서 너를 발견했어.

13 서준: 너는 어떻게 강에서부터 내 냄새를 맡을 수 있었지?

14 모기: 모기들은 열과 냄새를 매우 잘 감지해.

15 그래서 우리가 수백만 년 동안 살아남은 거야.

16 서준: 모든 모기가 너처럼 피를 마셔?

17 모기: 아니. 오직 나와 같은 암컷 모기만이 피를 마셔.

18 수컷 모기들은 과일과 식물의 즙만을 먹고 살아.

19 Seojun: That's _____. So _____ do you _____ blood?

    A. why   B. interesting   C. drink

20 Mrs. Mosquito: I need the _____ in blood _____ _____ my eggs.

    A. to   B. protein   C. lay

21 Seojun: _____ do you drink blood? Do you have _____ _____?

    A. teeth   B. how   C. sharp

22 Mrs. Mosquito: No, I _____ have _____.

    A. teeth   B. don't

23 But I have a _____ and _____ _____.

    A. mouth   B. pointed   C. long

24 _____ I can drink _____ blood _____.

    A. your   B. so   C. easily

25 Seojun: After you _____ me, I got a _____. It _____.

    A. bit   B. itches   C. bump

26 Mrs. Mosquito: I'm _____ _____ _____ that.

    A. hear   B. to   C. sorry

27 _____ _____ you _____ scratch it.

    A. sure   B. make   C. don't

28 Also, _____ it _____ alcohol _____.

    A. wipes   B. clean   C. with

29 Seojun: Alcohol wipes? I've _____ _____ that _____.

    A. tried   B. never   C. before

30 Mrs. Mosquito: It will _____ the _____.

    A. itchiness   B. reduce

31 Seojun: Okay, I'll _____ that at _____. Thanks.

    A. home   B. try

32 Mrs. Mosquito: I _____ _____ go. See you _____.

    A. have   B. soon   C. to

33 Seojun: _____ are you _____?

    A. going   B. where

34 Mrs. Mosquito: I'm _____ _____ _____ the river.

    A. back   B. going   C. to

35 Seojun: Wait! A _____ of people _____ _____ from your bites.

    A. suffered   B. lot   C. have

36 _____ _____ we _____ them?

    A. can   B. how   C. prevent

37 Mrs. Mosquito: Stay _____ and _____ long _____.

    A. wear   B. sleeves   C. cool

38 Seojun: Thanks. I'll _____ your advice _____ _____.

    A. mind   B. keep   C. in

19 서준: 그거 재미있네. 그럼 너는 왜 피를 마시는 거야?

20 모기: 알을 낳으려면 핏속의 단백질이 필요해.

21 서준: 너는 피를 어떻게 마시는 거야? 날카로운 이빨이 있니?

22 모기: 아니, 나는 이빨이 없어.

23 하지만 길고 뾰족한 입이 있지.

24 그래서 나는 너의 피를 쉽게 마실 수 있는 거야.

25 서준: 네가 나를 문 다음, 부어오른 자국이 생겼어. 가려워.

26 모기: 그 말을 들으니 미안하군.

27 그것을 긁지 않도록 해.

28 또한, 그것을 알코올 솜으로 닦아.

29 서준: 알코올 솜? 나는 전에 그것을 한 번도 해 보지 않았어.

30 모기: 그것은 가려움을 줄여 줄 거야.

31 서준: 알았어, 집에서 해 볼게. 고마워.

32 모기: 나는 이제 가야겠어. 다음에 보자.

33 서준: 너는 어디로 가는데?

34 모기: 강으로 돌아가려고.

35 서준: 기다려! 많은 사람이 모기에 물려서 괴로워하고 있어.

36 어떻게 하면 모기에 물리는 것을 막을 수 있지?

37 모기: 시원하게 지내고 소매가 긴 옷을 입어.

38 서준: 고마워. 너의 충고를 명심할게.

※ 다음 우리말과 일치하도록 빈칸에 알맞은 말을 쓰시오.

1 _____ was a _____ _____ _____.

2 Seojun _____ _____ _____ _____ in the park.

3 Soon, he _____ _____.

4 Seojun: I'm _____. I want _____ _____ _____ _____.

5 At that moment, _____ _____ flew _____ him and _____ his arm.

6 Mrs. Mosquito: Hey, catch me _____ _____ _____.

7 Seojun: Who are you? What _____ _____ _____ to me?

8 Mrs. Mosquito: I'm a mosquito. I've _____ _____ my dinner.

9 Seojun: _____ are you _____? _____ did you _____ me?

10 Mrs. Mosquito: I'm _____ a _____ _____.

11 I _____ _____ _____ some blood _____ _____ there.

12 Then I _____ _____ _____ and found you here.

13 Seojun: _____ could you _____ _____ from the river?

14 Mrs. Mosquito: Mosquitoes can _____ _____ and _____ very well.

15 That's _____ we _____ _____ for _____ of years.

16 Seojun: Do all mosquitoes drink blood _____ _____?

17 Mrs. Mosquito: No. Only _____ mosquitoes _____ _____ _____ _____.

18 Male mosquitoes only _____ _____ fruit and plant juice.

---

1 무더운 여름날의 저녁이었습니다.

2 서준이는 공원에 산책을 갔습니다.

3 곧, 그는 땀을 흘리고 있었습니다.

4 서준: 목말라. 뭔가 시원한 것을 마시고 싶어.

5 그때에, 뭔가 조그마한 것이 그에게로 날아와서 그의 팔을 물었습니다.

6 모기: 이봐, 나를 잡을 수 있으면 잡아 봐.

7 서준: 너는 누구니? 나한테 무슨 짓을 한 거지?

8 모기: 나는 모기야. 난 방금 저녁 식사를 마쳤어.

9 서준: 너는 어디에서 왔니? 너는 어떻게 나를 찾은 거야?

10 모기: 나는 근처 강에서 왔어.

11 나는 그곳에서 마실 피를 찾던 중이었지.

12 그러다가 땀 냄새를 맡았고, 여기서 너를 발견했어.

13 서준: 너는 어떻게 강에서부터 내 냄새를 맡을 수 있었지?

14 모기: 모기들은 열과 냄새를 매우 잘 감지해.

15 그래서 우리가 수백만 년 동안 살아남은 거야.

16 서준: 모든 모기가 너처럼 피를 마셔?

17 모기: 아니. 오직 나와 같은 암컷 모기만이 피를 마셔.

18 수컷 모기들은 과일과 식물의 즙만을 먹고 살아.

19 Seojun: That's _____. So why do you drink _____?

20 Mrs. Mosquito: I need _____ _____ in blood _____ _____ my eggs.

21 Seojun: _____ do you _____ _____? Do you have _____ _____?

22 Mrs. Mosquito: No, I don't have _____.

23 But I have _____ _____ and _____ _____.

24 _____ I _____ _____ your blood _____.

25 Seojun: _____ you _____ me, I _____ _____ _____. It _____.

26 Mrs. Mosquito: I'm _____ _____ _____.

27 _____ _____ you don't _____ _____.

28 Also, _____ _____ _____ alcohol wipes.

29 Seojun: Alcohol wipes? I've _____ _____ _____ _____.

30 Mrs. Mosquito: It will _____ _____ _____.

31 Seojun: Okay, I'll _____ _____ at home. Thanks.

32 Mrs. Mosquito: I _____ _____ _____. See you soon.

33 Seojun: _____ are you _____?

34 Mrs. Mosquito: I'm _____ _____ to the river.

35 Seojun: Wait! _____ _____ _____ people _____ _____ from your bites.

36 _____ _____ we _____ _____ _____?

37 Mrs. Mosquito: Stay _____ and _____ long _____.

38 Seojun: Thanks. I'll _____ your advice _____ _____.

20 모기: 알을 낳으려면 핏속의 단백질이 필요해.

21 서준: 너는 피를 어떻게 마시는 거야? 날카로운 이빨이 있니?

22 모기: 아니, 나는 이빨이 없어.

23 하지만 길고 뾰족한 입이 있지.

24 그래서 나는 너의 피를 쉽게 마실 수 있는 거야.

25 서준: 네가 나를 문 다음, 부어오른 자국이 생겼어. 가려워.

26 모기: 그 말을 들으니 미안하군.

27 그것을 긁지 않도록 해.

28 또한, 그것을 알코올 솜으로 닦아.

29 서준: 알코올 솜? 나는 전에 그것을 한 번도 해 보지 않았어.

30 모기: 그것은 가려움을 줄여 줄 거야.

31 서준: 알았어. 집에서 해 볼게. 고마워.

32 모기: 나는 이제 가야겠어. 다음에 보자.

33 서준: 너는 어디로 가는데?

34 모기: 강으로 돌아가려고.

35 서준: 기다려! 많은 사람이 모기에 물려서 괴로워하고 있어.

36 어떻게 하면 모기에 물리는 것을 막을 수 있지?

37 모기: 시원하게 지내고 소매가 긴 옷을 입어.

38 서준: 고마워. 너의 충고를 명심할게.

※ 다음 문장을 우리말로 쓰시오.

1 It was a hot summer evening.
➡ _____

2 Seojun went for a walk in the park.
➡ _____

3 Soon, he was sweating.
➡ _____

4 Seojun: I'm thirsty. I want something cold to drink.
➡ _____

5 At that moment, something tiny flew at him and bit his arm.
➡ _____

6 Mrs. Mosquito: Hey, catch me if you can.
➡ _____

7 Seojun: Who are you? What have you done to me?
➡ _____

8 Mrs. Mosquito: I'm a mosquito. I've just finished my dinner.
➡ _____

9 Seojun: Where are you from? How did you find me?
➡ _____

10 Mrs. Mosquito: I'm from a nearby river.
➡ _____

11 I was looking for some blood to drink there.
➡ _____

12 Then I smelled something sweaty and found you here.
➡ _____

13 Seojun: How could you smell me from the river?
➡ _____

14 Mrs. Mosquito: Mosquitoes can sense heat and smell very well.
➡ _____

15 That's why we have survived for millions of years.
➡ _____

16 Seojun: Do all mosquitoes drink blood like you?
➡ _____

17 Mrs. Mosquito: No. Only female mosquitoes like me drink blood.
➡ _____

18 Male mosquitoes only feed on fruit and plant juice.
➡ _____

19 Seojun: That's interesting. So why do you drink blood?
➡ _____

20 Mrs. Mosquito: I need the protein in blood to lay my eggs.
➡ _____

21 Seojun: How do you drink blood? Do you have sharp teeth?
➡ _____

22 Mrs. Mosquito: No, I don't have teeth.
➡ _____

23 But I have a long and pointed mouth.
➡ _____

24 So I can drink your blood easily.
➡ _____

25 Seojun: After you bit me, I got a bump. It itches.
➡ _____

26 Mrs. Mosquito: I'm sorry to hear that.
➡ _____

27 Make sure you don't scratch it.
➡ _____

28 Also, clean it with alcohol wipes.
➡ _____

29 Seojun: Alcohol wipes? I've never tried that before.
➡ _____

30 Mrs. Mosquito: It will reduce the itchiness.
➡ _____

31 Seojun: Okay, I'll try that at home. Thanks.
➡ _____

32 I have to go. See you soon.
➡ _____

33 Seojun: Where are you going?
➡ _____

34 Mrs. Mosquito: I'm going back to the river.
➡ _____

35 Seojun: Wait! A lot of people have suffered from your bites.
➡ _____

36 How can we prevent them?
➡ _____

37 Mrs. Mosquito: Stay cool and wear long sleeves.
➡ _____

38 Seojun: Thanks. I'll keep your advice in mind.
➡ _____

※ 다음 괄호 안의 단어들을 우리말에 맞도록 바르게 배열하시오.

1 (was / it / hot / a / evening. / summer)
➡ _____

2 (went / Seojun / a / for / walk / park. / the / in)
➡ _____

3 (he / soon, / sweating. / was)
➡ _____

4 (thirsty. / I'm // want / I / something / drink. / to / cold)
➡ Seojun: _____

5 (that / at / moment, / tiny / something / at / flew / him / and / arm. / his / bit)
➡ _____

6 (hey, / me / catch / can. / you / if)
➡ Mrs. Mosquito: _____

7 (are / who / you? // have / what / done / you / me? / to)
➡ Seojun: _____

8 (a / I'm / mosquito. // just / I've / dinner. / my / finished)
➡ Mrs. Mosquito: _____

9 (are / where / from? / you // did / how / find / me? / you)
➡ Seojun: _____

10 (from / I'm / river. / nearby / a)
➡ Mrs. Mosquito: _____

11 (was / I / looking / some / for / blood / there. / drink / to)
➡ _____

12 (I / then / smelled / sweaty / something / and / here. / you / found)
➡ _____

13 (could / how / smell / you / from / me / river? / the)
➡ Seojun: _____

14 (can / mosquitoes / sense / and / heat / smell / well. / very)
➡ Mrs. Mosquito: _____

15 (why / that's / have / we / for / survived / years. / of / millions)
➡ _____

16 (all / do / drink / mosquitoes / you? / like / blood)
➡ Seojun: _____

17 (no. // female / only / like / mosquitoes / me / blood. / drink)
➡ Mrs. Mosquito: _____

18 (mosquitoes / male / feed / only / fruit / on / and / juice. / plant)
➡ _____

1 무더운 여름날의 저녁이었습니다.

2 서준이는 공원에 산책을 갔습니다.

3 곧, 그는 땀을 흘리고 있었습니다.

4 서준: 목말라. 뭔가 시원한 것을 마시고 싶어.

5 그때에, 뭔가 조그마한 것이 그에게로 날아와서 그의 팔을 물었습니다.

6 모기: 이봐, 나를 잡을 수 있으면 잡아 봐.

7 서준: 너는 누구니? 나한테 무슨 짓을 한 거지?

8 모기: 나는 모기야. 난 방금 저녁 식사를 마쳤어.

9 서준: 너는 어디에서 왔니? 너는 어떻게 나를 찾은 거야?

10 모기: 나는 근처 강에서 왔어.

11 나는 그곳에서 마실 피를 찾던 중이었지.

12 그러다가 땀 냄새를 맡았고, 여기서 너를 발견했어.

13 서준: 너는 어떻게 강에서부터 내 냄새를 맡을 수 있었지?

14 모기: 모기들은 열과 냄새를 매우 잘 감지해.

15 그래서 우리가 수백만 년 동안 살아남은 거야.

16 서준: 모든 모기가 너처럼 피를 마셔?

17 모기: 아니. 오직 나와 같은 암컷 모기만이 피를 마셔.

18 수컷 모기들은 과일과 식물의 즙만을 먹고 살아.

19 (interesting. / that's // why / you / so / do / blood? / drink)
➡ Seojun: _____

20 (need / I / protein / the / blood / in / lay / to / eggs. / my)
➡ Mrs. Mosquito: _____

21 (do / how / you / blood? / drink // you / have / do / teeth? / sharp)
➡ Seojun: _____

22 (I / no, / have / teeth. / don't)
➡ Mrs. Mosquito: _____

23 (I / but / have / long / a / and / mouth. / pointed)
➡ _____

24 (I / so / drink / can / your / easily. / blood)
➡ _____

25 (you / me, / bit / after / got / I / bump. / a // itches. / it)
➡ Seojun: _____

26 (sorry / I'm / that. / hear / to)
➡ Mrs. Mosquito: _____

27 (sure / make / don't / you / it. / scratch)
➡ _____

28 (clean / also, / with / it / wipes. / alcohol)
➡ _____

29 (wipes? / alcohol // never / I've / before. / that / tried)
➡ Seojun: _____

30 (will / it / reduce / itchiness. / the)
➡ Mrs. Mosquito: _____

31 (I'll / okay, / that / try / home. / at // thanks.)
➡ Seojun: _____

32 (have / I / go. / to // soon. / you / see)
➡ Mrs. Mosquito: _____

33 (you / are / going? / where)
➡ Seojun: _____

34 (going / to / I'm / back / river. / the)
➡ Mrs. Mosquito: _____

35 (wait! // lot / a / of / have / people / from / suffered / bites. / your)
➡ Seojun: _____

36 (we / can / how / them? / prevent)
➡ _____

37 (cool / stay / wear / and / sleeves. / long)
➡ Mrs. Mosquito: _____

38 (thanks. // keep / I'll / advice / your / mind. / in)
➡ Seojun: _____

19 서준: 그거 재미있네. 그럼 너는 왜 피를 마시는 거야?

20 모기: 알을 낳으려면 핏속의 단백질이 필요해.

21 서준: 너는 피를 어떻게 마시는 거야? 날카로운 이빨이 있니?

22 모기: 아니. 나는 이빨이 없어.

23 하지만 길고 뾰족한 입이 있지.

24 그래서 나는 너의 피를 쉽게 마실 수 있는 거야.

25 서준: 네가 나를 문 다음, 부어오른 자국이 생겼어. 가려워.

26 모기: 그 말을 들으니 미안하군.

27 그것을 긁지 않도록 해.

28 또한, 그것을 알코올 솜으로 닦아.

29 서준: 알코올 솜? 나는 전에 그것을 한 번도 해 보지 않았어.

30 모기: 그것은 가려움을 줄여 줄 거야.

31 서준: 알았어. 집에서 해 볼게. 고마워.

32 모기: 나는 이제 가야겠어. 다음에 보자.

33 서준: 너는 어디로 가는데?

34 모기: 강으로 돌아가려고.

35 서준: 기다려! 많은 사람이 모기에 물려서 괴로워하고 있어.

36 어떻게 하면 모기에 물리는 것을 막을 수 있지?

37 모기: 시원하게 지내고 소매가 긴 옷을 입어.

38 서준: 고마워. 너의 충고를 명심할게.

※ 다음 우리말을 영어로 쓰시오.

1 무더운 여름날의 저녁이었습니다.

➡ _____

2 서준이는 공원에 산책을 갔습니다.

➡ _____

3 곧, 그는 땀을 흘리고 있었습니다.

➡ _____

4 서준: 목말라. 뭔가 시원한 것을 마시고 싶어.

➡ Seojun: _____

5 그때에, 뭔가 조그마한 것이 그에게로 날아와서 그의 팔을 물었습니다.

➡ _____

6 모기: 이봐, 나를 잡을 수 있으면 잡아 봐.

➡ Mrs. Mosquito: _____

7 서준: 너는 누구니? 나한테 무슨 짓을 한 거지?

➡ Seojun: _____

8 모기: 나는 모기야. 난 방금 저녁 식사를 마쳤어.

➡ Mrs. Mosquito: _____

9 서준: 너는 어디에서 왔니? 너는 어떻게 나를 찾은 거야?

➡ Seojun: _____

10 모기: 나는 근처 강에서 왔어.

➡ Mrs. Mosquito: _____

11 나는 그곳에서 마실 피를 찾던 중이었지.

➡ _____

12 그러다가 땀 냄새를 맡았고, 여기서 너를 발견했어.

➡ _____

13 서준: 너는 어떻게 강에서부터 내 냄새를 맡을 수 있었지?

➡ Seojun: _____

14 모기: 모기들은 열과 냄새를 매우 잘 감지해.

➡ Mrs. Mosquito: _____

15 그래서 우리가 수백만 년 동안 살아남은 거야.

➡ _____

16 서준: 모든 모기가 너처럼 피를 마셔?

➡ Seojun: _____

17 모기: 아니. 오직 나와 같은 암컷 모기만이 피를 마셔.

➡ Mrs. Mosquito: _____

18 수컷 모기들은 과일과 식물의 즙만을 먹고 살아.

➡ _____

19 ▶ 서준: 그거 재미있네. 그럼 너는 왜 피를 마시는 거야?

➡ Seojun: _____

20 ▶ 모기: 알을 낳으려면 핏속의 단백질이 필요해.

➡ Mrs. Mosquito: _____

21 ▶ 서준: 너는 피를 어떻게 마시는 거야? 날카로운 이빨이 있니?

➡ Seojun: _____

22 ▶ 모기: 아니, 나는 이빨이 없어.

➡ Mrs. Mosquito: _____

23 ▶ 하지만 길고 뾰족한 입이 있지.

➡ _____

24 ▶ 그래서 나는 너의 피를 쉽게 마실 수 있는 거야.

➡ _____

25 ▶ 서준: 네가 나를 문 다음, 부어오른 자국이 생겼어. 가려워.

➡ Seojun: _____

26 ▶ 모기: 그 말을 들으니 미안하군.

➡ Mrs. Mosquito: _____

27 ▶ 그것을 긁지 않도록 해.

➡ _____

28 ▶ 또한, 그것을 알코올 솜으로 닦아.

➡ _____

29 ▶ 서준: 알코올 솜? 나는 전에 그것을 한 번도 해 보지 않았어.

➡ Seojun: _____

30 ▶ 모기: 그것은 가려움을 줄여 줄 거야.

➡ Mrs. Mosquito: _____

31 ▶ 서준: 알았어, 집에서 해 볼게. 고마워.

➡ Seojun: _____

32 ▶ 모기: 나는 이제 가야겠어. 다음에 보자.

➡ Mrs. Mosquito: _____

33 ▶ 서준: 너는 어디로 가는데?

➡ Seojun: _____

34 ▶ 모기: 강으로 돌아가려고.

Mrs. Mosquito: _____

35 ▶ 서준: 기다려! 많은 사람이 모기에 물려서 괴로워하고 있어.

➡ Seojun: _____

36 ▶ 어떻게 하면 모기에 물리는 것을 막을 수 있지?

➡ _____

37 ▶ 모기: 시원하게 지내고 소매가 긴 옷을 입어.

➡ Mrs. Mosquito: _____

38 ▶ 서준: 고마워. 너의 충고를 명심할게.

➡ Seojun: _____

※ 다음 우리말과 일치하도록 빈칸에 알맞은 말을 쓰시오.

Let's check

1. Sora: You _____ _____, Minu. What's _____?

2. Minu: I _____ my hat. It was _____ _____.

3. Sora: I'm _____ _____ _____ _____.

4. _____ _____ you go to the _____ _____ _____ Center?

5. Minu: That's _____ _____ _____.

1. Sora: 속상해 보인다. 민우야. 무슨 일이니?
2. Minu: 내 모자를 잃어 버렸어. 내가 가장 좋아하는 거였는데.
3. Sora: 그것 참 안됐구나.
4. 분실물 센터에 가보는 게 어때?
5. Minu: 좋은 생각이다.

Let's Write

1. Summer _____ _____

2. _____

3. _____ you ever _____ _____ sunburn?

4. Here are some _____ _____ _____ _____ sunburn in summer.

5. 1. _____ sunscreen.

6. 2. _____ a hat.

7. _____ _____ and _____ the hot weather.

1. 여름철 건강관리 수칙
2. 햇볕 화상
3. 햇볕 화상으로 고통받은 적이 있나요?
4. 여기 여름에 햇볕 화상을 예방할 수 있는 유용한 팁이 있습니다.
5. 1. 선크림을 바르세요.
6. 2. 모자를 쓰세요.
7. 현명하게 무더운 날씨를 즐기세요.

Culture & Life

1. In summer, some people in Korea wear _____ and _____ pants _____ _____ _____.

2. They call them "_____ _____."

3. Refrigerator pants come in _____ _____.

4. Some of them _____ _____ _____.

1. 여름철 몇몇 한국 사람들은 시원함을 유지하기 위해 얇고 가벼운 바지를 입는다.
2. 그들은 그것을 '냉장고 바지'라고 부른다.
3. 화려한 무늬를 가진 냉장고 바지들이 나온다.
4. 어떤 것들은 매우 세련되어 보인다.

※ 다음 우리말을 영어로 쓰시오.

Let's check

1. Sora: 속상해 보인다, 민우야. 무슨 일이니?
➡ _____

2. Minu: 내 모자를 잃어 버렸어. 내가 가장 좋아하는 거였는데.
➡ _____

3. Sora: 그것 참 안됐구나.
➡ _____

4. 분실물 센터에 가보는 게 어때?
➡ _____

5. Minu: 좋은 생각이다.
➡ _____

Let's Write

1. 여름철 건강 관리 수칙
➡ _____

2. 햇볕 화상
➡ _____

3. 햇볕 화상으로 고통받은 적이 있나요?
➡ _____

4. 여기 여름에 햇볕 화상을 예방할 수 있는 유용한 팁이 있습니다.
➡ _____

5. 1. 선크림을 바르세요.
➡ _____

6. 2. 모자를 쓰세요.
➡ _____

7. 현명하게 무더운 날씨를 즐기세요.
➡ _____

Culture & Life

1. 여름철 몇몇 한국 사람들은 시원함을 유지하기 위해 얇고 가벼운 바지를 입는다.
➡ _____

2. 그들은 그것을 '냉장고 바지'라고 부른다.
➡ _____

3. 화려한 무늬를 가진 냉장고 바지들이 나온다.
➡ _____

4. 어떤 것들은 매우 세련되어 보인다.
➡ _____

MEMO

MEMO

적중100 plus
1학기 전과정
영어 기출 문제집

영어 기출 문제집

적중100 plus
1학기 전과정

1학기

정답 및 해설

지학 | 민찬규

중 2

영어 문제집

1학기

정답 및 해설

지학 | 민찬규

중 2

New Beginnings

시험대비 실력평가　　　　　　　p.08

01 private　02 ②　03 ⑤　04 ④
05 (1) am interested in　(2) is into　(3) heard from
　　(4) make changes　　06 ④

01 주어진 관계는 반의어를 나타낸다. public: 공공의, private: 사적인

02 planet: 행성, space: 우주

03 주어진 문장과 ⑤번에서 handle은 '손잡이'를 가리키지만 나머지 문장에서는 '다루다'를 의미한다.

04 nail은 '못' 또는 '손톱'을 뜻한다.

05 be interested in: ~에 관심이 있다, be into:~에 열중하다, hear from: ~로부터 소식을 듣다, make changes: 변화를 이루다

06 각각의 문장에서 tip은 '끝', '사례금', '정보'를 가리킨다. on the tip of one's tongue: 말이 (기억은 나지 않고) 혀끝에서 뱅뱅 도는

서술형 시험대비　　　　　　　p.09

01 false

02 homeroom teacher

03 planet

04 (1) Would you buy milk for me on your way home?
　　(2) It's time to use a new program to make changes.
　　(3) He doesn't take the computer class anymore.

05 (1) break my bad habit
　　(2) By the way
　　(3) comes true
　　(4) It's time to

06 (1) bite　(2) kind　(3) wish　(4) handles

07 (A) from, (B) By, (C) into

01 주어진 단어는 반의어 관계를 가리킨다. true: 사실인, 참인, false: 거짓의

02 학급을 담당하는 교사를 가리키는 말은 homeroom teacher(담임 선생님)이다.

03 별 주위를 도는 우주의 크고 둥근 물체를 가리키는 말은

planet(행성)이다.

05 break one's bad habit: 나쁜 습관을 그만 두다 by the way: 그건 그렇고, 그런데 come true: 이루어지다, 실현되다 It's time to ~: ~할 시간이다

06 bite: 물다, kind: 종류, wish: 바라다, handle: 손잡이

07 hear from: ~로부터 소식을 듣다. by the way: 그건 그렇고, 그런데, change into: ~로 변하다

교과서
Conversation

핵심 Check　　　　　　　p.10~11

1 You know what　　2 Guess what
3 (A) Look! (B) promise
4 (B) I'm going [planning] to
5 (A) I'm going to (B) decide
6 (A) I'm thinking of cooking

교과서 대화문 익히기

Check(√) True or False　　　　　　　p.12

(1) T　(2) F　(3) T　(4) F

교과서 확인학습　　　　　　　p.14~15

Listen & Talk 1 A
You konw what / you were interested in

Listen & Talk 1 B
homeroom teacher / fun / What does she teach / art

Listen & Speak 2 A
are thinking of starting / What kind of club / stars, planets / once a week / I'm interested in

Listen & Speak 2 B
I'm thinking of cooking / What about beef / I'll buy some for you on my way home

Real Life Communication A
I'm thinking of taking, painting class / decide / I want to go to an art high school / artist / comes true / do my best

Real Life Communication B
move / upset / I can understand her feelings / keep in touch with

01 You know what   02 (B) → (C) → (D) → (A)

03 Who's[Who is] your homeroom teacher this year?

04 ⑤

02 (B) 사실 확인 → (C) 구체적인 사실 설명 → (D) 반응 및 그리움 표현 → (A) 동의 표현

04 Jimin과 Tim은 각자 다른 반으로 다른 담임 선생님에 대해 이야기하고 있다.

01 ④   02 ③   03 (E) → (B) → (A) → (D) → (C)   04 ①   05 ④   06 keep in touch with   07 ③   08 ⓔ in → on   09 ⑤

10 How often are you going to meet?

11 They want to learn about stars and planets.

12 He is interested in space.

01 (A) 방학이 어떠하였는지를 묻고 있으므로 how, (B) amazing: 놀라운, 굉장한, amazed: 놀란, (C) be interested in: ~에 관심이 있다

02 ③ Brian은 Julia가 무에타이에 관심이 있는지 몰랐다.

03 (E) Emily의 계획에 대한 이유 질문 → (B) 이유 대답 → (A) 장래 희망 질문 → (D) 대답 및 관심사 표현 → (C) 반응 및 소망이 이루어지기를 기원

04 주어진 문장은 대화를 시작하기 전에 상대방의 주의를 끄는 말로 (A)에 들어가는 것이 알맞다. concert hall: 콘서트 홀, 연주회장

05 Ms. Kim은 새로 오신 선생님으로 작년에 수업이 어떠했는지 알 수 없다.

06 keep in touch with: ~와 연락하다

07 pleased: 기쁜, nervous: 긴장한, frustrated: 불안스러워하는, lonely: 외로운, excited: 흥분한

08 on one's way home: 집에 오는 길에

09 대화를 통해 Alex의 엄마가 지금 어디에 있는지 알 수 없다.

11 Sujin과 Jane은 우주 과학 동아리에서 별과 행성에 대해 배우고 싶어 한다.

12 민수는 우주에 관심이 있다

01 *muay thai*

02 She took *muay thai* lessons during the winter vacation.

03 She was interested in *muay thai*.

04 (E) → (D) → (C) → (B) → (A)

05 I'm thinking of learning yoga.

06 (A) stars and planets (B) once a week (C) Room 101

02 Julia는 겨울 방학 동안 무에타이 수업을 들었다.

03 Julia는 무에타이에 관심을 갖고 있다.

04 (E) 반응 및 Mr. Smith 선생님의 수업에 대한 설명 → (D) 상대방의 담임 선생님이 누구인지 질문 → (C) 대답 → (B) 무슨 과목 선생님인지 질문 → (A) 대답

06 오늘 Jane은 내게 새로운 동아리를 시작하는 것에 대해 이야기를 했다. Sujin과 그녀는 별과 행성에 관심이 있어서 우주과학 동아리를 만들고 싶어 했다. 그들은 일주일에 한 번 Room 101에서 만날 계획이었다. 이것은 좋은 생각이었다. 그래서 나는 동아리에 가입하기로 결심했다. 나는 우주에 대해 배우는 것을 매우 기대하고 있다.

교과서 Grammar

1 (1) One, the other   (2) One, Another, The others

   (3) Some books, other books[others]

2 (1) arrive, we will   (2) Unless, will be   (3) if

01 (1) will tell → tell   (2) Another → Other

   (3) practices → will practice   (4) other → the other

02 (1) rains   (2) One, the other   (3) Unless   (4) another, the others

03 (1) Some flowers are white, and others are yellow.

   (2) If you want this magazine, I will lend it to you.

   (3) You have two watches. One is here. Where is the other?

   (4) If you win, we will be happy.

01 (1) 조건의 부사절에서 현재형으로 미래를 나타낼 수 있다. (2) 복수 명사를 수식해야 하므로 other를 쓰는 것이 옳다. (3) If가 명사절을 이끌 경우 내용과 시제를 맞추어 준다. (4) 둘 중 남은 하나는 the other이다.

02 (1) 조건의 부사절에서 현재형으로 미래를 나타낼 수 있다. (2) 둘 중 하나는 one, 나머지 하나는 the other이다. (3) 일찍 일어나지 않으면 늦을 것이라는 의미가 자연스럽다. (4) 5개 중에서 제일 처음 가리키는 것은 one, 남은 것 중 다른 하나를 가리

킬 때는 another, 나머지 전체를 가리키는 말은 the others이다.

03 (1) 불특정 복수명사를 지칭할 때 some, 또 다른 것들을 묶어서 말할 때 others (2), (4) 조건의 부사절에서 현재형으로 미래를 나타낼 수 있다. (3) 둘 중 하나는 one, 남은 하나를 지칭할 때 the other

01 ①, ④   02 ⑤   03 ④   04 One, another, the other   05 ⑤   06 ④   07 ③   08 If you have time, will you do me a favor?   09 ③   10 Do you know if there is another one?   11 ③   12 ④   13 One, Another, The other   14 ⑤   15 ③   16 ⓐ: One ⓑ: Another ⓒ: Another ⓓ: Another ⓔ: The other   17 If she invites you, will you go to the party?   18 ③   19 Unless   20 ⑤   21 ③   22 ②   23 ⑤   24 Some people like blue and others like green.

01 빈칸이 이끄는 절은 현재시제이지만 주절은 미래이므로, 빈칸에는 시간이나 조건의 부사절이 들어가야 한다. 따라서 ①, ④번이 옳다.

02 둘 중 다른 하나를 가리키는 대명사는 the other이다.

03 조건의 부사절에서 현재시제로 미래를 나타낼 수 있다.

04 셋 중 가장 처음에 언급하는 것은 one, 또 다른 하나를 가리킬 때에는 another, 남은 하나는 the other를 써서 표현한다.

05 둘 중 하나를 one으로 지칭하면, 남은 하나는 the other이며, 조건의 부사절에서 현재시제로 미래를 표현할 수 있다.

06 other people을 대신하는 말이 들어가야 하므로 others라고 쓰는 것이 옳다.

07 ③번은 '~인지 아닌지'로 해석되는 명사절을 이끄는 접속사 if이다. 나머지는 모두 조건절을 이끄는 if이다.

08 do ~ favor: ~의 부탁을 들어주다

09 ① other cars라고 쓰는 것이 옳다. ② unless는 부정어가 있는 문장을 이끌지 않는다. not을 빼는 것이 옳다. ④ the other necklaces이므로 the others라고 쓰는 것이 옳다. ⑤ 이번 주말에 노트북을 살 것인지 궁금하다는 의미이다. 명사절을 이끄는 접속사 if이므로 will buy가 옳다.

10 if는 명사절을 이끌고 있다. 또 다른 복사기를 의미하므로 another를 쓰는 것이 옳다.

11 조건절과 명사절을 모두 이끌 수 있는 것은 if이다.

12 둘 중 하나는 one, 다른 하나는 the other로 지칭한다.

13 셋 중 가장 먼저 지칭하는 것을 one, 남은 것 중 또 다른 하나

another, 그리고 남은 마지막 하나는 the other로 지칭한다.

14 다른 하나를 사고 싶다는 것이므로 another가 옳다.

15 ① 조건의 부사절에서 현재시제로 미래를 나타내는 것이 옳다. ② other people 혹은 others라고 써야 한다. ④ 문맥상 Unless라고 쓰는 것이 옳다. ⑤ '또 다른 하나'를 가리키는 것이므로 another를 써야 한다.

16 첫 번째로 지칭하는 것을 one으로 하고 남은 하나씩의 손가락은 another로 지칭하고 마지막 손가락은 남은 하나이므로 the other를 쓴다.

17 조건의 부사절에서 현재시제가 미래시제를 대신한다. 따라서 If절은 현재시제를 쓴다.

18 손은 두 개이므로 '다른 손'은 the other로 지칭한다.

19 if … not은 unless와 같다.

20 동전은 두 개의 면을 가지고 있으므로, '다른 쪽 면'은 the other를 쓴다. 조건절의 시제가 현재라 할지라도 미래를 나타내고 있으므로, 주절에서는 의미에 맞게 미래시제를 쓴다.

21 Jenny의 자매 둘 중 한 명이 다른 한 명보다 더 크다는 의미이다. 둘 중 하나는 one, 남은 하나는 the other로 지칭한다. ②번에서 She를 Jenny로 생각한다면 others가 아니라 the others가 되어야 한다.

22 스타에게 사랑을 표현하는 여러 가지 방법 중에 어떤 학생들은 콘서트에서 소리를 지르고 또 어떤 학생들은 몇 시간을 기다리기도 한다는 의미이다. 따라서 불특정 복수명사를 지칭하는 some과 남은 몇몇을 무리지어 지칭하는 others를 쓴다.

23 둘 중에서 나머지 다른 하나는 the other로 지칭한다.

24 불특정 복수명사는 some, 다른 무리의 복수명사는 others로 지칭한다. other people을 줄여 others로 쓸 수 있다.

01 if I find it, I will tell you.

02 The other

03 Unless it rains

04 If I don't feel well tomorrow, I will stay at home. Unless I feel well tomorrow, I will stay at home.

05 I can speak two languages. One is Korean and the other is English.

06 comes, will go

07 If you see Jerry, you will like him.

08 One, another, the other

09 (1) Some, others
　(2) One, The other
　(3) three, One, Another, The other
　(4) One, The others
　(5) other

(6) another

(7) some, others

10 If you don't wear a helmet, you will be hurt.

If you cheat on the test, you will get caught.

If you have a car, will you take me to the airport?

11 the other chairs[the others]

12 ⓐit rains ⓑwill use ⓒ the other

13 There were two cookies in the cookie jar.

14 One, the other

01 시간·조건의 부사절에서 현재시제가 미래를 대신한다는 것에 유의하여 빈칸을 채운다. lip balm: 입술 크림

02 나머지 모든 아이들은 갈색 머리라는 의미이므로 남은 전체를 지칭하는 the other를 쓴다.

03 If ~ not은 Unless와 같다.

04 Unless는 If ~ not과 같다.

05 둘 중 하나가 one이면 다른 하나는 the other로 지칭한다.

06 조건의 부사절에서 현재시제로 미래를 나타낼 수 있다.

07 조건의 부사절에서 현재시제로 미래시제를 나타낼 수 있다.

08 세 가지 중 처음 가리키는 것이 one, 다른 하나는 another, 남아 있는 하나는 the other로 지칭한다.

09 불특정 복수명사를 some으로 지칭하며 다른 것을 묶어서 지칭할 때엔 other를 쓰고 'other+복수명사'를 묶어서 others로 표현한다. 둘 중 하나가 one이면 다른 하나는 the other이고 여러 개 중 하나를 one이라고 하고 나머지 전체를 가리킬 때에는 'the other+복수명사'를 쓰거나 줄여서 'the others'로 쓴다. another는 남은 것 중 또 다른 하나를 가리킬 때 사용한다.

10 Unless you wear a helmet을 써도 좋다. cheat: 부정행위를 하다 get caught: 들키다

11 나머지 전체를 지칭하는 것은 'the other+복수명사'이고, 'the other+복수명사'는 the others로 쓸 수 있다.

12 조건의 부사절에서 현재시제가 미래시제를 대신하므로 if절은 현재시제를, 주절은 내용에 맞게 미래시제를 써야 한다. 우산이 두 개 있으므로 다른 하나를 지칭할 때에는 the other를 쓴다.

13 지칭하는 대명사가 one과 the other이므로 쿠키가 두 개 있었다는 것을 알 수 있다.

14 둘 중 하나는 one, 다른 하나는 the other이다.

교과서
Reading

확인문제   p.28

1 F   2 T   3 T   4 F

확인문제   p.29

1 T   2 T   3 F   4 T   5 F   6 F

교과서 확인학습 A   p.30~31

01 made some interesting changes during

02 emailed each other, talked about

03 Dear   04 It, spring in

05 The last winter vacation, time

06 made, personal changes during 07 One

08 making   09 Making, own, is

10 The other change, breaking   11 often bit

12 don't anymore 13 feel great about, made

14 If, try to make, will feel, like   15 hear from

16 friend   17 Dear   18 In, it, in

19 about, changes

20 time to talk about

21 These days, into

22 two things with

23 One, dream car

24 If, is heavy, will change into   25 The other, for

26 hold, well, sick 27 three handles, to hold.

28 happy   29 By the way, to try

30 Take care.   31 wishes

교과서   p.32~33

1 My friend Eric and I made some interesting changes during the vacation.

2 We emailed each other and talked about our changes.

3 Dear Eric,

4 It's a beautiful spring in Seoul.

5 The last winter vacation was a great time for me.

6 I made two personal changes during the vacation.

7 One is my new hobby.

8 It's making cupcakes.

9 Making my own cupcakes is a lot of fun.

10 The other change is breaking one of my bad habits.

11 In the past, I often bit my nails.

12 Now I don't anymore.

13 I feel great about the changes I made.

14 If you try to make some changes, I'm sure you'll feel great like me.

15 I hope to hear from you soon.

16 Your friend, Junho.

17 Dear Junho,

18 In Sydney, it's fall in March.

19 You talked about your changes in your email.

20 Now, it's time to talk about my new changes.

21 These days, I'm into 3D printing.

22 I printed two things with a 3D printer.

23 One is a model of my dream car.

24 If the traffic is heavy, it will change into a flying car.

25 The other is a special cup for my grandfather.

26 He can't hold his cup well because he's sick.

27 My special cup has three handles, so it is easy to hold.

28 My grandfather is very happy.

29 By the way, I want to try your cupcakes some day, Junho.

30 Take care.

31 Best wishes, Eric

시험대비 실력평가

p.34~37

01 The other　02 ⑤　　03 the changes (that[which]) I made　04 ④　05 ④
06 ④　　07 ③　　08 ③　　09 (A) flying, (B)to try　　10 my special cup
11 ③　　12 ⑤　　13 ②　　14 my grandfather, three handles, cup　　15 ③
16 ③　　17 breaking one of my bad habits
18 ④　　19 (1) nail　(2) past　　20 I feel great.　　21 ②　　22 ④　　23 It has three handles.　　24 ⑤　　25 He wanted to help him because he couldn't hold his cup well.　　26 ⑤　　27 ⑤

01 두 개의 변화가 있었다고 하였고, 앞서 한 가지 변화에 관해 이야기하였으므로 나머지 하나는 The other로 받아준다.

02 hear from: ~로부터 연락을 받다 ① be thinking of ~ing: ~할 생각이다 ② on one's way home: 집에 오는 길에 ③ be interested in: ~에 흥미가 있다 ④ listen to: ~을 듣다 ⑤ come from: ~ 출신이다

03 앞서 언급한 두 가지 변화이므로 정관사 the를 써야 한다. 목적격 관계대명사 that이나 which는 생략할 수 있다.

04 밑줄 친 (A)는 날짜, 거리, 시간, 명암 등을 말할 때 쓰이는 비인칭 주어이며 해석되지 않는다. 따라서 Ⓐ, Ⓑ, Ⓔ가 옳다. Ⓒ:

인칭대명사 it(그것) Ⓓ: 가주어 It

05 (B) 두 개의 변화 중 하나를 지칭할 때 one, (C) 동명사구 주어는 단수 취급, (D) '습관들 중 하나'이므로 habits가 옳다.

06 글쓴이와 Eric은 이메일을 주고받았다고 하였다. 따라서 ④번은 옳지 않다.

07 be into: ~에 열중하다 change into: ~로 변하다

08 편찮으시기 때문에 컵을 잘 들 수 없다고 말하는 것이 가장 적절하다.

09 (A) '날 수 있는 차'라는 의미이므로 flying, (B) want는 to부정사를 목적어로 취하는 동사이다.

10 자신이 만든 특수 컵을 가리키는 말이다.

11 by the way: 그건 그렇고, 그런데

12 Eric은 준호의 컵케이크를 언젠가 먹어 보고 싶다고 하였다. 따라서 ⑤번은 일치하지 않는다.

13 편지의 서두에서 준호가 변화에 관하여 이야기했다고 하였다. 따라서 ②번이 가장 적절하다.

14 이 컵은 아주 특별해. 나는 그것을 나의 할아버지를 위해 만들었어. 그것은 세 개의 손잡이를 가지고 있어서 이 컵을 드는 것은 쉬워.

15 새로운 취미에 대하여 언급한 후, 그것은 컵케이크를 만드는 것이라고 말하고 컵케이를 만드는 것은 정말 재미있다고 말하는 것이 적절하다.

16 ⓐ 흥미를 유발하는 변화이므로 interesting, ⓑ talk about: ~에 관하여 이야기하다

17 be동사의 보어 자리이므로 break를 동명사로 변형하여 써서 문장을 만든다.

18 준호가 손톱을 왜 많이 물어뜯었는지는 알 수 없다.

19 (1) 손가락 끝을 덮고 있는 딱딱한 층은 손톱이다. (2) 현재 이전의 시간은 '과거'이다.

20 준호가 만들어낸 변화에 대해 기분이 어떤지 묻고 있다.

21 주어진 문장은 목적어로 쓰인 명사적 용법의 to부정사이다. ①, ③ 감정의 원인을 나타내는 부사적 용법, ② 동사의 목적어로 쓰인 명사적 용법, ④, ⑤ 앞에 나오는 명사를 수식하는 형용사로 사용된 to부정사

22 (A) it's time to V: V할 때이다 (B) change into: ~으로 변하다 (C) '들기 쉬운'이라는 의미로 to부정사가 부사로 쓰여 형용사 easy를 수식하고 있다.

23 세 개의 손잡이를 가지고 있다고 하였다.

24 be into: ~에 열중하다 be crazy about: ~에 푹 빠지다

25 Eric이 할아버지를 위해 특수 컵을 만든 이유는 할아버지가 컵을 잘 들지 못하셨기 때문에 그를 돕기 위해 만든 것이다.

26 할아버지가 행복해 하신다고 하였으므로 ⑤번은 일치하지 않는다.

27 (C) 두 가지 변화 중 첫 번째 변화를 소개 → (B) 남은 다른 하나의 변화를 소개하며 기분이 좋았음을 말함 → (A) 변화하려고 노력한다면 자신처럼 기분이 좋을 것이라고 말함.

01 We emailed each other.

02 ⓐOne ⓑThe other

03 Now I don't bite my nails anymore.

04 He lives in Seoul.

05 bad habit, break

06 making my own cupcakes, another

07 If you break one of your bad habits, you will feel great.

08 Because he made two personal changes during the vacation.

09 If you hold this cup, you will know it is easy to hold.

10 He wrote the letter in Sydney in March.

11 will be → is / 조건의 부사절에서 현재시제로 미래를 나타내기 때문이다.

12 am satisfied with, happy

13 The other is a special cup for my grandfather.

14 He is into 3D printing these days.

15 Because my special cup has three handles, it is easy to hold.

16 They talk about their new changes.

17 Junho can make cupcakes.

---

01 email은 명사와 동사로 모두 쓰일 수 있다. each other: 서로

02 둘 중 하나는 one, 남은 하나는 the other로 지칭한다.

03 더 이상 손톱을 깨물지 않는다는 의미이다. 동사 bite의 과거형은 bit이다.

04 준호는 서울에서 살고 있다.

05 Jenny: Junho야, 없애고 싶은 나쁜 습관이 있니? Junho: 예전에 있었지. 하지만 그걸 없앴어.

06 준호의 새로운 취미는 컵케이크를 만드는 것이라고 하였다. 또 다른 취미를 묻고 있으므로 another를 쓰는 것이 옳다.

07 조건의 부사절에서 현재시제로 미래를 나타내는 것에 유의하여 문장을 만든다. break a bad habit: 나쁜 습관을 그만두다

08 지난 겨울 방학이 준호에게 멋진 시간이었던 이유는 준호가 개인적인 변화를 만들었기 때문이다.

09 조건의 부사절에서 현재시제로 미래를 나타낼 수 있으며, hold, easy to hold 모두 위 글에서 찾을 수 있는 표현들이다.

10 부사(구)는 일반적으로 '장소-방법-시간' 순서로 쓴다. 편지의 내용으로 보아 Eric은 시드니에서 3월에 편지를 썼다.

12 be satisfied with: ~에 만족하다

13 나머지 다른 하나라고 하였으므로 정관사 the를 추가하여 문장을 만든다.

14 질문: Eric은 요즈음 무엇에 열중하고 있나요?

15 '특수 컵이 세 개의 손잡이를 가지고 있기 때문에 들기 편하다'는

문장으로 쓰면 된다.

17 Eric은 준호의 컵케이크를 먹어 보고 싶다고 하였다. 따라서 준호는 컵케이크를 만들 수 있다고 볼 수 있다.

01 (1) is into (2) on my way home (3) hear from

02 ①

03 (1) I decided to break my bad habit.

(2) I'll do my best to pass the test.

(3) He is into playing golf.

04 ③　　05 ①　　06 ⑤　　07 You know what?　　08 ⓑ for → during

09 ⑤　　10 (D) → (A) → (C) → (B)　　11 planet

12 ③　　13 ③　　14 It was a lot of fun.

15 They are going to learn art.　　16 ③

17 ⑤

18 ④　　19 I have three foreign friends. One is from Japan, and the others (are) from France.

20 ②　　21 ④　　22 Unless you do your best, you will not achieve anything.　　23 ⑤

24 If you don't wear warm clothes, you will catch a cold. / Unless you wear warm clothes, you will catch a cold.　　25 ④

26 If you go jogging every day, you will get healthier.

27 ②　　28 ③　　29 If you try to make some changes　　30 ④　　31 ⑤

32 handle　　33 Sydney, in 3D printing

34 Because it has three handles.

---

02 false: 거짓의

03 break one's bad habit: 나쁜 습관을 그만두다, do one's best: 최선을 다하다, be into: ~에 열중하다

04 bite는 '물다' 또는 '한 입, (물린) 상처'를 뜻한다. grab a bite: (간단히) 먹다 itch: 가려움 itchy: 가려운

05 주어진 문장과 ①번은 '종류'를 의미하며 나머지는 모두 '친절한'을 뜻한다.

06 ⑤번을 제외한 나머지는 모두 계획에 대해 이야기하고 있다.

08 for+일정한 기간, during+특정한 기간

09 Brian이 겨울 방학 동안에 어떤 수업을 들었는지는 알 수 없다.

10 (D) 저녁식사 계획 설명 → (A) 반응 → (C) 필요한 재료가 있는지 질문 → (B) 대답

11 별 주위를 도는 우주의 크고 둥근 물체를 가리키는 말은 planet(행성)이다.

12 be into: ~에 열중하다

13 ③ Jane과 Sujin은 일주일에 한 번 만나려고 한다.

14 작년에 Smith 선생님의 수업은 재미있었다.

15 새로 온 선생님은 미술 선생님이시다.

16 이탈리아는 또 다른 인기 있는 관광지이므로 another가 옳다.

17 현재시제로 미래를 표현하는 조건의 부사절이므로 comes를 쓰는 것이 옳다.

18 'other+복수명사'는 others로 쓸 수 있다.

19 셋 중 나머지 둘은 같은 곳에서 왔으므로 the others로 쓸 수 있다. the others are from France라고 해도 좋다.

20 ⓐ, ⓑ, ⓓ는 부사절을 이끄는 if로 '만약 ~라면'이라고 해석하고, ⓒ, ⓔ는 명사절을 이끄는 접속사 if이다.

21 'all comics'로 보아 나머지 모든 책을 가리키는 대명사가 나오는 것이 옳다. 따라서 the others라고 써야 한다.

22 Unless는 If ~ not과 같다. 조건의 부사절이므로 현재시제로 미래를 나타낼 수 있으며 주절의 시제는 내용과 일치시킨다.

23 둘 중 하나는 one, 남은 하나는 the other로 지칭한다. 딸이 둘이라고 하였으므로 the others가 아닌 the other가 옳다.

24 조건의 부사절에서는 현재시제로 미래를 나타내는 것에 유의한다. If ~ not은 Unless와 같다.

25 셋 중 하나는 one, 다른 하나는 another, 남은 하나는 the other로 지칭한다.

26 go Ving: V하러 가다

27 during은 '~ 동안'이라는 뜻으로 뒤에는 보통 숫자를 포함하지 않은 특정한 기간이 온다. ②번을 제외한 모든 곳에는 for가 들어간다.

28 one과 the other를 써서 변화를 설명하고 있으므로 '두 개의 변화'라고 보는 것이 옳다. 따라서 ③번이다. a couple of는 '둘의'라는 의미 외에도 '몇 개의'의 의미도 갖는다.

29 try to: ~하려고 노력하다

30 과거에 손톱을 물어뜯었다는 의미이다. 따라서 과거형 bit으로 쓰는 것이 옳다. ③은 The other change를 줄여서 쓴 말이다.

31 Eric의 할아버지가 왜 편찮으신지는 글을 읽고 답할 수 없다.

32 특히 손으로 쥘 수 있도록 만들어진 부분은 '손잡이(handle)'이다.

33 Eric은 시드니에 산다. 그는 3D 프린팅에 흥미가 있다.

34 Eric의 특수 컵이 들기에 쉬운 이유는 손잡이가 세 개 있어서이다.

단원별 예상문제
p.46~49

01 I met Mike on my way to the library.

02 ⑤　　　03 I hope your wish comes true.

04 She wants to be an artist in the future.

05 She is planning to take a painting class.

06 I'm thinking of keeping a diary in English.

07 ①　　　08 ②　　　09 ③

10 (D) → (E) → (C) → (B) → (A)　　　11 ③

12 ②　　　13 ⑤　　　14 lend me, will pay

15 One is blue. → Another is hot pink. → The other is yellow.

16 ③　　　17 ③　　　18 ⓑ making(또는 to make), ⓒ Making(또는 To make) ⓓ breaking(또는 to break)　　19 ④번 am not → don't　　20 ③

21 ③　　　22 ④　　　23 He printed a model of his dream car and a special cup for his grandfather.

24 He wants to try Junho's cupcakes some day.

25 ⑤

02 Alex와 엄마가 함께 부엌에서 이야기를 하고 있다는 설명은 대화의 내용과 일치하지 않는다.

04 Emily는 미래에 미술가가 되기를 원한다.

05 Emily는 예술 고등학교에 진학하기 위해 미술 수업을 들을 계획이다.

07 decide는 '결심하다'라는 뜻으로 determine과 바꾸어 쓸 수 있다. refuse: 거절하다, postpone: 미루다, delay: 미루다, bite: 물다

08 (A)의 '나도 그래.'와 바꾸어 쓸 수 있는 말은 'So am I.'이다

09 Jenny는 일본으로 이민을 가는 가게 되어서 지금 기분이 안 좋다.

10 (D) 방학이 어떠하였는지 질문→ (E) 대답 및 방학 동안에 한 일에 대한 구체적 설명 → (C) 놀라움 표현 → (B) 즐거웠음을 표현 → (A) 반응

11 다른 하나를 보여 달라는 의미이므로 another가 옳다.

12 책 읽기를 좋아한다면 언제든 빌릴 수 있는 책이 많이 있을 것이라는 의미로 조건절에서 현재가 미래를 대신하도록 문장을 쓸 수 있다. 따라서 ②번이 가장 적절하다.

13 첫 번째 문장은 다섯 명의 친구 중 둘을 제외한 나머지 모두가 오지 않았다는 것이므로 The others, 두 번째 문장은 어떤 학생들은 국어를 공부하고 다른 학생들은 영어를 공부한다는 말이므로 others를 쓴다.

14 be short of: ~이 부족하다 pay ~ back: (빌린 돈을) ~에게 갚다, ~에게 돌려주다

15 셋 중 하나는 one, 다른 하나는 another, 남은 하나는 the other로 지칭한다.

16 둘 중 남은 하나는 the other로 지칭하며, 조건의 부사절에서 현재시제로 미래를 표현한다. 단, 주절은 의미에 맞게 시제를 일치시킨다.

17 each other: 서로 ① 같은 스카프의 다른 색깔을 원하는 것이므로 another ② 둘 중 하나는 one, 남은 하나는 the other ③ 불특정 복수명사는 some, 다른 무리를 묶어서 other+복수명사 ④ 세 개의 인형 중 하나는 새 것이지만 나머지 둘은 낡았다는 의미이므로 the others, ⑤ 동사가 바로 따라오고 있으므로

other people을 대명사로 한 others

18 동사를 주어나 보어 자리에서 쓰기 위해서는 동명사나 to부정사 형태로 만들어 주어야 한다.

19 'I don't bite my nails anymore.'를 줄인 말이 들어간다. 따라서 don't라고 쓰는 것이 옳다.

20 편지 서두에 아름다운 봄이라고 하였다. used to: (과거에) ~하곤 했다

21 the other thing을 의미하는 대명사이므로 The other라고 쓰는 것이 옳다.

22 (A) 내용상 차가 '많을 때' 날 수 있는 차로 바뀐다고 말한 것이고, (B) 손잡이가 세 개 있어서 쥐기 쉬운 특수한 컵이라고 보는 것이 옳으며 (C) 편찮으시기 때문에 컵을 잘 들지 못한다고 하는 것이 적절하다.

23 Eric이 3D 프린터로 프린트한 것은 모형 드림 자동차와 할아버지를 위한 특수 컵이다.

24 Eric은 준호의 컵케이크를 먹어 보고 싶다고 하였다.

25 ⑤ Eric이 언제 준호의 컵케이크를 먹을지는 언급되지 않았다.

서술형 실전문제   p.50~51

01 I'm thinking of cooking bulgogi for dinner.?
02 He needs some vegetables and beef.
03 She is going to buy some beef on her way home.
04 One is making food, and the other is washing the dishes.
05 If you need it, you can have it.
   If you want her to help you, she will help you.
   If your alarm clock is out of order, I will buy you a new one.
06 If you don't listen carefully, you won't know what to do.
   Unless you listen carefully, you won't know what to do.
07 One, The others
08 finish, will you do, will clean, finish
09 personal
10 He feels great about them.
11 making, One, the other, breaking
12 If the traffic is heavy, it will change into a flying car.
13 It looks special.

02 Alex는 불고기를 요리하기 위해 야채와 소고기가 필요하다.
03 Alex의 엄마는 집에 오는 길에 소고기를 살 것이다.
04 두 사람이라고 하였으므로 한 사람은 one, 다른 한 사람은 the other로 지칭한다.

05 네가 그것을 필요로 한다면, 그걸 가져도 좋아. / 네가 그녀가 널 돕길 원하면, 그녀가 도와 줄 거야. / 너의 알람 시계가 고장 났다면, 내가 하나 사줄게.

06 '주의 깊게 들어라. 그렇지 않으면 너는 무엇을 해야 할지 모를 것이다.'라는 의미이다. If와 Unless를 이용하여 문장을 만든다.

07 두 번째 빈칸 뒤의 동사가 복수동사인 것으로 보아 나머지 고양이 두 마리의 눈 색깔을 지칭하는 것을 알 수 있다. 따라서 The others를 쓴다. The other cats를 써도 무방하다.

08 조건의 부사절에서 현재시제로 미래를 나타낸다.
09 person의 형용사형 personal로 고친다.
10 the changes를 대명사 them으로 받아준다.
11 spend+시간+Ving: V하느라 시간을 보내다
12 교통이 혼잡하다는 표현은 'heavy'를 쓰고, 반면에 한산하다고 표현할 때에는 'light'를 쓴다.
13 Eric은 특수한 컵을 만들었다고 하였으므로 '특별해 보인다.'고 답하면 된다.

창의사고력 서술형 문제   p.52

|모범답안|

01 (A) Jenny was going to move to Japan
   (B) Jenny was very upset
   (C) keep in touch
02 (1) There are two books on the table. One is a novel. The other is a textbook.
   (2) There are two cups. One is blue. The other is white.
   (3) There are two flowers in a vase. One is a tulip. The other is a rose.
   (4) There are two machines in the kitchen. One is a coffee machine. The other is a blender.
   (5) There are two teachers in the classroom. One teaches math. The other teaches English.
03 (1) If it is sunny tomorrow, I will go on a picnic.
   (2) If it is windy tomorrow, I'll wear my coat.
   (3) If it is rainy tomorrow, I will stay at home and watch a movie.
   (4) If it is hot tomorrow, I will have lots of ice cream.

01 오늘 나는 Jenny가 일본으로 이사를 갈 것이라고 들었다. 나는 Jenny가 이에 대해 전혀 이야기를 하지 않았기 때문에 너무 놀랐다. Sue는 Jenny가 매우 기분이 좋지 않다고 이야기 했다 왜냐하면 그녀의 가족이 지난주에야 이것에 대해 그녀에게 이야기했기 때문이다. 나는 그녀의 기분을 이해했다. 어쨌든 나는 그녀를 매우 그리워 할 것이고 그녀와 연락할 것이다.

01 false   02 ②   03 (1) truth   (2) nail   (3) personal

04 (1) come true   (2) take, class   (3) not, anymore   (4) break a bad habit   05 ②   06 artist

07 I'm thinking of taking a painting class[an art class].   08 ④

09 I'm interested in space, too.

10 They are going to meet once a week.

11 ④   12 ⑤   13 ②   14 ③

15 Kevin is different from the other boys.

16 If you take a taxi, it will take only 10 minutes.

17 ②   18 ③   19 ⑤

20 The other change   21 the changes he made

22 ⓐ: to talk ⓑ: flying   23 ⑤   24 ②

25 ③

---

01 주어진 관계는 반의어를 나타낸다. false: 거짓의, true: 사실인

02 특히 손으로 쥐어지도록 고안된 부분을 가리키는 말은 handle(손잡이)이다.

05 (A) You know what?: 너 그거 아니?, (B) because of+명사(구), because+주어+동사, (D) be interested in: ~에 관심이 있다

06 그림이나 회화 같은 예술 작품을 만들어내는 사람을 가리키는 말은 artist(예술가)이다.

07 think of: ~할 생각이다

09 be interested in: ~에 관심이 있다

10 동아리 회원들은 일주일에 한 번 만날 예정이다.

11 주어진 문장은 '그녀의 기분을 이해할 수 있다.'는 의미이므로 Jenny의 기분을 설명하는 문장 다음에 이어질 말로 적절하므로 (D)가 알맞다.

12 대화를 통해 왜 Jenny의 가족이 이사하려고 하는지는 알 수 없다.

13 ② Unless는 부정어를 이끌 수 없다.

14 둘 중에서 남은 하나는 the other를 쓴다.

15 나머지 전체를 지칭하는 것은 the other+복수명사이다.

16 take a taxi: 택시를 타다'

17 드레스를 두 벌 샀다고 하였으므로 파란색 드레스는 the other로 지칭하는 것이 옳다.

18 밑줄 친 ⓐ는 동명사로, 보어 역할을 하고 있다. 동명사는 명사로 쓰여 주어, 보어, 동사나 전치사의 목적어 역할을 한다. ③번은 '~하는 중'이라는 의미의 현재분사이다.

19 준호가 Eric에 대해 어떻게 느끼는지는 글을 읽고 답할 수 없다.

20 앞서 언급한 두 가지 변화 중 남은 한 가지 변화를 뜻하므로 The other change라고 쓴다.

21 이메일에서, 준호는 자신이 만든 변화들에 관하여 주로 이야기하고 있다.

22 ⓐ it's time toV: ~할 때이다 ⓑ '날 수 있는 자동차'라는 의미이므로 flying이 옳다.

23 빈칸에는 이유를 나타내는 because가 들어간다. ① while: 반면에 ② although: 비록 ~일지라도 ③ if: ~인지 아닌지 ④ unless: ~하지 않으면 ⑤ because: ~이기 때문에

24 '먹어 보고 싶다'는 의미로 쓰였으므로 ②번이 가장 적절하다.

25 ⓑ, ⓒ, ⓔ가 글의 내용과 일치한다.

Better Safe Than Sorry

시험대비 실력평가 p.60

01 empty 02 (1) Keep in mind (2) one by one (3) a little (4) Stay away from 03 ③

04 (1) escape (2) follow (3) slip (4) shake

05 ②, ③ 06 ② 07 ③

08 (1) more (2) often (3) slowly

01 주어진 단어의 관계는 반의어 관계이다. empty: 비어 있는, full: 가득 찬

02 keep in mind: ~을 기억하다, one by one: 하나씩, a little: 약간, stay away from: ~에서 떨어져 있다

03 ③ serious: 심각한

04 slip: 미끄러지다, shake: 흔들다, 흔들리다, escape: 탈출하다, follow: 따르다

05 주어진 문장에서 pole은 '막대기, 기둥'을 나타낸다. 이와 같은 의미로 쓰인 것은 ②, ③번이다. ①, ④번은 '극, 극지방'을 의미하며 ⑤ magnetic pole은 '자극'을 뜻한다.

06 갑자기 일어나 많은 사람들에게 많은 고통이나 손실을 야기하는 홍수, 토네이도, 화재, 비행기 사고 등과 같은 것을 가리키는 말은 disaster(재난)이다.

서술형 시험대비 p.61

01 safe

02 (1) I'm worried about the English exam.

(2) You should walk on the stairs.

(3) Watch your head when you get out of the car.
(When you get out of the car, watch your head.)

(4) You should watch your hand when you close the door.
(When you close the door, you should watch your hand.)

03 (A) about, (B) until, (C) another

04 (A) in (B) from (C) by

05 (1) feel better (2) took cover (3) earthquake, natural disaster

06 (1) Stay away from (2) Hold on to (3) get out of (4) take cover

01 주어진 단어의 관계는 반의어 관계이다. safe: 안전한, dangerous: 위험한

03 (A) be worried about:~에 대해 걱정하다, (B) until: ~까지, (C) another: 또 다른, one day: 언젠가

04 keep ~ in mind: ~을 기억하다, stay away from ~: ~에서 떨어져 있다, one by one: 하나씩

05 feel better: 기분이 나아지다, take cover: 숨다, natural disaster: 자연 재해

06 stay away from: ~에서 떨어져 있다, hold on to: ~을 꼭 잡다, get out of: ~에서 나가다, 떠나다, take cover: 숨다

교과서 Conversation

핵심 Check p.62~63

1 (A) I'm worried about

2 (A) Don't be anxious

3 (A) I'm concerned about

4 (B) You should

5 (B) Why don't you

6 (B) I think we need to

교과서 대화문 익히기

Check(√) True or False p.64

(1) T (2) T (3) T (4) F

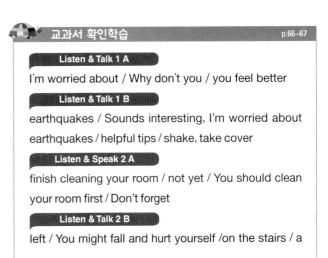

교과서 확인학습 p.66~67

Listen & Talk 1 A

I'm worried about / Why don't you / you feel better

Listen & Talk 1 B

earthquakes / Sounds interesting, I'm worried about earthquakes / helpful tips / shake, take cover

Listen & Speak 2 A

finish cleaning your room / not yet / You should clean your room first / Don't forget

Listen & Talk 2 B

left / You might fall and hurt yourself /on the stairs / a

<11>11</11>

little late / Better safe than sorry

a big fire / I was worried about the people there / safety / cover / with a wet towel, stay low, escape / keep that in mind

our picnic / until late afternoon / You should go another day / choose another day

---

 시험대비 기본평가 p.68

01 ③, ⑤   02 (E) → (C) → (B) → (D) → (A)   03 fall
04 Better safe than sorry.

01 'I'm worried about ~'은 '~을 걱정하다'는 표현으로 'I'm anxious about ~' 또는 'I'm concerned about ~'으로 바꾸어 쓸 수 있다.

02 (E) 걱정 표현 → (C) 제안 → (B) 제안에 대한 대답 → (D) 희망 표현 → (A) 동의

03 서 있는 자세에서 갑자기 밑으로 가는 것을 가리키는 말은 fall(넘어지다)이다.

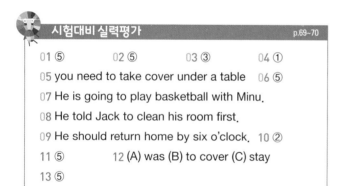 **시험대비 실력평가** p.69~70

01 ⑤   02 ⑤   03 ③   04 ①
05 you need to take cover under a table   06 ⑤
07 He is going to play basketball with Minu.
08 He told Jack to clean his room first.
09 He should return home by six o'clock.   10 ②
11 ⑤   12 (A) was (B) to cover (C) stay
13 ⑤

01 ⑤번을 제외한 나머지는 모두 '무슨 일이야?'라는 뜻이다.

02 ⑤번을 제외한 나머지는 모두 제안을 나타낸다.

03 Yujin은 다친 다리를 걱정하고 있으므로 anxious(걱정스러운)가 적절하다.

04 상대방의 'I'm worried about ~'에 대한 동의 표현으로 'So am I.'로 바꿀 수 있다.

07 Jack은 민우와 농구를 할 것이다.

08 아빠는 Jack에게 외출하기 전에 방청소를 먼저 하라고 말했다.

09 Jack은 6시까지 귀가해야 한다.

10 후회하는 것보다 안전한 것이 낫다는 ②번이 적절하다.

11 Tom은 안전한 것을 더 우선시 하였다.

12 (A) Everybody는 단수 취급하므로 was, (B) need to: ~할 필요가 있다. (C) 명령문은 동사로 시작하므로 stay

13 화재 시 몸을 낮게 유지해야 한다.

 **서술형 시험대비** p.71

01 (C) → (A) → (B) → (E) → (D)
02 Why don't you walk on the stairs?
03 Because Emily might fall and hurt herself.
04 There was a big fire at the city library yesterday.
05 Because they all followed the safety rules.
06 화재 시 젖은 수건으로 코와 입을 가리고 몸을 낮게 유지하여 탈출해야 한다는 것
07 You should watch your hands when you close the door.
   (When you close the door, you should watch your hands.)

01 (C) 방청소를 끝냈는지 질문 → (A) 대답 및 요청 → (B) 거절 및 충고 → (E) 반응 및 약속 → (D) 칭찬 및 상기시키기

02 'You should ~'는 충고하는 표현으로 'Why don't you ~'와 바꾸어 쓸 수 있다.

03 Emily가 계단에서 넘어지거나 다칠 수 있기 때문이다.

04 어제 시립 도서관에서 큰 불이 났다.

05 큰불에도 모든 사람들이 다치지 않은 이유는 그들 모두가 안전 규칙을 따랐기 때문이다.

 교과서
Grammar

핵심 Check p.72~73

1 (1) how to drive / how I should drive
  (2) when to leave / we should leave
  (3) who(m) to trust / who(m) I should trust
2 (1) who   (2) whose sister

시험대비 기본평가 p.74

01 (1) when quit → when to quit
  (2) and which → which   (3) to going → to go
  (4) who → which[that]
02 (1) how to read   (2) are   (3) whose
  (4) who(m) to ask
03 (1) I will let you know when to come.
  (2) Is there anything that you want to have?
  (3) I don't know how to use the machine.
  (4) I read a book which a famous writer wrote.

01 (1) '의문사+to부정사' 형태를 쓰는 것이 옳다. (2) and를 없애야 한다. (3) '의문사+to부정사' 형태이므로 'to+동사원형'이 옳다. (4) 관계대명사 who는 선행사가 사람일 때 쓴다.

02 (1) '의문사+to부정사' 형태를 쓰는 것이 옳다. (2) 선행사가 the boys이므로 복수 동사를 쓴다. (3) '개의 꼬리'를 의미하므로 소유격 관계대명사를 쓴다. (4) '누구에게 물어봐야 할지'라는 의미가 되어야 하므로 '의문사+to부정사'를 쓴다.

03 (1) '언제 오실지'이므로 when to come을 쓴다. (2) '묻고 싶은 것'이므로 관계사절이 anything을 수식하도록 문장을 쓴다. (3) '그 기계를 사용하는 방법'이므로 how to use the machine을 쓴다. (4) '어느 유명한 작가가 쓴 책'이므로 관계사절이 a book을 수식하도록 단어를 나열한다. 작가가 이미 책을 쓴 것이므로 write를 과거형으로 변형하여 쓰는 것에 유의한다.

시험대비 실력평가   p.75~77

01 ③   02 ③   03 ④

04 The man who is cleaning the house lives here.

05 ②   06 ①, ④, ⑤   07 ④.

08 Let me know where to get off.   09 ④

10 ⑤   11 ④   12 which[that] is on the desk   13 ③   14 ④   15 ④

16 I don't know what to order.   17 ⑤

18 ②   19 ②   20 who[that] asked me, where to go   21 ③   22 where to meet   23 ④, ⑤   24 what, should do

01 '어느 것'이라고 하였으므로 which를 쓰는 것이 옳다.

02 ①, ④, ⑤번에는 관계대명사 who가 들어가며 ②번에는 '의문사+to부정사' 형태로 의문사 who가 들어간다. ③번은 소유격 관계대명사 whose의 자리이다.

03 '어디서'와 '시작하다'를 이용하여 where to start를 쓰면 된다.

04 '그 집을 청소하는 그 남자는 여기에 산다.'라는 문장으로 이어주면 된다.

05 '의문사+to부정사'는 '의문사+주어+should~'와 같다. 따라서 ②번이 옳다.

06 빈칸은 목적격 관계대명사 whom의 자리이다. whom을 대신하여 who, that을 쓸 수 있다.

07 위 문장은 '언제 시작할지' 혹은 '어떻게 시작할지'라는 의미가 될 수 있고, 아래 문장은 주격 관계대명사 자리이므로 ④번이 옳다.

08 해석: 어디에서 내릴지 알려주세요.

09 '어느 것을 살지'라는 의미에 부합하며, 사물을 선행사로 받아주는 관계대명사는 which이다.

10 모두 명사절을 이끄는 접속사 that이지만 ⑤번은 관계대명사

that이다.

11 ⓐ '의문사+to부정사' 형태이어야 하므로 how to make, ⓓ the key that was on the sofa라고 쓰는 것이 옳다.

12 the pen은 사물이고, 두 번째 문장에서 the pen을 가리키는 대명사 it이 주어 역할을 하므로 주격 관계대명사 which나 that을 써서 문장을 만든다.

13 주어가 the man이므로 tells가 옳다.

14 ① when to ask 혹은 when they should ask라고 쓰는 것이 옳다. ② friend가 선행사이므로 whom[that] 혹은 who라고 써야 한다. ③ where to go 혹은 where I should go라고 쓰는 것이 옳다. ⑤ 선행사가 a puppy이므로 are가 아닌 is이다.

15 목적격 관계대명사는 생략할 수 있다. ④번은 주격 관계대명사이다.

16 '무엇을 주문해야 할지'라고 하였으므로 의문사 what을 사용하여 문장을 만든다.

17 선행사가 사물이므로 첫 번째 빈칸에는 관계대명사 that 혹은 which가 들어가는 것이 옳으며 영화는 이미 만들어진 것이고 the film이 주어이므로 단수동사 was를 써야 한다.

18 '의문사+to부정사'는 '의문사+주어+should ~'와 같다. 따라서 ②번이 옳다.

19 사람과 사물을 모두 선행사로 받을 수 있는 것은 관계대명사 that이다.

20 선행사가 the man이므로 관계대명사 who나 that을 쓰고, '어디로 가야 할지'는 '의문사+to부정사'를 쓴다.

21 ①, ②, ⑤ 선행사를 사물로 하는 목적격 관계대명사 which 혹은 that, ④ 주격 관계대명사 who를 쓰는 것이 옳다.

22 where we should meet이라고 써도 무방하다.

23 I bought a book from the boy who(또는 that) was talking with my sister.에서 '주격 관계대명사+be동사'를 생략할 수 있으므로 ④, ⑤번이 옳다

24 '의문사+to부정사'는 '의문사+주어+should ~'와 같다.

서술형 시험대비   p.78~79

01 (1) who is visiting a place for pleasure and interest
　(2) which were painted by your mom
　(3) who want to be rich
　(4) which is veryuseful for you

02 (1) where to find the bathroom
　(2) what to do next
　(3) which class to sign up for

03 what to do after graduation.

04 who(m)

05 How to say hello varies in different cultures.

06 There are children who are playing in the garden.

07 where to go

08 The apartment which was empty is no longer available.

The boy who cut his finger is now in the hospital.

Do you want to buy the pictures which are very expensive?

Bruno Mars is a singer who is very popular all over the world.

I must thank the people who congratulated me.

An artist is a person who draws or paints pictures as a job.

09 who[that], what to do

10 who[that] are doing / doing

11 who[that] read it how to think

12 who[that] helped me

13 Did you finish the book which[that] you were reading?

14 I don't know what to say.

I don't know what I should say.

01 (1) 선행사가 someone이므로 관계대명사 who 또는 that을 쓰는 것이 옳다. (2) 선행사가 사물이므로 which나 that을 써서 문장을 하나로 만든다. (3) 선행사가 사람이므로 관계대명사 who를 쓴다. (4) a tip이 사물이므로 관계대명사 which 혹은 that을 사용한다.

02 (1) 그녀는 내게 어디에서 화장실을 찾아야 할지 물어보았다. (2) 다음에 무엇을 할지는 네가 결정하기에 달려 있어. (3) 어느 수업에 등록할지 아직 결정하지 못했어.

03 '무엇을 해야 할지'이므로 what to do를 쓴다.

04 위 문장에는 '누구에게 말을 걸어야 할지'라는 의미로 who [whom]가 들어가고, 아래 문장에는 목적격 관계대명사 whom이 들어간다. whom 대신에 who를 쓸 수 있다.

05 '안녕이라고 말하는 방식'이므로 how to say hello라고 쓴다. vary: 다양하다

06 who 대신에 that을 써도 무방하다.

07 대화의 내용으로 미루어 보아, '어디로 가야 하는지 아느냐?'는 물음에 대한 답임을 알 수 있다.

08 available: 이용할 수 있는 cut one's finger: 손가락을 베다 congratulate: 축하하다

09 주격 관계대명사 who를 대신하여 that을 써도 무방하다.

10 '주격 관계대명사+be 동사'는 생략 가능하다.

11 '그것을 읽는 사람들'이므로 who read it이 people을 수식하게 만든다.

12 '나를 도와준 그 경찰관에게 감사하다고 했어'라는 의미이다.

13 finish: ~을 끝내다

14 '의문사+to부정사'는 '의문사+주어+should 동사원형'과 같다.

Reading

확인문제 p.80

1 T 2 F 3 T 4 F

확인문제 p.81

1 F 2 T 3 T 4 F 5 T

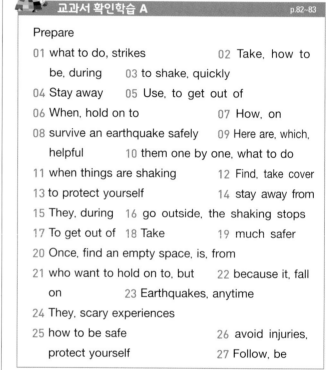

교과서 확인학습 A p.82~83

Prepare

01 what to do, strikes

02 Take, how to be, during

03 to shake, quickly

04 Stay away

05 Use, to get out of

06 When, hold on to

07 How, on

08 survive an earthquake safely

09 Here are, which, helpful

10 them one by one, what to do

11 when things are shaking

12 Find, take cover

13 to protect yourself

14 stay away from

15 They, during

16 go outside, the shaking stops

17 To get out of

18 Take

19 much safer

20 Once, find an empty space, is, from

21 who want to hold on to, but

22 because it, fall on

23 Earthquakes, anytime

24 They, scary experiences

25 how to be safe

26 avoid injuries, protect yourself

27 Follow, be

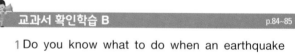

교과서 확인학습 B p.84~85

1 Do you know what to do when an earthquake strikes?

2 Take this quiz and think about how to be safe during this kind of natural disaster.

3 When things start to shake, run outside quickly.

4 Stay away from windows.

5 Use the stairs to get out of buildings.

6 When you are outside, hold on to a pole or a tree.

7 How did you do on the quiz?

8 Can you survive an earthquake safely?

9 Here are some safety tips which can be helpful in an earthquake.

10 Let's check them one by one and learn what to do.

11 Don't run outside when things are shaking.

12 Find a table or a desk and take cover under it.

13 You can hold on to the legs to protect yourself.

14 Also, stay away from windows.

15 They can break during an earthquake and hurt you.

16 You can go outside when the shaking stops.

17 To get out of buildings, don't use the elevator.

18 Take the stairs.

19 It's much safer.

20 Once you are outside, find an empty space that is far from buildings.

21 There may be people who want to hold on to a pole or a tree, but think again.

22 That's a bad idea because it can fall on you.

23 Earthquakes can strike anytime.

24 They can be scary experiences for everyone.

25 So learn how to be safe in an earthquake.

26 You can avoid injuries and protect yourself.

27 Follow these tips and be safe!

시험대비 실력평가　p.86~89

01 ⑤	02 what to do	03 ②	04 shake
05 ⑤	06 ③	07 are	08 ③, ④
09 ③	10 a quiz	11 ⑤	12 a table or a desk
13 ④	14 whose legs, under it		
15 ③	16 ⑤	17 ③, ④	18 ④
19 the shaking stopped	20 ③		21 empty

22 There are many situations which can be dangerous.　23 ③　24 safe

25 A wet floor and broken glass can be dangerous to people.　26 ②　27 ③　28 ②

29 ③　30 ⑤　31 how to get / take the stairs　32 We should look for an empty space(far from buildings).

01 안전 지침이 있다는 주어진 글에 이어 (D)에서 them이 주어진 글의 safety tips를 가리키므로 다음에 오고 (B)에서 설명을 시작하며 (A)에서 the legs가 (B)의 탁자나 책상의 다리를 말하므로 다음에 나오고 (C)의 They가 (A)의 windows를 가리키므로 다음에 나온다.

02 '의문사+주어+should+동사원형'은 '의문사+to부정사'와 같다.

03 '이러한 종류의 자연 재해가 발생하는 동안'이라는 의미가 가장 적절하다.

04 앞뒤 혹은 아래위로의 짧고 빠른 움직임은 '흔들림, 떨림'이다.

05 퀴즈는 지진이 발생했을 때 무엇을 해야 하는지를 확인하는 문제이다.

06 survive는 '살아남다, 생존하다'라는 의미이다.

07 some safety tips가 주어이므로 복수동사 are를 쓴다.

08 ⓒ에는 주격 관계대명사 which 혹은 that이 들어간다.

09 ⓓ에는 '하나씩'이라는 의미로 one by one을 완성하는 전치사 by가 들어간다. ① at: 시간 앞에 쓰이면서 '~에'라고 해석 ② be interested in: ~에 흥미가 있다 ③ by: 교통수단 앞에서 쓰이며 '~로'라고 해석 ④ be crowded with: ~으로 붐비다 ⑤ look forward to: ~를 고대하다

10 이 글 앞에, 우리가 풀어야 하는 퀴즈가 있었다.

11 빈칸에는 '하나씩'이라는 의미가 들어가는 것이 가장 적절하다. ① 사례별로 ② 나란히 ③ 조금씩, 서서히 ④ 하나씩

12 탁자나 책상을 가리키는 대명사이다.

13 ④번 뒤 문장의 주어인 They가 가리키는 것은 창문이다.

14 스스로를 보호하기 위해서, 당신은 다리를 붙잡을 수 있는 탁자나 책상을 찾아서 그 아래에 숨어야 한다.

15 ⓒ는 to부정사가 '~하기 위하여'라는 의미의 부사로 쓰이고 있다. ① 목적보어 ② 진주어 ③ 부사적 용법 중 목적(~하기 위하여) ④ 목적어 ⑤ something을 수식하는 형용사로 각각 쓰이고 있다.

16 창문으로부터 멀리 떨어져야 할 이유로 창문이 깨져 다칠 수 있기 때문이라고 하였다.

17 사람을 선행사로 받는 관계대명사 who가 들어가야 하며, who를 대신하여 that이 쓰일 수 있다.

18 (A) '건물에서 나가기 위해서'라는 목적을 나타내는 to부정사, (B) 비교급을 강조하는 much, (C) 부사절을 이끄는 접속사 because가 들어가는 것이 옳다.

19 흔들림이 멈추었을 때 밖으로 나가라고 하였다.

20 건물과 멀리 떨어진 공터를 찾아야 한다고 하였으므로 ③번 '건물 가까이에서 가만히 서 있어야 한다.'는 내용과 일치하지 않는다.

21 사람이 없거나 아무것도 담고 있지 않는 상태는 '비어 있는'이다.

22 which를 대신하여 that을 써도 좋다.

23 '의문사+to부정사'는 '의문사+주어+should 동사원형'으로 바꿔 쓸 수 있다.

24 위험한 상황에서 무엇을 해야 할지 배우고 안전하자는 의미이다. dangerous의 반의어인 safe를 쓰는 것이 옳다.

25 젖은 바닥과 깨진 유리가 위험할 수 있다고 하였다.

26 바닥이 젖어 있으면 닦아야 한다고 하였다.

27 hold on to: ~을 붙잡다 fall on: ~위로 떨어지다

28 빈칸 (C)에는 방법을 나타내는 how가 들어간다. ②번에는

How+형용사+명사+주어+동사!의 감탄문이 들어가며 나머지는 모두 What이 쓰인다.

29 기둥이나 나무가 넘어질 수 있으므로 그것들을 붙잡는 것은 나쁜 생각이라고 보는 것이 옳다. 따라서 **bad**라고 써야 한다.

30 ① outside ② empty ③ far from ④ safe의 반의어이다.

31 had better+동사원형: ~하는 편이 낫다

32 밖으로 나오면 (건물에서 떨어진) 공터를 찾으라고 하였다.

서술형 시험대비
p.90~91

01 how to be safe

02 an earthquake

03 to shake (또는 shaking)

04 strike

05 Here are some safety tips.
They can be helpful in an earthquake.

06 some safety tips

07 what we should do

08 ⓐ are ⓑ learn ⓒ to protect

09 Also, stay away from windows which can break during an earthquake and hurt you.

10 Because tables and desks can protect us when things fall.

11 Find an empty space that(또는 which) is far from buildings.

12 When the shaking stops

13 Taking the stairs, using the elevator

14 it can fall on us

15 Don't use the elevator.
Don't hold on to a pole or a tree.

16 how to be safe during an earthquake

17 learn how to be safe in an earthquake

01 '어떻게 해야 안전할 수 있는지'라는 의미이다. 의문사+to부정사 형태를 활용하여 답을 쓴다.

02 '이러한 종류의 자연 재해'는 지진을 가리킨다.

03 start는 to부정사와 동명사를 모두 목적어로 취하는 동사이다.

04 어떤 사람이나 사물에 손상이나 해를 끼치게 위해 갑작스럽게 나쁜 방식으로 영향을 미치는 것은 strike이다.

05 선행사가 some safety tips이므로 대명사로 쓸 경우 They를 쓰는 것에 유의한다.

06 몇몇 안전 지침을 가리키는 대명사이다.

07 '의문사+to부정사'는 '의문사+주어+should+동사원형'과 같다.

08 ⓐ some safety tips가 주어이므로 are, ⓑ 무엇을 해야 할지 배워 보자는 것이 자연스러우므로 learn이며 check와 병렬 관

계이므로 learn을 그대로 쓴다. ⓒ '스스로를 보호하기 위해서' 라고 해석해야 하므로 to부정사를 사용하여 빈칸을 채운다.

09 They가 가리키는 것이 windows이므로 사물을 가리키는 주격 관계대명사 which를 써서 문장을 만든다. that을 써도 무방하다.

10 질문: 탁자 아래에 숨는 것이 왜 도움이 되나요?

11 주격 관계대명사 which 혹은 that을 사용하여 하나의 문장으로 만든다.

12 흔들림이 멈추면 밖으로 나갈 수 있다고 하였다.

13 계단을 이용하는 것이 엘리베이터를 이용하는 것보다 훨씬 더 안전하다.

14 기둥이나 나무가 넘어질 수 있으므로 이것을 붙잡고 있는 것은 좋은 생각이 아니라고 하였다.

15 승강기를 이용하지 말고 기둥이나 나무도 붙잡지 말라고 하였다.

16 위 글은 지진이 발생하는 동안 지켜야 할 안전 수칙에 관하여 이야기하고 있다.

17 지진은 모두에게 무서운 경험이기 때문에 지진으로부터 안전을 지키는 법을 배워야만 한다.

영역별 핵심문제
p.93~97

01 ④   02 ①   03 ①   04 ⑤

05 (1) Keep in mind   (2) one by one   (3) ake a rest
(4) Why don't you

06 (1) You should hold on to your hat.
(2) I tried to stay away from crowded places.
(3) My younger brother took cover behind the car.

07 ①   08 ⑤   09 ⑤

10 Remember to be home by six o'clock.

11 ⑤   12 (A) interesting, (B) worried, (C) cover   13 They are worried about earthquakes these days.   14 I should take cover under a table. 15 ③   16 safety   17 ⑤

18 ③   19 what to say   20 ③

21 ⑤   22 ④   23 ②, ③

24 You should know how to use your money wisely.

25 ⑤   26 Where is the ketchup which(또는 that) was in the refrigerator?   27 ⑤

28 what to write about   29 ③   30 ③

31 safety tips which, can be helpful[useful]   32 ③

33 ④   34 ②   35 ④

01 홍수, 가뭄, 지진, 폭풍우를 포함할 수 있는 것은 disaster(재난) 이다.

02 위험하거나 해롭지 않은 상태를 가리키는 말은 safety(안전)이 다.

03 ① slippery: 미끄러운

04 cover: (비용을) 감당하다, 감싸다; 표지

05 keep in mind: ~을 기억하다, one by one: 하나씩, take a rest: 휴식을 취하다, Why don't you ~?: ~하는 게 어때?

06 hold on to: ~을 꼭 잡다, stay away from: ~에서 떨어져 있다, take cover: 숨다

07 주어진 문장은 무엇이 문제인지에 대한 질문의 답변으로 적절하므로 (A)가 적합하다.

08 대화에서 Yujin이 왜 의사에게 안 갔는지는 나와 있지 않다.

09 (A)에 들어갈 말로 ⑤번을 제외한 나머지는 모두 충고하는 표현이다.

10 'Don't forget ~'은 '~할 것을 잊지 마.'라는 의미로 'Remember ~'와 바꾸어 쓸 수 있다.

11 Jack은 방청소를 먼저 한 후 외출할 것이다.

12 (A) sound interesting: 흥미롭다 (B) be worried about ~: ~에 대해 걱정하다 (C) take cover: 숨다, 피난하다

13 Brian과 Jane은 요즘 지진에 대해 걱정한다.

14 프로그램에 따르면 지진 발생시, 탁자 아래로 숨어야 한다.

15 영화가 시작하기까지 20분이 남았으므로 뛰자는 Emily의 제안에 다칠 수 있다는 내용이 이어져야 하므로 (C)가 알맞다.

16 비록 Tom과 Emily는 영화관에 조금 늦었지만 그들은 안전(safety)보다 중요한 것은 없다고 동의하였다.

17 목적격 관계대명사 whom은 who나 that이 대신할 수 있으며 생략 가능하다. ⑤ 전치사 뒤의 관계대명사는 생략할 수 없다.

18 ③번은 who 대신 소유격 관계대명사 whose를 써야 한다.

19 '의문사+to부정사'는 '의문사+주어+should 동사원형'과 같다.

20 '책의 표지'라는 의미이므로 첫 번째 문장에는 소유격 관계대명사 whose가 들어가는 것이 옳으며, 두 번째 문장에는 bought의 목적어가 비어 있으므로 목적격 관계대명사 which나 that이 들어가는 것이 옳다.

21 where to wash 혹은 where I should wash라고 쓰는 것이 옳다.

22 목적격 관계대명사로 사용되면서 동시에 '어느 드레스'라는 의미로 쓰일 수 있는 which가 공통으로 들어간다.

23 주격 관계대명사가 쓰이는 자리이다. 사람을 선행사로 취하고 있으므로 who나 that을 쓰는 것이 옳다.

24 '돈을 현명하게 쓰는 법'이므로 how를 사용하여 문장을 만든다.

25 모두 관계대명사 who이지만, ⑤번은 의문대명사 who로 '누구'라고 해석된다. betray: 배신하다

26 냉장고 안에 있던 케첩이 어디 있는지를 묻는 문장으로 쓰면 된다.

27 what do you think about ~?: ~에 대해 어떻게 생각하니? what to do: 무엇을 해야 할지

28 '의문사+to부정사'를 이용하여 빈칸을 채운다. write about: ~에 대하여 쓰다

29 ⓐ는 '안전할 방법'이고 ⓑ는 '퀴즈가 어땠는지'를 묻는 말이다. 따라서 둘 다 how가 들어가야 한다.

30 글쓴이는 안전 지침에 관하여 이야기하기를 원한다.

31 which를 대신하여 that을 써도 무방하다.

32 지진 발생 시에 유의해야 할 점을 열거하고 있으므로 ⓐ에는 '더욱이, 또한'에 해당하는 moreover를 쓰는 것이 옳다. ① 그러나 ② 그러므로 ④ 마찬가지로 ⑤ 반면에

33 ④ 탁자 아래로 숨으라고 하였다.

34 ⓐ는 '~하기 위하여'라는 의미의 부사적 용법으로 쓰인 to부정사이다. 각 to부정사의 용법은 ① want의 목적어로 쓰인 명사적 용법 ② '~하기 위하여'라는 의미의 부사 ③ anything을 수식하는 형용사 ④ 진주어로 쓰인 명사적 용법 ⑤ 목적격보어로 쓰인 명사적 용법이다.

35 밖에 있을 때 공터를 찾으라고 하였으므로 ④번이 옳다.

단원별 예상문제   p.98~101

01 (B) → (C) → (D) → (A)

02 is a person who tells the actors what to do

03 I'm worried about my leg.

04 I hope you feel better soon.   05 ①

06 (A) earthquakes   (B) some helpful tips   (C) we need to take cover under a table

07 ⓑ to clean → cleaning   08 ③

09 You should keep that in mind.

10 ④   11 ③   12 ②   13 where to go   14 ②   15 ④   16 ②

17 The person who(또는 that 또는 whom) I talked with gave me good advice.   18 ④

19 ③   20 Find a table or a desk and take cover under it   21 ⑤   22 ①, ④

23 ③   24 how to protect   25 ⑤

01 (B) 걱정 표현 → (C) 고마움 표현 → (D) 충고하기 → (A) 대답

02 영화감독은 배우들에게 무엇을 할지 말해주는 사람이다.

03 be worried about: ~에 대해 걱정하다

05 useful: 유용한, handy: 편리한, friendly: 친근한, generous: 관대한, convenient: 편리한

06 오늘 나는 지진에 대한 프로그램을 보았다. 나는 요즘 지진에 대해 걱정하기 때문에 이는 매우 흥미로웠다. 내가 프로그램을 보고 있는 동안, 나는 Brian과 이야기를 나누었고 그에게 지진 안전에 대한 유용한 정보를 주었다. 프로그램은 우리 주변에 무언가가 흔들리기 시작할 때 우리는 탁자 아래로 숨을 필요가 있다고 하였다.

07 finish는 동명사를 목적어로 취하기 때문에 cleaning이 알맞

08 ③ 대화를 통해 왜 Jack이 방청소를 나중에 하고 싶어 했는지 알 수 없다.

10 주어진 문장은 안전 규칙에 관한 내용이므로 (D)에 위치해야 한다.

11 각각 지시부사, 관계대명사, 명사절 접속사로 쓰이는 that이 들어가야 한다.

12 ②번의 아래 문장은 'I know the man. I admire him.'을 하나로 만든 문장이다. 따라서 위 문장과 다르다.

13 '어디로 가야 할지'를 설명해주겠다는 의미로 볼 수 있다.

14 ⓐ which는 전치사 to의 목적어였던 the music을 받아주는 관계대명사이다. ⓑ 목적격 관계대명사가 생략되어 있으나 빠져도 무방하다. ⓒ 주격 관계대명사가 빠져 있다. people who don't have their own gardens로 쓰는 것이 옳다. ⓓ 목적격 관계대명사가 생략된 채로 두 문장이 이어지고 있으므로 대명사 it을 빼는 것이 옳다. ⓔ be into ~: ~에 관심이 많다

15 ④ how to protect yourself 혹은 how you should protect yourself라고 쓰는 것이 옳다.

16 사람과 사물을 모두 선행사로 받을 수 있는 것은 관계대명사 that이다.

17 give someone advice: ~에게 조언을 해주다

18 ④번은 '차의 핸들'이 고장 난 것이므로 소유격 관계대명사 whose가 쓰이며, 나머지는 모두 that이 들어갈 수 있다.

19 (A) some safety tips를 가리키므로 복수명사를 지칭하는 them, (B) 주어와 목적어가 같을 때 목적어로 재귀대명사 사용, (C) 명사가 잇따라 나오므로 전치사 during을 쓴다. while 은 접속사로 부사절을 이끈다.

20 'A: 물건들이 흔들리기 시작해. 지진이 오려나봐. 어디에 숨어야 할지 모르겠어. B: 책상이나 탁자를 찾아서 그 밑에 숨어.'

21 주어진 문장의 They가 가리키는 것은 Earthquakes이다.

22 since와 as는 모두 '~ 때문에'라는 의미로 사용될 수 있는 접속사이다.

23 사람들이 무언가를 붙잡는 이유는 글에 나와 있지 않다.

24 답변에서 조언을 따라함으로써 스스로를 보호할 수 있다고 하였으므로 '내 스스로를 보호할 방법을 모르겠어.'라고 말했다고 볼 수 있다.

25 ⓐ 계단을 이용하는 것을 가리키는 대명사이다. ⓑ which로 대체 가능하다. ⓒ '~일지도 모른다'는 가능성을 의미하고 있다. ⓓ hold on to: ~을 꼭 붙잡다.

서술형 실전문제 p.102~103

01 ⓑ worrying → worried

02 She is concerned about her leg.

03 She is going to go see a doctor.

04 I like the people whom I work with. / I like the people with whom I work.

05 what to do after graduation. / what I should do after graduation.

06 (1) I want to have the cheese cake.
It is sold only online.
(2) Where is the cap?
It was in the closet.

07 (A) I'm worried about you.
(B) You should watch your hands when you use a knife.

08 how to dance

09 There may be people.
They want to hold on to a pole or a tree.

10 기둥이나 나무를 꼭 붙잡으려는 것

11 (C) strike (D) avoid (E) protect (F) Follow

12 We should use the stairs because it is much safer.

13 We can learn how to be safe in an earthquake.

14 It's because they can break and hurt us.

15 which[that], helpful[useful]

01 be worried about: ~에 대해 걱정하다

02 Yujin은 그녀의 다리를 걱정하고 있다.

03 Yujin은 방과 후에 의사에게 갈 것이다.

04 'I like the people. I work with them.'을 하나로 만든 문장이다.

05 graduation: 졸업

06 is sold: 판매되다 closet: 옷장

08 대화의 흐름을 보아 춤추는 방법을 알려줄 수 있는지를 묻는 말이 들어가는 것이 옳다.

09 They 대신 People을 써도 좋다.

10 Holding on to a pole or a tree를 의미하는 것이다.

11 strike: 발생하다

12 계단을 이용하는 것이 훨씬 더 안전하다고 하였다.

13 위 글에서 무엇을 배울 수 있는지 묻고 있다. 지진에서 안전할 수 있는 방법을 배울 수 있는 지문이다.

14 창문에서 떨어져 있어야 하는 이유는 창문이 깨져서 우리를 다치게 할 수 있기 때문이다.

15 글쓴이가 독자들에게 주는 조언은 유용하다.

창의사고력 서술형 문제 p.104

|모범답안|

01 (A) the people there
(B) they all followed the safety rules
(C) cover my nose and mouth with a wet towel

02 (1) Do you know how to prepare for natural disasters?

(2) I want to learn how to cook spaghetti.

(3) Tell me when to go to the theater.

(4) I don't know what to buy.

(5) Let's decide when to meet.

03 (1) A pilot is a person who flies a plane.

(2) A nurse is a person who takes care of patients.

(3) An architect is a person who designs buildings.

(4) A dentist is a person whose job is to examine and treat people's teeth.

(5) A farmer is a person who owns or manages a farm.

01 나는 어제 시립 도서관에 큰 불이 났다고 들었다. 나는 Brian과 그것에 대해 이야기를 나누었다. 나는 거기 있는 사람들에 대해 걱정했었다. Brian은 그들 모두 안전 규칙을 따랐기 때문에 안전하다고 이야기해 주었다. 솔직히, 나는 화재 시 무엇을 해야 하는지 알지 못했다. Brian은 젖은 수건으로 코와 입을 가리고 몸을 낮게 유지하여 탈출해야 한다고 이야기해 주었다. 나는 그것을 명심했다. 또한, 나는 안전 규칙에 대해 좀 더 알아볼 것을 다짐했다.

단원별 모의고사
p.105~108

01 ③　　　　02 ①　　　　03 ③

04 (C) → (A) → (D) → (E) → (B)

05 (1) How can we prepare for a natural disaster?

(2) When an earthquake strikes, buildings can shake and fall down.

(3) Don't run on the stairs. You might fall or get hurt.

06 earthquake　　　　07 ②, ③

08 물건들이 흔들리기 시작하면 탁자 아래에 숨는 것

09 (A) play basketball with Minu

(B) clean his room

(C) be home by six o'clock

10 ⑤　　　11 ⓐ → accident　　　12 ②

13 ④　　　14 ②, ⑤　　　15 decide what to eat

16 is the day that comes before　　　17 ③

18 ④　　　19 Taking, how to be safe, strikes

20 ④　　　21 ③　　　22 ③　　　23 We can hold on to the legs of the table.

24 drinking　　　25 ⑤

01 앞뒤로 또는 위 아래로 짧고 빠른 움직임을 나타내는 말은 shake(흔들림)이다

02 주어진 문장에서 fall은 '떨어지다'를 뜻한다. 이와 같은 의미로 쓰인 것은 ①번이다. ②, ③, ④번은 '가을', ⑤번은 '폭포'를 의미한다.

03 take a break: 휴식을 취하다, break: 부서지다, (기록을) 깨다

04 (C) 영화가 몇 시에 시작하는지 질문 → (A) 대답 → (D) 반응 및 뛰자고 제안 → (E) 거절 및 충고하기 → (B) 동의

05 prepare for: ~을 준비하다, ~을 대비하다, natural disaster: 자연 재해, strike: 발생하다, stairs: 계단, get hurt: 다치다

06 종종 큰 피해를 야기하는 지구 표면의 한 부분이 흔들리는 것을 가리키는 말은 earthquake(지진)이다.

07 tip은 '조언, 정보'를 뜻하며 이와 바꾸어 쓸 수 있는 것은 information(정보), guidance(지침)이다.

09 Jack은 Minu와 농구하기로 되어 있었다. 아빠는 그에게 외출하기 전에 방청소를 먼저 할 것을 충고했지만 Jack은 이를 미루고 싶어 했다. 하지만 아빠는 이를 먼저 할 것을 요구했고, 그래서 Jack은 그의 방을 청소하기로 결정했다. 농구하러 나가면서 Jack은 6시까지 귀가할 것을 약속했다.

10 수진은 친구에게 전화를 해서 다른 날에 소풍을 가려고 한다.

11 accidental: 우연한, accident: 사고

12 바닥이 미끄럽다는 상대방의 말에 너의 침실 실내화가 마음에 든다는 대답은 어색하다.

13 주어진 문장의 빈칸에는 주격 관계대명사 who 또는 that이 들어간다. 관계대명사 that은 who, whom, which를 대신하여 쓰일 수 있다. ④번에는 소유격 관계대명사 whose가 들어간다.

14 눈이 크다는 표현은 'She has big eyes.' 혹은 'Her eyes are big.'이다.

15 '무엇을 먹을지'이므로 what to eat이라고 쓰는 것이 옳다.

16 월요일은 화요일 앞에 오는 날이다.

17 위 문장에는 주격 관계대명사, 아래 문장에는 소유격 관계대명사가 들어가야 한다. 소유격 관계대명사 뒤에는 관사가 없는 명사가 온다.

18 (A) '빠르게'라는 의미가 옳으므로 부사 quickly, (B) stay away from: ~에서 떨어져 있다, (C) '건물 밖으로 나오기 위해서'이므로 부사로 쓰인 to부정사를 쓰는 것이 옳다.

19 이 퀴즈를 푸는 것은 지진이 발생할 때 우리가 어떻게 해야 안전할 수 있는지를 생각하도록 돕는다.

20 퀴즈는 자연 재해가 발생하는 동안 해야 하는 일을 제대로 알고 있는지를 확인하는 것이다.

21 지진 발생 시 주의해야 하는 사항을 첨가하여 이야기하고 있으므로 '게다가'라는 의미의 연결어가 들어가는 것이 옳다.

22 ⓑ, ⓒ, ⓔ가 글의 내용과 일치한다

23 스스로를 보호하기 위하여 탁자나 책상의 다리를 잡을 수 있다고 하였다.

24 전치사의 목적어 역할을 하도록 동명사를 쓰는 것이 옳다.

25 Darlene이 지진 발생 후 15일 후에 발견되었다고 나와 있을 뿐 지진이 며칠 동안 지속되었는지는 언급되지 않았다.

19

Happy Others, Happier Me

06 어떤 것에 관한 정보를 제공하는 글귀나 사진들이 위에 있는 종이나 나무 등을 가리키는 말은 sign(표지판)이다.

시험대비 실력평가   p.112

01 ②	02 ③	03 ①	04 danger
05 ①	06 (1) confusing	(2) decide	(3) soap
(4) secret			

01 국가, 마을, 강 등을 보여주는 지구의 표면 또는 그것의 일부의 그림이나 도면을 나타내는 것은 map(지도)이다.

02 say: (글이) 쓰이다, 말하다

03 sign: 표지판

04 주어진 단어의 관계는 반의어 관계이다. danger: 위험, safety: 안전

05 주어진 문장에서 'free'는 '무료의'를 의미한다. 이와 같이 쓰인 문장은 ①번이다. 나머지는 '자유로운'을 의미한다.

06 confusing: 혼란스러운, secret: 비결, soap: 비누, decide: 결정하다, 결심하다

서술형 시험대비   p.113

01 impossible

02 (A)good (B)help (C)try (D)tip (E)glad

03 (1) He put up a 'For Sale' sign in front of his house.

  (2) I finished this work earlier thanks to his help.

  (3) We have to do our homework on our own.

04 (1) Thanks to (2) the other day (3) give out

05 (1) give out (2) come up with (3) put up (4) One day

06 sign

01 주어진 단어의 관계는 반의어 관계이다. possible: 가능한, impossible: 불가능한

03 (1) put up: ~을 세우다 in front of: ~ 앞에 (2) thanks to: ~ 덕택에 (3) on one's own: 자기 스스로

04 thanks to: ~ 덕분에, the other day: 며칠 전에, give out: ~을 나누어 주다

05 give out: 나누어 주다, come up with: 제시하다, put up: 세우다, 설치하다, one day: 어느 날

Conversation

핵심 Check   p.114~115

1 me help you   2 Do you need any help

3 deep / Don't worry, help you

4 glad you like it   5 My pleasure

6 for saying so

교과서 대화문 익히기

Check(√) True or False   p.116

(1) T   (2) F   (3) T   (4) F

교과서 확인학습   p.118~119

Listen & Speak 1 A

give out / Let me help you then / volunteer club activity / mean / It means that, each other, better place

Listen & Speak 1 B

my mentee / Do you teach her every weekend / You are a good mentor

Listen & Speak 2 A

this is for you / How did you know that / the other day / How nice / I'm glad you like it

Listen & Talk 2 B

I read a story about a special boy in India / Why is he special / had to work / I'm glad you like it

Real Life Communication

Are you feeling better / on my own / Let me help you. join my study group / we can learn better when we teach each other / Thanks for helping me

Let's Check 1

looks heavy. Let me help you / Where is the bus stop around here / No problem

시험대비 기본평가 — p.120

01 ② 02 ④ 03 ⓒ which → that

04 ④

01 'Let me help you.'는 '내가 도와줄게.'라고 도움을 제안하는 표현이다.

02 Henry는 Sujin과 같이 버스 정류장으로 가고 있다.

03 명사절을 이끄는 접속사 that이 적절하다.

시험대비 실력평가 — p.121~122

01 ② 02 Let me help you. 03 ④

04 smile 05 ③ 06 ⑤ 07 (A) her

mentee (B) her old books (C) she felt happy (D)

she was a good mentor 08 She suggested

joining her study group to him.

09 Because she thought that they can learn better

when they teach each other.

10 (B)→ (D) → (A) → (C) 11 a massage

12 He gave Aram a massage.

03 ④번은 유감을 나타낸다.

04 스티커는 웃음의 중요성을 강조한다.

05 주어진 문장의 앞에서 그가 많은 학생들을 집에서 가르치는 이유를 설명하고 있으므로 (C)번이 알맞다.

06 Yujin이 인도에 있는 많은 학생들을 돕기 위해 무엇을 했는지는 알 수 없다.

07 오늘 나는 지민이 인상 깊었다. 그녀는 매주 아동 센터에서 그녀의 멘티를 가르친다. 게다가 그녀는 그녀의 멘티에게 그녀가 보던 책을 주려고 하였다. 그녀는 멘티를 가르칠 때 행복을 느낀다고 말했다. 나는 그녀가 좋은 멘토라고 생각했다. 상자가 무거워 보여서 나는 그녀를 도와주었다. 나는 타인을 돕는 것이 세상을 더 나은 곳으로 만들어 준다고 생각한다.

08 Emily는 Brian에게 그녀의 공부 모임에 함께 할 것을 제안했다.

09 Emily가 공부 모임을 시작한 것은 서로 가르칠 때 더 잘 학습할 수 있다고 생각했기 때문이다.

10 (B) 고민 이야기 및 조언 구함 → (D) 도움 및 방법 제안 → (A) 시도할 계획 나타내기 및 고마움 표현 → (C) 칭찬에 대해 응답하기

12 Jack은 Aram의 기분이 나아지도록 마사지를 해 주었다.

서술형 시험대비 — p.123

01 I feel happy when I teach her.

02 (m)entor

03 many children in his town

04 (A) a special boy in India

(B) he was special

(C) couldn't go to school and had to work

05 She is going to give out free stickers.

06 서로에게 미소 지을 때 세상은 더 좋은 곳이 될 것이다.

02 경험이 별로 없거나 종종 어린 사람에게 도움이나 조언을 주거나 가르치는 사람을 가리키는 말은 mentor(멘토)이다.

04 오늘 Yujin은 나에게 인도의 어느 특별한 소년에 관한 이야기를 해주었다. 나는 왜 그녀가 그가 특별하다고 하는지 궁금했다. Yujin은 그 소년이 그의 마을에서 학교에 갈 수 없고 일을 해야 하는 많은 아이들을 자기 집에서 매일 가르친다고 이야기했다. 그것은 정말 좋은 이야기였다.

05 Sora는 Tom을 돕기 위해 무료 스티커를 나누어 줄 것이다.

교과서

Grammar

핵심 Check — p.124~125

1 (1) which(또는 that) (2) who(m)(또는 that)

2 (1) persuaded, to shake (2) expect, to eat (3) told, not to be

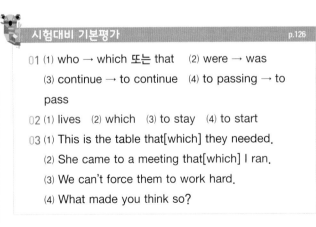

시험대비 기본평가 — p.126

01 (1) who → which 또는 that (2) were → was

(3) continue → to continue (4) to passing → to pass

02 (1) lives (2) which (3) to stay (4) to start

03 (1) This is the table that[which] they needed.

(2) She came to a meeting that[which] I ran.

(3) We can't force them to work hard.

(4) What made you think so?

01 (1) 사물이 선행사이므로 which 또는 that, (2) The building이 주어이므로 단수동사 was, (3), (4) enable과 allow는 to부정사(to+동사원형)를 목적격보어로 취하는 동사이다.

02 (1) 주어가 The man이므로 단수동사 lives를 쓴다. (2) 사물을 선행사로 취하는 목적격 관계대명사 which를 쓰면 된다.

(3), (4) tell과 encourage는 5형식으로 쓰일 때 to부정사를 목적격보어로 사용한다.

03 (1) 'They needed the table.'을 관계절로 만든다. (2) 'I ran a meeting.'을 관계사절로 만든다. (3) force는 to부정사를 목적격보어로 취하는 동사이다. (4) '네가 생각하게 만들다'이므로 make를 사역동사로 사용한다.

01 ③, ④   02 ④   03 ④   04 He didn't allow me to use all the money that I have.
05 ⑤   06 ③   07 ⑤   08 which you should do, to boil   09 ③   10 ②
11 ⑤   12 Do you remember those people who(m) you met on holiday?   13 ⑤
14 ④   15 ③   16 to help me with math
17 ⑤   18 which I did yesterday
19 we will force you to
20 The only thing that you should not do is to cut in while others are talking.   21 ⑤   22 ④
23 taught us to love

01 사물을 선행사로 받아주면서, 이끄는 문장에 동사의 목적어가 비어 있으므로 목적격 관계대명사 which가 들어간다. which를 대신하여 that을 쓸 수 있다.

02 'My mom bought the shoes for me.'를 관계절로 만든 것이다. 따라서 ④번이 옳다.

03 사역동사 make는 원형부정사를 목적격보어로 취한다.

04 '내가 가진 모든 돈'이므로 I have가 all the money를 수식하도록 문장을 만든다. 관계대명사 which를 써도 좋다.

05 목적격 관계대명사를 생략할 수 있다. ⑤번은 명사절을 이끄는 접속사로 생각할 수 없다. go bad: 상하다

06 '작은 가게들'이 주어이므로 복수동사 are를 쓴다. be crowded with: ~으로 붐비다

07 allow, encourage는 to부정사를 목적격보어로 취하는 동사이며, decide와 refuse는 to부정사를 목적어로 취하는 동사이다. ⑤번은 전치사 in의 목적어로 동명사가 들어간다.

08 목적격 관계대명사 which를 대신하여 that을 써도 무방하다.

09 cause는 to부정사를 목적격보어로 취하는 동사이다. 따라서 to stop이 옳다.

10 ⓐ The toys가 주어이므로 동사는 are를 쓴다. ⓑ, ⓔ want, require는 to부정사를 목적격보어로 취하는 동사이므로 각각 to do the job, to hand in the reports라고 쓰는 것이 옳다. ⓒ look for~ : ~을 찾다

11 빈칸에는 to부정사를 목적격보어로 취하는 동사가 들어가야 한

12 who(m)을 대신하여 that을 써도 무방하며 목적격 관계대명사이므로 생략해도 좋다.

13 <보기>의 that은 관계대명사로 동사의 목적어가 빠져 있는 불완전한 문장을 이끈다. 따라서 ⑤번이 관계대명사이다. 나머지는 모두 명사절을 이끄는 접속사 that으로 완전한 문장을 이끈다.

14 선행사가 사람이 아니므로 관계대명사 which를 쓰고, persuade는 to부정사를 목적격보어로 취하는 동사이므로 to tell, '내가 돈을 지불하게 만들었다'는 사역동사로 쓰인 make이므로 원형부정사 pay를 쓰는 것이 적절하다.

15 불완전한 문장을 이끄는 관계대명사와 완전한 문장을 이끄는 명사절 접속사로 모두 쓰일 수 있는 것은 that이다.

16 수학을 도와줄 멘토가 필요하다고 하였으므로 help me with math를 어법에 맞게 to help me with math로 쓰면 된다.

17 모두 목적격 관계대명사가 들어가지만 ⑤번에는 주격 관계대명사가 들어간다.

18 목적격 관계대명사 which 대신 that을 써도 좋다.

19 force는 to부정사를 목적격보어로 취하여 '목적어가 V하게 강요하다'라는 의미로 쓰인다.

20 'The only thing is to cut in while others are talking. You should not do it.'을 목적격 관계대명사를 이용하여 하나로 합친 문장이다.

21 need는 5형식으로 쓰일 때 to부정사를 목적격보어로 취한다. 따라서 to do라고 쓰는 것이 옳다.

22 would like는 5형식으로 쓰일 때 to부정사를 목적격보어로 취한다. to부정사는 'to+동사원형' 형태이다.

23 '우리가 삶을 사랑하도록'이므로 teach를 5형식으로 사용하며, 목적격보어로 to부정사를 쓴다. 시제에 유의한다.

01 are, know, to believe, to clean, to focus
02 Hannah's cousin taught her how to play the piano.
03 What do you want me to do
04 the girl to turn down the music.
05 (1) Kyle has the money.
       He found it on the street.
   (2) Is this the book?
       You are looking for it.
06 James advises Olivia to see a doctor.
07 I want to get the job that I applied for.
08 allows him to go shopping with Ann on Monday.
09 to play the guitar for her.
10 The technology that they have developed

enables us to drive a car safely.

11 I like the cat that John found at the park.

12 cause people to have headaches.

13 (1) Osaka is the city which my sister visited last week.

   (2) Robert is an actor whom we like very much.

   (3) My dad gave me the wallet which I really wanted to have.

14 that I can do is to be quiet

15 told me to have

01 관계사절의 수의 일치는 선행사에 달려 있다. people이 선행사이므로 be동사는 are를 쓴다. let은 목적격보어로 원형부정사를 취하는 사역동사이며, expect, get, order는 to부정사를 목적격보어로 취하는 5형식 동사이다.

02 teach+목적어+how 'to부정사'의 형을 취한다.

03 want는 to부정사를 목적격보어로 취하는 동사이다.

04 ask는 to부정사를 목적격보어로 취하는 동사이다.

05 동사와 전치사의 목적어를 목적격 관계대명사로 만들었으므로 the money, the book을 동사와 전치사의 목적어로 하여 문장을 둘로 나눈다.

06 James는 Olivia에게 병원으로 가서 진찰 받을 것을 권하고 있다.

07 apply for: ~에 지원하다

08 allow는 to부정사를 목적격보어로 취하는 동사이다.

09 Emma가 자신을 위해 기타를 연주해 줄 수 있는지 내게 묻고 있다. to부정사를 목적격보어로 취하는 동사 ask를 이용하여 빈칸을 채운다.

10 enable은 to부정사를 목적격보어로 취하는 동사이며, the technology가 주어이므로 enable을 단수동사로 만드는 것에 유의한다.

11 'John이 공원에서 발견했던 고양이'이므로 목적격 관계대명사가 이끄는 문장 'John found at the park'가 the cat을 수식하도록 문장을 만드는 것이 옳다.

12 cause는 목적격보어로 to부정사를 취하는 동사이다. '사람들에게 두통을 일으키는 것'이므로 목적어로 people, 목적격보어로 to have를 사용하여 문장을 만든다.

13 (1), (3) which를 대신하여 that을 쓸 수 있다. (2) whom을 대신하여 who, that을 쓸 수 있으며, 모두 목적격 관계대명사이므로 생략이 가능하다.

14 The only thing이 주어이므로 단수 동사를 쓰는 것에 유의한다.

15 tell은 5형식으로 쓰일 때 to부정사를 목적격보어로 취한다.

Reading

p.132

확인문제

1 T 2 T 3 F 4 F 5 F

p.133

확인문제

1 T 2 F 3 F 4 T 5 F

교과서 확인학습 A

p.134~135

01 are, which 02 to hear, them 03 You Love
04 had 05 However, nobody
06 came up with 07 stuck, to 08 put up, that said 09 were using 10 When, whom they loved, smiling 11 a big success
12 During, disappeared 13 because, happiness to 14 Arrow Man 15 A few years ago, were, confusing 16 enough information 17 ask others to explain
18 Where, on, go to 19 often took, wasted 20 decided to solve
21 lots of red arrow stickers 22 rode, around, stuck, on 23 asked him to do
24 wanted to help
25 Thanks to, easily, save time

교과서 확인학습 B

p.136~137

1 Here are two stories which I read yesterday.

2 Do you want to hear about them?

3 Call Someone You Love

4 New York had many pay phones on its streets.

5 However, nobody really used them.

6 One day, a man came up with an idea.

7 He stuck coins to one of the phones.

8 He also put up a sign that said, "Call Someone You Love."

9 Soon, many people were using the phone.

10 When they were talking to someone whom they loved, they didn't stop smiling.

11 His idea became a big success.

12 During the day, all the coins disappeared.

13 The man was very happy because his small idea

gave happiness to many people.

14 The Red Arrow Man

15 A few years ago, the maps at bus stops in Seoul were very confusing.

16 They didn't have enough information.

17 People had to ask others to explain the maps.

18 "Where is this bus stop on the map? Does this bus go to Gwanghwamun?"

19 Many people often took the wrong bus and wasted their time.

20 One day, a young man decided to solve this problem.

21 He bought lots of red arrow stickers.

22 Every day he rode his bicycle around the city and stuck the stickers on the bus maps.

23 Nobody asked him to do this.

24 He just wanted to help others.

25 Thanks to his effort, people could understand the maps easily and save time.

시험대비 실력평가
p.138~141

01 two stories which I read yesterday

02 ⑤   03 who, whom, that   04 ②

05 ③   06 ④   07 ③

08 It said, "Call Someone You Love."   09 ②

10 wasted

11 화살표 모양의 스티커를 사서 서울 시내를 돌아다니며 버스 지도에 스티커를 붙이는 것

12 ③   13 ③   14 Because there wasn't enough information on the maps.   15 ④

16 ⓐ to hear ⓒ talking   17 ⑤

18 disappear   19 ④   20 ②   21 which, stuck coins to   22 ③

23 (B)—(A)—(C) 24 ②   25 explain → to explain

26 ③   27 ⑤   28 They didn't have enough information.   29 ③   30 Seoul, right, save their time

01 어제 내가 읽은 두 개의 이야기를 가리키는 대명사이다.

02 길거리에 공중전화가 많이 있었지만 아무도 사용하지 않았다는 의미이므로 However를 쓰는 것이 옳다.

03 사람을 선행사로 받아주는 목적격 관계대명사 whom이 들어가야 한다. whom을 대신하여 who 혹은 that을 써도 좋다.

04 4형식 동사를 3형식으로 전환할 때 동사 give는 간접목적어 앞에 전치사 to를 붙인다.

05 한 남자가 표지판을 설치하자 곧 많은 사람들이 전화기를 사용하기 시작했다고 이어지는 것이 옳으며, ③번 뒤 문장의 they가 가리키는 것은 주어진 문장의 many people이다.

06 (A) hear about: ~에 관하여 듣다, hear from: ~로부터 소식을 듣다 (B) pay phones를 가리키고 있으므로 복수명사를 지칭하는 them (C) 명사를 이끌고 있으므로 전치사 During, While은 접속사로 부사절을 이끈다.

07 어떤 남자가 공중전화 하나에 동전들을 붙였다고 하였다.

08 표지판에는 '당신이 사랑하는 사람에게 전화 하세요'라고 쓰여 있었다.

09 빈칸 ⓐ에는 좁은 장소 앞에 쓰이는 전치사 at이 들어간다. ① turn off: ~을 끄다 turn on: ~을 켜다 ② be surprised at: ~에 놀라다 ③ pick somebody up: ~을 (차에) 태우러 가다 ④ take care of: ~을 돌보다 ⑤ wait for: ~을 기다리다

10 시간을 낭비했다는 의미이다.

11 간단하게 '버스 지도에 스티커를 붙이는 것'이라고 써도 좋다.

12 청년의 노력 덕분에 사람들이 지도를 쉽게 이해할 수 있게 되었다는 의미이다. Depending on: ~에 따라

13 (A) 셀 수 있는 명사를 수식하는 것은 a few, (B) 지도가 혼란을 유발하는 것이므로 confusing, (C) 사람들의 시간을 가리키는 것이므로 복수 명사를 지칭하는 their를 쓰는 것이 옳다.

14 사람들이 서울에서 버스를 잘못 탔던 이유는 지도에 충분한 정보가 없었기 때문이었다.

15 아무도 이 청년에게 이 일을 하라고 요청하지 않았다고 하였다.

16 ⓐ want는 to부정사를 목적어로 취한다. ⓑ '누군가에게 전화하고 있을 때'라는 의미이므로 진행형을 만들어 주는 것이 옳다.

17 ⓑ 길거리 위에 공중전화가 있다는 의미이므로 전치사 on을 쓴다. ① be interested in: ~에 흥미가 있다 ② be satisfied with: ~에 만족하다 ③ pay attention to: ~에 주목하다 ④ take care of: ~을 돌보다 ⑤ depend on: ~에 의지하다

18 '보여지는 것을 멈추다'는 '사라지다'이다.

19 (A)는 관계대명사 that이다. ④번은 명사절을 이끄는 접속사 that이다.

20 Soon은 '곧'이란 의미로 before long과 같다. For a long time: 오랫동안 Hardly: 거의 ~하지 않는 Still: 그럼에도 불구하고 Lately: 최근에

21 which를 대신하여 that을 써도 무방하다.

22 'nobody really used them'은 아무도 실제로 그것을 사용하지 않았다는 의미로 'not everyone used the pay phone'과는 의미가 다르다. 후자는 모두가 공중전화를 사용한 것은 아니었다는 의미로 누군가는 사용했다는 뜻이다.

23 공중전화(pay phones)가 있지만 → (B) 누구도 그것들(them)을 사용하지 않아 한 남자가 좋은 아이디어를 떠올리고 동전을 붙여 둠 → (A) 또한(also) 표지판을 설치하자 곧 많은 사람들이 전화기를 사용함 → (C) 그들이(they) 통화할 때 계속 미소를

지음

24 지도에 정보가 부족하다고 하였고, 사람들이 다른 사람들에게 지도를 설명해 달라고 요청해야 하므로 '혼란스러운(confusing)'이 들어가는 것이 옳다.

25 ask가 5형식으로 쓰일 때는 to부정사를 목적격보어로 취한다.

26 지도상에서 정류장을 확인하고 지도 위에 스티커를 붙이는 것이다. 전치사 on은 '~(위)에'라는 의미로 어떤 것의 표면에 닿거나 그 표면을 형성하는 것을 나타낼 때 쓰인다.

27 내용상 청년은 다른 사람을 돕기 위해 스티커를 붙였다고 볼 수 있으며, 또한 청년의 노력 덕분에 사람들이 지도를 쉽게 이해할 수 있게 되었다고 하였으므로 bother는 help를 쓰는 것이 옳다.

28 서울의 버스 지도가 가진 문제는 충분한 정보가 없다는 것이다.

29 광화문으로 가는 버스 번호는 위 글에 나와 있지 않다.

30 버스를 잘못 타서 시간을 낭비했다고 했으므로, 청년의 노력 덕분에 서울 사람들은 버스를 제대로 타서 시간을 절약할 수 있었다고 말할 수 있다.

서술형 시험대비
p.142~143

01 (A) happy (B) happiness

02 Here are two stories. / I read them yesterday.

03 Call Someone Who(m) You Love

04 pay phones (on its streets)

05 they kept smiling

06 coins, which(또는 that) nobody really used

07 who, coins

08 A: stick, B: stuck coins, to use, someone whom

09 put up a sign

10 The maps at bus stops in Seoul

11 who asked him to do this

12 they(또는 the maps) didn't have enough information.

13 He stuck red arrow stickers on them.

14 His effort enabled people to understand the maps easily.

15 which, was red

16 confusing, them, waste

17 wanted the maps at bus stops to have enough information.

18 It's because he just wanted to help others.

01 (A) be동사의 보어가 들어가야 하므로 형용사 happy (B) 목적어가 들어가야 하므로 happiness로 쓰는 것이 옳다.

02 목적격 관계대명사를 이용하여 하나로 만들어진 문장이다. two stories가 선행사이므로 복수명사 them을 이용하여 문장을 둘로 나눈다.

03 목적격 관계대명사 whom이 생략되어 있다. whom을 대신하여 who 혹은 that을 써도 좋다.

04 길거리에 있는 공중전화를 가리키는 대명사이다.

05 didn't stop Ving는 'V하는 것을 멈추지 않았다'는 의미이므로 keep Ving를 써서 '계속 V하다'로 쓸 수 있다.

06 누구도 사용하지 않았던 공중전화기 중 하나에 동전들을 붙여 놓은 것을 의미한다.

07 who를 대신하여 that을 써도 좋다.

08 whom을 대신하여 who 또는 that을 써도 무방하다.

09 B as well as A: A 뿐만 아니라 B도

10 서울의 버스 정류장에 있는 지도들을 가리키는 말이다.

11 who를 대신하여 that을 써도 좋다.

12 사람들이 다른 사람들에게 지도를 설명해 달라고 요청해야 했던 이유는 지도에 충분한 정보가 없었기 때문이었다.

13 청년은 버스 지도에 스티커를 붙였다.

14 enable은 목적격보어로 to부정사를 취하는 동사이다.

15 청년이 산 스티커의 색깔은 빨간색이었다. 관계대명사 which를 대신하여 that을 써도 무방하다.

16 don't have to V: V할 필요가 없다

17 want는 to부정사를 목적격보어로 취하는 동사이다. '정류장의 지도가 정보를 갖는 것'이므로 목적어로 the maps at bus stops를 쓰고 목적격보어로 to have ~를 쓴다.

18 남자가 매일 스티커를 지도에 붙인 이유는 다른 사람들을 돕고 싶어서였다.

영역별 핵심문제
p.145~149

01 ② 02 ② 03 (1) waste your time (2) on your own (3) stopped playing

04 mentee 05 (1) come up with (2) The other day (3) on your own 06 ⑤ 07 ②

08 volunteer 09 ⑤ 10 ① 11 ④, ⑤

12 ⑤ 13 ② 14 He made a basket with plastic bags for his mom.

15 She talked about it when they were having dinner the other day.

16 (D) → (C) → (E) → (B) → (A)

17 ④ 18 ⓐ which 또는 that ⓑ to save

19 ③ 20 ① 21 ④ 22 ask her to copy 23 ⑤ 24 ⑤ 25 ⑤

26 whom(또는 that) they loved 27 ②

28 ④번 used → using 29 ⑤

30 (A) to explain (B) to solve (C) to do 31 ①

32 ④ 33 ③ 34 People often took the wrong bus and wasted their time.

25

01 사물들을 차갑게 유지하기 위해 사용되는 장치나 공간을 가리키는 말은 refrigerator(냉장고)이다.

02 ② effort: 노력

03 waste one's time: ~자신의 시간을 낭비하다, on one's own: 자기 스스로, stop ~ing: ~하기를 멈추다

04 주어진 단어의 관계는 상대어 관계이다. mentor: 멘토, mentee: 멘티

05 come up with: ~을 생각해 내다, the other day: 며칠 전에, 지난번, come across: ~을 우연히 만나다 on one's own: 자기 스스로

06 주어진 문장을 포함한 나머지는 모두 '휴식'을 의미하지만 ⑤번은 '나머지'를 의미한다.

07 ②번은 '그러면 내가 도와줄게.'라는 의미로 도움을 제안할 때 쓴다. 나머지는 도와달라는 의미로 쓴다.

08 보수를 받지 않고 무언가를 해주는 사람을 가리키는 말은 volunteer(자원봉사자)이다.

10 주어진 문장은 상자에 든 것이 무엇인지 묻는 질문에 대한 대답이므로 (A)가 알맞다.

11 amazing: 놀라운 discouraged: 낙심한

12 Mike는 지역 아동 센터에서 책을 읽을 것이라는 설명은 대화 내용과 일치하지 않는다.

13 이어지는 대답으로 어떻게 새 바구니를 필요로 하는지 알게 된 것을 설명하는 내용이 이어져야 하므로 ⓑ가 적절하다.

14 Alex는 엄마를 위해 비닐봉지로 바구니를 만들었다.

15 Alex와 엄마는 며칠 전 저녁을 먹으며 새 바구니에 대해 이야기했었다.

16 (D) 이야기 주제 언급 → (C) 주인공이 특별한 이유 질문 → (E) 이야기 내용 설명 → (B) 반응 → (A) 칭찬에 답하기

17 warn은 '~하지 말라고 경고하다'라는 의미로 쓰일 때 to부정사를 목적격보어로 취한다. leak: (물 따위가) 새다

18 ⓐ에는 두 개의 문장을 이어주는 주격 관계대명사를 써야 하며, ⓑ에는 내용상 '물을 절약하도록 조언한다'는 내용이 들어가는 것이 옳다. advise는 to부정사를 목적격보어로 취하므로 to save를 쓴다.

19 want는 to부정사를 목적격보어로 취하는 동사이며, 두 번째 빈칸에는 목적격 관계대명사 which 혹은 that이 들어가는 것이 옳다.

20 목적격 관계대명사로 쓰이면서 동시에 '어느, 어떤'이라고 해석되는 의문사는 which이다.

21 ④ would like는 5형식으로 쓰일 때 to부정사를 목적격보어로 취한다. 따라서 to accept라고 쓰는 것이 옳다.

22 ask가 5형식으로 쓰일 때는 목적격보어로 to부정사를 취한다. '그녀가 복사하는 것'이므로 목적어로 her, 목적격보어로 to copy를 쓴다.

23 주어가 The bananas이므로 복수 동사를 쓰는 것이 옳다.

24 주격 관계대명사는 생략할 수 없다.

25 say는 to부정사를 목적격보어로 취할 수 없다.

26 글의 내용상 그들이 사랑하는 사람에게 전화하고 있다고 보는 것이 옳다.

27 (A) 공중전화기가 많지만 아무도 쓰지 않는다는 것이 옳으므로 nobody, (B) come up with: (생각을) 떠올리다, come down with: (병으로) 앓아눕다 (C) 낮 동안에 모든 동전이 사라졌다는 것이 내용상 적절하다.

28 사람들이 그 전화기를 사용했다는 것이므로 현재분사를 써서 수동태가 아닌 진행형으로 표현하는 것이 옳다.

29 사람들이 몇 통의 전화를 했는지는 글을 읽고 알 수 없다.

30 ask는 5형식으로 쓰일 때 to부정사를 목적격보어로 취한다. decide는 to부정사를 목적어로 취하는 동사이다.

31 ①번에 이어지는 문장에서 the stickers는 청년이 산 lots of red arrow stickers를 의미한다.

32 ④는 (교통수단 등을) 타다[이용하다]는 의미로 쓰였다. ① 넣다, ② 선택하다, 사다, ③ 가지고 가다, ④ 타다, ⑤ 잡다

33 사람들이 버스를 잘못 타는 일이 종종 있었다고 했을 뿐 사람들이 항상 버스를 잘못 탔다는 것은 글의 내용과 맞지 않는다.

34 버스 정류장 지도로 인해서 사람들은 종종 버스를 잘못 타서 시간을 낭비하였다.

단원별 예상문제   p.150~153

01 ①   02 ⑤   03 ⑤
04 ①, ⑤   05 I'm glad (that) you like it. 06 ⑤
07 (A)many children in his town   (B)couldn't go to school and had to work
08 How about joining my study group?
09 ⓓ disagree → agree   10 ⑤   11 ④
12 ②   13 ③   14 The car that I want to buy is minivan.
15 ⑴ He gave some candies to the little kids who(m) he saw.
⑵ There was a festival which many people took part in.
⑶ The dish which you broke was not that expensive.
16 to close the window   17 ③
18 that, which 19 ②   20 ④
21 the man was very happy 22 (D)-(A)-(C)-(B)
23 **빨간 화살표 스티커를 버스 지도에 붙이다.** 24 ⑤
25 People could understand the maps easily and save time.

01 주어진 문장은 도움을 제공하고자 하는 표현으로 Tom의 고민에 대한 대답으로 적절하므로 (A)번이 적절하다.

02 ⓐ는 '무료의'라는 의미로 이와 같은 의미로 쓰인 것은 ⑤번이다.

03 왜 Hojun이 봉사활동을 하러 나오지 않았는지는 알 수 없다.

04 (A)는 '정말 멋있구나!'라는 표현으로 ①, ⑤번과 바꾸어 쓸 수 있다.

07 인도의 소년이 특별한 이유는 그의 마을에서 학교에 갈 수 없고 일을 해야 하는 많은 아이들을 매일 그의 집에서 가르쳤기 때문이다.

08 'Why don't you ~?'는 '~하는 게 어때?'라고 제안하는 표현으로 'how about ~?'으로 바꾸어 쓸 수 있다.

09 이어지는 대화에서 좋은 구성원이 되기 위해 열심히 노력한다고 하였으므로 상대방의 의견에 동의하는 'I agree.'가 적절하다.

10 ⑤ Brian은 혼자서 병원에서 공부하려고 노력했었다.

11 ask는 to부정사를 목적격보어로 취하는 동사이다. 목적격 관계대명사 which 혹은 that과 to부정사가 짝지어지는 것이 옳다.

12 '내가 답변하는 것'이므로 목적어로 me, 목적격보어로 to answer를 써서 문장을 만든 ②번이 가장 적절하다.

13 주어가 복수 명사 men이므로 수의 일치는 복수 동사로 하는 것이 옳으므로 are를 쓴다.

14 'The car is minivan. I want to buy it.'을 하나로 합친 문장이다. 목적격 관계대명사를 이용하여 문장을 쓴다.

15 관계대명사 who(m), which를 대신하여 that을 쓸 수 있으며 목적격 관계대명사이므로 생략해도 좋다.

16 창문이 열려 있어 추웠다고 하였다. 창문 옆에 앉아 있던 Jimmy에게 창문을 닫아 달라고 요청하는 말을 쓰는 것이 옳다.

17 <보기>의 that은 동격의 명사절을 이끄는 접속사이다.

18 사물을 선행사로 받아주는 주격 관계대명사가 쓰인다.

19 ⓐ와 ⓓ가 글의 내용과 일치한다.

20 두 가지 이야기를 읽었다고 하였으므로 다른 한 가지 이야기가 이어질 것이라고 보는 것이 옳다.

21 그 남자가 행복한 이유는 많은 사람들에게 행복을 주었기 때문이라고 하였다. so는 결과를 이끄는 접속사이다.

22 (D)에서 They는 주어진 문장의 the maps를 가리키고, (A)는 사람들이 지도에 대한 설명을 요구하는 글이며, (C)는 이에 대한 해결책을 한 남자가 떠올려 스티커를 사서 (B) 그 스티커를 붙이고 다녔다는 순서가 가장 적절하다.

23 do this=stick the stickers on the bus maps

24 매일 스티커를 붙였다고 하였다. 따라서 주말마다 붙였다는 것은 글의 내용과 일치하지 않는다.

25 남자의 노력이 있은 후 사람들은 지도를 쉽게 이해하고 시간을 절약할 수 있었다.

서술형 실전문제
p.154~155

01 She is going to give her old books to her.

02 Jimin feels happy when she teaches her mentee.

03 He is going to carry the box.

04 to open

05 Do you have the book which we checked out from the library?

06 My mom allowed me to stay out late.

07 asks Jimmy to get in line

08 Is the book which you are reading interesting?

09 you were talking to[with]

10 ④번 to smile → smiling

11 sticking coins / to call, they love

12 his small idea gave happiness to many people

13 that he bought to solve the problem

14 They had to ask others to explain the maps.

01 지민은 오늘 멘티에게 그녀가 보던 책을 줄 것이다.

02 지민은 멘티를 가르칠 때 행복을 느낀다.

03 Mike는 지민을 도와주기 위해 상자를 날라 줄 것이다.

04 입을 벌리라고 했지만 너무 무서워서 벌릴 수 없었다는 의미가 되므로 tell의 목적격보어로 to부정사를 사용하여 답을 쓴다.

05 check out: (도서관에서 책을) 대출하다

06 3인칭 단수 주어에 let을 썼으므로 과거 시제임을 알 수 있다. 따라서 allowed를 쓴다. let+목적어+V: 목적어가 V하게 허락하다

07 Paul은 Jimmy에게 줄을 서라고 요청하였다. ask는 to부정사를 목적격보어로 취하는 동사이다.

08 which를 대신하여 that을 써도 무방하다.

09 목적격 관계대명사를 생략해야 빈칸에 맞게 답을 쓸 수 있다. talk to[with]: ~와 이야기하다

10 stop to V: ~하기 위해 멈추다, stop Ving: ~하던 것을 멈추다

11 뉴욕 사람들 누구도 공중전화를 사용하지 않는 것에 대하여 좋은 생각을 떠올린 한 남자와의 대화이다. enable은 목적격보어로 to부정사를 취한다.

12 그의 생각이 많은 사람들에게 행복을 주었기 때문에 남자는 행복했다.

13 that을 대신하여 which를 써도 무방하다.

14 사람들은 올바른 버스를 타기 위해서 다른 사람들에게 지도를 설명해 달라고 요청해야 했다.

|모범답안|

01 (A)on my own   (B)joining her study group.
    (C)we can learn better when we teach each
    other   (D)be a good member

02 (1) A painter is an artist who paints pictures.
  (2) A purse is a small bag which people keep their
    money in.
  (3) A baker is a person whose job is to bake and
    sell bread.
    (4) A chair is a piece of furniture which people
      sit on.

03 (1) She asked me to go there with her.
  (2) The teacher encourages me to try again.
  (3) They forced him to tell the truth.
  (4) Computers enables us to live convenient lives.
  (5) I allowed my friend to use my pen. / We told
    them to stay calm.

01 나는 학교에 다시 돌아오게 되어 행복했다. Emily는 나를 매우 따뜻하게 반겨주었다. 우리는 공부를 포함한 많은 것들에 대해 이야기했다. 내가 병원에 있는 동안 나는 혼자 공부하려고 노력했지만 어려웠다. 내가 이것에 관해 Emily에게 이야기했을 때 그녀는 나를 도와주었다. 그녀는 내게 그녀의 스터디 모임에 가입할 것을 제안했다. 그녀는 우리가 서로 가르칠 때 더욱 잘 배울 수 있다고 생각했기 때문에 스터디 모임을 시작했다. 나는 그녀의 생각에 동의했다. 나는 좋은 구성원이 되기로 결심했다. 나는 정말로 그녀에게 고마웠다.

01 outside   02 ①

03 (1) Bats mostly sleep during the day.
  (2) I used a pay phone to call my mom.
  (3) He came up with a great idea at the meeting.

04 ②   05 ②   06 ⑤

07 (A)on (B)that (C)like   08 ⑤   09 ⑤

10 She was looking for the bus stop.

11 He helped Sujin by carrying her bag to the bus
stop.

12 ⑤   13 ①   14 to eat   15 ⑤

16 I want to make a movie which many people will
love.

17 The teacher told us to be on time.   18 ④

19 ③, ⑤   20 ②   21 Thanks to a man's
idea, many people in New York became happy when
they called someone they loved.   22 ⑤

23 ②   24 ③   25 people to understand

01 주어진 단어의 관계는 반의어 관계이다. inside: 안쪽에, outside: 바깥에

02 더 경험이 있는 사람에 의해 조언을 받거나 도움을 받는 사람을 가리키는 말은 mentee(멘티)이다.

04 'How+형용사(+주어+동사)!'의 감탄문이다.

05 엄마는 Alex의 선물을 받고 기뻐하였으므로 happy(행복한)가 적절하다.

06 대화를 통해 Alex가 어디에서 바구니 만드는 법을 배웠는지는 알 수 없다.

07 (A) on own's own: 혼자서, (B) 명사절을 이끄는 접속사 that이 알맞다. (C) 명사절의 주어 you 다음이므로 동사 like가 알맞다.

08 나머지는 모두 감사함에 대한 대답을 나타내며 ⑤번은 비난을 거부하는 표현이다.

09 Emily와 Brian이 공부 모임에서 무엇을 배웠는지는 알 수 없다.

10 Sujin은 버스 정류장을 찾고 있었다.

11 Henry는 버스 정류장까지 Sujin의 가방을 들어주며 그녀를 도왔다.

12 ⑤ 그 말을 들으니 기쁘다는 대답이 자연스럽다.

13 사람과 사물을 모두 선행사로 받아줄 수 있는 관계대명사는 that이다.

14 엄마는 내가 야채를 먹기를 원한다는 말이 들어가는 것이 적절하다. want는 to부정사를 목적격보어로 취한다.

15 make는 목적격보어로 원형부정사를 취하는 사역동사이다.

16 which를 대신하여 that을 써도 좋다.

17 tell은 to부정사를 목적격보어로 취하는 동사이다.

18 (A)는 동명사이다. 모두 동명사이지만 ④번은 현재진행형을 만드는 현재분사이다.

19 이유를 나타내는 접속사가 들어가는 것이 적절하다.

20 한 남자가 뉴욕에서 사용되지 않는 공중전화기에 동전을 붙여두었다고 하였다.

21 한 남자의 아이디어 덕분에, 뉴욕에 있는 많은 사람들이 그들이 사랑하는 사람들에게 전화했을 때 행복해졌다.

22 much는 셀 수 없는 명사를 수식하는 수량형용사이다.

23 (A) 주어가 the maps이므로 복수 동사 were, (B) 빈도부사는 일반동사 앞에 위치하므로 often took, (C) 스티커들을 지도들에 붙였다는 의미이므로 them이 옳다.

24 ⓐ 서울 버스 정류장의 지도에 정보가 부족한 것이 문제였고, ⓓ 청년은 문제를 해결하기 위하여 화살표 스티커를 붙이고 다녔으며, ⓔ 사람들이 종종 버스를 잘못 탔던 이유는 지도에 정보가 부족했기 때문이었다.

25 help는 원형부정사나 to부정사를 모두 목적격보어로 취할 수 있다. 따라서 other people understand를 답으로 써도 좋다.

For a Healthy Summer

06 eye disease: 눈병

Conversation 교과서

핵심 Check
p.166~167

1 (1) sorry to hear   (2) too bad   (3) That's terrible

2 (1) Make sure   (2) Don't forget   (3) I'll keep that in mind

---

시험대비 실력평가
p.164

01 female   02 ①   03 ③

04 (1) bump   (2) itches   (3) scratch

05 (1) At that moment   (2) went for a walk   (3) feed on

06 (1) sweaty   (2) pointed   (3) protein   (4) tiny   (5) standing

07 ④

01 주어진 관계는 반의어 관계를 나타낸다. male: 수컷의, 남성의, female: 암컷의, 여성의

02 날카로운 무언가로 당신의 피부를 문지르는 것을 나타내는 말은 scratch(긁다)이다.

03 sweat: 땀

06 tiny: 아주 작은 sweaty: 땀을 흘리는 protein: 단백질 standing: 괴어 있는 pointed: 뾰족한

07 주어진 문장에서 pointed는 '뾰족한'을 의미하며 이와 같은 의미로 쓰인 것은 ④번이다.

교과서 대화문 익히기

Check(√) True or False
p.168

(1) T   (2) F   (3) T   (4) T

서술형 시험대비
p.165

01 empty   02 mosquito

03 (1) buzzing   (2) prevent   (3) lay   (4) strange

04 (1) do better   (2) keep, in mind   (3) suffering from

05 (1) Why don't we stay here for a while?

(2) I'd love to go back to Korea.

(3) Many people suffered from food poisoning.

06 (1) If you take the bone from the dog, he will bite you.

(2) I don't like summer because I get too hot and sweaty.

(3) To prevent an eye disease, always wash your hands with soap.

01 주어진 관계는 반의어 관계를 나타낸다. empty: 텅 빈, full: 가득 찬

02 사람이나 동물의 피부를 물어 그들의 피를 빠는 작은 날아다니는 곤충을 가리키는 말은 mosquito(모기)이다.

03 whether: ~인지 아닌지 frog: 개구리

04 suffer from: ~으로 고통 받다

05 go back to: ~으로 돌아가다, food poisoning: 식중독

교과서 확인학습
p.170~171

Listen & Speak 1-A (1)

worried / worried, my cat is sick / I'm sorry to hear that / I will

Listen & Speak 1-A (2)

How / lost by / I'm sorry to hear that, you do better next time

Listen & Speak 1-B

I can't / Why not / to stop swimming for a while / hear that, next weekend / hope so

Listen & Speak 2-A (1)

sunburn / a lot, without sunscreen / Make sure

Listen & Speak 2-A (2)

Just make sure you, wear a hat / I will

Listen & Speak 2-B

any / the sink / fruit flies / put, trash / Make sure you don't put fruit waste in the trash can / keep, in mind, empty our trash can

Real Life Communication

what happened / mosquito bites / I'm sorry to hear that, How / went camping / Don't scratch them / itchy / with, make sure you wear long sleeves

01 ②　　　　02 (B) → (C) → (D) → (A)　　03 ④

04 ⑤

01 이어지는 대화로 유감을 표현하고 있으므로 ②번이 적절하다.

02 (B) 쇼핑가고 싶은지 질문 → (C) 거절 및 이유 설명 → (D) 당부하기 → (A) 대답

03 ④번은 안도감을 나타낸다.

04 Brian이 Jimin을 의사에게 데려가려 했다는 설명은 대화의 내용과 일치하지 않는다.

01 ⑤

02 The doctor told me to stop swimming for a while.

03 ①, ③

04 How about taking her to an animal doctor?

05 ②

06 Just keep in mind that you should wear a hat.

07 ⑤　　　　08 ⑤　　　　09 empty

10 (A)fruit waste　(B)Empty your trash can

11 ②　　　　12 I'm sorry to hear that.

01 don't have to: ~할 필요가 없다

02 tell은 목적격보어로 to부정사가 나오며 'stop+~ing'는 '~하기를 멈추다'라는 뜻이다.

03 제안을 나타내는 표현으로는 Let's+동사원형 ~. / Why don't we+동사원형 ~? / How about -ing ~? 등이 있다.

04 Why don't you~? = How about -ing ~? = ~하는 게 어때?

05 Jimin의 고양이가 아프기 때문에 걱정스러운(anxious)이 적절하다. ① pleased: 즐거운 ③ nervous: 긴장된, ④ excited: 흥분된, 신난 ⑤ encouraged: 격려 받은

07 Hojun이 Alex와 야구 경기할 때 모자를 쓸 것이라는 것은 대화의 마지막에 나타난다.

08 주어진 문장은 상대방의 당부의 말에 대한 대답으로 적절하므로 (E)가 적절하다.

09 용기 등에 있는 모든 것을 없애는 것을 가리키는 말은 empty (비우다)이다.

10 초파리를 막기 위해 쓰레기통에 과일 쓰레기를 버리지 말아야 하며 쓰레기통을 더 자주 비워야 한다.

11 축구 경기에서 졌다는 것으로 보아 낙담한(discouraged)이 적절하다.

01 I'm sorry to hear that.

02 Make sure you wear sunscreen next time.

03 Because he went swimming at the beach without sunscreen.

04 He got the mosquito bites at the camp.

05 you clean the mosquito bites with cool water

06 (B) → (D) → (C) → (A) → (E)

02 make sure: 반드시 ~해라

05 모기에 물렸을 때는 찬물로 모기 물린 곳을 닦아 주어야 한다.

06 (B) 찾고 있는 물건 위치 설명 및 이유 질문 → (D) 이유로 쓰레기통에 초파리가 많다고 설명 → (C) 쓰레기통에 무엇을 버렸는지 질문 → (A) 대답 → (E) 당부하기

교과서
Grammar

1 (1) something strange　(2) something, to play with

　(3) cold to drink

2 (1) Have, made　(2) have been　(3) has been

　(4) have travel(l)ed

01 (1) wrong anything → anything wrong

　(2) to eat healthy → healthy to eat

　(3) have talked → talked

　(4) played → has played

02 (1) has not[hasn't] polished (2) Have, seen

　(3) have not[haven't] told (4) has just read

　(5) has worn

03 (1) I need something cold to drink.

　(2) We have been to France twice.

　(3) Do you have anything fun to read?

　(4) Have you ever played this game?

01 (1), (2) -thing으로 끝나는 대명사는 형용사의 수식을 뒤에서 받으며, to부정사와 동시에 수식을 받을 때는 '-thing+형용사+to부정사'의 어순으로 수식받는다. (3) 과거를 나타내는 부사구 last month가 있으므로 현재완료를 쓸 수 없다. (4) 아이였을 때부터 연주해 온 것이므로 현재완료 시제를 써야 한다.

02 (1), (3), (4), (5)에서 쓰인 already, yet, just, many times

는 모두 현재완료 시제와 함께 쓰이는 어구이다. (2) 오늘 그녀를 본 적이 있는지 묻는 말이므로 현재완료를 쓰는 것이 옳다.

03 (1) -thing으로 끝나는 대명사는 형용사의 수식을 뒤에서 받는다. to부정사의 to를 추가해야 한다. (2) '가 본 적이 있다'는 have been to이다. (3) '-thing+형용사+to부정사' 순서로 수식한다. (4) 경험을 물을 때에는 현재완료 시제를 사용한다.

시험대비 실력평가　　　　　p.179~181

01 ②　　　　02 ③　　　　03 ④
04 She told me something important.　　05 ③
06 ④　　　　07 ③
08 They have already arrived.　　09 ③
10 ⑤　　　11 ③　　　12 dangerous to do
13 ②　　　14 ④　　　15 ⑤
16 I need someone diligent to work with.　17 ④
18 ⑤　　　　19 ③
20 I want to do something different.　　21 ④
22 ②　　　　23 ③
24 I need something new to play with.

01 지난해 이래로 만난 적이 없다는 계속 용법의 현재완료가 들어가는 것이 가장 적절하다.

02 has been to: ~에 가 본 적이 있다

03 Ron이 현재 휴가를 갔다는 말에 어디에 가서 없느냐고 물을 수 있다. has gone to: ~에 가서 (지금) 없다

04 -thing으로 끝나는 대명사는 형용사의 수식을 뒤에서 받는다.

05 너에게 소개할 사람이므로 someone to introduce to you라고 쓰는 것이 옳으며 형용사는 someone 바로 뒤에 놓는다. introduce A to B: A를 B에게 소개하다

06 주어진 문장은 현재완료의 '경험' ①, ② 완료 ③, ⑤ 계속 ④ 경험

07 ① nothing interesting ② been to ④ Did you see ⑤ something to talk about이라고 쓰는 것이 옳다.

08 김씨 가족이 몇 시에 오느냐는 질문에 이미 도착했다고 하였으므로 현재완료와 already를 사용하여 문장을 만든다.

09 '한 시간 전'이라는 과거를 나타내는 부사어구가 있으므로 과거 동사, '오랜 시간'이라는 기간이 나오므로 전치사 for, '여러 번'이라고 하였으므로 읽은 경험을 나타내는 현재완료 시제가 가장 적절하다.

10 ⑤ something warm to eat이 옳다.

11 ③ 어제 새 차를 샀다고 하였으므로 'She bought a new car yesterday.'라고 쓰는 것이 옳다. 현재완료는 과거를 나타내는 어구와 함께 쓸 수 없다.

12 -thing으로 끝나는 대명사는 형용사의 수식을 뒤에서 받으며, to부정사와 동시에 수식을 받을 때에는 '-thing+형용사+to부정사' 어순으로 수식받는다.

13 벌써 끝냈느냐는 질문에 아직 끝내지 못했다고 답하는 것이 가장 자연스럽다.

14 피아노를 배운 것은 과거의 일이므로 learned를 쓴다.

15 의문문이므로 anyone을 쓰고, -one으로 끝나는 대명사이므로 뒤에서 형용사의 수식을 받는다. '아직 아무도 못 만났다'는 의미이므로 현재완료를 쓰는 것이 적절하다.

16 -one으로 끝나는 대명사이므로 '형용사+to부정사' 어순으로 수식한다.

17 12살 이래로 쭉 알아왔다는 의미이므로 현재완료 시제를 쓰고, Julia가 Grace를 잘 아는 것은 현재 상태를 나타내는 것이므로 knows를 쓴다.

18 형용사가 -thing, -one, -body로 끝나는 단어를 수식할 때는 형용사가 뒤에 위치한다. ⑤ special everything → everything special

19 그녀는 나가고 없다는 의미의 결과 용법의 현재완료 문장으로 만들 수 있다.

20 -thing으로 끝나는 대명사는 형용사의 수식을 뒤에서 받는다.

21 의문문이므로 anyone을 써야 한다. ~을 돌보다: take care of / look after

22 since+특정한 때, for+기간, 부정문과 함께 쓰이는 것은 yet이다.

23 지금까지 '10년 동안'이라고 하였으므로 현재완료 시제를 써서 '계속'을 나타내는 것이 옳다.

24 -thing으로 끝나는 대명사이므로 '형용사+to부정사'의 어순으로 수식하는 것에 유의한다.

서술형 시험대비　　　　　p.182~183

01 It has rained since last night.
02 have you had, have had
03 nothing to eat
04 Have you ever been, did you go
05 Have you ever met anyone famous?
06 (1) has had　(2) has gone　(3) happened
　　(4) has been　(5) taught
07 I don't want to do anything to hurt her feelings.
08 interesting to see
09 ⓐ Is there anything warm to drink?
　　ⓑ I have just made some coffee.
10 Amelia has been[lived] in this city for 5 years. /
　　Amelia has been[lived] in this city since 2016.
11 she arrived in / has been
12 Have you ever been to the museum?
13 There is nothing important to read in the magazine.
14 Is there anything comfortable to sit on?
15 warm to wear
16 How long have you learned English? /
　　I have learned English for eight months.

31

01 어젯밤 이후로 계속 비가 오고 있다는 문장을 쓰면 된다.

02 'since March'로 미루어 보아, 자동차를 얼마나 오랫동안 소유해 왔는지를 물었고 이에 3월부터 소유하고 있다고 답할 수 있다.

03 집에 음식이 하나도 없으므로 '먹을 것이 아무것도 없다'는 표현을 쓸 수 있다.

04 베트남에 가 본 적이 있느냐는 질문에 가봤다고 답하자, 언제 갔었느냐는 질문이 이어지고 있다. '가 본 적이 있느냐'는 질문은 현재완료를 써서 답할 수 있고, '언제 갔었느냐'는 질문은 과거시제로 표현한다.

05 경험을 묻고 있으므로 현재완료 시제를 쓰고 –one으로 끝나는 대명사이므로 형용사가 뒤에서 수식을 하도록 문장을 만든다.

06 과거를 나타내는 어구인 '~ ago', 'in+년도'는 현재완료와 함께 쓸 수 없음에 유의한다.

07 -thing으로 끝나는 대명사이므로 to부정사가 뒤에서 수식하도록 문장을 만들 수 있다.

08 글의 흐름상 흥미로운 볼거리를 찾고 있다고 볼 수 있다. -thing으로 끝나는 대명사는 '형용사+to부정사' 어순으로 뒤에서 수식받는다.

09 -thing으로 끝나는 대명사이므로 '형용사+to부정사' 어순으로 뒤에서 수식하며, '지금 막 커피를 끓였다'고 하였으므로 현재완료를 써서 나타낸다.

10 for+기간, since+특정 시점

11 도착한 것은 과거 시제로 표현하고, 이틀간 머문 것은 현재완료 시제로 표현할 수 있다.

12 경험을 묻고 있으므로 현재완료 시제를 쓴다.

13 -thing으로 끝나는 대명사이므로 to부정사가 뒤에서 수식하도록 문장을 만들 수 있다.

14 의문문이므로 anything을 쓰며, -thing으로 끝나는 대명사이므로 '형용사+to부정사'의 어순으로 수식하는 것에 유의한다.

15 답변으로 미루어 보아 '따뜻한 입을 무언가'가 필요하다고 말했음을 유추할 수 있다.

16 현재완료의 '계속' 용법을 이용하여 묻고 답하는 문제이다. 8개월째 영어를 배우고 있다고 하였으므로 기간을 나타내는 전치사 for를 써서 문장을 쓰는 것이 옳다

교과서
Reading

확인문제   p.184

1 T   2 T   3 F

확인문제   p.185

1 T   2 F   3 F   4 T   5 F

교과서 확인학습 A   p.186~187

01 It, evening   02 went for a walk

03 sweating   04 thirsty, cold to drink

05 something tiny, at, bit

06 if you can   07 have you done

08 just finished   09 from, How, find

10 from, nearby   11 was looking for, to drink

12 something sweaty   13 smell me

14 sense heat, smell

15 why, have survived   16 like you

17 female, drink blood   18 feed on

19 interesting   20 the protein, to lay

21 How, sharp teeth   22 teeth.

23 a long, pointed mouth   24 So, easily

25 bit, got a bump, itches   26 to hear that

27 Make sure, it   28 clean it

29 never tried that before   30 the itchiness

31 try that   32 have to go   33 Where, going

34 going back   35 have suffered   36 prevent them

37 cool, wear, sleeves

38 keep, in mind

교과서 확인학습 B   p.188~189

1 It was a hot summer evening.

2 Seojun went for a walk in the park.

3 Soon, he was sweating.

4 I'm thirsty. I want something cold to drink.

5 At that moment, something tiny flew at him and bit his arm.

6 Hey, catch me if you can.

7 Who are you? What have you done to me?

8 I'm a mosquito. I've just finished my dinner.

9 Where are you from? How did you find me?

10 I'm from a nearby river.

11 I was looking for some blood to drink there.

12 Then I smelled something sweaty and found you here.

13 How could you smell me from the river?

14 Mosquitoes can sense heat and smell very well.

15 That's why we have survived for millions of years.

16 Do all mosquitoes drink blood like you?

17 No. Only female mosquitoes like me drink blood.

18 Male mosquitoes only feed on fruit and plant juice.

19 That's interesting. So why do you drink blood?

20 I need the protein in blood to lay my eggs

21 How do you drink blood? Do you have sharp teeth?

22 No, I don't have teeth.

23 But I have a long and pointed mouth.

24 So I can drink your blood easily.

25 After you bit me, I got a bump. It itches.

26 I'm sorry to hear that.

27 Make sure you don't scratch it.

28 Also, clean it with alcohol wipes.

29 Alcohol wipes? I've never tried that before.

30 It will reduce the itchiness.

31 Okay, I'll try that at home. Thanks.

32 I have to go. See you soon.

33 Where are you going?

34 I'm going back to the river.

35 Wait! A lot of people have suffered from your bites.

36 How can we prevent them?

37 Stay cool and wear long sleeves.

38 Thanks. I'll keep your advice in mind.

시험대비 실력평가

p.190~193

01 sweating   02 ③   03 ③   04 ⑤

05 She was looking for some blood to drink there.

06 ③

07 It happened in a park on a hot summer evening.

08 ③   09 drink blood   10 ③

11 ⑤   12 ④

13 they need the protein in blood to lay their eggs.

14 ②   15 ⑤

16 Cleaning the bump with alcohol wipes

17 ⑤   18 ③   19 ⑤   20 ⑤

21 your bites   22 I will keep your advice in mind.

23 ⑤   24 how to prevent

25 We have lived in Korea for six years.   26 ③

27 ④   28 She is going to visit Jeju.

01 덥거나 긴장할 때 피부에서 투명한 액체를 만들어 내는 것은 '땀을 흘리다(sweat)'이고, 빈칸에는 '땀을 흘리고 있었다'는 과거진행형으로 쓰는 것이 옳다.

02 ⓑ는 조건의 부사절 접속사이다. '~라면'이라고 해석되며, ③번은 '~인지 아닌지'라고 해석되는 명사절 접속사이다.

03 모기의 답변으로 보아 서준이가 모기에게 어디에서 왔는지를 묻는 것이 가장 적절하다.

04 서준이와 함께 저녁식사를 한 것은 아니다.

05 모기는 강에서 마실 피를 찾던 중이었다고 하였다.

06 (A), (C) -thing으로 끝나는 부정대명사는 형용사의 수식을 뒤에서 받으며 '형용사+to부정사' 순서로 수식받는다. (B) fly at: ~을 향해 날아가다

07 무더운 여름날 저녁 공원에서 발생한 이야기이다.

08 '~에서, ~에서부터'라는 의미를 동시에 지니는 전치사는 from이다.

09 모기의 답변에서 암컷 모기만이 피를 마신다고 하였으므로 '모든 모기가 너처럼 피를 마셔?'라고 물었음을 알 수 있다.

10 ④는 부사적 용법 중 '목적'에 해당한다. ① 형용사 ② 명사 - 진주어 ③ 부사적 용법 중 '목적' ④ 명사 - hope의 목적어 ⑤ 명사 – 주어

11 수컷 모기가 식물 즙을 먹고 산다고 나와 있을 뿐, 암컷 모기도 식물 즙을 먹을 수 있는지는 알 수 없다.

12 ① feed on ② lay ③ sweaty ④ buzz ⑤ protein을 풀이한 말이다.

13 암컷 모기는 알을 낳기 위해 핏속에 있는 단백질이 필요해서 피를 마신다고 하였다.

14 길고 뾰족한 입을 가지고 있기 때문에 피를 쉽게 마실 수 있다는 의미가 적절하다. ② since: ~이기 때문에

15 ⓐ에서 쓰인 현재완료는 '경험'을 나타낸다. 경험적 용법으로 쓰인 것은 ⑤번이다.

16 알코올 솜으로 부어오른 자국을 닦는 것을 가리키는 대명사이다.

17 모기가 서준이를 문 것은 과거의 일이므로 bit이라고 쓰는 것이 옳다.

18 ③ 모기가 서준이를 어디에서 물었는지는 알 수 없다.

19 ⓐ에 쓰인 현재완료 용법은 '경험'이다. ⑤번은 '경험'을 나타내는 현재완료이다.

20 suffer from: ~로부터 고통받다, pick up: ~을 줍다, give up: 포기하다, be surprised at: ~에 놀라다, look forward to: ~을 고대하다 come from: ~에서 오다

21 모기에 물린 것을 의미한다.

22 keep ~ in mind: ~을 명심하다

23 'Thanks'라고 하였으므로 ⑤번은 옳지 않다.

24 모기는 서준이에게 모기 물리는 것을 예방하는 방법에 관하여 조언하고 있다.

25 우리가 6년 전에 한국으로 이사 와서 여전히 한국에 살고 있다고 하였으므로 '한국에서 6년 동안 살고 있다'는 현재완료 문장을 쓸 수 있다.

26 ③ 내일 제주로 간다고 하였다.

27 (B) '~에 가 본 적이 있다'는 경험을 나타내는 표현은 been to, (C) 감정을 느낄 때에는 과거분사형 형용사, (D) finish는 동명사를 목적어로 취하는 동사이다.

28 여름 방학 첫날 이 글을 쓴 Kate는 다음 날 제주로 간다고 하였다. 따라서 여름 방학 둘째 날에 제주로 갈 예정이라고 할 수 있다.

01 I want something cold to drink.

02 if you can catch me

03 She has bitten his arm.

04 sweat

05 reducing the itchiness

06 I have never tried that before.

07 to scratch it / to clean it with alcohol wipes

08 pointed

09 interesting

10 feed on, why

11 She needs the protein in blood.

12 fruit and plant juice, blood

13 A lot of people have suffered from your bites.

14 Staying cool and wearing long sleeves

15 She is from the river.

16 ⑤번 → advice

---

01 -thing으로 끝나는 부정대명사는 '형용사+to부정사' 순서로 후치 수식받는다.

02 자신을 잡을 수 있으면 잡아 보라는 의미이다.

03 글에 따르면 모기는 서준이의 팔을 물었다.

04 무더운 여름에 걷는 것은 서준이가 땀을 흘리게 만들었다.

05 알코올 솜으로 부어오른 자국을 닦는 것은 가려움을 줄이는 데 도움이 될 것이다.

06 try는 '한 번 해보다'라는 의미이다.

07 서준이의 이야기를 듣고서, 모기는 그것을 긁지 말라고 말했다. 또한 서준이에게 그것을 알코올 솜으로 닦으라고 조언해 주었다. tell과 advise는 모두 to부정사를 목적보어로 취하는 동사임에 유의한다.

08 모기의 입은 길고 뾰족하다고 하였다.

09 흥미를 '유발'할 때에는 interesting을 쓴다.

10 모기들이 무엇을 먹는지, 그리고 암컷 모기들이 왜 피를 마시는지에 관하여 이야기하고 있다.

11 알을 낳기 위해 암컷 모기는 핏속의 단백질이 필요하다고 하였다.

12 수컷 모기는 과일과 식물의 즙을 먹지만 암컷 모기는 피를 먹으며 산다고 하였다.

13 많은 사람들이 모기에 물려 괴로워하는 것은 과거부터 현재까지 이어지는 일이므로 현재완료 시제를 쓰는 것에 유의한다.

14 시원하게 지내고 소매가 긴 옷을 입는 것이 사람들이 모기에 물리지 않게 예방할 수 있다. 주어 자리이므로 동명사나 to부정사를 이용하여 답을 쓰는 것이 옳으며 빈칸 개수에 맞게 동명사를 쓸 수 있다. prevent A from B: A가 B하지 않도록 예방하다[막다]

15 강으로 돌아간다고 말하고 있으므로 모기는 강에서 왔음을 알

수 있다.

16 명사를 쓰는 것이 옳다.

---

01 thin　　　　　02 ④

03 (1) stay away from　(2) took, to　(3) lost, by

04 (1) Birds feed on insects.

　(2) The queen ant's job is to lay eggs.

　(3) I sensed danger.

05 ②　　　　06 ①　　　　07 ③　　　　08 happen

09 mosquito bites　　　　10 ④

11 ⓒ → Make 12 ⑤　　　　13 sunburn

14 She told him to wear sunscreen next time.

15 (A)going swimming this weekend

　(B)her eye problem　(C)stop swimming for a while

16 His class played soccer with Minsu's class.

17 He hoped to do better next time.　　　　18 ⑤

19 ③　　　　20 ⑤　　　　21 ⑤

22 Did you find anything strange?　　　　23 ①, ④

24 ④　　　　25 has died → died　　　　26 ④

27 The movie hasn't started yet.　　　　28 ④

29 ③　　　　30 ④

31 She smelled something sweaty from a nearby river.

32 ④　　　　33 ④

34 a long and pointed mouth　　　　35 bump

36 He will clean the bump with alcohol wipes.

---

01 주어진 관계는 반의어 관계를 나타낸다. thick: 두꺼운, thin: 얇은

02 맞거나 물려서 부푼 피부의 한 부분을 나타내는 말은 bump(혹, 타박상)이다.

03 stay away from: ~로부터 떨어져 있다 lose (~) by …(점, 골 등) 차로 (경기에서) 지다

04 feed on: …을 먹고살다 queen ant: 여왕개미

05 sleeve: 소매

06 주어진 문장에서 lay는 '(알을) 낳다'라는 의미로 이와 같이 쓰인 것은 ①번이다. ②, ③번은 '놓다', ④, ⑤번은 '누워 있었다'를 나타낸다. (lie의 과거)

07 suffer from: ~로 고통 받다, stay away from: ~로부터 떨어져 있다

08 특히 계획됨 없이 발생하다를 가리키는 것은 happen(발생하다)이다.

10 준수는 모기에 물리지 않기 위해 찬물로 샤워를 해야 한다는 설명은 대화의 내용과 일치하지 않는다.

11 ⓒ는 명령문이므로 동사원형 Make가 적절하다.

12 위 대화를 읽고 수진이가 쓰레기를 줄이기 위해 무엇을 해야 하는지는 알 수 없다.

---

13 너무 많은 햇빛으로 당신의 피부가 쓰리고 붉어진 상태를 가리키는 말은 sunburn(햇볕에 탐, 그을림)이다.

14 Emma는 Tim에게 다음에는 자외선 차단제를 바르라고 말하였다.

15 오늘 나는 유진에게 이번 주에 수영을 가자고 제안했다. 불행하게도, 그녀는 눈에 문제가 있기 때문에 나와 함께 갈 수 없었다. 그녀는 당분간 수영을 그만해야 한다고 말했다. 나는 그 이야기를 듣고 유감이었다. 나는 우리가 다음 주말에 함께 갈 수 있기를 바랐다.

18 '~에 관하여 생각하다'는 think about이다.

19 over a week는 기간이므로 for를 쓰는 것이 옳다. go see a doctor: 병원에 가다, 진찰을 받다

20 Jessica has been sick since last week.이라고 쓰는 것이 옳다.

21 과거를 나타내는 어구는 현재완료 시제와 함께 쓰일 수 없다.

22 의문문이므로 anything을 쓰고, -thing으로 끝나는 대명사이므로 형용사가 뒤에서 수식하도록 문장을 만드는 것에 유의한다.

23 주어진 문장은 Grace가 병원을 벌써 퇴원했다는 뜻이다. 과거에 병원에 있었으나 지금은 병원에 없다는 의미이다.

24 주어진 문장의 현재완료는 '완료' 용법으로 쓰였다. ④번은 '계속' 용법이다.

25 2년 전이라는 과거를 나타내는 부사어구가 있으므로 현재완료 시제를 쓸 수 없다.

26 과거를 나타내는 부사어구인 the other day(지난번)와 현재완료 시제는 함께 쓸 수 없다.

27 '아직 시작하지 않았다'고 하였으므로 현재완료 시제와 yet을 사용하여 문장을 만든다.

28 ⓐ는 비인칭 주어로 날씨, 날짜, 요일, 거리, 명암 등을 나타낼 때 쓰이며 해석되지 않는다. ④번은 인칭대명사 it으로 '그것'이라고 해석된다

29 ⓑ는 완료 용법으로 쓰였다. ③번은 경험을 나타내는 현재완료이다.

30 ④ 서준이가 어디 출신인지는 알 수 없다.

31 모기는 근처 강에서 마실 피를 찾던 중 땀 냄새를 맡았다고 하였다.

32 it이 가리키는 것은 a bump이다.

33 ④ 서준이는 알코올 솜을 쓰는 방법을 궁금해 하지는 않는다.

34 길고 뾰족한 입 덕분에 피를 쉽게 마실 수 있다.

35 맞거나 물려서 볼록하게 올라온 피부의 일부분은 혹이나 타박상이라고 한다.

36 서준이는 집에 가서 알코올 솜으로 부어오른 곳을 닦을 것이다.

단원별 예상문제 p.202~205

01 ③

02 과일 쓰레기를 쓰레기통에 넣지 말아야 한다는 것

03 ⑤　　04 ⑤

05 lost by three goals, do better

06 ⓒ → because　　07 Her cat is sick.

08 She is going to take her cat to an animal doctor.

09 He suggested going swimming this weekend.

10 Because she had an eye problem.

11 She needs someone strong to help her.　12 ③

13 ④　　14 ③

15 has won / Have you seen / saw

16 ⑤　　17 cold to drink　　18 ④

19 ③　　20 sensing heat and smell

21 ③　　22 ③　　23 ⑤　　24 ④

25 Cleaning the area with alcohol wipes can reduce the itchiness.

01 for a while: 당분간, go for a walk: 산책하러 가다

03 ⑤ Sujin이는 쓰레기통에 과일 쓰레기를 버리면 안 된다.

04 축구 경기가 어땠는지 묻는 질문으로 'How', lose by: ~ 차이로 (경기에서) 지다, do better: 더 잘하다

06 'because+주어+동사', 'because of+명사구'

07 Jimin의 고양이가 아프다.

08 Jimin은 고양이를 수의사에게 데려갈 것이다.

09 Tom은 Yujin에게 이번 주말에 수영하러 갈 것을 제안하였다.

10 Yujin은 눈에 문제가 있기 때문에 수영을 갈 수 없었다.

11 -one으로 끝나는 부정대명사이므로 '형용사+to부정사' 어순으로 뒤에서 수식하는 것에 유의한다.

12 주어진 문장과 ③의 빈칸에는 since가 들어간다. 나머지는 모두 for가 들어간다.

13 경험을 나타내는 현재완료로 표현할 수 있다. have gone to는 '~에 가고 없다'는 의미의 결과 용법이다.

14 ⓑ, ⓓ, ⓔ가 옳은 문장이다. ⓐ anyone strange, ⓒ Where were you last night?

15 현재도 조각가로 활동하고 있으므로 작품으로 상을 받은 것은 현재완료 시제를 써서 나타내는 것이 옳다.

16 ⑤번은 현재완료의 용법 중 '경험'에 해당한다. 나머지는 모두 '계속' 용법이다.

17 차가운 우유가 있다고 답하는 것으로 보아 '마실 시원한 것'을 원한다고 했음을 짐작할 수 있다.

18 (A) '그래서'라는 의미로 결과를 나타내는 것은 That's why (B) 기간을 나타내는 어구를 이끄는 것은 전치사 for (C) '(알을) 낳다'는 lay이다.

19 오직 암컷 모기만 피를 마신다고 하였다.

20 모기들은 열과 냄새를 감지하는

21 길고 뾰족한 입이 있어서 그 결과 피를 쉽게 마실 수 있다는 의미가 가장 자연스럽다.

22 ⓐ에서 쓰인 현재완료의 용법은 '경험'이다. have gone to는 '~에 가고 없다'는 의미로 결과를 나타낸다.

23 모두 부어오른 자국을 가리키는 말이지만 ⑤번은 알코올 솜으로 닦는 것을 가리킨다.

24 ④ 모기의 입이 얼마나 긴지는 알 수 없다.

25 알코올 솜으로 닦는 것이 가려움을 줄여줄 수 있다고 하였다. 주어 자리이므로 동명사 혹은 to부정사를 써서 문장을 만들 수 있다.

p.206~207

서술형 실전문제

01 It's under the sink.

02 Because there are a lot of fruit flies around the trash.

03 She should not put fruit waste in the trash and should empty the trash can more often.

04 I have nothing special to do.

05 (E) → (B) → (A) → (C) → (D)

06 have seen, have never spoken, Have you ever spoken / met

07 I need someone funny to talk with.

08 I have never lied to you.

09 for, since

10 anything dangerous

11 something sweaty

12 She smelled him from the river.

13 They can sense heat and smell very well.

14 female, male

15 ⑤번 → drink

16 Unlike male mosquitoes, female mosquitoes feed on blood.

01 under the sink라고 아버지가 답하고 있다.

02 Why?라는 아버지의 질문에 답하는 Sujin의 말을 쓴다.

03 대화의 마지막 부분에 두 가지가 나와 있다.

04 오늘을 위한 특별한 계획이 있느냐는 질문이다. '특별히 할 일은 없어.'라고 답할 수 있다.

05 (E) 수영하러 가자는 제안에 → (B) 그리고 싶지만 갈 수 없다고 대답하고 → (A) 이유를 묻고 → (C) 이유 설명하며 → (D) 유감을 나타내는 순서가 적절하다.

06 '몇 번 만난 적이 있다'거나 '말해 본 적 있다'는 현재완료 시제를 이용하여 '경험'을 나타내는 문장으로 쓸 수 있다. '지난달에 파티에서 만났다'는 것은 과거의 일이므로 과거 시제를 쓴다.

07 talk with: ~와 함께 이야기하다

08 lie to ~: ~에게 거짓말을 하다

09 for+기간, since+특정 시점

10 부정문이므로 anything을 쓰고 -thing으로 끝나는 대명사이므로 형용사의 수식을 뒤에서 받는다.

11 -thing으로 끝나는 부정대명사는 형용사의 수식을 뒤에서 받는다.

12 모기는 강에서 서준이의 냄새를 맡았다고 하였다.

13 모기들은 열과 냄새를 매우 잘 감지하기 때문에 수백만 년 동안

살아남은 것이라고 하였다.

14 사람을 물어 피를 마시는 것은 암컷 모기라고 하였다.

15 주어가 복수명사 female mosquitoes이므로 복수 동사를 쓰는 것이 옳다.

16 해석: 수컷 모기와는 달리 암컷 모기는 피를 먹고 산다.

p.208

창의사고력 서술형 문제

|모범답안|

01 (A) packing for the school trip tomorrow
   (B) take an umbrella.

02 (1) I have already sent an e-mail to my friend.
   (2) I have played the violin since I was five.
   (3) I have been to Alaska once.
   (4) I have found the solution to the problem.

03 (1) I want something cold to drink.
   (2) I need something cool to wear.
   (3) I want someone funny to play with in a pool.
   (4) I want something scary to watch at night in the summer.

01 Sue는 내일 수학여행을 위해 가방을 싼 후 그녀의 목록을 다시 확인하고 있었다. 왜냐하면 그녀는 아무것도 놓치고 싶지 않았기 때문이다. 그때, Mike가 내일 비가 올지도 모르기 때문에 그녀에게 우산을 가져가도록 상기시켜 주었다.

p.209~212

단원별 모의고사

01 (1) go for a walk (2) At that moment
   (3) lose by (4) Keep in mind   02 ③

03 ⑤   04 ⑤

05 Make sure you take an umbrella with you.

06 ⑤   07 (A) To prevent, (B) sweating

08 She can hold a green tea bag on the itchy area.

09 ②   10 (A) mosquito bites, (B) itchy, (C) clean them with cool water, (D) I wear long sleeves

11 (C) → (B) → (D) → (A)

12 (that) you don't watch TV   13 ②

14 Claire has studied medicine at the university for two years.

15 ③   16 ②

17 I have something more important to do.

18 something tiny flew at him   19 ③

20 ③   21 some blood to drink   22 ②

23 ⑤   24 She is fourteen years old now.

25 since

02 주어진 문장은 수영하러 갈 수 없는 이유를 설명하고 있으므로 (C)가 적절하다.

03 ⑤ Yujin은 다음 주말에 수영을 가길 원하지만 계획을 세운 것은 아니므로 대화의 내용과 일치하지 않는다.

04 worried: 걱정하는, worrying: 걱정시키는, 'because+주어+동사', 'because of+명사구', 감정의 이유를 나타내는 to부정사가 알맞다.

06 위 대화를 통해 Sue가 무엇을 빼먹었는지 알 수 없다.

07 (A)에는 문맥상 '~을 예방하기 위해'라는 의미가 되어야 하므로 To prevent, (B)에는 avoid가 동명사를 목적어로 취하므로 sweating이 적절하다.

09 주어진 문장은 유감을 표현하므로 모기에 많이 물렸다는 Junsu의 말에 이어지는 대답으로 적합하므로 (B)가 알맞다.

10 나는 얼굴에 모기에 물린 상처로 고통 받고 있다. 나는 지난 주말 캠핑 가서 이 상처를 얻었다. 그것들은 정말로 가렵다. Ms. Wheeler는 내게 차가운 물로 물린 곳을 닦으라고 조언해 주었다. 더욱이, 나는 내가 캠핑 갈 때 긴 소매를 입어야 한다는 것을 명심하고 있다.

11 (C) 축구 경기에 대해 질문 → (B) 경기 결과 설명 → (D) 유감 표현 및 격려 → (A) 희망 표현

12 Make sure (that)~. : 꼭 ~하도록 해라.

13 ② since last Friday라고 해야 올바르다.

14 2년 전에 의학 공부를 시작하여 현재도 하고 있으므로 '2년 동안 공부하고 있다'는 현재완료 문장으로 쓸 수 있다.

15 오후 내내 찾았으나 지금에서야 발견하여 '어디에 있었느냐'고 묻고 있다. 따라서 ③번이 가장 적절하다.

16 -thing으로 끝나는 대명사를 to부정사가 뒤에서 수식하고, '방금 점심을 먹었다'는 표현이 가장 적절하다.

17 -thing으로 끝나는 대명사이므로 '형용사+to부정사' 어순으로 뒤에서 수식하는 것에 유의한다.

18 -thing으로 끝나는 부정대명사는 형용사의 수식을 뒤에서 받는다.

19 ③ 모기는 서준이의 다리가 아닌 팔을 물었다.

20 모기는 강 근처에서 마실 피를 찾고 있었다.

21 모기는 마실 피가 필요하다고 하였다.

22 많은 훌륭한 곳을 방문한 적이 있다는 경험을 나타내는 문장이다.

23 ⑤ 짐 싸는 것을 끝냈다고 하였다.

24 8살에 이사 와서 6년 동안 살고 있다고 하였으므로 현재 Kate는 14살이다.

25 8살에 이사 왔다고 하였으므로 8살 이래로 쭉 살아왔다고 쓸 수 있다.

교과서 파헤치기

Lesson 1

1 beef, 소고기   2 during, ~ 동안
3 homeroom teacher, 담임 선생님   4 decide, 결정하다
5 email, 이메일을 보내다   6 bite, 물다   7 nail, 손톱
8 wish, 소망   9 handle, 손잡이   10 personal, 개인적인
11 planet, 행성   12 hobby, 취미   13 try, 시도하다
14 art, 미술   15 traffic, 교통   16 print, 인쇄하다

단어 TEST Step 1   p.02

01 행성	02 물다; 물린 자국	03 사실, 진실
04 곧	05 청소하다, 깨끗하게 하다	
06 친애하는	07 깨뜨리다, 부수다	08 ~ 동안
09 소고기	10 이메일을 보내다	11 장난감
12 손잡이	13 달리기	14 거짓말을 하다
15 손톱	16 틀린, 거짓의	17 소망
18 확실한, 확신하고 있는		19 시도하다
20 방학	21 담임 선생님	22 화난, 속상한
23 건강한, 튼튼한	24 결정하다	25 똑똑한, 명석한
26 개인적인	27 취미	28 인쇄하다
29 교통	30 조언, 정보	31 가을
32 우주	33 더 이상 ~하지 않다	
34 ~할 생각이다	35 그건 그렇고, 그런데	
36 요즈음에	37 ~로 변하다	38 실현되다
39 ~에 열중하다	40 최선을 다하다	41 서로
42 집에 오는 길에	43 ~에 흥미가 있다	

단어 TEST Step 2   p.03

01 soon	02 traffic	03 tip
04 false	05 smart	06 spring
07 print	08 art	09 healthy
10 fall	11 space	12 decide
13 kind	14 cupcake	15 personal
16 hold	17 care	18 hobby
19 upset	20 funny	21 vegetable
22 lie	23 planet	24 break
25 bite	26 truth	27 vacation
28 beef	29 false	30 handle
31 nail	32 toy	33 each other
34 on one's way home		35 be into
36 make changes	37 come true	38 by the way
39 not ~ anymore	40 do one's best	41 those days
42 change into	43 be interested in	

대화문 TEST Step 1   p.05~06

Listen & Speak 1 A

how, winter vacation / You know what, during the vacation / you were interested in / really fun / want to try

Listen & Speak 1 B

know what, homeroom teacher / His sciene class, a lot of fun / this year / new teacher / What does she teach / teaches art

Listen & Speak 2 A

are thinking of starting / What kind of club / learn about stars, planets, thinking, starting / Sounds, How often, going / once a week / will, meet / want to join our club / I'm interested in, too

Listen & Speak 2 B

made, I'm thinking, of cooking, for dinner / sounds great / at home / What about beef / vegetables, don't have, I'll buy some for you on my way home

Real Life Communication A

know what, I'm thinking of taking, painting class / decide to take / I want to go to an art high school / Are, thinking of becoming / interested in painting / comes true / do my best

Real Life Communication B

going to move / didn't tell me about / learned about, upset / I can understand her feelings, going to miss / keep in touch with

---

대화문 TEST Step 2   p.07~08

Listen & Speak 1 A

Brian: Julia, how was your winter vacation?
Julia: It was great. You konw what? I took muay thai lessons during the vacation.
Brian: That's amazing. I didn't know that you were interested in muay thai.
Julia: Yes. It was really fun.

Brian: Really? I want to try it.

Jimin: You know what, Tim?

Mr. Smith is my homeroom teacher this year.

Tim: That's great, Jimin. His science class last year was a lot of fun.

Jimin: Who's your homeroom teacher this year?

Tim: It's Ms. Kim. She's a new teacher.

Jimin: What does she teach?

Tim: She teaches art.

Jane: Minsu, Sujin and I are thinking of starting a club.

Minsu: Really? What kind of club?

Jane: We want to learn about stars and planets. So, we're thinking of starting a space science club.

Minsu: Sounds good. How often are you going to meet?

Jane: Maybe once a week.

Minsu: I see. Where will you meet?

Jane: In Room 101. Minsu, do you want to join our club?

Minsu: Yes, I'm interested in space, too.

Alex: Mom, I made bulgogi at school today. I'm thinking of cooking bulgogi for dinner.

Mom: That sounds great, Alex.

Alex: Do we have any vegetables at home, Mom? What about beef?

Mom: We have some vegetables, but we don't have beef. I'll buy some for you on my way home

Alex: Great.

Emily: You know what, Junsu? I'm thinking of taking a painting class.

Junsu: Really? Why did you decide to take a painting class, Emily?

Emily: Because I want to go to an art high school.

Junsu: Are you thinking of becoming an artist in the future?

Emily: I hope so. I'm interested in painting pictures.

Junsu: That's great. I hope your wish comes true.

Emily: Thanks. I'll do my best.

Sue: You know what? Jenny's family is going to move to Japan.

Jack: Is that right? Jenny didn't tell me about it.

Sue: She learned about it just last week and she's very upset now.

Jack: I can understand her feelings. I am going to miss her so much.

Sue: Me, too. She said she would keep in touch with us.

01 made, changes during

02 emailed, other, about   03 Dear Eric

04 It, spring in   05 last, vacation, time for

06 made, personal, during

07 One, my, hobby

08 making cupcakes   09 Making, own, is

10 other change, breaking, habits   11 past, bit, nails

12 don't anymore

13 feel, about, made   14 If, try, fell, like

15 hope, hear from   16 Your friend

17 Dear Junho   18 In, it, fall

19 talked about, changes

20 time to talk about

21 These days, into

22 printed, things with   23 One, of, dream

24 traffic, heavy, change into

25 other, special, for

26 hold, because, sick

27 handles, so, to hold   28 My, happy

29 By, to try, some   30 Take care

31 Best wishes

01 made some interesting changes during the vacation

02 emailed each other, talked about our changes

03 Dear   04 It, beautiful spring in

05 The last winter vacation, time

06 made, personal changes during

07 One, new hobby

08 making cupcakes

09 Making, own, is, lot

10 The other change, breaking, habits

11 past, often bit my nails   12 don't anymore

13 feel great about, changes, made

14 If, try to make, sure, will feel, like

15 hope to hear from   16 Your friend

17 Dear   18 In, it, in March

19 talked about, changes

20 time to talk about

21 These days, into 3D printing

22 printed two things with

23 One, model of, dream car

24 If, is heavy, will change into a flying car

25 The other, special cup for

26 can't hold, well because, sick

27 three handles, easy to hold

28 My, happy

29 By the way, to try, some day

30 Take care

31 Best wishes

---

1 내 친구 Eric과 나는 방학 동안 흥미로운 변화가 있었다.

2 우리는 서로에게 이메일을 보냈고 우리의 변화에 관해 이야기했다.

3 안녕 Eric,

4 서울은 아름다운 봄이야.

5 지난 겨울 방학은 나에게 멋진 시간이었어.

6 나는 방학 동안 두 가지 개인적인 변화가 있었어.

7 하나는 나의 새로운 취미야.

8 그것은 컵케이크를 만드는 거야.

9 나만의 컵케이크를 만드는 것은 정말 재미있어.

10 나머지 다른 변화는 나의 나쁜 습관 중 하나를 없애는 거야.

11 예전에 나는 종종 손톱을 물어뜯곤 했어.

12 이제 나는 더 이상 그러지 않아.

13 나는 내가 만든 변화가 정말 기분 좋아.

14 만약 네가 변화하려고 노력한다면, 너도 나처럼 기분이 좋을 거라고 확신해.

15 곧 소식 전해 줘.

16 너의 친구 준호가.

17 안녕 준호,

18 시드니에서는 3월이 가을이야.

19 너는 이메일에서 너에게 일어난 변화들을 말해 주었지.

20 이제 나의 새로운 변화를 말해 줄 차례야.

21 요즘, 나는 3D 프린팅에 빠져 있어.

22 나는 3D 프린팅 2가지를 인쇄했어.

23 하나는 나의 꿈의 자동차의 모형이야.

24 교통이 혼잡할 때, 그것은 날 수 있는 차로 바뀌어.

25 나머지 다른 하나는 우리 할아버지를 위한 특수 컵이야.

26 할아버지는 편찮으셔서 컵을 잘 들지 못하셔.

27 나의 특수 컵은 손잡이가 3개 있어서 들기 쉬워.

28 할아버지는 아주 행복해 하셔.

29 그건 그렇고, 너의 컵케이크를 언젠가 먹어 보고 싶다, 준호야.

30 잘 지내.

31 행운을 빌어, Eric.

---

1 My friend Eric and I made some interesting changes during the vacation.

2 We emailed each other and talked about our changes.

3 Dear Eric

4 It's a beautiful spring in Seoul.

5 The last winter vacation was a great time for me.

6 I made two personal changes during the vacation.

7 One is my new hobby.

8 It's making cupcakes.

9 Making my own cupcakes is a lot of fun.

10 The other change is breaking one of my bad habits.

11 In the past, I often bit my nails.

12 Now I don't anymore.

13 I feel great about the changes I made.

14 If you try to make some changes, I'm sure you'll feel great like me.

15 I hope to hear from you soon.

16 Your friend, Junho.

17 Dear Junho,

18 In Sydney, it's fall in March.

19 You talked about your changes in your email.

20 Now, it's time to talk about my new changes.

21 These days, I'm into 3D printing.

22 I printed two things with a 3D printer.

23 One is a model of my dream car.

24 If the traffic is heavy, it will change into a flying car.

25 The other is a special cup for my grandfather.

26 He can't hold his cup well because he's sick.

27 My special cup has three handles, so it is easy to hold.

28 My grandfather is very happy.

29 By the way, I want to try your cupcakes some day, Junho.

30 Take care.

31 Best wishes, Eric.

Real Life Communication - Step 2

1. what, thinking of keeping

2. Why, decide to do

3. because, be good at

4. great

My Writing Portfolio

1. Dear
2. smart, funny
3. However, don't you
4. One, The other, become healthier
5. Here are, wishes
6. nicer to others, make these changes
7. Love

Culture Link

1. my pet dog
2. two brothers
3. One, The other
4. two boys
5. One, The other
6. two habits
7. watching, sleeping

구석구석지문 TEST Step 2   p.20

Real Life Communication - Step 2

1. A: You know what? I'm thinking of keeping a diary in English.
2. B: Why did you decide to do that?
3. A: It's because I want to be good at English writing.
4. B: That's great.

My Writing Portfolio

1. Dear me,
2. You are very smart and funny.
3. However, you still want to make two changes, don't you?
4. One is to have more good friends. The other is to become healthier.
5. Here are my tips for your wishes.
6. If you are nicer to others and eat more vegetables, you'll make these changes.
7. Love, Me

Culture Link

1. Bobo is my pet dog.
2. She has two brothers.
3. One is black. The other is white.
4. She has two toys.
5. One is a ball. The other is a plastic duck.
6. She has two habits.
7. One is watching TV. The other is sleeping on my chair.

단어 TEST Step 1   p.21

01 흔들림, 떨림; 흔들다		02 해결하다
03 비어 있는, 빈	04 넘어지다	05 따르다, 따라가다
06 이상한, 낯선	07 공간	
08 다치게 하다, 아프게 하다		09 바닥, 마루
10 상처, 부상	11 기둥, 장대	12 칼
13 낮은	14 약	15 안전
16 놀라운	17 깨다, 부수다, 부서지다	
18 두려운, 무서운	19 결정하다, 결심하다	
20 미끄러지다	21 발생하다	22 젖은
23 보호하다	24 탈출하다	25 심각한
26 걱정, 근심; 걱정하다		27 방지하다, 막다, 피하다
28 아픈	29 위험한	30 미끄러운
31 지진	32 잊어버리다	33 재난, 재해
34 살아남다, 생존하다		
35 (~에서) 나가다, 떠나다		36 숨다
37 약간, 좀	38 ~에서 떨어져 있다	
39 ~에 대해 걱정하다		40 ~을 꼭 잡다
41 ~을 기억하다	42 (기분이) 나아지다	43 휴식을 취하다

단어 TEST Step 2   p.22

01 cover	02 wipe	03 escape
04 serious	05 disaster	06 forget
07 floor	08 sore	09 avoid
10 stair	11 by	12 worry
13 survive	14 prepare	15 elevator
16 slippery	17 dangerous	18 protect
19 situation	20 earthquake	21 throat
22 program	23 safety	24 empty
25 slip	26 break	27 injury
28 solve	29 wet	30 strange
31 rule	32 space	33 shake
34 medicine	35 take a rest	36 be worried about
37 feel better	38 hold on to	39 stay away from
40 keep ~ in mind		41 one by one
42 Why don't you ~?		43 get out of

단어 TEST Step 3   p.23

1 solve, 해결하다   2 protect, 보호하다

3 forget, 잊어버리다   4 safety, 안전   5 wipe, 닦다

6 empty, 비어 있는, 빈   7 fall, 넘어지다

8 shake, 흔들림, 떨림   9 pole, 기둥, 막대

10 earthquake, 지진   11 follow, 따르다, 따라가다

12 avoid, 방지하다, 막다, 피하다   13 hurt, 다치게 하다

14 injury, 상처, 부상   15 disaster, 재난, 재해

16 break, 깨다, 부수다

대화문 TEST Step 1
p.24~25

Listen & Speak 1 A

wrong / I'm worried about, hurts a lot / Why don't you go see / going to go / you feel better / hope so, too

Listen & Speak 1 B

are, watching / program about earthquakes / Sounds interesting, I'm worried about earthquakes / Me, too / helpful tips / does, say / start to shake, take cover / didn't know

Listen & Speak 2 A

going out to play / finish cleaning your room / not yet, later / You should clean your room first / clean, play basketball / Don't forget, by six o'clock

Listen & Speak 2 B

What time / left . Let's run / You might fall and hurt yourself, should walk on the stairs / right, a little late / Better safe than sorry

Real Life Communication

a big fire, city library / heard about, I was worried about the people there / Don't worry, followed, safety rules / What / cover, with a wet towel, stay low, escape / didn't know / keep that in mind, helpful some day

Let's Check

raining, worried about our picnic / until late afternoon, You should go another day / call, choose, another day

대화문 TEST Step 2
p.26~27

Listen & Speak 1 A

Tom: Yujin, what's wrong?

Yujin: I'm worried about my leg. It hurts a lot.

Tom: Why don't you go see a doctor?

Yujin: I'm going to go after school today.

Tom: I hope you feel better soon.

Yujin: I hope so, too.

Listen & Speak 1 B

Brian: What are you watching?

Jane: It's a program about earthquakes.

Brian: Sounds interesting. I'm worried about earthquakes these days.

Jane: Me, too. This program has some helpful tips.

Brian: Really? What does it say?

Jane: When things start to shake, you need to take cover under a table.

Brian: Oh, I didn't know that.

Listen & Speak 2 A

Jack: Dad, I'm going out to play basketball with Minu.

Dad: Did you finish cleaning your room?

Jack: No, not yet. Can I do it later?

Dad: No. You should clean your room first.

Jack: Okay. I'll clean my room and then play basketball.

Dad: Good. Don't forget to be home by six o'clock.

Jack: Okay.

Listen & Speak 2 B

Emily: What time is the movie?

Tom: It starts at 4:30.

Emily: Oh, no. We only have 20 minutes left. Let's run!

Tom: No! You might fall and hurt yourself. You should walk on the stairs.

Emily: You're right. We can be a little late.

Tom: Yes. Better safe than sorry.

Real Life Communication

Brian: There was a big fire at the city library yesterday.

Mina: Yes, I heard about it. I was worried about the people there.

Brian: Don't worry. Everybody was okay. They all followed the safety rules.

Mina: Really? What are the rules?

Brian: You need to cover your nose and mouth with a wet towel. Then stay low and escape.

Mina: Oh, I didn't know that.

Brian: You should keep that in mind. It might be helpful some day.

Let's Check

Sujin: It's raining. I'm worried about our picnic in the afternoon.

Mom: It is going to rain until late afternoon today. You should go another day.

Sujin: You're right, Mom. I'll call my friend and choose another day.

01 what to, when, strikes
02 Take, how, during, disaster
03 things, shake, outside   04 Stay away
05 Use, out of   06 outside, hold, pole
07 How, on   08 survive, safely
09 Here, safety, which, helpful
10 check, by, what
11 run, when, shaking
12 Find, take cover
13 hold on, to protect
14 stay away from
15 break, earthquake, hurt
16 go outside, shaking stops
17 get out, don't use   18 Take, stairs
19 much safer   20 Once, find, empty, far
21 may, hold, pole, but
22 because, fall on
23 can strike anytime
24 scary experiences, everyone
25 how, safe, earthquake
26 avoid injuries, protect
27 Follow, tip, safe

01 what to do, earthquake strikes
02 Take, how to be, during, natural disaster
03 to shake, quickly   04 Stay away from
05 Use, to get out of
06 When, outside, hold on to
07 How, on the quiz
08 survive, an earthquake safely
09 Here are, which, helpful in an earthquake
10 Let's, them one by one, what to do
11 Don't, when things are shaking
12 Find, take cover under
13 hold, to protect yourself
14 stay away from windows
15 They, break, during
16 go outside, the shaking stops
17 To get out of, don't use   18 Take, stairs
19 much safer
20 Once, find an empty space, is far from
21 who want to hold on to, but think
22 because it, fall on
23 Earthquakes, strike anytime

24 scary experiences for everyone
25 how to be safe
26 can avoid injuries, protect yourself
27 Follow these tip, be

1 지진이 발생할 때 해야 할 일을 알고 있습니까?
2 이 퀴즈를 풀며 이러한 종류의 자연 재해가 발생하는 동안 어떻게 해야 안전할 수 있는지를 생각해 보세요.
3 물건들이 흔들리기 시작하면, 빨리 밖으로 뛰어나가세요.
4 창문으로부터 멀리 떨어지세요.
5 건물에서 나갈 때는 계단을 이용하세요.
6 밖에 나가서는 기둥이나 나무를 붙들고 있으세요.
7 퀴즈가 어떠셨나요?
8 당신은 지진에서 안전하게 살아남을 수 있나요?
9 여기에 지진 발생 시 도움이 될 수 있는 안전 지침이 있습니다.
10 하나하나 확인하면서 무엇을 해야 하는지를 배워 봅시다.
11 물건이 흔들리기 시작할 때 밖으로 뛰어나가지 마세요.
12 탁자나 책상을 찾아서 그 밑에 숨으세요.
13 자신을 보호하기 위해 탁자나 책상 다리를 붙들고 있으세요.
14 또한, 창문으로부터 멀리 떨어지세요.
15 지진이 일어나는 동안 창문들이 깨져 다칠 수 있으니까요.
16 흔들림이 멈추었을 때 밖으로 나가도 됩니다.
17 건물에서 나가기 위해 엘리베이터를 이용하지 마세요.
18 계단을 이용하세요.
19 그것이 훨씬 더 안전합니다.
20 일단 밖으로 나가면, 건물로부터 멀리 떨어진 공터를 찾으세요.
21 기둥이나 나무를 꼭 잡고 있으려는 사람들이 있을 수 있지만, 다시 생각해 보세요.
22 그것이 당신 위로 넘어질 수 있으므로 그것은 좋지 않은 생각입니다.
23 지진은 언제든지 발생할 수 있습니다.
24 지진은 모두에게 무서운 경험일 것입니다.
25 따라서 지진이 날 때 안전을 지키는 법을 배우세요.
26 부상을 방지하고 자신을 보호할 수 있습니다.
27 이 지침을 따르고 안전을 지키세요!

1 Do you know what to do when an earthquake strikes?
2 Take this quiz and think about how to be safe during this kind of natural disaster.
3 When things start to shake, run outside quickly.

4 Stay away from windows.

5 Use the stairs to get out of buildings.

6 When you are outside, hold on to a pole or a tree.

7 How did you do on the quiz?

8 Can you survive an earthquake safely?

9 Here are some safety tips which can be helpful in an earthquake.

10 Let's check them one by one and learn what to do.

11 Don't run outside when things are shaking.

12 Find a table or a desk and take cover under it.

13 You can hold on to the legs to protect yourself.

14 Also, stay away from windows.

15 They can break during an earthquake and hurt you.

16 You can go outside when the shaking stops.

17 To get out of buildings, don't use the elevator.

18 Take the stairs.

19 It's much safer.

20 Once you are outside, find an empty space that is far from buildings.

21 There may be people who want to hold on to a pole or a tree, but think again.

22 That's a bad idea because it can fall on you.

23 Earthquakes can strike anytime.

24 They can be scary experiences for everyone.

25 So learn how to be safe in an earthquake.

26 You can avoid injuries and protect yourself.

27 Follow these tips and be safe!

Real Life Communication B

1. A: I heard about your accident. I was worried about you.

2. B: Thanks. I hurt my hand, but it's not serious. I'll be okay.

3. A: Good. You should watch your hands when you close the door.

4. B: You're right. I will.

Culture & Life

1. When an earthquake struck in Italy in 2016, people found Georgia thanks to Leo, a dog.

2. Leo found the eight-year-old girl 16 hours after the earthquake struck.

Culture & Life Project

1. Here are the items for our survival bag.

2. We packed some food and water.

3. We need them to survive.

4. We also packed some matches that might be helpful in disasters.

5. We put medicine in the bag, too.

6. We might need it for injuries.

Real Life Communication B

1. heard about, was worried about

2. hurt, not serious

3. should watch, when, close

4. right, will

Culture & Life

1. When, struck, thanks to

2. found, after the earthquake struck

Culture & Life Project

1. Here are, our survival bag

2. packed some food

3. need, to survive

4. packed, matches, in disasters

5. put, in, too

6. need, injuries

10 refrigerator, 냉장고   11 arrow, 화살표

12 mentee, 멘티   13 sign, 표지판

14 rest, 쉬다, 휴식하다   15 map, 지도   16 mentor, 멘토

단어 TEST Step 1   p.40

01 쉬다, 휴식하다	02 피하다	03 공중전화
04 활동	05 화살, 화살표	06 위험
07 (글·글씨 등이) 쓰이다		08 노력
09 성공	10 가능한	11 자원 봉사 동아리
12 ~하려고 계획하다		13 해결책
14 멘티	15 훌륭한, 굉장한	16 거리
17 설명하다	18 혼란스러운	19 냉장고
20 필요로 하다	21 잊어버리다	22 쓰레기
23 비밀, 비결; 비밀의		24 사라지다
25 다른	26 틀, 테	27 바깥의, 외부의
28 아동 센터	29 동전	30 해결하다
31 지도	32 무료의	33 비닐봉지
34 표지판	35 (생각을) 찾아내다, 제시하다	
36 낮 동안	37 자기 스스로	
38 시도하다, 한번 해 보다		39 설치하다, 세우다
40 ~하는 것을 멈추다		41 ~ 덕분에
42 ~해야 한다	43 (과거의) 어느 날	

단어 TEST Step 2   p.41

01 sticker	02 basket	03 coin
04 sign	05 confusing	06 secret
07 solve	08 few	09 bus stop
10 children's center		11 disappear
12 frame	13 free	14 soap
15 glad	16 hear	17 map
18 different	19 mentor	20 outside
21 plastic bag	22 trash	23 refrigerator
24 explain	25 effort	26 decide
27 avoid	28 trash	29 danger
30 rest	31 success	32 pay phone
33 solution	34 forget	35 the other day
36 give out	37 come up with	38 during the day
39 stop -ing	40 on one's own	41 put up
42 thanks to	43 give it a try	

단어 TEST Step 3   p.42

1 few, 몇몇의   2 confusing, 혼란스러운   3 start, 시작하다

4 disappear, 사라지다   5 free, 무료의   6 secret, 비밀의

7 activity, 활동   8 hear, 듣다   9 success, 성공

대화문 TEST Step 1   p.43~44

Listen & Speak 1 A

planned to give out / think, forgot / Let me help you
then, going, give out / part, volunteer club activity /
mean / It means that, smile at each other, become a
better place / wonderful idea

Listen & Speak 1 B

in the box / my mentee, going to give / Do you teach
her every weekend / feel happy, teach / You are a
good mentor, looks heavy, Let, help

Listen & Speak 2 A

this is for you, made, with / How did you know that.
needed / talked about, the other day / How nice,
many different colors / I'm glad you like it

Listen & Speak 2 B

I read a story about a special boy in India, hear about
/ Why is he special / couldn't go, had to work, taught,
every day / great story / I'm glad you like it

Real Life Communication

Are you feeling better / tried to, on my own, but / Let
me help you, join my study group / study group / we
can learn better when we teach each other / try hard,
Thanks for helping me / welcome, glad, like

Let's Check 1

looks heavy, Let me help you / Where is the bus
stop around here / over there, carry / very kind / No
problem, going, too

대화문 TEST Step 2   p.45~46

Listen & Speak 1 A

Tom: Hojun and I planned to give out free stickers
today, but I think he forgot.

Sora: Really? Let me help you then. Why are you
going to give out stickers?

Tom: It's part of our volunteer club activity.

Sora: I see. What does this sticker mean?

Tom: It means that when we smile at each other, the
world will become a better place.

Sora: That's a wonderful idea.

Mike: Jimin, what are all these things in the box?

Jimin: They're for my mentee at the children's center. I'm going to give her my old books today.

Mike: Do you teach her every weekend?

Jimin: Yes. I feel happy when I teach her.

Mike: You are a good mentor. Oh, the box looks heavy. Let me help you.

Jimin: Thanks.

Alex: Mom, this is for you. I made it with plastic bags

Mom: That's very cute, Alex. How did you know that I needed a new basket?

Alex: You talked about it when we were having dinner the other day.

Mom: How nice! I really like this basket. It has many different colors.

Alex: I'm glad you like it.

Yujin: I read a story about a special boy in India. Do you want to hear about it?

Jack: Sure. Why is he special, Yujin?

Yujin: Many children in his town couldn't go to school and had to work . So he taught them in his house every day.

Jack: That's a great story

Yujin: I'm glad you like it.

Emily: Welcome back, Brian. Are you feeling better?

Brian: Yes, thanks. I tried to study on my own in the hospital, but it was hard.

Emily: Let me help you. Why don't you join my study group?

Brian: Did you start a study group? That's wonderful.

Emily: Thanks. I think that we can learn better when we teach each other.

Brian: I agree. I'll try hard to be a good member. Thanks for helping me.

Emily: You're welcome. I'm glad you like my idea.

Henry: Your bag looks heavy. Let me help you.

Sujin: Thanks. Where is the bus stop around here?

Henry: It's over there. I'll carry your bag to the bus stop for you.

Sujin: You're very kind.

Henry: No problem. I am going that way, too.

01 are, which, read

02 want, hear about 03 Call, You Love

04 had, pay, on, streets

05 However, nobody, used 06 One, up with

07 stuck, to, of 08 put up, that

09 many, were using

10 When, talking, whom, smiling

11 His, became, success

12 During, all, disappeared

13 because, gave happiness 14 Arrow Man

15 few, ago, were, confusing

16 didn't, enough information

17 had, others, explain

18 Where, on, go to

19 often took, wasted

20 One, decided to solve

21 bought lots, arrow

22 rode, around, stuck, on 23 asked, to do

24 just, help others

25 Thanks, could, easily, save

01 are, which, read

02 to hear about 03 Call, You Love

04 had, pay, phones

05 However, nobody, used 06 came up with

07 stuck coins to 08 put up, that said, Call, Love

09 many, were using

10 When, were talking, whom they loved, didn't stop smiling 11 became a big success

12 During the day, disappeared

13 because, gave happiness to

14 Red Arrow Man

15 A few years ago, were, confusing

16 didn't have enough information

17 ask others to explain

18 Where, on the map, go to

19 often took the wrong bus, wasted

20 decided to solve

21 lots of red arrow stickers

22 Every day, rode, around, stuck, on

23 asked him to do 24 wanted to help

25 Thanks to his effort, could understand, easily, save time

1 여기 내가 어제 읽은 이야기가 두 개 있어.

2 들어볼래?

3 당신이 사랑하는 누군가에게 전화하세요.

4 뉴욕에는 길거리에 공중전화가 많이 있었다.

5 그러나 아무도 그것들을 실제로 사용하지는 않았다.

6 어느 날, 한 남자에게 좋은 아이디어가 떠올랐다.

7 그는 공중전화 하나에 동전들을 붙였다.

8 그는 또한 "당신이 사랑하는 사람에게 전화하세요."라고 쓰인 표지판을 설치했다.

9 곧, 많은 사람들이 그 전화기를 사용하고 있었다.

10 그들이 사랑하는 누군가에게 전화하고 있을 때, 그들은 미소 짓기를 멈추지 않았다.

11 그의 아이디어는 커다란 성공이었다.

12 낮 동안, 모든 동전이 사라졌다.

13 그 남자는 자신의 작은 아이디어가 많은 사람에게 행복을 가져다 주었기 때문에 매우 행복했다.

14 빨간 화살표 청년

15 몇 년 전, 서울의 버스 정류장의 지도는 매우 혼란스러웠다.

16 지도에는 충분한 정보가 없었다.

17 사람들은 다른 사람들에게 지도를 설명해 달라고 요청해야 했다.

18 "이 버스 정류장은 지도의 어디에 있는 건가요? 이 버스가 광화문으로 가나요?"

19 많은 사람이 종종 버스를 잘못 타서 시간을 낭비하곤 했다.

20 어느 날, 한 젊은 청년이 이 문제를 해결해 보기로 했다.

21 그는 빨간 화살표 스티커를 많이 샀다.

22 매일 그는 자전거를 타고 서울 시내를 돌아다니며 버스 지도에 스티커를 붙였다.

23 아무도 그 청년에게 이 일을 하라고 요청하지 않았다.

24 그는 단지 다른 사람들을 돕고 싶었다.

25 그의 노력 덕분에, 사람들은 지도를 쉽게 이해하고 시간을 절약할 수 있었다.

1 Here are two stories which I read yesterday.

2 Do you want to hear about them?

3 Call Someone You Love

4 New York had many pay phones on its streets.

5 However, nobody really used them.

6 One day, a man came up with an idea.

7 He stuck coins to one of the phones.

8 He also put up a sign that said, "Call Someone You Love."

9 Soon, many people were using the phone.

10 When they were talking to someone whom they loved, they didn't stop smiling.

11 His idea became a big success.

12 During the day, all the coins disappeared.

13 The man was very happy because his small idea gave happiness to many people.

14 The Red Arrow Man

15 A few years ago, the maps at bus stops in Seoul were very confusing.

16 They didn't have enough information.

17 People had to ask others to explain the maps.

18 "Where is this bus stop on the map? Does this bus go to Gwanghwamun?"

19 Many people often took the wrong bus and wasted their time.

20 One day, a young man decided to solve this problem.

21 He bought lots of red arrow stickers.

22 Every day he rode his bicycle around the city and stuck the stickers on the bus maps.

23 Nobody asked him to do this.

24 He just wanted to help others.

25 Thanks to his effort, people could understand the maps easily and save time.

Real Life Communication B

1. not good at, What

2. Let me help, Why don't

3. give it a try

4. problem, glad

Let's Write

1. Be

2. in the second grade

3. want to help, with

4. can meet, after school

5. ask, to be

6. think, can be

7. whom my mentee can trust

Culture & Life

1. see, inside

2. wash their hands, to get

3. Washing, can prevent

4. Thanks to, fewer, getting sick

Real Life Communication B

1. A: I'm not good at science. What can I do?
2. B: Let me help you. Why don't you start with easier books?
3. A: Okay, I'll give it a try. Thanks for the tip.
4. B: No problem. I'm glad you like it.

Let's Write

1. Be a Mentor!
2. My name is Semi and I'm in the second grade.
3. I want to help my mentee with her homework.
4. I can meet my mentee after school.
5. I'll ask my mentee to be on time.
6. I think a good mentor can be a good friend.
7. So I want to become a good friend whom my mentee can trust.

Culture & Life

1. Do you see toys inside the bars of soap?
2. Children in South Africa wash their hands more often to get the toys.
3. Washing your hands can prevent many health problems.
4. Thanks to this idea, fewer children are getting sick.

Lesson 4

01 이상한	02 뾰족한	03 땀; 땀을 흘리다
04 벌레	05 긁다	06 목마른
07 놓치다, 빼먹다	08 단백질	09 비우다
10 (옷의) 소매, 소맷자락		11 암컷의, 여성의
12 예방하다, 방지하다		13 느끼다, 감지하다
14 식중독	15 모기	16 위, 복부, 배
17 피	18 일어나다, 발생하다	
19 땀에 젖은	20 가렵다	21 (알을) 낳다
22 걱정[근심]하는	23 자외선 차단제	24 수컷의, 남성의
25 충고, 조언	26 100만, 다수	27 아주 작은
28 (가방을) 싸다	29 윙윙거리다	30 줄이다
31 가려운	32 혹, 타박상	33 쓰레기
34 유용한	35 그때에	
36 ~에서 떨어져 있다, 멀리하다		37 ~을 먹고살다
38 ~으로 고통받다	39 ~을 명심하다	
40 ~(점, 골 등) 차로 (경기에서) 지다		41 산책 가다
42 당분간	43 ~하고 싶다	

01 worried	02 sunscreen	03 bug
04 reduce	05 trash	06 million
07 food poisoning		08 female
09 sweaty	10 itch	11 male
12 lay	13 sweat	14 sunburn
15 sharp	16 miss	17 scratch
18 pointed	19 strange	20 protein
21 sleeve	22 blood	23 empty
24 mosquito	25 stomach	26 thirsty
27 bump	28 useful	29 prevent
30 tiny	31 advice	32 pack
33 buzz	34 itchy	35 for a while
36 suffer from	37 do better	38 feed on
39 keep ~ in mind		40 go for a walk
41 at that moment		
42 stay away from		43 take ~ to ...

1 bug, 벌레　2 bite, 물린 상처　3 prevent, 방지하다, 막다
4 miss, 놓치다, 빼먹다　5 bump, 혹, 타박상
6 scratch, 긁다　7 lay, (알을) 낳다　8 protein, 단백질
9 buzz, 윙윙거리다　10 happen, 일어나다, 발생하다

11 reduce, 줄이다　　12 itch, 가렵다

13 pack, (가방을)싸다　　14 sunburn, 햇볕에 탐, 그을림

15 mosquito, 모기　　16 sense, 느끼다, 감지하다

대화문 TEST Step 1

p.62~63

Listen & Speak 1–A (1)

look worried, wrong / worried, my cat is sick / I'm sorry to hear that, Why don't you take / I will

Listen & Speak 1–A (2)

How, class / lost by / I'm sorry to hear that, you do better next time / hope so, too

Listen & Speak 1-B

Let's go swimming / love to, I can't / Why not / to stop swimming for a while / sorry to hear that, can go next weekend / hope so

Listen & Speak 2–A (1)

look at, sunburn / hurts a lot, went swimming, without sunscreen / Make sure, wear sunscreen

Listen & Speak 2–A (2)

go shopping / going to play / Just make sure you wear a hat, going to be very hot / I will

Listen & Speak 2–B

any / under the sink / fruit flies around / put, trash / fruit waste / Make sure you don't put fruit waste in the trash can / keep, in mind, should also empty our trash can / good idea

Real Life Communication

what happened / a lot of mosquito bites / I'm sorry to hear that, How / went camping / Don't scratch them / itchy / with, make sure you wear long sleeves, go camping / thank you

대화문 TEST Step 2

p.64~65

Listen & Speak 1–A (1)

Brian: You look worried, Jimin. What's wrong?

Jimin: I'm worried because my cat is sick.

Brian: I'm sorry to hear that. Why don't you take her to an animal doctor?

Jimin: Okay, I will.

Listen & Speak 1–A (2)

Jane: How was the soccer game with Minsu's class, Alex?

Alex: We lost by three goals.

Jane: I'm sorry to hear that. I hope you do better next time.

Alex: I hope so, too.

Listen & Speak 1-B

Tom: Let's go swimming this weekend, Yujin.

Yujin: I'd love to, but I can't.

Tom: Why not?

Yujin: I have an eye problem. The doctor told me to stop swimming for a while.

Tom: I'm sorry to hear that. Maybe we can go next weekend.

Yujin: I really hope so.

Listen & Speak 2–A (1)

Emma: Tim, look at your face! You got sunburn.

Tim: Yes, it hurts a lot. I went swimming at the beach without sunscreen.

Emma: Oh dear! Make sure you wear sunscreen next time.

Listen & Speak 2–A (2)

Mom: Hojun, do you want to go shopping with me?

Hojun: Sorry, Mom. I'm going to play baseball with Alex this afternoon.

Mom: Okay. No problem. Just make sure you wear a hat. It's going to be very hot this afternoon.

Hojun: Okay, I will.

Listen & Speak 2–B

Sujin: Dad, do we have any bug spray?

Dad: Yes, it's under the sink. Why?

Sujin: There are a lot of fruit flies around the trash.

Dad: Oh no! What did you put in the trash?

Sujin: Some fruit waste.

Dad: Fruit flies love sweet things. Make sure you don't put fruit waste in the trash can.

Sujin: I'll keep that in mind. I think we should also empty our trash can more often.

Dad: That's a good idea.

Real Life Communication

Ms. Wheeler: Junsu, what happened to your face?

Junsu: I got a lot of mosquito bites.

Ms. Wheeler: I'm sorry to hear that. How did it happen?

Junsu: It happened when I went camping last weekend.

Ms. Wheeler: Oh dear. Don't scratch them!

Junsu: I know, but they're really itchy.

Ms. Wheeler: Clean them with cool water. That'll help. Also, make sure you wear long sleeves when you go camping.

Junsu: Okay, thank you.

01 It, hot, evening   02 for, walk in

03 Soon, sweating

04 thirsty, something cold, drink

05 At, something tiny, bit

06 catch, if, can   07 have you done

08 just finished   09 from, How, find

10 from, nearby   11 looking for, to

12 something sweaty, found

13 could, smell, from

14 sense heat, smell

15 why, survived for   16 all, like you

17 female, drink blood   18 feed on, plant

19 interesting, why, drink   20 protein, to lay

21 How, sharp teeth   22 don't, teeth

23 long, pointed mouth

24 So, your, easily

25 bit, bump, itches   26 sorry to hear

27 Make sure, don't

28 clean, with, wipes

29 never tried, before

30 reduce, itchiness   31 try, home

32 have to, soon   33 Where, going   34 going back to

35 lot, have suffered

36 How can, prevent

37 cool, wear, sleeves   38 keep, in mind

01 It, hot summer evening

02 went for a walk   03 was sweating

04 thirsty, something cold to drink

05 something tiny, at. bit

06 if you can   07 have you done

08 just finished   09 Where, from, How, find

10 from, nearby river

11 was looking for, to drink

12 smelled something sweaty

13 How, smell me

14 sense heat, smell

15 why, have survived, millions   16 like you

17 female, like me drink blood   18 feed on

19 interesting, blood

20 the protein, to lay

21 How, drink blood, sharp teeth   22 teeth

23 a long, pointed mouth

24 So, can drink, easily

25 After, bit, got a bump, itches

26 sorry to hear that

27 Make sure, scratch it

28 clean it with   29 never tried that before

30 reduce the itchiness   31 try that

32 have to go   33 Where, going   34 going back

35 A lot of, have suffered

36 How can, prevent them

37 cool, wear, sleeves   38 keep, in mind

1 무더운 여름날의 저녁이었습니다.

2 서준이는 공원에 산책을 갔습니다.

3 곧, 그는 땀을 흘리고 있었습니다.

4 서준: 목말라. 뭔가 시원한 것을 마시고 싶어.

5 그때에, 뭔가 조그마한 것이 그에게로 날아와서 그의 팔을 물었습니다.

6 모기: 이봐, 나를 잡을 수 있으면 잡아 봐.

7 서준: 너는 누구니? 나한테 무슨 짓을 한 거지?

8 모기: 나는 모기야. 난 방금 저녁 식사를 마쳤어.

9 서준: 너는 어디에서 왔니? 너는 어떻게 나를 찾은 거야?

10 모기: 나는 근처 강에서 왔어.

11 나는 그곳에서 마실 피를 찾던 중이었지.

12 그러다가 땀 냄새를 맡았고, 여기서 너를 발견했어.

13 서준: 너는 어떻게 강에서부터 내 냄새를 맡을 수 있었지?

14 모기: 모기들은 열과 냄새를 매우 잘 감지해.

15 그래서 우리가 수백만 년 동안 살아남은 거야.

16 서준: 모든 모기가 너처럼 피를 마셔?

17 모기: 아니. 오직 나와 같은 암컷 모기만이 피를 마셔.

18 수컷 모기들은 과일과 식물의 즙만을 먹고 살아.

19 서준: 그거 재미있네. 그럼 너는 왜 피를 마시는 거야?

20 모기: 알을 낳으려면 핏속의 단백질이 필요해.

21 서준: 너는 피를 어떻게 마시는 거야? 날카로운 이빨이 있니?

22 모기: 아니, 나는 이빨이 없어.

23 하지만 길고 뾰족한 입이 있지.

24 그래서 나는 너의 피를 쉽게 마실 수 있는 거야.

25 서준: 네가 나를 문 다음, 부어오른 자국이 생겼어. 가려워.

26 모기: 그 말을 들으니 미안하군.

27 그것을 긁지 않도록 해.

28 또한, 그것을 알코올 솜으로 닦아.

29 서준: 알코올 솜? 나는 전에 그것을 한 번도 해 보지 않았어.

30 모기: 그것은 가려움을 줄여 줄 거야.

31 서준: 알았어, 집에서 해 볼게. 고마워.

32 모기: 나는 이제 가야겠어. 다음에 보자.

33 서준: 너는 어디로 가는데?

34 모기: 강으로 돌아가려고.

35 서준: 기다려! 많은 사람이 모기에 물려서 괴로워하고 있어.

36 어떻게 하면 모기에 물리는 것을 막을 수 있지?

37 모기: 시원하게 지내고 소매가 긴 옷을 입어.

38 서준: 고마워. 너의 충고를 명심할게.

본문 TEST Step 4 - Step 5 · p.72~75

1 It was a hot summer evening.

2 Seojun went for a walk in the park.

3 Soon, he was sweating.

4 I'm thirsty. I want something cold to drink.

5 At that moment, something tiny flew at him and bit his arm.

6 Hey, catch me if you can.

7 Who are you? What have you done to me?

8 I'm a mosquito. I've just finished my dinner.

9 Where are you from? How did you find me?

10 I'm from a nearby river.

11 I was looking for some blood to drink there.

12 Then I smelled something sweaty and found you here.

13 How could you smell me from the river?

14 Mosquitoes can sense heat and smell very well.

15 That's why we have survived for millions of years.

16 Do all mosquitoes drink blood like you?

17 No. Only female mosquitoes like me drink blood.

18 Male mosquitoes only feed on fruit and plant juice.

19 That's interesting. So why do you drink blood?

20 I need the protein in blood to lay my eggs

21 How do you drink blood? Do you have sharp teeth?

22 No, I don't have teeth.

23 But I have a long and pointed mouth.

24 So I can drink your blood easily.

25 After you bit me, I got a bump. It itches.

26 I'm sorry to hear that.

27 Make sure you don't scratch it.

28 Also, clean it with alcohol wipes.

29 Alcohol wipes? I've never tried that before.

30 It will reduce the itchiness.

31 Okay, I'll try that at home. Thanks.

32 I have to go. See you soon.

33 Where are you going?

34 I'm going back to the river.

35 Wait! A lot of people have suffered from your bites.

36 How can we prevent them?

37 Stay cool and wear long sleeves.

38 Thanks. I'll keep your advice in mind.

구석구석지문 TEST Step 1 · p.76

Let's check

1. look upset, wrong

2. lost, my favorite

3. sorry to hear that

4. Why don't, Lost and Found

5. a good idea

Let's Write

1. Health Guide

2. Sunburn

3. Have, suffered from

4. useful tips to prevent

5. Wear

6. Wear

7. Be smart, enjoy

Culture & Life

1. thin, light, to stay cool

2. refrigerator pants

3. colorful patterns

4. look very stylish

구석구석지문 TEST Step 2 · p.77

Let's check

1. Sora: You look upset, Minu. What's wrong?

2. Minu: I lost my hat. It was my favorite.

3. Sora: I'm sorry to hear that.

4. Why don't you go to the Lost and Found Center?

5. Minu: That's a good idea .

Let's Write

1. Summer Health Guide

2. Sunburn

3. Have you ever suffered from sunburn?

4. Here are some useful tips to prevent sunburn in summer.

5. 1. Wear sunscreen.

6. 2. Wear a hat.

7. Be smart and enjoy the hot weather.

Culture & Life

1. In summer, some people in Korea wear thin and light pants to stay cool.

2. They call them " refrigerator pants."

3. Refrigerator pants come in colorful patterns.

4. Some of them look very stylish.

MEMO

적중 100 + 특별부록

Plan B

우리학교
최신기출

지학 · 민찬규 교과서를 배우는

학교 시험문제 분석 · 모음 · 해설집

전국단위 학교 시험문제 수집 및 분석
출제 빈도가 높은 문제 위주로 선별
문제 풀이에 필요한 상세한 해설

중2-1
영어

지학 · 민찬규

◎ 선택형 문항의 답안은 컴퓨터용 수정 싸인펜을 사용하여 OMR 답안지에 바르게 표기하시오.
◎ 서술형 문제는 답을 답안지에 반드시 검정 볼펜으로 쓰시오.
◎ 총 30문항 100점 만점입니다. 문항별 배점은 각 문항에 표시되어 있습니다.

[부산 ○○중]

1. 다음 대화의 밑줄 친 부분의 의도로 알맞은 것은?
(3점)

A: You know what? Mr. Smith is my homeroom teacher this year.
B: That's great, Jimin. His science class last year was a lot of fun.
A: Who's your homeroom teacher this year?
B: It's Ms. Kim. She's a new teacher.

① 칭찬하기
② 주의 끌기
③ 당부하기
④ 도움 제안하기
⑤ 계획 알려주기

[울산 ○○중]

2. 다음 중 영어 표현과 우리말 뜻이 바른 것은? (3점)

① a little: 많이
② be into ~: ~에 열중하다
③ by the way: 그래서
④ these days: 그 때에
⑤ get out of ~: ~ 안으로 들어가다

[부산 ○○중]

3. 다음 대화의 흐름상 빈칸에 들어갈 말로 가장 적절한 것은?
(4점)

A: I want to fly like you.
B: Try to eat more. You can make big changes some day.
A: _____ I love eating.
B: Great. Then you won't be the same. You can fly like me soon.

① I'm into eating these days.
② I'm worried about my legs.
③ You should try to do more exercise.
④ I don't know how to cook spaghetti.
⑤ Let me help you to solve this problem.

[충북 ○○중]

4. 다음 우리말에 맞는 영어 문장을 주어진 표현을 사용하여 작성하시오.
(4점)

• 만약 내일 비가 오지 않는다면, 나는 나의 친구들과 축구를 할 것이다.

조건
'if' 또는 'unless'를 반드시 사용할 것.

→ _____

[영등포구 ○○중]

5. 다음 대화의 (A)~(C)를 순서대로 바르게 배열한 것은?
(3점)

Julia, how was your winter vacation?

(A) Yes. It was really fun.
(B) That's amazing. I didn't know that you were interested in *muay thai*.
(C) It was great. You know what? I took *muay thai* lessons during the vacation.

Really? I want to try it.

① (C) - (B) - (A)
② (C) - (A) - (B)
③ (B) - (C) - (A)
④ (B) - (A) - (C)
⑤ (A) - (B) - (C)

[6~7] 다음 대화를 읽고 물음에 답하시오.

Emily: You know what, Junsu? I'm thinking of taking a painting class.

Junsu: Really? Why did you decide to take a painting class, Emily?

Emily: Because I want to go to an art high school.

Junsu: Are you thinking of _____ an artist in the future?

Emily: I hope so. I'm interested in painting pictures.

Junsu: That's great. I hope your wish comes true.

Emily: Thanks. I'll do my best.

6. 위 대화의 주제로 가장 적절한 것은? (4점)

① 꿈 실현의 중요성

② 진로에 대한 이야기

③ 예술고 진학의 어려움

④ 그림 수업 중 주의 사항

⑤ 수업에 영향을 주는 요소

7. 위 대화의 빈칸에 들어갈 표현으로 적절한 것은?

(2점)

① become ② became

③ becoming ④ to become

⑤ be becoming

8. 다음 대화의 내용과 일치하는 것은? (4점)

Yujin: Minsu, Sujin and I are thinking of starting a club.

Minsu: Really? What kind of club?

Yujin: We want to learn about stars and planets. So, we're thinking of starting a space science club.

Minsu: Sounds good. How often are you going to meet?

Yujin: Maybe twice a week.

Minsu: I see. Where will you meet?

Yujin: In Room 103. Minsu, do you want to join our club?

Minsu: Yes, I'm interested in space, too.

① Minsu is thinking of starting a club.

② Sujin is interested in writing essays in English.

③ Yujin is going to meet Sujin once a week.

④ Sujin doesn't want to join a space science club.

⑤ Minsu will learn about stars and planets with Sujin and Yujin.

9. 다음 두 사람의 대화가 자연스럽지 않은 것은? (3점)

① A: Wow! Mr. Smith is my homeroom teacher this year.

 B: That's great. His class last year was a lot of fun.

② A: What was your plan last weekend?

 B: I'm thinking of going hiking with my friend.

③ A: Julia, how was your winter vacation?

 B: It was great. I took sports lessons to be healthier.

④ A: You know what? I took *muay thai* lessons during the vacation.

 B: That's amazing. I didn't know that you were interested in *muay thai*.

⑤ A: Do we have any vegetables at home, Mom?

 B: We have some vegetables, but we don't have beef. I'll buy some for you on my way home.

10. 다음 대화에서 우리말에 알맞은 영어 한 문장을 쓰시오. **(4점)**

A: You know what? 나는 일찍 자려고 생각 중이야.

B: Why did you decide to do that?

A: It's because I want to go jogging in the morning.

B: That's great.

조건
- 반드시 주어진 단어를 모두 사용할 것.
- 어법에 맞게 변형하여 사용할 것.

early, bed, think

→ _____

11. 다음 표의 설명에 맞게 문장을 완성하시오. **(5점)**

<Directions>
- 한 문장당 취미 하나씩 표현할 것.
- 두 가지 중 각각을 지칭하는 표현을 활용할 것.

Momo has two hobbies.
(1) _____.
(2) _____.

12. 다음 중 어법상 옳은 것은? **(3점)**

① If it rain tomorrow, I will stay home.

② If it doesn't rain tomorrow, I will go hiking.

③ I stay home if it will rain tomorrow.

④ Unless it doesn't rain tomorrow, I will play soccer with my friends.

⑤ If she go shopping, I'll go with her.

13. 다음 그림을 보고 주어진 우리말에 알맞은 표현을 영어 한 문장으로 쓰시오. **(4점)**

- 나는 나의 숙제를 일찍 끝낸다면, 내 방 청소를 할 것이다.

조건
- If절이 들어가는 완전한 영어 문장으로 쓸 것.

→ _____

14. 다음 두 사람의 대화가 자연스럽게 이어지도록 빈칸에 들어갈 가장 알맞은 것은? **(4점)**

A: You know what? Jenny's family is going to (A)_____ to Japan.

B: Is that right? Jenny didn't tell me about it.

A: She learned about it just last week and she's very upset now.

B: I can understand her feelings. I am going to (B)_____ her so much.

A: Me, too. She said she would keep in (C)_____ with us.

	(A)	(B)	(C)
①	keep	tell	mind
②	start	find	reach
③	move	miss	touch
④	leave	see	heart
⑤	reach	imagine	control

[15~20] 다음 글을 읽고 물음에 답하시오.

My friend Eric and I made some interesting changes (가)_____ the vacation. We emailed each other and talked about our changes.

Dear Eric,
It's a beautiful spring in Seoul. The last winter vacation was a great time for me. I made two personal changes during the vacation. One is my new hobby. It's making cupcakes. (A)[Making / Made] my own cupcakes is a lot of fun. The other change is (나)_____ one of bad habits.

Ⓐ

If you try to make some changes, I'm sure you'll feel great like me. I hope to hear from you soon.
Your friend, Junho

Dear Junho,
In Sydney, it's fall in March. You talked about your changes in your email. Now, ⓐ_____ talk about my changes.
ⓑ_____, I'm into 3D printing. I printed two things with a 3D printer. One is a model of my dream car. If the traffic is heavy, it (B)[will change / changed] into a flying car. (C)[The other / Another] is a special cup for my grandfather. He can't hold his cup well because (D)[he's / his] sick. My special cup has three handles, so it is easy to hold. My grandfather is very happy. By the way, I want to try your cupcakes some day, Junho.
Take care.
Best wishes, Eric

15. 위 글의 흐름에 맞도록 빈칸 Ⓐ에 들어갈 말을 순서에 맞게 배열한 것은? (2점)

㉠ Now I don't anymore.
㉡ I feel great about the changes I made.
㉢ In the past, I often bit my nails.

① ㉠ - ㉡ - ㉢   ② ㉠ - ㉢ - ㉡
③ ㉢ - ㉠ - ㉡   ④ ㉢ - ㉡ - ㉠
⑤ ㉡ - ㉠ - ㉢

16. 위 글의 (A)~(D)에서 올바른 것을 바르게 연결한 것은? (4점)

	(A)	(B)	(C)	(D)
①	Making	changed	Another	his
②	Making	will change	The other	he's
③	Making	will change	The other	his
④	Made	changed	Another	he's
⑤	Made	will change	The other	he's

17. 위 글의 (가)~(나)에 들어갈 말로 알맞게 연결된 것은? (3점)

	(가)	(나)
①	for	erasing
②	during	cleaning
③	for	cleaning
④	for	breaking
⑤	during	breaking

18. 위 글의 빈칸 ⓐ와 ⓑ에 들어갈 말을 주어진 단어를 활용하여 우리말에 맞게 쓰시오. (4점)

ⓐ ~할 시간이다 (time)
ⓑ 요즈음에는 (day)

ⓐ _____, ⓑ _____

19. 위 글의 내용과 일치하는 것은? (3점)

① Junho is having winter vacation now.

② Junho is interested in 3D printing.

③ Junho gave Eric some cupcakes that he made.

④ Eric and Junho have different weathers.

⑤ Eric's grandfather is getting healthier.

20. 다음은 위 글의 Junho가 Eric에게 보낸 답장이다. 적절하지 않은 문장은? (3점)

Dear Eric,
Thank you for your email. I am happy that you are making new changes just like me. ⓐI feel so sorry for your grandfather. ⓑ Because we all hope for him to get better, he will be healthy again. ⓒI think your idea of making him a special cup is great. ⓓThe model of your dream car will be useful because it can become small in heavy traffic. ⓔI am enjoying making cupcakes much more. It's great to hear from each other. Take care!

Junho

① ⓐ   ② ⓑ   ③ ⓒ   ④ ⓓ   ⑤ ⓔ

[부산 ○○중]

[21~22] 다음 글을 읽고 물음에 답하시오.

The last winter vacation was a great time for me. I made two personal changes during the vacation. ⓐOne is my new hobby. ⓑIt's making cupcakes. ⓒMaking my own cupcakes is a lot of fun. ⓓNow I also know how to make gimbap. ⓔThe other change is breaking one of my bad habits. In the past, (A)_____ _____. Now I don't anymore. I feel great about the changes I made.

21. 위 글의 ⓐ~ⓔ 중 글의 흐름상 어색한 것은? (2점)

① ⓐ   ② ⓑ   ③ ⓒ   ④ ⓓ   ⑤ ⓔ

22. 위 글의 빈칸 (A)에 '나는 종종 내 손톱을 물어뜯었어.' 라는 뜻이 되게 영어로 쓰시오. (4점)

• In the past, _____.

보기

bite, my, often, nails

<Directions>
• 완전한 문장으로 쓰시오.
• <보기>의 단어를 모두 활용하고, 필요시 단어의 형태를 바꾸시오.

→ _____

[강원 ○○중]

[23~24] 다음 글을 읽고 물음에 답하시오.

It's a beautiful spring in Seoul. The last winter vacation was a great time for me. I ⓐmade two personal changes during the vacation. One ⓑis my new hobby. (A)It is making cupcakes. Making my own cupcakes ⓒare a lot of fun. The other change is breaking one of my bad habits. In the past, I often ⓓbit my nails. Now I don't anymore. I feel great about the changes I made. If you ⓔtry to make some changes, I'm sure you'll feel great like me. I hope to hear from you soon.

23. (A)It이 가리키는 것을 우리말로 쓰시오. (3점)

→ _____

24. 위 글의 ⓐ~ⓔ 중 어법상 적절하지 않은 것은? (3점)

① ⓐ   ② ⓑ   ③ ⓒ   ④ ⓓ   ⑤ ⓔ

[25~27] 다음 글을 읽고 물음에 답하시오.

Dear Junho,
In Sydney, it's fall in March. You talked about your changes in your email. Now, <u>it's time to</u> talk about my new changes. <u>These days</u>, I'm into 3D printing. I printed two things with a 3D printer. One is a model of my dream car. (교통이 혼잡하면 그것은 날 수 있는 차로 바뀔 거야.) The other is a special cup for my grandfather. He can't hold his cup well because he's sick. My special cup has three handles, so it is easy to hold. My grandfather is very happy. <u>By the way</u>, I want to try your cupcakes <u>some day</u>, Junho. Take care.

Best wishes,
Eric

25. 위 글의 괄호 안의 우리말에 맞게 영작하시오. (5점)

→ _____

26. What did Eric make with a 3D printer? (4점)

• He made (1)_____
and (2)_____ with
a 3D printer.

(1) _____

(2) _____

27. 위 글의 밑줄 친 부분의 의미로 <u>어색한</u> 것은? (2점)

① it's time to: ~할 때다
② These days: 요즈음에
③ I'm into: 나는 ~ 안에 있다
④ By the way: 그건 그렇고
⑤ some day: 언젠가

[28~30] 다음 글을 읽고 물음에 답하시오.

Dear Eric,
(A) ⓐ_____'s a beautiful spring in Seoul. The last winter vacation was a great time for me. (B) One is my new hobby. ⓐ_____'s making cupcakes. Making my own cupcakes is a lot of fun. (C) The other change is breaking one of my bad habits. In the past, I often bit my nails. (D) Now I don't anymore. I feel great about those changes. If you try to make some changes, I'm sure you'll feel great like me. (E) I hope to hear from you soon.

Your friend,
Junho

28. 위 글의 내용상 아래의 문장이 들어갈 위치로 가장 알맞은 곳은? (3점)

I made two personal changes during the vacation.

① (A) ② (B) ③ (C) ④ (D) ⑤ (E)

29. 위 글의 빈칸 ⓐ에 공통으로 알맞은 표현은? (2점)
① It   ② That   ③ This
④ One   ⑤ Other

30. 위 글의 내용으로 바르지 <u>않은</u> 것은? (3점)
① Junho made changes this winter.
② Junho wants to hear from Eric.
③ Junho likes his changes that he made.
④ Junho doesn't bite his nails anymore.
⑤ Junho's new hobby is making cupcakes.

◎ 선택형 문항의 답안은 컴퓨터용 수정 싸인펜을 사용하여 OMR 답안지에 바르게 표기하시오.
◎ 서술형 문제는 답을 답안지에 반드시 검정 볼펜으로 쓰시오.
◎ 총 29문항 100점 만점입니다. 문항별 배점은 각 문항에 표시되어 있습니다.

[영등포구 ○○중]

1. 다음 우리말을 참고하여 빈칸에 알맞은 말을 써 넣으시오. (4점)

• We have some vegetables, but we don't have beef. I'll buy some for you ⓐ_____ _____ _____ home. (내가 집에 가는 길에)

• ⓑYou _____ _____, Tim?(너 그거 아니, Tim?) Mr. Smith is my homeroom teacher this year.

ⓐ _____ _____ home

ⓑ You _____ _____, Tim?

[강동구 ○○중]

2. 다음 그림의 나비와 애벌레의 대화가 자연스럽게 이루어지도록 할 때, 보기의 단어들 중 빈칸 어디에도 들어갈 수 <u>없는</u> 단어들만 묶어 놓은 것은? (4점)

> **보기**
> anymore, away, fly, into, make, avoid, some

🐛 I want to _____ like you.

🦋 Try to eat more. You can _____ big changes _____ day.

🐛 I'm _____ eating these days. I love eating.

🦋 Great. Then you won't be the same _____. You can _____ like me soon.

① away, make ② into, avoid
③ anymore, fly ④ away, avoid
⑤ make, some

[울산 ○○중]

3. 다음 중 짝지어진 대화가 <u>어색한</u> 것은? (3점)

① A: How often are you going to meet?
  B: Maybe for two hours.

② A: The floor is slippery.
  B: You should watch your step.

③ A: What is your plan for this weekend?
  B: I'm thinking of visiting my grandparents.

④ A I'm worried about my sore throat.
  B: Why don't you take some medicine?

⑤ A: You know what? Our soccer team won the match last week.
  B: Oh, really? That's great.

[강원 ○○중]

4. 다음 문장이 들어갈 곳으로 가장 적절한 것은? (3점)

> What about beef?

Alex: Mom, I made *bulgogi* at school today. I'm thinking of cooking *bulgogi* for dinner. (A)
Mom: That sounds great, Alex. (B)
Alex: Do we have any vegetables at home, Mom? (C)
Mom: We have some vegetables, but we don't have beef. (D) I'll buy some for you on my way home. (E)
Alex: Great.

① (A) ② (B) ③ (C) ④ (D) ⑤ (E)

5. 다음은 소녀와 소년의 대화이다. 주어진 대화에 이어질 말의 순서를 가장 적절하게 배열한 것은?　(4점)

> G: You know what? Mr. Smith is my homeroom teacher this year.
> B: That's great!
>
> G: Girl, B: Boy

> (A) Who's your homeroom teacher this year?
> (B) She teachers art.
> (C) What does she teach?
> (D) His science class last year was a lot of fun.
> (E) It's Ms. Kim. She's a new teacher.

① (A) - (C) - (B) - (D) - (E)
② (C) - (B) - (D) - (E) - (A)
③ (C) - (B) - (E) - (A) - (D)
④ (D) - (A) - (E) - (C) - (B)
⑤ (D) - (C) - (B) - (A) - (E)

6. 다음 빈칸에 들어갈 말로 가장 적절한 것은?　(3점)

> B: How was your winter vacation?
> G: It was great. _____ I took *muay thai* lessons during the vacation.
> B: That's amazing. I didn't know that you were interested in *muay thai*.
> G: Yes. It was really fun.
> B: Really? I want to try it.
>
> *G: Girl, B: Boy

① You know what?
② It is right, isn't it?
③ Don't you know him?
④ What's wrong with you?
⑤ How did you know that?

7. 다음 대화의 내용으로 <u>어색한</u> 것은?　(3점)

> Emily: You know what, Junsu? I'm thinking of taking a painting class.
> Junsu: Really? Why did you decide to take a painting class, Emily?
> Emily: Because I want to go to an art high school.
> Junsu: Are you thinking of becoming an artist in the future?
> Emily: I hope so. I'm interested in painting pictures.
> Junsu: That's great. I hope your wish comes true.
> Emily: Thanks. I'll do my best.

① Emily wants to go to an art high school.
② Emily plans to take a painting class.
③ Emily's hope is to be an artist in the future.
④ Emily is interested in taking pictures.
⑤ Junsu hopes that Emily becomes an artist.

8. 다음 대화를 읽고 빈칸에 들어갈 표현으로 <u>어색한</u> 것은?　(4점)

> B: Mom, I made *bulgogi* at school today. I'm thinking of cooking *bulgogi* for dinner.
> W: That sounds great, Alex.
> B: Do we have any vegetables at home, Mom? What about beef?
> W: We have some vegetables, but we don't have beef. I'll buy for you on my way home.
> B: Great.

↓

> B: Mom, I'm thinking of ⓐ_____ *bulgogi* for ⓑ_____. Do you have any ⓒ_____ at home?
> W: No, I'll ⓓ_____ some on my way ⓔ_____.

① ⓐ cooking　② ⓑ dinner
③ ⓒ vegetables　④ ⓓ buy
⑤ ⓔ home

9. 다음 대화를 읽고 대화의 내용과 일치하지 <u>않는</u> 것은?　　(4점)

A: Minsu, Sujin and I are thinking of starting a club.
B: Really? Sumi, can you tell me what kind of club it is?
A: We want to learn about stars and planets. So, we're thinking of starting a space science club.
B: Sounds good. How often are you going to meet?
A: Maybe once a week.
B: I see. Where will you meet?
A: In Room 101. Minsu, do you want to join our club?
B: Yes. I'm interested in space, too.

① Sumi and Sujin are planning to start a space science club.
② Sujin and Sumi want to learn about stars and planets.
③ Maybe Sumi is going to meet Sujin in her club once a week.
④ If Minsu join Sujin and Sumi's club, he will meet them in Room 101.
⑤ Minsu is interested in space but he is not going to join Sumi's space science club.

10. 다음 대화의 빈칸에 가장 알맞은 표현은?　　(2점)

A: You know what? _____
B: Why did you decide to do that?
A: It's because I want to be good at English writing.
B: That's great.

① I'm thinking of saving money.
② I'm thinking of keeping a diary in English.
③ I'm planning to go to bed early.
④ I'm going to get up early.
⑤ I'm thinking of taking a painting class.

11. 다음 글을 'one, the other' 구문과 괄호 안에 주어진 표현을 이용하여 완성하시오.　　(5점)

• Bobo is my pet dog. She has two habits.
(1) _____
(2) _____
(watching TV / sleeping on my chair)

(1) _____
(2) _____

12. 다음 중 어법상 바른 것은?　　(4점)

① If you go jogging every morning, you got healthier.
② If you don't wear warm clothes, catch a cold.
③ She feels sleepy all day if she will sleep only three hours at night.
④ If she goes shopping, I'll go with her.
⑤ If you won't get up now, you'll be late for school.

13. 빈칸에 들어갈 말이 바르게 짝지어진 것은?　　(4점)

• Bobo is my pet dog. She has two brothers. _____ is black. _____ is white.

① One — Another
② The other — One
③ Another — The other
④ One — The others
⑤ One — The other

[14~17] 다음 글을 읽고 물음에 답하시오.

My friend Junho and I made some interesting changes ⓐduring the vacation. We emailed ⓑeach other and talked about our changes.

Dear Junho,
In Sydney, it's fall in March. You talked about your changes in your email. Now, ⓒit's time to talk about my new changes. These days, I'm into 3D printing. I printed two things with a 3D printer. One is a model of my dream car. (A)_____ _____. The other is a special cup for my grandfather. He can't hold his cup well (B)_____ he's sick. My special cup has three handles, (C)_____ it is easy to hold. My grandfather is very happy. ⓓBy the way, I want to try your cupcakes some day, Junho. Take care.
ⓔBest wishes,
Eric

14. 위 글의 ⓐ~ⓔ 중 뜻풀이가 잘못된 것은? (2점)

① ⓐduring: ~ 동안
② ⓑeach other: 서로
③ ⓒit's time to: ~할 때다
④ ⓓBy the way: 언젠가
⑤ ⓔBest wishes: 행운을 빌며

15. 위 글을 읽고 질문에 답할 수 없는 것은? (4점)

① Did Junho email Eric?
② Did Eric change his habits?
③ How many things did Eric make with a 3D printer?
④ Did Eric already eat Junho's cupcakes?
⑤ Does Eric's grandfather like the special cup?

16. 위 글의 빈칸 (A)에 '만약 교통이 혼잡하면, 그것은 날 수 있는 차로 바뀔 것이다.'라는 뜻이 되게 영어로 쓸 때, 〈보기〉의 어구를 모두 배열하시오. (4점)

> 보기
>
> heavy / a flying car / it / will / is / the traffic / change into

→ If _____.

17. 위 글의 (B)와 (C)에 들어갈 말로 가장 적절한 것은? (3점)

	(B)	(C)
①	because	when
②	but	when
③	because	so
④	but	so
⑤	for example	so

18. 밑줄 친 부분 중 내용상 어색한 것은? (4점)

Dear Junho,
In Sydney, ⓐit's fall in March. You talked about your changes in your email. Now, it's time to talk about my new changes. These days, I'm into 3D printing. ⓑI printed three things with a 3D printer. One is a model of my dream car. ⓒIf the traffic is heavy, it will change into a flying car. The other is a special cup for my grandfather. He can't hold his cup well ⓓbecause he's sick. My special cup has three handles, so ⓔit is easy to hold. My grandfather is very happy. By the way, I want to try your cupcakes some day, Junho. Take care.
Best wishes,
Eric

① ⓐ　② ⓑ　③ ⓒ　④ ⓓ　⑤ ⓔ

[19~22] 다음 글을 읽고 물음에 답하시오.

> Dear Junho,
>
> In Sydney, it's fall in March. You talked about your changes in your email. ⓐ_____, it's time to talk about my new changes. (A) These days, I'm ⓑ_____ 3D printing. (B) I printed two things with a 3D printer. (C) If the traffic is heavy, it will change ⓑ_____ a flying car. (D) The other is a special cup for my grandfather. He can't hold his cup well because he's sick. (E) My special cup has three handles, ⓒ_____ _____.
>
> My grandfather is very happy.
>
> ⓓ_____, I want to try your cupcakes some day, Junho.
>
> Take care.
>
> Best wishes,
>
> Eric

19. 위 글의 (A)~(E) 중 다음 문장이 들어갈 위치로 가장 알맞은 것은? (3점)

> One is a model of my dream car.

① (A)　② (B)　③ (C)　④ (D)　⑤ (E)

20. 위 글의 빈칸 ⓐ, ⓓ에 들어갈 가장 알맞은 것끼리 짝지은 것은? (3점)

	ⓐ	ⓓ
①	Now	By the way
②	Of course	Now
③	However	Of course
④	By the way	However
⑤	From now on	These days

21. 빈칸 ⓑ에 공통으로 들어갈 알맞은 것은? (2점)

① at　② into　③ on
④ to　⑤ with

22. 빈칸 ⓒ에 들어갈 가장 알맞은 것은? (4점)

① so it is difficult to hold
② but it is not easy to hold
③ so it is not difficult to hold
④ however it is heavy to hold
⑤ and they aren't easy to hold

[23~24] 다음 글을 읽고 물음에 답하시오.

> In Sydney, it's fall in March. You talked about your changes in your email. Now, it's time to talk about my ⓐnew changes. These days, I'm into 3D printing. I printed two things with a 3D printer. (A)하나는 나의 꿈의 차 모형이다. If the traffic is ⓑlight, it will change into a flying car. (B)다른 하나는 나의 할아버지를 위한 특별한 컵이다. He can't hold his cup well because he's ⓒsick. My special cup has three handles, so it is ⓓeasy to hold. My grandfather is very ⓔhappy. By the way, I want to try your cupcakes some day, Junho. Take care.

23. 위 글의 흐름상 적절하지 않은 표현은? (2점)

① ⓐ　② ⓑ　③ ⓒ　④ ⓓ　⑤ ⓔ

24. 위 글의 (A), (B)의 우리말과 일치하도록 주어진 단어를 모두 이용하여 영어 한 문장으로 쓰시오. (5점)

(1) (A) 하나는 나의 꿈의 차 모형이다. (model, dream)

→ _____

(2) (B) 다른 하나는 나의 할아버지를 위한 특별한 컵이다. (special, grandfather)

→ _____

[25~27] 다음 글을 읽고 물음에 답하시오.

My New Changes
My friend Eric and I made some interesting changes during the vacation. We emailed (A)_____ and talked about our changes.
Dear Eric,
It's a beautiful spring in Seoul. The last winter vacation was a great time for me. I made two personal changes during the vacation. One is my new hobby. It's making cupcakes. Making my own cupcakes is a lot of fun. (B)_____ change is breaking one of my bad habits. In the past, I often (C)_____ my nails. <u>Now I don't anymore.</u> I feel great about the changes I made. If you try to make some changes, I'm sure you'll feel great like me. I hope to hear from you soon.
Your friend,
Junho

25. 위 글의 빈칸 (A)~(C)에 들어갈 가장 알맞은 것끼리 짝지은 것은? (4점)

	(A)	(B)	(C)
①	one another	Another	bit
②	each other	The other	bit
③	each other	The other	bite
④	one another	Another	bite
⑤	one by one	Another	bitten

26. 위 글의 밑줄 친 <u>Now I don't anymore</u>의 의미로 가장 알맞은 것은? (3점)

① Now I don't bite my nails anymore.
② Now I don't make changes anymore.
③ Now I don't break my bad habit anymore.
④ Now I don't feel great about my changes anymore.
⑤ Now I don't want to change my bad habit anymore.

27. 위 글의 내용과 일치하는 것은? (3점)

① 지금 서울은 겨울이다.
② Eric은 방학 동안 변화가 없었다.
③ 준호는 더 이상 손톱을 물어뜯지 않는다.
④ 준호는 방학 동안 한 가지 개인적인 변화가 있었다.
⑤ 방학 이전에 준호의 취미는 컵케이크를 만드는 것이었다.

[28~29] 다음 글을 읽고 물음에 답하시오.

Dear Junho,
(A) In Sydney, it's fall in March. You talked about your changes in your email. (B) These days, I'm into 3D printing. I printed two things with a 3D printer. (C) One is a model of my dream car. If the traffic is heavy, it will change into a flying car. (D) The other is a special cup for my grandfather. He can't hold his cup well because he's sick. (E) My special cup has three handles, so it is easy to hold. My grandfather is very happy. By the way, I want to try your cupcakes some day, Junho. Take care.
Best wishes,
Eric

28. 위 글에서 다음 문장이 들어갈 알맞은 위치는? (3점)

Now, it's time to talk about my new changes.

① (A) ② (B) ③ (C) ④ (D) ⑤ (E)

29. 위 글을 읽고 대답할 수 <u>없는</u> 것은? (4점)

① Who sent the email?
② Who received the email?
③ What is Eric into these days?
④ How is the weather in Sydney?
⑤ Why did Eric make a special cup with three handles?

2학년 영어 1학기 중간고사(2과) 1회

반		점수
이름		

문항수 : 선택형(26문항) 서술형(8문항)　　20 ． ． ．

◎ 선택형 문항의 답안은 컴퓨터용 수정 싸인펜을
사용하여 OMR 답안지에 바르게 표기하시오.
◎ 서술형 문제는 답을 답안지에 반드시 검정
볼펜으로 쓰시오.
◎ 총 34문항 100점 만점입니다. 문항별 배점
은 각 문항에 표시되어 있습니다.

[부산 ○○중]

1. 다음 중 영영 풀이가 <u>어색한</u> 것은? (3점)

① wisdom: good sense and judgment

② empty: having nothing inside

③ disaster: to prevent something bad from
happening

④ be into: to like and be interested in
something

⑤ injury: a wound or damage to part of your
body

[강동구 ○○중]

2. 다음 빈칸에 들어갈 가장 알맞은 말은? (2점)

> • These stairs are wet and _____. Watch
> your step.

① slippery　　② serious　　③ hurt

④ stormy　　⑤ wisdom

[영등포구 ○○중]

3. 다음 중 짝지어진 대화가 <u>어색한</u> 것은? (2점)

① A: What's wrong?
　 B: I'm worried about my leg.

② A: What are you watching?
　 B: It's a program about earthquakes.

③ A: Why don't you go see a doctor?
　 B: I'm going to go after school today.

④ A: What time is the movie?
　 B: It starts at the theater.

⑤ A: We should walk on the stairs.
　 B: You're right.

[충북 ○○중]

**4. 다음 A와 B의 대화가 어울리도록 보기의 표현을 바르
게 배열한 것은?** (4점)

> A: I'm worried about my dog. He seems
> sick.
> B: (A) _____
> A: I'm worried about my weight. I weigh 80
> kilograms now.
> B: (B) _____
> A: I'm worried about my English grade. I
> got a 65% on the last test.
> B: (C) _____

보기
> ⓐ Maybe you should ask your classmates to
> help you study.
> ⓑ You should take him to the vet.
> ⓒ You should join a gym.
> ⓓ Why don't you take some medicine?
> ⓔ Why don't you take some rest?

　　(A)　(B)　(C)　　　　　　(A)　(B)　(C)
① ⓓ － ⓒ － ⓐ　　　② ⓑ － ⓒ － ⓐ

③ ⓑ － ⓔ － ⓐ　　　④ ⓔ － ⓒ － ⓐ

⑤ ⓑ － ⓐ － ⓒ

[영등포구 ○○중]

5. 대화의 내용상 밑줄 친 부분이 <u>어색한</u> 것은? (2점)

> B: Dad, I'm ⓐ<u>going out</u> to play basketball
> with Minsu.
> M: Did you ⓑ<u>finish cleaning</u> your room?
> B: ⓒ<u>Yes, not yet</u>. Can I do it later?
> M: No. You should clean your room first.
> B: Okay. ⓓ<u>I'll clean</u> my room and then play
> basketball.
> M: Good. ⓔ<u>Don't forget</u> to be home by six
> o'clock.
> B: Okay.

① ⓐ　　② ⓑ　　③ ⓒ　　④ ⓓ　　⑤ ⓔ

[6~7] 다음 대화를 읽고 물음에 답하시오.

G: What time is the movie? (A)
B: It starts at 4:30. (B)
G: Oh, no. (C) We only have 20 minutes left. Let's run!
B: No! You might fall and hurt yourself. (D)
G: (E) You're right. We can be a little late.
B: Yes. Better safe than sorry.
(G: Girl / B: Boy)

6. 위 대화의 (A)~(E) 중 다음 문장이 들어갈 알맞은 곳은? (3점)

You should walk on the stairs.

① (A)　② (B)　③ (C)　④ (D)　⑤ (E)

7. 위 대화의 내용과 일치하는 것은? (2점)

① 그들은 뛰지 않기로 했다.
② 그들은 정시에 도착할 것이다.
③ 현재 영화가 시작하기 30분 전이다.
④ 소년은 과거에 다쳐 본 적이 있다.
⑤ 소녀는 소년의 조언을 듣지 않고 있다.

8. 다음 대화의 내용과 일치하지 않는 것은? (3점)

Brian: There was a big fire at the city library yesterday.
Mina: Yes, I heard about it. I was worried about the people there.
Brian: Don't worry. Everybody was okay. They all followed the safety rules.
Mina: Really? What are the rules?
Brian: You need to cover your nose and mouth with a wet towel. Then stay low and escape.
Mina: Oh, I didn't know that.
Brian: You should keep that in mind. It might be helpful some day.

① 어제 도서관에 화재가 발생했다.
② Mina는 화재가 일어난 것을 이미 알고 있었다.
③ 사람들이 화재에서 모두 안전했다.
④ 탈출할 때에는 몸을 낮게 숙인 채 나가야 한다.
⑤ 화재 발생 시에는 마른 수건으로 코와 입을 먼저 막아야 한다.

9. 대화의 내용상 밑줄 친 부분이 어색한 것은? (2점)

B: Dad, I'm ⓐgoing out to play basketball with Minsu?
M: Did you ⓑfinish cleaning your room?
B: ⓒYes, not yet. Can I do it later?
M: No. You should clean your room first.
B: Okay. ⓓI'll clean my room and then play basketball.
M: Good. ⓔDon't forget to be home by six o'clock.
B: Okay.

① ⓐ　② ⓑ　③ ⓒ　④ ⓓ　⑤ ⓔ

10. 다음 빈칸 (A), (B)에 들어갈 단어가 바르게 짝지어진 것은? (3점)

B: What are you watching?
G: It's a program about earthquakes.
B: Sounds interesting. I'm (A)_____ about earthquakes these days.
G: Me, too. This program has some (B)_____ tips.
B: Really? What does it say?
G: When things start to shake, you need to take cover under a table.
B: Oh, I didn't know that.

	(A)	(B)		(A)	(B)
①	late	– help	②	kind	– help
③	worried	– helpful	④	kind	– helpful
⑤	worried	– scary			

11. 다음 대화의 빈칸에 내용과 어울리는 충고하기 표현을 이용하여 문장을 완성하시오. (4점)

G: What time is the movie?

B: It starts at 4:30.

G: Oh, no. We only have 20 minutes left. Let's run!

B: No! You might fall and hurt yourself. _____ on the stairs.

G: You're right. We can be a little late.

B: Yes. Better safe than sorry.

→ _____

12. What will the boy do first after this dialog? (2점)

B: Dad, I'm going out to play basketball with Minu.

M: Did you finish cleaning your room?

B: No, not yet. Can I do it later?

M: No, you should clean your room first.

B: Okay. I'll clean my room and then play basketball.

M: Good. Don't forget to be home by six o'clock.

B: Okay.

→ He'll _____ .

13. 다음 문장 중 어법상 바른 것은? (4점)

① He didn't tell me why to do next.

② Junha learned what to make gimbap.

③ Sera couldn't choose what to wear for the party.

④ Could you tell me what to solve this problem?

⑤ Hajun asked what to write the report.

14. 다음 우리말에 맞도록 관계대명사를 이용하여 두 문장을 한 문장으로 바꿔 쓰시오. (4점)

• Look at the man and his dog.

• They are running over there.

• 저쪽에서 뛰고 있는 남자와 그의 개를 봐라.

→ _____

15. 다음 주어진 두 문장을 주격 관계대명사를 이용하여 하나의 문장으로 바꾸시오. (3점)

• I watched a TV show.

• The TV show was about natural disasters.

→ _____

16. 다음 그림의 상황에 맞게 주어진 단어를 모두 이용하여 영어 한 문장으로 쓰시오. (5점)

(1)  (2)

(1) _____

당신은 문을 닫을 때 당신의 손을 조심해야 한다. (should, hands, watch, when)

(2) _____

당신은 차에서 나올 때 당신의 머리를 조심해야 한다. (should, get out of)

- 15 -

[17~21] 다음 글을 읽고 물음에 답하시오.

Do you know what to do when an earthquake strikes? Take this quiz and think about how to be safe during this (가)kind of natural disaster.

(중략)

How did you do on the quiz? Can you survive an earthquake safely? Here ⓐis some safety tips ⓑwhich can be helpful in an earthquake. Let's check them one by one and learn what to do.

Don't run outside when things are shaking. Find a table or a desk and take cover (A)_____ it. You can hold on to the legs ⓒto protect yourself. Also, stay away (B)_____ windows. They can break during an earthquake and hurt you.

You can go outside when the shaking stops. To get out (C)_____ buildings, don't use the elevator. Take the stairs. It's ⓓvery safer. Once you are outside, find an empty space that is far from buildings. There may be people ⓔwho want to hold on to a pole or a tree, but think again. That's a bad idea because it can fall on you.

17. 위 글에 대한 내용과 일치하지 않는 것은? (2점)

① 창문으로부터 멀리 떨어져 있어야 한다.

② 건물로부터 멀어져 있는 공터로 가야 한다.

③ 건물 밖으로 나갈 때에는 계단을 이용한다.

④ 물건이 흔들리기 시작하면 밖으로 대피해야 한다.

⑤ 지진 발생 중에 큰 기둥을 잡고 있는 것은 위험하다.

18. 위 글의 (가)와 같은 의미로 쓰이지 않은 것은? (정답 2개) (4점)

① He is such a kind person.

② She likes music of all kinds.

③ What kind of movie do you like?

④ It was really kind of you to help me.

⑤ Exercises of this kind are very popular.

19. 위 글의 빈칸 (A)~(C)에 들어갈 말이 바르게 짝지어진 것은? (3점)

	(A)	(B)	(C)
①	under	from	into
②	over	for	into
③	under	from	of
④	over	for	of
⑤	under	for	of

20. 위 글의 밑줄 친 ⓐ~ⓔ 중 어법상 어색한 것은? (정답 2개) (3점)

① ⓐ   ② ⓑ   ③ ⓒ   ④ ⓓ   ⑤ ⓔ

21. 위 글에서 다음 질문에 대한 답을 찾아 쓰시오. (3점)

Q: Why is holding on to a tree a bad idea?
A: It's because _____.

→ _____

22. 다음 빈칸에 들어갈 가장 알맞은 말은? (2점)

There are many situations which can be dangerous. Here are some tips. Let's learn what to do and be safe! Broken glass can be dangerous. People might step on the broken glass. So you should _____ the broken glass.

① wash   ② make   ③ clean up

④ paint   ⑤ keep

[23~28] 다음 글을 읽고 물음에 답하시오.

Can you survive an earthquake ⓐsafe? Here are some safety tips which can be helpful in an earthquake. Let's check them one by one and learn ⓑwhat to do.
(A) Don't run outside when things are shaking. (B) Find a table or a desk and take cover under it. (C) Also, stay away from windows. (D) They can break during an earthquake and hurt you. (E)
You can go outside when the shaking stops. ⓒGet out of buildings, don't use the elevator. Take the stairs. It's much safer. Once you are outside, find an empty space that is far from buildings. There may be people ⓓwhich want to hold on to a pole or a tree, but think again. That's a bad idea because it can fall on you.
Earthquakes can ㉠발생하다 anytime. They can be scary ㉡경험들 for everyone. So learn ⓔwhat to be safe in an earthquake. You can ㉢피하다 injuries and protect yourself. Follow these tips and be safe!

23. 위 글의 ⓐ~ⓔ 중 문법적으로 올바른 것은? (3점)

① ⓐ ② ⓑ ③ ⓒ ④ ⓓ ⑤ ⓔ

24. 위 글의 (A)~(E) 중 다음 문장이 들어갈 곳으로 올바른 곳은? (4점)

You can hold on to the legs to protect yourself.

① (A) ② (B) ③ (C) ④ (D) ⑤ (E)

25. 위 글의 지진 대비 수칙의 내용과 일치하는 것은? (2점)

① You should stay far from the windows.
② You should take elevators during an earthquake.
③ You should hold a tree to be safe.
④ You should go outside when things start to shake.
⑤ You should stand up next to the desk to protect yourself.

26. 위 글의 밑줄 친 ㉠~㉢의 우리말에 알맞은 어휘로 바르게 연결된 것은? (3점)

	㉠	㉡	㉢
①	break	memories	forget
②	work	experiences	avoid
③	strike	experiences	avoid
④	strike	memories	avoid
⑤	work	memories	forget

27. 위 글을 읽고 대답할 수 없는 질문은? (4점)

① What should you find when you are outside of buildings?
② What should you do when you are in an elevator during an earthquake?
③ What should you use to go outside when the shaking stops?
④ Where should you take cover when things start to shake?
⑤ Why is it a bad idea to hold on to a pole when the shaking stops?

28. 다음 질문에 대한 답을 영어 문장으로 작성하시오. (2점)

Q: Why is holding on to a pole a bad idea?
A: It's because _____.

→ _____

[29~34] 다음 글을 읽고 물음에 답하시오.

Do you know how to prepare for natural disasters? An important tip is to prepare a disaster survival bag. Here are some key items to put in your bag.
ⓐWater and food are important. ⓑEating healthy food every morning is necessary. ⓒ Try to include food that is easy to prepare. ⓓSleeping bags are useful in disasters, too. ⓔPack enough medicine for at least a week. You will need them for injuries. Matches, a radio, some money, toilet paper, and soap are all necessary items in dangerous situations. A cell phone may not work in a disaster, but it can be a good idea to have a cell phone and a charger with you.
Also, remember to put your bag in a place that is easy to find. Everyone's situation will be different, so (A)_____. (B) 만약 당신이 이러한 조언들을 따른다면, 당신은 재난들에 대비하고 안전할 수 있을 것이다.

29. 위 글의 밑줄 친 ⓐ~ⓔ 중 글의 흐름과 관련이 없는 문장은? (2점)

① ⓐ　② ⓑ　③ ⓒ　④ ⓓ　⑤ ⓔ

30. 위 글의 빈칸 (A)에 들어갈 말로 가장 적절한 것은? (3점)

① everyone should prepare a large bag
② everyone should prepare a different bag for their own situation
③ everyone should remember disaster safety tips
④ everyone should have good ideas for earthquakes
⑤ everyone should put a charger with a cell phone in a disaster survival bag

31. 밑줄 친 (B)의 우리말에 맞게 다음 단어들을 한 번씩 사용하여 바르게 배열하시오. (3점)

be / follow / you / you / If / ready / tips / disasters / these / for / will

→ _____ and stay safe.

32. 위 글의 주제로 적절한 것은? (3점)

① Safety tips for outside activities
② How to prepare for injuries
③ Kinds of foods to prepare for an earthquake
④ How to prepare a disaster survival bag
⑤ Why is preparing a disaster survival bag important?

33. 위 글에서 재난 대비 가방에 넣을 것으로 제시되지 않은 것은? (2점)

① 손전등　　② 비누　　③ 라디오
④ 침낭　　⑤ 일주일치의 약

34. 위 글의 조언에 따른 재난 대비로 적절하지 않은 것은? (4점)

① I will pack a disaster survival bag and put it in the place that is easy to find.
② I will put food that is easy to prepare in my disaster survival bag.
③ I will avoid putting matches in my disaster survival bag because they can be dangerous.
④ I will include a radio in my disaster survival bag to listen to the news.
⑤ I will include some medicine enough for a week in my disaster survival bag.

2학년 영어 1학기 중간고사(2과) 2회

문항수 : 선택형(24문항) 서술형(5문항)   20 . . .

◎ 선택형 문항의 답안은 컴퓨터용 수정 싸인펜을
  사용하여 OMR 답안지에 바르게 표기하시오.
◎ 서술형 문제는 답을 답안지에 반드시 검정
  볼펜으로 쓰시오.
◎ 총 29문항 100점 만점입니다. 문항별 배점
  은 각 문항에 표시되어 있습니다.

[충북 ○○중]

1. 다음 문장 중 보기의 단어를 이용하여 문장을 완성할 수 없는 것은? (3점)

보기
empty / experience / disaster / prepare / tips

① A flood is one type of natural _____.

② A fire can be a scary _____ for anyone.

③ Here are a few _____ to survive an earthquake.

④ Please drive safely to _____ yourself and your family.

⑤ When I entered the room, nobody was there. It was _____.

[강동구 ○○중]

2. 다음 대화가 자연스럽게 이어지도록 순서대로 바르게 배열한 것은? (4점)

B: Dad, I'm going out to play basketball with Minu.
ⓐ No. You should clean your room first.
ⓑ Okay. I'll clean my room and then play basketball.
ⓒ No, not yet. Can I do it later?
ⓓ Good. Don't forget to be home by six o'clock.
ⓔ Did you finish cleaning your room?
F: Okay.

① ⓐ - ⓑ - ⓒ - ⓓ - ⓔ
② ⓑ - ⓒ - ⓓ - ⓐ - ⓔ
③ ⓒ - ⓐ - ⓑ - ⓔ - ⓓ
④ ⓓ - ⓐ - ⓑ - ⓔ - ⓒ
⑤ ⓔ - ⓒ - ⓐ - ⓑ - ⓓ

[강원 ○○중]

3. 다음 대화에서 나타난 상황으로 가장 적절한 것은? (3점)

B: There was an accident at Lotte supermarket.
G: Yes, I heard about it. How about the people there? Were they okay?
B: Don't worry. Everybody was okay. They all followed the safety rules.
G: Really? What are the rules?
B: You need to cover your nose and mouth with a wet towel. Then stay low and escape.
G: Oh, I didn't know that.
B: You should keep that in mind. It might be helpful some day.

① fire   ② flood
③ tsunami   ④ snowstorm
⑤ earthquake

[부산 ○○중]

4. 다음 중 대화의 내용이 어색한 것은? (3점)

① A: Why did you decide to take a painting class?
   B: Because I want to go to an art high school.

② A: How often are you going to meet?
   B: Maybe once a week.

③ A: Minsu, do you want to join our club?
   B: Yes, I'm interested in space, too.

④ A: Do we have any vegetables at home, Mom?
   B: No, I'll buy some for you.

⑤ A: Are you thinking of becoming an artist in the future?
   B: That's great. I hope your wish comes true.

5. 다음 대화의 빈칸에 가장 알맞은 표현은? (3점)

G: What time is the movie?
B: It starts 4:30.
G: Oh, no. We only have 20 minutes left. Let's run!
B: No! You might fall and hurt yourself.
_____
G: You're right. We can be a little late.
B: Yes. Better safe than sorry.

① You should take an umbrella.
② You should wear a helmet.
③ You should walk on the stairs.
④ You should run fast on the road.
⑤ You should ride a bike.

6. 다음 대화의 밑줄 친 (A)를 주어진 단어를 이용하여 알맞게 영어 한 문장으로 쓰시오. (4점)

Tom: Yoojin, what's wrong?
Yoojin: (A)난 내 감기에 대해 걱정이야.
Tom: You should take some medicine.
Yoojin: I'm going to go see a doctor after school today.
Tom: I hope you feel better soon.
Yoojin: I hope so, too.

worry

→ _____

7. 다음 대화의 내용으로 바른 것은? (4점)

Brian: There was a big fire at the city library yesterday.
Mina: Yes, I heard about it. I was worried about the people there.
Brian: Don't worry. Everybody was okay. They all followed the safety rules.
Mina: Really? What are the rules?
Brian: You need to cover your nose and mouth with a wet towel. Then stay low and escape.
Mina: Oh, I didn't know that.
Brian: You should keep that in mind. It might be helpful some day.

① People need dry towels to cover their noses in a fire.
② People should cover their mouths and not run to be safe in a fire.
③ Mina already knew that a fire took place at the city library yesterday.
④ People should stay low and hide under a table in a fire.
⑤ Mina already knew the safety rules about a fire before Brian told her the rules.

8. 다음 대화의 빈칸에 공통으로 들어갈 가장 알맞은 표현은? (3점)

B: What are you watching?
G: It's a program about _____.
B: Sounds interesting. I'm worried about _____ these days.
G: Me, too. This program has some helpful tips.
B: Really? What does it say?
G: When things start to shake, you need to take cover under a table.
B: Oh, I didn't know that.

① floods   ② snowstorms
③ storms   ④ heavy rains
⑤ earthquakes

9. 다음 대화가 자연스럽게 이어지도록 배열한 것은? (3점)

B: Yujin, what's wrong?
ⓐ Why don't you go see a doctor?
ⓑ I hope you feel better soon.
ⓒ I'm worried about my leg. It hurts a lot.
ⓓ I'm going to go after school today.
G: I hope so, too.

① ⓐ-ⓒ-ⓓ-ⓑ
② ⓒ-ⓓ-ⓐ-ⓑ
③ ⓒ-ⓐ-ⓓ-ⓑ
④ ⓓ-ⓒ-ⓐ-ⓑ
⑤ ⓒ-ⓐ-ⓑ-ⓓ

10. 다음 대화의 밑줄 친 우리말 (A), (B)에 맞는 영어 문장을 완성하시오. (4점)

A: Tomorrow is Jina's birthday.
B: I know, but (A)나는 무엇을 사야 할지 결정하지 못했어. How about you?
A: I'm going to buy her a pair of pretty gloves.
B: That's a good idea.
A: But (B)나는 그것들을 사기 위해 어디로 가야 할지 모르겠어.

(A): I didn't _____.

(B): _____ to buy them.

11. 다음 빈칸에 who가 들어갈 수 있는 문장은? (3점)

① Chris helped an old man _____ was carrying a heavy bag.
② I'm reading a book _____ is about amazing sea animals.
③ This is the movie _____ is about earthquakes.
④ Mina wore a cap _____ was red.
⑤ I lost my sweater _____ was green and soft.

12. 다음 주어진 두 문장을 관계대명사를 이용하여 영어 한 문장으로 쓰시오. (that은 사용하지 말 것) (5점)

(1) • My student bought many books.
    • They were very helpful.

→ _____

(2) • The boy likes playing Poketmon games.
    • He lives in Wonju now.

→ _____

13. 다음 중 어법상 옳은 것은? (4점)

① Do you know why to do next?
② Hajun asked what to write the report.
③ I didn't know what to say to her.
④ Look at the man and his dog that is running over there.
⑤ These are the animals which lives in the water.

14. 다음 중 문법적으로 <u>어색한</u> 문장은? (3점)

① Jake is the boy who has black eyes.
② I like my teacher that teaches English.
③ I sold my computer who was expensive.
④ Junha learned how to solve the problem.
⑤ Sara couldn't decide what to buy for the party.

[15~17] 다음 글을 읽고 물음에 답하시오.

Don't run outside when things are shaking. Find a table or a desk and <u>take cover</u> under ⓐ<u>it</u>. You can hold on to the legs. Also, <u>stay away from</u> windows. ⓑ<u>They</u> can break during an earthquake and hurt you.

You can go outside when the shaking stops. <u>To get out of buildings</u>, don't use the elevator. Take the stairs. ⓒ<u>It</u>'s <u>much</u> safer. Once you are outside, find an empty space that is far from buildings. There may be people who want to hold on to a pole or a tree, but think again, ⓓ<u>That</u>'s a bad idea because it can fall on you.

Earthquakes can strike anytime. ⓔ<u>They</u> can be scary experiences for everyone. So learn how you should be safe in an earthquake. You can avoid injuries. Follow these tips and be safe!

15. 위 글의 내용으로 <u>어색한</u> 것은?　(3점)

① You shouldn't move outside when things are shaking.

② You can hold on to your own legs when an earthquake strikes.

③ You should use the stairs to get out of the building during an earthquake.

④ You should be far from the windows during an earthquake.

⑤ You shouldn't hold on to a pole or a tree when an earthquake strikes.

16. 위 글의 밑줄 친 표현이 가리키는 것이 <u>어색한</u> 것은?
　　　　　　　　　　　　　　　　　(4점)

① ⓐit: a table or a desk

② ⓑThey: legs

③ ⓒIt: taking the stairs

④ ⓓThat: holding on to a pole or a tree

⑤ ⓔThey: earthquakes

17. 위 글의 밑줄 친 표현을 바르게 설명한 것은? (3점)

① take cover: 숨다

② stay away from: ~에서 뛰어내리다

③ To get out of buildings: 건물에서 나오는 것은

④ much: 많이

⑤ space: 우주

[18~19] 다음 글을 읽고 물음에 답하시오.

How did you do on the quiz? Can you _____ an earthquake safely? Here are some safety tips which can be helpful in an earthquake. Let's check ⓐ<u>them</u> one by one and learn what to do.

Don't run outside when things are shaking. Find a table or a desk and _____ cover under it. You can hold on to the legs to _____ yourself. Also, stay away from windows. ⓑ<u>They</u> can break during an earthquake and _____ you.

18. 위 글의 빈칸 어디에도 사용할 수 <u>없는</u> 것은? (4점)

① take　　② survive　　③ protect

④ follow　　⑤ hurt

19. 위 글의 ⓐ, ⓑ가 가리키는 것으로 바르게 짝지어진 것은?　　　　　　　　　　　(3점)

	ⓐ	ⓑ
①	safety tips	legs
②	an earthquake	windows
③	safety tips	a desk or a table
④	safety tips	windows
⑤	an earthquake	legs

[20~22] 다음 글을 읽고 물음에 답하시오.

How did you do on the quiz? Can you survive an earthquake safely? Here are some safety tips ⓐ<u>who</u> can be helpful in an earthquake. Let's check them one (A)_____ one and learn what to do.

Don't run outside when things are ⓑ<u>shake</u>. Find a table or a desk and take cover under it. You can hold on to the legs ⓒ<u>protect</u> yourself. Also, stay away from windows. They can break during an earthquake and hurt you.

You can go outside when the shaking stops. ⓓ<u>To get</u> out of buildings, don't use the elevator. Take the stairs. It's ⓔ<u>very</u> safer. Once you are outside, find an empty space that is far from buildings. There may be people who want to hold on to a pole or a tree, but think again. That's a bad idea because it can fall (B)_____ you.

Earthquakes can strike anytime. They can be scary experiences for everyone. So learn how to be safe in an earthquake. You can avoid injuries and protect yourself. Follow these tips and be safe!

20. 위 글의 ⓐ~ⓔ 중 어법에 맞는 것은?　(3점)

① ⓐ who　　② ⓑ shake　　③ ⓒ protect

④ ⓓ To get　　⑤ ⓔ very

21. 위 글의 빈칸 (A), (B)에 들어갈 말이 바르게 짝지어진 것은?　(3점)

	(A)	(B)
①	by	from
②	to	on
③	at	by
④	on	at
⑤	by	on

22. 위 글의 내용과 일치하지 <u>않는</u> 것은?　(4점)

① You can't go outside before the shaking stops.

② You should not use the elevator to get out of the building.

③ You can take cover under the table to protect yourself.

④ You should not hold on to a tree or a pole to protect yourself.

⑤ You can stay near the windows when an earthquake strikes.

23. 다음 글의 밑줄 친 부분의 의미가 바르지 <u>않은</u> 것은?　(3점)

Do you know <u>what to do</u> when an earthquake strikes? Take this quiz and think about <u>how to be safe</u> during this kind of natural disaster.

1. When things start to shake, run outside quickly.
2. <u>Stay away from</u> windows.
3. Use the stairs to <u>get out of</u> buildings.
4. When you are outside, <u>hold on to</u> a pole or a tree.

① what to do: 무엇을 해야 할지

② how to be safe: 얼마나 안전할지

③ Stay away from: ~에서 멀리 떨어져 있다

④ get out of: ~에서 나가다

⑤ hold on to: ~을 꼭 잡다

24. 다음 빈칸에 들어갈 알맞은 말은?　(2점)

• I know a girl _____ speaks French very well.

① whose　　② what　　③ which

④ who　　⑤ whom

- 23 -

[25~28] 다음 글을 읽고 물음에 답하시오.

How to be safe during an earthquake.
Can you survive an earthquake safely? Here are ⓐsome safety tips which can be helpful in an earthquake. Let's check them (ⓑ하나씩) and learn what to do.

Don't run outside when things are shaking. Find a table or a desk and take cover under it. You can hold on to the legs to protect yourself. Also, stay away from windows. They can break during an earthquake and hurt you. You can go outside when the shaking stops. To get out of buildings, don't use the elevator. Take the stairs. It's much safer. Once you are outside, find an empty space that is far from buildings. There may be people who want to hold on to a pole or a tree, but think again. That's a bad idea because it can (ⓒ~ 위에 떨어지다) you.

(A) Earthquakes can strike anytime. (B) They can be scary experiences for everyone. (C) You can avoid injuries and protect yourself. (D) Follow these tips and be safe! (E)

25. 위 글에서 언급한 ⓐsome safety tips에 해당하는 내용을 2개 고르면? (4점)

① Don't use the stairs to get out of buildings.
② When things start to shake, take cover under a table or a desk.
③ Stay away from windows.
④ When you are outside, hold on to a pole or a tree.
⑤ Use the elevator to get out of buildings.

26. 위 글의 빈칸 ⓑ, ⓒ에 들어갈 우리말에 해당하는 알맞은 표현을 순서대로 쓰시오. (4점)

ⓑ: _____ ⓒ: _____

27. 위 글의 (A)~(E) 중 글의 흐름상 다음 문장이 들어갈 위치로 가장 알맞은 곳은? (3점)

So learn how to be safe in an earthquake.

① (A) ② (B) ③ (C) ④ (D) ⑤ (E)

28. 위 글을 읽고 질문에 답할 수 없는 것은? (4점)

① When the shaking stops, how can you get out of buildings?
② Why do natural disasters occur recently?
③ Why do you need to stay away from windows?
④ Once you are outside, what should you look for?
⑤ Why is taking cover under a table or a desk helpful?

29. 다음 글의 밑줄 친 (A)를 주어진 단어들을 반드시 전부 이용하여 우리말에 맞게 영작하시오. (4점)

(A)지진이 발생할 때 해야 할 일을 알고 있습니까? Take this quiz and think about how to be safe during this kind of natural disaster.

When things start to shake, run outside quickly.
Stay away from windows.
Use the stairs to get out of buildings.
When you are outside, hold on to a pole or a tree.

what / when / you / know / do /
Do / to / an earthquake / strikes

→ _____?

2학년 영어 1학기 기말고사(3과) 1회

문항수 : 선택형(25문항) 서술형(6문항) 20 . . .

◎ 선택형 문항의 답안은 컴퓨터용 수정 싸인펜을
  사용하여 OMR 답안지에 바르게 표기하시오.
◎ 서술형 문제는 답을 답안지에 반드시 검정
  볼펜으로 쓰시오.
◎ 총 31문항 100점 만점입니다. 문항별 배점
  은 각 문항에 표시되어 있습니다.

[울산 ○○중]

1. 다음의 영영 풀이에 해당하는 단어가 <u>아닌</u> 것은?
(3점)

- the physical or mental energy that is
  needed to do something
- known about by only a few people and
  kept hidden from others
- an experienced person who advises and
  helps a less experienced person
- a piece of paper, metal, or wood with
  words or a picture that gives people
  information, warnings, or instructions

① sign   ② mentor   ③ effort

④ secret   ⑤ success

[울산 ○○중]

**2. 다음 주어진 문장에 들어갈 단어로 알맞은 것을 보기에
서 고르면?**
(3점)

보기
ⓐ keep   ⓑ sense   ⓒ success
ⓓ buzz   ⓔ save

• Frogs can _____ a coming storm.

① ⓐ   ② ⓑ   ③ ⓒ   ④ ⓓ   ⑤ ⓔ

[충북 ○○중]

3. 다음 대화 중 <u>어색한</u> 것은?
(2점)

① A: I can't open the window. Can anybody
     help me?
   B: Let me help you.
② A: The box looks heavy. Let me help you.
   B: Thanks. You're very kind.
③ A: This bag you made me is wonderful.
   B: I'm glad you like it.
④ A: Thanks. I really like this picture frame.
   B: You're welcome. I'm glad you like it.
⑤ A: We lost the game by three goals.
   B: I'm glad you like it.

[충북 ○○중]

**4. 다음 (A)~(C)의 대화가 자연스럽게 이어지도록 〈보
기〉의 표현을 바르게 배열한 것은?**
(4점)

B: Hojun and I planned to give out free
   stickers today, but I think he forgot.
G: Really? (A)_____
   then. Why are you going to give out
   stickers?
B: It's part of our volunteer club activity.
G: I see. (B)_____?
B: It means that when we smile at each
   other, (C)_____.
G: That's a wonderful idea.

보기
ⓐ L(l)et me help you
ⓑ W(w)hat does she mean
ⓒ T(t)he world will become a worse place
ⓓ W(w)hat does this sticker mean
ⓔ T(t)he world will become a better place
ⓕ I need your help

	(A)	(B)	(C)
①	ⓐ	ⓑ	ⓒ
②	ⓐ	ⓓ	ⓔ
③	ⓐ	ⓑ	ⓔ
④	ⓕ	ⓓ	ⓔ
⑤	ⓕ	ⓑ	ⓐ

5. 다음 중 도움을 제안하는 말이 <u>아닌</u> 것은? (3점)

① Let me help you.

② Can I help you?

③ Let me give you a hand.

④ Can I ask you for help?

⑤ Do you need some help?

6. 다음 대화의 내용과 일치하지 <u>않는</u> 것은? (4점)

B: Mom, this is for you. I made it with plastic bags.

W: That's very cute, Alex. How did you know that I needed a new basket?

B: You talked about it when we were having dinner the other day.

W: How nice! I really like this basket. It has many different colors.

B: I'm glad you like it.

① Alex made something for his mom with plastic baskets.

② Alex already knew the thing his mom needed.

③ Alex's mom really liked the new basket Alex gave her.

④ Alex's mom wanted to have a new basket.

⑤ The new basket that Alex made for his mom is colorful.

7. 다음 대화의 빈칸에 들어갈 알맞은 단어를 고르면? (3점)

B: Hojun and I planned to give out free stickers today, but I think he forgot.

G: Really? Let me _____ you then. Why are you going to give out stickers?

B: It's part of our volunteer club activity.

G: I see.

① think ② down ③ help

④ see ⑤ explain

8. 다음 대화의 순서로 가장 적절한 것은? (2점)

(A) No problem. I'm glad you like it.

(B) Let me help you. Why don't you start with easier books?

(C) I'm not good at science. What can I do?

(D) Okay, I'll give it a try. Thanks for the tip.

① (B)-(A)-(C)-(D) ② (B)-(D)-(A)-(C)

③ (C)-(A)-(B)-(D) ④ (C)-(B)-(D)-(A)

⑤ (D)-(A)-(B)-(C)

9. 다음 대화의 내용과 일치하는 것은? (4점)

Emily: Welcome back, Brian. Are you feeling better?

Brian: Yes, thanks. I tried to study on my own in the hospital, but it was hard.

Emily: Why don't you join my study group?

Brian: Did you start a study group? That's wonderful.

Emily: Thanks. I think that we can learn better when we teach each other.

Brian: I agree. I'll try hard to be a good member. Thanks for helping me.

Emily: You're welcome. I'm glad you like my idea.

① Emily was in the hospital.

② Brian is happy to help Emily.

③ Brian will join the study group.

④ Emily made a study group last year.

⑤ Emily will teach Brian every weekend.

10. 다음 빈칸에 문맥상 공통으로 들어갈 가장 알맞은 단어를 고르면? (4점)

> • Everyone needs _____ from everyone.
> • As you grow older, you will discover that you have two hands: one is to _____ yourself, the other is to _____ others.

① attack   ② debate   ③ help
④ opinion   ⑤ happiness

11. 다음 대화 중 자연스럽지 <u>않은</u> 것을 고르면? (3점)

① A: Let me help you set the table.
   B: Thank you for helping me.

② A: What's wrong with the computer? It's too slow.
   B: Okay. No problem.

③ A: How nice! I really like this basket. It has many different colors.
   B: I'm glad you like it.

④ A: I'm scheduled to go to the dentist tomorrow.
   B: Don't forget to call the dentist before you go.

⑤ A: I lost my hat. I'm so upset.
   B: That's too bad. Let's go to the Lost and Found Center.

12. 주어진 단어를 배열하여 문장을 완성할 때 세 번째로 오는 것은? (2점)

> what / mean / this / sticker / does
> 이 스티커는 무엇을 의미하니?

① what   ② mean   ③ this
④ sticker   ⑤ does

13. 다음 중 어법상 <u>어색한</u> 문장은? (4점)

① I got a present which I wanted to have it.
② A fisherman is a person who catches fish.
③ A camera is a thing which takes pictures.
④ I know a boy who can speak Spanish very well.
⑤ The movie I saw yesterday was very exciting.

14. 다음 두 문장을 관계대명사를 이용하여 우리말에 맞도록 한 문장으로 영작하시오. (4점)

> (A) • Sam is an actor.
>   • We like him very much.
> → Sam은 우리가 매우 많이 사랑하는 배우이다.
> (B) • I love the cat.
>   • John found it at the park.
> → 나는 John이 공원에서 발견한 그 고양이를 사랑한다.

(A): _____

(B): _____

15. 다음 중 빈칸에 to가 들어갈 수 <u>없는</u> 것은? (4점)

① I saw you _____ talk to the teacher.
② I want you _____ drink more water.
③ The man asked us _____ be quiet.
④ Mike told me _____ have a good weekend.
⑤ The doctor allowed him _____ go swimming.

[16~18] 다음 글을 읽고 물음에 답하시오.

Here are two stories which I read yesterday. Do you want ⓐhear about them?
1. Call Someone You Love
2. Be a Mentor
3. The Red Arrow Man
4. The Happy Refrigerator Project
5. Secret Steps

Call Someone You Love
New York had many pay phones on its streets. (A) However, nobody really used them. One day, a man came up with an idea. (B) He stuck coins to one of the phones. (C) Soon, many people were ⓑuse the phone. When they were talking to someone (가)_____ they loved, they didn't stop ⓒsmile. (D) His idea became a big success. During the day, all the coins disappeared. (E) The man was very happy because his small idea gave happiness to many people.

16. 위 글의 빈칸 (가)에 들어갈 알맞은 표현을 〈보기〉에서 모두 고른 것은? (3점)

> **보기**
>
> who / whom / which / that

① who, that
② who, whom
③ who, whom, that
④ which, that
⑤ who, whom, which, that

17. 위 글의 밑줄 친 ⓐ~ⓒ에 알맞은 표현으로 가장 적절한 것은? (3점)

	ⓐ	ⓑ	ⓒ
①	hearing	to use	to smile
②	hearing	to use	smiling
③	to hear	using	to smile
④	to hear	to use	smiling
⑤	to hear	using	smiling

18. 위 글의 흐름으로 보아 주어진 문장이 들어가기에 가장 적절한 곳은? (3점)

> He also put up a sign that said, "Call Someone You Love."

① (A) ② (B) ③ (C) ④ (D) ⑤ (E)

[19~20] 다음 글을 읽고 물음에 답하시오.

A few years ago, the maps at bus stops in Seoul were very ⓐconfusing. They didn't have enough information. People had to ask others to explain the maps. "Where is this bus stop on the map? Does this bus go to Gwanghwamun?" Many people often took the ⓑright bus and ⓒwasted their time. One day, a young man decided to ⓓsolve this problem. He bought lots of red arrow stickers. Every day he rode his bicycle around the city and stuck the stickers on the bus maps. Nobody asked him to do this. He just wanted to help others. Thanks to his effort, people could understand the maps easily and ⓔsave time.

19. 위 글의 내용과 일치하는 것은? (3점)

① The maps became more confusing because of the arrows.
② The young man voluntarily stuck the stickers just to help others.
③ The young man rode his bike around the city to buy a lot of stickers.
④ Thanks to the young man, people could take the right subway and save time.
⑤ The young man asked others to help him while he put the stickers on the maps.

20. 위 글의 밑줄 친 ⓐ~ⓔ 중, 문맥상 낱말의 쓰임이 적절하지 않은 것은? (2점)

① ⓐ ② ⓑ ③ ⓒ ④ ⓓ ⑤ ⓔ

[21~25] 다음 글을 읽고 물음에 답하시오.

The Red Arrow Man

A few years ago, the maps at bus stops in Seoul were very confusing. They didn't have enough information. People had to ask others to explain the maps. "Where is this bus stop on the map? Does this bus go to Gwanghwamun?" Many people often took the wrong bus and wasted their time.

One day, a young man decided to solve this problem. He bought lots of red arrow stickers. Every day he rode his bicycle around the city and stuck the stickers on the bus maps.

Nobody ⓐ_____ _____ _____ do this. He just ⓑ_____ _____ _____ others. ⓒThanks to his effort, people could understand the maps easily and save time.

21. 위 글의 ⓐ에 들어갈 말을 to부정사를 이용하여 완성하시오. (3점)

Nobody ⓐ_____ _____ _____ do this. [아무도 그에게 이것을 하라고 요청하지 않았다.]

조건
• 빈칸에 들어갈 말만 적을 것.

→ _____

22. 위 글의 ⓑ에 들어갈 말을 to부정사를 이용하여 완성하시오. (3점)

He just ⓑ_____ _____ _____ others. [그는 단지 다른 사람들을 돕기를 원했다.]

조건
• 빈칸에 들어갈 말만 적을 것.

→ _____

23. 위 글에서 ⓒ에 해당하는 구체적인 사건을 찾아 적으시오. (4점)

→ _____

24. 위 글에서 〈보기〉의 영어 뜻풀이에 해당하는 영어 단어를 찾아 각각 적으시오. (4점)

보기
(1)_____ : unclear and difficult to understand
(2)_____ : a mark used to show direction or position

(1): _____   (2): _____

25. Why was the maps at bus stops in Seoul confusing? Answer in English. (4점)

→ _____

26. 다음 글의 제목으로 가장 적절한 것은? (3점)

Do you enjoy reading? Is a big library hard to visit? Then these little libraries are good news for you. You can check out books for free from the little libraries in the streets and return them anytime.

① Little Free Libraries
② Libraries Hard to Visit
③ Good News and Bad News
④ Reading Books in the Streets
⑤ Reading: A Way to Succeed in Life

[27~29] 다음 글을 읽고 물음에 답하시오.

Here are two stories ⓐwho I read yesterday. Do you want to hear about (ㄱ)them?

New York had many pay phones on its streets. And nobody really used (ㄴ)them. One day, a man came up with an idea. He stuck (ㄷ)coins to one of the phones. He also put up a sign that said, "Call Someone You Love." Soon, many people ⓑare using the phone. When they ⓒwere talking to someone whom they loved, (ㄹ)they didn't stop smiling. His idea became a big ⓓsuccessful. People spent the coins calling someone they loved. During the day, all of (ㅁ)them disappeared. The man was very happy because his small idea gave ⓔhappiness to many people.

27. 위 글의 밑줄 친 ⓐ~ⓔ 중 어법상 적절한 것으로 묶인 것은? (3점)

① ⓐ, ⓑ ② ⓑ, ⓒ ③ ⓑ, ⓓ
④ ⓒ, ⓔ ⑤ ⓓ, ⓔ

28. 위 글의 밑줄 친 (ㄱ)~(ㅁ) 중 가리키는 대상이 같은 것끼리 짝지어진 것은? (3점)

① (ㄱ), (ㄴ) ② (ㄱ), (ㄹ) ③ (ㄷ), (ㅁ)
④ (ㄷ), (ㄹ) ⑤ (ㄹ), (ㅁ)

29. 위 글을 읽고 답할 수 없는 것은? (2점)

① How many stories did the writer read yesterday?
② What did the sign say?
③ Who did people want to call?
④ Why was the man very pleased?
⑤ How many pay phones were placed in New York?

[30~31] 다음 글을 읽고 물음에 답하시오.

All across Canada, police officers are giving 'tickets' to kids. However, the 'tickets' are for young people who did good things. They can get free pizza or ice cream with them. Jarvis Kievill got a 'ticket.' He wore his helmet while riding a bike. He took home a free pizza from a restaurant that day. In Calgary, a boy got a 'ticket.' He looked both ways before he crossed the road. A girl got a 'ticket' for picking up trash on the street. Ward Clapham first came up with this idea. He was a 28-year-old police officer in Richmond, Vancouver. (A) One day he thought, 'How can young kids build good habits? How can police officers get closer to people?' (B) Finally, he had an idea: Giving tickets to kids for doing the right things. (C) "We started small and the program began to grow. Many local businesses joined our program." says Ward. (D) After the program, there are fewer problems that police officers have to handle. (E) A small idea made a big difference.

30. 위 글의 흐름상 (A)~(E) 중 주어진 문장이 들어갈 가장 알맞은 곳을 고르면? (4점)

Also, people felt friendlier towards officers.

① (A) ② (B) ③ (C) ④ (D) ⑤ (E)

31. 위 글의 내용과 일치하지 않는 것을 2개 고르면? (4점)

① 밴쿠버의 교통 법규를 어기는 청소년을 교육하기 위해 시작된 프로그램이다.
② 캐나다 일부 지역에서는 바른 행동을 하는 아이들에게 '티켓'을 준다.
③ 캘거리에서 한 소년은 길을 건너기 전 길 양쪽을 살펴보고 건너서 티켓을 받았다.
④ Ward Clapham은 아이들에게 좋은 습관을 기를 수 있도록 하기 위해 이 생각을 내놓았다.
⑤ 이 프로그램의 규모가 커지면서 많은 지역 사업장들이 이 프로그램에 동참했다.

2학년 영어 1학기 기말고사(3과) 2회

반		점수
이름		

문항수 : 선택형(23문항) 서술형(5문항) 20 . . .

◎ 선택형 문항의 답안은 컴퓨터용 수정 싸인펜을 사용하여 OMR 답안지에 바르게 표기하시오.
◎ 서술형 문제는 답을 답안지에 반드시 검정 볼펜으로 쓰시오.
◎ 총 28문항 100점 만점입니다. 문항별 배점은 각 문항에 표시되어 있습니다.

[충북 ○○중]

1. 다음 중 빈칸에 들어갈 어구를 〈보기〉에서 고를 때 완성할 수 <u>없는</u> 문장은? (단, 중복 사용 불가) (4점)

보기
mentor / put up / prevent / come up with / suffer

① I can help you. I am a good _____ who can help you with history.
② Make sure you brush your teeth after meals to _____ tooth problems.
③ In summer, many people _____ from sunburn.
④ I like your creative idea. How did you _____ it?
⑤ The TV drama was a _____. A lot of people are into it.

[울산 ○○중]

2. 다음 주어진 문장에 들어갈 단어로 알맞은 것을 〈보기〉에서 고르면? (3점)

보기
ⓐ waste ⓑ cost ⓒ spend
ⓓ lose ⓔ save

• He will take a taxi to _____ time.

① ⓐ ② ⓑ ③ ⓒ ④ ⓓ ⑤ ⓔ

[울산 ○○중]

3. 다음 대화의 내용과 일치하는 것은? (4점)

Alex: Mom, this is for you. I made it with plastic bags.
Mom: That's very cute, Alex. How did you know that I needed a new basket?
Alex: You talked about it when we were having dinner the other day.
Mom: How nice! I really like this basket. It has many different colors.
Alex: I'm glad you like it.

① Alex는 종이 봉지로 바구니를 만들었다.
② 엄마는 빨래를 담을 바구니를 구입했다.
③ 엄마는 Alex가 준 가방을 마음에 들어한다.
④ Alex는 무늬가 화려하고 튼튼한 바구니를 만들었다.
⑤ 엄마는 지난번 저녁 먹을 때 바구니가 필요하다고 말했다.

[영등포구 ○○중]

4. 다음 우리말과 의미가 같도록 주어진 단어를 알맞게 배열하여 문장을 완성하시오. (3점)

• "나는 네가 그것을 좋아한다니 기뻐."
(you / glad / I'm / it / like)

= _____

[울산 ○○중]

5. 다음 대화의 ⓐ~ⓔ 중 흐름상 <u>어색한</u> 것은? (3점)

B: Jimin, what are all these things in the box?
G: They're for my ⓐmentee at the children's center. I'm going to ⓑgive her my old books today.
B: Do you teach her every weekend?
G: Yes. I feel ⓒupset when I teach her.
B: You are a good ⓓmentor. Oh, the box looks ⓔheavy. I'll carry it for you.
G: Thanks.

① ⓐ ② ⓑ ③ ⓒ ④ ⓓ ⑤ ⓔ

6. 다음 대화를 읽고 요약한 글의 내용이 적절하지 <u>않은</u> 것은? (4점)

> G: I read a story about a special boy in India. Do you want to hear about it?
> B: Sure. Why is he special, Yujin?
> G: Many children in his town couldn't go to school and had to work. So he taught them in his house every day.
> B: That's a great story.
> G: I'm glad you like it.
> *B: Jinsu

> ⓐYujin read a story about a special boy in India. ⓑJinsu wanted to hear about the story. ⓒMany children in the boy's town had to work, so they couldn't go to school. ⓓThe special boy taught them in school. ⓔJinsu said, "The story is good." And Yujin was happy he liked it.

① ⓐ   ② ⓑ   ③ ⓒ   ④ ⓓ   ⑤ ⓔ

7. 다음 두 사람의 대화 내용으로 알 수 <u>없는</u> 것을 고르면? (4점)

> Boy: Hojun and I planned to give out free stickers today, but I think he forgot.
> Girl: Really? Let me help you then. Why are you going to give out stickers?
> Boy: It's part of our volunteer club activity.
> Girl: I see. What does this sticker mean?
> Boy: It means that when we smile at each other, the world will become a better place.
> Girl: That's a wonderful idea.

① What is the boy going to give out?

② Why doesn't Hojun give out free stickers with the boy?

③ Why is the boy going to give out stickers?

④ What does the boy think about his volunteer club activity?

⑤ What does the sticker mean?

8. 다음 대화가 자연스럽게 이어지도록 (A)~(D)를 바르게 배열한 것은? (3점)

> Yujin: I read a story about a special boy in India. Do you want to hear about it?
> (A) I'm glad you like it.
> (B) That's a great story.
> (C) Sure. Why is he special, Yujin?
> (D) Many children in his town couldn't go to school and had to work. So he taught them in his house every day.

① (A)-(C)-(B)-(D)   ② (B)-(D)-(C)-(A)

③ (C)-(D)-(A)-(B)   ④ (C)-(D)-(B)-(A)

⑤ (D)-(C)-(B)-(A)

9. 대화를 읽고, (1)과 (2)의 <u>어색한</u> 부분을 바르게 고쳐 문장 전체를 쓰시오. (4점)

> Yujin: I read a story about a special boy in India. Do you want to hear about it?
> Brian: Sure. Why is he special, Yujin?
> Yujin: Many children in his town couldn't go to school and had to work. So he taught them in his house every day.
> Brian: That's a great story
> Yujin: I'm happy to hear that.

(1) Brian told Yujin a great story about a special boy.

조건
• 총 10 단어로 작성할 것.

→ _____

(2) Many children taught a special boy every day.

조건
• 총 8 단어로 작성할 것.

→ _____

[10~11] 다음 대화를 읽고 물음에 답하시오.

Emily: Welcome back, Brian. Are you feeling ⓐbetter?

Brian: (A) Yes, thanks. I tried to study on my own in the hospital, but it was ⓑhard.

Emily: (B) Why don't you join my study group?

Brian: (C) Did you start a study group? That's wonderful.

Emily: Thanks. I think that we can learn ⓒbetter when we teach ⓓeach other. (D)

Brian: I agree. I'll try ⓔhard to be a good member. ⓕThanks for helping me.

Emily: (E) You're welcome. I'm glad you like my idea.

10. 위 대화의 밑줄 친 ⓐ~ⓕ에 대한 설명으로 바른 것은? (4점)

① ⓐ는 ⓒ와 같은 의미이다.

② ⓑ와 ⓔ는 서로 다른 의미로 사용되었다.

③ ⓒ는 'good'의 비교급이다.

④ ⓓ의 의미는 '각각 다른'이다.

⑤ ⓕ는 '~에 대해 감사하다'란 의미로 'thanks to'와 바꿔 사용할 수 있다.

11. 위 대화의 흐름으로 보아 주어진 문장이 들어가기에 가장 적절한 곳은? (3점)

Let me help you.

① (A) ② (B) ③ (C) ④ (D) ⑤ (E)

12. 다음 중 밑줄 친 부분을 생략할 수 없는 것은? (3점)

① Jimin is the girl who I met last weekend.

② This is Kim Hongdo who painted Ssirreum.

③ This is King Sejong who many Koreans loved.

④ I want to make a movie which many people will love.

⑤ My dad gave me the watch that I really wanted to have.

13. 다음 그림을 보고 대화의 빈칸에 들어갈 말을 완성하시오. (4점)

Boy: (1) I _____ for you. [너를 위해 내가 이 케이크를 구웠어.]

Girl: Thanks! It's wonderful.

Boy: You're welcome. (2) I'm _____ _____. [나는 네가 그것을 좋아한다니 기뻐.]

조건
• 문장 전체를 각각 적을 것.

(1): _____

(2): _____

14. 문장의 빈칸에 들어갈 단어의 알맞은 형태는? (3점)

• The doctor advised me _____.

① exercise ② exercises ③ exercised

④ to exercise ⑤ exercising

[15~17] 다음 글을 읽고 물음에 답하시오.

A few years ago, the maps at bus stops in Seoul were very confusing. They didn't have enough information. (A)[explain / had / people / to / others / ask / the maps / to]. "Where is this bus stop on the map? Does this bus go to Gwanghwamun?" Many people often took the wrong bus and wasted their time. One day, a young man decided to solve this problem. He bought lots of red arrow stickers. Every day he rode his bicycle around the city and stuck the stickers on the bus maps. (B)아무도 그에게 이것을 하라고 요청하지 않았다. He just wanted to help others. Thanks to his effort, people could understand the maps easily and save time.

15. 위 글의 (A)의 주어진 단어를 배열하여 알맞은 문장을 완성한 것은? (3점)

① People had others ask to explain to the maps.

② Others had people to explain to ask the maps.

③ People had to explain others to ask the maps.

④ People had to ask others to explain the maps.

⑤ Others ask people had to explain to the maps.

16. 위 글의 밑줄 친 우리말 (B)를 〈조건〉에 맞도록 영작하시오. (4점)

조건
• 'nobody', 'ask', 과거시제를 반드시 사용할 것.

→ _____

17. 다음은 위 글의 내용을 요약한 것이다. 빈칸 (A)~(C)에 들어갈 말로 가장 적절한 것은? (4점)

The bus (A)_____ in Seoul were very confusing. A young man stuck red arrow stickers on the maps to (B)_____ others. Thanks to his effort, people could (C)_____ time.

	(A)	(B)	(C)
①	maps	help	save
②	stops	ask	save
③	maps	ask	waste
④	stops	help	save
⑤	maps	help	waste

[18~19] 다음 글을 읽고 물음에 답하시오.

New York had ⓐmany pay phones on its streets. However, nobody really used them. One day, (A)a man came up with an idea. He ⓑstuck coins to one of the phones. He also ⓒput up a sign said, "Call Someone You Love." Soon, many people were using the phone. When they were talking to ⓓsomeone whom they loved, ⓔthey didn't stop smiling. His idea became a big success. During the day, all the coins disappeared. The man was very happy because his small idea gave happiness to many people.

18. (A)a man에 대한 설명과 일치하는 것은? (4점)

① He was a selfish person.

② He called someone he loved.

③ He was happy to earn money with his idea.

④ He asked people to use the pay phones, but failed.

⑤ He made many people happy with his small idea.

19. 위 글의 ⓐ~ⓔ 중 어법상 어색한 것은? (3점)

① ⓐ   ② ⓑ   ③ ⓒ   ④ ⓓ   ⑤ ⓔ

22. 위 글의 (B)에 들어갈 말로 가장 적절한 것은? (3점)

[20~22] 다음 글을 읽고 물음에 답하시오.

① he could make a lot of money

② many people were paying for the pay phones

③ his idea gave happiness to many people

④ his idea became popular all across America

⑤ he thinks using pay phones is very good

New York had many pay phones on its streets. (A)_____
Soon, many people were using the phone. When they were talking to someone whom they loved, they didn't stop smiling. His idea became a big success. During the day, all the coins disappeared. The man was very happy because (B)_____.

[23~24] 다음 글을 읽고 물음에 답하시오.

20. 위 글의 (A)에 들어갈 ⓐ~ⓓ의 순서로 올바른 것은? (3점)

ⓐ One day, a man came up with an idea.

ⓑ He also put up a sign that said, "Call Someone You Love."

ⓒ However, nobody really used them.

ⓓ He stuck coins to one of the phones.

① ⓐ - ⓒ - ⓓ - ⓑ

② ⓐ - ⓑ - ⓒ - ⓓ

③ ⓐ - ⓓ - ⓒ - ⓑ

④ ⓒ - ⓐ - ⓓ - ⓑ

⑤ ⓒ - ⓓ - ⓐ - ⓑ

The Red Arrow Man
(A) A few years ago, the maps at bus stops in Seoul were very (a)_____. They didn't have enough information. People had to ask others (b)_____ the maps. "Where is this bus stop on the map? Does this bus go to Gwanghwamun?" Many people often took the wrong bus and wasted their time. (B) One day, a young man decided (c)_____ this problem. (C) Every day he rode his bicycle around the city and stuck the stickers on the bus maps. Nobody asked him to do this. He just wanted to help others. (D) Thanks to his effort, people could understand the maps easily and save time. (E)

23. 위 글의 빈칸에 들어갈 말이 바르게 짝지어진 것은? (4점)

	(a)	(b)	(c)
①	confused	to explain	solve
②	confused	explain	to solve
③	confusing	explaining	solve
④	confusing	to explain	to solve
⑤	confusing	explain	to solve

21. 위 글에 대한 설명으로 올바른 것은? (4점)

① A lot of people in New York always used pay phones.

② People could not call someone they loved because they were busy.

③ The man stuck coins to all of the pay phones in New York.

④ The man stuck coins to the pay phone to become rich.

⑤ The man's idea of sticking the coins became a big success.

24. 위 글에서 다음 문장이 들어갈 가장 알맞은 위치는? (3점)

He bought lots of red arrow stickers.

① (A)   ② (B)   ③ (C)   ④ (D)   ⑤ (E)

[25~27] 다음 글을 읽고 물음에 답하시오.

Call Someone You Love

New York had many pay phones on its streets. However, nobody really used them. One day, a man came up with an idea. He stuck coins to one of the phones. He also put up a sign that said, "Call Someone You Love." Soon, many people were using the phone. When they were talking to someone whom they loved, they didn't stop (A)[to smile / smiling]. His idea became a big success. During the day, all the coins (B)[appeared / disappeared]. The man was very happy because his small idea gave happiness to many people.

The Red Arrow Man

A few years ago, the maps at bus stops in Seoul were very (C)[confusing / confused]. They didn't have enough information. People had to ask others to explain the maps. "Where is this bus stop on the map? Does this bus go to Gwanghwamun?" Many people often took the wrong bus and wasted their time. One day, a young man decided (D)[solving / to solve] this problem. He bought lots of red arrow stickers. Every day he rode his bicycle around the city and stuck the stickers on the bus maps. Nobody asked him to do this. He just wanted to help others. @그의 노력 덕분에, 사람들은 지도를 쉽게 이해하고 시간을 절약할 수 있었다.

25. 위 글의 괄호 (A)~(D) 안에서 들어갈 말로 가장 알맞은 것을 고르면? (4점)

	(A)	(B)	(C)	(D)
①	to smile	disappeared	confused	to solve
②	to smile	appeared	confusing	to solve
③	smiling	disappeared	confused	solving
④	to smile	appeared	confused	solving
⑤	smiling	disappeared	confusing	to solve

26. 위 글의 내용과 일치하지 않는 것을 2개 고르면? (4점)

① Only a few people were using the phone to call someone they loved.

② Because the man's small idea gave happiness to many people, he was very happy.

③ The bus maps in Seoul didn't have enough information.

④ Because of the man's wrong information about the maps at bus stops, people took the wrong bus and wasted their time.

⑤ Because the man just wanted to help others, he stuck red arrow stickers on the bus maps.

27. 위 글의 밑줄 친 우리말 @에 해당하는 영어 문장을 조건에 맞게 완성하시오. (5점)

조건
• effort, could, easily, save, maps를 한 번씩만 사용하여 총 13 단어의 문장으로 쓸 것.
• 반드시 우리말 내용과 어법에 맞게 쓸 것.

→ _____

28. 다음 중 어법상 어색한 것은? (3점)

① Jisu likes the teacher who teaches English.

② I have a sister who is a doctor.

③ We met a tall man whom exercises every day.

④ Amy is an actor whom we like the most.

⑤ We love the cat which we found at the park.

◎ 선택형 문항의 답안은 컴퓨터용 수정 싸인펜을 사용하여 OMR 답안지에 바르게 표기하시오.
◎ 서술형 문제는 답을 답안지에 반드시 검정 볼펜으로 쓰시오.
◎ 총 27문항 100점 만점입니다. 문항별 배점은 각 문항에 표시되어 있습니다.

[충북 ○○중]

1. 다음 두 단어의 관계가 같은 것끼리 짝지어진 것은?
(3점)

ⓐ happy - happiness　ⓑ succeed - success
ⓒ itchy - itchiness　ⓓ advise - advice
ⓔ survive - survival

① ⓐ, ⓑ　　② ⓑ, ⓒ　　③ ⓒ, ⓓ
④ ⓑ, ⓓ　　⑤ ⓒ, ⓔ

[울산 ○○중]

2. 다음 〈보기〉에서 설명하는 단어로 가장 알맞은 것은?
(3점)

보기
as much as is necessary

① tiny　　② sweaty　　③ effort
④ enough　　⑤ confusing

[충북 ○○중]

3. 다음 대화가 자연스럽게 이어지도록 바르게 배열한 것은?
(4점)

B: Let's go swimming this weekend, Yujin.
G: I'd love to, but I can't.
ⓐ I really hope so.
ⓑ I have an eye problem. The doctor told me to stop swimming for a while.
ⓒ I'm sorry to hear that. Maybe we can go next weekend.
ⓓ Why not?

① ⓐ-ⓒ-ⓓ-ⓑ　　② ⓓ-ⓑ-ⓒ-ⓐ
③ ⓓ-ⓑ-ⓐ-ⓒ　　④ ⓑ-ⓓ-ⓐ-ⓒ
⑤ ⓐ-ⓒ-ⓑ-ⓓ

[울산 ○○중]

4. 다음 중 주어진 단어와 그 뜻이 바르게 연결된 것은?
(4점)

① tiny – extremely big
② feed on – to use things
③ female – a man or a boy
④ at that moment – then
⑤ million – the number 100,000

[충북 ○○중]

5. 다음 대화의 내용으로 알 수 없는 질문은?　(4점)

Ms. Wheeler: Junsu, what happened to your face?
Junsu: I got a lot of mosquito bites.
Ms. Wheeler: I'm sorry to hear that. How did it happen?
Junsu: It happened when I went camping last weekend.
Ms. Wheeler: Oh dear. Don't scratch them!
Junsu: I know, but they're really itchy.
Ms. Wheeler: Clean them with cool water. That'll help. Also, make sure you wear long sleeves when you go camping.
Junsu: Okay, Thank you.

① What happened to Junsu?
② What did Junsu do last weekend?
③ What does Ms. Wheeler advise Junsu to do?
④ Did mosquitoes bite Junsu's face?
⑤ Why should Junsu not scratch the mosquito bites?

6. 다음 중 짝지어진 대화가 <u>어색한</u> 것은? (3점)

① A: I got a lot of mosquito bites.

B: Make sure you wear sunscreen next time.

② A: Let's go swimming on Sunday, Yumi.

B: I'd love to, but I can't.

③ A: You look worried, Jinsu. What's wrong?

B: I'm worried because my sister is sick.

④ A: Maybe we can go shopping next weekend.

B: I really hope so.

⑤ A: How was the soccer game with Tom's class?

B: We lost by two goals.

7. 다음 (1), (2) 대화의 빈칸에 들어갈 수 <u>없는</u> 단어들만 묶어 놓은 것은? (대·소문자 무시) (4점)

(1)
B: You look worried, Jimin. What's _____?
G: I'm worried because my cat is sick.
B: I'm sorry to hear _____. Why _____ you take her to an animal doctor?
G: Okay, I will.

(2)
M: Let's go swimming this weekend, Yujin.
G: I'd love _____, but I can't.
M: _____ not?
G: I have an eye problem. The doctor told me to _____ swimming for a while.

① do, wrong   ② don't, to

③ do, go   ④ stop, why

⑤ prevent, that

8. 다음 대화의 Mr. Kim의 말에 이어질 대화의 순서가 바르게 나열된 것은? (4점)

Mr. Kim: Junsu, what happened to your face?
Junsu: _____
Mr. Kim: _____
Junsu: _____
Mr. Kim: _____
Junsu: I know, but they're really itchy.

(A) I'm sorry to hear that. How did it happen?
(B) I got a lot of mosquito bites.
(C) Oh dear. Don't scratch them!
(D) It happened when I went camping last weekend.

① (A)-(B)-(C)-(D)   ② (B)-(A)-(D)-(C)

③ (B)-(C)-(A)-(D)   ④ (C)-(A)-(D)-(B)

⑤ (D)-(C)-(A)-(B)

9. 다음 대화의 내용과 일치하는 것은? (4점)

G: Dad, do we have any bug spray?
M: Yes, it's under the sink. Why?
G: There are a lot of fruit flies around the trash.
M: Oh no! What did you put in the trash?
G: Some fruit waste.
M: Fruit flies love sweet things. Make sure you don't put fruit waste in the trash can.
G: I'll keep that in mind. I think we should also empty our trash can more often.
M: That's a good idea.

*G: girl

① Fruit flies don't love fruit waste.

② The girl needs a bug spray because of the sink.

③ The girl will put fruit waste in the trash can again.

④ There are lots of fruit flies because of fruit waste.

⑤ Dad told the girl to use a bug spray more often.

10. 다음 중 어색한 대화는? (4점)

① A: You look worried. What's wrong?

　B: I am worried because my cat is sick.

② A: I got a bad sunburn at the beach yesterday.

　B: Oh dear! Does it hurt?

③ A: Mom, I made this basket for you.

　B: Oh, how nice!

④ A: Dad, I'm going to play tennis with Minsu this afternoon.

　B: Okay. Make sure you wear sunscreen.

⑤ A: Do you want to hear the story about a boy in India?

　B: I'm sorry to hear that.

11. 다음 대화가 자연스럽게 이루어지도록 빈칸에 들어갈 가장 알맞은 것을 고르면? (4점)

A: How was the soccer game with Minsu's class, Alex?

B: (A)_____ three goals.

A: That's too bad. I hope you do better next time.

B: (B)_____, too.

	(A)	(B)
①	We lose with	I am sure
②	We lost by	I hope so
③	We got loser to	I'd like to
④	We were lost in	I will do better
⑤	We got lost from	I'll do my best

12. 다음 주어진 우리말에 맞는 문장을 각각 영작하시오. (5점)

(A) Susan은 3년 동안 캐나다에서 살아왔다.

(B) 너는 얼마나 오랫동안 영어를 공부해 왔니?

(A) _____

(B) _____

13. 다음 중 어법상 적절한 문장으로 짝지어진 것은?

ⓐ I read the book last night.

ⓑ It rained since last week.

ⓒ We studied English together yesterday.

ⓓ Have you ever been to Australia before?

ⓔ When have you cooked this spaghetti?

ⓕ When I was young, I have lived with my aunt.

① ⓐ, ⓒ, ⓓ　　　　② ⓒ, ⓔ, ⓕ

③ ⓑ, ⓒ, ⓓ　　　　④ ⓑ, ⓒ, ⓔ

⑤ ⓒ, ⓓ, ⓕ

14. 다음 의미상 두 문장을 한 문장으로 바꾼 것들 중 잘못 바꾼 것을 고르면? (4점)

① I lost my smartphone and I don't have it now.

→ I have lost my smartphone.

② His family came here ten years ago and they still live here.

→ His family has lived here for 10 years.

③ My friend went to New York, so he is not here now.

→ My friend has been to New York.

④ It was very hot yesterday, and it is still very hot now.

→ It has been very hot since yesterday.

⑤ My grandfather died 5 years ago, and he is not living now.

→ My grandfather has been dead for 5 years.

[15~16] 다음 글을 읽고 물음에 답하시오.

Seojun: After you bit me, I got a bump. It itches.

Mrs. Mosquito: I'm sorry to hear that. Make sure you don't scratch ⓐit. Also, clean ⓑit with alcohol wipes.

Seojun: Alcohol wipes? I've never tried that before.

Mrs. Mosquito: ⓒIt will reduce the itchiness.

Seojun: Okay, I'll try ⓓthat at home. Thanks.

Mrs. Mosquito: I have to go. See you soon.

Seojun: Where are you going?

Mrs. Mosquito: I'm going back to the river.

Seojun: Wait! A lot of people have suffered from your bites. How can we prevent ⓔ them?

Mrs. Mosquito: 시원하게 지내 그리고 소매가 긴 옷을 입어.

Seojun: Thanks. I'll keep your advice in mind.

15. 위 글의 밑줄 친 ⓐ~ⓔ가 가리키는 대상이 적절하지 않은 것은? (4점)

① ⓐ: a bump

② ⓑ: a bump

③ ⓒ: A bump

④ ⓓ: cleaning with alcohol wipes

⑤ ⓔ: mosquito bites

16. 위 글의 밑줄 친 우리말과 일치하도록 주어진 단어를 배열하여 영작할 때 (라)에 오는 단어는? (3점)

- 시원하게 지내 그리고 소매가 긴 옷을 입어.
  (long, stay, and, sleeves, cool, wear)
  → (가)_____ (나)_____ (다)_____
     (라)_____ (마)_____ (바)_____.

① wear   ② stay   ③ long

④ cool   ⑤ sleeves

[17~18] 다음 글을 읽고 물음에 답하시오.

Seojun: Where are you from? How did you find me?

Mrs. Mosquito: I'm from a nearby river. I was looking for some blood to drink there. Then I smelled something sweaty and found you here.

Seojun: How could you smell me from the river?

Mrs. Mosquito: Mosquitoes can sense heat and smell very well. That's why (A)우리가 수백만 년 동안 살아남았다.

Seojun: Do all mosquitoes drink blood like you?

Mrs. Mosquito: No. Only female mosquitoes like me drink blood. Male mosquitoes only feed on fruit and plant juice.

Seojun: That's interesting. So why do you drink blood?

Mrs. Mosquito: I need the protein in blood to lay my eggs.

Seojun: How do you drink blood? Do you have sharp teeth?

Mrs. Mosquito: No, I don't have teeth. But I have a long and pointed mouth. So I can drink your blood easily.

17. 위 글의 우리말 (A)를 가장 바르게 표현한 것은? (4점)

① we has survived for millions of years

② we were surviving for thousands of years

③ we survived for hundreds of years

④ we have survived for millions of years

⑤ we have survived for hundreds of years

18. 위 글을 읽고 답할 수 없는 질문은? (4점)

① How did Mrs. Mosquito find Seojun?

② What do male mosquitoes feed on?

③ Why do female mosquitoes drink blood?

④ How do female mosquitoes drink blood?

⑤ Where do female mosquitoes lay their eggs?

[19~21] 다음 글을 읽고 물음에 답하시오.

Seojun: After you bit me, I got a bump. ⓐIt itches.

Mrs. Mosquito: I'm sorry to hear that. Make sure you don't scratch ⓑit. Also, clean ⓒit with alcohol wipes.

Seojun: Alcohol wipes? I've never tried ⓓthat before.

Mrs. Mosquito: ⓔIt will reduce the itchiness.

Seojun: Okay, I'll try ⓕthat at home. Thanks.

Mrs. Mosquito: I have to go. See you soon.

Seojun: Where are you going?

Mrs. Mosquito: I'm going back to the river.

Seojun: Wait! A lot of people have suffered from your bites. How can we prevent ⓖthem?

Mrs. Mosquito: Stay cool and wear long sleeves.

Seojun: Thanks. I'll keep your advice in mind.

---

19. 위 글의 밑줄 친 ⓐ~ⓖ가 가리키는 대상이 잘못된 것만 묶은 것은? (5점)

ⓐ = A bump, ⓑ = a bump, ⓒ = a bump, ⓓ = cleaning with alcohol wipes, ⓔ = Alcohol wipe, ⓕ = cleaning with alcohol wipes, ⓖ = mosquitoes

---

① ⓐ, ⓓ ② ⓑ, ⓕ ③ ⓒ, ⓓ

④ ⓔ, ⓖ ⑤ ⓓ, ⓕ

20. 위 글을 통해 알 수 없는 것을 고르면? (3점)

① 모기는 강에서 왔다.

② 모기는 서준이에게 가려움을 줄여 주는 방법을 알려주고 있다.

③ 모기에게 물렸을 땐 긁지 않고 물린 부위를 알코올 솜으로 깨끗이 닦는다.

④ 모기를 없애는 방법은 습한 곳을 피하고 긴소매를 입는 것이다.

⑤ 앞으로 서준이는 모기에게 물리지 않도록 예방할 것으로 기대된다.

21. 위 글을 다음과 같이 요약할 때 빈칸에 들어갈 가장 알맞은 것을 고르면? (4점)

Mrs. Mosquito (A)_____ Seojun on (B)_____ to reduce the itchiness, and to (C)_____ mosquito bites.

	(A)	(B)	(C)
①	worries	whom	cut
②	warns	where	get
③	orders	why	stop
④	suggests	what	block
⑤	advises	how	prevent

22. 다음 글의 내용을 요약할 때 빈칸 (A)~(E)에 들어갈 단어가 <u>잘못된</u> 것은? (4점)

It was a hot summer evening. Seojun went for a walk in the park. Soon, he was sweating.

Seojun: I'm thirsty. I want to drink something.

At that moment, a mosquito flew at him and bit his arm.

Mrs. Mosquito: Hey, catch me if you can.

Seojun: Who are you? What have you done to me?

Mrs. Mosquito: I'm a mosquito. I'm from a nearby river. I've just finished my dinner.

↓

One summer (A)_____ in a (B)_____, Seojun met a mosquito from a nearby (C)_____. The mosquito (D)_____ Seojun's (E)_____.

---

① (A): evening ② (B): park

③ (C): river ④ (D): caught

⑤ (E): arm

[23~26] 다음 글을 읽고 물음에 답하시오.

It was a hot summer evening. Seojun went for a walk in the park. Soon, he was sweating.

Seojun: I'm thirsty. I want something cold to drink. At that moment, something tiny flew at him and bit his arm.

Mrs. Mosquito: Hey, catch me if you can.

Seojun: Who are you? What have you done to me?

Mrs. Mosquito: I'm a mosquito. I've just finished my dinner. (A)

Seojun: Where are you from? How did you find me?

Mrs. Mosquito: I'm from a nearby river. (B) I was looking for some blood to drink there. Then I smelled something sweaty and found you here.

Seojun: How could you smell me from the river?

Mrs. Mosquito: Mosquitoes can sense heat and smell very well. (C)

Seojun: Do all mosquitoes drink blood like you?

Mrs. Mosquito: No. Only female mosquitoes like me drink blood. Male mosquitoes only feed on fruit and plant juice.

Seojun: That's interesting. _____ why do you drink blood? (D)

Mrs. Mosquito: I need the protein in blood to lay my eggs.

Seojun: How do you drink blood? Do you have sharp teeth? (E)

Mrs. Mosquito: No, I don't have teeth. But I have a long and pointed mouth. _____ I can drink your blood easily.

Seojun: I learned a lot about you. Thank you.

---

23. 위 글의 내용을 다음과 같이 요약할 때 빈칸에 필요하지 <u>않은</u> 단어는? (4점)

One summer evening in a park, a mosquito _____ at Seojun from a nearby _____. The mosquito _____ Seojun's arm. After Seojun _____ with the mosquito, he learned a lot about mosquitoes.

① river ② bit ③ flew
④ talked ⑤ fought

24. 위 글의 흐름으로 보아, (A)~(E) 중 다음 문장이 들어가기에 가장 적절한 곳은? (4점)

That's why we have survived for millions of years.

① (A) ② (B) ③ (C) ④ (D) ⑤ (E)

25. 위 글을 읽고 대답할 수 <u>없는</u> 질문은? (4점)
① Where is Mrs. Mosquito from?
② How did Mrs. Mosquito find Seojun?
③ How can we prevent mosquito bites?
④ What has Mrs. Mosquito done to Seojun?
⑤ What does Mrs. Mosquito's mouth look like?

26. 위 글의 빈칸에 공통으로 들어갈 접속사는? (3점)
① But ② As ③ When
④ So ⑤ Because

27. 다음 중 어법상 옳은 것은? (4점)
① I have visited many great places last summer.
② This is King Sejong whom many Koreans loved.
③ He is Kim Hongdo whom painted Ssireum.
④ Sam is an actor which we like very much.
⑤ Jisu and I have never be to China before.

◎ 선택형 문항의 답안은 컴퓨터용 수정 싸인펜을 사용하여 OMR 답안지에 바르게 표기하시오.
◎ 서술형 문제는 답을 답안지에 반드시 검정 볼펜으로 쓰시오.
◎ 총 28문항 100점 만점입니다. 문항별 배점은 각 문항에 표시되어 있습니다.

[영등포구 ○○중]

1. 다음 중 밑줄 친 표현의 쓰임이 어색한 것은? (3점)

① You talked about it when we were having dinner the other day.

② We lost the soccer game on three goals.

③ Do you teach your mentee every weekend?

④ Many children in his town couldn't go to school and had to work.

⑤ Did you pack for the school trip tomorrow?

[울산 ○○중]

2. 다음 주어진 영영 풀이에 해당하는 단어는? (3점)

• the part of a piece of clothing that covers all or part of your arm

① male   ② sleeve   ③ bump
④ blood   ⑤ sunburn

[울산 ○○중]

3. 다음 Jane의 말에 이어질 대화의 순서가 바르게 나열된 것은? (2점)

Jane: How was the soccer game with Minsu's class, Alex?
(A) I'm sorry to hear that. I hope you do better next time.
(B) We lost by three goals.
(C) I hope so, too.

① (A) - (B) - (C)   ② (A) - (C) - (B)
③ (B) - (A) - (C)   ④ (B) - (C) - (A)
⑤ (C) - (A) - (B)

[충북 ○○중]

4. 다음 대화를 읽고 초파리를 예방하는 방법 두 가지를 본문에서 찾아 영어 문장으로 쓰시오. (5점)

G: Dad, do we have a bug spray?
M: Yes, it's under the sink. Why?
G: There are a lot of fruit flies around the trash.
M: Oh no! What did you put in the trash?
G: Some fruit waste.
M: Fruit flies love sweet things. Make sure you don't put fruit waste in the trash can.
G: I'll keep that in mind. I think we should also empty our trash can more often.
M: That's a good idea.

How to Prevent Fruit Flies
1. _____
2. _____

[충북 ○○중]

5. 다음 중 대화가 가장 어색한 것은? (2점)

① A: I'm worried because my cat is sick.
   B: I'm sorry to hear that.

② A: I think I have food poisoning.
   B: I'm sorry to hear that.

③ A: We won the game by three goals.
   B: I'm sorry to hear that. You'll win next time.

④ A: Let's have dinner.
   B: Make sure you wash your hands before dinner.

⑤ A: Let's go camping this weekend.
   B: Make sure you avoid sweating to prevent mosquito bites.

[6~7] 다음 대화를 읽고 물음에 답하시오.

G: Dad, do we have any bug spray?
M: Yes, it's under the sink. Why?
G: There are a lot of fruit flies around the trash.
M: Oh no! What did you put in the trash?
G: Some fruit waste.
M: Fruit flies love sweet things. (A)반드시 과일 쓰레기를 넣지 않도록 해 in the trash can.
G: I'll keep that in mind. I think we should also empty our trash can more often.
M: That's a good idea.

(G: girl)

6. 위 대화를 읽고 답할 수 <u>없는</u> 질문은? (3점)

① Why does the girl need a bug spray?
② Where is a bug spray?
③ What do fruit flies like?
④ How can they prevent fruit flies?
⑤ How do they reduce fruit waste?

7. 위 대화의 밑줄 친 우리말 (A)를 영작하시오. (단, 'make sure' 구문을 반드시 사용할 것.) (4점)

→ _____

8. 다음 대화를 읽고 질문에 대한 답을 주어진 표현으로 시작하여 영어 문장을 완성하시오. (5점)

Ms. Wheeler: Junsu, what happened to your face?
Junsu: I got a lot of mosquito bites.
Ms. Wheeler: I'm sorry to hear that. How did it happen?
Junsu: It happened when I went camping last weekend.
Ms. Wheeler: Oh dear. Don't scratch them!
Junsu: I know, but they're really itchy.
Ms. Wheeler: Clean them with cool water. That'll help. Also, make sure you wear long sleeves when you go camping.
Junsu: Okay, thank you.

Q1. What does Ms. Wheeler tell Junsu to do when he has mosquito bites?
→ She tells him (1)_____. And she also tells him (2)_____.

Q2. What does Ms. Wheeler advise Junsu to do when he goes camping?
→ She advises him (3)_____.

(1): _____

(2): _____

(3): _____

9. 다음 대화 (1), (2)의 빈칸에 공통으로 들어갈 가장 알맞은 단어를 고르면? (3점)

(1)
W: Tim, look at your face! You got sunburn.
B: Yes, it hurts a lot. I went swimming at the beach without sunscreen.
W: Oh dear! Make sure you _____ sunscreen next time.

(2)
W: Hojun, do you want to go shopping with me?
B: Sorry, Mom. I'm going to play baseball with Alex this afternoon.
W: Okay. No problem. Just make sure you _____ a hat. It's going to be very hot this afternoon.
B: Okay, I will.

① stay   ② wear   ③ avoid
④ prevent   ⑤ bite

10. 다음 대화의 내용과 일치하는 것은? (3점)

> G: Dad, do we have any bug spray?
> M: It's under the sink. Why?
> G: There are a lot of fruit flies around the trash.
> M: Oh no! What did you put in the trash?
> G: Some fruit waste.
> M: Fruit flies love sweet things. Make sure you don't put fruit waste in the trash can.
> G: I'll keep that in mind. I think we should empty our trash can more often.
> M: That's a good idea.

① 방충제는 싱크대 옆에 있다.
② 소녀는 과일 쓰레기를 싱크대에 버렸다.
③ 쓰레기통 주변에 모기가 많이 있다.
④ 소녀는 쓰레기통을 더 자주 비워야 할 것 같다고 말했다.
⑤ 소녀의 아버지는 소녀에게 과일 쓰레기를 쓰레기통에 버릴 것을 당부했다.

11. 다음 중 어법상 올바른 것을 두 개 고르면? (4점)

① I've known the girl when I was 5 years old.
② Tom has lived in Jeju Island last month.
③ Minji has been to China once.
④ I have studied for the test five days ago.
⑤ I have already finished my breakfast.

12. 다음 중 어법상 바른 것은? (3점)

① It has rained since last week.
② I have read the book last night.
③ When have you cooked this spaghetti?
④ I have never gone to China before.
⑤ We have studied English together yesterday.

13. 다음 우리말에 맞게 주어진 영어 단어를 배열하여 영어 문장을 완성할 때, ★에 들어갈 알맞은 단어는? (3점)

> • 그 공원에는 즐길 특별한 무언가가 있다.
> → There _____ _____ _____
>   ___★___ _____ in the park.
>   (is, to, special, enjoy, something)

① to   ② is   ③ enjoy
④ special   ⑤ something

14. 다음 Amy가 경험한 것을 보고 〈보기〉와 같이 현재완료를 사용하여 (1), (2)를 영작하시오. (4점)

What Amy has done	
eat Indian food	O
(1) see a UFO	O
(2) have a pet	X

O: Amy가 경험한 것.
X: Amy가 경험하지 않은 것.

보기

> She has eaten Indian food.

(1): _____
(2): _____

15. 다음 우리말과 일치하도록 괄호 안의 주어진 단어를 사용하여 영작하시오. (4점)

> • 나는 나를 도울 힘센 누군가가 필요해.
> (me, strong, to, help, someone, need, I)

→ _____

[16~21] 다음 글을 읽고 물음에 답하시오.

It was a hot summer evening. Seojun went for a walk in the park. Soon, he was sweating.

Seojun: I'm thirsty. I want (A)_____ cold to drink.

At that moment, (A)_____ tiny flew at him and bit his arm.

Mrs. Mosquito: Hey, catch me if you can.
Seojun: ⓐ_____
Mrs. Mosquito: I'm a mosquito. I've just finished my dinner.
Seojun: ⓑ_____
Mrs. Mosquito: I'm from a nearby river. I was looking for some blood to drink there. Then I smelled (A)_____ sweaty and found you here.
Seojun: ⓒ_____
Mrs. Mosquito: Mosquitoes can sense heat and smell very well. That's why we have survived for millions of years.
Seojun: ⓓ_____
Mrs. Mosquito: No. Only female mosquitoes like me drink blood. Male mosquitoes only feed (B)_____ fruit and plant juice.
Seojun: ⓔ_____
Mrs. Mosquito: I need the protein in blood to lay my eggs.
Seojun: How do you drink blood? Do you have sharp teeth?
Mrs. Mosquito: No, I don't have teeth. But I have a long and pointed mouth. So I can drink your blood (C)_____.
Seojun: After you (D)_____ me, I got a bump. It (E)_____.
Mrs. Mosquito: I'm sorry to hear that. Make sure you don't scratch it. Also, clean it with alcohol wipes.
Seojun: Alcohol wipes? I've never tried that before.
Mrs. Mosquito: It will reduce the (F)_____.

Seojun: Okay, I'll try that at home. Thanks.
Mrs. Mosquito: I have to go. See you soon.
Seojun: Where are you going?
Mrs. Mosquito: I'm going back to the river.
Seojun: Wait! (G)많은 사람들이 너에게 물려서 고통받고 있어. How can we prevent them?
Mrs. Mosquito: Stay cool and wear long sleeves.
Seojun: Thanks. I'll keep that in mind.

16. 위 글의 내용과 일치하는 것은? (3점)
① Seojun came from a nearby river.
② Seojun got a bump because of Mrs. Mosquito.
③ Mrs. Mosquito drinks fruit and plant juice.
④ Mrs. Mosquito has sharp teeth.
⑤ Mrs. Mosquito uses alcohol wipes for itching.

17. 위 글의 ⓐ~ⓔ에 각각 들어갈 질문으로 올바른 것은? (4점)
① ⓐ Do all mosquitoes drink blood like you?
② ⓑ Who are you? What have you done to me?
③ ⓒ How could you smell me from the river?
④ ⓓ That's interesting. So why do you drink blood?
⑤ ⓔ Where are you from? How did you find me?

18. 위 글을 읽고 알 수 있는 사실은? (4점)
① Male mosquitoes lay eggs.
② Male mosquitoes drink blood.
③ Female mosquitoes drink fruit and plant juice.
④ Female mosquitoes have sharp teeth.
⑤ Female mosquitoes need protein.

19. 위 글의 (A)~(B)에 들어갈 단어로 적절한 것을 각각 쓰시오. (4점)

(A) _____, (B) _____

20. 위 글의 (C)~(F)에 알맞은 말로 연결된 것은? (4점)

	(C)	(D)	(E)	(F)
①	easy	bite	itches	itchy
②	easy	bit	itchy	itch
③	easily	bit	itchy	itchiness
④	easily	bit	itches	itchiness
⑤	easily	bite	itchy	itch

21. 위 글의 (G)의 우리말과 의미가 같도록 주어진 단어를 모두 알맞게 배열하여 문장을 완성하시오. (필요한 경우 단어를 변형하시오.) (4점)

people / bites / lot / suffer / a / your / of / have / from

→ _____

[울산 ○○중]

22. 다음 글의 밑줄 친 ⓐ~ⓔ 중, 문맥상 낱말의 쓰임이 적절하지 <u>않은</u> 것은? (3점)

Do you see toys ⓐ<u>inside</u> the bars of soap? Children in South Africa wash their hands ⓑ<u>more often</u> to ⓒ<u>get</u> the toys. Washing your hands can ⓓ<u>prevent</u> many health problems. Thanks to this idea, ⓔ<u>more</u> children are getting sick.

① ⓐ ② ⓑ ③ ⓒ ④ ⓓ ⑤ ⓔ

[충북 ○○중]

[23~25] 다음 글을 읽고 물음에 답하시오.

It was a hot summer evening. Sejin ⓐ<u>went</u> for a walk in the park. Soon, he was sweating.

Seojun: I'm thirsty. I want (A)_____.

At that moment, something tiny ⓑ<u>flew</u> at him and ⓒ<u>bit</u> his arm.

Mrs. Mosquito: Hey, catch me if you can.
Seojun: Who are you? What have you ⓓ<u>did</u> to me?
Mrs. Mosquito: I'm a mosquito. I've just ⓔ<u>finished</u> my dinner.

23. 위 글의 밑줄 친 부분 중 쓰임이 <u>어색한</u> 것은? (3점)

① ⓐ went   ② ⓑ flew

③ ⓒ bit   ④ ⓓ did

⑤ ⓔ finished

24. 위 글의 빈칸 (A)에 들어갈 표현으로 알맞은 것은? (4점)

① something to drink cold

② cold something to drink

③ something cold to drink

④ cold something drinking

⑤ something to cold drink

25. 위 글을 참고하여 다음 질문에 대한 답을 완성하시오. (4점)

Q: What has the mosquito done to Seojun?   A: The mosquito _____.

→ _____

[26~28] 다음 글을 읽고 물음에 답하시오.

It was a hot summer evening. Seojun went for a walk in the park. Soon, he was sweating.

Seojun: I'm thirsty. I want some cold water to drink.

At that moment, <u>조그마한 무언가가 그에게 날아와서 그의 팔을 물었다</u>.

Mrs. Mosquito: Hey, catch me if you can.

Seojun: Who are you? What have you done to me?

Mrs. Mosquito: I'm a mosquito. I've just finished my dinner.

Seojun: Where are you from? How did you find me?

Mrs. Mosquito: I'm from a nearby river. I was looking for some blood to drink there. Then I smelled something sweaty and find you here.

Seojun: How could you smell me from the river?

Mrs. Mosquito: Mosquitoes can sense heat and smell very well. That's _____ we have survived for millions of years.

Seojun: Do all mosquitoes drink blood like you?

Mrs. Mosquito: No. Only female mosquitoes like me drink blood. Male mosquitoes only feed on fruit and plant juice.

Seojun: That's interesting. So why do you drink blood?

Mrs. Mosquito: I need the protein in blood to lay my eggs.

Seojun: How do you drink blood? Do you have sharp teeth?

Mrs. Mosquito: No, I don't have teeth. But I have a long and pointed mouth. So I can drink your blood easily.

26. 위 글의 빈칸에 들어갈 한 단어와 공통으로 사용할 수 없는 문장을 고르면?　　　　　　　(4점)

① The work may be a little dangerous. That's _____ he is careful with it.

② Making good friends is very important in our life. That's _____ we should be thoughtful in choosing our friends.

③ He doesn't have money enough to buy a new car. That's _____ he's looking for work to get money.

④ He has a lot of information that you want to get. That's _____ I've asked you to meet him.

⑤ I hope we can meet again soon. That's _____ I had lots of fun in England with you.

27. 위 글에 대하여 답할 수 <u>없는</u> 질문을 고르면? (4점)

① How did the mosquito find Seojun?

② What has the mosquito done to Seojun in the park?

③ Why do all mosquitoes need the protein in blood?

④ How can the mosquito drink blood without teeth?

⑤ Do male mosquitoes drink blood like female mosquitoes?

28. 위 글의 밑줄 친 우리말에 해당하는 영어 문장을 조건에 맞게 쓰시오.　　　　　　　　　(5점)

조건

1. 반드시 and, at, tiny 단어를 사용할 것.
2. 총 9 단어로 답할 것.
3. 반드시 우리말 내용과 어법, 시제에 맞게 쓸 것.

조그마한 무언가가 그에게 날아와서 그의 팔을 물었다.

→ _____

정답 및 해설

Lesson 1 (중간) 1회

01 ② **02** ② **03** ①

04 Unless it rains tomorrow, I'll play soccer with my friends. 또는 If it doesn't rain tomorrow, I'll play soccer with my friends.

05 ① **06** ② **07** ③ **08** ⑤ **09** ②

10 I'm thinking of going to bed early.

11 (1) One is going camping with friends.
(2) The other is watching movies.

12 ②

13 If I finish my homework early, I will clean my room.

14 ③ **15** ③ **16** ② **17** ⑤

18 ⓐ it's time to ⓑ These days   **19** ④ **20** ④

21 ④ **22** I often bit my nails. **23** 나의 새로운 취미

24 ③

25 If the traffic is heavy, it will change into a flying car.

26 (1) a model of his dream car
(2) a special cup for his grandfather

27 ③ **28** ② **29** ① **30** ①

01 'You know what?'을 이용하여 대화를 시작하기 전에 상대방의 주의를 끄는 말을 할 수 있다.

02 ① a little: 약간의 ③ by the way: 그런데 ④ these days: 요즘 ⑤ get out of: ~에서 나오다

03 뒤에서 'I love eating.'이라고 했으므로 ①번이 적절하다.

04 if는 'If+주어+동사(현재 시제) ~, 주어+will+동사원형 ….'의 형태로 '만약 ~한다면, …할 것이다.'라는 뜻의 '조건'을 나타낸다. Unless는 'If ~ not'의 의미로 쓰인다.

05 방학이 어땠는지 묻자 (C) 좋았다며 무에타이 수업을 들었다고 하고 (B) 놀랍다며 관심있는 줄 몰랐다고 하자 (A) 아주 재미있다고 하는 순서가 자연스럽다.

06 장차 화가가 되고 싶다는 것이 주요 내용이다.

07 of의 목적어로 동명사가 적절하다.

08 'We want to learn about stars and planets. So, we're thinking of starting a space science club.'이라고 했고 'do you want to join our club?'이라고 하자 'Yes, I'm interested in space, too.'라고 했다.

09 지난 주말의 계획이 무엇이었는지 물었는데 친구와 하이킹을 갈 생각이라고 앞으로의 계획을 말하는 것은 어색하다.

10 'be thinking of ~ing'는 '~하려고 생각 중이다'라는 뜻이다. go to bed early: 일찍 자다

11 둘 중의 처음 하나를 언급할 때는 one을 쓰고 나머지 다른 하나는 the other로 쓴다.

12 ① rain → rains
③ stay → will stay, will rain → rains
④ doesn't rain → rains
⑤ go → goes

13 if는 'If+주어+동사(현재 시제) ~, 주어+will+동사원형 ….'의 형태로 '만약 ~한다면, …할 것이다.'라는 뜻의 '조건'을 나타낸다. 조건절 If의 동사는 미래 시제가 아닌 현재 시제를 사용하는 것에 주의한다.

14 (A) 이사한다는 move (B) 그리워한다는 miss (C) keep in touch with: 연락을 취하다

15 ⓒ 과거에 나는 종종 손톱을 물어뜯곤 했다.
ⓐ 이제 나는 더 이상 그러지 않는다.
ⓑ 내가 만든 변화가 정말 좋다.

16 (A) 주어가 필요하므로 동명사 Making (B) 'If+주어+동사(현재 시제) ~, 주어+will+동사원형 ….'의 형태이므로 will change (C) 둘 중의 처음 하나를 언급할 때 one을 쓰고 나머지 하나는 the other로 쓰므로 The other (D) he's = he is

17 (가) 숫자를 포함하지 않는 특정한 기간이 나오므로 during, 보통 for는 숫자를 포함한 구체적 기간이 나온다. (나) 나쁜 습관을 없애는 것이므로 breaking이 적절하다.

18 ⓐ It's time to ~: ~할 시간이다
ⓑ These days: 요즈음

19 'It's a beautiful spring in Seoul.', 'In Sydney, it's fall in March.'라고 했다.

20 'If the traffic is heavy, it will change into a flying car.'라고 했다.

21 본인의 두 가지 변화를 말하는 중에 ⓓ의 '김밥 만드는 법도 안다'라는 말은 어색하다.

22 과거의 일이므로 bite를 bit로 써야 한다.

23 앞 문장의 my new hobby를 가리킨다.

24 Making이 주어이므로 is가 적절하다.

25 if는 'If+주어+동사(현재 시제) ~, 주어+will+동사원형

….’의 형태로 ‘만약 ~한다면, …할 것이다.’라는 뜻의
‘조건’을 나타낸다.

26 ‘One is a model of my dream car.’, ‘The other is a special cup for my grandfather.’라고 했다.

27 be into ~: ~에 열중하다

28 (B) 다음에 One이 나오고 (C) 다음에 The other가 나오므로 주어진 문장은 (B)에 들어가는 것이 적절하다.

29 첫 번째 ⓐ에는 비인칭주어 It, 두 번째 ⓐ에는 인칭대명사 It이 적절하다.

30 ‘The last winter vacation was a great time for me.’라고 했다.

Lesson 1 (중간) 〔2회〕

---
01 ⓐ on my way ⓑ know what **02** ④ **03** ①
04 ③ **05** ④ **06** ① **07** ④ **08** ③ **09** ⑤ **10** ②
11 (1) One is watching TV.
(2) The other is sleeping on my chair.
12 ④ **13** ⑤ **14** ④ **15** ②
16 If the traffic is heavy, it will change into a flying car.
17 ③ **18** ② **19** ③ **20** ① **21** ② **22** ③ **23** ②
24 (1) One is a model of my dream car.
(2) The other is a special cup for my grandfather.
25 ② **26** ① **27** ③ **28** ② **29** ④
---

01 ⓐ on one’s way: ~하는 중에, 도중에 ⓑ ‘You know what?’을 이용하여 대화를 시작하기 전에 상대방의 주의를 끄는 말을 할 수 있다.

02 순서대로 배열하면 fly, make, some, into, anymore, fly이다.

03 얼마나 자주 만날지 물었는데 두 시간 동안이라고 답하는 것은 어색하다.

04 (C) 뒤에서 ‘We have some vegetables, but we don’t have beef.’라고 했으므로 (C)가 적절하다.

05 Smith 선생님이 금년 담임이라는 말에 잘됐다고 하자 (D)에서 그의 과학 수업이 재미있었다고 하고 (A)에서 상대방의 담임을 묻고 (E)에서 김 선생님이라고 하자 (C)에서 가르치는 과목을 묻고 (B)에서 미술이라고 답하는 순서가 자연스럽다.

06 ‘You know what?’은 ‘있잖아.’ 또는 ‘너 그거 아니?’라는 뜻으로, 상대방이 자기의 말에 귀를 기울이도록 주의를 끌기 위한 표현이다. 이다음에는 말하고자 하는 새로운

사실이 나온다.

07 Emily가 사진 찍는 것에 관심이 있다는 말은 없다.

08 ⓒ는 vegetables가 아니라 beef가 적절하다.

09 ‘Minsu, do you want to join our club?’이라는 말에 ‘Yes. I’m interested in space, too.’라고 했다.

10 ‘It’s because I want to be good at English writing.’이라고 했다.

11 둘 중의 처음 하나를 언급할 때는 one을 쓰고 나머지 다른 하나는 the other로 쓴다.

12 ① got → will get
② catch → you will catch
③ feels → will feel, will sleep → sleeps
⑤ won’t → don’t

13 둘 중의 처음 하나를 언급할 때는 one을 쓰고 나머지 다른 하나는 the other로 쓴다.

14 By the way: 그런데, 그나저나

15 Eric이 습관을 바꿨다는 말은 없다.

16 if는 ‘If+주어+동사(현재 시제) ~, 주어+will+동사원형 ….’의 형태로 ‘만약 ~한다면, …할 것이다.’라는 뜻의 ‘조건’을 나타낸다. 조건절 If의 동사는 미래 시제가 아닌 현재 시제를 사용하는 것에 주의한다.

17 (B) 뒤에 이유가 나오므로 because (C) 뒤에 결과가 나오므로 so가 적절하다.

18 뒤에 두 가지가 나오므로 ⓑ three를 two로 바꿔야 한다.

19 주어진 문장의 One에 주목한다. (C) 앞에서 two things라고 했고 (D) 다음에 The other가 나오므로 (C)가 적절하다.

20 ⓐ Now: 이제 ⓓ By the way: 그런데(화제 전환)

21 be into: ~에 열중하다 change into: ~으로 바뀌다

22 앞에서 ‘손잡이가 3개 있다’고 했으므로 ‘들기 어렵지 않다’가 적절하다.

23 ⓑ는 교통이 ‘혼잡하면’이 적절하다.

24 둘 중의 처음 하나를 언급할 때는 one을 쓰고 나머지 하나는 the other로 쓴다.

25 (A) each other: (둘 사이의) 서로
(B) 둘 중의 처음 하나를 언급할 때 one을 쓰고 나머지 하나는 the other로 쓴다.
(C) bite의 과거형은 bit이다.

26 앞에서 ‘I often bit my nails.’라고 했으므로 ①번이 적절하다.

27 ‘In the past, I often bit my nails. Now I don’t anymore.’라고 했다.

28 (B) 다음부터 Eric 자신의 이야기가 나오므로 (B)가 적절

하다.

29 Sydney의 날씨 이야기는 없다.

Lesson 2 (중간) 〔1회〕

01 ③ **02** ① **03** ④ **04** ② **05** ③ **06** ④ **07** ①
08 ⑤ **09** ③ **10** ③ **11** You should walk
12 clean his room **13** ③
14 Look at the man and his dog that are running over there.
15 I watched a TV show which[that] was about natural disasters.
16 (1) You should watch your hands when you close the door.
(2) You should watch your head when you get out of the car.
17 ④ **18** ①, ④ **19** ③ **20** ①, ④
21 it can fall on you **22** ③ **23** ② **24** ③ **25** ①
26 ③ **27** ② **28** it can fall on you **29** ② **30** ②
31 If you follow these tips, you will be ready for disasters
32 ④ **33** ① **34** ③

01 disaster: a sudden event such as a flood, storm, or accident which causes great damage or suffering

02 조심하라고 했으므로 'slippery(미끄러운)'가 적절하다.

03 ④번은 '시간'을 묻고 있는데 '장소'로 답하고 있다.

04 (A) 개가 아프다고 했으므로 수의사에게 데려가라는 ⓑ
(B) 체중에 대해 걱정하므로 체육관에 등록하라는 ⓒ
(C) 영어 성적에 대해 걱정하므로 반 친구들에게 도움을 요청하라는 ⓐ가 적절하다.

05 뒤에서 'Can I do it later?'라고 했으므로 ⓒ 'No, not yet.'이 적절하다.

06 '계단에서는 걸어야 한다.'고 충고하고 있으므로 앞에서 '넘어져 다칠 수 있다'한 (D)가 적절하다.

07 'You're right. We can be a little late.'라고 했다.

08 'You need to cover your nose and mouth with a wet towel.'이라고 했다.

09 뒤에서 'Can I do it later?'라고 했으므로 ⓒ 'No, not yet.'이 적절하다.

10 be worried about: ~에 대해 걱정하다, helpful: 도움이 되는

11 넘어져 다칠 수 있다고 했으므로 should를 이용하여

'You should walk'로 충고할 수 있다.

12 'I'll clean my room and then play basketball.'이라고 했다.

13 ① why → what, why+to부정사는 사용하지 않는다.
② what → how ④ what → how ⑤ what → how

14 선행사가 'the man and his dog'이므로 주격 관계대명사로 that을 써야 한다.

15 'a TV show'를 선행사로 하여 주격 관계대명사로 which나 that을 쓴다.

16 'You should'를 이용하여 충고한다.
(1) watch your hands: 손을 조심하다
(2) get out of: ~에서 나오다

17 'Don't run outside when things are shaking.'이라고 했다.

18 (가)와 ②, ③, ⑤: 종류 ①, ④: 친절한

19 (A) 밑에 숨어야 하므로 under
(B) stay away from: ~에서 떨어져 있다
(C) get out of: ~에서 나가다

20 ⓐ some safety tips가 주어이므로 are ⓓ 비교급을 수식하므로 much, even 등으로 써야 한다.

21 'That's a bad idea because it can fall on you.'라고 했다.

22 앞에서 깨진 유리를 밟을 수 있다고 했으므로 ③번이 적절하다.

23 ⓐ safely ⓒ To get ⓓ who ⓔ how

24 주어진 문장의 the legs가 (B) 앞의 a table or a desk의 legs이므로 (B)가 적절하다.

25 'Also, stay away from windows.'라고 했다.

26 ㉠ strike: (재난·질병 등이 갑자기) 발생하다
㉡ experience: 경험 ㉢ avoid: 피하다

27 지진이 있는 동안 엘리베이터에 있을 때 무엇을 해야 하는지는 알 수 없다.

28 'That's a bad idea because it can fall on you.'라고 했다.

29 재난에 대비해서 가방에 넣어두어야 할 것들을 언급하고 있는데 매일 아침에 건강한 음식을 먹는 것은 중요하다는 언급은 어색하다.

30 모든 사람의 상황이 다르다고 했으므로 ②번이 적절하다.

31 follow these tips: 이러한 조언들을 따르다, be ready for: ~할 준비가 되다

32 'An important tip is to prepare a disaster survival bag. Here are some key items to put in your bag.'이라고 했다.

33 손전등은 언급되지 않았다.

34 'Matches, a radio, some money, toilet paper, and soap are all necessary items in dangerous situations.'라고 했다.

Lesson 2 (중간)

---

01 ④ **02** ⑤ **03** ① **04** ⑤ **05** ③

06 I'm worried about my cold.　　　**07** ③ **08** ⑤

09 ③

10 (A) decide what to buy
(B) I don't know where to go

11 ①

12 (1) My student bought many books which were very helpful.
(2) The boy who lives in Wonju now likes playing Poketmon games.

13 ③ **14** ③ **15** ② **16** ② **17** ① **18** ④ **19** ④

20 ④ **21** ⑤ **22** ⑤ **23** ② **24** ④ **25** ②, ③

26 ⓑ one by one ⓒ fall on　　**27** ③ **28** ②

29 Do you know what to do when an earthquake strikes?

---

01 ① disaster ② experience ③ tips ④ protect ⑤ empty

02 농구하러 나가겠다고 하자 ⓔ 방 청소를 끝냈는지 묻고 ⓒ 안 했다며 나중에 할 수 있는지 되묻고 ⓐ 먼저 끝내라고 하자 ⓑ 알았다며 청소하고 농구하겠다고 하자 ⓓ 좋다며 6시까지 돌아오라고 하는 순서가 적절하다.

03 'You need to cover your nose and mouth with a wet towel. Then stay low and escape.'로 보아 'fire(화재)'가 적절하다.

04 화가가 될 생각인지 물었는데 너의 희망이 이루어지기를 바란다는 대답은 어색하다.

05 'You might fall and hurt yourself.'라고 했으므로 ③번이 적절하다.

06 be worried about: ~에 대해 걱정하다

07 'Yes, I heard about it.'이라고 했다.

08 When things start to shake, you need to take cover under a table.'로 보아 'earthquakes(지진)'임을 알 수 있다.

09 무엇이 잘못되었는지 묻자 ⓒ 다리가 아프다고 하고 ⓐ 병원에 가 보라고 하자 ⓓ 방과 후에 갈 거라고 하고 ⓑ 곧

좋아지길 바란다고 하는 순서가 적절하다.

10 (A) what to buy: 무엇을 사야 할지
(B) where to go: 어디로 가야 할지

11 ① an old man이 선행사이므로 주격 관계대명사로 who가 적절하다. ②, ③, ④, ⑤는 모두 which나 that이 적절하다.

12 (1) 'many books'를 선행사로 하여 주격 관계대명사 which를 쓴다.
(2) 'The boy'를 선행사로 하여 주격 관계대명사 who를 쓴다.

13 ① what to do: 무엇을 할지, why+to부정사는 사용하지 않는다. ② what → how ④ that is → that are ⑤ lives → live

14 'my computer'가 선행사이므로 ③번은 who를 which나 that으로 고쳐야 한다.

15 'Find a table or a desk and take cover under it. You can hold on to the legs.'라고 했다.

16 ⓑ의 They는 windows를 가리킨다.

17 ② stay away from: ~에서 떨어져 있다
③ To get out of buildings: 건물에서 나오기 위해
④ much: 훨씬
⑤ space: 공간

18 순서대로 survive, take, protect, hurt가 들어간다.

19 ⓐ 앞에서 언급한 safety tips를 가리킨다.
ⓑ 앞에서 언급한 windows를 가리킨다.

20 ⓐ which[that] ⓑ shaking ⓒ to protect
ⓔ much[even/far/a lot/still]

21 (A) one by one: 하나씩 (B) fall on: ~ 위에 떨어지다

22 'Also, stay away from windows.'라고 했다.

23 how to be safe: 안전한 방법

24 'a girl'이 선행사이므로 주격 관계대명사로 who가 적절하다.

25 'Find a table or a desk and take cover under it. Also, stay away from windows.'라고 했다.

26 ⓑ one by one: 하나씩 ⓒ fall on: ~ 위에 떨어지다

27 주어진 문장의 So에 주목한다. '지진은 언제든지 발생할 수 있고 모두에게 무서운 경험일 수 있다.'고 한 뒤 '따라서 지진에서 안전을 지키는 법을 배우라.'고 하는 것이 적절하다.

28 왜 최근에 자연재해가 발생하는지는 알 수 없다.

29 know의 목적어로 'what to do: 의문사+to부정사'를 쓴다.

---

01 ⑤ **02** ② **03** ⑤ **04** ② **05** ④ **06** ① **07** ③
08 ④ **09** ③ **10** ③ **11** ② **12** ③ **13** ①
14 (A) Sam is an actor who[whom/that] we love very much.
(B) I love the cat which[that] John found at the park.
15 ① **16** ③ **17** ⑤ **18** ③ **19** ② **20** ②
21 asked him to   **22** wanted to help
23 Every day he rode his bicycle around the city and stuck the stickers on the bus maps.
24 (1) confusing (2) arrow
25 Because they didn't have enough information.
26 ① **27** ④ **28** ③ **29** ⑤ **30** ⑤ **31** ①, ②

---

01 순서대로 • effort • secret • mentor • sign의 영영풀이이다.

02 sense: 감지하다

03 경기에 졌다고 하는데 그걸 좋아해서 기쁘다고 하는 것은 어색하다.

04 (A) Hojun이가 잊었다고 생각한다고 했으므로 도와주겠다는 ⓐ, (B) 의미를 설명하고 있으므로 ⓓ, (C) 서로에게 웃어 주면 세상이 더 나은 곳이 될 것이라는 게 어울리므로 ⓔ가 적절하다.

05 ④번은 도와달라는 의미이다.

06 'Mom, this is for you. I made it with plastic bags.'라고 했다.

07 'Let me help you.'는 도움을 제안하는 표현이다.

08 (C)에서 과학을 잘 못한다며 조언을 구하자 (B)에서 도와주겠다며 쉬운 책부터 시작하라고 하고 (D)에서 해보겠다며 고맙다고 하고 (A)에서 좋아하니 기쁘다고 하는 순서가 적절하다.

09 'I'll try hard to be a good member.'라고 했다.

10 문맥에 맞는 단어는 help(도움)이다.

11 컴퓨터가 무엇이 잘못되었는지 묻는데 문제없다고 하는 것은 어색하다.

12 문장을 완성하면 'What does this sticker mean?'이다.

13 ①번은 목적격 관계대명사가 있으므로 it을 삭제해야 한다. I got a present which I wanted to have.

14 (A) an actor를 선행사로 하여 목적격 관계대명사로 who나 whom 또는 that을 쓴다.
(B) the cat을 선행사로 하여 목적격 관계대명사로

which나 that을 쓴다.

15 ①번은 지각동사의 목적격 보어로 동사원형이 나와야 한다.

16 사람이 선행사이고 목적격 관계대명사가 필요한 자리이다.

17 ⓐ want의 목적어로 to부정사 ⓑ were 다음에 진행형으로 현재분사 ⓒ stop의 목적어로 동명사가 적절하다.

18 주어진 문장의 also로 보아 (C) 앞에서 공중전화 하나에 동전들을 붙이고 이어서 한 것이므로 (C)가 적절하다.

19 'Nobody asked him to do this. He just wanted to help others.'라고 했다.

20 ⓑ는 문맥상 wrong이 적절하다.

21 asked의 목적어로 him을 쓰고 목적격 보어로 to부정사를 쓴다.

22 wanted의 목적어로 to부정사 to help를 쓴다.

23 'Every day he rode his bicycle around the city and stuck the stickers on the bus maps.'라고 했다.

24 (1) 명확하지 않고 이해하기 어려운
(2) 방향이나 위치를 보여주기 위해 사용되는 기호

25 They(The maps at bus stops) didn't have enough information.이라고 했다.

26 'You can check out books for free from the little libraries in the streets and return them anytime.'에서 ①번이 적절함을 알 수 있다.

27 ⓐ which[that] ⓑ were using ⓓ success

28 (ㄱ) two stories (ㄴ) pay phones (ㄷ), (ㅁ) coins (ㄹ) many people

29 뉴욕에 공중전화가 얼마나 많이 있었는지는 알 수 없다.

30 주어진 문장의 Also로 보아 (E) 앞의 내용에 추가하고 있으므로 (E)가 적절하다.

31 'Giving tickets to kids for doing the right things.', 'All across Canada, police officers are giving 'tickets' to kids.'라고 했다.

---

01 ⑤ **02** ⑤ **03** ⑤ **04** I'm glad you like it.
05 ③ **06** ④ **07** ④ **08** ④
09 (1) Yujin told Brian a great story about a special boy.
(2) A special boy taught many children every day.
10 ② **11** ② **12** ②

13 (1) I baked this cake for you.

(2) I'm glad you like it.

14 ④ **15** ④ **16** Nobody asked him to do this.

17 ① **18** ⑤ **19** ③ **20** ④ **21** ⑤ **22** ③ **23** ④

24 ③ **25** ⑤ **26** ①, ④

27 Thanks to his effort, people could understand the maps easily and save time.

28 ③

---

01 ① mentor ② prevent ③ suffer ④ come up with ⑤ success가 들어간다.

02 save: 절약하다, (낭비하지 않고) 아끼다

03 'You talked about it when we were having dinner the other day.'라고 했다.

04 네가 그것을 좋아하다: you like it, 나는 기뻐: I'm glad

05 ⓒ는 happy 정도가 되어야 적절하다.

06 'So he taught them in his house every day.'라고 했다.

07 소년이 자원봉사 동아리 활동에 대해 어떻게 생각하는지는 알 수 없다.

08 이야기를 들어 보겠느냐고 묻자 (C)에서 그렇다며 무엇이 특별한지 묻고 (D)에서 설명하고 (B)에서 멋진 이야기라고 호응하고 (A)에서 좋아한다니 기쁘다고 하는 순서가 적절하다.

09 (1) Yujin이 Brian에게 말해 줬다.

(2) special boy가 아이들을 가르쳤다.

10 ⓐ 기분이 보다 좋은 ⓑ 어려운 ⓒ 더 잘(well의 비교급) ⓓ 서로 ⓔ 열심히 ⓕ ~에 대해 감사하다 thanks to: ~ 덕분에

11 혼자 공부하려고 했는데 어려웠다고 하자 '내가 도와줄게'라고 하고 스터디 모임에 함께 하자고 제안하는 것이 적절하다.

12 주격 관계대명사는 생략하지 않는다.

13 (1) 뒤에 for가 있으므로 동사(baked)+직접 목적어(this cake) 순서로 쓴다.

(2) I'm glad와 you like it. 사이에 접속사 that을 써도 된다.

14 advised의 목적격 보어로 to부정사가 적절하다.

15 ask의 목적격 보어로 to explain을 쓴다.

16 ask의 목적격 보어로 to부정사를 쓴다.

17 (A) the maps at bus stops

(B) He just wanted to help others.

(C) people could understand the maps easily and

save time

18 'The man was very happy because his small idea gave happiness to many people.'라고 했다.

19 sign과 said 사이에 주격 관계대명사 that[which]이 필요하다.

20 뉴욕에 공중전화가 많이 있었다.

ⓒ 그러나 아무도 그것들을 실제로 사용하지 않았다.

ⓐ 한 남자에게 좋은 아이디어가 떠올랐다.

ⓓ 그는 공중전화 하나에 동전들을 붙였다.

ⓑ 그는 또한 "당신이 사랑하는 사람에게 전화하세요."라고 쓰인 표지판을 설치했다.

21 'His idea became a big success.'라고 했다.

22 'When they were talking to someone whom they loved, they didn't stop smiling.'라고 했다.

23 (a) the maps가 주어이므로 confusing (b) ask의 목적격 보어로 to explain (c) decided의 목적어로 to solve가 적절하다.

24 스티커를 사야 붙일 수 있으므로 (C)가 적절하다.

25 (A) stop의 목적어로 smiling, (B) 문맥상 disappeared, appear: 나타나다 (C) 감정을 불러일으키는 것이므로 confusing (D) decided의 목적어로 to solve가 적절하다.

26 'many people were using the phone.', '그의 노력 덕분에, 사람들은 지도를 쉽게 이해하고 시간을 절약할 수 있었다.'

27 그의 노력 덕분에: Thanks to his effort. 지도를 쉽게 이해하다: understand the maps easily 시간을 절약하다: save time

28 ③ We met a tall man who[that] exercises every day.

Lesson 4 (기말) 1회

01 ④ **02** ④ **03** ② **04** ④ **05** ⑤ **06** ① **07** ③

08 ② **09** ④ **10** ⑤ **11** ②

12 (A) Susan has lived in Canada for three years.

(B) How long have you studied English?

13 ① **14** ③ **15** ③ **16** ① **17** ④ **18** ⑤ **19** ④

20 ④ **21** ⑤ **22** ④ **23** ⑤ **24** ③ **25** ③ **26** ④

27 ②

---

01 ⓐ, ⓒ: 형용사 - 명사 ⓑ, ⓓ, ⓔ: 동사 - 명사

02 '필요한 만큼 많은'은 'enough(충분한)'이다.

03 못 간다고 하자 ⓓ에서 이유를 묻고 ⓑ에서 의사가 수영을 하지 말라고 했다고 설명하고 ⓒ에서 다음 주말에 가자고 하고 ⓐ에서 그러길 바란다는 순서가 적절하다.

04 tiny – extremely small, feed on – to eat something as food, female – relating to the sex that can produce young or lay eggs, million – the number 1,000,000

05 왜 준수가 모기에 물린 곳을 긁으면 안 되는지는 알 수 없다.

06 모기에 물렸다는데 자외선 차단제를 바르라는 것은 어색하다.

07 순서대로 (1) wrong, that, don't (2) to, Why, stop

08 무슨 일인지 묻자 (B)에서 모기에게 물렸다고 답하고 (A)에서 유감을 표하며 어떻게 그 일이 일어났는지 묻고 (D)에서 캠핑 가서 생겼다고 답하자 (C)에서 긁지 말라고 하는 순서가 적절하다.

09 'There are a lot of fruit flies'라고 했고 'What did you put in the trash?'에 'Some fruit waste.'라고 했다.

10 이야기를 들어보겠느냐는 물음에 유감을 표하는 것은 어색하다.

11 (A) lose by: ~ 차이로 지다
　　(B) I hope so: 그러기를 바란다

12 '~해 왔다'를 현재완료로 나타낸다.

13 ⓑ It has rained since last week.
　　ⓔ When did you cook this spaghetti?
　　ⓕ When I was young, I lived with my aunt.

14 ③ My friend has gone to New York.

15 ⓒ의 It은 'Cleaning with alcohol wipes'를 가리킨다.

16 영작하면 'Stay cool and wear long sleeves.'이다.

17 수백만 년 동안: for millions of years 살아남았다: have survived

18 암컷 모기가 어디에 알을 낳는지는 알 수 없다.

19 ⓔ: Cleaning with alcohol wipes
　　ⓖ: mosquito bites

20 모기를 없애는 방법은 나와 있지 않다.

21 모기는 서준이에게 가려움을 줄이는 방법과 모기에 물리는 것을 막는 방법을 충고해 준다.

22 'It was a hot summer evening. Seojun went for a walk in the park.', 'I'm from a nearby river.'와 'a mosquito flew at him and bit his arm'이라고 했다.

23 순서대로 flew, river, bit, talked가 들어간다.

24 'That's why'로 보아 그 앞에 살아남은 이유가 있어야 하므로 (C)가 적절하다.

25 모기에 물리는 것을 어떻게 방지할지는 나와 있지 않다.

26 so: (접속사로 '이유'나 '결과'를 나타내어) 그래서

27 ① have visited → visited ③ whom → who ④ which → who[whom/that] ⑤ be → been

Lesson 4 (기말)

2회

01 ② **02** ② **03** ③

04 (1) Don't put fruit waste in the trash can.
　　(2) Empty our trash can more often.

05 ③ **06** ⑤

07 Make sure you don't put fruit waste

08 (1) not to scratch them
　　(2) to clean them with color water
　　(3) to wear long sleeves

09 ② **10** ④ **11** ③, ⑤ **12** ① **13** ①

14 (1) She has seen a UFO.
　　(2) She has never had a pet.

15 I need someone strong to help me. **16** ② **17** ③

18 ⑤ **19** (A) something (B) on **20** ④

21 A lot of people have suffered from your bites.

22 ⑤ **23** ④ **24** ③ **25** has bitten his arm **26** ⑤

27 ③ **28** Something tiny flew at him and bit his arm.

01 by three goals: 3골 차이로

02 '팔의 일부 또는 전체를 가리는 옷의 일부'는 'sleeve(소매)'이다.

03 축구 경기가 어땠는지 묻자 (B)에서 3골 차로 졌다고 답하고 (A)에서 다음에는 더 잘하길 바란다고 하자 (C)에서 그러길 바란다고 하는 순서가 적절하다.

04 'Make sure you don't put fruit waste in the trash can.', 'I think we should also empty our trash can more often.'이라고 했다.

05 이겼다고 했는데 유감을 표하는 것은 어색하다.

06 어떻게 과일 쓰레기를 줄이는지는 나와 있지 않다.

07 'make sure'는 '당부'하는 표현이다.

08 tell과 advice의 목적격 보어로 to부정사를 쓰는 것에 주의한다.
　　(1) 'Don't scratch them!'이라고 했다.
　　(2) 'Clean them with cool water.'라고 했다.
　　(3) 'Also, make sure you wear long sleeves when

you go camping.'이라고 했다.

09 wear: (옷·모자·장갑·신발·장신구 등을) 입고[쓰고/끼고/신고/착용하고] 있다, 바르다

10 'I think we should empty our trash can more often.'이라고 했다.

11 ① I've known the girl since I was 5 years old.
② Tom lived in Jeju Island last month.
④ I studied for the test five days ago.

12 ② I read the book last night.
③ When did you cook this spaghetti?
④ I have never been to China before.
⑤ We studied English together yesterday.

13 영작하면 'There is something special to enjoy'이다.

14 현재완료는 'have/has+(not/never)+과거분사'의 형태이다.

15 '-thing, -body, -one'으로 끝나는 부정대명사는 '형용사(+to부정사)'가 뒤에서 수식한다.

16 'After you bit me, I got a bump.'라고 했다.

17 ⓐ Who are you? What have you done to me?
ⓑ Where are you from? How did you find me?
ⓓ Do all mosquitoes drink blood like you?
ⓔ That's interesting. So why do you drink blood?

18 'I need the protein in blood to lay my eggs.'라고 했다.

19 (A) something은 형용사가 뒤에서 수식한다.
(B) feed on: ~을 먹고 살다

20 (C) 동사를 수식하는 부사 easily
(D) 과거이므로 bit
(E) 동사가 필요하므로 itches
(F) 명사가 필요하므로 itchiness

21 a lot of: 많은 have suffered from: ~으로 고통받아 오다

22 앞에서 손을 닦으면 많은 건강 문제를 막을 수 있다고 했으므로 ⓔ의 more는 fewer로 고쳐야 한다.

23 현재완료형으로 ⓓ는 done이 되어야 한다.

24 '-thing'으로 끝나는 대명사는 '형용사+to부정사'가 뒤에서 수식한다.

25 something tiny flew at him and bit his arm이라고 했다.

26 'That's why' 다음에는 결과가 이어진다. 'That's because' 다음에는 원인(이유)이 이어진다. ①~④: why ⑤: because

27 'Only female mosquitoes like me drink blood.'라고 했다.

28 조그마한 무언가: something tiny, 그에게 날아와서: flew at him, 그의 팔을 물었다: bit his arm